9TH EDITION | WEEKEND ADVENTURES

IN SAN FRANCISCO & NORTHERN CALIFORNIA

CAROLE TERWILLIGER MEYERS

CAROUSEL PRESS

BERKELEY, CALIFORNIA

Published by: **CAROUSEL PRESS**
P.O. Box 6038
Berkeley, CA 94706-0038
(510) 527-5849
editor@carousel-press.com
www.carousel-press.com

Distributed to the book trade by Publishers Group West

This book was previously published under the titles *Weekend Adventures in Northern California* (1997 and 2001 editions), *Weekend Adventures for City-Weary People: Overnight Trips in Northern California* (1984, 1989, and 1993 editions), and *Weekend Adventures for City-Weary Families: A Guide to Overnight Trips in Northern California* (1977 and 1980 editions).

Library of Congress Cataloging-in-Publication Data

Meyers, Carole Terwilliger.
 Weekend adventures in San Francisco & northern California / by Carole Terwilliger Meyers -- 9th ed.
   p. cm.
 Includes indexes.
 ISBN-13: 978-0-917120-21-3
 ISBN-10: 0-917120-21-3
1. California, Northern--Guidebooks. 2. San Francisco (Calif.)--Guidebooks. 3. Family recreation--California, Northern--Guidebooks. 4. Family recreation--California--San Francisco--Guidebooks. I. Title.

F867.5.M48 2009
917.94'60454--dc22

                         2008038088

The information in this book was correct at press time. However, the author and publisher hereby disclaim any liability due to changes, errors, or omissions, and cannot be held responsible for the experiences of readers while traveling. Also, all recreational activities include an element of risk. The publisher and author disclaim all responsibility for any injury, harm or illness that may occur through use of information in this book. Specific information is gathered in the year before publication and included to give an approximate idea of what to expect; phone numbers are included so that readers can call to determine current details. All establishments listed in this book are mentioned to alert the reader to their existence; they are endorsed by neither the author nor publisher. No business has paid to be included.

Blog update: Sign up for the author's free e-mail update at www.carousel-press.com.
Reader feedback: Text errors and typos, listing changes, exciting new discoveries, praise, even complaints—we want to hear about it all.
Special sales: Bulk purchases of Carousel Press titles are available to corporations at special discounts. Custom editions can be produced to use as premiums and promotional items.

Manufactured in the United States of America

Mixed Sources
Product group from well-managed
forests and other controlled sources
www.fsc.org Cert no. SW-COC-002283
© 1996 Forest Stewardship Council

10 9 8 7 6 5 4 3 2 1

"This lady is organized . . . well-researched guide."
San Francisco Chronicle Book Review

". . . almost overwhelmingly full of detailed information. Excellent."
San Diego Union-Tribune

"This guidebook is a gem. It has it all . . . well-known and unusual activities are
presented in an organized manner. Buy this book, enjoy Meyers' insights, and plan for a memorable
vacation in Northern California."
The Bloomsbury Review

"Businesses have come and gone. What's unchanged is her attention to detail and
enthusiasm for this lovely chunk of California. This book is a valuable resource."
Mike Cleary, radio personality

". . . covers its territory like white on rice."
John Briggs, reader, Portland, OR

"We had a great time on our California vacation. Weekend Adventures was essential both during
planning and execution. Thank you for a wonderful guide!"
Joleen Chambers, parent, Annapolis, MD

"Carole Terwilliger Meyers writes intelligently about family fun.
She finds places kids like that adults can stomach. And vice versa."
Alice Kahn, author

"The guide is very well organized . . . Highly recommended."
Pacific Sun

". . . a gold mine of travel tips."
The Montclarion

"My 9-year-old has been working on a California history project, and your book has been invaluable.
I am amazed you packed in so much interesting history! Weekend Adventures contains
a lot of important, brief (a real asset when dealing with 4th-grade assignments) historical facts about
many of the places and attractions covered, and our copy has become
porcupined with a wild assortment of sticky notes."
Helen Chang, parent, Fremont, CA

"Carole is the doyenne-empress-goddess of family travel in the Bay Area. She invented it."
Peter Beren, co-author of The Writer's Legal Companion

"Enjoyable to read . . . and loaded with photos."
Small Press

". . . easy-to-follow format."
Booklist

"This hefty guide is full of opinionated reporting by author Carole Terwilliger Meyers. It covers a lot of
ground. The writing is sharp and informative. Clearly, Meyers knows her stuff."
June Sawyers, Chicago Tribune

Also by Carole Terwilliger Meyers:

FamilyFun Vacation Guide: California & Hawaii

Bay Area Family Fun (an annotated map)

The Family Travel Guide: An Inspiring Collection of Family-Friendly Vacations (Editor)

Miles of Smiles: 101 Great Car Games & Activities

San Francisco Family Fun

How to Organize a Babysitting Cooperative and Get Some Free Time Away From the Kids

Eating Out With the Kids in San Francisco and the Bay Area

Getting in the Spirit: Annual Bay Area Christmas Events

Eating Out with the Kids in the East Bay

for Gene

CONTENTS

INTRODUCTION

We residents of the Bay Area are fortunate to live within easy driving distance of a wealth of exciting vacation possibilities—mountains, ocean, rivers, snow. Our biggest recreational problem is deciding, from among the many possibilities, where we should go and what we should do.

The destinations in this book radiate out from San Francisco. Most make good weekend or mid-week trips, and all can be adapted easily to longer stays.

Because it is frustrating to discover after you're home that an area where you've just vacationed has an interesting attraction you didn't know about, and because it also isn't much fun finding out too late that there is a better or cheaper (depending on what you're after) lodging you could have booked into or a restaurant you would have enjoyed trying, this book is designed so that you can determine quickly what is of special interest in the area you are planning to visit. Listings are all special in some way—bargain rates, family-friendly, aesthetically pleasing, historically interesting,

etc. Toll-free numbers, phone numbers, and websites are provided for obtaining further information.

Parents especially need to have this information in advance. I know because one of the worst trips I ever experienced was the first trip my husband and I took with our first baby. I hadn't planned ahead. We took off for the Gold Rush Country and went where the winds blew us—just like before we were parents. That was a mistake. We wound up in a hotel that had no compassion for a colicky baby or his parents, and we ate a series of memorably bad meals. Now my husband and I can laugh about that trip, but at the time it wasn't funny. That fateful trip turned me into a travel writer. Since then, I've never gone anywhere without exhaustively researching it beforehand. And I've never had a bad trip since that I can blame on lack of information.

With all of this in mind, I've written this book to help make your trip-planning easier, allowing you to get the most out of your weekends away.

1

CREDITS

Book design and layout: Betsy Joyce
Maps: Eureka Cartography
Printing: McNaughton & Gunn, Inc.

Images by:

COVER: Shutterstock.com

INSIDE PAGES:
Carole Terwilliger Meyers: *p.62; p.86; p.98; p.158; p.201; p.202; p.211; p.222; p.244, top & bottom; p.252; p.255, bottom; p.257; p.260; p.262; p.274; p.275; p.276; p.309, bottom; p.328; p.329; p.333; p.345; p.359; p.382; p.384; p.385; p.391; p.405; p.412; p.416, top; p.427; p.445, top; p.449; p.469.*

California State Department of Parks and Recreation: *p.89; p.97; p.119:* Pete Amos; *p.125; p.136; p.140:* John Kaestner; *p.143, bottom; p.144; p.266; p.268; p.304; p.349, top; p.365:* Larry Paynter; *p.460, top; p.465.*

Redwood Empire Association: *p.148; p.156:* Ansel Adams; *p.164; p.255, top; p.273:* Ansel Adams; *p.421:* Balloon Aviation of Napa Valley; *p.432.*

Provided by site described: *p.22; p.23; p.25; p.26; p.30; p.38; p.50; p.56; p.61; p.64; p.67; p.101; p.110, top; p.114; p.129; p.134; p.152, top; p.178; p.183; p.186; p.190; p.193; p.195; p.209; p.210:* Rob Stark; *p.216:* Jane Oka; *p.218:* Michael Morgan; *p.234; p.242; p.259; p.264:* Pat Cudahy; *p.281; p.286, bottom:* Peg Skorpinski; *p.287; p.291; p.298; p.299; p.300, top; p.312, bottom; p.314; p.316; p.321; p.323, bottom; p.324; p.325; p.354; p.389; p.394; p.396, bottom; p.400:* Clarence Chu; *p.402; p.410; p.419; p.431; p.445, bottom; p.450; p.452:* David Martinez.

Shutterstock.com: *p.7, top; p.17; p.19, bottom; p.27, bottom; p.40; p.59, bottom; p.70; p.143, top; p.167; p.177; p.215; p.271; p.279; p.302; p.318; p.406; p.408; p.439; p.440; p.455; p.467.*

Other: *p.7, bottom:* Carl Wilmington, San Francisco CVB; *p.8:* San Francisco CVB; *p.9: top:* Hanford Associates; *bottom:* George Olson, Dudell & Associates; *p.11:* Alameda Naval Air Station Public Affairs Office; *p.12:* Arne Folkedal, San Francisco Ballet; *p.16:* Robert Stinnel, Red & White Fleet; *p.19, top:* Herb Bettin, San Francisco CVB; *p.21:* San Francisco CVB; *p.24:* Richard Barnes, SFMOMA; *p.27, top:* Nancy Rodger, Exploratorium; *p.33:* San Francisco Recreation and Park Department; *p.34:* San Francisco CVB; *p.35:* Michael Shay, San Francisco Zoological Society; *p.36:* Ron Scherl, Steve Silver Productions; *p.52:* Park Hyatt San Francisco; *p.59, top:* Fortune Public Relations; *p.83:* Katy Greene; *p.94:* Terry Pimsleur & Co.; *p.99:* Hostelling International; *p.106:* Janet Anderson; *p.110, bottom:* California Artichoke Advisory Board; *p.146:* Clerin Zumwalt, Audubon Canyon Ranch; *p.152, bottom:* Sharon Taussig, Sonoma County CVB; *p.205:* Valley Guild, Steinbeck Library; *p.230:* Petaluma Visitors Program; *p.267:* Humboldt County CVB; *p.286, top:* California Alumni Association; *p.300:* Harre W. Demoro; *p.303:* Robert Bone, Sacramento CVB; *p.309, top:* unknown; *p.312, top:* Dunsmuir Historic Estate; *p.313:* Sonoma Valley Visitors Bureau; *p.323, top:* unknown; *p.331:* John F. Reginato, Shasta-Cascade Wonderland Assoc.; *p.336:* B.F. Loomis, Poimiroo & Partners; *pp.337 & 342:* John F. Reginato, Shasta-Cascade Wonderland Assoc.; *p.349, bottom:* Gold Prospecting Expeditions; *p.352:* City Hotel; *p.353:* 39th District Agricultural Assoc.; *p.368: unknown; p.375:* Yosemite Concession Services; *p.376:* John Poimiroo, Yosemite Concession Services; *p.377:* Yosemite Research Library; *p.379:* Yosemite Concession Services; *p.383:* Mono Lake Committee; *p.386:* Sanger District Chamber of Commerce; *p.396, top:* Santa Cruz County Conference & Visitors Council; *pp.399 & 401:* Hal Schell; *p.409:* unknown; *p.416, bottom:* Smothers Winery; *p.433:* Penn, Dr. Wilkinson's Hot Springs; *p.441, p. 443 top & bottom, p.447:* Lake Tahoe Visitors Authority; *p.444:* unknown; *p.448:* Greater Reno Chamber of Commerce; *p.456:* Royal Gorge Nordic Ski Resort; *p. 460, bottom, & p.461, top & bottom:* Yosemite Concession Services; *p.463:* Shasta-Cascade Wonderland Assoc.; *p.464:* John M. Giosso, San Francisco Recreation & Park Dept.; *p.466:* Rapid Shooters, Mariah Wilderness Expeditions.

BACK COVER: Author photo taken at AT&T Park concession.

GUIDELINES FOR INTERPRETING LISTINGS

This book is organized by geographical area. Each chapter has most of the following subsections:

A LITTLE BACKGROUND

Historical and general background information about the area; what kinds of activities to expect.

VISITOR INFORMATION

Address phone number, and website of visitor bureau or chamber of commerce.

GETTING THERE

The quickest, easiest driving route from San Francisco; scenic driving routes; other transportation options.

STOPS ALONG THE WAY

Noteworthy places for meals or sightseeing.

ANNUAL EVENTS

The area's best events. When no phone number is listed, contact the visitor bureau or chamber of commerce for information.

WHAT TO DO

Activities and sights in the area that are of special interest, listed alphabetically and including the following information when available: Address, phone number; website. Days and hours open; months closed; if reservations are required. Admission fee; parking fee.

WHERE TO STAY

Lodging facilities, listed alphabetically and including the following information when available: Street address, toll-free reservations number, phone number; website (where e-mail address can usually be obtained). Number of stories if more than 3; number of rooms; price range per night for two people (see price code below); months closed. If facility is unsuitable for children under a specified age. If no TVs are provided; if kitchens, gas or wood-burning fireplaces, or wood-burning stoves are provided; if any baths are shared. Recreational facilities available: pool; hot tub; sauna; fitness room; full-service spa; tennis courts; golf course. If an afternoon or evening snack is included; if breakfast is included; if there is a restaurant; if there is room service. If pets are *not* permitted. (This is complicated. Lodgings that do permit pets have varied restrictions—small dogs are ok, but not large dogs, etc.—and they usually charge a fee. Most lodgings do allow service guide dogs.) If there is an overnight parking fee.

$=under $100 $$=$100-$199 $$$=$200-$299
$$$+=more than $300

WHERE TO EAT

Reliable restaurants, listed alphabetically and including the following information when available: Address, phone number, website. Meals served (B, L, D, SunBr), days open; price range (see price code below). If reservations are advised (note that a "no reservations" policy sometimes changes to "reservations accepted" at dinner or when the party is 6+). If credit cards are not accepted. If valet parking is available.

$ =   inexpensive. Average entrée might cost up to $10.
$$ =   moderate. Average entrée might cost up to $20.
$$$ =   expensive. Average entrée might cost up to $30.
$$$+=   very expensive. Average entrée might cost more than $30.

Always call for current details. Remember that some restaurants and attractions close on major holidays. Also, note that some attractions and hotels post special offers on their website and offer AAA or senior citizen discounts.

3

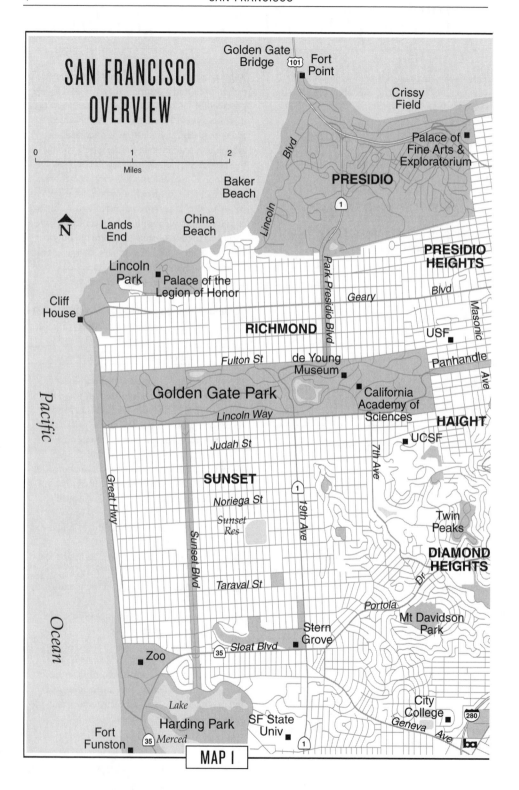

SAN FRANCISCO OVERVIEW

Golden Gate Bridge — 101 — Fort Point

Crissy Field

Palace of Fine Arts & Exploratorium

PRESIDIO

Baker Beach

0   1   2
Miles

N

Lands End

China Beach

Pacific

PRESIDIO HEIGHTS

Lincoln Park — Palace of the Legion of Honor

Cliff House

Blvd

Lincoln

Park Presidio Blvd

Geary   Blvd

Masonic

RICHMOND

USF

Fulton St   de Young Museum

Panhandle

Ave

Golden Gate Park

California Academy of Sciences

HAIGHT

Lincoln Way

UCSF

Judah St

7th Ave

SUNSET

Noriega St

1

Sunset Res

19th Ave

Twin Peaks

DIAMOND HEIGHTS

Ocean

Great Hwy

Sunset Blvd

Taraval St

Dr

Portola   Mt Davidson Park

Stern Grove

35   Sloat Blvd

Zoo

Lake

City College

280

Harding Park   SF State Univ

Geneva   Ave

Fort Funston   35   Merced

1

ba

MAP 1

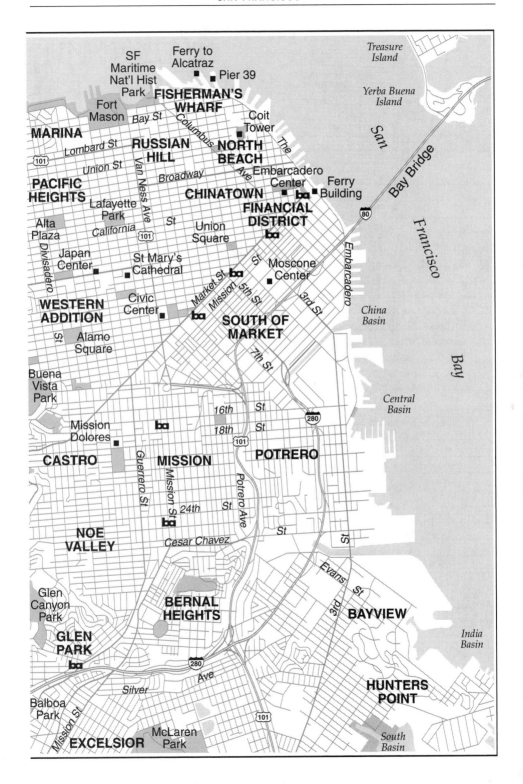

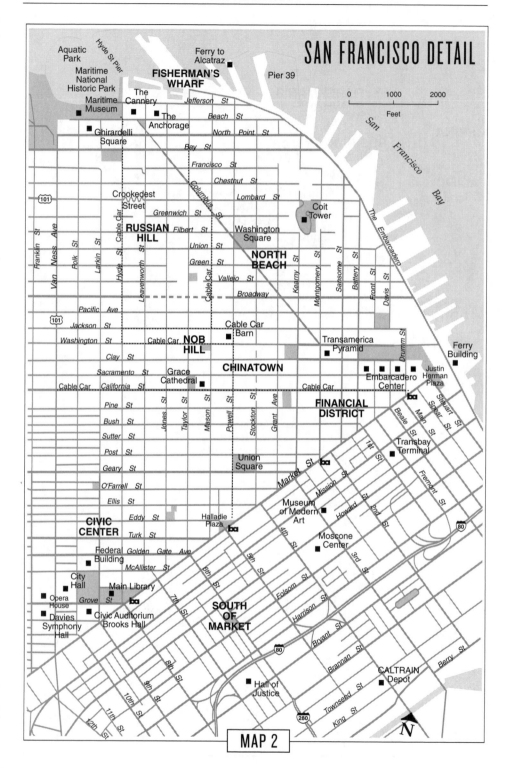

SAN FRANCISCO DETAIL

Aquatic Park
Maritime National Historic Park
FISHERMAN'S WHARF
Ferry to Alcatraz
Pier 39
Hyde St Pier
The Cannery
Maritime Museum
The Anchorage
Ghirardelli Square
Jefferson St
Beach St
North Point St
Bay St
Francisco St
Chestnut St
Crookedest Street
Columbus St
Lombard St
Coit Tower
Greenwich St
RUSSIAN HILL
Filbert St
Washington Square
Union St
NORTH BEACH
Green St
Vallejo St
Broadway
0   1000   2000
Feet
San Francisco Bay
The Embarcadero
Franklin St
Van Ness Ave
Polk St
Larkin St
Hyde St
Leavenworth St
Cable Car
Kearny St
Montgomery St
Sansome St
Battery St
Front St
Davis St
101
Pacific Ave
Jackson St
101
Washington St
Clay St
Sacramento St
Cable Car
California St
Cable Car
Cable Car Barn
NOB HILL
CHINATOWN
Grace Cathedral
Transamerica Pyramid
Embarcadero Center
Ferry Building
Justin Herman Plaza
Drumm St
Pine St
Bush St
Sutter St
Post St
Geary St
O'Farrell St
Ellis St
Jones St
Taylor St
Mason St
Powell St
Stockton St
Grant Ave
FINANCIAL DISTRICT
Cable Car
Transbay Terminal
Beale St
Main St
Spear St
Steuart St
Union Square
Market St
1st St
CIVIC CENTER
Eddy St
Turk St
Federal Building
Golden Gate Ave
McAllister St
City Hall
Opera House
Davies Symphony Hall
Main Library
Grove St
Civic Auditorium
Brooks Hall
Halladie Plaza
Museum of Modern Art
Moscone Center
Mission St
Howard St
Folsom St
Harrison St
Bryant St
Brannan St
Townsend St
King St
2nd St
3rd St
4th St
5th St
6th St
7th St
8th St
9th St
10th St
11th St
12th St
SOUTH OF MARKET
Hall of Justice
CALTRAIN Depot
Berry St
Fremont St
80
80
280
N

MAP 2

SAN FRANCISCO

"Postcard Row"

A LITTLE BACKGROUND

You wouldn't think such a place as San Francisco could exist. The wonderful sunlight there, the hills, the great bridges, the Pacific at your shoes. Beautiful Chinatown. Every race in the world. The sardine fleets sailing out. The little cable-cars whizzing down the city hills. The lobsters, clams, & crabs . . . Every kind of seafood there is. And all the people are open and friendly.

— Dylan Thomas

San Francisco has only one drawback. 'Tis hard to leave.

— Rudyard Kipling

One day if I do go to heaven, I'm going to do what every San Franciscan does who goes to heaven. I'll look around and say, 'It ain't bad, but it ain't San Francisco.'

— Herb Caen, June 14, 1996

You tell people you live in California and surf, and they have a picture of a 'Gidget' movie. In San Francisco, however, it's more like some kind of German Expressionist film—all foggy, cold and dark, and nobody around. Just me and the sharks.

— Chris Isaak, 1999

Though the quotes above aren't heard often, the saying attributed to Mark Twain, "The coldest winter I ever spent was a summer in San Francisco," is familiar to most people. Scholars dispute that the words were Twain's, but no one who has spent a summer in San Francisco will dispute the comment.

Measuring just 7 miles by 7 miles square, this relatively small big city is known for its morning and evening fog in summer. Locals coming in from the suburbs have learned always to bring along wraps. In summer, it is easy to spot tourists. They are the ones wearing

7

shorts . . . or white shoes, another no-no among locals. Perhaps these visitors are confusing San Francisco with the image of Southern California's warm beaches. That is a mistake.

In general, the climate is temperate, ranging between 40 and 70 degrees. The best weather usually occurs in September and October.

VISITOR INFORMATION

San Francisco Convention & Visitors Bureau Visitor Information Center

900 Market St./Powell St., Halladie Plaza, (415) 391-2000; www.onlyinsanfrancisco.com. M-F 9-5, Sat-Sun 9-3; closed Sun Nov-May.

Get a free copy of *The San Francisco Book*—filled with sightseeing, shopping, and dining information—and *Visitor Planning Guide*. For visitors with disabilities, *Access San Francisco* is also available. Make lodging reservations through the bureau by calling (888) 782-9673. At the center, agents can communicate in 12 languages.

For a recorded listing of the day's events, call (415) 391-2001. For the same information in French, call (415) 391-2003; German (415) 391-2004; Spanish (415) 391-2122; Japanese (415) 391-2101; Italian (415) 391-2002.

ANNUAL EVENTS

— JANUARY —

Chinese New Year Festival & Parade

Or in February or March, depending on the lunar

calendar. (415) 982-3071; www.chineseparade.com. Free.

First held in 1851 and again every year since, this popular event is composed of a beauty pageant, an outdoor carnival in Chinatown, and the famous parade featuring a spectacular block-long golden dragon (this parade is one of the few illuminated night parades in the U.S.).

— FEBRUARY —

Pacific Orchid Exposition

Or in March. Fort Mason Center; (415) 665-2468; www.orchidsanfrancisco.org. $14, 65+ $8, under 13 free.

Thousands of gorgeous blooming orchid plants are on display at this stunning show of amateur and professional collections—the largest of its kind on the West Coast. In addition to the plants entered for judging and show, thousands more are available for purchase. Lectures by international orchid experts are scheduled. Sponsored by the San Francisco Orchid Society.

— MARCH —

St. Patrick's Day Parade

(415) 675-9885; www.sfstpatricksdayparade.com. Free.

This traditional parade is the city's largest and has been held annually for more than 150 years.

San Francisco Flower & Garden Show

Cow Palace; (800) 569-2832, (415) 771-6909; www.gardenshow.com. $9-$20, 6-17 $4; parking $8.

The area's top garden designers display their talents with more than 20 full-size gardens. Garden items and blooming plants—including bonsai and orchids—are for sale, and how-to seminars and a children's area are included with admission.

— APRIL —

Grand National Rodeo, Horse & Stock Show

Cow Palace, in Daly City; (415) 404-4111; www.grandnationalrodeo.com. $27-$42, seniors & under 13 free-$17.

This is the largest such show held west of the Mississippi. A rodeo and horse show is scheduled each day, and ticket holders are invited to come early for a variety of related activities: dairy animal auctions; judging contests; displays of unusual livestock breeds, including literally tons of premium steers, woolly sheep, and prime swine. Kids especially enjoy the pony rides and baby animals.

Northern California Cherry Blossom Festival

Japan Center; (415) 563-2313; www.nccbf.org. Free.

Japanese cultural events at this elaborate celebration of spring include traditional dancing, martial arts demonstrations, taiko drum and koto performances, and tea ceremonies. A Japanese food bazaar operates continuously, and demonstrations of the Japanese arts of doll making, calligraphy, and flower arranging are usually scheduled. The festival culminates with a colorful 2-hour, Japanese-style parade.

San Francisco Decorator Showcase

(415) 447-5830; www.decoratorshowcase.org. $25-$30.

Strict quality control gives this show house a reputation for being the best in the West—perhaps even the best in the entire country. Proceeds benefit San Francisco University High School.

San Francisco International Film Festival

(415) 561-5000; www.sffs.org. $8+.

Known for honoring the finest in cinematic achievement, this oldest film festival in the Western Hemisphere presents recent productions from around the world. Some children's films are usually included.

— MAY —

Bay to Breakers

(415) 359-2800; www.baytobreakers.com. Entry fee $39-$49, under 18 $33-$45.

The world's largest, and perhaps zaniest, footrace began in 1912 as a way of uniting residents and boosting morale after the 1906 earthquake. It is routed through the Financial District, up the Hayes Street hill, and on through Golden Gate Park to the Great Highway. Outrageous outfits are de rigueur and in the past have included everything from a band of running Elvises to spawning salmon and even the Golden Gate Bridge. All participants receive a commemorative t-shirt.

Carnaval San Francisco

(415) 920-0125; www.carnavalsf.com. Free.

This spectacular Mardi Gras-like revel is a multicultural celebration of life. It includes a parade and a 2-day outdoor festival.

Cinco de Mayo Festival

(415) 206-0577. Free.

Commemorating the Battle of Puebla, Mexico on May 5, 1862—which marked the defeat of the powerful French Napoleonic Army by a small, poorly equipped Mexican force—this is the largest such festival in the U.S. It attracts visitors and performers from throughout Latin America and includes a free parade.

— JUNE —

North Beach Festival
(415) 989-2220; www.sfnorthbeach.org/festival. Free.

This granddaddy of street fairs was established by a committee of Beat generation artists in 1954 and is said to be the country's very first. It features Italian foods, sidewalk cafes, traditional Italian sword fighting demonstrations, bocce ball games, and a variety of entertainment.

San Francisco Lesbian Gay Bisexual Transgender Pride Parade & Celebration
(415) 864-FREE; www.sfpride.org. Free.

Though other cities now also hold annual gay pride celebrations, San Francisco's self-described "queerific" event is considered the biggest and wildest. The parade is a don't-miss. A popular highlight is the Women's Motorcycle Contingent, also known as "Dykes on Bikes," which leads the parade every year.

Stern Grove Festival
Through mid-Aug. 19th Ave./Sloat Blvd.;
(415) 252-6252; www.sterngrove.org. Free. No pets.

Featuring the finest of Bay Area performing arts, this program is the country's oldest free summer performing arts festival and has been held in the Grove's natural outdoor amphitheater each summer since 1938. It is traditional to bring a picnic lunch and the Sunday newspaper and spend the pre-performance wait indulging in food, drink, and relaxation. Bring a blanket to sit on and a jacket in case the weather turns chilly.

The city's **croquet lawns** *((415) 776-4104)* are available here year-round for play.

— JULY —

Cable Car Bell-Ringing Competition
Month sometimes changes. Union Square; (415) 673-MUNI or 311; www.sfmta.com. Free.

Competition for "Ding Dong Daddy" is held in both pro and amateur divisions. The previous year's champion defends his title, and amateurs (who include some well-known Bay

Area personalities) ring on behalf of non-profit organizations. Judges are selected from among the area's musical and theatrical elite.

Fourth of July Waterfront Festival
Pier 39, Fisherman's Wharf, San Francisco Municipal Pier; (415) 705-5500; www.pier39.com. Free.

Continuous entertainment begins in the early afternoon. The celebration culminates after sunset with the West Coast's largest fireworks display.

— AUGUST —

American Craft Show in San Francisco
Fort Mason Center; (800) 836-3470; www.craftcouncil.org. $12, under 12 free. Valet parking.

Produced by the American Craft Council, this is the largest juried craft fair in the West. It features the latest work of more than 250 of the nation's premier craft artists.

—SEPTEMBER—

San Francisco Blues Festival
Great Meadow at Fort Mason; (415) 979-5588; www.sfblues.com. $35-$40, under 10 free. No pets.

Known for its all-star lineup, this upbeat affair has been called "one of the best blues events in the world." Indeed, it is the oldest blues festival in America and features a breathtaking background view of the Golden Gate Bridge. John Lee Hooker once sang of this indigenous American music form, "The blues is a healer. It healed me and it'll heal you." This show is definitely good for what ails you.

San Francisco Fringe Festival
Union Square; (415) 931-1094; www.sffringe.org. Free-$8.

Independent theater companies from around the world are invited here to present eclectic, cutting-edge performances over a period of 12 days. No show lasts more than an hour, and venues are concentrated around Union Square so that patrons can easily walk from performance to performance. Tickets are available only at the performance.

San Francisco International Dragon Boat Festival

Off Treasure Island; (415) 262-0155; www.sfdragonboat.com. Free.

Racing dragon boats is said to be the second most popular sport in the world. According to legend, the races began over 2,300 years ago, in 288 B.C., when fishermen rowed into China's Mi Lo river trying to rescue an exiled poet as he drowned himself in protest against a corrupt government. Though the fishermen thrashed their oars in the water to scare away evil spirits, the poet died anyway. Nowadays, dragon boat racing commemorates the poet's heroic spirit. This traditional race attracts world-class teams, in addition to amateur and local high school crews, and is the largest competitive dragon boat festival in the U.S. Dragon boating is the most popular team sport in the world, with more than 60 million participants. Dragon boat teams consist of 1 steerer, 1 drummer who sets the pace, and up to 20 paddlers on a fiberglass or teak hull boat. Many wear traditional Chinese costume. The long, narrow, modern fiberglass boats are adorned with colorful dragon figureheads. Shuttle buses are available between Treasure Island and the Autumn Moon Festival in Chinatown held the same weekend.

— OCTOBER —

Columbus Day Celebration

(415) 703-9888; www.sfcolumbusday.org. Free.

San Francisco's is the only Columbus Day celebration in the country that includes a re-enactment of Columbus's landing in San Salvadore. When landing at Aquatic Park, the person acting as Columbus wears a handmade Italian replica of the great navigator's clothing.

The **Blessing of the Fishing Fleet** takes place the next day at Fisherman's Wharf. (The three most dangerous areas for fishing are the tip of South America, the tip of South Africa, and the bay outside the Golden Gate Bridge. This event honors those who were lost, with flowers dropped in the procession from the church to the bay.)

The **Italian Heritage Parade and Festival** usually takes place the next weekend.

Fleet Week

(650) 599-5057; www.fleetweek.us. Free.

To celebrate the anniversary of the Navy's birthday and honor the men and women of the U.S. Navy and Marines, the City of San Francisco throws a gigantic party each year and the public is invited. Past events have included demonstrations of high-speed boat maneuvering, parachute drops, and a fly-by of World War

ll vintage aircraft. **The Blue Angels**, the Navy's premier precision flying team, also perform in a breathtaking culmination. Viewing is best from Crissy Field, the Marina Green, Aquatic Park, Pier 39, and the Marin Headlands. As part of the celebration, all Navy ships moored at the piers are usually open for public visits. Fleet Week originated in 1908 when President Teddy Roosevelt's "Great White Fleet" of battleships sailed under the Golden Gate. Mayor Dianne Feinstein established it as an annual event in 1981.

San Francisco Jazz Festival
(800) 850-SFJF, (415) 398-5655; www.sfjazz.org. Free–$55.

The *Chicago Tribune* calls this "the biggest and most acclaimed jazz festival in the United States."

— DECEMBER —

A Christmas Carol
Geary Theater; (415) 749-2ACT; www.act-sf.org. $25–$80.

Dickens' popular seasonal ghost tale, which celebrates the rebirth of the human spirit and death of indifference, is sure to rekindle any lagging Christmas enthusiasm in grumpy holiday Scrooges. American Conservatory Theater's

lively production enhances the story with a musical score of carols, songs, and dance. It is interesting to note that Dickens' story is credited with actually reviving the celebration of Christmas, which at the time his book was published in 1843 had slipped to the status of a quaint, almost obsolete custom. It is also considered responsible for some English social reform. Fortunately for all of us, his story still manages to wake up the spirit of human kindness.

Chanticleer
See p. 37.

Golden Gate Park Christmas Tree Lighting
Golden Gate Park; (415) 831-2700; www.parks.sfgov.org. Free.

San Francisco's official Christmas tree, a 100-foot Monterey cypress located at the east entrance to Golden Gate Park, is decorated each Christmas season with more than 3,000 lights. The mayor is usually present to flip the switch. Santa also makes an appearance, and the audience is led in singing carols.

Great Dickens Christmas Fair
Cow Palace; (800) 510-1558; www.dickensfair.com. $17–$22, 62+ $19, 5-11 $10; parking $8. No pets.

See *A Christmas Carol* brought to life at this re-creation of Christmas in Victorian London. After playing spirited parlour games, purchasing some fine yuletide gifts, and feasting on period food and drink, even the grumpiest Scrooge will capture the season's spirit. Entertainment is continuous and includes parades, theatrical performances, and caroling—even dancing with Mr. and Mrs. Fezziwig and guests at their celebrated party. And as if this isn't enough, Her Majesty Queen Victoria and consort Prince Albert always attend. Visitors are encouraged to dress in period costume.

Guardsmen Christmas Tree Sale

Fort Mason Center; (415) 771-7747; www.guardsmen.org. Trees $25-$200.

Claiming to have the largest enclosed Christmas tree lot in Northern California, the Guardsmen sell more than 5,000 trees each year. This sale is famous for having the best selection of noble firs but also stocks a variety of other trees, including Douglas fir, Frazer fir, and Scotch pine. Just visiting the lot is a thrill—it resembles a small forest—and is particularly nice on a rainy day. Trees range from tabletop size to 14 feet. Garlands, wreaths, holly, mistletoe, and ornaments are also on sale. Proceeds fund educational programs for disadvantaged Bay Area children.

Nutcracker

War Memorial Opera House; (415) 865-2000; www.sfballet.org. $18-$198.

The San Francisco Ballet has presented the *Nutcracker* since 1944, when it blazed the path for all subsequent U.S. Nutcrackers by dancing the first full-length production. A new version is introduced every 10 to 15 years, the most recent in 2004. It is always an extravagant interpretation, with hundreds of thousands of dollars worth of scenery and handmade costumes, and each performance features a cast of more than 175 dancers comprised of the company's dancers plus children from the Ballet School.

Union Square Window Displays

Each year the biggest department stores—Macy's, Saks Fifth Avenue, Neiman Marcus—treat the public to elaborate window decorations, some with moving mechanical displays. A visit to the commercial, but gorgeous, Christmas wonderland at Macy's, known as

Bayberry Row—is always special, and Santa is also found here. The lobby of the Westin St. Francis Hotel is always festively decorated and worth a walk-through, and street entertainers, vendors, and carolers provide further diversion.

WHAT TO DO

TOURS: By Boat

Blue and Gold Fleet Bay Tours

Depart from Pier 39, Fisherman's Wharf, (415) 705-8200; www.blueandgoldfleet.com. Daily from 10:45am. $21, 62+ & 12-18 $17, 5-11 $13.

This 1-hour narrated cruise of the bay goes out under the world's most beautiful bridge—the Golden Gate—and also passes close to Alcatraz Island. Other boat tours include Angel Island, Six Flags Discovery Kingdom, Sausalito, and Tiburon.

Hornblower Cruises and *The San Francisco Spirit*

Both offer scenic dining cruises. For descriptions, see page 73.

Ruby Sailing Yacht

At foot of Mariposa St./near 3rd St., (415) 861-2165; www.rubysailing.com. Daily at 12:30 & 6, May-Nov; at other times by appt. $35, under 10 $20. Reservations required.

Captain Joshua Pryor built the 64-foot steel sloop *Ruby* himself in 1979. He also sails her himself. A 2½-hour lunch cruise circles Alcatraz, and guests can dine on deli sandwiches either on the deck or below in the salon. An evening trip sails to Sausalito and includes hors d'oeuvres. Beer and wine are available at additional charge.

Whale-Watching Tours

Depart from Fort Mason Center, Marina District, (800) 326-7491, (415) 474-3385; www.oceanic-society.org. Sat-Sun & some F & M; Jan to mid-May. $80-$85. Must be 10 or older. Reservations required.

Sponsored by the non-profit Oceanic Society Expeditions, these all-day trips have a professional naturalist on board to instruct about the whales and interpret their behavior. Half-day trips depart from Princeton-by-the-Sea (see page 91).

Farallon Islands Nature Cruises *(Sat-Sun & some F; June-Nov. $95. Must be 10 or older. Reservations required.)* take participants 25 miles across the Pacific Ocean from the Golden Gate Bridge to this National Wildlife Refuge. These islands support the largest seabird rookery in the eastern Pacific south of Alaska and are the habitat of 200,000 nesting sea birds—including tufted puffins, loons, and auklets—as well as sea lions and seals.

TOURS: By Bus

Gray Line Tours
(888) 428-6937, (415) 434-8687; www.grayline sanfrancisco.com. Fares vary; under 5 free on parent's lap. Reservations required 1 day in advance.

Day tours are available of San Francisco, Muir Woods/Sausalito, Yosemite, Monterey/ Carmel, and the Wine Country. Dinner tours of San Francisco are also scheduled.

Three Babes and a Bus
Depart from Union Square, (800) 414-0158, (650) 341-7060; www.threebabes.com. Sat 8:30pm-1:30am. $39. Must be 21 or older. Reservations advised.

These babes and their bus pick up guests and take them out to party in four of the city's hottest dance clubs. The fee includes cover charges and VIP entry, and participants needn't worry about parking, taxi fares, or drinking and driving.

TOURS: By Car

49-Mile Drive
This planned driving route through San Francisco is marked with signs and a blue line in the road and hits most of the high points. For a free map, contact the San Francisco Convention and Visitors Bureau (see page 8).

GoCar Rentals
2715 Hyde St./Beach St., Fisherman's Wharf, (800) 91-GoCar, (415) 441-5695; www.gocartours.com. Also at 321 Mason St/O'Farrell St., near Union Square. $49/1st hr., $39/2nd hr., $29/hr. thereafter up to 5 hours total, then no additional charge; daily collision damage waiver (CDW) $9.

The world's first computer-guided story-telling cars, these open-air, three-wheel vehicles with a motorcycle engine guide passengers to the city's sights. They tell when to turn, where

to turn, and if the car is in the wrong lane. And they are so much *fun*, this really is the *only* way to go. Made in Holland, each seats two and can go up to 35 m.p.h., though under 30 feels best. The onboard Global Positioning System provides a custom narration leading drivers on either, or both, of two routes—the waterfront/ Golden Gate Park or downtown/Union Square—explaining the sights along the way. The sporty cars can be parked in any legal motorcycle or car parking spot, allowing time for exploration or a snack. Typical rentals last about 2 hours. However, because the price per hour goes down every hour, it makes sense to rent it for the whole day and pack in a lot of sightseeing. The itinerary is available in five languages (English, French, German, Spanish, and Italian).

Mr. Toad's Vintage Car Tours
Departs from Mason St./Jefferson St., Fisherman's Wharf, (877) 4MR-TOAD, (415) 205-3303; www.mrtoadstours.com. Schedule varies. $32+, 62+ $26+, 4-12 $15+.

This family-owned and operated sightseeing company features brand-new, environmentally friendly, custom-built pre-1930s vehicles. They include a 1929 Model A "woody," a 1912 Rambler, and a 1925 Yellowstone bus. Choose from an 80-minute "Hop Around the City" tour, or a 2.5-hour "Postcard San Francisco" tour that makes four or five stops. Why the name? The owner says, "Thanks to our propane-powered engines, our vehicles have 60% fewer ozone-forming emissions than gasoline. We figure that toads are green, and so are we!"

TOURS: By Fire Engine

San Francisco Fire Engine Tours & Adventures
Depart from The Cannery, Fisherman's Wharf. (415) 333-7077; www.fireenginetours.com. W-M at 1; some additional tours. $45, 13-17 $35, under 13 $25. Reservations advised.

This happy, exhilarating 75-minute excursion takes sightseers over the Golden Gate Bridge in a bright-red 1955 Mack fire engine. Because it can get chilly in the open-air truck, authentic insulated fire-fighter jackets are available for passengers to bundle up in. Children get a lesson in fire safety through original sing-along songs. After, the tour guides go back to their home inside a vintage firehouse.

TOURS: On Foot

San Francisco is a walker's paradise. The city's naturally intriguing streets become even more so when walked with a knowledgeable guide. Even natives learn something new on such as tour.

City Guides
(415) 557-4266; www.sfcityguides.org. Free.

Sponsored by the San Francisco Public Library, these informative tours last approximately 1½ hours and cover most areas of the city. Among the many options are: Alamo Square, City Hall, Coit Tower Murals, Haight-Ashbury, Historic Market Street, Japantown, Mission Murals, Nob Hill, North Beach, Pacific Heights Mansions, Presidio Walk, Union Square.

Dashiell Hammett Tour
Civic Center; www.donherron.com. Schedule varies. $10, under 15 free.

While dashing off trivia and anecdotes, guide Don Herron leads walkers to landmarks from *The Maltese Falcon* and to all Hammett's known San Francisco residences. Herron, who is always appropriately attired in trench coat and fedora, has operated this tour since 1977. Said to be the longest ongoing literary tour in the country, it lasts 4 hours and covers approximately 3 miles.

Golden Gate Park Walking Tours
For description, see page 34.

Local Tastes of the City Tours
(888) 358-TOUR, (415) 665-0480; www.sffoodtour.com. Daily at 10, 2, & 6. $59, 15-18 $39, 8-14 $15.

These slow, easy walks are designed to uncover the soul of Chinatown or North Beach and to expose and help preserve the area's food artisans. The enthusiastic guide also tosses in a bit of enlightening history, architecture, and politics. Stops are made at local bakeries, restaurants, and cafes for tastings and sometimes to observe production. Participants might meet an

Asian calligrapher whose family has honed the craft for thousands of years, a baker using old family recipes, or a crab fisherman whose family has been in the business for generations. Each tour ends with an optional restaurant meal.

Mission Trail Mural Walk
Depart from 2981 24th St./Harrison St., Mission District, (415) 285-2287; www.precitaeyes.org. Sat-Sun at 1:30. $10-$12, 13-17 $5, under 12 $2.

Sponsored by the Precita Eyes Mural Arts Center, this 2-hour walk is led by a professional muralist and views more than 75 of the 300-plus murals found in the Mission District. The afternoon walk includes a slide show and talk by a professional muralist.

Pacific Heights Walking Tour
For description, see page 22.

Victorian Home Walk
Pacific Heights, (415) 252-9485; www.victorianwalk.com. Daily at 11; leaves from Union Square. $20.

Learn the differences between the three Victorian house styles—Italianate, Stick, and Queen Anne. This educational walking tour goes where tour buses and mini vans are prohibited. After a short public bus ride, explorations begin with the interior of a Queen Anne B&B and end with the exterior of the *Mrs. Doubtfire* Queen Anne. The 2½-hour tour is over mostly flat terrain in Pacific Heights and Cow Hollow and provides the chance to get off the beaten path and focus on a quiet city neighborhood. After, participants are on their own to lunch on Union Street or take a public bus back to Union Square via North Beach and Chinatown.

Wok Wiz Walking Tours
Chinatown, (650) 355-9657; www.wokwiz.com. Daily at 10am. $40 with lunch, $30 without lunch; under 11 $35/$25. Reservations required.

Led by cookbook author and TV chef Shirley Fong-Torres and her staff, the basic Chinatown Tour involves no hills and takes participants behind the scenes and into the heartbeat of this colorful and historic neighborhood. A dim sum lunch is optional. More theme tours are available.

For more Chinatown walks, see page 17.

TOURS: Factory

Anchor Brewing Company

1705 Mariposa St./DeHaro St., Potrero Hill,
(415) 863-8350; www.anchorbrewing.com. Tour &
tasting M-F in aft. Free. Reservations required.

    This compact brewery was founded in the
1890s, when it started producing the locally
popular Anchor Steam beer. It is San Francisco's
only remaining brewery. The tour concludes
with a tasting. Children are welcome but, of
course, may not taste.

HISTORICAL SITES

Alcatraz Island

www.nps.gov/alcatraz. Depart from Pier 33, on The
Embarcadero betw. Chestnut & Bay sts., (415)-981-
ROCK; www.alcatrazcruises.com. Daily departures;
schedule varies. $24.50, 62+ $23.25, 5-11 $15.25,
includes audio tour. Reservations advised.

    Before Alcatraz opened to the public in
1973, it served as a fort in the 19th century and
as a federal penitentiary from 1934 to 1963.
Native Americans occupied it from 1969 to
1971. During the time it was a maximum security prison, it was home to some of the country's most hardened criminals, including Al
Capone, George "Machine Gun" Kelly, and
Robert "The Birdman" Stroud. Now it is run by
the National Park Service as part of the Golden
Gate National Recreation Area—the largest
urban park in the world—and is the most

visited landmark in the U.S. And it is as good as
it's cracked up to be—the boat ride, the tour,
and the 360-degree bay view. After a short,
scenic ride to this infamous island (its name
translates as "island of the pelicans"), visitors
follow a self-guided audio tour of the cell block,
narrated in part by former inmates and guards.
It is interesting to note that the 84-foot-tall
lighthouse still operates (when the original
214-foot-tall lighthouse was built here in 1854,
it was the first on the West Coast). Picnicking
is not permitted. Wear comfortable shoes, dress
warmly, and expect cool, windy weather—
even in summer. If the standard tour is sold out
(once Alcatraz was hard to get out of; now it
is hard to get in to), consider the more expensive Island Hop, which makes a stop at Angel
Island and then at Alcatraz, or the Night Tour,
which provides the opportunity to see this
fascinating site without crowds. Note that the
full-service restaurants at Pier 39 provide a
discounted parking validation for the Pier 39
garage.

Cable Cars

(415) 673-MUNI; www.sfmta.com,
www.cablecarmuseum.org/ride.html. Daily 6am-1am.
$5, under 5 free.

    Before these beloved objects were devel-
oped by Andrew Hallidie in 1873, horses had
to pull cars up the city's steep hills. Now, 26
"single-enders" operate on the two Powell Street
routes and 12 "double-enders" operate on
California Street. (Single-ended cable cars have
controls only at one end and need to use a
turntable at the end of the line to reverse
direction. Double-ended cars have controls at
both ends and need only a crossover track to
turn back.) Catch the Powell-Hyde line at the
turnaround located at the base of Powell Street
(at Market Street) and ride it up and over the
hills all the way to Aquatic Park. This line goes
down the steepest hill and affords the most
breathtaking views. The Powell-Mason line
ends at Bay Street at Fisherman's Wharf. The
less-used California Street line begins at Market
Street and runs along California Street, passes
Chinatown and then climbs over Nob Hill,
ending at Van Ness Avenue. Riders can also
board at designated stops along the routes.

Chinatown

Bounded by Broadway, Bush St., Kearny St., &
Powell St.; www.sanfranciscochinatown.com.

With a population of approximately 80,000 residents and covering 24 square blocks, San Francisco's Chinatown is the largest Chinese community outside of Asia. The most memorable way to enter the area is on foot through the ornate dragon-crested archway located at Grant Avenue and Bush Street. Designed to the Taoist principles of Feng Shui, the gate features Foo dogs to scare away evil spirits, dragons for fertility and power, and fish for prosperity. A walk along pedestrian-crowded Grant Avenue, the city's oldest street, is quite an experience. For good souvenir hunting, stop in at one of the many shops. Favorite items with children include golden dragon-decorated velvet slippers, rice candy in edible wrappers, and silk coin purses.

• Chinese Culture Center of San Francisco

750 Kearny St./Washington St., 3rd fl.,
(415) 986-1822; www.c-c-c.org. Tu-Sun 10-4; closed
last 2 wks. in Dec. Free.

This two-room gallery displays rotating exhibits of historical and contemporary Chinese art by both native Chinese and Chinese-Americans.

Cultural and culinary tours of Chinatown sponsored by the Chinese Culture Foundation are scheduled year-round. All require reservations and work best with children 8 and older. The **Heritage Walk** *(W at 10:30, Sat at 10:30 & 1. $20, under 12 $12.)* stresses the history and cultural achievements of the area. Stops might include a Chinese temple and historical society. The **Culinary Walk** *(By appt. $60, under 12 $30.)* introduces Chinese cuisine with stops in markets and at a fortune cookie factory, herb shop, and tea shop. It concludes with a dim sum lunch.

• Chinese Historical Society of America, Museum and Learning Center

965 Clay St./Powell St., (415) 391-1188; www.chsa.org.
Tu-F 12-5, Sat 11-4. $3, seniors $2, 6-17 $1; free 1st
Thur of month.

Situated within a building designed by Julia Morgan for the YWCA, this museum's new location displays approximately 50,000 artifacts relating to Chinese immigration and Chinese Americans. Among the items displayed are a Chinese fishing junk and a water cannon used in gold mining.

• Dim Sum

Translated variously as meaning "touch of heart," "touch your heart," "heart's desire," and "heart's delight," dim sum items originally were served for breakfast during China's Tang Dynasty (618 to 907 A.D.) A meal of these appetizers makes an interesting change of pace for breakfast or lunch, and there is no better place to try the cuisine than here—San Francisco is said to have more dim sum parlors than any other city in the U.S.

Dim sum includes steamed buns, fried dumplings, and turnovers, as well as delicacies such as steamed duck beaks and chicken feet. It is great fun to pick and choose from items brought around to tables Hong Kong-style on carts or trays. Be aware that it can be difficult to find out what a particular item is composed of, as sometimes servers don't speak English or understand it very well.

Sometimes tea arrives automatically and is then usually complimentary. When diners are given a choice of styles, usually there is a charge. The three most common kinds are mild green, semi-fermented oolong, and strong fermented black. Chrysanthemum combines black tea with dried flowers, and jasmine combines oolong with dried flowers. For a tea refill, do as the Chinese do and signal the waiter by turning over the lid on the teapot. Some establishments also offer other drinks.

Note that although crossed chopsticks usually are considered an omen of bad luck, in dim sum houses they signal the server that the diner is finished.

Though this quaint custom is rapidly dying, the bill in some restaurants is determined by how many serving plates remain on the table at meal's end. (This concept is reminiscent of the tiny hill town of San Gimignano in Italy, which once had 70 bell towers. A family's wealth there was measured by the height of its bell tower.) To keep a running tab, just make a stack of the serving plates and steamers as they are emptied. Most teahouses charge about $2 to $4.50 per plate, and tips are usually divided by the entire staff.

• **Dim Sum restaurants**
  • **Gold Mountain** See page 72.
  • **New Asia** See page 78.
Excellent dim sum spots that are not located in Chinatown include:
  • **Ton Kiang** See page 85.
  • **Yank Sing** See page 86.

• **Fortune Cookie Factories**
Always fun is a walk through the narrow Chinatown streets and alleys to find a fortune cookie factory. Though workers aren't often pleased to see tourists, it is usually possible to get at least a glimpse of the action by peeking in through a door or window. Nowadays, the traditional hand-folding of cookies is giving way to intricate machines invented in San Francisco in the 1970s by Edward Louie. Proprietors are usually glad to sell cookies, and bags of broken "misfortune" cookies can be purchased at bargain prices.
  • **Golden Gate Fortune Cookies Co.**
56 Ross Alley/Washington St., (415) 781-3956. Daily 9-8:30. Free.
Tucked away in a picturesque alley in the heart of Chinatown, this is the only fortune cookie factory in town that still makes cookies by hand. It also sells delicious mini-almond cookies.
  • **Mee Mee Bakery**
1328 Stockton St./Broadway, (415) 362-3204; www.meemeebakery.com. Daily 8-6.
Located at the border of Chinatown and North Beach, this factory has been baking fortune cookies since 1948—longer than anyone else in town. It also sells x-rated, giant, and chocolate and strawberry versions as well as mini-almond cookies.

• **Herb shop**
  • **Superior Trading Co.**
835 Washington St./Grant Ave., (415)495-7988; www.superiortrading.com. Daily 9:30-6.
This somewhat mysterious shop measures out aromatic herbs on scales. Unless actually planning to purchase something, it is best just to peek in the window.

• **Restaurants**
Though locals often claim good Chinese restaurants aren't found in Chinatown, in reality some are.
  • **Brandy Ho's Hunan Food** See page 63.
  • **Far East Cafe** See page 70.
  • **House of Nanking** See page 73.
  • **The Pot Sticker** See page 81.
  • **R&G Lounge** See page 81.
  • **Sam Wo** See page 81.

• **Temple**
Though there are many temples in Chinatown, only one seems to welcome visitors.
  • **Tien Hau Temple**
125 Waverly Pl./Washington St., 4th fl. Daily 10-5 & 7-9pm. Donations appreciated.
Named after the goddess of the heavens and seas—who protects sailors, prostitutes, actors, and writers—this temple is located in the heart of Chinatown on a lane known for its ornate, colorfully-painted balconies. Built in 1852 and the oldest Taoist temple in the U.S., it is easy to find—just follow the scent of incense up the narrow wooden stairs. Bear in mind that the temple still is used for worship, and reverent behavior is expected.

City Lights Books
261 Columbus Ave./Broadway, North Beach, (415) 362-8193; www.citylights.com. Daily 10am-midnight.
Founded in 1953 by beatnik poet Lawrence Ferlinghetti, who still looks after the business, this multi-level independent bookstore was the first in the country to specialize in paperbacks. Many obscure titles are in its eclectic collection, providing great browsing. Don't miss stepping into the small press poetry alcove or traipsing down the creaky wooden stairs into the large subterranean space. Not content just to sell books, the proprietors published Allen Ginsberg's *Howl* and continue to publish unusual books. The bookstore was given landmark status in 2001.

Coit Tower

At top of Lombard St., North Beach, (415) 362-0808. Daily 10-6:30. $4.50, 65+ $3.50, 6-12 $2.

This 210-foot-tall tower (approximately 18 stories) located atop fashionable Telegraph Hill offers a magnificent 360-degree view that includes the Golden Gate and Bay bridges and Lombard Street. Resembling the nozzle of a fire hose, it was built in 1933 as a memorial to the city's volunteer fire department. Colorful murals painted on the ground floor walls in 1934 depict area activities during the Depression. They were controversial at the time because of left-wing political content. The admission fee includes an attendant-operated elevator ride to the top. Parking is extremely limited.

Visitors can take the 39 Coit bus up, then walk down the **Filbert Street Steps** (keep an eye and ear out for the wild parrots that live in this area—made famous by Mark Bittner's book, *The Wild Parrots of Telegraph Hill*—and for Napier Lane—made famous by Armistead Maupin's novel, *Tales of the City*) and see some charming 19th-century cottages as well as the Grace Marchant Garden, exiting onto Levi Plaza near Battery Street.

Crookedest Street in the World

Lombard St. betw. Hyde St. & Leavenworth St., Russian Hill.

This famous curvy street is one way downhill. Drivers must maneuver over a bumpy brick-paved road with eight tight turns while trying not to be distracted by the magnificent view. Get here by driving up the steep incline on the west side of Lombard Street, or, for an easier time of it, drive up from the south side of Hyde Street.

The **other crookedest street** is Vermont Street between 22nd and 23rd streets on Potrero Hill. Though it has only six turns, they are said to be tighter than Lombard's.

The **shortest crooked street** is Octavia Street between Jackson and Washington streets in Pacific Heights. It is a charming, brick-paved mini-Lombard.

The city's **steepest streets** are Filbert Street between Hyde and Leavenworth streets (with a 31.5% grade), 22nd Street between Church and Vicksburg streets (also with a 31.5% grade), and Jones Street between Union and Filbert streets (with a 29% grade).

Ferry Building Marketplace

For description, see page 70.

Fisherman's Wharf

For description, see page 39.

Fort Mason

Laguna St./Marina Blvd., Marina District, (415) 441-3400; www.fortmason.org. Parking approx. $2/hr.

In addition to housing the park headquarters for the Golden Gate National Recreation Area, this complex of buildings is home to theaters, art galleries, museums, and myriad other facilities. Highlights include:

• **Book Bay Bookstore**

Bldg. C, (415) 771-1076; www.friendssfpl.org. Daily 11-5.

Thousands of bargain books, records, and tapes are on sale here, and the West's largest **Used Book Sale** is held each September. Proceeds benefit the San Francisco Public Library.

• **Greens** restaurant

For description, see page 72.

• **Magic Theatre**

For description, see page 37.

• **Museo ItaloAmericano**

For description, see page 24.

• **Young Performers Theatre**

For description, see page 39.

Fort Point National Historic Site

Located directly under the south anchorage of the Golden Gate Bridge, at end of Marine Dr., The Presidio; take Lincoln Blvd. to Long Ave., turn left, at bottom follow road along water to fort; (415) 556-1693; www.nps.gov/fopo. F-Sun 10-5; cannon demonstration at 12, tour at 3. Free.

Built in 1861, this is the only Civil War-era fort on the West Coast. Its four tiers once held 126 cannons; now several 10,000 pound-plus originals and replicas are displayed. It is perhaps even more famous as the site in Hitchcock's *Vertigo* where Kim Novak's character jumped into the bay.

Candlelight Fort Tours *(Nov-Feb; 6:30-8pm. Must be age 15+. Reservations required.)* occur each winter. Participants see the fort from the viewpoint of a Civil War soldier. What was it like in the 1860s to live in drafty quarters heated by fireplaces and lighted by candles? What kind of food did the soldiers eat and how was it prepared? A walk through the 1870 gun emplacements located south of the fort concludes each tour.

Golden Gate Bridge

The bridge does not have a physical address. To stop at the plaza, turn right at the last S.F. exit off Hwy. 101 just before the toll plaza. The sign reads "Golden Gate National Recreation Area view area." At the stop sign, turn left into the southeast parking lot. (415) 921-5858; www.goldengatebridge.org. $5 toll for southbound vehicles, free for northbound vehicles; free for pedestrians and bicyclists.

Once called "the bridge that couldn't be built," this magnificent example of man's ingenuity and perseverance is one of San Francisco's most famous sights. Though it is no longer the longest suspension bridge in the world, it measures 6,450 feet, or approximately 1.7 miles, and its 746-foot-high towers remain the tallest ever built. Many visitors are disappointed to discover that the bridge is not a golden color. Its dull red-orange protective coating is known officially as International Orange and was chosen by the bridge's architect, Irving Morrow, to make it visible in dense fog. In fact, the bridge takes its colorful name from the strait of San Francisco, which in 1846 John C. Fremont dubbed the Golden Gate because of its resemblance to the harbor of Constantinople, known as the Golden Horn. Crossing it is a must—by car, foot, or bicycle. The round-trip is about 2 miles, and views are breathtaking.

Grace Cathedral

1100 California St./Taylor St., Nob Hill, (415) 749-6300; www.gracecathedral.org. Daily 8-6; tour M-F 1-3, Sat 11:30-1:30, Sun 12:30-2. Free.

Located atop Nob Hill, this majestic French Gothic cathedral stands 265 feet tall and is the largest in the western U.S. It is graced with more than 60 opulent stained-glass windows, and its gilded bronze entrance doors are exact replicas of Lorenzo Ghiberti's "Doors of Paradise" at the Baptistry in Florence, Italy. Concerts using the cathedral's renowned 7,286-pipe organ are scheduled often, sometimes accompanied by the 44-bell carillon. The cathedral's reverberant acoustics and architecturally magnificent interior make these memorable experiences.

Walking **labyrinths**—a unique tool for meditation and enlightenment and said to be a metaphor for entering one's center—are located both inside the cathedral and outside on a plaza. (A labyrinth is different from a maze,

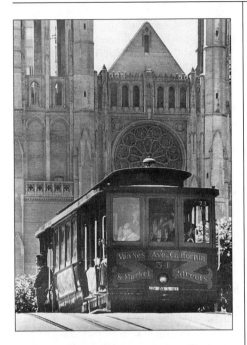

rough around the edges, and Haight Street is now lined with an assortment of colorful boutiques and inexpensive restaurants and coffeehouses. Wavy Gravy describes his neighborhood as "a coexistence between the punks and the hippies, a little cutting-edge U.N. in action." See also page 41.

Visiting here permits the chance to see some of the area's magnificent Victorian houses, including the one at 710 Ashbury Street, where the Grateful Dead once resided, and the mansion at 2400 Fulton Street, where the Jefferson Airplane lived. Janis Joplin once lived with Country Joe McDonald in apartment 3 at 112 Page Street, Big Brother & the Holding Company formed at 1090 Page Street, and the first free medical clinic in the U.S. still operates at 558 Clayton Street. On a more somber note, the notorious Manson "family" once lived at 636 Cole Street.

Historical houses

San Francisco is known for its abundance of beautiful turn-of-the-century Victorian houses. At last count there were more than 14,000. One of the pleasures of living here is visiting people who actually reside in them. Visitors to the city interested in capturing a taste of that delight can visit two historic homes that are open to the public.

To see some of the city's "painted ladies," as the many colorfully painted Victorian homes sometimes are called, visit the area around Alamo Square at Hayes and Steiner streets. Nicknamed "Postcard Row," 710 to 720 Steiner holds six Queen Anne Victorians known as the Six Sisters and is often photographed commercially from the top of the park with the skyline in the distance. "Postcard Row" appears in the opening credits of TV's *Full House*. Another good area is along the Golden Gate Park Panhandle, particularly on the Fell Street side, where well-maintained mansions are plentiful. (It is interesting to note that the Panhandle was originally the carriage entrance to the park and that it holds approximately 50 species of the park's oldest trees.)

And, of course, everyone wants to see the house used in exterior scenes for *Mrs. Doubtfire*. Check it out in Pacific Heights at 2640 Steiner Street. Interior scenes were filmed in a studio so there is no need to peek in windows.

which is a puzzle and designed to confuse.) Patterned after one at Chartres cathedral, these were the first permanent labyrinths laid in the Western hemisphere in 600 years.

Annual **Cathedral Choir Christmas Concerts** include the Grace Cathedral Choir of Men and Boys singing both traditional and new carols. They are wondrous, inspirational events. A Festival of Lessons and a Midnight Mass are traditional on Christmas Eve, and a celebratory New Year's Eve event is scheduled each year. Also, every few years the cathedral is the unusual, yet appropriate, setting for a screening of the original 1923 silent film classic *The Hunchback of Notre Dame* with live organ accompaniment.

Down the hill, **Old St. Mary's Cathedral** *(660 California St., Chinatown, (415) 288-3800; www.oldsaintmarys.org.)* was built of brick in 1853 and was the West Coast's first Roman Catholic cathedral.

Haight-Ashbury
Haight St. betw. Stanyan St. & Masonic St.

It's almost possible to step back in time here to the Summer of Love. A few locals still don bell-bottoms, tie-dyed shirts, and love beads, and these items are still for sale in some shops. Not yet gentrified, the area is a little

• Haas-Lilienthal House
2007 Franklin St./Jackson St., Pacific Heights,
(415) 441-3004; www.sfheritage.org. House tour:
W & some Sat 12-3, Sun 11-4; $8, 62+ & under 12 $5.
No baby strollers. Walking tour: Sun at 12:30; $8, 62+
& under 12 $5.

In 1886 architect Peter R. Schmidt built this 24-room, 7½-bathroom Queen Anne Victorian home of fir and redwood for Bertha and William Haas, a mercantile grocer. It cost $18,500 (average homes then cost about $2,000). The house survived the infamous 1906 earthquake relatively unscathed, with a small bulge in the plaster the only visible damage. It also escaped the fire that followed, though Mr. Haas's downtown offices were destroyed. Family members occupied the house until 1972. Most of the furnishings are original to the house, including a lovely and extensive set of matching art nouveau pieces in the main bedroom. Children often find the doll house in the second-floor nursery especially interesting.

The **Pacific Heights Walking Tour** of the surrounding neighborhood focuses on the exteriors of some of San Francisco's finest Victorian and Edwardian homes.

• Octagon House
2645 Gough St./Union St., Cow Hollow,
(415) 441-7512. 2nd & 4th Thur & 2nd Sun of month,
12-3; closed Jan. By donation.

Built in 1861, when this architectural style was a fad throughout the country, this eight-sided house is now one of only two left in San Francisco. The National Society of The Colonial Dames of America in California has restored and furnished it and turned it into the only museum of Colonial and Federal decorative arts on the West Coast. Items displayed date from 1700 to 1830. Of special interest is a display featuring the signatures of 54 of the 56 signers of the Declaration of Independence. The house's well-groomed garden and adjacent **Allyne Park** are both perfect for a stroll.

Market Street Railway F-Line
Runs for 5 mi. along Market St., from Castro St. to
The Embarcadero, and along the waterfront to Jones
St. at Fisherman's Wharf, (415) 956-0472; www.street
car.org. Daily 6am-1am. $1.50, 65+ & 5-17 50¢.

Vintage electric trolley cars from around the world, San Francisco's own historic streetcar fleet, and even New Orleans' famous streetcar named Desire are all part of this line.

Mission San Francisco de Asis
3321 16th St./Dolores St., Mission District, (415) 621-
8203; www.missiondolores.org. Daily 9-4, in summer
to 4:30. $5, 65+ & 5-12 $3, audio tour $5.

Known commonly as **Mission Dolores**, this relatively small mission is sixth in California's chain of 21. The mission church, completed in 1791, is the oldest intact building in the city and is still used for services. Its cool adobe and redwood interior offers pleasant respite from the occasional hot San Francisco day. Of special interest is the ceiling, painted in Ohlone tribal patterns and colors originally produced by vegetable dyes. A picturesque enclosed cemetery garden is landscaped to period correctness. It contains an Ohlone tule reed house, and all the plants growing here were once used in some way by resident Native Americans. The mission's cemetery is one of only two remaining in San Francisco (the other is at the Presido), and, although only 200 tombstones are visible, 5,000 people are actually buried on the mission site. A small museum completes the complex.

Presidio of San Francisco
Lombard St./Lyon St., (415) 561-4323;
www.nps.gov/prsf, www.presidio.gov. Daily 10-5. Free.

Used as a military garrison by Spain, Mexico, and the U.S., the Presidio was established by Spain in 1776, taken over by Mexico in 1822, and then taken over by the U.S. as an Army post in 1846. It played a role in every major military conflict for the next century and a half and also was critical in providing refuge to the 1906 earthquake victims. The Presidio is undergoing continuous major changes as it transforms from an Army post into a recreational area. Hiking and biking trails are available. Begin a visit of the Main Post at the Visitor Center in the Officers' Club. And don't miss the charming Pet Cemetery or the poignant San Francisco National Cemetery.

• Crissy Field Center
603 Mason St./Halleck St., at the shoreline of The Presidio, (415) 561-7690; www.crissyfield.org. Visitor Center & warming hut: Daily 9-5. Free.

The post's former landing strip is now a spectacular shoreline park, with several boardwalks leading through the scenic dunes and restored tidal marsh. A large grassy expanse for unstructured play and a nature center are part of the facility, and picnic tables are available. A former torpedo depot, the Visitor Center cafe is a model of sustainability. It uses recycled products, and the deli menu is prepared with mostly local organic products. A warming hut also has a small cafe and provides remarkable views of the Golden Gate Bridge.

MUSEUMS

Many museums are concentrated in the Yerba Buena area South of Market: San Francisco Museum of Modern Art, Museum of Craft and Folk Art, Museum of the African Diaspora, Cartoon Art Museum, California Historical Society, and Contemporary Jewish Museum.

Art Museums

Asian Art Museum
200 Larkin St./Fulton St., Civic Center, (415) 581-3500; www.asianart.org. Tu-Sun 10-5, Thur to 9. $12, 65+ $8, 13-17 $7; free on 1st Sun of month; free audio tour.

Newly relocated in the 1917 Beaux-Arts building that was the city's main library until 1994—the redesign was done by architect Gae Aulenti, who also converted a derelict Paris train station into the celebrated Musée d'Orsay—this is the largest museum in the Western world devoted exclusively to Asian art. And with more than 15,000 objects from 40 Asian countries spanning a period of more than 6,000 years, it is the best Asian collection in the U.S. (At any one time it displays 2,500 objects in its 33 galleries representing 7 Asian cultural regions.) The museum also holds the largest collection of Indian sculpture outside India. Combining East and West, the building represents San Francisco's past and future. Children especially enjoy viewing the Indonesian rod puppets.

Cartoon Art Museum
655 Mission St./3rd St., South of Market, (415) CARTOON; www.cartoonart.org. Tu-Sun 11-5. $6, 62+ $4, 6-12 $2; pay what you wish on 1st Tu of month.

This museum showcases important developments in cartoon history from the early 18th century to the present. One of only two such museums in the country, its aim is "to preserve this unique art form and to enrich the public's knowledge of its cultural and aesthetic value."

Fine Arts Museums of San Francisco
www.famsf.org.

• de Young
50 Hagiwara Tea Garden Dr., in Golden Gate Park, (415) 750-3600; www.deyoungmuseum.org. Tu-Sun 9:30-5:15, F to 8:45. $10, 65+ $7, 13-17 $6; free on 1st Tu of month; tickets may be used on the same day for free entrance to the Legion of Honor.

Housed now in a monumental new building that seems as if it grew organically right out of the park, the city's premier museum holds a significant collection of American paintings, sculpture, and decorative arts from the 17th through 21st centuries, as well as the country's best collection of American trompe l'oeil paintings from the late 1800s. The permanent collection of art from Africa, Oceania, Mesoamerica, and Central and South America features outstanding works from ancient to modern times

and an extraordinary collection of New Guinea art. Some contemporary art is displayed and a sculpture garden is adjacent to the café, which serves delicious fare and has both indoor and outdoor seating. Do visit the 9th floor of the tower for a breath-taking 360-degree view.

For three days every March the museum galleries are decorated stunningly with fresh flowers. For **Bouquets to Art**, members of Bay Area flower clubs and professional florists design arrangements inspired by museum paintings. Some mimic the paintings, other pick up the colors or feeling; overall, they enliven the galleries.

• Legion of Honor
100 34th Ave./Clement St., in Lincoln Park, Outer Richmond District, (415) 750-3600; www.legionofhonor.org. Tu-Sun 9:30-5:15. $10, 65+ $7, 13-17 $6; free on 1st Tu of month; tickets may be used on the same day for free entrance to the deYoung.

Situated on a scenic knoll overlooking the Golden Gate Bridge, this is the only museum in the country exhibiting primarily French art. Rodin's earliest casting of his sculpture, "The Thinker," greets visitors as they approach the entrance to this impressive neoclassical marble structure—a ¾ replica of the Palais de la Legion d'Honneur in Paris, where Napoleon established his new Order of the Legion of Honor in the 18th century. The museum's collection of Rodins is outstanding and were cast by the artist, and a small glass pyramid in the entry seems to make a nod to the larger one at Paris's Louvre. This museum also holds the city's collection of European and ancient art, and it presents free organ concerts on weekends at 4 p.m. The museum was given to the city of San Francisco on Armistice Day in 1924 and is dedicated to the memory of California men who died in World War I. A cafe offers simple food with a French flair as well as a dining room and terrace with a view.

The entrance to the **Holocaust Memorial** is on the north side of the parking circle. A semicircular stairway leads down to an area where cast bronze, white-painted pieces created by sculptor George Segal are displayed.

For a scenic drive, leave via Lincoln Avenue, on the north side of the museum. Follow it to its conclusion at Lombard Street. This route has several vista points of the Golden Gate Bridge. It passes by Baker Beach,

goes through the elegant Sea Cliff residential area, and continues into the Presidio.

Museo ItaloAmericano
Fort Mason Center, Bldg. C, Laguna St./Marina Blvd., Marina District, (415) 673-2200; www.museoitaloamericano.org. Tu-Sun 12-4. Free.

This small museum is dedicated to displaying the works of Italian and Italian-American artists.

Museum of Craft & Folk Art
51 Yerba Buena Lane/betw. Mission & Market sts. near 3rd St., South of Market, (415) 227-4888; www.mocfa.org. Tu-F 11-6, Sat-Sun 10-5 . $5, 62+$4, under 18 free.

Located on a pedestrian-only street, this museum is a showcase for high quality contemporary crafts and folk art. Exhibits change every two months.

A few doors down, **Beard Papa** *(99 Yerba Buena Lane, (415) 978-9972; www.beardpapasf.com. M-Sat 10-8, Sun 10-6:30; $.)* offers a menu of sweets, including what they claim are the world's best cream puffs. Puffs are stuffed with custard in a variety of flavors, and éclairs are also on the menu.

San Francisco Museum of Modern Art
151 3rd St./Howard St., South of Market, (415) 357-4000; www.sfmoma.org. Thur-Tu 11-5:45, Thur to 8:45; in summer from 10am. $11.50, 62+ $8, under 13 free; half-price Thur 6-9; free 1st Tu of month; audio tours $3-$6.

Located within a striking contemporary building designed by Mario Botta of Lugano, Switzerland, this museum was the first in the

West devoted entirely to 20th-century art. Its collection includes abstract art, photography, and the work of acclaimed contemporary artists. The most efficient way to see everything is to take the elevator to the fifth floor and work down.

The museum gift shop has an array of exceptional merchandise and a particularly noteworthy section for children, and casual **Caffe Museo** *((415) 357-4500.)* offers a menu of scrumptious meals and light snacks.

Floating Museums

The collection of historic ships berthed along the San Francisco waterfront is the largest (by weight) in the world.

San Francisco Maritime National Historical Park
Fisherman's Wharf, (415) 447-5000; www.nps.gov/safr. Visitor Center: 499 Jefferson St.; daily 9:30-5, in summer to 7; free.

• Maritime Museum
900 Beach St./foot of Polk St., across from Ghirardelli Square.

This museum is closed for repairs until 2009.

• Hyde Street Pier
2905 Hyde St./Jefferson St. Daily 9:30-5; in summer to 5:30. $5, under 17 free.

The vessels moored on this scenic pier represent the late 19th century—a time of rapid growth for San Francisco begun by the 1849 Gold Rush and an era during which the city was an important shipping center. Visitors can board four:

• *Balclutha* A Cape Horn sailing ship built in Scotland in 1886, this 301-foot steel-hulled merchant ship carried whiskey, wool, and rice, but mainly coal, to San Francisco. On her return sailing to Europe she carried grain from California. Typical of Victorian British merchant ships, she is described colorfully by the men who sailed her as a "blue water, square-rigged, lime juice windbag." She is the last of the Cape Horn fleet and ended her sailing career as an Alaskan salmon ship. She opened to the public in 1955. A fascinating way to experience this ship is at a **chantey sing** *((415) 561-7171. Adult program 1st Sat of month,*

Balclutha

8pm-12; children's program 3rd Sat at 2. Free. Reservations required.) held in her cozy hold. Participants should dress warmly and bring a cushion to sit on, a mug for hot cider to wet the whistle, and a chantey or two to share.

• *C.A. Thayer* A fleet of 900 ships once carried lumber from the north coast forests to California ports. This is one of only two that still exist. A three-mast lumber schooner built in Fairhaven (near Eureka) in 1895, she was the very last commercial sailing ship in use on the West Coast and made her last voyage in 1950 as a fishing ship.

• *Eureka* Originally named the *Ukiah*, this double-ended, wooden-hulled ferry was built in Tiburon in 1890 to carry railroad cars and passengers across the bay. She was rebuilt in 1922 to carry automobiles and passengers and renamed the *Eureka*. Later she served as a commuter ferry (the largest in the world) between San Francisco and Sausalito, and yet later as a ferry for train passengers arriving in San Francisco from Oakland. She held 2,300 people plus 120 automobiles. Her 4-story "walking beam" steam engine is the only one still afloat in the U.S. A model demonstrates its operation, and a ranger-guided tour through the engine room is sometimes available. Two decks are open to the public. The lower deck houses a display of antique cars, and the main deck features original benches and a historical photo display.

Chantey sing in Balclutha

• **Hercules** This ocean-going tugboat was built in 1907.

More ships are moored at the pier but are not usually open for boarding. The ***Alma***, a scow schooner built in 1891 at Hunters Point, is a specialized cargo carrier and the last of her kind still afloat. The ***Eppleton Hall***, built in England in 1914 and used in the canals there to tow coal barges, is the only vessel in the collection not directly associated with West Coast maritime history.

Non-floating displays at the pier include a late 19th-century ark (houseboat), a restored donkey engine that is sometimes operated for visitors, and the reconstructed sales office of the Tubbs Cordage Company.

S.S. Jeremiah O'Brien

Pier 45, foot of Taylor St., Fisherman's Wharf, (415) 544-0100; www.ssjeremiahobrien.com. Daily 10-4. $8, 62+ $5, 6-14 $4.

This massive 441-foot-long vessel is the last unaltered Liberty Ship from World War II still in operating condition. Between 1941 and 1945, in an all-out effort to replace the cargo ships being sunk in huge numbers by enemy submarines, 2,751 Liberty Ships were built to transport troops and supplies. Shipyards operated around the clock. Assembled from pre-fabricated sections, each ship took only

between 6 and 8 weeks to build. Shockingly large, the *O'Brien* was built in South Portland, Maine in 1943. She was in operation for 33 years and sailed from England to Normandy during the D-Day invasion. In 1978 she was declared a national monument. Since then, dedicated volunteers—many of whom served on similar ships—have worked to restore her to her original glory. Visitors have access to almost every part of the ship, including the sleeping and captain's quarters, wheelhouse, and guns, as well as the catwalks in the eerie 3-story engine room. The triple expansion steam engine operates on the third weekend of each month.

An annual fund-raising **Seamen's Memorial Cruise** occurs in May, and **Fleet Week Cruises** occur in October.

USS Pampanito

Pier 45, foot of Taylor St., Fisherman's Wharf, (415) 775-1943; www.maritime.org. Daily from 9am, closing time varies. $9, 62+ $5, 6-12 $3.

This 312-foot-long World War II submarine built in Portsmouth, New Hampshire in 1943 is credited with sinking six Japanese ships and damaging four others. She also rescued a group of British and Australian POWs from the South China Sea. The self-guided tour through her cramped belly and meticulously restored compartments is enhanced with a recorded audio tour that provides narrative by former crew members and helps listeners imagine what it must have been like for men to be cooped up in this small space for months at a time.

Science Museums

California Academy of Sciences
55 Concourse Dr., (415) 379-8000; www.calacademy.org. M-Sat 9:30-5, Sun 11-5. $24.95, 65+ & 12-17 $19.95, 7-11 $14.95; free on 3rd W of month.

This oldest scientific institution in the West was founded in 1853 following the Gold Rush. Newly rebuilt, it combines an aquarium, planetarium, natural history museum, and scientific research facilities under one roof. Visitors can explore the outer reaches of the galaxy in the world's largest all-digital planetarium, get a bird's-eye view of the humid canopy of a Costa Rican rainforest, and enjoy the view beneath the waves at the world's deepest display of living corals. The new building is topped with a 2.5-acre living roof and employs a wide range of energy-saving materials and technologies. More than 38,000 live animals fill the aquarium and natural history exhibits, one of the most diverse collections of live animals at any museum or aquarium in the world.

Exploratorium
3601 Lyon St./Marina Blvd., Marina District, (415) EXP-LORE; www.exploratorium.edu. Tu-Sun 10-5. $14, 65+ & 13-17 $11, 4-12 $9; free on 1st W of month.

Located inside the cavernous **Palace of Fine Arts** *(www.nps.gov/archive/prsf/places/palace.htm)*, which was designed by architect Bernard Maybeck in 1915 as part of the Panama-Pacific Exposition (an early World's

Palace of Fine Arts

Fair celebrating the opening of the Panama Canal) and said to be the world's largest artificial ruin, this museum makes scientific and natural phenomena understandable through a collection of more than 650 hands-on exhibits. *Scientific American* described it as the best science museum in the world. Indeed, visitors can step through a miniature tornado or encase themselves in bubbles. To the shrieking delight of youngsters, a walk-in Shadow Box allows reverse images to remain on a wall. Teenage "Explainers" wearing easy-to-see orange vests wander the premises ready to assist. The **Tactile Dome** *((415) 561-0362. $17, includes museum admission. Must be 7 or older. Reservations required.)* is a geodesic dome with 13 chambers through which visitors walk, crawl, slide, climb, and tumble in complete darkness using only their sense of touch to guide them. Plan a pleasant picnic outside by the picturesque reflecting pond populated with ducks and even a few swans.

The **Wave Organ** *(1 Yacht Rd., behind Golden Gate Yacht Club, (415) 561-0360; www.exploratorium.edu/visit/wave_organ.html. Free.)* is located across Marina Boulevard at the eastern tip of the breakwater forming the Marina Yacht Harbor. This unusual musical instrument—designed by Exploratorium artist Peter Richards in collaboration with stonemason George Gonzales—consists of more than 20 pipes extending down through the breakwater into the bay and provides a constant symphony of natural music. Listeners can relax in a small granite-and-marble amphitheater and view the San Francisco skyline. It's the perfect spot for a picnic. The organ plays most effectively at high tide.

Miscellaneous Museums

Beat Museum

540 Broadway/Columbus, North Beach, 800-KER-OUAC, (415) 399-9626; www.thebeatmuseum.org. Tu-Sun 10-10. $5, seniors $4.

The late, beloved *San Francisco Chronicle* columnist Herb Caen is credited with coining "beatnik" in 1956 to describe the followers of the Beat Movement who hung out in the coffeehouses of North Beach. This cool museum has existed before in a variety of venues, including a traveling bus. Now in the back of the former Figone hardware store, it displays book collections, manuscripts, and ephemera from Beat legends such as Jack Kerouac, Allen Ginsberg, and Lawrence Ferlinghetti. The merchandise in the front retail store is almost as interesting as the artifacts in the museum itself.

Boudin Museum

For description, see page 63.

Cable Car Barn and Museum

1201 Mason St./Washington St., Chinatown, (415) 474-1887; www.cablecarmuseum.com. Daily 10-5; in summer to 6. Free.

Located inside the lovely brick cable car barn and powerhouse dating from the 1880s, this museum lets visitors see the huge, noisy cable-winding machinery powering the underground cable that moves the cable cars along at 9½ miles per hour. Two retired cable cars—including one from the original 1873 fleet—and assorted artifacts are on display, and an informative film with vintage footage explains how the cable cars actually work. To complete the experience, catch a cable car across the street and take a ride downtown or to Fisherman's Wharf.

California Historical Society Museum

678 Mission St./3rd St., South of Market, (415) 357-1848; www.californiahistoricalsociety.org. W-Sat 12-4:30. $3, 62+ & students $1, under 5 free.

Founded in 1871, this society has a collection of artifacts documenting California's history from the 16th century through the present. That adds up to more than 500,000 photographs and 150,000 manuscripts, as well as thousands of books, maps, paintings, and ephemera. Among the gems in this small museum, housed within the former Hundley Hardware Building are Emperor Norton's cane and a stereoscope—the precursor to today's 3-D films.

The Contemporary Jewish Museum

736 Mission St./3rd St., South of Market, (415) 655-7800; www.thecjm.org. Thur 1-8:30, F-Tu 11-5:30. $10, 65+ $8, under 19 free, Thur after 5 $5.

Retaining the original brick façade and some interior catwalks and trusses from the historic 1907 PG&E Jessie Street Power Substation building, this brand new museum has a very modern angular interior. Designed to explore Jewish culture, history, art, and ideas, the structure is filled with symbolism—for instance, the auditorium design is based on a map of Jerusalem. The museum has no permanent collection. A free cell phone tour is available, and a Family tour and drop-in art program occur each Sunday.

Café on the Square serves a contemporary kosher-style Jewish menu of mostly vegetarian items. A vast entry courtyard in front—an open space that seems quite luxurious because it is surrounded by high-rises—is city operated.

Musée Mécanique

Pier 45, Taylor St./The Embarcadero, Fisherman's Wharf, (415) 346-2000; www.museemecaniquesf.com. M-F 10-7, Sat-Sun 10-8. Free admission; games 25¢-50¢.

This "mechanical museum" filled with old arcade games—some date to the 17th century—is the world's largest collection of antique coin-operated machines. For just a quarter it is possible to operate a miniature steam shovel and collect 90 seconds worth of gumballs or to see naughty Marietta sunbathing in 3-D realism. Highlights include several player pianos, a mechanical horse ride, and jolly Laughing Sal with her original soundtrack (she was rescued from the Fun House at the now torn down Playland-at-the-Beach). But the roller coaster made of toothpicks and the machines that make pressed-penny souvenirs are also quite special. Beeping modern video games are in the back, where they belong. Don't miss the Arm Wrestler—the strength-tester beaten by Julie Andrews in the Disney film *The Princess Diaries*.

Museum of the African Diaspora

685 Mission St./3rd St., South of Market,
(415) 358-7200; www.moadsf.org. W-Sat 11-6,
Sun 12-5. $10, 65+ $5, under 13 free.

This museum celebrates the global influence of the African Diaspora on art and culture (this refers to the settling of native Africans far from their ancestral homelands). One particularly intriguing permanent exhibit depicts human adornment a la Michael Jackson's famous face-morphing "Black or White" music video.

North Beach Museum

1435 Stockton St./Columbus, on 2nd fl. of U.S. Bank,
North Beach, (415) 566-4497. M-F 9-5, Sat 9-12. Free.

Nostalgic photographs depicting this area's past are displayed along with an assortment of interesting artifacts.

Randall Museum

199 Museum Way/Roosevelt Way, near 14th St.,
Corona Heights, (415) 554-9600;
www.randallmuseum.org. Tu-Sat 10-5. Free.

Located below Buena Vista Park, between Upper Castro and Haight-Ashbury, this small children's museum has an indoor Live Animal Exhibit inhabited by uncaged but tethered hawks and owls and other small, accessible animals. Most are recovering from injuries inflicted in the wild. A highlight is the Touching Pen, where children can handle domesticated animals such as rabbits, chickens, and ducks. Permanent exhibits include a replica of a 1906 earthquake refugee shack and an operating seismograph. Nature walks and classes are scheduled regularly. An Outdoor Learning Environment has gardens kids dig exploring, including a native California plants garden which attracts local birds and butterflies. Picnickers can relax on a lush carpet of green known as the Great Lawn while taking in an expansive view of San Francisco below.

On Saturday, the Golden Gate Model Railroad Club shows off its **model railroad** *((415) 346-3303; www.ggmrc.org. Sat 11-4. Free.)* in the museum's basement.

Ripley's Believe It or Not! Museum

175 Jefferson St./Taylor St., Fisherman's Wharf,
(415) 771-6188; www.ripleysf.com. Sun-Thur 10-10,
F-Sat to midnight. $14.99, 5-12 $8.99.

Among the 250-plus exhibits from Ripley's personal collection of oddities are a cable car made from 270,000 matchsticks and an authentic shrunken torso from Ecuador once owned by Ernest Hemingway. All this, plus two floors filled with more curiosities. It's unbelievable!

San Francisco Art Institute

800 Chestnut St./Jones St., Russian Hill,
(415) 771-7020; www.sfai.edu. Free.

The oldest arts organization west of the Mississippi, this institution trained painter Richard Diebenkorn, photographer Annie Leibovitz, and sculptor John Gutzon Borglum (he carved Mount Rushmore). The campus holds the Diego Rivera Gallery and its famous 1931 Diego Rivera mural *(Daily 9am-7:30pm.)*; the Walter and McBean galleries *(Tu-Sat 11-6.)*; and a picturesque Spanish mission-style courtyard with a goldfish pond. To fit in, dress in bohemian style and include plenty of black.

For a bargain organic meal, stop in at the **cafe** *((415) 749-4567. B-L-D M-F to 4:30; $.)*, where a spectacular bay view is thrown in for free.

San Francisco Fire Museum

655 Presidio Ave./Bush St., Presidio Heights,
(415) 558-3546; www.sffiremuseum.org. Schedule
varies. Free.

Antique fire apparatus found in this small museum includes engines from the hand-drawn, horse-drawn, and motorized eras of fire fighting. Of special interest is an ornate hand-pulled engine dating from 1849 that is San Francisco's—and California's—first fire engine. In addition, historical photographs, memorabilia, and artifacts combine to tell the story of fire fighting in San Francisco, beginning in 1849 with the volunteer department and emphasizing the 1906 earthquake and fire. Visitors are welcome to stop in next door at fire station #10 to see what modern rigs are looking like.

Wax Museum at Fisherman's Wharf

145 Jefferson St./Taylor St., Fisherman's Wharf,
(800) 439-4305, (415) 202-0402;
www.waxmuseum.com. Sun-Thur 10-9, F-Sat 9-10.
$12.95, 55+ & 12-17 $9.95, under 12 $6.95.

Exhibits feature more than 200 wax figures, including a depiction of the Last Supper, a scene of U.S. presidents, and a Gallery of Stars.

The Chamber of Horrors intrigues the daring with its "blood"-stained floors and ghoulish figures, but it is easily by-passed if young children are in tow.

Wells Fargo History Museum

420 Montgomery St./California St., Financial District, (415) 396-2619; www.wellsfargohistory.com/museums. M-F 9-5. Free.

In homage to the Old West, this museum displays an authentic stagecoach complete with strongbox. Samples of various kinds of gold found in the state, a telegraph exhibit, and, of course, a re-creation of an old banking office are also displayed. The oldest bank in the West—Wells Fargo—is the sponsor, and the museum rests on the site of the bank's first office.

PARKS-ZOO

Angel Island State Park

San Francisco departures from Pier 39 at Fisherman's Wharf & the Ferry Bldg. on The Embarcadero; schedule varies; $14.50, 6-12 $6.50. East Bay departures from Jack London Square; Sat-Sun only; fares vary. Both (415) 705-8200; www.blueandgoldfleet.com. Tiburon departures from 21 Main St.; (415) 435-2131; www.angelislandferry.com; schedule varies; $13.50, 5-11 $6, bikes $1. State Park: (415) 435-5360; www.parks.ca.gov; daily 8am-sunset; free; no dogs.

Visitors Center: Sat-Sun 11-3:30, Apr-Oct only. Tram: schedule varies; $13.50, 62+ $12.50, 6-12 $9.50, under 5 free when seated on lap.

Half the fun of a trip to Angel Island is the scenic ferry ride over. Visitors disembark at Ayala Cove, as did the first explorers who sailed into the bay. Picnic tables and barbecue facilities are nearby, as is a pleasant little beach for sunbathing. Packing along a picnic is highly recommended, but the island does have its own **Cove Cafe**. Approximately 12 miles of well-marked trails and paved roads allow hikers to completely circle the 740-acre island—the largest on the bay. Some lead to old military ruins that are reminders of the island's past as a detention center for immigrants from 1910 to 1940 (the island was once called the "Ellis Island of the West"), as a prisoner-of-war processing facility, and as a Nike missile defense base from 1955 to 1962. A 3.2-mile loop trail leads from the cove to the top of 781-foot-high Mount Livermore, where a picnic area and 360-degree view await. A park map is available at the Visitors Center, and guided tours are scheduled. Except for Park Service vehicles, cars are not permitted on the island. Open-air trams circle the island via the 5-mile perimeter road, and bikes may be brought over on the ferry or rented on the island. **Sea Trek Ocean Kayaking** *((415) 488-1000; www.seatrekkayak.com.)* schedules tours, and primitive environmental campsites are available.

Beaches

San Francisco is *not* the place to visit to go to the beach. Los Angeles is where *that* California is. Still, the city does have a few good spots to soak up some rays, weather willing. The water, however, is usually either too cold or too dangerous for swimming.

• Aquatic Park

Foot of Polk St., Fisherman's Wharf, (415) 447-5000; www.nps.gov/safr. Open 24 hrs. Free.

Located in the people-congested area across the street from Ghirardelli Square, this is a good spot for children to wade and there are great views of the bay.

• Baker Beach

Off Lincoln Blvd./25th Ave., The Presidio, (415) 561-4323; www.nps.gov/prsf/places/bakerbch.htm. Daily sunrise-sunset. Free.

The surf here is unsafe and the temperature often chilly, yet plenty of people are usually sunning and strolling and the views of the Golden Gate Bridge are spectacular.

Battery Chamberlin is located adjacent. Rangers conduct demonstrations of the world's last remaining 50-ton "disappearing gun" on the first weekend of the month, and environmental programs are sometimes offered.

• China Beach

End of Seacliff Ave./28th Ave., Richmond District, (415) 561-4700. Daily dawn-dusk. Free.

Located in an exclusive residential area, this secluded cove is a surprising find. Visitors park on a bluff, then walk down steep stairs to a sheltered, sandy beach. The surf is gentle, so swimming and wading are possible, and changing rooms and restrooms are available in summer.

Fort Funston

South end of Great Highway/Skyline Blvd., (415) 239-2366; www.nps.gov/goga. Daily sunrise-sunset. Free.

Acquired by the U.S. Army in 1900, these bluffs were once a link in the coastal artillery batteries lining the coast. Nike anti-aircraft missiles guarded the area from the 1950s until the fort's closure in 1963. The missile silos were located underneath the main parking area. Now part of the Golden Gate National Recreation Area, this fort's former barracks houses the Ranger Station and Environmental Science Center. A short, paved loop trail offers stunning coastal views. An observation platform on a bluff above the ocean provides a bird's-eye view of hang-gliders practicing their sport and is a great vantage point for whale-watching in winter.

Golden Gate National Recreation Area (GGNRA)

(415) 561-2700; www.nps.gov/goga.

The GGNRA is the world's second-largest urban national park and is one of the most heavily visited national parks in the U.S. Located in three California counties—San Francisco, Marin, and San Mateo—its total area is more than 114 square miles, or 2½ times the size of San Francisco. These Bay Area sites are part of the GGNRA: Alcatraz, Baker Beach, China Beach, the Cliff House, Crissy Field, Fort Baker, Fort Funston, Fort Mason, Fort Point, Gerbode Valley, Lands End, Marin Headlands, Muir Woods, Ocean Beach, Olema Valley, The Presidio, Stinson Beach, Sutro Heights Park, Sweeney Ridge, Tennessee Valley, Mori Point, and Tomales Bay. Also within the boundaries but not administered by the GGNRA: Angel Island State Park, Audubon Canyon Ranch, Mount Tamalpais State Park, Samuel P. Taylor State Park, and various ranches in the Tomales Bay-Lagunitas Creek area.

Golden Gate Park

Bounded by Fulton St., Stanyan St., Lincoln Way, & Great Highway; (415) 831-2700; www.parks.sfgov.org. Daily dawn-dusk. Free.

One of the world's great metropolitan parks, Golden Gate Park encompasses 1,017 acres. It is nearly 200 acres larger than Manhattan's Central Park, after which it was patterned originally. Once just sand dunes, it is now one of the largest man-made parks in the world. Miles of trails wind through the park, and on Sundays many of the roads are closed to automobile traffic.

• Annual Events
• Comedy Day
August-October, date varies. www.comedyday.com. Free.

Just bring a blanket, a picnic, and a smile. Laughs are provided by national headliners and local professional comedians, who in the past have ranged from upstarts—who just naturally seem to try harder—to such established

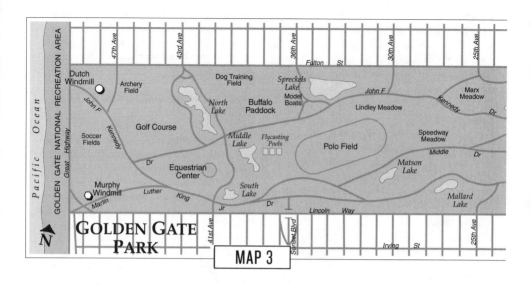

luminaries as Robin Williams, Bob Goldthwait, and Father Guido Sarducci.

• Free Shakespeare in the Park
September. (800) 978-PLAY, (415) 422-2222; www.sfshakes.org. Free.

Performances are staged in the park and at other Bay Area locations.

• Opera in the Park
September. (415) 777-7120; www.chronicleevents.com. Free.

Designed to make opera accessible to everyone, this event is a great way for reluctant listeners to give this art form a try.

• Band Concourse
On Tea Garden Drive, across from Academy of Sciences, (415) 831-5500; www.goldengate parkband.org. Sun at 1; Apr-Oct only. Free.

Formed in 1882, the Golden Gate Park Band is the oldest continuously operating municipal band in the U.S. Bring a picnic.

• Beach Chalet Visitors Center
For description, see page 61.

• Biking/Skating
On Sundays, part of John F. Kennedy Drive is closed to automobiles. Car traffic is replaced with bikers, skaters, and pedestrians. Skate and bike rentals are available at shops along Stanyan and Fulton streets.

• Buffalo Paddock
At W end of Kennedy Dr., W of 36th Ave. across from Anglers Lodge.

Bison have lived here since the 1880s. Foreign visitors seem particularly impressed with viewing this small herd of authentic buffalo.

• California Academy of Sciences
For description, see page 27.

• Conservatory of Flowers
On JFK Dr., (415) 666-7001; www.conservatoryof flowers.org. Tu-Sun 9-4:30. $5, 65+ & 12-17 $3, 5-11 $1.50; free 1st Tu of month.

Modeled after the Palm House in London's Kew Gardens, this impressive example of Victorian architecture was erected here in 1879. This tropical greenhouse consists of a central dome flanked by two wings and is the oldest remaining building in the park and the oldest wood-and-glass conservatory in the U.S. The conservatory's oldest and largest plant—a 35-foot-tall imperial philodendron from southeastern Brazil (Philodendron speciosum)— is located in the dome, where it has been displayed since 1901. Other noteworthy specimens include primitive cycads (from the dinosaur era), a collection of 2,500 rare cool-growing orchids that exist almost nowhere else, and two ponds featuring giant Amazon water lilies that were displayed first in the U.S. here. Outside, giant flowerbeds are tilted at a 45-degree angle so that their floral messages can be seen from the street. Known as "carpet bedding," this old European gardening technique is costly and time-consuming and now almost extinct.

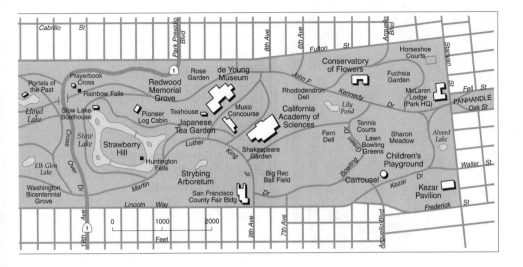

• de Young museum
See page 23.

• Dutch Windmill
In NW corner of park; www.goldengatepark windmills.org.

Completed in 1903, this 75-foot-high windmill once pumped up well water. In February and March, the **Queen Wilhelmina Tulip Garden** bursts forth in riotous color with more than 10,000 tulip bulbs.

• Japanese Tea Garden and Teahouse
Next to de Young museum, (415) 752-1171 . Daily 9-6 or dusk. Garden: $4, 65+ & 6-12 $1.50. Tea: $2.95/person; no reservations; no cards.

A stroll through this garden is pleasurable at any time of day, any time of year, and in almost any kind of weather. Climb the steep arch of the "wishing bridge" (actually a drum bridge), make a wish, and drop a coin in the pond below; then stroll the winding paths, which are plentiful because the Japanese believe that evil travels in a straight line. Steep steps lead to a miniature red pagoda, and an undulating dragon hedge is nearby. A spectacular display occurs annually during the last week of March, when the **cherry blossoms** bloom.

Everyone seems to enjoy stopping for refreshment at the inviting open-air stone teahouse, where tea and Asian cookies are served by waitresses clad in traditional Japanese kimonos. It is pleasant and relaxing to observe

nature while leisurely sipping jasmine or green tea and munching on exotic cookies. An interesting note: Makoto Hagiwara, who designed the garden in 1893 for the Mid-Winter Exposition, is credited with inventing the fortune cookie in America in 1909 and introducing it here in 1914.

• Koret Children's Quarter
320 Bowling Green Dr., betw. King & Kennedy drives, E of California Academy of Sciences; www.parks.sfgov.org. Daily dawn-dusk.

Constructed in 1887, this was the very first public playground in a U.S. park. Today it is equipped with creative modern play structures.

Located adjacent, an antique **Carrousel** *(415) 831-2770. F-Sun 10-4:30; daily in summer. $1.50, 6-12 50¢.)* makes its rounds within a protective hippodrome enclosure. Built in 1914 by Herschel-Spillman, it has 62 beautifully painted hand-carved animals and its original Gebruder band organ.

• San Francisco Botanical Garden at Strybing Arboretum
Entrance adjoins San Francisco County Fair Bldg., (415) 661-1316; www.sfbotanicalgarden.org. M-F 8-4:30, Sat-Sun 10-5; tour daily at 1:30, Sat-Sun also at 10:30. Free.

Known for its magnolia and rhododendron collections, this 55-acre garden displays more than 7,500 plant species. Many are unique to this climate, and most are labeled. Noteworthy among the 24 specialty gardens are the Japanese-style Moon-viewing Garden, the Arthur Menzies Garden of California Native Plants, the Redwood Trail, the Garden of Fragrance, the Meso-American Cloud Forest, and the Primitive Plant Garden.

Many garden events take place in the adjacent **San Francisco County Fair Building** *((415) 753-7090)*. The **Mother's Day Rose Show** displays a splendid variety of climbing, miniature, and old roses. It is the largest such show in Northern California, and cuttings perfect for presenting to Mom are for sale.

• Shakespeare Garden
Behind California Academy of Sciences.

This formal, manicured garden is planted with the 150 flowers mentioned in William's plays. An attractive wrought-iron archway marks the entrance, where a brick pathway bordered by crabapple trees leads into the garden. Benches and grassy expanses invite lingering.

• Stow Lake Boathouse
(415) 752-0347. Daily 10-4; in summer to 5. Paddle & rowboats $14-$19/hr. No cards.

A boat on Stow Lake, the largest of the park's 11 lakes, makes both an unusual, and memorable, picnic spot. Find a pleasant cove with little water movement, and then be careful about tossing bread to the ducks and seagulls as they can sink a boat with their enthusiasm. Though the water is shallow and it's not possible to get far from shore, it is comforting to know that cushions in the boats double as life preservers. Life vests are also available upon request at no additional charge. Because boats are often wet inside, consider bringing along a blanket to sit on. Also, **Wheel Fun Rentals** *((415) 668-6699; www.wheelfunrentals.com/listlocations/28.)* rents four-wheel surrey bikes and one-person chopper bikes.

• Walking Tours
(415) 263-0991; www.sfpt.org. Free.

All walks are led by volunteers from the San Francisco Parks Trust and require no reservations, and, except for the 45-minute Japanese Tea Garden tour, all last about 90 minutes.

• The **Japanese Garden Tour** covers the history and design of this serene landscape garden.

• The **East End Historical Walk** takes participants down the favorite paths of John McLaren and includes Conservatory Valley and the **National AIDS Memorial Grove** *(www.aidsmemorial.org)*.

• Participants on the **Strawberry Hill Tour** enjoy a spectacular view of the Golden Gate Bridge and San Francisco from atop the hill. They see Huntington Falls, explore the Pioneer Log Cabin, and visit the Redwood Memorial Grove and the Rose Garden.

• Designed especially for parents of young children, **Stroller Walks** cover various areas of the park.

Mountain Lake Park

Entrance at Lake St./Funston Ave., Richmond District, (415) 831-2700; www.parks.sfgov.org.

Well-hidden from the street, this delightful park has a lakeside path, a basketball court, tennis courts, a par course that begins at 9th Avenue, and a large, well-equipped playground off 12th Avenue. There are even ducks to feed. It is interesting to note that spring-fed Mountain Lake supplied all of the city's water between 1852 and 1870.

Playgrounds

• DiMaggio Playground

Columbus Ave./Greenwich St., North Beach, (415) 831-2700; www.parks.sfgov.org.

This simple spot is where the late baseball legend Joe DiMaggio played in his youth. Kids love it here.

• Julius Kahn Playground

End of Pacific St./Spruce St., Pacific Heights, (415) 831-2700; www.parks.sfgov.org.

"JK"—as it is popularly known—has lots of wide-open space as well as swings, sandboxes, and tennis courts.

San Francisco Zoo

Sloat Blvd./47th Ave., by Great Highway, Outer Sunset, (415) 753-7080; www.sfzoo.org. Daily 10-5. $11, 65+ & 12-17 $8, 3-11 $5; parking $6.

Of special note are the new Grizzly Gulch bear exhibit; the ½-acre Gorilla Preserve, which is one of the world's largest gorilla habitats; the 3-acre African Savanna habitat for giraffes, zebras, and antelope as well as a host of African bird species; and the Lipman Family Lemur Forest featuring species of this endangered primate. Also, the zoo's collection of extremely endangered snow leopards is one of the most successful breeding groups in the world, and the lions and tigers are particularly interesting to visit when they are fed each afternoon from 2 to 3 p.m.—except on Monday, when they fast (this is the only remaining scheduled public feeding of lions and tigers in North America).

A separate **Children's Zoo** *(Daily 11-4:30.)* has a petting area with sheep and goats. Its **Insect Zoo** is populated with the likes of 6- to 8-inch-long walking sticks and giant Madagascar hissing cockroaches, and it has a functioning honeybee hive. An adjacent butterfly garden features native plants labeled with the type of butterfly they attract. Kids also especially enjoy the main zoo's large playground, a recently restored antique **carousel** *($2)* built in 1921 by the William Dentzel Carving Company, and the circa 1904 **Little Puffer** steam train *($2)*. The perfect souvenir is a plastic Storybox Key *($3)* that children can insert in boxes throughout the zoo to hear information about the animals.

A popular **Valentine's Day tour** teaches about the birds and the bees from the perspective of various other species and is scheduled annually in February. Each year in September, members of the Zoological Society *($80/year/family.)* are invited to **Night Tour**. Entertainment, demonstrations, behind-the-scenes tours, and admission are all free, and a picnic dinner is available for a small charge. Support the zoo and find out just what happens here after dark.

Sutro Heights Park

On 48th Ave., betw. Geary Blvd. & Anza St., Outer Richmond District, (415) 561-4700; www.nps.gov/goga, www.parksconservancy.org.

Formerly the estate of Adolph Sutro, this magnificent park has expansive views of the southern coastline. It is perfect for a picnic, but hold on to little kids as drop-offs can be sudden and dangerous.

PERFORMING ARTS

Moving pictures got their start in 1878 when
Leland Stanford placed a $20,000 bet. He hired
photographer Eadweard Muybridge to prove
that the four hooves of a running horse are all
off the ground at the same time. Still photos
were mounted on a carousel and spun so that
the horse appeared to be moving. Stanford won
$20,000, and the world's first moving picture
later debuted in San Francisco.

American Conservatory Theatre (A.C.T.)

*405 Geary St., in Geary Theater, 1 blk. from Union
Square, (415) 749-2ACT; www.act-sf.org. Schedule
varies. $11-$61; the evening after openings is
Pay What You Wish night.*

Nationally recognized for its groundbreak-
ing productions of classical and contemporary
works, this company's conservatory was the first
U.S. training program not affiliated with a college or university. Danny Glover, Annette
Bening, Denzel Washington, Benjamin Bratt,
and Winona Ryder are among the distinguished
former students. See also page 12.

Asia SF

*201 9th St./Howard St., South of Market,
(415) 255-ASIA; www.asiasf.com. D daily; $$
($20/person min.; no cover). Reservations advised.*

This place seems to have everything going
for it: good food, great entertainment, central
location, easy parking, reasonable prices. All the
waitresses here are actually Asian men who
dress as women. These "gender illusionists" also
perform hourly—dancing and lip-synching atop
a 40-foot-long runway at the back of the bar.
This means everyone gets to see *almost* every-
thing. The wait to get in can be long, but a
dance club downstairs offers more diversion at
no additional charge. And though the show is
the main draw, the East-West fusion food is
tasty (appetizers include several kinds of spring
roll, chicken satay, and a refreshing Thai
cucumber salad; an ahi burger and steamed sea
bass dish are among the entrees) and the mixed
drinks are fun—Trina's Pussycat made with
Malibu rum and Chambord—and include some
sake cocktails and a few non-alcoholic specials.
For desert, the tray trio of yummy miniature
cones filled with Thai iced tea, kiwi sorbet, and
buko ice creams is the way to go.

Beach Blanket Babylon

*678 Green St./Powell St., in Club Fugazi, North Beach,
(415) 421-4222; www.beachblanketbabylon.com.
W-Thur at 8, F-Sat at 6:30 & 9:30, Sun at 2 & 5.
$25-$78.*

Going strong since 1974, this fast-moving
and humorous musical revue is known for its
colorful, creative costumes and elaborate over-
size headdresses. It is the longest running musi-
cal revue in the nation. The show changes peri-
odically, adding new surprises. Family-friendly
Sunday matinees are the only performances
open to minors (under age 21; best for 12+).
No alcohol is served then, there is no profanity
or violence, and sexual puns are toned down.
Performances sell out regularly, so reserve tick-
ets early and arrive when the doors open.

Biscuits & Blues

*401 Mason St./Geary St., 2 blks. from Union Square,
(415) 292-BLUE; www.biscuitsandblues.com. Shows
Tu-Sun at 8pm. Cover $12.50-$17.50. Reservations
advised.*

Spicy Southern cooking—including fried
chicken and the famous namesake biscuits—is
dished up along with hefty portions of the
blues in this intimate subterranean venue.
Sundays bring on family-friendly jazz and a
dinner special with all the fixin's.

Castro Theatre
429 Castro St./Market St., Castro District, (415) 621-6120; www.castrotheatre.com. $7-$9.

This landmark 1922 movie palace seats 1,420 people. It presents an eclectic program of classic and new films, and a Wurlitzer organ plays "San Francisco" every night as the film is about to begin.

Chanticleer
(800) 407-1400, (415) 392-4400, (415) 252-8589; www.chanticleer.org. $25-$44.

This internationally acclaimed, locally based 12-man a cappella ensemble performs four Bay Area concert sets each year in between touring and recording. Performances in local churches during the Christmas holidays are positively ethereal.

Comedy Clubs

• Cobb's Comedy Club
915 Columbus Ave./Lombard St., North Beach, (415) 928-4320; www.cobbscomedy.com. Sun-Thur at 8, F-Sat at 8 & 10:15. Cover $10-$35 + 2-drink min. Minors 16 & 17 welcome with parent or legal guardian. Validated parking nearby.

This popular club features live stand-up, plus a full bar and dinner menu. Dining in guarantees best seating, but all seating is good. The pre-show dinner menu includes delicious, well-spiced entrees such as achiote-rubbed chicken and grilled halibut. A cafe menu served during the show includes popcorn shrimp and calamari, crispy Dungeness crab rolls, a focaccia burger, and an ice cream sundae topped with housemade butterscotch and fudge. This building has been a nightclub since it went up in 1923, and USO shows here wowed World War II troops with big band music.

• The Punch Line
444 Battery St./Washington St., Financial District, (415) 397-7573; www.punchlinecomedyclub.com. Daily at 8, F & Sat also at 10. Cover $8-$45 + 2-drink min.

This is the oldest comedy club in San Francisco and Dave Chappelle's favorite club in the world.

Donald Pippin's Pocket Opera
At various Bay Area venues, (415) 972-8930; www.pocketopera.org. $31-$37, under 18 $20.

Bright and witty, this talented troupe skill-fully performs sometimes dramatic, sometimes hilarious, but always enjoyable opera that is easy to understand. One of these performances is a great introduction to opera for anyone. Though most shows are appropriate for children, some are produced especially for them.

EXIT Theatreplex
156 Eddy St./Taylor St., (415) 673-3847; www.theexit.org. Schedule & prices vary.

This venue for independent theatre has four stages. Many shows are produced by independent theater companies that take their own reservations and run their own box offices.

Lamplighters Music Theatre
Performances at Yerba Buena Center for The Arts, 701 Mission St./3rd St., South of Market, (415) 227-4797; www.lamplighters.org. $11-$44.

This company has produced and performed light opera and musical theater—particularly Gilbert & Sullivan—since 1952. Performances are also scheduled in Walnut Creek and Napa.

Magic Theatre
Bldg. D, in Fort Mason Center, Marina District, (415) 441-8001; www.magictheatre.org. Sept-June. $20-$45.

Founded in 1967 at the legendary, long-gone Steppenwolf bar in Berkeley, this is the only major Bay Area theatre company dedicated solely to producing new plays. It has presented more than 250 premieres by some of the greatest writers of our time, including the 2001 world premiere of Sam Shepard's *The Late Henry Moss*—starring Sean Penn, Nick Nolte, Woody Harrelson, and Cheech Marin—and the 2004 world premiere of David Mamet's *Dr. Faustus.*

Post Street Theatre
See page 47.

San Francisco Ballet
301 Van Ness Ave./Grove St., in War Memorial Opera House, Civic Center, (415) 861-5600; wwww.sfballet.org. Feb-May. $15-$265.

This is the country's oldest professional ballet company. See also page 13.

San Francisco Ballet, 1957

San Francisco Mime Troupe

At neighborhood parks throughout Bay Area, (415) 285-1717; www.sfmt.org. July 4-Aug. Free.

Since 1964, this Tony Award-winning troupe has presented sometimes caustic, always entertaining commentary on current events, political leaders, and the state of our world. The troupe's original productions combine music, satire, and comedy. In spite of the description, children and families attend in large numbers and generally enjoy the spectacle.

San Francisco Opera

301 Van Ness Ave./Grove St., in War Memorial Opera House, Civic Center, (415) 864-3330; www.sfopera.com. Sept-Dec, June-July. $15-$275.

This is the nation's second-oldest opera company (the oldest being the Met in NYC).

San Francisco Symphony

201 Van Ness Ave./Grove St., in Davies Symphony Hall, Civic Center, (415) 864-6000; www.sfsymphony.org. Sept-June. $15-$125.

In addition to classic programs, the symphony presents special "Music for Families" concerts *(www.sfskids.com)* designed to introduce children to classical music, and a July "Summer in the City" concert series that showcases classical favorites as well as Broadway and popular music.

Supperclub

657 Harrison St./3rd St., South of Market, (415) 348-0900; www.supperclub.com. D Tu-Sun; $$$+; price varies depending of night of week. Reservations advised. Valet parking.

Surprises and naughty fun await diners here, where a bit of San Francisco butts heads with a bit of Roman decadence. It's best not to know too much before arrival. Ideally, the experience begins with a drink in the circular bar area before the doors open to the club, and a Black Cherry Drop is a great way to go. Diners are led to their spot among a bank of beds that flank ¾ of the all-white room. After taking off their shoes and climbing up on the beds, they can snuggle into pillow backrests. The rest of the room is left open for watching theater—the video screen that is reminiscent of a '60s light show, the DJs doing their thing, the bartenders shaking away, the chefs scurrying in the exhibition kitchen, and the night's entertainment. The set menu (dietary restrictions are accommodated) multi-course dinner consists of sophisticated cuisine served to loungers on a bed tray. Scheduled entertainment might include anything from a delightful designer fashion show to a bit of divalicious drag queen debauchery. One night, anyone who wanted to be spanked was accommodated, and every night a foot massage is available for an additional fee. After dinner, guests have the choice of staying on past bedtime for the club scene or exiting through the oversize, shiny-brass double doors and seeing the envious looks of those who are still waiting for entry outside behind velvet ropes.

Teatro ZinZanni: Love, Chaos & Dinner

At Pier 29, The Embarcadero/Battery, (415) 438-2668; www.zinzanni.org. W-Sun. $116-$140/person + drinks & tip. Reservations essential.

Had one too many microwaved dinners downed in front of *Seinfeld* reruns? (Not that there's anything *wrong* with that.) Then it's definitely time for a night out at this circus for adults. Sequins and feather boas are the dress of choice when entering the gorgeous antique, art nouveau-style mirrored spiegeltent from Belgium that contains this theatrical wonderment. In between five preset courses—delivered to tables with great fanfare by both performers and waitstaff—the talented international cast entertains with a mixture of European cabaret, circus acts, comedy, and theatrical antics. Though not an inexpensive ticket, it is well worth the splurge for a break from the usual or to celebrate a special occasion. Everyone leaves with a smile.

TIX Bay Area/Half-Price Tickets
On Powell Street, betw. Geary St./Post St., Union Square, (415) 433-7827; www.tixbayarea.org. Tu-Thur 11-6, F 11-7, Sat 10-7, Sun 10-3.

Day-of-performance and week-of-performance half-price tickets are available for many theatre, dance, and music events. Sunday and Monday events are available on Saturday. Full-price tickets through Ticketmaster are also available.

Yoshi's
1330 Fillmore St./Eddy St., on the ground floor of the Fillmore Heritage Center, (415) 655-5600; http://sf.yoshis.com/sf/jazzclub.

For description, see page 317.

Young Performers Theatre
Fort Mason, Bldg. C, Laguna St./Marina Blvd., Marina District, (415) 346-5550; www.ypt.org. Sat at 1, Sun at 1 & 3:30. $10, under 13 $7.

A combination of professional adult performers and young actors in training, this company uses imaginative stage settings and costumes. The fast-moving productions are usually short as well, making them a good introduction to theatre for children ages 4 through 10. Past productions have included *Charlie and the Chocolate Factory, Wind in the Willows,* and *The Secret Garden.*

SHOPPING/NEIGHBORHOODS

Castro District
Castro St., betw. 17th & 20th sts., including Collingwood and Hartford sts.

San Francisco is known as the gay capital of the U.S., and this neighborhood is definitely the gay capital of the city. It is a great place for people-watching. Boutiques, bars, and restaurants flourish in this neighborhood filled with lovely Victorian homes.

• Castro Theatre
For description, see page 37.

• Cliff's Variety
479 Castro St./18th St., (415) 431-5365; www.cliffsvariety.com.

Everything anyone might need—from Halloween wigs to kitchen scrubbers—are found in the aisles here, plus a selection of toys that adults covet.

Chestnut Street
Betw. Fillmore St. & Scott St., Marina District, (415) 869-8661; www.chestnutshop.com.

This trendy neighborhood shopping area is popular with the many young professionals who live nearby.

Chinatown
See page 17.

Clement Street
Betw. Arguello Blvd. & 24th St., Richmond District.

The seven blocks between Arguello Boulevard and 7th Street are heavy with Asian restaurants, produce markets, and bakeries. In fact, this whole stretch is quite exotic and could be called Chinatown West.

Embarcadero Center
Bounded by Battery St./Sacramento St./Drumm St./Clay St., The Embarcadero, (800) 733-6318, (415) 772-0700; www.embarcaderocenter.com. Shops open M-F 10-7, Sat 10-6, Sun 12-5; restaurants open later. Validated parking: 4 hrs. free M-F after 5pm, Sat-Sun after 10am.

This enormous complex of high-rise buildings holds more than 100 shops and restaurants on its lower floors, countless offices on the upper floors, and both the Le Meridien San Francisco and Hyatt Regency hotels. A movie theater complex keeps things busy late into the night.

Justin Herman Plaza is home to the **Vaillancourt Fountain**, nicknamed "#10 on the Richter" and described by an art critic as "something deposited by a dog with square intestines." A brochure mapping out a self-guided Sculpture Tour to the center's treasure-trove of art is available.

Fisherman's Wharf
Jefferson St./The Embarcadero, (415) 674-7503; www.fishermanswharf.org.

Yes, it's commercial, and yes, locals stay away. But wandering around here is lots of fun, and the locals are missing out on something because they have trouble seeing beyond the parking restrictions. Feasting on fresh

Dungeness crab or on clam chowder in a
Boudin sourdough bowl are definitely San
Francisco treats. To avoid parking hassles, arrive
via cable car or an historic street car on the
F Line.

• The Cannery at Del Monte Square
*Bounded by Beach St./Leavenworth St./Hyde
St./Jefferson St., (415) 771-3112; www.thecannery.com.
Shops open M-Sat at 10, Sun at 11; closing times vary.*

This charming red brick shopping complex, constructed in 1907, was once the world's
largest fruit and vegetable cannery. It now holds
many unique shops, and free entertainment by
street performers is scheduled daily under century-old olive trees in an inviting courtyard.

• Cost Plus World Market
*2552 Taylor St./North Point St., (415) 928-6200,
(800) COST-PLUS; www.costplusworldmarket.com.
M-Sat 9-9, Sun 10-8.*

The original store in a chain that now
numbers 299, this gigantic importer has long
been a favorite shopping stop for visitors. Back
in the '60s, it was where everyone stocked up on
"hippie" supplies: batik bedspreads, incense,
candles. Current imports from around the
world include inexpensive jewelry, kitchenware,
and baskets.

• Ghirardelli Square
*900 North Point St./Larkin St., (415) 775-5500;
www.ghirardellisq.com. Shop hours vary; usually
M-Sat 10-9, Sun 10-6.*

Built in 1900 as a chocolate factory and
converted into a festive marketplace in 1964,
this beautiful brick complex was the nation's
first quaint upscale shopping center. It is now a
National Historic Landmark and home to an
assortment of shops and restaurants. Musicians
entertain on the courtyard stage each weekend
(daily in summer). Don't miss indulging at the
Ghirardelli Chocolate Manufactory (see page
71) or dining with a view at **McCormick &
Kuleto's Seafood Restaurant** (see page 77).

Each September, a **Chocolate Festival**
caters to those loco for cocoa.

• PIER 39
*Beach St./The Embarcadero, Fisherman's Wharf,
(415) 705-5500; www.pier39.com. Most shops open
daily 10-8:30. Parking lot across street; $7/hr.,
less with validation.*

This popular spot offers myriad diversions
in addition to more than 110 shops and 12

restaurants. Among the boutiques is one that
specializes in puppets, another in chocolate, and
another in charms, and the **California Welcome
Center** *((415) 981-1280; www.visitcwc.com.)* dispenses free visitor information. Restaurants
include **Bubba Gump Shrimp Co.** (see page 63)
and **Neptune's Palace** (see page 78). Restaurant
menu boards are posted around the pier, providing a chance to analyze offerings and prices.

Street performers entertain daily. The
Riptide Arcade is packed with cutting-edge
video games and located at the bay end next to
a contemporary two-tiered **carousel** *(Sun-Thur
10-9, F-Sat 10-10. $2.)* that is hand-painted with
famous San Francisco landmarks and trimmed
with 1,800 lights. Also here is the **Turbo Ride**
((415) 392-TURBO. $12.95, 3-11 $9.95.)—a
simulated thrill ride that synchronizes hydrauli-
cally powered seats to the action on a giant
movie screen. **Sea lions** have taken up permanent residence on the west side of the pier and
are seen there basking, barking, and belching
on floating docks. **Aquarium of the Bay**
*((415) 623-5300, tickets (888) SEA-DIVE;
www.aquariumofthebay.com. M-F 10-6, Sat-Sun
10-7, in summer daily 9-8. $14.95, 65+ & 3-11
$8.)* uses moving sidewalks to transport visitors
through transparent acrylic tunnels for a
diver's-eye view of the fishes, sharks, and other
sea life residing in San Francisco Bay.

Each year in February, the **Tulipmania
Festival** displays approximately 39,000 tulips
throughout the pier. These harbingers of spring
are a lot of work to grow here, because in this
climate fresh bulbs must be planted each year.
Free tours are scheduled.

Haight-Ashbury

Haight Street betw. Stanyan St. & Fillmore St.

Though Bill Graham Presents has trade-marked the term "Summer of Love" and not many hippy-dippy flower children are seen here anymore, strolling along Haight Street is still like groovy, man. Street people, teeny boppers, and used clothing stores abound, as do unusual boutiques, galleries, restaurants, and nightclubs. It is *the* place to get pierced and buy tie-dye. What makes it clear the times they are a changin', though, is that now a Gap is ensconced on the famous corner. For more information, see page 21.

Japan Center

Three square blocks bounded by Post St., Geary St., Laguna St., & Fillmore St., (415) 922-6776; www.sfjapantown.org. Most shops open daily 10-5, restaurants to 9. Some businesses validate for center garages.

This 5-acre cultural center houses shops, restaurants, art galleries, traditional Japanese baths, a Japanese-style market, a movie theater complex, and a hotel. The mostly indoor mall allows shoppers to walk from one building to another without going outside to cross streets. A five-tiered, 100-foot-tall **Peace Pagoda** that was a gift from Japan is illuminated at night, and an eternal flame, brought from the Sumiyoshi Shrine in Osaka, burns above a reflecting pool.

Restaurants scattered throughout the complex open exotic avenues of food exploration. Especially noteworthy are: **Benihana** (see page 62); **Isobune Sushi** (see page 73); **Mifune** (see page 78).

The traditional Japanese public baths at **Kabuki Springs & Spa** *(1750 Geary Blvd., (415) 922-6000; www.kabukisprings.com. Daily 10-10.)* include large Japanese-style hot and cold deep tubs, a whirlpool bath, a dry sauna, a steam room, and showers. Bathing suits must be worn during co-ed hours. A variety of treatments and massage are available, including expert shiatsu and Thai.

The **Nihonmachi Street Fair** *((415) 771-9861; www.nihonmachistreetfair.org. Free.)* is held on the first weekend in August. In addition to a food bazaar, it features contemporary ethnic bands and performing arts.

Union Square

(415) 781-7880; www.unionsquaresf.net.

World-class shopping is found on the streets surrounding this large square, which was a sand dune before it opened in 1847. The square itself is the scene of art shows and a good choice for people-watching. Charming flower carts are still found on the sidewalks, and a fragrant gardenia corsage costs just a few dollars. Do take time to wander down charming pedestrians-only Maiden Lane and to explore other blocks leading off from the square. At Christmas, many larger stores have elaborate window displays, and the square holds one of the city's largest and prettiest trees.

• **Britex Fabrics**
146 Geary St./Stockton St., (415) 392-2910; www.britexfabrics.com. M-Sat 10-6, Sun 12-5.

Even people who can't thread a needle enjoy browsing the four floors of magnificent fabrics and notions in this unique San Francisco store. It is the largest fabric store in the West.

• **Crocker Galleria**
50 Post St./Kearny St., 2 blks. to Union Square, (415) 393-1505; www.shopatgalleria.com. M-F 10-6, Sat 10-5.

This "covered street" links Post and Sutter streets. More than 35 shops and restaurants on three floors are situated under a spectacular arched skylight. The design was influenced by Milan's famous Galleria Vittorio Emmanuelle. A roof garden makes a delightful spot to enjoy a take-out lunch.

• **Department stores** include **Macy's** *(233 Geary St., (415) 397-3333; www.macys.com.)*, **Neiman Marcus** *(150 Stockton St., (877) 634-6264, (415) 362-3900; www.neimanmarcus.com.)*, and **Saks Fifth Avenue** *(384 Post St., (800) 799-1939, (415) 986-4300; www.saksfifthavenue.com.)*. All have restaurants.

• **Gump's**
135 Post St./Kearny St., 2 blks. to Union Square, (800) 766-7628, (415) 982-1616; www.gumps.com. M-Sat 10-6, Sun 12-5.

Opened in 1861, this is the oldest store in San Francisco. Known for stocking fine oriental imports, it carries the city's largest selection of fine china and crystal and has an eye-popping collection of American crafts.

• **Maiden Lane**
Off Stockton St., betw. Post St. & Geary St.

Closed to cars during business hours, this charming alley holds many unusual shops. One not to miss is **Xanadu Gallery** at #140 *((415) 392-9999; www.xanadugallery.us. Tu-Sat 10-6.),* which specializes in art and antiquities from around the world. When this small, circular space was designed by Frank Lloyd Wright in 1948 to display fine china and silver, it was considered radical because it had no display window. Similar to the design of New York's Guggenheim Museum, for which this building was a prototype, a ramp spirals up to the mezzanine along curving walls.

• **Shreve & Co.**
200 Post St./Grant St., 1 blk. to Union Square, (800) 5-SHREVE, (415) 421-2600; www.shreve.com. M-Sat 10-6, Sun 12-5.

Opened in 1852, just 4 years after gold was discovered in California, this esteemed jewelry shop is one of San Francisco's oldest stores.

• **Westfield San Francisco Centre**
865 Market St., (415) 512-6776; http://westfield.com/sanfrancisco. M-Sat 9:30-9, Sun 10-7.

Opened in 1988, this swanky 9-story indoor shopping complex is now the largest urban shopping center west of the Mississippi and is one of the few vertical malls in the U.S. A must-see 4-story spiral escalator—the only one in the U.S.—wends its way up through a sun-lit atrium into the word's largest **Nordstrom** *((415) 243-8500; www.nordstrom.com.).* A subterranean food court provides refreshment, and free balloons and "kiddie cruiser" strollers are available at the information center. A new section includes the world's second-largest **Bloomingdale's** *(845 Market St., (415) 856-5300; www.bloomingdales.com)*—the largest is in Manhattan—and an assortment of restaurants.

Union Street
Betw. Gough St. & Divisadero St., Pacific Heights, (415) 441-7055; www.unionstreet.com.

Many of the upscale shops and restaurants that fill this trendy area are inside vintage Victorian and Edwardian buildings. Flower stands add a seasonal burst of color on the four blocks running between Fillmore and Octavia streets—where the heaviest concentration of shops occurs—but boutiques continue on in both directions and down side streets. This area is referred to as Cow Hollow, in reference to the fact that it was once the city's dairy community.

For the annual **Union Street Arts Festival** *(June. (800) 310-6563; www.unionstreet festival.com. Free.),* the street is closed off from Gough to Steiner. It begins with a Saturday morning Waiter Race in which competing servers must open a bottle of wine, pour two glasses, and carry them on their tray intact to the top of Green Street and back again. Music, food, and crafts booths round out the fun.

Upper Fillmore Street
Betw. Jackson St. & Ellis St., Pacific Heights, (415) 775-8366; www.fillmorestreetsf.com.

This is the second-wealthiest neighborhood in the U.S. (Greenwich, Connecticut is first). The popular shopping street is lined with trendy boutiques, restaurants, and coffeehouses. Thrift stores keep it real. Don't miss **Mrs. Dewson's Hats** *(#2050, (415) 346-1600; www.mrsdewsonhats.com.),* where the former mayor shops, and **D & M Wine and Liquor Co.** *(#2200, (415) 346-1325; www.dandm.com.),* for the most mind-boggling selection of whiskeys and champagnes in town.

MISCELLANY

Entertainment Complexes

• **Metreon**
101 4th St./Mission St., South of Market, (415) 369-6000; www.westfield.com/metreon. Daily 10-10; movies later.

Originally built by Sony, this 4-story urban entertainment complex has a futuristic-style interior. It has a 15-screen movie theater, an IMAX theater that is the largest west of the Mississippi and that also shows 3-D specials and screens feature films, and the Portal One gaming arcade with virtual bowling. Shops include **Sony Style**, which showcases the latest in electronics, and **PlayStation**, where every game in this line is available for play before purchase. **Jillians** *((415) 369-6100; www.jilliansonline.com.)*—a spacious sports bar with a 50-foot-long video wall and a bank of large half-moon booths—and an assortment of casual restaurant venues, including **Sanraku** *((415) 369-6166; www.sanraku.com. L-D daily.)*

for traditional Japanese fare (also see page 82), keep visitors from starving.

• Yerba Buena Gardens

Mission St./4th St., South of Market, (415) 820-3550; www.yerbabuenagardens.com. Daily 6-10. Free.

Situated atop the Moscone Convention Center, this complex holds a variety of attractions designed for the education and recreation of young people. It also features an outdoor stage, two cafes, a butterfly garden, a redwood grove, public sculptures, a waterfall, and a multi-language memorial to Dr. Martin Luther King, Jr. Expansive lawns, fountains, a maze and play circle, and robotic sculpture invite open-air relaxation.

• Ice Skating and Bowling Center

750 Folsom St., (415) 777-3727; www.skatebowl.com. Schedules vary. Ice Skating: $8, 55+$5.50, under 13 $6.25, skate rental $3. Bowling: $4-$7/game, shoe rental $3.

• Yerba Buena Center for the Arts

701 Mission St./3rd St., (415) 978-ARTS; www.ybca.org. Gallery: Tu-Sun 12-5, 1st Thur 12-8; $5, 65+ & students $3; free 1st Tu of month.

This center presents art shows and live entertainment emphasizing the diverse artists and communities of the region.

• Zeum

221 4th St./Howard St., (415) 777-2800; www.zeum.org. W-F 1-5, Sat-Sun 11-5; also Tu in summer. $8, seniors $7, 3-18 $6.

The entire family can explore creativity and innovation through the arts and media at this high tech museum. Creating videos, viewing performances in a state-of-the-art theater, and learning about animation as art are all part of the program. A playground with a giant slide provides outside fun.

A beautifully restored 1906 Looff **carousel** *(Daily 11-6. $3/2 rides.)* at the entrance formerly made rounds at the defunct Playland-at-the-Beach. It boasts 65 heavily jeweled, hand-carved animals—including camels, rams, giraffes, and a rare gray horse whose mouth is carved with closed lips—and now twirls inside a glass pavilion.

Glide Memorial United Methodist Church

330 Ellis St./Taylor St., 4 blks. from Union Square, (415) 771-6300; www.glide.org. Services on Sun at 9 & 11am.

Arrive early because this rollicking service packs 'em in, often up to the dark, carved-beam rafters, where the balcony seating is up close and personal with colorful stained-glass windows. The service is sometimes still conducted by Reverend Cecil Williams and is always enhanced by a choir of *real* people in *real* clothes and a live band. This is a place of smiles, hugging, and joyous sounds. Enjoy it, and leave inspired. Services are attended by everyone from recovering drug addicts to celebrities that include the likes of Sharon Stone, Maya Angelou, and Bono.

Spectator Sports

• Baseball

• San Francisco Giants

AT&T Park, 24 Willie Mays Plaza, King St./3rd St., China Basin, (415) 972-2000; www.sfgiants.com. Apr-Sept. $13-$48. Tours: (415) 972-2400; $10, 55+ $8, under 13 $6.

Located on the city's scenic waterfront, this new ballpark was designed to be a state-of-the-art old-fashioned ballpark. It features unobstructed views from every seat and plenty of restrooms. A unique public promenade parallels the waterfront from right field to center field, and fans can watch the game through portholes in the fence there at no charge.

• Football

• San Francisco 49ers

Candlestick Park, 490 Jamestown Ave., 8 mi. S of downtown. (415) 656-4900; www.49ers.com. Sept-Dec. $25-$84.

WHERE TO STAY

According to a 2007 survey, the average hotel room in San Francisco costs $182.28 per night.

The San Francisco Convention & Visitors Bureau has a reservations service in partnership with more than 220 participating hotels. For assistance, call (800) 637-5196 or (415) 391-2000, or visit their website at www.only insanfrancisco.com.

Union Square

This is a choice area to stay in, especially if traveling *without* a car (hotels listed here charge between $22 and $56 per night for parking). All of these hotels are within a few blocks of down-town, the theater district, and the cable car line. Many are quaint establishments that provide an European-style small hotel experience.

Chancellor Hotel

433 Powell St./Post St., ½ blk. from Union Square, (800) 428-4748, (415) 362-2004; www.chancellor hotel.com. 15 stories; 137 rooms; $$-$$$. Restaurant; room service. No pets. Self-parking $22, valet $35.

Built in 1914, this European-style small hotel opens right onto the cable car line and greets guests at check-in with freshly baked cookies. Rooms are small but have charm and are fitted with double-paned windows that deaden street sound. A pillow menu offers everything from soothing to tantalizing, and bathrooms have extra-deep tubs and a compli-mentary rubber ducky souvenir.

Luques Restaurant *((415) 248-2475. B-L daily.)* serves breakfast until 2:30 p.m. and offers an intriguing list of specials: Order a "Do Your Own Thing" and you get to choose any scram-ble or omelette. The bar stays open late serving drinks.

Clift Hotel

495 Geary St./Taylor St., 2 blks. from Union Square, (800) 65-CLIFT, (415) 775-4700; www.clifthotel.com. 17 stories; 329 rooms; $$$-$$$+. Fitness room. 2 restaurants; room service. Valet parking $40.

The ultra-cool updated redo of this his-toric luxury hotel dating from 1915 has been described as "like Helen Hayes has turned into Madonna." Even if not staying here, it warrants at least a stop in the chic lobby for a drink and to sit in the oversized Alice-in-Wonderland chair. Hefty rates put it on the lodging list of the world's rich and famous, including Mick Jagger. Service is high priority for the staff, and everyone gets the royal treatment—celebrity or not. Even kids. A family plan includes two connecting rooms, and the desk loans toys for toddlers, magazines for teens, and children's books, board games, Nintendo games, and movies. The concierge has loaner strollers and can help plan family sightseeing trips. At bedtime, snacks such as cookies and milk or popcorn and soda are available from room service. Pets receive a basket of treats, sleeping pillow, and food bowl upon arrival.

Just off the lobby, the classic art deco **Redwood Room** cocktail lounge was lined in 1933 with redwood panels from a single 2,000-year-old giant redwood tree. It is a great spot to sip an exotic cocktail while waiting for seating in **Asia De Cuba** (see page 61).

Donatello Hotel

501 Post St./Mason St., 1 blk. from Union Square, (800) 227-3184, (415) 441-7100; www.thedonatello sf.com. 15 stories; 94 rooms; $$-$$$. Hot tub; 2 saunas; fitness room. Restaurant; room service. No pets. Valet parking $28.

Named after the Italian Renaissance sculp-tor, this European-style luxury hotel has the largest standard guest rooms in town. More than 300 pieces of original art decorate the hotel, and the lobby features 18th- and 19th-century antiques, imported Venetian chande-liers, and Italian marble quarried from the same site where Michelangelo selected the marble for his statue of David. The 15th-floor Penthouse Club Lounge has a wood-burning fireplace and a wraparound terrace with sweeping city views and is free to guests.

Grand Hyatt San Francisco

345 Stockton St./Post St., on Union Square, (800) 233-1234, (415) 398-1234; www.grand sanfrancisco.hyatt.com. 36 stories; 685 rooms; $$$-$$$+. Fitness room. Restaurant; room service. No pets. Valet parking $48.

This hotel is well known locally for its Ruth Asawa-designed bronze fountain depicting scenes of San Francisco. Room amenities include a TV in the bathroom. The hotel restaurant is on the 36th floor, and the flagship **Levi Strauss Store** *(300 Post St./Stockton St., (800) USA-LEVI, (415) 501-0100; www.levi.com. M-Sat 10-8, Sun 11-6.)* operates on the ground level.

Handlery Union Square Hotel

351 Geary St./Powell St., ½ blk. from Union Square, (800) 843-4343, (415) 781-7800; www.handlery.com. 8 stories; 377 rooms; $$-$$$. Heated pool; sauna. Restaurant; room service. No pets. Valet parking $38.

This family-owned and -operated hotel dates from 1908. Comfortable rooms equipped with modern amenities are available in both a historical section and in a more contemporary club section. The courtyard pool is a rare find downtown—only five hotels in the entire city have an outdoor pool—and permits sunbathing to the sounds of nearby cable cars. A plethora of packages add to the already good value.

Modeled after the great grills of the 1930s and '40s, the clubby, comfortable **Daily Grill** *(347 Geary St., (415) 616-5000; www.dailygrill.com. B-L-D daily; $-$$.)* operates off the lobby and has plenty of booths and a full bar.

Hilton San Francisco

333 O'Farrell St./Mason St., 2 blks. from Union Square, (800) HILTONS, (415) 771-1400; www.hilton.com. 46 stories; 1,907 rooms; $$-$$$+. Heated pool; hot tub; full-service spa; fitness room. 2 restaurants; room service. Self-parking $45, valet $49.

Occupying a full block and incorporating three buildings, this is the largest hotel on the West Coast. It features a dramatic sunken marble lobby, and the hotel's 46th-floor restaurant has a million dollar view.

Hotel Adagio

550 Geary St./Taylor St., 3 blks. from Union Square, (800) 228-8830, (415) 775-5000; www.thehotel adagio.com. 16 stories; 171 rooms; $$$. Fitness room. Restaurant; room service. No pets. Valet parking $33.

Built in 1929 as the El Cortez Hotel, this Spanish Colonial Revival building now holds a clean-lined contemporary hotel. Its aim is to be relaxed, debonair, urbane, handsome, and sophisticated. If it were a magazine, it would be *Metropolitan Home*. In guest rooms a drape serves as the closet door, and even on the top floors windows open to fresh air. Guests are well advised to take advantage of a free tour led by the hotel's special Golden Gate Greeter corps.

Cortez *(415) 292-6360; www.cortez restaurant.com. B-L-D daily; $$-$$$.)* operates off the lobby with a menu of Mediterranean small plates and delicious cocktails.

Hotel Beresford

635 Sutter St./Mason St., 2 blks. from Union Square, (800) 533-6533, (415) 673-9900; www.beresford.com. 7 stories; 114 rooms; $-$$. Continental breakfast. Valet parking $24-$35.

This European-style small hotel has a cozy Victorian decor and pleasant rooms.

With cross-timbered walls, the hotel's

White Horse Restaurant and Pub *(D Tu-Sat; $$.)* is an authentic replica of a vintage pub in Edinburgh.

Hotel Carlton

1075 Sutter St./Hyde St., near Polk St., 5½ blks. from Union Square, (800) 922-7586, (415) 673-0242; www.carltonhotel.com. 9 stories; 161 rooms; $$. Evening wine; restaurant; limited room service. Self-parking $25, valet $30.

Inspired by the fact that 60% to 80% of its guests are from abroad, the hotel within this renovated 1927 building strives to make guests feel like they are visiting a well-traveled aunt's home. If it were a magazine it would be *National Geographic Traveler*. Decor is "international vintage," with travel photographs and antiques from around the world used throughout. One-of-a-kind furnishings grace the lobby. Guest rooms feature a color scheme of cream-saffron-persimmon-blue that was inspired by a vintage Indian sari, and original architectural details include intricate hand-carved ceiling moldings and banisters topped with wrought-iron pinecones. Most rooms have a view of city lights, and adjoining rooms are available. The exceptional staff here brings travelers back again and again. A complimentary shuttle is provided to the Financial District on weekdays.

Saha restaurant *((415) 345-9547; www.sahasf.com. B M-F, D Tu-Sat, SunBr; $$.)* operates off the lobby and serves a delicious Arabic fusion cuisine that includes knaffe (ahi with kalamata olive-walnut relish and fig sauce) and fattoush (chopped salad with cucumbers, tomatoes, Feta, olives, mint, cilantro, sumac and more).

Hotel Diva

440 Geary St./Mason St., 2 blks. from Union Square, (800) 553-1900, (415) 202-8787; www.hoteldiva.com. 7 stories; 116 rooms; $$-$$$. Fitness room. Restaurant; room service. Valet parking $35.

Built in 1913, this hotel features cutting-edge contemporary design. The trip begins with the exterior window in the lobby, designed to resemble a frozen layer of glass, and with a Sidewalk of Fame out front bearing the hand imprints of famous divas, including Lily Tomlin, Angelica Huston, and Carol Channing. Movies and music videos roll continuously on a large flat-screen TV above the reception desk, and the elevator's cobalt blue-leather padding matches the carpeting. With a 1920s ocean liner decor, rooms feature beds with sculptured steel headboards, buffed steel and maple wood furniture, more cobalt blue carpeting, and black granite bathrooms. Two-room suites each have a wall bed in the living area (the Murphy Bed Company was founded in San Francisco in 1900) and are especially comfortable and well priced for families.

Hotel Mark Twain

345 Taylor St./Ellis St., 4 blks. from Union Square, (877) 854-4106, (415) 673-2332; www.hotelmark twain.com. 9 stories; 118 rooms; $-$$$+. Fitness room. Restaurant; room service. No pets. Valet parking $27.

The past: In January 1949, Billie Holiday was busted here in room 203 as she tried to flush away some opium. She was found not guilty by a jury.

The present: Now a sophisticated boutique hotel, some rooms here feature iPod docking stations and laptop computer pillows. Room 203 is now the Billie Holiday Suite.

Invitingly decorated like an old-time train station cafe, **Fish and Farm** *(399 Taylor St., (415) 474-FISH; www.fishandfarmsf.com. D Tu-Sun; $$$.)* adjoins and serves a sustainably farmed, contemporary surf & turf menu.

Hotel Monaco

501 Geary St./Taylor St., 2 blks. from Union Square, (866) 622-5284, (415) 292-0100; www.monaco-sf.com. 7 stories; 201 rooms; $$-$$$+. Hot tub; sauna; steam room; full-service spa; fitness room. Evening snack; restaurant; room service. Valet parking $45.

Built in 1910, this landmark American beaux arts building is completely renovated. The inviting lobby has high, high ceilings with hand-painted domes, as well as an impressive 2-story French inglenook fireplace and a grand staircase with the original bronze filigree railing and marble steps—both are remains from the hotel's prior incarnation as the Bellevue Hotel. Each sumptuously decorated room features a canopy bed, and guests can borrow a companion goldfish during their stay.

The magnificent **Grand Cafe** *((415) 292-0101; www.grandcafe-sf.com. B-L M-Sat, D daily, SunBr; $$-$$$. Reservations advised. Valet parking.)* operates within the hotel's restored turn-of-the-19th-century ballroom that was

designed after La Coupole in Paris. This immense, open dining room features a 30-foot-high ceiling, ornate columns, majestic art deco-style ceiling lamps, original murals, and fanciful decorative art. Seating is in intimate booths arranged in asymmetrical formations that give all diners a good view. The menu is composed of French brasserie fare. The **Petite Cafe** bar in front is a pleasant setting for a quick sandwich or pizza.

Hotel Nikko San Francisco

222 Mason St./O'Farrell St., 2 blks. from Union Square, (866) NIKKO-SF, (415) 394-1111; www.hotelnikkosf.com. 25 stories; 532 rooms; $$$-$$$+. Indoor heated pool; hot tub; sauna; fitness room. Restaurant; room service. Valet parking $45.

Featuring clean architectural lines and a slick, marble-rich decor, this luxury hotel has San Francisco's only atrium-style, glass-enclosed rooftop lap pool. The spacious fitness center is equipped with a traditional kamaburo dry sauna and deep Japanese soaking tub. Rooms are elegantly contemporary.

Since this hotel caters to a large Japanese business clientele, breakfast in elegant **ANZU** *(2nd fl., (415) 394-1100; www.restaurant anzu.com. B-L M-Sat, D daily, SunBr; $$$. Reservations advised. Valet parking validated.)*—the name means "apricot" in Japanese—features both American and Japanese fare.

The **Rrazz Room** presents cabaret entertainment in an intimate setting on the hotel's lobby level.

Hotel Rex

562 Sutter St./Powell St., 2 blks. from Union Square, (800) 433-4434, (415) 433-4434; www.thehotel rex.com. 7 stories; 94 rooms; $$-$$$. Evening wine; restaurant; room service. No pets. Valet parking $30.

Aspiring to become the Algonquin Hotel of the West Coast and designed as a focal point for the arts, this theme hotel has a clubby, writer-friendly ambiance. If it were a magazine it would be *The New Yorker*, and it aims to be warm, witty, and smart. Hand-painted lampshades are featured throughout, and the elevator is papered with pages from the city's 1945 Social Register. Wall colors are warm, with guest rooms in shades of citrus, and back rooms face a lovely garden. Sketches of Martha Graham in the '30s hang in a lobby furnished with period pieces, including an authentic clock-face table, and literary events are scheduled regularly. Appetizers and drinks are purveyed each evening in the wood-paneled lobby bar.

Hotel Triton
342 Grant Ave./Bush St., 3 blks. from Union Square, (800) 433-6611, (415) 394-0500; www.hotel triton.com. 7 stories; 140 rooms; $$-$$$+. Fitness room. Evening wine; restaurant; room service. Valet parking $33.

Situated across the street from the ornate dragon-gate entrance to Chinatown and in the heart of the "French Quarter," this playfully decorated hotel is sophisticated, casual, amusing, and chic all at the same time. Original art adorns public areas and guest room walls, much of it painted by local artist Chris Kidd, and bathrooms are positively slick. The Carlos Santana Suite sports hand-painted angels on the ceiling, plus concert posters and photos of the musician on the walls, and it is stocked with meditation candles, incense, and a prayer pillow. Suites honoring Jerry Garcia and whale-artist Wyland are also available, and another very special suite has an in-room hot tub. Guests who miss their pets can borrow a goldfish, and sessions with a tarot card reader can be arranged. A must-have souvenir rubber ducky inscribed with the hotel logo is for sale in the room honor bar.

Cafe de la Presse (see page 64) operates next door.

Hotel Union Square
114 Powell St./Ellis St., 1 blk. from Union Square, (800) 553-1900, (415) 202-8787; www.hotel unionsquare.com. 6 stories; 131 rooms; $$-$$$. Valet parking $35.

Built in 1913 for the Pan American Exposition, this hotel is decorated in a tailored contemporary style and situated just steps from the cable car turnaround. It is where Dashiell Hammett wrote *The Maltese Falcon*, and a large corner suite is named for him. Special features include a massive Egyptian mosaic mural in the lobby and, on the 6th-floor landing, a hand-carved wood mermaid that once graced the bow of a ship.

The Inn at Union Square
440 Post St./Powell St., ½ blk. from Union Square,
(800) 288-4346, (415) 397-3510; www.union square.com. 6 stories; 30 rooms; $$-$$$+. Evening wine; continental breakfast. No pets. Valet parking $28-$40.

This small European-style hotel pampers guests with evening turndown, a complimentary overnight shoeshine, and a morning newspaper at the door.

JW Marriott San Francisco
500 Post St./Mason St., 1 blk. from Union Square, (800) 605-6568, (415) 771-8600; www.jwmarriott unionsquare.com. 21 stories; 338 rooms; $$$+. Restaurant; room service. Fitness room. Valet parking $39.

The luxurious rooms in this tranquil hotel feature a gorgeous marble bathroom and a bed topped with a cozy feather comforter. Swanky window-walled interior elevators traverse the 17-story central atrium.

Kensington Park Hotel
450 Post St./Powell St., 2 blks. from Union Square, (800) 553-1900, (415) 202-8787, (415) 788-6400; www.kensingtonparkhotel.com. 12 stories; 89 rooms; $$-$$$. Restaurant. Valet parking $35.

This Gothic-style, circa 1924 hotel is decorated tastefully with Queen Anne antique mahogany furnishings and period art.

Afternoon tea and sherry is served in the lobby, and stylish **Farallon** restaurant (see page 70) is adjacent.

The intimate **Post Street Theatre** (*(415) 771-6900; www.poststreettheatre.com. $35-$75.*) presents live performances in a beautifully restored space on the hotel's second floor. It is a gem, with carved coffered ceilings and antique tiles.

King George Hotel
334 Mason St./Geary St., 1 blk. from UnionSquare, (800) 288-6005, (415) 781-5050; www.kinggeorge.com. 9 stories; 153 rooms; $$-$$$. Room service. No pets. Self-parking $28, valet $36.

Thomas Edison was an original investor in this stylishly colorful hotel, built in 1914, and it was he who convinced management to switch from gaslight to electricity.

A moderately priced continental breakfast and traditional afternoon tea are served in **The Windsor Tearoom** (*B daily, tea Sat-Sun 1-4; $. No reservations.*) and open to non-guests. Room service is provided by '50s-style **Lori's Diner** *(336 Mason St./Geary St., (415) 392-8646; www.lorisdiner.com. B-L-D daily; $.)*, which is located next door and never closes.

Larkspur Hotel Union Square
524 Sutter St./Powell St., 1 blk. from Union Square, (800) 919-9779, (415) 421-2865; www.larkspurhotel unionsquare.com. 8 stories; 114 rooms; $$-$$$+. Evening wine; room service. Self-parking $27, valet $40.

Built in 1914 for the Panama-Pacific Exposition, this small classic hotel has a cozy ambiance. Guest room decor features contemporary furnishings.

The intimate **Bar 1915** serves a continental breakfast in the morning and features a light menu and beer and wine in the evening.

Marines' Memorial Club & Hotel
609 Sutter St./Mason St., (800) 5-MARINE, (415) 673-6672; www.marineclub.com. 12 floors; 138 rooms; $$-$$$+. Evening cocktails; full breakfast; restaurant. Indoor pool; fitness room. Parking $22.50.

Established as a memorial to Marines who served in the Pacific during World War II, this private club and hotel offers rooms to non-members on a space-available basis. The club also has a small military museum on the first floor and a library.

The **Leatherneck Steakhouse** *(x254. B & D daily, L M-F; $$.)*, with its expansive city view, and the atmospherically decorated **Flying Leatherneck Lounge** both operate on the 12th floor.

Marines' Memorial Theatre *((415) 771-6900; www.marinesmemorialtheatre.com.)* is located on the second floor. Opened in 1926, this theater once hosted national radio broadcasts featuring greats Jack Benny, Bob Hope, Bing Crosby, and Frank Sinatra. From 1955 to 1965 it housed the legendary Actors' Workshop, and the American Conservatory Theatre began here in 1967. New productions are scheduled regularly.

Orchard Garden Hotel
466 Bush St./Stockton St., 4 blks. from Union Square, (888) 717-2881, (415) 399-9807; www.theorchard gardenhotel.com. 10 stories; 86 rooms; $$$-$$$+. Fitness room. Restaurant; room service. Self-parking $30, valet $40. No pets.

Well-situated in the "French Quarter," this hotel gives vigilant attention to green practices. Anyone with environmental illnesses should be quite happy, and everyone can breathe deeply, and easily, while inside. However, once you hit the street, all bets are off. Unfortunately, the hotel can't control what goes on outside. In-room green features include a key card energy control system, trash recycling system, chemical-free cleaning products, compact fluorescent light bulbs, FSC-certified maple wood furniture, organic bath products and sustainable amenities, water-efficient bathroom fixtures, and individual climate control.

Casual **Roots Restaurant** *((415) 659-0349; www.therootsrestaurant.com. L-D daily; $$-$$$)* features innovative American-Mediterranean cuisine that is prepared with locally sourced organic and sustainable ingredients. Vegetarian items are options, and still or sparkling water—filtered and bottled in house—is available. Cocktails are served late into the night at the bar.

Just up the street, the **Orchard Hotel** *(665 Bush St./E. of Powell St., 2 blks. from Union Square, (415) 362-8878; www.theorchard hotel.com. 10 stories; 104 rooms; $$-$$$+. Fitness room. Restaurant; room service. Self-parking $30, valet $40.)* sister property is a slightly older, well-maintained boutique hotel. And, like most sisters, they are very similar but also different. This hotel features a classic Pan-Asian-style decor and platform beds.

Petite Auberge
863 Bush St./Mason St., 4 blks. from Union Square, (800) 365-3004, (415) 928-6000; www.petite aubergesf.com. 5 stories; 26 rooms; $$-$$$. Some fireplaces. Afternoon snack, full breakfast. No pets. Valet parking $30.

Located on the lower slopes of Nob Hill, this charming B&B operates within a small, ornate, baroque-style building and rooms are furnished with French country antiques. Breakfast is served in a cheery room decorated with a wrap-around painted mural depicting a French market scene and also sports a view of a tiny garden. Special features include a beveled-glass door leading to the entry, curved bay windows, and an unusual vintage elevator. A sister property, the White Swan Inn, is just a few doors away.

Serrano Hotel

405 Taylor St./O'Farrell St., 3 blks. from Union Square, (877) 294-9709, (415) 885-2500; www.serranohotel.com. 17 stories, 236 rooms; $$$-$$$+. Fitness room. Afternoon wine; restaurant; room service. Valet parking $40; hybrids park free.

Located in the theater district, this 1920s Spanish revival building has an ornate, architecturally interesting lobby with tall ceilings. The decor is stylish and comfortable in a regal sort of way. Eclectic furnishings have Moroccan touches and whimsical accents, and bright jewel tones and sumptuous fabrics are used throughout. A game library with a variety of board games is available to guests in the lobby, and a few are placed in each room; most can be purchased to go. Complimentary amenities include morning coffee and afternoon wine served fireside in the lobby, overnight shoeshine service, a morning newspaper, and weekday morning town car service to the Financial District.

Ponzu *(401 Taylor St./O'Farrell St., (415) 775-7979; www.ponzurestaurant.com. B-D daily; $$.)* serves a menu of California-Asian appetizers and specialty cocktails in its bar, where everything is bargain priced during the Feng Shui Happy Hour scheduled daily from 5 to 7 p.m.—making it perfect for a quick before- or after-theatre stop.

Sir Francis Drake Hotel

450 Powell St./Sutter St., 1 blk. from Union Square, (800) 227-5480, (415) 392-7755; www.sirfrancis drake.com. 21 stories; 417 rooms; $$-$$$+. Fitness room. 2 restaurants; room service. Valet parking $35-$37.

When built in 1928, this Gothic-Renaissance building was the tallest in town and the last word in hotels. Innovations at the time included an indoor golf course, ice water on tap, and radios in every guest room. The grand two-level lobby retains its magnificent original marble walls, recessed mirrors, and murals depicting the life of explorer Sir Francis Drake, and cable cars still stop at the front door. Rooms are tastefully contemporary, and afternoon tea and drinks are served in the mezzanine lobby lounge. The most famous of the hotel's doormen—who all wear a colorful bright-red Beefeater uniform—is Tom Sweeney, who is known for his terrific memory for faces.

Height is no longer its claim to fame,

though it remains famous for its glamorous art deco **Harry Denton's Starlight Room** *((415) 395-8595; www.harrydenton.com. Daily 6pm-2am; free-$15. Sunday's a Drag brunch: 2 shows at noon & 2pm; $30. Reservations advised.)* rooftop bar, offering fancy cocktails, light supper, and dancing to a full orchestra as well as a panoramic city view. **Scala's Bistro** (see page 82) operates on the sidewalk level.

Villa Florence Hotel

225 Powell St./Geary St., 1 blk. from Union Square, (800) 553-4411, (415) 397-7700; www.villaflorence.com. 7 stories; 183 rooms; $$-$$$. Restaurant. Parking $33-$40.

Built in 1908, this hotel has the feel of an Italian-style villa.

A popular Italian restaurant, **Kuleto's** (see page 75), operates off the lobby.

The Westin St. Francis

335 Powell St./Geary St., on Union Square, (800) WESTIN 1, (415) 397-7000; www.westinstfrancis.com. 32 stories; 1,195 rooms; $$-$$$+. Fitness room; full-service spa. 3 restaurants; room service. Valet parking $49-$56.

Built in 1904, this legendary landmark hotel has a superb location opening right onto Union Square. Every president since William Howard Taft has walked through its lobby, as have Ernest Hemingway and Queen Elizabeth II, and Jennifer Lopez lived here during the filming of *The Wedding Planner*. The hotel consists of both a 12-story historical section—where elegant rooms feature tall ceilings, elegant crystal chandeliers, and antique crystal-ball doorknobs—and a newer 32-story tower with five outside glass elevators that go non-stop from the lobby to the 32nd floor in less than 30 seconds. All rooms are equipped with the chain's famous fluffy Heavenly Beds®—they feel like sleeping in a cloud and can be ordered for home delivery—and the Heavenly Bath® featuring a shower head that emits a soft rain. Upon check-in, children 12 and under get a free Westin Kids Club packet filled with an assortment of age-appropriate amenities and the extension numbers for bedtime stories galore. Kids also get their own section of the room service menu featuring inexpensive favorites such as a hot dog and a jumbo chocolate chip cookie. Westin Heavenly Cribs, strollers, highchairs, bottle warmers, potty seats, and step stools can be placed in the room at no additional charge. And dogs get their own Heavenly Dog Bed, too. Silver and gold charms, including a cable car, are sold in a lobby boutique and make great souvenirs.

Michael Mina restaurant (see page 77) has replaced Compass Rose.

White Swan Inn

845 Bush St./Mason St., 4 blks. from Union Square, (800) 999-9570, (415) 775-1755; www.whiteswaninnsf.com. 4 stories; 26 rooms; $$-$$$+. All fireplaces. Fitness room. Evening snack, full breakfast. No pets. Valet parking $34.

Built after the 1906 earthquake in 1915, this charming hotel resembles an English manor house—with curved bay windows, warm dark woods, and handsome antique furnishings. The cheery reception area, cozy living room, and book-lined library all have fireplaces and are inviting places to relax. Guest rooms are large, and each has a separate sitting area. They are individually decorated with English floral wallpapers and furnished with a mahogany bed fitted with a warming European-style wool mattress cover. Amenities include evening turndown and a morning newspaper. Breakfast is served in a dining room just off a tiny English garden. A sister inn, Petite Auberge, is just a few doors away.

Nob Hill

After its steep slopes were conquered by Andrew Hallidie's development of the cable car in 1873, Nob Hill became one of the city's most exclusive residential areas. It was known as the "Hill of Palaces" because it held so many opulent mansions. Unfortunately, all of them burned down in the fire that followed the 1906 earthquake, save the brownstone shell of what is now the private Pacific Union Club. Because of its spectacular views and steep streets, Nob Hill has been the setting for many films. Most memorable, perhaps, is *Bullitt* with Steve McQueen.

Fairmont San Francisco

950 Mason St./California St., (800) 441-1414, (415) 772-5000; www.fairmont.com/sanfrancisco. 24 stories; 591 rooms; $$$-$$$+. Fitness room; full-service spa. 3 restaurants; room service. No pets. Valet parking $51.

Situated at the top of one of San Francisco's highest hills, this elegant landmark hotel welcomes guests with a gargantuan gilded lobby appointed with marble Corinthian columns, alabaster marble floors, and a valuable art collection. The hotel has hosted many international heads of state, including former President Clinton, and numerous celebrities, and in 1973 it was the first in the U.S. to have a concierge—Tom Wolfe, who is still here. It has starred in movies—*Vertigo, Shoot the Moon, Sudden Impact*—and its lobby and grand staircase were the setting for the *Hotel* TV series. The spacious guest rooms feature goose-down pillows and twice-daily maid service, and the cable cars—which stop in front of the hotel—can be heard from some. The hotel's crown is the historic eight-room Penthouse Suite. The most opulent and expensive in the U.S., it rents for $12,500 per night and features a 2-story circular library, 24-karat-gold-plated bathroom fixtures, and a game room with a stained-glass skylight.

Afternoon tea is served in **The Laurel Court Restaurant** (*(415) 772-5260. Daily 2:30-4:30. $36.*). In the Tiki-hut atmosphere of **The Tonga Room Restaurant & Hurricane Bar** (*(415) 772-5278. D daily; $$. Reservations advised.*), a simulated tropical rainstorm occurs every 30 minutes. It is *the* place to stop in the evening for an exotic drink, and is a bargain during the happy hour buffet (M-F 5-7; buffet $9/person + drink.). A live dance band floating aboard a boat in the room's indoor lagoon—a converted swimming pool dating from 1929—entertains beginning at 8 p.m. (W-Sun. $5 cover.).

The Huntington Hotel

1075 California St./Taylor St., Nob Hill, (800) 227-4683, (415) 474-5400; www.huntingtonhotel.com. 136 rooms; $$$+. Indoor pool & hot tub; fitness room; full-service spa. Restaurant; room service. No pets. Valet parking $39.

Perched atop Nob Hill, this hotel's posh rooms feature an English-style decor composed of leather, silk, damask, and velvet. It is a popular spot with visiting authors, and many rooms have a spectacular view.

The **Nob Hill Spa** *((415) 345-2888; www.nobhillspa.com.)* is in the space formerly occupied by the legendary restaurant L'Etoile. One of the city's most luxurious spas, it sports an indoor infinity pool with a view of downtown through 18-foot high windows, saunas, steam rooms, and a Jacuzzi. Three treatment rooms have a fireplace, and one is designed especially for couples. Rumor has it that Courtney Love experienced the "Nirvana" treatment here.

Named after the nation's four most famous 19th-century railroad tycoons—C.P. Huntington, Charles Crocker, Leland Stanford, and Mark Hopkins—**The Big 4 Restaurant** *((415) 771-1140; www.big4restaurant.com. B-L-D daily.)* is known for its wild game focus, with occasional menu selections including buffalo, ostrich, venison, antelope, and alligator.

InterContinental Mark Hopkins San Francisco

One Nob Hill, 999 California St./Mason St., (800) NOB-HILL, (415) 392-3434; www.intercontinental. com/sanfrancisco. 19 stories; 380 rooms; $$$-$$$+. Fitness room. Restaurant; room service. Valet parking $51.

Built on the spot where once stood the mansion of Mark Hopkins, who founded the Central Pacific Railroad, this hotel opened in 1926. Combining an architectural style that is part French château, part Spanish Renaissance, it has a central tower and two wings affording spectacular city views.

The tower is crowned by the legendary **Top of the Mark** *((415) 616-6916; www.topofthemark.com. Cocktails F-Sat 4pm-1am, Sun-Thur 5-midnight. B-L M-Sat, D F-Sat at 7:30, SunBr; reservations advised. Live music cover charge $10.),* which has an extraordinary 360-degree view of the city and features live entertainment and dancing most evenings. It is said that proposing marriage by presenting a diamond engagement ring in the bottom of a drink glass is played out more frequently here than anywhere else in the world. A plaque on the wall by the bar commemorates this as being a favorite spot for World War II Marines to have a last drink before sailing off to battle in the Pacific, believing that this was good luck and would bring them home. Wives and sweethearts gathered here in the northwest corner, dubbed "The Weepers' Corner," to gaze out the windows as their men sailed out. Service men also had a tradition of buying a bottle and leaving it with the bartender so the next soldier from their squadron could enjoy a free drink.

The Ritz-Carlton, San Francisco

600 Stockton St./California St., (800) 241-3333, (415) 296-7465; www.ritzcarlton.com. 9 stories; 336 rooms; $$$+. Indoor heated pool; hot tub; 2 steam rooms; fitness room; full-service spa. 2 restaurants; room service. Valet parking $59.

Occupying a full square block about halfway up Nob Hill, just off the California Street cable car line, this branch of the classy chain is set within a restored 1909 neoclassical landmark building. The interior features Italian marble, silk wall coverings, Bohemian crystal chandeliers, Persian carpets, and antique furnishings. A museum-quality collection of 18th- and 19th-century European and American art and antiques is displayed throughout.

The Terrace offers the only outdoor hotel dining in San Francisco. In fair weather, its dressy al fresco Sunday Jazz Brunch *($78, 5-12 $39.)* is sublime. Diners sit outside on a red brick courtyard that is surrounded by a colorful flower garden and protected on three sides by the building's "U" shape. Inside, a battery of buffet tables offer delicacies that include caviars, smoked salmon, imported cheeses, fresh fruits, tasty cold salads, and hot entrees such as eggs Benedict, blintzes, and fish and meat courses.

Also, a heavily laden pastry table and a killer dessert table are included along with coffee and freshly squeezed orange juice. Everything is carefully prepared and elegantly presented by a well-trained kitchen staff. **The Dining Room** *((415) 773-6168. D Tu-Sat; $$$. Reservations advised.)* serves an elegant dinner, and **The Lobby Lounge** presents a relaxing afternoon tea *((415) 773-6198. F 2:30-4:30, Sat-Sun 1-4:30; $36-$49. Reservations advised.).* Special teas for children include an **Easter Bunny Tea**, with service by the Easter Bunny, and **Teddy Bear Teas** during the weeks leading up to Christmas.

The Stanford Court, A Renaissance Hotel

905 California St./Powell St., (800) HOTELS-1, (415) 989-3500; www.stanfordcourt.com. 8 stories; 393 rooms; $$-$$$+. Fitness room. Restaurant; room service. Valet parking $45.

Built on the site where once stood Leland Stanford's house—described as "a mansion that dominated the city like the castle of a medieval hill town"—this grand hotel is blessed with striking turn-of-the-19th-century detail, a beaux arts fountain in the carport, and a lobby dome of Tiffany-style stained glass. Guest room pampering includes marble bathrooms with heated towel racks, and complimentary amenities include coffee and newspaper delivered to the room in the morning, an overnight shoeshine, and downtown limousine service.

Financial District

Hyatt Regency San Francisco

5 Embarcadero Center/Market St., (800) 233-1234, (415) 788-1234; http://sanfranciscoregency.hyatt.com. 17 stories; 805 rooms; $$$-$$$+. 2 restaurants; room service. No pets. Valet parking $49.

This elegant hotel resembles a pyramid. Every room has a view of either the city or the bay, and nifty glass elevators run the 17-story height of what is the world's largest atrium lobby. Conveniently, one end of the California Street cable car line is just outside the front door.

Mandarin Oriental, San Francisco

222 Sansome St./Pine St., (800) 622-0404, (415) 276-9888; www.mandarinoriental.com. 48 stories; 158 rooms; $$$+. Fitness room. 2 restaurants; room service. Valet parking $45.

Located in the heart of the Financial District, this luxury hotel's lobby and restaurants occupy the first two floors of a skyscraper. Guest rooms are in twin towers on the top 11 floors of the 48-story building. This translates into quiet rooms with stupendous views. Furnishings are contemporary, with an oriental flair, and upon check-in a pot of hot jasmine tea is delivered to the room. All bathrooms are stocked with fine English soaps and lotions, and some bathtubs feature a city view—permitting bathers to literally soak up the sights.

An afternoon Asian tea service, with snacks in a bento box and tea in a cast-iron pot, is presented in **MO BAr** *((415) 986-2020. Daily 2:30-5pm; $28).* Appointed sumptuously with silk-themed art created especially for the restaurant, **Silks** *((415) 986-2020. B daily, L M-F, D Tu-Sat; $$$. Reservations advised. Valet parking.)* offers an excitingly sophisticated menu of California cuisine with an Asian accent.

South of Market

Referred to by old-timers as "South of the Slot," signifying its location south of the streetcar tracks on Market Street, this colorful area was city center in the mid-1800s. Rapidly being refurbished, it is now home to several art museums and to the Moscone Convention Center.

Four Seasons Hotel San Francisco

757 Market St./3rd St., (800) 332-3442, (415) 633-3000; www.fourseasons.com/sanfrancisco. 12 stories; 277 rooms; $$$+. Fitness room; full-service spa. Restaurant; room service. Valet parking $39.

Occupying the first 12 floors of a 40-story building, this sleek property features a muted decor and displays a collection of contemporary art by mostly California artists. South-facing rooms have views over the city and bay. Bathrooms are spacious, with a deep soaking tub and Italian marble vanities, and beds are made with down duvets and pillows. Kids get pint-sized bathrobes, and guests have complimentary access to the building's ultra trendy **The Sports Club/LA** fitness center and day spa. A visit to the **bar** for a specialty cocktail and bowl of the chef's fabulous wasabi-covered peanuts is a must.

Harbor Court Hotel

165 Steuart St./Mission St., (866) 792-6283, (415) 882-1300; www.harborcourthotel.com. 8 stories; 131 rooms; $$$-$$$+. Evening wine; restaurant. Valet parking $40.

This historic 1907 landmark building has an attractive vintage brick façade and offers some rooms with spectacular views of the bay and Treasure Island. Guests get discounted use of the YMCA full-service fitness center next door.

Hotel Griffon

155 Steuart St./Mission St., (800) 321-2201, (415) 495-2100; www.hotelgriffon.com. 5 stories; 62 rooms; $$-$$$+. Continental breakfast; restaurant; room service. No pets. Valet parking $40.

Among the guest rooms in this stylish boutique hotel are eight with expansive bay views plus five penthouse suites. All feature whitewashed brick walls, tall ceilings, and window seats. Guests have discounted access to a nearby fitness center with an indoor pool and hot tub.

Hotel Palomar

12 Fourth St./Market St., (877) 294-9711, (415) 348-1111; www.hotelpalomar-sf.com. 196 rooms; $$$-$$$+. Fitness room. Restaurant; room service. Valet parking $47.

Featuring a sophisticated interior design, this well-located hotel operates on the 5th through 9th floors of a completely refurbished 1907 landmark building. Original modern art is sprinkled throughout. In Spanish, its name means "where the dove comes to rest," and a quiet retreat is what is offered the weary traveler.

The cool, chic, very trendy **The Fifth Floor** restaurant *((415) 348-1555; www.fifth floorrestaurant.com. D M-Sat; $$$. Reservations advised. Valet parking.)* features tailored furnishings, dramatic lighting, and faux zebra carpet.

Hotel Vitale

8 Mission St./The Embarcadero, (888) 890-8868, (415) 278-3700; www.hotelvitale.com. 8 stories; 199 rooms; $$$-$$$+. Fitness room; full-service spa. Restaurant; room service. Valet parking $42.

According to owner Chip Conley, this luxury hotel is popular with "the post W, pre-Four Seasons crowd." Designed to be modern, urbane, revitalizing, fresh, and nurturing, if it were a magazine it would be *Dwell* meets *Real Simple*. Building materials include luxurious natural stone and wood, and a particularly nice feature has the hallway lights shining down through a leaf-embossed Plexiglas cover that casts leafy shadows on the walls. Each room's doorway holds a fragrant sprig of lavender, and the fog-colored room decor includes a puffy cloud-like bed. About half the rooms have a bay view, and seven suites feature 270-degree "infinity views." All have a flat screen TV. A free rooftop yoga class is scheduled each morning, and passes are provided to a nearby YMCA.

Americano Restaurant & Bar serves light Italian fare with a Northern California twist, offers a great bay view, and features a series of paintings depicting "American Dreamers" (all are friends of the chef).

Palace Hotel

2 New Montgomery St./Market St., (800) 325-3535, (415) 512-1111; www.sfpalace.com. 8 stories; 552 rooms; $$$+. Indoor pool; hot tub; sauna; fitness room; full-service spa. 3 restaurants; room service. Valet parking $48.

When this grande dame hotel opened in 1875, it was the largest and most luxurious in the world. It also was the first hotel in the world with electrical lighting and the first to install an elevator, known then as a "rising room." Though that original hotel burned to the ground after the 1906 earthquake, it was rebuilt in 1909 as the present structure. A dubious claim to fame from its past is the fact that this is where President Harding, who was staying in the Presidential Suite, died in 1923. Nowadays anyone with $3,000 can stay in the Presidential Suite, and the list of those who have includes Sophia Loren and Whoopi Goldberg.

Tours are given of the public rooms by City Guides; make reservations through the concierge.

One of the most elegant public rooms is the **Garden Court**. Filled with tall marble columns, Austrian crystal chandeliers, and enormous potted palms, its most glorious feature is a 25,000-pane stained-glass dome said to be worth more than $7 million, and it is the only *room* on the National Register of Historic Places. **Afternoon tea** *((415) 546-5089; www.gardencourt-restaurant.com. Sat 1-3; $48+; also B-L daily. Reservations advised.)* here is an elegant affair, with fussy sandwiches, rose petal jam, and a classical harpist providing background ambiance. A special **Prince** and **Princess Tea** *($32/child. Reservations required.)* welcomes children 10 and under with a crown or scepter and includes kid-friendly hot chocolate and peanut butter & jelly finger sandwiches. The **Pied Piper Bar** and adjoining **Maxfield's Restaurant** *(www.maxfields-restaurant.com)* hold three noteworthy murals: Maxfield Parrish's "Pied Piper of Hamelin" (commissioned in 1909) and two Antonio Sotomayers—one depicting Mark Twain and the other madam Sally Stanford. And since Green Goddess dressing was first created here, do try it on the house salad.

San Francisco Marriott
55 Fourth St./Mission St., (800) 228-9290, (415) 896-1600; www.marriott.com/sfodt. 39 stories; 1,500 rooms; $$-$$$+. Indoor pool & hot tub; sauna; steam room; fitness room. 2 restaurants; room service. No pets. Valet parking $52.

Referred to by locals as the "Jukebox Marriott" in recognition of its distinctive architectural design, this well-positioned mega hotel is the second-largest in San Francisco. It opened at 9 a.m. on October 17, 1989 and closed at 5:04 p.m. the same day, just after the strongest earthquake since 1906 hit this city. Fortunately, it sustained only cosmetic damage. Most rooms have a sweeping view of the city, and a panoramic view is available from the 39th-floor **View** lounge.

W San Francisco
181 3rd St./Howard St., (877) W-HOTELS, (415) 777-5300; www.whotels.com/sanfrancisco. 31 stories; 410 rooms; $$$-$$$+. Indoor lap pool & hot tub; fitness room. 1 restaurant; room service. Valet parking $49.

Situated next door to the San Francisco Museum of Modern Art, this sleek and stylish hotel greets guests with a 3-story-high octagonal lobby that buzzes with activity most evenings. Rooms feature stunning city views and fluffy down duvets.

Super sleek **XYZ** restaurant *((415) 817-7836; www.xyz-sf.com. B-L M-F, D daily, Sat-SunBr; $$$. Reservations advised. Valet parking.)* features a wide open, yet cozy, dining room, with several ¾-circular booths providing very private seating.

Fisherman's Wharf

The major chains are well represented in this very popular area.

Argonaut
495 Jefferson St./Hyde St., Fisherman's Wharf, (866) 415-0704, (415) 563-0800; www.argonaut hotel.com. 4 stories; 252 rooms; $$-$$$+. Fitness room. Evening wine hour; restaurant; room service. Valet parking $39.

Located in a 1907 warehouse that once was the largest fruit and vegetable cannery in the world, this well-situated, stylish hotel is leased from the National Park Service. All lease money goes toward preservation of the historic ships at the San Francisco Maritime National Historical Park, which is just across the street and whose visitor center and interactive museum is located on the hotel's ground floor. In line with its nautical theme, the primary-colored lobby has a fleet of deck chairs to lounge in, and the hotel's early 20th-century architectural features include natural brick walls and the building's original massive Douglas fir wood beams that are more than 1-foot square. Nautical room decor includes an oversize porthole-like mirror and captain's-style swivel desk chair. Some rooms have a view of the Golden Gate Bridge or Alcatraz, and suites are equipped with brass telescopes.

The brick-walled **Blue Mermaid Chowder House & Bar** *(471 Jefferson St./Hyde St., (415) 771-2222; www.bluemermaidsf.com. B-L-D daily; $$.)* continues the nautical theme and offers ocean-themed cocktails and a variety of chowders and traditional seafood items, among them excellent deep-fried calamari and fish & chips.

Best Western Tuscan Inn

425 North Point St./Mason St., (800) 648-4626, (415) 561-1100; www.tuscaninn.com. 4 stories; 221 rooms; $$-$$$+. Evening wine; restaurant; room service. Valet parking $36.

This pleasantly appointed small hotel is reputed to be popular with filmmakers. Complimentary hot drinks and biscotti are available each morning.

Appealing **Cafe Pescatore** *(2455 Mason St./North Point St., (415) 561-1111. B-L-D daily; $-$$. Reservations advised.)* has windows that open to the sidewalk in warm weather and features a menu of fresh fish, pizza baked in a wood-burning oven, and pastas.

Hilton San Francisco Fisherman's Wharf

2620 Jones St./Bay St., (800) HILTONS, (415) 885-4700; www.hilton.com. 234 rooms; $$-$$$. Fitness room. Restaurant; room service. No pets. Self-parking $28, valet $35.

This motel claims to have the largest guest rooms at Fisherman's Wharf. Since the property gobbled up and adjoined itself to the former Ramada, rooms vary in size. Beds are made with cotton sheets and comforters, and bathrooms have granite counters.

Holiday Inn Fisherman's Wharf San Francisco

1300 Columbus Ave./North Point St., (800) HOLIDAY, (415) 771-9000; www.holiday-inn.com/sfo-fishermans. 5 stories; 585 rooms; $$-$$$. Heated pool; fitness room. 3 restaurants; room service. Self-parking $35.

This well-located hotel comprises two buildings across the street from each other and takes up almost two entire blocks. A coin-operated laundry is available.

Hyatt at Fisherman's Wharf

555 North Point St./Jones St., (800) 233-1234, (415) 563-1234; www.fishermanswharf.hyatt.com. 5 stories; 313 rooms; $$-$$$+. Heated lap pool; hot tub; sauna; fitness room. Restaurant; room service. No pets. Valet parking $39.

This attractive hotel recycles the historic façade of a former marble works building that was here and incorporates it into a modern interpretation of the building's original design. Decor is spare and modern, the color scheme is chocolate brown, and all bathrooms have ceiling-mounted sunflower showerheads. Washers and dryers are available, and the particularly family-friendly restaurant has a children's menu and a games area with shuffleboard and a pool table.

Marriott San Francisco Fisherman's Wharf

1250 Columbus Ave./Bay St., (800) 228-9290, (415) 775-7555; www.marriott.com/sfofw. 5 stories; 285 rooms; $$-$$$. Fitness room; sauna. Restaurant; room service. Valet parking $43.

Comfortable public spaces include a relaxing lobby lounge equipped with a fireplace.

Radisson Hotel Fisherman's Wharf

250 Beach St./Powell St., (877) 497-1212, (415) 392-6700; www.radissonfishermanswharf.com. 4 stories; 355 rooms; $$-$$$+. Heated pool; fitness room. No pets. Self-parking $30.

Covering an entire block, this lodging has many rooms with bay and city views. The pool is located within an enclosed, landscaped courtyard, and several restaurants operate within the same building.

Sheraton Fisherman's Wharf

2500 Mason St./Beach St., (800) 325-3535, (415) 362-5500; www.sheratonatthewharf.com. 4 stories; 529 rooms; $$$-$$$+. Heated pool; fitness room. 2 restaurants; room service. Valet parking $43.

This huge hotel takes up an entire city block. It has spacious rooms, an "outdoor living room" with firepits, and that rarest of San Francisco amenities—a heated swimming pool.

Suites at Fisherman's Wharf

2655 Hyde St./North Point St., (800) 227-3608, (415) 771-0200; www.shellhospitality.com. 24 suites; $$-$$$. All kitchens. No pets. Self-parking $23.

Staying here is like living in an apartment building and makes it possible to feel like a local rather than a visitor. In addition to offering most of the comforts of home, this lodging is located 1 block from Ghirardelli Square and is right on the Hyde Street cable car line. It has a rooftop observation deck with a spectacular view of the bay and the Golden Gate Bridge, and a newspaper is delivered to the door each morning.

Chinatown and North Beach

Royal Pacific Motor Inn

661 Broadway/Columbus Ave., (800) 545-5574,
(415) 781-6661; http://royalpacific.ypguides.net.
5 stories; 74 rooms; $-$$. Sauna; fitness room.
No pets. Free parking.

Situated on the Chinatown-North Beach
border, this bargain motel is right in the thick
of it.

San Remo Hotel

2237 Mason St./Chestnut St., (800) 352-REMO, (415)
776-8688; www.sanremohotel.com. 62 rooms; $-$$.
All shared baths. Restaurant. No pets. No parking.

Tucked away in a quiet residential neighborhood between Fisherman's Wharf and North
Beach, this family-owned and -operated
Italianate Victorian hotel was built by the
founder of Bank of America just after the big
earthquake in 1906. The reception area and the
charming, comfortable, European-style rooms
are upstairs, reached via a steep and narrow
staircase. With their lace-covered windows and
mish-mash of antique furnishings, rooms are
situated off a warren of narrow hallways made
cheery by well-placed skylights and many have
views of famous city landmarks. With the
exception of a rooftop penthouse featuring a
great bay view, all rooms share baths; half have
sinks in the room.

Downstairs, venerable **Fior d'Italia** *((415)*
986-1886; www.fior.com. L-D M-Sat; $$-$$$.
Reservations advised. Valet parking.), which has
moved locations six times since it first opened
in 1886 and is the oldest traditional northern
Italian restaurant in the U.S., continues to serve
a very good four-course, fixed price dinner in a
dining room featuring white-painted embossed
tin ceilings.

SW Hotel

615 Broadway/Columbus Ave., (888) 595-9188,
(415) 362-2999; www.swhotel.com. 4 stories;
81 rooms; $$-$$$+. Continental breakfast. No pets.
Self-parking $23.

This sleek, quiet hotel features Ming-style
beds with colorful floral spreads.

Washington Square Inn

1660 Stockton St./Filbert St., (800) 388-0220,
(415) 981-4220; www.wsisf.com. 15 rooms; $$-$$$+.
Evening snack, continental breakfast. No pets.
Self- parking $20-$25, valet $35.

This charming North Beach gem features a
super location that permits easy coffeehouse
hopping, and it is just a few blocks from an
uncrowded cable car stop. Each room is decorated individually and furnished with English
and French antiques. Several choice rooms in
the front have bay windows overlooking
Washington Square Park and the beautiful Sts.
Peter & Paul Church, the bells from which are
heard tolling the hour. Amenities include
down pillows and comforters, and a morning
newspaper is delivered to the room. Wine and
hors d'oeuvres are served in the cozy lobby, and
breakfast can be delivered to the room.

Japantown

Surprisingly, this quiet part of town is just 10
blocks from bustling Union Square. Both of
these hotels have an exotic Asian flavor.

Best Western Hotel Tomo

1800 Sutter St./Buchanan St., (888) 466-9990,
(800) 528-1234, (415) 921-4000;
www.jdvhotels.com/tomo. 8 stories; 125 rooms; $$.
Restaurant. No pets. Self-parking $15.

Made over in "J-pop" style, this hotel is self
described as quirky, optimistic, practical, warm,
and inviting. Rooms are large, and many have
dramatic city views. Each holds a stuffed car-
toon character from a Japanese comic book and
features a cartoon wall mural, and some are
equipped with steam baths.

Hotel Kabuki

1625 Post St./Laguna St., (800) 533-4567,
(415) 922-3200; www.jdvhotels.com/kabuki.
13 stories; 218 rooms; $$-$$$. Fitness room. Evening
snack; restaurant; room service. Self-parking $15,
valet $28.

This exotic hotel offers serene western-style rooms with Japanese touches as well as two traditional Japanese-style suites with futon feather beds on tatami mats. Tea is delivered shortly after arrival, and the hotel hosts an evening sake hour. All rooms have deep furo bathing tubs, and some suites have a private redwood sauna. The serene lobby overlooks a Japanese garden large enough to stroll in.

O Izakaya Lounge *((415) 614-5431. B&D daily, L Sat-Sun; $$.)*—a Japanese-style tavern with vintage Japanese baseball decor and a flat-screen TV tuned to games from across the Pacific—serves small plates featuring tempura and yakimono (grilled meats) and features a selection of more than 20 sakes.

Pacific Heights/Presidio Heights

Chateau Tivoli Bed & Breakfast

1057 Steiner St./Golden Gate Ave., Alamo Square,
(800) 228-1647, (415) 776-5462; www.chateau
tivoli.com. 9 rooms; $-$$$. Afternoon snack,
continental breakfast (champagne brunch Sat-Sun).
No pets. No parking.

Mark Twain and Enrico Caruso were once guests in this opulent landmark 1892 mansion. The charming Jack London room has a sitting area in a sunny cupola and also a bathroom with ceiling eaves, dark wood wainscoting, and a clawfoot tub. The gorgeous Aimee Crocker room sports a canopy bed with draped netting and an ornate painted ceiling.

Hotel Drisco

2901 Pacific Ave./Broderick St., (800) 634-7277, (415)
346-2880; www.hoteldrisco.com. 4 stories; 43 rooms;
$$$-$$$+. Fitness room. Afternoon snack, evening
wine, continental breakfast. No pets. No parking.

Built in 1903, before the '06 quake, this Edwardian-style building is in a quiet residential neighborhood. It maintains its original dark-wood interior trim and is elegantly decorated and furnished. Turn-of-the-19th-century millionaires are said to have kept their mistresses lodged here. Later, President Eisenhower bunked here due to its close proximity to the Presidio. Rooms are spacious and comfortable, and the suites have good views.

Hotel Majestic

1500 Sutter St./Gough St., (800) 869-8966,
(415) 441-1100; www.thehotelmajestic.com. 5 stories;
58 rooms; $$-$$$. Restaurant; room service.
No pets. Valet parking $20.

Built originally as a private mansion in 1902 and converted to a hotel in 1904, this small Edwardian hotel survived the 1906 earthquake and fire and is the longest continuously operating hotel in San Francisco. It is restored to its original grandeur—with gorgeous vintage marble, exotic woods, and rich brocades and wallpapers—and sports bay windows and high ceilings. It offers a cozy, soothing retreat from the world outside. Each sumptuously decorated room has either a canopied four-poster bed or a two-poster bed with a bonnet canopy, and fine French and English antiques are used throughout. Many rooms have clawfoot tubs. Why, even rock stars have been known to head straight for their posh room immediately after a concert to cocoon. Julia Roberts, The GoGos, and numerous Nobel laureates have slept here, and the hotel was once the permanent residence of actresses Joan Fontaine and Olivia de Havilland.

Named for a butterfly, the lobby bar, **Avalon**, displays a collection of rare butterflies from South America and Africa.

Laurel Inn

444 Presidio Ave./California St., (800) 552-8735,
(415) 567-8467; www.thelaurelinn.com. 4 stories;
49 rooms; $$$. Some kitchens. Afternoon snack,
continental breakfast. Self-parking $15.

Located far from the usual tourist haunts, in a nice residential area near Sacramento Street shopping, this motel has spacious rooms and a stylish 1950s-modern decor. East-facing rooms have good city views, and it's hard to beat the price.

Haight-Ashbury

Stanyan Park Hotel

750 Stanyan St./Waller St., (415) 751-1000;
www.stanyanpark.com. 36 rooms; $$-$$$+. Some
kitchens. Afternoon snack, continental breakfast.
No pets. No parking.

Located at the edge of Golden Gate Park, this 1904 Victorian mansion survived the great quake of '06. It has been renovated into a pleasant hotel with attractively decorated rooms.

By the Sea

Ocean Park Motel
2690 46th Ave./Wawona St., Sunset District, (415) 566-7020; www./oceanparkmotel.ypguides.net. 25 rooms; $-$$. Some kitchens. Hot tub. Free parking.

Located near the ocean and just a block from the zoo, this landmark streamline moderne gem dates from the '30s and was San Francisco's first motel. It maintains its original nautical decor and interior cedar paneling, and some windows are shaped like portholes. Rooms are attractive and homey, and several spacious family suites are available. Amenities include a playground, a barbecue area, and mature gardens with Monterey pine and cypress trees.

Miscellaneous

Hostels
www.sfhostels.com. $. Continental breakfast. No pets.

For more description, see page 468.

• **Union Square:**
312 Mason St./Geary St., (415) 788-5604. 6 stories; 270 beds; 40 private rooms.

This is in a prime location with an on-site laundry.

• **Civic Center:**
685 Ellis St./Larkin St., (415) 474-5721. 7 stories; 262 beds; 10 private rooms.

All rooms in this beautifully restored vintage hotel have an en suite bathroom. Amenities include a restaurant-quality guest kitchen.

• **Fisherman's Wharf:** *Fort Mason, Bldg. 240, Bay St./Franklin St., (415) 771-7277. 144 beds; 5 private rooms. Restaurant.*

This former Civil War barracks is situated on a peaceful knoll with a magnificent view of the bay.

Motel Row
A plethora of lodgings lines the 20-block corridor stretching along Lombard Street from Van Ness Avenue to the Presidio.

WHERE TO EAT

San Francisco has far too many good restaurants to permit listing them all here. Those included are excellent in some way. Don't be reluctant to try places discovered while wandering. If the people dining inside look animated and happy, give it a try. It is amazing how infrequently a bad meal is served in this food-fanatical town. Even hotel restaurants (described briefly in the "Where to Stay" section), which are often best overlooked in other cities, are usually good here. They don't call San Francisco "Food City" for no reason. In fact, it is said there are more restaurants per resident in San Francisco than in any other city in the U.S.

And do try some of the local food specialties. The fortune cookie, Irish coffee, and martini were all invented here. Pisco punch, an unusual drink made with Peruvian brandy, dates back to the Gold Rush. Sourdough bread is credited to Isidore Boudin, a French immigrant who in 1849 got some sourdough from a gold prospector and mixed it in with his French bread to produce the world's first sourdough French bread. The Lactobacillus sanfrancisco sour culture has been kept alive in a mother dough for more than 150 years now, and was saved during the 1906 earthquake when a family member scooped it into a bucket before running out into the street. Dry salami is made by several local companies, including Molinari and Cariani, which both date back to the 1890s. The original **Swensen's Ice Cream shop** still operates at Hyde and Union streets dishing out its Sticky Chewy Chocolate and Turkish Coffee specialties, though vanilla remains the favorite. It's It—an ice cream sandwich made with oatmeal cookies, vanilla ice cream, and a coating of chocolate—was developed in 1928 at long-gone Playland-at-the-Beach. The confection is sold now in grocery stores. Another frozen delight, the Popsicle, was created on one very cold San Francisco night in 1905 when 11-year-old Frank Epperson carelessly left out some powdered soda, water, and a stirring stick. Green Goddess salad dressing was created in 1923 at the Palace Hotel by chef Philip Roemer, who named it after a play of the same name by William Archer. Double Rainbow is the ice cream of choice, Anchor Steam the beer, Calistoga (from the Wine Country) the mineral water,

Ghirardelli the chocolate, Torani the flavored syrup, and Tom's the cookie.

Note that a state law makes it illegal to smoke in any California restaurant or bar, or in any public place of business. Valet parking averages around $7 to $10.

For some combined dining/theater experiences, see the "Performing Arts" section.

Acquerello

1722 Sacramento St./Van Ness Ave., Russian Hill, (415) 567-5432; www.acquerello.com. D Tu-Sat; $$$+. Reservations advised.

Formerly a church, the romantic, intimate dining room of this upscale Italian gem features a rustic, pitched Moorish wood ceiling. It is the kind of place where the Mayor might be seated at the next table. Menu selections include a four-course tasting menu with wines. Definitely not the usual, the delicious preparations are derived from a refined style of Italian cuisine known as cucina della nonna, or "grandmother's cooking," and feature complex reduced sauces achieved through slow, home-style cooking. An exquisite example is tortelloni stuffed with brandy-plumped figs and ground pork in a nut dough. The kitchen sends out occasional complimentary little treats—perhaps a tiny citrus appetizer cocktail or a plump, perfect scallop sitting on mashed potatoes splashed with truffle oil. Service is elegant and formal, with meals served on fine china and crystal enhanced by paper doilies.

Alborz

1245 Van Ness Ave./Sutter St., Pacific Heights, (415) 440-4321. L-D daily; $-$$. Reservations advised.

This simple but comfortable spot offers a wall of windows looking onto the street. It has an exceptional Persian menu and starts diners off with a complimentary basket of delicious lavash flat bread and Feta cheese. Excellent appetizers include kasik bodemjan (roasted eggplant baked with onion, garlic, mint, and yogurt), mast-o-khiar (cucumber and mint mixed with delicious, rich, housemade yogurt), and salad shirazi (a mixture of diced tomatoes, cucumbers, and onions in a lemony dressing). For entrees, any of the juicy kabobs are excellent, but don't overlook the more complex house specialties—the richly flavored fes enjoon consists of chicken breast cooked in a delicious thick, sweet walnut-pomegranate sauce. The perfect ending is, of course, baklava.

Alioto's

#8 Fisherman's Wharf, at bottom of Taylor St./Jefferson St., (415) 673-0183; www.aliotos.com. L-D daily; $$-$$$. Validated parking.

Historical photos of the Wharf line the stairway up to the restaurant, where the view here is about as San Francisco as you can get— the fishing boats, the bay, The Bridge—and plenty of oversize booths and window-front tables provide comfortable seating. Fresh seafood is always a good choice, but the many Sicilian regional specialties are also worth trying. Spicy deviled crab served in a scallop shell, pan-fried sole picatta, and potato gnocchi with creamy tomato sauce are particularly tasty. Portions are bountiful, and both European wines and New World wines are served Old

World-style in volume-marked glasses. The charming little Calamari Room off the main dining room can be reserved for parties of six to ten people.

Downstairs, the **Cafe Eight** fast-service seafood deli serves up sandwiches, seafood salads, and brick-oven pizzas, and a sidewalk crab stand operates out front.

Ana Mandara

891 Beach St./Polk St., in Ghirardelli Square, Fisherman's Wharf, (415) 771-6800; www.anamandara.com. L M-F, D daily; $$$. Reservations advised. Valet parking.

Located within a stunning high-ceilinged, open dining room, this delightful restaurant's name translates as "beautiful refuge" and is the title of a 700-year old legend based on a warrior and a princess who were star-crossed lovers. It is co-owned by TV's *Nash Bridges* stars Don Johnson and Cheech Marin and a few others. The elaborate decor and theatrical ceiling lights that mimic a star-studded evening sky sometimes do double-duty as stage sets. Full-grown potted palms and antique Vietnamese artifacts complete the effect, making this space resemble a Vietnamese village. And then there's the food. Though portions are small, the modern Vietnamese cuisine is delicious. Appetizers include crispy spring rolls filled with crab and shrimp, and among the main dishes are marinated grilled quail and fresh fish steamed in banana leaves. Elegant cocktails and beers provide the perfect accompaniment. Vietnamese coffee and green tea grown on the chef's family plantation in Vietnam are available with dessert. A luxurious bar area awaits upstairs.

Ananda Fuara

1298 Market St./9th St., Civic Center, (415) 621-1994; www.anandafuara.com. L-D M-Sat, L only on W, SunBr occassionally; $. No reservations. No cards.

The translation of this cheery, all-vegetarian restaurant's name is "Fountain of Supreme Bliss." It is owned by the peace teacher and poet Sri Chinmoy and operated by his students. Female servers wear saris, and fresh flowers grace every table. The varied menu should please everyone, even vegans—who eat no dairy or eggs—and carnivores—we know what *they* eat! Menu winners include appetizer vegan samosas filled with a potato-pea curry, a

hearty soup of the day, and a house specialty "neatloaf" sandwich made with a baked mixture of grains and spices. A selection of salads, wraps, sandwiches, pizzas, baked potatoes, and entrees is also available. Drinks include a decaffeinated Indian-spiced hot Yogi Tea that is simply the best.

Andalé

2150 Chestnut St., Marina District, (415) 749-0506; www.andalemexican.com.

For description, see page 180.

Antica Trattoria

2400 Polk St./Union St., Russian Hill, (415) 928-5797; www.anticasf.com. D Tu-Sun; $$.

Located on the quiet north end of Polk, in a neighborhood filled with boutiques and lovely Victorian buildings, this inviting spot features one large open room that is paneled with dark wood topped with walls painted a warm shade of rusty red. The talented owner-chef presents a changing seasonal menu of authentic Italian dishes. One delicious dinner enjoyed here included tartufata (butter lettuce salad tossed with a highly flavored truffle vinaigrette and chopped hard-boiled eggs); black pepper pappardelle with a reduced wild boar ragout; and vitello alla Milanese (crispy breaded veal scaloppini topped with caper aioli and served with perfectly roasted brussels sprouts). The affogato sundae (white chocolate gelato topped with espresso, amaretto, and hazelnuts) and the panna cotta with huckleberries in a Zinfandel sauce are primo.

Aqua

252 California St./Battery St., Financial District, (415) 956-9662; www.aqua-sf.com. L M-F, D daily; $$$+. Reservations essential. Valet parking at D.

Featuring a large dining room with a tall, tall ceiling, this sophisticated space is enhanced by gorgeous oversize flower arrangements. It is chic, bustling, and romantic all at the same time and delivers food of equal caliber. Creative, full-flavored, impeccably fresh seafood items dominate the menu, and it seems impossible to choose a wrong dish. Presentations are dazzling, with colorful flavored oils often drizzled around the perimeter of plates, and some dishes involve "table theater," with the waiter dramatically mixing and preparing items at table. Non-fish entrees include duck, foie gras, and a vegetarian tasting menu. Desserts include a daily soufflé and a variety of cheeses. A seven-course tasting menu with optional wine pairings is perfect for those who just cannot decide.

Asia De Cuba

495 Geary St./Taylor St., in Clift Hotel, Union Square, (415) 929-2300; www.clifthotel.com. B-L-D daily; $$$. Reservations advised. Valet parking.

This sumptuous dining room has a high ceiling and walls draped in merlot velvet. Perfect starters from the Cuban-inspired menu are a fancy cocktail—perhaps a tart mojito— and a platter of lobster pot stickers. Calamari salad and miso-cured butterfish are also delicious. For dessert, who can resist the Bay of Pigs banana split or the Suspiros Calientes— fortune cookie ice cream with sticky buns and toffee sauce that is described by the chef as "like giving your lover a kiss on the neck"?

B44

44 Belden Pl./Bush St., Financial District, (415) 986-6287; www.b44.ypguides.net. L M-F, D daily; $$-$$$. Reservations advised.

The best way to enjoy the Catalan menu at this engaging bistro is to pick several appetizers per person—the piquillo peppers stuffed with crab meat and the fresh white shrimp sautéed with crispy garlic and served in a little iron frying pan are both superb—and share a moist paella or entree. A sherry or Catalan wine is the perfect accompaniment. A refined chocolate banana pie or rice-and-cinnamon ice cream provide a not too sweet ending. Seating is in an open dining room with industrial-style decor and a full bar, or, in good weather, outside European-style in an alley closed to traffic. A restroom visit is enhanced by a video display depicting the annual "human tower" festival that dates back to the 14th century in owner-chef Daniel Olivella's Spanish hometown of Vilafranca del Penedes, located near Barcelona.

Beach Chalet Brewery & Restaurant

1000 Great Highway/Ocean Beach, in Golden Gate Park, (415) 386-VIEW; www.beachchalet.com. B-L-D daily, Sat-SunBr; $-$$. Reservations advised. Free parking lot adjoins.

Designed in 1925 by San Francisco architect Willis Polk, this historic colonnaded

Spanish stucco building with terra-cotta roof tiles is at the western end of Golden Gate Park, across the street from the Pacific Ocean. In the past it has served as a tea house and as an Army signal station, but now the upstairs is a wildly popular brewpub bistro with ocean views from every table. Target a visit for breakfast or lunch, when the menu is less pricey and the views can be enjoyed uninterrupted by sun-shielding shades. Don't miss the sampler of house-brewed, English-style ales or the full-flavored, though essentially fizz-less, housemade root beer. Two standouts on the eclectic, bistro-style menu are a hamburger made with flavorful Niman Ranch ground chuck and an herb-crusted rotisserie-roasted chicken with garlic mashed potatoes. Sausage dishes are usually available, and the kitchen is famous for its achiote-spiced chicken wings. Desserts include the ultimate vertical dessert—the pastry chef's signature Chocolate Sandcastle, whimsically composed of a flourless chocolate truffle cake placed vertically between two chocolate castle-shaped cookies. A nickel from each beer sold goes to charity, and live music is scheduled Tuesday through Saturday evenings and Sunday afternoons.

The more informal **Park Chalet** cafe operates downstairs in the back and has a large outside area dotted with comfy oversize Adirondack chairs.

Downstairs in the front, the **Golden Gate Park Visitors Center** *((415) 751-2766. Daily 9am-10:30pm.)* displays natural history exhibits and provides information about the Beach Chalet's colorful WPA wall frescoes depicting life in San Francisco during the Depression.

Benihana

1737 Post St., in Kintetsu Mall at Japan Center,
(415) 563-4844; www.benihana.com. L-D daily;
$$-$$$. Reservations advised.

Diners at this branch of the well-known
Japanese restaurant chain sit at a community
table with a large grill imbedded in the middle.
Once the seats are filled with diners, the chef
dramatically prepares each order as everyone
watches. Though there are no karate yells from
the chefs, they wouldn't seem out of place. The
chefs are adept performers with their razor-
sharp knives, and the show is spectacular.

Betelnut Pejiu Wu

2030 Union St./Buchanan St., Cow Hollow,
(415) 929-8855; www.betelnutrestaurant.com. L-D
daily; $$. Reservations advised. Validated parking.

With a menu of native dishes from
throughout Asia and a streamlined interior fea-
turing lacquered walls and some very comfort-
able half-moon booths, this always-bustling,
casual spot is modeled after the beer houses
found in Asia. Though most dishes are full-fla-
vored and satisfying, exceptional items include
minced chicken in lettuce cups, red-cooked
pork in a spicy-sweet sauce, and tea-smoked
duck. Portions are small and meant to be
shared tapas-style. Beer is the perfect drink—
especially with a plate of sun-dried anchovies,
peanuts, and chilies to munch on—but exotic
mixed drinks are also divine, and a rare Chinese
tea can provide a satisfying conclusion.

Unreserved seats are often available in the
Dragonfly Lounge bar, where large windows
overlook sidewalk traffic and exotic flap fans
keep things cool, and at an auspicious long red
bar facing the open kitchen.

Bill's Place

2315 Clement St./25th Ave., Outer Richmond District,
(415) 221-5262; www.billsplace.qpg.com. L-D daily;
$. Reservations accepted.

A variety of hamburgers named after
celebrities star on the menu here along with hot
dogs and sandwiches, and breakfast is available
until 1 p.m. Choice shoulder chuck is ground in
the kitchen daily for the tasty burgers. Sides
include perfect french fries made from fresh
potatoes and made-from-scratch soup, potato
salad, and coleslaw. Milkshakes are served in
old-fashioned metal canisters. Seating is at

tables or at a counter with swivel stools, and a
collection of Presidential china decorates the
walls. In mild weather, a pleasant outdoor patio
landscaped with a waterfall and Japanese garden
is inviting.

Bittersweet

2123 Fillmore St./California St., Upper Fillmore,
(415) 346-8715; www.bittersweetchocolatecafe.com.
For description, see page 318.

Blowfish Sushi To Die For

2170 Bryant St./19th St., South of Market, (415) 285-
3848; www.blowfishsushi.com. L M-F, D daily; $$-$$$.
For description, see page 194.

Boudin at the Wharf

160 Jefferson St./Taylor St., Fisherman's Wharf,
(415) 928-1849; www.boudinbakery.com. L-D daily;
$-$$$. Museum: daily 11:30-6:30; free.

After watching the bakers through a sidewalk window, where they sometimes respond to
questions via a two-way speaker, visitors can
choose between informal dining downstairs—
both inside and outside on a heated deck—and
finer dining upstairs in **Bistro Boudin** (it is
pronounced either "boo-deen" or "bow-
deen")—with a dead-on view of Alcatraz.
Among the best items are an ever-popular clam
chowder in a sourdough bowl, meaty crab
cakes, and pizzas.

Upstairs, the **Boudin Museum** is an homage to sourdough bread-making with some interesting city history mixed in (Boudin is the oldest continuously run business in San Francisco). The busy first-floor bakery can be observed below from a glass-walled catwalk, and a tasting room completes the tour. Take home the perfect souvenir—a loaf of bread in the shape of a darling turtle or alligator.

Boulevard

1 Mission St./Stewart St., The Embarcadero, (415) 543-6084; www.boulevardrestaurant.com. L M-F, D daily; $$$. Reservations advised. Valet parking.

Co-owned by chef Nancy Oakes and acclaimed local restaurant designer Pat Kuleto, this sumptuous restaurant offers a feast for both the palate and the eyes and is one of the most popular restaurants in town. Diners enter the gorgeous 1889 French-style building via a revolving door. The belle époque-style interior features stunning mosaic tiled floors as well as sensuous blown-glass light fixtures and pressed tin and ironwork accents. Some tables have three-landmark views—of the Ferry Building, Embarcadero Center, and the Bay Bridge. Large, serious forks foreshadow the exciting, full-flavored dishes to follow. One flawless meal here began with a Chinese-seasoned appetizer of two perfect prawns intertwined over a plump rock shrimp dumpling. The entree was a thick, honey-cured pork loin served with roasted potatoes and baby spinach. A pear tart with caramel sauce and vanilla bean ice cream provided the perfect finish.

Brandy Ho's Hunan Food

217 Columbus Ave./Pacific St., Chinatown, (415) 788-7527; www.brandyhoshunan.com. L-D daily; $.

Hot and spicy Chinese Hunan peasant cuisine is prepared to order here in an atmospheric high-ceilinged old building. Seating is at granite-top tables and at a counter overlooking busy cooks in the noisy open kitchen. Medium-hot is plenty spicy, and everything is prepared without MSG. The lengthy menu offers an array of enticing choices, including tasty onion cake, deep-fried dumplings, and gon-pou shrimp. House-smoked meats, whole fish, and a variety of noodle and rice dishes are also available. Lunch specials are particularly well priced.

Bubba Gump Shrimp Co.

On Beach St., at Pier 39, Fisherman's Wharf, (888) 561-GUMP, (415) 781-GUMP; www.bubbagump.com. L-D daily; $$. No reservations. Validated parking in Pier 39 garage.

The second link in the chain licensed by Paramount Pictures (the first is in Monterey), this theme restaurant is based on the shrimping scenes in the movie *Forrest Gump*. Located on the second-story level at the end of the pier, it resembles a seafood shack. Not surprisingly, the menu has many shrimp selections, most of them deep-fried, as well as fresh fish entrees and baby back ribs. The bar serves up fun drinks, including several kinds of margaritas (the Delta Sunset is particularly tasty) and some non-alcoholic, good-for-you drinks—a peanutty-chocolate Alabama Sweet Smoothie and a frothy pink Run Forrest Run. Dessert should, of course, be a box of chocolates, and that *is* an option. As a bonus, magnificent views of the bay are enjoyed from most tables. An adjacent shop sells everything Gump. (Winston Groom lived in San Francisco when he wrote *Forrest Gump*—the book. In fact, he named the main character after this city's famous department store.) For more description, see page 117.

Buca di Beppo

855 Howard St./4th St., South of Market, (415) 543-POPE; www.bucadibeppo.com. L-D daily; $$. Reservations advised.

The party begins upon entering the door at this festive, happy, old-time southern Italian spot, whose name translates as "Joe's basement." Choose from a warren of small subterranean rooms, or pick one of the comfortable booths in the boisterous upstairs bar, where kids can wiggle and squirm until their heart's content. Then study the menu posted on the wall while being entertained by favorite Italian tunes from the '50s. Another primo seating spot is the Kitchen Table; it seats up to five, and everything coming out of the kitchen parades by. Portions are huge and meant for sharing. Lord have mercy on anyone who orders a "large" of anything here, and on the poor soul who arrives without a BIG appetite. The oblong, thin-crusted, Neapolitan-style pepperoni pizza measures 2 feet long by 1 foot wide and is nothing short of great; it's served high on a footed tray so as not to crowd a tall bowl of spaghetti with one

very large, fist-sized meatball and perhaps a tasty salad, too. Or skip the pizza and order the satisfying garlic bread. Kids have been known to grow saucer eyes when they find out soft drink orders include *unlimited* refills.

The Buena Vista Cafe

2765 Hyde St./Beach St., Fisherman's Wharf, (415) 474-5044; www.thebuenavista.com. B-L-D daily; $. No reservations.

In 1952 the owner of this legendary bar challenged local travel writer Stanton Delaplane to help him re-create the Irish coffee served at Shannon Airport in Ireland. The biggest problem was getting the cream to float. Once mastered, the result is history, and this cozy bar now dispenses more Irish whiskey than any other spot in the country. A decaf version is available. (The official recipe according to its inventor, the late Joe Sheridan, is: Cream as rich as an Irish brogue; coffee as strong as a friendly hand; sugar sweet as the tongue of a rogue; and whiskey smooth as the wit of the land.) It is de rigueur to stop at this cozy spot and find out what all the fuss is about. Delicious casual meals have been served since the 1890s and currently include hamburgers and sandwiches as well as hot entrees with fresh vegetables. A window seat provides views of the action across the street at the cable car turnaround and of the bay and Golden Gate Bridge.

Cafe Bastille

22 Belden Pl./Bush St., Financial District, (415) 986-5673; www.cafebastille.com. L-D M-Sat, SunBr; $-$$. Reservations advised for D; no reservations for L.

Located in the middle of a quaint alley in the "French Quarter," this Very French bistro provides a quick fix for Francophiles. Seating is either at a long row of tight tables with a wall bench on one side and a chair on the other, or

in the Bohemian atmosphere of a crowded cellar. In warm weather, tables are set up outside in the alley. The Americanized menu includes salads, sandwiches, a pizzetta, crêpes, and more substantial entrees such as boudin noir (black sausage) and quiche. Authentic French desserts include crème caramel, chocolate mousse, and a fabulous crêpe topped with chocolate sauce, toasted almonds, and whipped cream. Live music is scheduled upstairs Tuesday through Saturday.

Cafe Claude

7 Claude Lane/Bush St., near Grant Ave., Financial District, (415) 392-3505; www.cafeclaude.com. L M-Sat, D daily; $-$$$. Reservations advised.

Located in a narrow alley, this restaurant is about as Parisian as you can get without an 11-hour flight. In the main dining room, banquettes line walls, and all the furnishings and fittings were bought in France from a restaurant that went out of business and then reassembled here. Additional seating is available upstairs and outside in an alley. The onion soup, pâté plate, pan bagnat, and coq au vin are all exceptional, especially when accompanied by a robust cote du Rhone. For dessert, stick to the classics—a tarte tatin, crème brûlée, or refreshing pastis. Live jazz is scheduled Thursday through Saturday evenings.

Cafe de la Presse

352 Grant Ave., (415) 398-2680; www.cafedela presse.com. B-L-D daily; $$. Reservations accepted.

Large windows offering views of the sidewalk make *the* place to be for breakfast. Dine then on croissants and lattes as well as waffles, pancakes, and oatmeal. Lunch brings on a refreshing Nicoise salad, a good old American hamburger, and a classic croque monsieur. A perfect brasserie dinner consists of a warm fingerling potato salad topped with goat cheese and olive tapenade, grilled sea bass with mashed potatoes made delicious with a sauce Vierge, and Ile Flottante (Floating Island)—the lightest-ever meringue floating in vanilla crème Anglaise dessert. Three beers are on tap at the impressive horseshoe-shaped bar, and 25 wines are poured by the glass. Seating options include casual tables up front, a more formal section centered around a mammoth dessert table topped with a gigantic floral arrangement in the back, and outdoor sidewalk-side tables that entice on nice days. International newspapers and magazines are for sale in the cafe's small gift shop. The surrounding neighborhood is filled with French cafes and has become popular with French visitors.

Café Zoetrope
916 Kearny St./Columbus, North Beach, (415) 291-1700; www.cafecoppola.com. L-D Tu-Sun; $$.

An original Francis Ford Coppola production, this flagship cafe site is located in the historical wedge-shaped Sentinel Building that houses Mr. Coppola's American Zoetrope production company. The Roman trattoria-style menu includes Neapolitan pizzas, Argentine picadas (like tapas), salads, and some pastas and sauces from the Coppola product line.

Caffe Puccini
411 Columbus Ave./Vallejo St., North Beach, (415) 939-7033. Daily 6:30am-11pm; $. No reservations.

This delightful European-style cafe offers great coffees as well as tasty housemade tarts and cakes to go with them. Diners order at a counter and carry items to their table, perhaps sitting under a mirrored wall lined with a banquette or at one of the tiny tables that fill the rest of the angular room and spill out to the sidewalk. Housemade pastas and panini are also available.

Caffé Roma
526 Columbus Ave./Green St., North Beach, (415) 296-7942; www.cafferoma.com. M-Thur 6am-7pm, F 6-8, Sat 6-11, Sun 7-8.

This atmospheric coffee house is the perfect spot for a slow cuppa cap. It is especially fragrant when the immense 50-pound coffee roaster, which takes up a corner of the shop and is visible from the sidewalk, is in action. The roaster is the size of a small car and turns round and round like a clothes dryer.

Caffe Trieste
601 Vallejo St./Grant Ave., North Beach, (415) 392-6739; www.caffetrieste.com. Daily 6:30am-11pm; $. No reservations. No cards.

This very cool, effortlessly authentic, always buzzing coffeehouse was a favorite hangout with the Beat Generation and frequented by Jack Kerouac, Allen Ginsberg, and friends. Bill

Cosby and Steve Allen also hung here, Pavorotti sang here, and it is where Francis Ford Coppola wrote part of *The Godfather* script. Photos on the wall attest to this. It is also credited with having the first espresso machine on the West Coast. In traditional Italian style, the owners perform live opera every Saturday afternoon.

Calzone's
430 Columbus Ave./Green St., North Beach, (415) 397-3600; www.calzonesf.com. L-D daily; $-$$. Reservations accepted.

Reflecting the colors of the Italian flag, walls reaching up to a high ceiling here are painted dark green and decorated with colorful Italian cooking products. Diners seated at marble tables downstairs enjoy up-close views of sidewalk traffic, while some upstairs diners are entertained by overviews of the downstairs diners. Favorite appetizers are light and crunchy deep-fried calamari and fresh tomato bruschetta. Misshapen pizzas are baked in a wood-fired brick oven, and delicious calzone (pizza turnovers) are also available. Housemade lasagna and gnocchi, a hamburger, and freshly made fettuccine ribbons, orzo, and angel hair pastas are also on the menu.

For dessert, **Stella Pastry and Cafe** (446 Columbus Ave., (415) 986-2914; www.stellapastry.com. Daily 7:30am-7pm.) is just next door. It is famous for its trademarked sacripantina cake, described by *Gourmet* magazine as "a San Francisco concoction of cream, air, and magic . . ."

Capp's Corner
1600 Powell St./Green St., North Beach, (415) 989-2589; www.cappscorner.com. L-D daily; $$. Reservations advised.

After entering saloon-style swinging doors, diners are in what is reputed to be the liveliest and noisiest of the few remaining North Beach family-style restaurants. When there is a wait for a table, a seat at the Victorian-era bar can make time fly. In the cozy, friendly interior dining room, where photos of prior happy diners decorate the walls, noisy family groups rub elbows with swinging singles while enjoying hearty Italian food. A bountiful three-course dinner includes minestrone soup, green salad, and entree (steak, osso bucco, lasagna, cannelloni, etc.).

Carnelian Room

555 California St./Montgomery St., 52nd fl. in Bank of America bldg., Financial District, (415) 433-7500; www.carnelianroom.com. D daily, SunBr; $$$. Reservations advised.

In a luxurious setting atop San Francisco's tallest building, this elegant restaurant presents a fine-dining menu and has a wine cellar holding 40,000 bottles. It also provides diners a feast for their eyes, with walnut paneling and fine art on one side and breathtaking bay views on the other. A three-course, fixed-price menu that changes with the season offers items such as sweet pea ravioli with Meyer lemon-mint broth, peppercorn-crusted ahi tuna with ginger mashed potatoes, and a banana pecan tart. Men are requested to wear jackets in the dining room. A bar lounge permits enjoying the view without dining.

Cha-Am

701 Folsom St./3rd St., South of Market, (415) 546-9710; www.chaamthaisf.com. L M-F, D daily; $.

For description, see page 292

Chaya Brasserie

132 The Embarcadero/Mission St., (415) 777-8688; www.thechaya.com. L M-F, D daily; $$$. Reservations advised. Valet parking.

This restaurant features magnificent views of the bay and Bay Bridge that are especially pretty at night. French-style parquet floors, Japanese-style bamboo ceilings, and dramatic contemporary art hanging on natural brick walls work to make it part French brasserie and part Japanese teahouse, or "chaya." The Franco-Japanese menu offers up items such as grilled free-range chicken with Maine lobster tail and wild-rice risotto. A full sushi bar dining area is also an option. Martinis are strong and popular, and desserts are a highlight—a warm Valrhona chocolate cake with raspberry sauce is to die for.

The Cheesecake Factory

251 Geary St./Powell St., 8th fl. in Macy's, Union Square, (415) 391-4444; www.thecheesecake factory.com. L-D daily; $-$$. No reservations.

Reached via an express elevator inside Macy's, this wildly popular rooftop restaurant overlooks Union Square. The eclectic menu is extensive—appetizers, pizza, specialty dishes, pastas, fish and seafood, steaks and chops, salads, sandwiches, and breakfast items are all options—and, as might be expected from the name, it features a head-spinning selection of cheesecakes. With a menu so large it is bound like a book, it is a great spot for either a snack (the avocado egg rolls are great) or a full meal. And then there are the fabulous espresso drinks and frozen, smoothies. Kids like the bite-size burgers on mini-buns known as "roadside sliders" and the sweet-corn tamale cakes—both on the appetizer menu. The delicious problem here is deciding.

Chez Papa

1401 18th St./Missouri St., Potrero Hill, (415) 824-8210; www.chezpapasf.com. L M-Sat, D daily; $$. D reservations advised.

There is usually a line out the door at this tiny, cozy French-style brasserie. A comfortable banquette lines the wall, and the din of happy dinners can be positively deafening—making it a great place to go if talking is not of primary interest. The menu is broken into starters and small plates—a soothing bowl of puréed cauliflower soup, a plate of seared scallops and fava beans—and larger entrees—a roasted chicken or fragrant lamb daube. It doesn't really matter. The entire menu is delectable.

Chez Papa Resto

414 Jessie St./5th St., on Mint Plaza, South of Market, (415) 546-4134; www.chezpapasf.com. L M-F, D daily, Sat-SunBr; $$$. Reservations advised.

Located just across the street from San Francisco Centre, this spot serves authentic French Provencal cuisine in a comfortable room with high ceilings, large windows, and chic black walls. The professional staff is mostly French and from the South of France, so charming accents ring out throughout a meal. However, the cool temperatures that keep diners inside and not out on the umbrella- and heater-equipped front patio is all San Francisco. Menu stars include a butter lettuce salad with mustard vinaigrette, a tasty and tender braised lamb daube, any of several roasted fishes, and grease-less pommes frites with aioli.

Chinatown restaurants

See page 18.

Second Cliff House, circa 1896

Citizen Cake

399 Grove St./Gough St., Hayes Valley,
(415) 861-2228; www.citizencake.com. B-L Tu-F,
D Tu-Sat, Sat-SunBr; $$-$$$. Reservations advised.
Valet parking F-Sat.

It *is* nice being seated in the sleek, modern, industrial-style interior here, with its soothing view through tall windows. Lunch choices might include a Cuban marinated pork-Havarti cheese sandwich on scrumptious housemade bread, or a puffy Molinari pepperoni pizza. A French-style coffee bowl of hot chocolate prepared with Scharffen Berger bittersweet chocolate and topped with a marvelous housemade marshmallow makes a great dessert, but something from the celebrated pastry kitchen is a must—maybe a vanilla cupcake with white chocolate frosting or a sticky toffee pudding or a blood orange cremesicle parfait. And don't forget a bag of mixed cookies to take home. When leaving, do view the glassed-in demonstration pastry kitchen and then stop in at the art gallery next door.

Cliff House

1090 Point Lobos Ave., Outer Richmond District,
(415) 386-3330; www.cliffhouse.com.

Perched solidly at the edge of the Pacific on Point Lobos bedrock, this historic treasure holds the only ocean-front restaurant in San Francisco. It has been around for quite some time, since 1863 to be exact, but in four different renditions—it twice burned to the ground and it went through a major update completed in 2004. Though all the changes the structure has always housed a restaurant, and it has been part of the Golden Gate National Recreation Area since 1977. Elegant **Sutro's** *(L-D daily; $$$. Reservations advised.)* is housed in a new 2-story wing with floor-to-ceiling windows and features an American seafood menu. Hardwired remote control Venetian blinds control the glare. The more casual **Bistro** *(B-L-D daily; $$. No reservations.)* serves a less expensive menu that includes omelettes, sandwiches, and fish and chips.

While here, visit the **Camera Obscura** *((415) 750-0415; www.giantcamera.com. Daily 11-5, weather permitting. $3, seniors & 2-12 $2.).* Leonardo daVinci's 16th-century invention was probably a popular tourist attraction in the 1700s and 1800s. This reproduction was built here in 1946 and was once part of Playland-at-the-Beach. It uses a 10-inch mirror and two opposing plano-convex lenses to focus a live image of the shoreline outside onto a 6-foot parabolic screen inside. Rotating slowly, it presents magnified views of Ocean Beach, Seal Rocks, and crashing Pacific waves. The personalized tour is both entertaining and educational.

Visible from shore, barking sea lions and brown pelicans share space out on historic **Seal Rocks.** They can be seen with just the naked eye or viewed through an antique telescope. However, there are now more birds than seals since the seals got smart and moved to Pier 39—where there are no sharks and more food.

Scenic trails leading to the **Sutro Baths ruins**—it was once the world's largest indoor swimming pool complex—and to **Land's End** begin on the bluffs above to the east.

Cordon Bleu

1574 California St./Polk St., Nob Hill, (415) 673-5637. L Tu-Sat, D Tu-Sun; $. No reservations. No cards.

One of the oldest Vietnamese restaurants in the city and under the same management since 1976, this petite venue has just a few counter seats and tiny tables. From the counter, diners can sip a complimentary mug of hot tea while watching their meal being prepared. Satisfying one-plate meals consist of a large scoop of rice topped with light tomato-based meat sauce and a choice of a deep-fried imperial roll, a tasty barbecued beef satay (listed on the menu as shish kebab), or barbecued chicken.

Landmark's Lumiere movie theater *(1572 California St./Polk St., (415) 267-4893; www.landmarktheatres.com.)* is right next door, and a host of shops are just around the corner.

Delancey Street Restaurant

600 The Embarcadero/Brannan St., (415) 512-5179; http://delanceystreetfoundation.org/enterrestaurant. php. L Tu-F, D Tu-Sun, Sat-SunBr; $-$$. Reservations advised. Valet parking.

The comfortable open room here lets in plenty of light and even a glimpse of the bay. Though that is enough to lure in plenty of diners, this special restaurant is also a training school of the Delancey Street Foundation—the country's largest and most acclaimed self-help residential organization for former hard-core criminals. It is completely self-supporting. All tips are considered donations, and all restaurant profits go directly to caring for the residents. Interestingly, no resident who has finished the 2-year training program has ever gone on to commit a serious crime. In this win-win atmosphere, it seems impossible to leave unsatisfied. Lunch is a particular bargain, with plenty of well-priced, well-executed sandwiches, a hot dog, a hamburger, and an assortment of heart-healthy items—including a Chocolate Decadence dessert that claims only 200 calories and 6 grams of fat. The menu changes daily and features international home-style dishes and also items reflecting the current residents' backgrounds.

E&O Trading Company

314 Sutter St./Grant Ave., 2 blks. from Union Square, (415) 693-0303; www.eotrading.com. L M-Sat, D daily; $$. Reservations advised.

The sleek, quiet exterior here belies the warm, roaring interior designed to resemble an Indonesian trading company warehouse. Live guitar music keeps things jumping in the busy bar and is heard throughout the restaurant. Seating for meals is found both upstairs, where some diners have views of the street and others can watch the action down in the bar, and downstairs adjoining the bar, where there is additionally a counter with tall stools overlooking the kitchen. (An intriguing bamboo birdcage collection hangs near the bar.) Tropical sodas prepared with housemade fruit syrups are the perfect accompaniment to the mild-mannered but complexly flavored Indonesian fare. Sharing a variety of items from the southeast Asian menu is the way to go. A feast can be composed of lamb naan (a stuffed bread); Cambodian lettuce cups filled with spicy chicken and vegetables; Thai crab cakes with a tangy red curry sauce; papaya-avocado salad with spicy Asian greens; and delicious Hawaiian walu fish with black-and-tan sesame seed crust served atop a bed of rice atop green long beans. Noteworthy small dishes—the menu's strong point—include crispy Indonesian corn fritters and satays with spicy peanut sauce. Desserts are made in-house. For more description, see page 224.

Elite Cafe

2049 Fillmore St./California St., Upper Fillmore, (415) 67-ELITE; www.theelitecafe.com. D daily, Sat-SunBr; $$$. Reservations advised. Valet parking.

Parties of four get the best seats here, in enclosed wooden booths left from the restaurant's prior life as an old-time Chinese restaurant. In addition to Cajun martinis and other exotic bar drinks, the menu offers a selection of contemporary spicy Cajun-Creole dishes that includes gumbo, jambalaya, and blackened salmon.

Ella's

500 Presidio Ave./California St., Presidio Heights, (415) 441-5669; www.ellassanfrancisco.com. B-L M-F, Sat-SunBr; $. Reservations accepted for L.

This cheery spot changes its menu weekly and serves a close to perfect weekend brunch. Grin and bear the wait. It is worth it for the oh-so-simple fluffy scrambled eggs that come with faultless home fries and an oversize baking soda biscuit with strawberry preserves. The waffles, pancakes, and chicken hash are also primo. And parents will be happy to know it is kid central here on weekends, with pacifiers, toys, and baby carriers everywhere. The limited lunch menu includes soups, sandwiches, salads, hot entrees, and a delicious gingery punch made with fresh OJ. After, it's just a block over to Sacramento Street for some chi-chi shopping.

El Mansour

3119 Clement St./32nd Ave., Outer Richmond District, (415) 751-2312; www.elmansour.com. D Tu-Sun; $$$. Reservations advised.

Upon entering the double doors of this Moroccan restaurant, diners are encased in another world. Cloth is draped from the ceiling in the intimate dining room, giving occupants the illusion of being inside a sultan's tent. Floors covered with plush oriental carpets and hassock seating at low tables of inlaid wood add to the sensuous feeling. After diners select an entree from the fixed-price menu, a waiter in a long caftan appears to perform a ritual hand washing. Hands are gathered over a large metal pot placed in the middle of the table, then splashed with warm water. When the first course arrives—a tasty lentil soup—diners drink it right from the bowl, since no eating utensils are provided unless requested. A house-made Moroccan bread accompanies it. The next course is a salad plate of spicy marinated rounds of carrots and cucumbers plus a delicious mixture of tomatoes and green peppers and eggplant puree meant to be scooped up with the bread. Then comes bastela—a fragrant pie containing a sweet chicken and almond mixture wrapped in flaky filo pastry and sprinkled with powdered sugar. Entree choices include seafood, rabbit, couscous, and shish kabob, as well as succulent roasted chicken and tender stewed lamb topped with almonds, honey, or prunes. Tangines (stews) are another option. Dessert is fried bananas with honey and a repeat of the hand-bathing ritual. And finally the waiter pours mint tea, skillfully and beautifully, from up high. Belly dancers perform nightly.

Enoshima Sushi

2280 Chestnut St./Scott St., Marina District, (415) 563-0162; www.enoshimasushi.com. L-D M-Sat; $.

What's lacking in atmosphere here is more than made up for in delicious bargain fare and fast service. The extensive menu offers a surprisingly large choice of traditional Japanese items: teriyaki, tempura, sashimi, sukiyaki, nabe, sushi, donburi, udon noodles, and more. For dessert try mochi ice cream.

Enrico's

504 Broadway/Kearny St., North Beach, (415) 982-6223; www.enricossf.com. L-D daily; $$. Reservations advised. Valet parking.

Enrico Banducci has passed on. He was the well-known original owner of this landmark restaurant that was the city's first coffeehouse and a favorite with beatniks. So, too, has the coffeehouse atmosphere passed on. Nowadays the tip amounts to what the tab once did, and the only beat you'll see is a beet in the salad. But the outdoor patio now sports some classy and comfortable couches and is heated in cool weather, and it is still one of the best spots around for people watching. In the large, open interior room, a large bar takes up one side of the room and a sea of tables and wall-hugging banquettes populate the other. The restaurant becomes a supper club on the evenings live jazz is scheduled. Items on the short menu include a Caesar salad, petite burgers, pizza, and a grilled flat iron steak with frites.

Espetus Churrascaria

1686 Market St./Gough St., (415) 552-8792; www.espetus.com. L-D daily; $$$. Reservations advised.

Operating within a glass-walled corner building, this authentic Brazilian steakhouse provides comfortable seating at well-spaced tables. Fine paintings by renowned Brazilian artist Edgar Cliquet depict Brazilian scenes. Meals are a set price ($18.95-$29.95 for lunch, $39.95 for dinner) and include as much as you can eat. Skewers of meats cooked over an open fire are brought around to each table by skilled carvers and sliced onto diners' plates. Meats include filet mignon and other cuts of beef as well as pork, lamb, chicken, housemade sausage, and shrimp. The salad bar is a cornucopia of delights. It offers tangy Brazilian potato salad and coleslaw and also some typical Brazilian side dishes. Two kinds of sangria, signature cocktails, and Brazilian beers are available in addition to wine, and desserts include a tasty passion fruit mousse and a classic tres leches pudding cake.

Farallon

450 Post St./Powell St., Union Square, (415) 956-6969; www.farallonrestaurant.com. D daily; $$$+. Reservations advised. Valet parking.

The long bar entryway of this spectacular restaurant leads under gorgeous lighting fixtures posing as jellyfish, past curving stairs slathered with "caviar," and on into a magnificent back room. An elaborate painted mosaic, successfully designed to look aged, covers the three Gothic arches of the main dining room ceiling (it was once the ceiling for the Elks Club salt-water swimming pool on the floor below) along with gargantuan belle époque sea urchin light fixtures. No table in the tiered main room is bad, and many are attached to exquisitely comfortable velvet-covered booths. The fish-centered menu of impeccably fresh seasonal "coastal cuisine" changes daily and includes innovative preparations of fish, a large selection of raw items (including house-prepared caviar), and usually a lobster dish. Raw shellfish appetizers and roasted fish entrees are usually available, along with a token chicken and beef item. Luscious desserts have included Tahitian vanilla bean fritters with apricot coulis and a Bing cherry Napoleon.

Far East Cafe

631 Grant Ave./Sacramento St., Chinatown, (415) 982-3245; www.fareastcafesf.com. L-D daily; $$. Reservations advised.

Looking much as it did when it opened in 1920, this intriguing restaurant has seven private wooden booths with curtains for a door. These wonderful, cozy enclosures provide the ultimate in privacy. The extensive a la carte menu includes sizzling rice soup, fried won tons, cashew chicken, deep-fried squab, and a variety of chow mein and chop suey dishes, and the family-style Cantonese dinner is always a good choice. Exotic shark's fin, bird's nest, and seaweed soups are also available.

Ferry Building Marketplace

At foot of Market St./The Embarcadero, (415) 693-0996; www.ferrybuildingmarketplace.com. M-F 10-6, Sat 9-6, Sun 11-5. No dogs. Valet parking.

Bay views punctuate the long (it's the length of two football fields), 2-story-high, sky lighted interior corridor of this landmark 1898 building—a sort of indoor Main Street—filled with food-related stalls and shops. All the best, most delicious organic produce and gourmet delicacies are easy to collect and carry home: Acme baked goods, Peet's coffee, Cowgirl Creamery cheeses, Frog Hollow Farm stone fruit, Scharffen Berger chocolates. Shops specializing in caviar and in mushrooms are also in the mix, as are a branch of **Book Passage** (see page 224) and **Culinaire**, an antique shop specializing in food- and wine-related objects. Restaurants include **The Slanted Door** (see page 82). Decorated with a collection of bamboo birdcages, the exotic **Imperial Tea Court** *((800) 567-5898, (415) 788-6080; www.imperialtea.com. $5-$8/person.)* serves some of the world's most acclaimed, and expensive, teas. Sit down at one of the beautiful rosewood tables and relax while a selected tea is prepared. Like it? It's available for purchase, as are an assortment of tea accouterments. A **farmers' market** *((415) 291-3276;_www.ferryplazafarmersmarket.com. Tu 10-2 & Sat 8-2.)* operates informally around the exterior of the building.

Fog City Diner

1300 Battery St./The Embarcadero, (415) 982-2000; www.fogcitydiner.com. L M-F, D daily, Sat-SunBr; $$. Reservations advised.

Glitzy with chrome and glowing with neon, this inviting diner offers comfy black leather booths and good views all around. The updated comfort food includes jalapeño corn bread, tasty crab cakes, chicken schnitzel with homey garlic mashed potatoes, and, of course, a good old American hamburger. Opt for a side of housemade bread and butter pickles, some crispy onion rings made with Anchor Steam beer batter, and a house-invented Barbados Cosmopolitan cocktail, and you're ready to rock 'n roll (however, there's no jukebox in *this* diner). Do save room for ice cream—perhaps a fabulous sundae of the day, a milkshake or malted, or maybe a black cow (root beer float).

Forbes Island

At Pier 39, Fisherman's Wharf, (415) 951-4900; www.forbesisland.com. D W-Sun; $$$. Reservations required. Boat shuttle $3/person; validated parking at Pier 39 garage.

After the short 5-minute voyage over to the world's only floating island, owner/host Forbes Thor Kiddoo conducts a short tour. He provides a quick glimpse of a replica 40-foot lighthouse and of some *real* sand and palm trees, then it's down the steps to the partially submerged, oriental-carpeted dining room decorated with antique nautical artifacts and paintings. The smallish menu—a selection of California cuisine with a French twist—is prepared in a tiny galley and includes an excellent Caesar salad, a divine rack of lamb with 2-inch-thick chops, and a *very* French apple tarte tatin. For a romantic occasion, consider requesting the single teeny table in the diminutive wine cellar. Cigars can be enjoyed outside overlooking the sea lions basking on nearby docks. And don't miss seeing the women's lounge.

Foreign Cinema

2534 Mission St./21st St., Mission District, (415) 648-7600; www.foreigncinema.com. D daily, Sat-SunBr; $$-$$$. Reservations advised. Valet parking at D.

Operating within the dramatically remodeled interior of a former department store in which everything was ripped out and left bare and trendy, this wildly popular spot attracts the hordes down its long, votive-lit corridor to party and feast. Seating is either on an open-air patio (covered by a clear plastic canopy in cool weather), where diners can watch the foreign flick of the week, or in the roaring main dining room with its 20-foot-tall ceiling. Specialties include an expansive oyster bar, baked cheese with roasted potatoes, curry-roasted chicken, and chocolate pot de crème. Several communal tables are available for walk-ins.

Gary Danko

800 North Point St./Hyde St., Fisherman's Wharf, (415) 749-2060; www.garydanko.com. D daily; $$$+. Reservations advised. Valet parking.

Simply the best is found here, from buttery foie gras to smoked sturgeon on buckwheat blini to winter root vegetable soup to juniper-crusted venison to sweet Meyer lemon soufflé cake. A fixed-price dinner includes some of the owner-chef's signature dishes—glazed oysters with leeks, salmon medallions topped with horseradish mousse, seasonal flambéed fruit prepared tableside—and a cheese cart presents enticing artisanal cheeses. It is the perfect place to celebrate a special occasion. Large flower arrangements greet diners in the entryway, and two sophisticated, intimate dining rooms keep the atmosphere cozy and lively. Worthy of mention, too, is the serene, spa-like ladies room.

Ghirardelli Chocolate Manufactory & Soda Fountain

900 North Point, in Ghirardelli Square, Fisherman's Wharf, (415) 771-4903; www.ghirardelli.com. Sun-Thur 10am-11pm, F-Sat to 12; $. No reservations.

A small working chocolate factory using original equipment from the early 1900s still operates for show in the back of this classic ice cream parlor. All of the chocolate sauces and syrups are made on site, as is the fudge sold in the shop. After selecting from the mouth-watering menu, ice cream-lovers take a seat and await the fulfillment of their ice cream fantasy. Special concoctions include The Alcatraz Rock (rocky road and vanilla ice cream covered with a shell of chocolate, chopped almonds, whipped cream, and a whole cherry) and The Earthquake Sundae, which serves four or more people (eight flavors of ice cream with eight different toppings accented with bananas, whipped cream, chopped almonds, and cherries). Hot fudge sundaes, sodas, and milkshakes are also available. Ghirardelli chocolate goodies, including a 5-pound chocolate bar, are sold in an adjoining shop.

Gold Mountain

644 Broadway/Stockton St., Chinatown, (415) 296-7733. Dim sum M-F 10:30-3, Sat-Sun 9-3; $. Reservations advised.

In the 19th century, Chinese immigrants nicknamed San Francisco "Gold Mountain," in reference to its promise of a new life and fortune. This gigantic, bustling restaurant now promises everyone delicious dim sum (see page 17), which is served on floors two and three. It is so big that the waiters use walkie-talkies to communicate. Though floor two alone seats 280 people, there still usually is a wait. Once seated, if carts don't arrive fast enough, flag down someone who looks in charge and order directly from the kitchen. Crisp taro balls and roast duck are particularly good here.

Gordon Biersch Brewery Restaurant

2 Harrison St./The Embarcadero, (415) 243-8246; www.gordonbierschrestaurants.com. L-D daily; $. Reservations accepted.

This brewpub is located on the waterfront in the historic Hills Bros. Coffee Building. Outdoor seating and brewery tours are available. For more description, see page 198.

Greens

Laguna St./Marina Blvd., at Fort Mason Center, Bldg. A, The Marina, (415) 771-6222; www.greens restaurant.com. L Tu-Sat, D M-Sun, SunBr; $$-$$$. Reservations essential. Free parking lot adjoins.

With high ceilings, large windows framing the Golden Gate Bridge, and colorful modern art hanging on the walls, this trendy, all-vegetarian restaurant packs 'em in. Starters on the ever-changing menu might include a fragrant and flavorful black bean chili or a delicate watercress salad with pears and walnuts. Entrees include pastas and sandwiches. Desserts are uncomplicated but delicious—perhaps a pear-almond upside down cake or a fabulous apricot tart with pistachio nuts and toasted almond ice cream. On Saturday nights, a fixed-price three-course dinner is the only menu option. Greens is run by the San Francisco Zen Center, and many of the fresh herbs and vegetables are grown at the center's West Marin farm.

Greens To Go *((415) 771-6330. M-Thur 8-8, F-Sat 8-5, Sun 9-4.)* operates off the entry and packs up many menu items as well as the delicious house breads, pastries, and desserts.

Hard Rock Cafe

On Beach St., at Pier 39, Fisherman's Wharf, (415) 956-2013; www.hardrock.com. L-D daily; $-$$. Reservations accepted Sept-May. Validated parking in Pier 39 garage.

Sitting in one of the roomy booths here allows first-rate people watching. Wall decorations include George Harrison's and Pete Townsend's guitars, Grateful Dead stuff, and a large Fillmore poster collection. And, as might be expected from the name, rock & roll is played non-stop. The American-style food is quite good, the service attentive, and the prices reasonable. The house salad is crisp, cold romaine lettuce, and the housemade Thousand Island dressing is tangy with fresh onion. Hamburgers are served on whole-wheat sesame buns and are just plain good. The menu also offers an assortment of sandwiches, housemade chili, grilled fresh fish, and rich, old-fashioned desserts. A plethora of souvenir items can be ordered at the table and added to the tab.

Henry's Hunan

924 Sansome St./Broadway, North Beach, (415) 956-7727; www.henryshunanrestaurant.com. L-D daily; $-$$. Reservations accepted.

Once upon a time this was a tiny, obscure restaurant located in Chinatown. It seated 29 people. Then it was described in *The New Yorker* as "the best Chinese restaurant in the world." Lines formed, and it was no longer possible to just saunter in and sit down at one of the few tables or at the counter, where half the pleasure was in watching the cooks in action. To satisfy demand, the restaurant moved to this huge warehouse, which seats 314 and permits instant seating once again. The kitchen uses unsaturated oils, lean meats, and skinned chicken, and it uses no MSG or sugar; salt-free dishes are available. The unusual Diana's Special consists of spicy meat sauce and lettuce sandwiched between two deep-fried flour pancakes. Harvest pork (a traditional dish fed to farm workers and pallbearers to give them strength), hot and sour chicken, and bean sprout salad are all especially good, as is the cold chicken salad mixed with shredded cucumbers, shiny noodles, and peanut dressing. Specialties include excellent fresh seafood dishes and unusual house-smoked ham, chicken, and duck cured over hickory wood, tea leaves, and orange peels. The distinctive hot bean sauce—a combination of fermented black beans, powdered red peppers, garlic, oil, and vinegar—is available to go.

Hornblower Cruises

Pier 33, Bay St./The Embarcadero, (888) HORN-BLOWER, (415) 788-8866; www.hornblower.com. D daily, $83-$114; Sat-SunBr, $72; 4-12 half price, under 4 free. Reservations required.

Diners at brunch are seated as they board, and the maitre d' announces to each table when it is their turn to visit the bounteous buffet. Magnificent views of San Francisco and the bay are enjoyed as the boat goes out under the Golden Gate Bridge, past Sausalito and Angel Island, and beside Alcatraz. Live music plays in the background, and the Captain makes the rounds to greet everyone. After dining, there is time to tour the vessel. The dinner-dance cruise is more formal, with waiters serving four-course dinners. Special events are also often scheduled. Note that though highchairs and booster seats are not available, parents are welcome to bring on board strollers with wheel locks, and children are given crayons and coloring books to keep them busy.

The *San Francisco Spirit* offers a similar Sunday Brunch cruise *(Pier 9/The Embarcadero, (800) 2-YACHTS, (415) 788-9100; www.signaturesf.com. SunBr $76; 4-12 $26, under 4 free. Reservations required.).*

House of Nanking

919 Kearny St./Jackson St., Chinatown, (415) 421-1429. L-D daily; $-$$. No reservations.

It seems everyone knows about this exceptional restaurant, so expect lines. Seating is at small Formica tables and at a counter crammed into two small rooms separated by a busy kitchen. Though the menu is not descriptive, most everything is delicious—especially the pot stickers, steamed vegetable dumplings Nanking, onion pancakes, and Nanking scallops or crispy chicken with sesame vegetables (both are deep-fried tempura-style and topped with a tasty garlic sauce). Chow meins feature large housemade noodles; rice noodles are also available.

A stress-reducing option is to decide on the number of dishes desired and let the server (who is often the owner-chef) select a balanced menu. After dining here, one restaurant critic reflected upon the idea that it must be written somewhere that the more abysmal the decor and unfriendly the service in a Chinese restaurant, the more exquisite the food.

House of Prime Rib

1906 Van Ness Ave./Washington St., (415) 885-4605; www.houseofprimerib.ypguides.net. D daily; $$$. Reservations advised. Valet parking.

The specialty of the house in this posh, clubby spot has been the same since 1949—the finest aged prime rib served right from the cart and carved to order tableside. (In fact, the only other entree on the menu is grilled fresh fish.) Choose a City Cut (for small appetites), an English Cut (several thin slices), or a King Henry VIII Cut (for those with king-size appetites). The complete dinner includes a chilled green salad prepared at the table and presented with *chilled* forks, bread and butter, either mashed potatoes with gravy or a baked potato, fresh horseradish sauce, creamed fresh spinach, and Yorkshire pudding. Come here hungry.

Il Fornaio

1265 Battery St./Greenwich St., in Levi's Plaza, near The Embarcadero, (415) 986-0100; www.ilfornaio.com. L M-F, D daily, Sat-SunBr. Reservations advised. Valet parking.

Diners have a choice of sitting inside beneath tall ceilings at tables covered elegantly with white cloths or outside on a more casual patio at marble tables sheltered by a glass windbreak. Outside seating is prime in good weather and permits enjoying an adjacent park fountain that sounds like a rushing waterfall. Items on the traditional Italian menu lend themselves to sharing, and a salad, pasta, and main course making a generous meal for two. Several pizzas and risottos are also options. Breads and desserts are housemade.

Isobune Sushi

1737 Post St., in Kintetsu Mall at Japan Center, (415) 563-1030. L-D daily; $. No reservations.

At this small sushi bar, items circle the counter on little floating boats. Customers remove what looks interesting.

Jackson Fillmore

2506 Fillmore St./Jackson St., Pacific Heights,
(415) 346-5288; www.jacksonfillmoresf.com. D Tu-Sun;
$$. Reservations advised; accepted for 3+.

Those who show up at this trattoria without reservations usually find themselves standing in a line that stretches out the door; complimentary bruchetta and wine are sometimes provided to take off the edge. Even those *with* reservations can wind up sitting at cramped tables or on a stool at the counter. However, the exceptional antipastos and pastas make it all worthwhile. Cloud-like gnocchi, fresh fish items, and truffle dishes are options, and a hot zabaglione classico fresh from the stove makes a heavenly dessert.

Jeanty at Jack's

615 Sacramento St./Montgomery St., Financial
District, (415) 693-0941; www.jeantyatjacks.com.
L M-F, D daily; $$$. Reservations advised.

This charming French bistro operates in a delightful multi-level space. A delicious dinner might start with a complexly spiced tomato soup in a bowl topped with puff pasty, then move on to a delicate sole meunière atop mashed potatoes. For dessert, it's hard to go wrong with a soothing rice pudding topped with tiny brandied cherries.

John's Grill

63 Ellis St./Powell St., Union Square, (415) 986-DASH;
www.johnsgrill.com. L-D daily; $-$$. Reservations
advised for D.

This restaurant opened in 1908 and was a setting in Dashiell Hammett's *The Maltese Falcon*. It is a national literary landmark. The cozy interior features original gaslight fixtures, some original period furnishings, and mahogany-paneled walls covered with photos of famous patrons and historical San Francisco scenes. The lunch menu offers a variety of salads as well as a hamburger, several pastas, and that hard-to-find Hangtown fry (an early California dish prepared with oysters and eggs). Dinner brings on extensive seafood selections. One of the most popular dishes is straight out of the book—Sam Spade's Chops (broiled rack of lamb with a baked potato and sliced tomatoes).

Katia's: A Russian Tea Room

600 5th Ave./Balboa St., Sunset District,
(415) 668-9292; www.katias.com. L W-F, D W-Sun; $$.
Reservations taken.

Located in the heart of San Francisco's Russian neighborhood, among side streets lined with noteworthy vintage houses, this intimate restaurant offers traditional thick beet-and-cabbage borscht, breaded ground chicken cutlets Pozharski, and golubtsi—cabbage leaves stuffed with ground beef. For dessert, try boiled cheese dumplings topped with exquisite fresh sour cream. Live guitar music is scheduled on Saturday evenings.

Across the street, teeny, tiny **Globus** (*332 Balboa St., (415) 668-4723; www.globusbooks. com. W-Sun 12-5.*) specializes in Slavic books.

Khan Toke Thai House

5937 Geary Blvd./24th Ave., Outer Richmond District,
(415) 668-6654. D daily; $-$$. Reservations advised.

Diners remove their shoes before entering a maze of lushly decorated small dining rooms. The richly embellished tables are low to the ground. Some have floor pillows for reclining, while others have wells in the floor beneath into which legs can dangle. Many of the unusual Thai herbs used in preparing dishes for the extensive, well-executed menu are grown in a courtyard behind the restaurant. The extensive menu is heavy with delicious choices, and a large selection of vegetarian items is available.

Kokkari

200 Jackson St./Front St., Financial District,
(415) 981-0983; www.kokkari.com. L M-F, D M-Sat;
$$$. Reservations advised. Valet parking at D.

Named for a small fishing village on the island of Samos in the Aegean Sea, this stylish restaurant serves sophisticated versions of Greek cuisine. Starters include traditional spanakotiropita (spinach-filled filo pies) and pikilia (an array of delicious classic spreads served with grilled housemade pita and rice-filled dolmathes). Entrees include fabulous grilled lamb chops with memorably good baked potato wedges, a grilled whole striped bass, and what might be the best rendition of moussaka west of Athens. Among the delectable desserts are a creamy rice pudding with poached peaches and cherries, and an expansive array of Greek cookies and baklava—they taste even better with a cup of strong stone-ground Greek coffee prepared in a giant urn over hot sand, or with a glass of ouzo selected from ten varieties. Seating here is a decided bonus and includes both comfortable booths and upholstered chairs.

A sister restaurant, Evvia, is located in Palo Alto (see page 181).

Kuleto's Italian Restaurant
221 Powell St./Geary St., in Villa Florence Hotel, Union Square, (415) 397-7720; www.kuletos.com. B-L-D daily; $$. Reservations advised. Valet parking.

Northern Italian cuisine is served here in elegant surroundings that feature high vaulted ceilings and Italian marble floors. The 40-foot bar was hand-carved in England and brought here around the Horn. It was formerly at the Palace Hotel, where it survived the 1906 earthquake. Counter seating in the back is often available at the last minute and provides the additional treat of watching the skilled kitchen staff in action. Breads and pastries are housemade, as are pastas, which, along with grilled items, are particularly good. Don't miss sampling the signature appetizer—radicchio e pancetta alla griglia. The 100% cold-pressed extra virgin California olive oil used by the restaurant is attractively bottled for purchase and makes a good souvenir.

La Méditerranée
2210 Fillmore St./California St., Upper Fillmore, (415) 921-2956; www.cafelamed.com.

For description, see page 293.

La Taqueria
2889 Mission St./25th St., Mission District, (415) 285-7117. L-D daily; $. No reservations. No cards.

For fast food Mexican-style, step through one of the two arches here and head to the order counter. Then pick a table, and kick back. Entertainment is provided by a colorful folk mural decorating one wall, by cooks in the open kitchen busily preparing orders, and by a jukebox with Mexican music. The menu is simple: either a taco made with two steamed corn tortillas or a burrito made with a flour tortilla. Fillings are a choice of pork, beef, sausage, chicken, or vegetarian (beans and cheese). Pinto beans and fresh tomato salsa round things out; avocado and sour cream cost a bit more.

Depending on the season, delicious housemade fresh fruit drinks include strawberry, cantaloupe, orange, banana, and pineapple.

Pick up a walk-away dessert next door at **Dianda's Italian-American Pastry** *(2883 Mission St./25th St., (415) 647-5469. M-Sat 6-6, Sun 6-4:30.)*, where everything is made from scratch and the cannoli are particularly good.

Le Colonial
20 Cosmo Pl./off Taylor & Post, 2 blks. from Union Square, (415) 931-3600; www.lecolonialsf.com. D daily; $$$. Reservations advised. Valet parking.

Hidden away on the back-alley site, this is a branch in an upscale chain of Vietnamese restaurants. With a tropical decor evoking 1920s Vietnam—vintage black-and-white photos of turn-of-the-century Saigon adorn the walls while quiet ceiling fans gently stir the air—the outdoor verandah and elegant interior dining rooms offer sanctuary from street bustle. Drinks are exotic, appetizers include several kinds of spring rolls, and fresh tropical fruit and housemade sorbets and cookies are winning desserts. An inviting upstairs lounge serves an hors d'oeuvres menu and sometimes schedules live music.

Liverpool Lil's
2942 Lyon St./Lombard St., the Presidio, (415) 921-6664; www.liverpoollils.com. L M-F, Sat-SunBr, D daily; $-$$.

This atmospheric pub is often packed to its authentic rafters. On-tap brews are refreshing, and two TVs are tuned to sports. A limited menu—a decent hamburger, fish & chips, a few finger foods—is served in the cozy front alcoves and in a sidewalk area outside that is inviting on a warm day. A full dinner menu is available in the popular back dining room.

Lovejoy's Tea Room
1351 Church St./Clipper St., Noe Valley, (415) 648-5895; www.lovejoystearoom.com.W-Sun 11-6; $-$$. Reservations for 4+.

As cozy as anything encountered in England, this tiny, absolutely charming spot provides a welcome retreat from city streets. The menu offers all things English—toasted crumpets, scones, tea sandwiches, sausage rolls, pasties. Tea service ranges from a simple cream tea to an expansive high tea, and a special Wee

Tea is served to children. And diners can shop while they sip: Everything is for sale—from tea cups to furniture. I say, old chap, what fun!

Luna Park

694 Valencia St./18th St., Mission District, (415) 553-8584; www.lunaparksf.com. L M-F, D daily, Sat-SunBr; $$. Reservations advised.

A visit to this loud and lively little bistro should begin at the bar with a mojito cocktail. After enjoying the bartender's show of smashing the aromatic mint and mixing it with plenty of light rum and very little seltzer, it's time to claim a table amid the merlot-colored walls and peruse the enticing menu. Winners include a fabulously flavorful, really, really good grilled artichoke with lemon aioli, a smashing breaded pork cutlet stuffed with mushrooms and Gruyère cheese, and gooey upscale s'mores made by slathering housemade graham crackers with molten marshmallow and bittersweet chocolate from petite fondue pots.

Magic Flute

3673 Sacramento St./Spruce St., Presidio Heights, (415) 922-1225; www.magicfluteristorante.com. L M-F, D W-Sat, Sat-SunBr; $-$$. Reservations advised.

Situated within a vintage Victorian on a low-key, high-quality shopping street, this pleasant spot offers comfortable indoor tables as well as outdoor garden seating. The work of local artists colorfully decorates the sponge-painted walls. Among the lunch items on the California-Italian menu are salads and pastas as well as a great cheeseburger and a portobello focaccia sandwich. A few of these items stay on the brunch menu, when egg dishes are added. The housemade desserts include a killer double fudge chocolate cake and a rich, rich tiramisu.

Mama's on Washington Square

1701 Stockton St./Filbert St., North Beach, (415) 362-6421; www.mamas-sf.com. B-L Tu-Sun; $. No reservations. No cards.

Diners wait in a usually long line to enter this cozy, cheery spot on a corner of Washington Square. However, once inside the hassle is over. Orders are placed at a counter from which the kitchen action is visible, and then diners are seated by their server. Breakfast choices include blueberry pancakes, thick French toast made from various breads, a variety of omelettes, and tasty Florentine eggs prepared with fresh spinach. Lunch brings on salads, sandwiches, hamburgers, hot dogs, and a zucchini and cheese frittata. Delicious desserts and fresh strawberry creations—even out of season—are a house specialty.

Mario's Bohemian Cigar Store Cafe

566 Columbus Ave./Union St., North Beach, (415) 362-0536. L-D daily; $. No reservations.

Cigars are no longer sold in this cozy retreat across from Washington Square, but hot focaccia sandwiches are. The meatball and eggplant are both made with grilled onions and melted Swiss cheese and are delicious. The short menu also offers panini and a few hot entrees. For drinks, try a specialty coffee or maybe a comforting steamed almond milk. Tables are available inside and out, and a vintage oak bar with stools is the perfect perch for singles.

Marnee Thai

2225 Irving St./23rd Ave., Sunset District, (415) 665-9500; www.marneethaisf.com. L-D W-M; $. Reservations advised.

Exceptional Thai cuisine is served in a tiny room completely covered with attractive, sound-absorbing woven fibers. Especially good are the mild yellow curry dishes prepared with potatoes in a complex mixture of spices softened with coconut milk, and the stir-fried chicken with cashew nuts (tossed on after the dish is cooked, allowing them to retain their crunchiness). A side order of delicious peanut sauce and a palate-refreshing cucumber salad are recommended. Allow time before or after for shopping the produce markets scattered among the mostly Asian businesses along this bustling street.

A branch is at 1243 9th Ave. *(at Irving St, Inner Sunset District, (415) 731-9999. L-D daily.).*

Marrakech

419 O'Farrell St./Taylor St., 3 blks. from Union Square, (415) 776-6717; www.marrakechsanfrancisco.com. D daily; $$. Reservations accepted.

After passing through the doors of this oasis in the urban jungle, diners enter the enveloping womb-like warmth of an exotic Middle Eastern bazaar. Resembling a posh adult playpen, the main room has comfortable padded benches and round tables circling the perimeter with low stools providing supplemental seating. Traditional Moroccan foods include a kaleidoscope plate of colorful vegetable salads, a flaky bastella pastry filled with a sweet chicken-toasted almond mixture, and couscous. Main course choices include a simple but divine chicken with lemon and olives as well as several rabbit, lamb, and shrimp dishes. Belly dancing is scheduled nightly.

Masa's

648 Bush St./Powell St., in Executive Vintage Court Hotel, Nob Hill, (415) 989-7154; www.masas restaurant.com. D Tu-Sat; $$$+. Closed 1st 2 wks. of Jan & 1st wk. of July. Reservations required. Valet parking.

This highly acclaimed, elegant, and very expensive restaurant serves a menu of contemporary French cuisine at luxuriously set tables. Six- and nine-course tasting menus with optional wine pairings and a six-course vegetarian menu are available. Tidbits are sent out from the kitchen throughout, and a dessert cart laden with housemade lollipops, candies, and cookies provides a sweet conclusion. A dress code requests that ladies wear cocktail attire and that men wear jackets.

McCormick & Kuleto's Seafood Restaurant

900 North Point, in Ghirardelli Square, Fisherman's Wharf, (888) 344-6861, (415) 929-1730; www.mccormickandkuletos.com. L-D daily; $$-$$$. Reservations advised. Validated parking in Ghirardelli Square garage.

Though most tables in this splendidly appointed seafood restaurant have spectacular views, the half-circle booths on the second of three tiers are choice. High ceilings, floor-to-ceiling leaded glass windows, and fantastical light fixtures add to an overall elegant ambiance. Designed to please every appetite, the extensive menu changes daily. Starters include delicious crab cakes; sweet, crisp rock shrimp popcorn; and a satisfying, nicely seasoned clam chowder. Among the many seafood dishes, which are fresh whenever possible, are an excellent pan-fried petrale sole with caper-lemon butter and a delicious blackened sea bass with a side of homey mashed potatoes. Pastas, salads, sandwiches, and a variety of meats round it out. A more casual lounge area offers the same

incredible view with a less expensive, less extensive menu and the additional option of a hamburger.

Mel's Drive-In

2165 Lombard St./Fillmore St., Marina District, (415) 921-2867; www.melsdrive-in.com. B-L-D daily; $. No reservations. Free parking lot adjoins.

Long ago when Mel's was a *real* drive-in, carhops brought trays out to clamp on windows for in-car dining. Now the eating goes on inside the restaurant. Seating is at a long counter, in booths, or at tables with chairs, and an oldie but goodie can be played for two bits on a computerized mini-jukebox. (An interesting aside: Jukeboxes were invented in San Francisco in 1888.) Dress is just-off-the-jogging-trail casual. Menu items include the Famous Melburger with all the trimmings, a variety of veggie burgers, fries with the skins still on, and, of course, BIG onion rings. All this plus salads, soups, and sandwiches galore. For more substantial appetites, the menu offers a chicken pot pie, meat loaf served with lumpy mashed potatoes and gravy, and the day's blue-plate special. Among the drinks are flavored cokes and thick, old-fashioned milkshakes served in the mixer tin. Desserts include chocolate fudge cake, banana cream pie, and a banana split. Kids love that their meals are served in boxes that look like cars, and teens call this place "cool."

A branch at 3355 Geary Boulevard *(at Stanyan St., Presidio Heights, (415) 387-2244),* the exact location of one of the three original Mel's. More branches are at 801 Mission St. *(at 4th St., South of Market, (415) 227-4477)* and at 1050 Van Ness Ave. *(at Geary St., (415) 292-6357).*

Michael Mina

335 Powell St./Geary St. , in The Westin St. Francis hotel, on Union Square, (415) 397-9222; www.michael mina.net. D daily; $$$+. Reservations essential.

This spare, trendy, hot, hot restaurant specializes in serving the very best modern American cuisine. Service is elegant, and the white Royal Doulton dinnerware is designed by Mina. The choice is between a three-course seasonal menu and a larger tasting menu. Most items consist of a primary ingredient presented three different ways, allowing for an interplay of contrasting sauces and techniques. Seasonal offerings might include: tempura langoustine with maroon carrots and ginger, with pineapple quince and galangal, and with green papaya and mango; for dessert: peanut butter pudding cake and a peanut butter shake, banana bread pudding and banana pot de creme, devil's food cake and a caramel sundae. The wine list is grand—2,500 bottles—and prices range from $25 to $14,000. And the bill here is as breathtaking as the food presentation.

Mifune

1737 Post St., in Kintetsu Mall at Japan Center, (415) 922-0337; www.mifune.com. L-D daily; $. No reservations.

This branch in a well-established Japanese chain specializes in serving two types of easily digested, low-calorie fresh noodles: udon—fat, white flour noodles; and soba—thin, brown buckwheat noodles. Before walking through the noren (a slit curtain), peruse the plastic food displays in the exterior windows. Noodle toppings include chicken, beef, and shrimp tempura as well as exotic raw egg, sweet herring, and seaweed. Sesame spice salt is on each table for pepping up the blander items. A child's Bullet Train plate consists of cold noodles with shrimp-and-vegetable tempura and is served in a ceramic replica of the famous Japanese train.

Millennium

580 Geary St./Jones St., in The Hotel California, 3 blks. from Union Square, (415) 345-3900; www.millenniumrestaurant.com. D daily; $$$. Reservations advised. Valet parking.

Specializing in richly flavored vegan and vegetarian cuisine, this stylish restaurant has an exciting, eclectic menu that also interests non-vegetarians—especially those watching their fat intake. No animal products are used, most items are prepared with little or no oil, and organic ingredients are used whenever possible. House-brined olives and pickles make nice munchies. Entree selections might include a crisp sesame-shitake phyllo spring roll or a fabulous portobello mushroom prepared Moroccan-style. Delicious desserts adhere to the program, too, and usually include an irresistible chocolate item and several lighter sorbets. Beverages include an exclusively organic wine list as well as cocktails and organic beers from a full bar, housemade herbal elixirs, and plenty of non-alcoholic drinks.

Once a month, on the Sunday evening closest to the full moon, an Aphrodisiac Overnight Package is available that includes a dinner of aphrodisiac delights and a hotel room for the night.

Morton's of Chicago

400 Post St./Powell St., 1 blk. from Union Square, (415) 986-5830; www.mortons.com. D daily; $$$. Reservations advised. Valet parking.

The first Morton's steakhouse opened in Chicago in 1978. This clubby subterranean outpost, decorated with historical photographs on the wall, is the place to go when a red meat attack occurs. The minimum 14-ounce cut of tender, tasty, prime grain-fed beef served here—the steaks get as big as a colossal 48 ounces, though that is meant for two—requires a substantial cutting tool, and so a large Bowie-style knife is at each place setting to assist. Noteworthy side dishes include a heavenly lobster bisque, sautéed wild mushrooms, and a gigantic baked Idaho potato. Lamb chops, fresh fish, and fresh Maine lobster are also on the menu. Though it might be impossible, save room for one of the decadent desserts, which include an exquisite Hot Chocolate Cake and a New York cheesecake brought in from the Bronx (the only menu item not prepared on site). According to one happy diner, the reason it gets so noisy here is "so you don't hear your arteries slamming shut." Leave guilt at home.

Neptune's Palace

At Pier 39, Fisherman's Wharf, (415) 434-2260; www.pier39restaurants.com. L-D daily; $$$. Reservations advised.

Situated at the far end of the pier, this airy spot stands out with a magnificent bay view of Alcatraz and a seafood menu featuring a rich clam chowder and a selection of dishes prepared with mussels, shrimp, and lobster.

A companion facility, the adjacent, more casual **Sea Lion Cafe**, offers a simple menu of soups, salads, and sandwiches as well as fresh seafood, plus it has a great view of the sea lions.

New Asia

772 Pacific Ave./Stockton St., Chinatown, (415) 391-6666. Dim sum daily 9-3; $. No reservations.

Even with a reputed 1,000 seats—the staff uses walkie-talkies to communicate across the vast, noisy interior—this busy dim sum (see page 17) spot usually requires a wait for seating in its popular ground level dining room. However, immediate seating is often available upstairs. Hesitation when offered a choice of eight teas usually is translated by the server into "green," because that tea is the most popular. Delicate shrimp dumplings, deep-fried taro balls filled with sweet poi, and cloud-like pork bows are all especially good. A to-go counter operates off the waiting area.

In December this restaurant is the site of the annual **Kung Pao Kosher Comedy** show (*(415) 522-3737; www.koshercomedy.com. $40-$60.*).

North Beach Pizza

1499 Grant Ave./Union St., North Beach, (415) 433-2444; www.northbeachpizza.com. L-D daily; $. No reservations.

Lacking pretension and finesse, this cozy corner restaurant serves an unfussy kind of pizza with an excellent crust in a relaxed, easy atmosphere. The pepperoni and cheese and the spicy hot sausage versions are both particularly tasty, and a salad tossed with creamy house Italian dressing is the perfect accompaniment. An outstanding cannelloni is among the pasta choices, and both barbecued ribs and chicken plus a submarine sandwich are also on the menu.

A branch is one block down the street at #1310.

One Market

1 Market St./Steuart St., The Embarcadero, (415) 777-5577; www.onemarket.com. L M-F, D M-Sat; $$$. Valet parking.

Situated in a scenic corner of an attractive historic building dating from 1917, this popular restaurant has great bay views and an airy, substantial interior that is a delight to be in. Celebrity chef Bradley Ogden's all-American menu includes crab cakes and barbecued oysters as appetizers. For entrees, the changing menu might offer tender Yankee pot roast with roasted turnips and potatoes, or succulent rosemary-roasted chicken breast with wild mushrooms and three kinds of garlic mashed potatoes. For dessert, expect old favorites—a signature butterscotch pudding—and new takes on old favorites—strawberry shortcake with orange

ice cream—plus stellar cookies and fruit sorbets.

Perry's

1944 Union St./Laguna St., Cow Hollow, (415) 922-9022; www.perryssf.com. B-L M-F, D daily, Sat-SunBr; $$. Reservations advised.

Consistency is a strong point at this popular watering hole. Drinks are strong and tasty, and the cafe food is always just as remembered. A good hamburger comes on a Kaiser roll with a side of thin, greaseless fried potato rounds, and the corned beef hash is neatly chopped and topped with two poached eggs. Chops, steaks, and fresh fish flesh out the menu. For dessert, try the housemade apple brown Betty. Seating areas include sidewalk tables, the boisterous bar area, a dark but quiet back room, and a sunny back porch.

Picnic Pick-Ups

• A. G. Ferrari Foods

468 Castro St./18th St., Castro District, (415) 255-6590; www.agferrari.com. M-Sat 10-9:30, Sun 11-7. Also at 688 Mission St./3rd St., South of Market, (415) 344-0644.

For description, see page 295.

• Lucca Delicatessen

2120 Chestnut St./Steiner St., Marina District, (415) 921-7873; www.luccadeli.com. M-F 9-6:30, Sat-Sun 9-6. No cards.

Owned by the same family since 1929, this deli prices its made-to-order sandwiches by weight. Housemade salads, handmade bread sticks, and a large selection of Italian wines are also available.

• A North Beach picnic

Molinari Delicatessen (*373 Columbus Ave./Vallejo St., (415) 421-2337. M-Sat 8-5:30.*) has been on its present corner since 1912 and claims to be the oldest Italian deli in town. It can provide the makings for a great picnic. Dash into one of the Chinese markets for some fresh fruit, then into **Victoria Pastry Co.** (*1362 Stockton St./ Vallejo St., (415) 781-2015; www.victoriapastry.com. M-F 7-7, Sat 7-9, Sun 8-6.*) for a sweet—perhaps a cannoli or their specialty St. Honoré cake, or maybe some pignoli or brutti ma buoni cookies. Then head to grassy Washington Square. And that's picnicking North Beach-style!

• Say Cheese
856 Cole St./Carl St., Cole Valley, (415) 665-5020.
M-Sat 10-7, Sun 10-5.

Almost 300 kinds of cheese are available in this very small shop, as are made-to-order sandwiches, salads, pâtés, crackers, cheese spreads, and fresh cookies.

• Sweet Things
3585 California St./Spruce St., in Cal-Mart in Laurel Village, Laurel Heights, (415) 221-8583; www.sweetthings.com. M-Sat 8-7, Sun 9-6.

For description, see page 223.

• Vivande Porta Via
2125 Fillmore St./California St., Upper Fillmore, (415) 346-4430; www.vivande.com. Deli daily 10-7. L-D daily; reservations advised.

All items here are prepared in the heavenly smelling open kitchen and are, in keeping with the literal meaning of the deli's name, "food to carry away." The Italian fare varies, but main dishes might include succulent roasted chicken or chicken turnovers in a flaky crust. Salads include caponata (eggplant with raisins and pine nuts) and several fresh pastas. Sandwiches are made to order, and tempting dolci (sweets) beckon from a display case (try the hazelnut meringues labeled as "brutti ma buoni," which translates as "ugly but good"). Seating is also available for dining on the premises.

Plouf
40 Belden Pl./Bush St., Financial District, (415) 986-6491; www.ploufsf.com. L M-F, D M-Sat; $$. Reservations advised.

Specializing in steamed mussels and offering eight different versions, this seafood bistro is so contemporary French that after just a few minutes diners feel like they've been beamed onto the French Riviera. One waiter witnessed here could do no wrong. Dressed in a white-and-black-striped shirt and sporting a charming, authentic French accent, he brought a huge iron pot full of mussels pastis with a side of perfect thin, crisp pommes frites, and he regularly removed bowls of discarded shells. More seafood items are on the menu—including fish & chips with garlic aioli and malt vinegar—along with a variety of meats and a seafood pasta. Good wine choices straight out of France include Muscadet, Sancerre, and Burgundy. For dessert, profiteroles—little cream puff shells filled with banana ice cream and topped with warm chocolate and caramel sauces—are the way to go. Outside, tables fill the pedestrians-only alley just as they do in the south of France. However, because the weather here isn't as divine as it is there, heat lamps attempt to take off the chill. The dining room features a high, pressed-tin ceiling and a romantic fireplace, and it has booths as well as a bank of intimate bench-and-chair tables for two. In sync with the name, which translates as "splash," stuffed sport fish decorate the walls.

Polly Ann Ice Cream
3138 Noriega St./39th Ave., Outer Sunset District, (415) 664-2472; www.pollyann.com. Daily 11-10; $.

Claiming to be the only ice cream store in the world where both dogs and babies get a free ice cream cone, this small shop is notable for yet other reasons. Where else is there a constantly changing choice of more than 500 flavors of ice cream? Where else does the owner make all of his own ice cream and smile happily as he declares, "Tonight I think I'll make watermelon"? At least 49 flavors are available every day. Some are seasonal, and some are trendy—like Batman (black vanilla with lemon swirls) and Star Wars (blue vanilla with rainbow marshmallows). Among the many unusual flavors are sunflower seed, vegetable, red bean, chocolate-peanut butter, and American beauty made with rose petals. Believe it or not, some very traditional flavors are also available, and vanilla is always the number one best seller. According to the owner, "Anything is possible." And those who just can't decide can spin a big wheel and let fate determine the flavor.

Postrio
545 Post St./Mason St., in the Prescott Hotel, Union Square, (415) 776-7825; www.postrio.com. B&D daily; $$$. Reservations advised for D. Valet parking.

Owned by Los Angeles celebrity chef Wolfgang Puck, and referred to inelegantly by some as Puck's Place, this grand spot is entered via a dramatic staircase leading down into an attractive contemporary dining room. It is a place to see, to be seen, and to enjoy a fabulous meal. The complex California-style cuisine and desserts are generally excellent, and, as would be expected in any restaurant owned by Mr. Puck, a bar menu with great wood-oven pizzas is also available.

The Pot Sticker

150 Waverly Pl./Washington St., Chinatown,
(415) 397-9985. L-D daily; $. Reservations accepted.

Situated in a picturesque alley that is famous for its historic buildings sporting ornate painted balconies, this spot is known for hand-made noodles and dumplings. Dishes are lightly sauced and have lots of vegetables. Good choices include hot-and-sour soup, Mongolian beef, and princess chicken. Dramatic Hunan crispy whole fish is served with a hot sauce.

Ramblas

557 Valencia St./6th St., Mission District,
(415) 565-0207; www.ramblastapas.com. D daily,
SunBr; $$. Reservations advised.

In a deep room featuring kitchen and street views, this festive tapas bar serves a variety of the tasty Spanish tidbits and they just might be better than those found in Spain. The marinated olives, boquerones (white anchovies), piquillos (sweet red peppers filled with goat cheese), empanadillas (little turnovers filled with chorizo and spinach), and gambas (shrimp baked in garlic and olive oil) are all exquisite. Several paellas are also available. Drinks include ThirstyBear draft beers, fruity Sangria, and a minty mojito, and desserts include both flan and cinnamony churros with warm chocolate sauce. Live flamenco guitar is scheduled on Monday and Tuesday evenings.

R&G Lounge

631 Kearny St./Clay St., Chinatown, (415) 982-7877;
www.rnglounge.com. L-D daily; $$. Reservations
advised.

This restaurant has three levels: a casual downstairs that is popular with families and that features a fish tank in the center of the room; a small, quiet area behind the bar; and a larger banquet area upstairs outfitted with round tables topped with lazy Susans. The same menu and prices apply in all areas. Cantonese-style fresh seafood is the house specialty, including a signature salt-and-pepper roasted crab, but most everything is delicious.

Restaurant LuLu

816 Folsom St./4th St., South of Market,
(415) 495-5775; www.restaurantlulu.com. L-D daily;
$$$. Reservations advised. Valet parking at L M-F,
at D daily.

This casual restaurant operates in the large, open, high-ceilinged room of a converted 1910 warehouse. The house specialty is simply prepared foods of the French and Italian Riviera served family style. Almost anything from the wood-fired rotisserie or oven is tasty, but the delicate fritto misto with artichokes, the crisp rosemary-scented roast chicken, the thin-crust pizza, and the iron skillet-roasted mussels are simply fabulous. Among the nightly specials are rabbit on Tuesdays and suckling pig on Fridays.

Rose Pistola

532 Columbus Ave./Union St., North Beach,
(415) 399-0499; www.rosepistola.com. L-D daily; $$$.
Reservations advised. Valet parking.

In a modern setting with sleek decor, this comfortable Italian trattoria produces top-notch Ligurian-style fare. The enticing menu changes twice daily and includes wood-fired pizza, housemade pastas such as pappardelle with pork sugo, entrees such as delicate whole petrale sole grilled with white beans and fennel, and vegetable sides such as grilled broccoli di cicco. Appetizers usually include a creative bruschetta, and desserts something tasty and beautiful like a blood orange panna cotta atop an oat cake. Meals begin with house-cured olives and ciabatta bread, and sometimes service is by the effervescent waiter, Harry, who brings joy to the experience at no extra charge. Service is family-style. A full bar serves colorful cocktails, and live jazz adds to the atmosphere on weekends.

Sam Wo

813 Washington St./Grant Ave., Chinatown, (415) 982-
0596. L-D daily; $. No reservations. No cards.

People once came here for the experience of being insulted by, and to watch the reaction of others being insulted by, Edsel Ford Fong—the infamous waiter who reigned over the second floor. Unfortunately for those of us who actually became fond of him, Fong passed away in 1984. It is doubtful a replacement could ever be found. So now the main reason to come here is for the fresh housemade noodles and the unusual layout of the tiny dining rooms. Entering this "jook joint" through the cramped and busy kitchen and climbing the narrow stairs to the second and third floors is not unlike entering a submarine, only going up instead of down. Diners sit on stools at tables unexpectedly topped with real marble. Waiters shout orders down an ancient hand-operated dumbwaiter via which finished dishes later arrive. The house specialty, noodle soup, is available in 12 varieties, and won ton soups and chow fun dishes are also on the menu. The roasted pork rice noodle roll is especially good. No soft drinks, milk, or coffee are available, and no fortune cookies arrive with the amazingly inexpensive check. It is worth knowing this place stays open until 3 a.m. every day but Sunday.

Sanppo

1702 Post St./Buchanan St., Japantown, (415) 346-3486. L-D Tu-Sat, D daily; $$. No reservations.

This cozy Japanese restaurant serves a tasty traditional menu. Appetizers include gomaae spinach (uncooked and sprinkled with sesame seeds), harusame salad (sweet potato noodles mixed with lettuce, onion, and a creamy dressing), and housemade gyoza, (similar to Chinese pot stickers). Entrees include a light tempura, deep-fried fresh oysters, and nasu hasamiyaki (grilled slices of ginger-marinated beef and eggplant). A large selection of noodle dishes is also available.

Sanraku

704 Sutter St./Taylor St., near Union Square, (415) 771-0803; www.sanraku.com. L M-F, D daily; $-$$. Reservations accepted.

Service is delightfully welcoming in this tiny Japanese restaurant. Choose freshly made delicacies from the small sushi bar, or better yet order it combined with a teriyaki, tempura, or donburi entree. Shrimp tempura consists of a generous portion of perfectly deep-fried shrimp and assorted vegetables. Dinners come with tea, a green salad, soup, rice, and fresh fruit dessert. A branch is at the Metreon.

Scala's Bistro

432 Powell St./Sutter St., 1 blk. from Union Square, (415) 395-8555; www.scalasbistro.com. B-L-D daily; $$-$$$. Reservations essential.

San Francisco tourists are the luckiest in the world. They can step out of their hotel into a restaurant like this. Diners in the main room of sit under a dramatic 25-foot-high ceiling featuring its original ornate tin work. When the

elegant dining room is full, seating in the bar is an alternative; an elegant cocktail helps dim any disappointment, and it is possible to dine there as well. The menu of rustic Italian dishes changes regularly. Starters might include a tasty bruschetta topped with wild mushrooms and arugula, or a crab cake with blood orange aioli. Sharing a primi dish—perhaps delicate pesto-ricotta-filled ravioli topped with lemon cream sauce—and a secondi—long-cooked short ribs Bourguignonne with celery-root mash is superb—is a good way to go. Diner's usually have room for dessert because mini versions are available, including a Bostini cream pie made with orange chiffon cake topped with creamy vanilla custard and then drizzled with warm chocolate glaze.

Shanghai 1930

133 Steuart St./Mission St., The Embarcadero, (415) 896-5600; www.shanghai1930.com. L M-F, D M-Sat; $$-$$$. Reservations advised. Valet parking.

Stepping down the curving red-carpeted staircase here leading into the cozy womb of the spacious **Blue** bar promises the beginning of a mysterious Chinatown adventure. The adventure gets even better in the subterranean dining room ringed with comfy booths. In fact, the restaurant is modeled after the between-wars atmosphere in Shanghai, when the Chinese city was known as the "Paris of the Orient." The members-only private cigar club located behind frosted glass doors in the **Guanxi Lounge** brings on visions of exotic opium dens. But back to the restaurant. Live jazz from the bar carries into the dining room (*From 7pm M-W, 8pm Thur-Sat.*), adding a delicious dreamy quality. Favorite dishes from the extensive, intriguing menu—all are served artistically arranged—include minced duck in lettuce petals, sweet tangerine beef with celery hearts, hot-and-red firecracker chicken, and striking Jade & Ebony (succulent black mushrooms and jade-green baby bok choy). For dessert don't miss sesame seed-covered bananas, flambéed table-side and served with a trio of sorbets. A creative cocktail is the drink of choice.

The Slanted Door

1 Ferry Plaza/Market St., in Ferry Building, The Embarcadero, (415) 861-8032; www.slanteddoor.com. L-D daily; $$-$$$. Reservations essential.

Delicious Vietnamese-inspired food made from quality organic ingredients is served here in a sleek, stylish setting with a bay view. Best bets from the open kitchen include soft spring rolls, rice noodle stir-fry, caramelized shrimp, and spicy baby spinach-eggplant with coconut sauce. Mick Jagger got some satisfaction from the grapefruit and jicama salad, shaking beef, and spicy green beans when he dined here. And that's just the tip of the culinary iceberg. A large selection of precious hot teas and unusual ales is also available.

South Park Cafe

108 South Park Ave./2nd St., South of Market, (415) 495-7275; www.southparkcafesf.com. L M-F, D Tu-Sat; $$-$$$. Reservations advised.

With large windows overlooking the small and popular park that fills the center oval of this unique street (it was originally designed to resemble London's Berkeley Square), this tiny butter-yellow French bistro is a great place to sit down for a pleasant meal. The changing menu includes both unusual and traditional dishes. Though French-owned, it is reminiscent of a New York City cafe.

Steps of Rome Trattoria

362 Columbus Ave./Grant St., North Beach, (415) 986-6480; www.stepsofrome.com. D W-M; $$. Reservations accepted.

Reminiscent of a charming little New York City Italian restaurant, this spot has several tables in a street-level room, plus more up narrow stairs in a second-floor dining room—all with sidewalk views. The menu is a choice of delicious housemade pastas and more substantial meat entrees, but the kitchen seems willing to produce any reasonable request. Desserts are exceptional and include a cliché tiramisu as well as a memorable creamy panna cotta with fruit sauce. Service is attentive and cheerful and the food quality surprisingly good considering a barker often brings people in.

Just a few doors down, the related, though more informal, **Steps of Rome Caffe** *(348 Columbus Ave./Grant Ave., (415) 397-0435; www.stepsofrome.com. M-F 10am-2am, Sat-Sun to 3am.)* offers less expensive dining in a coffeehouse atmosphere. The cafe's red-lips logo was designed by Ruby Mazur, who designed the Rolling Stones' lips-and-tongue logo.

St. Francis Fountain

2801 24th St./York St., Mission District, (415) 826-4200. B-L-D daily; $. No reservations.

Here since 1918, this informal cafe retains its old-time wooden booths and a counter with swivel stools, and it claims to be the oldest ice cream parlor in San Francisco. Specialties include a Guinness float and a hot vanilla shake. The menu features typical diner fare, including pancakes, waffles, soups, salads, sandwiches, and burgers, plus many vegan options.

The Stinking Rose

325 Columbus Ave./Broadway, North Beach, (415) PU-1-ROSE; www.thestinkingrose.com. L-D daily; $$. Reservations advised.

A warren of unusual rooms awaits garlic lovers here, as does some delicious food made with as much garlic as possible. A don't-miss item is the bagna calda, consisting of tender, soft, almost sweet cloves of garlic served with bread for spreading. Among the winning dishes are wild mushroom-roasted eggplant lasagna, 40-clove garlic chicken, and delectable Silence of the Lamb Shank with Chianti glaze and fava beans. For dessert, the truly adventurous can try garlic *ice cream*! For those who still haven't had enough, a tiny shop in front sells all things garlic.

Tadich Grill

240 California St./Battery St., Financial District, (415) 391-1849. L-D M-Sat; $$$. No reservations.

Begun in another location in 1849 as a coffee stand, this San Francisco institution has been here since 1967 and is California's oldest restaurant in continuous operation. With dark wood walls, a long wooden dining counter, and private enclosed booths, it has an old-fashioned clubby feel and is a cozy place to be on a rainy day. The wait to get in can be long, but persevere. Then be wise and order simple, unsauced dishes. Pan-fried seafood is particularly good and served with housemade tartar sauce. Steaks and chops are on the menu, and Hangtown fry—scrambled eggs, bacon, and oysters—is available, and the housemade rice pudding has been on the menu for more than 100 years.

Taiwan

445 Clement St./6th Ave., Inner Richmond District, (415) 387-1789. L-D daily; $. No reservations.

For description, see page 297.

Tartine Bakery

600 Guerrero St./18th St., Mission District, (415) 487-2600; www.tartinebakery.com. M 8-7, Tu-W 7:30-7, Thur-F 7:30-8, Sat 8-8, Sun 9-8; $.

This small bakery-cafe is famous for its huge loaves of country-style bread made with organic ingredients and wild yeasts. The bread is used for toast at breakfast and in sandwiches at lunch. A line generally snakes out the door, and seating space is limited and parking space difficult to find. Still, everything is so delicious that patrons seem not to mind. Pastries include an exquisite sugary morning bun, a jewel of an éclair, and the flakiest of croissants. Loaves of bread are available for purchase only after 4 p.m. The best plan of attack is to have one person get in the order line while another holds a table, preferably while sipping a drink purchased quickly at the back counter. One of the oversize sandwiches—the croque monsieur is popular and ready immediately, while other hot pressed sandwiches require a 10-minute wait—and a dessert pastry can easily fill two diners. Organic ingredients, local eggs, and Niman Ranch meats are used.

ThirstyBear Restaurant & Brewery

661 Howard St./3rd St., South of Market, (415) 974-0905; www.thirstybear.com. L M-Sat, D daily; $-$$. Reservations accepted.

This brewpub has several seating areas in a large, open room of concrete floors and aged brick walls, plus an upstairs area with pool tables. Ordering a 3-ounce taster of each of the nine different organic house brews, which include the popular Polar Bear pilsner and Brown Bear English-style ale, is a good idea. It will probably be impossible to pick a favorite until all are sampled, and by then most people forget which is which and have to start over—or come back again. Cocktails, single malt scotches, and housemade Sangria are also options. The menu features modern rustic Spanish cuisine, including tapas—boquerones (fresh Spanish anchovies) and gambas (sautéed garlic prawns)—plus paellas and desserts (don't miss the classic Spanish churros with chocolate dipping sauce).

Live **flamenco performances** are scheduled on Sunday evenings (No cover. Reservations recommended.).

Ti Couz Crêperie

3108 16th St./Valencia St., Mission District, (415) 25-CREPE. M & F 11am-11pm, Sat-Sun 10am-11pm, Tu-Thur 5pm-11pm; $. No reservations.

Always busy as a beehive, this Brittany-style French crêperie whips up a vast variety of the delicious pancakes. Choose either a savory buckwheat delight—perhaps a jambon and fromage (ham and cheese) or a champignon (mushroom with sauce)—or a whole-wheat sweet concoction (the orange butter version is light, while the popular chocolate with banana is more substantial). A few soups, salads, seafood items, and crêpe ice cream cones are also on the menu. Fresh citrus juices, and occasionally fresh peach juice, make refreshing accompaniments, but a full bar is also available. Seating options are as ample as the menu, but the best choice is likely the counter from which the cooks can be viewed in action.

Tommaso's

1042 Kearny St./Broadway, North Beach, (415) 398-9696; www.tommasosnorthbeach.com. D Tu-Sun; $$. No reservations.

In 1935, when this spot was known as Lupo's, it was the first restaurant to bring pizza from New York City to the West Coast. (Pizza was introduced to the U.S. at the Lombardy Pizza Restaurant in New York City in 1905.)

And for quite a while it was the only restaurant in the entire U.S. to prepare all of its baked foods in a genuine oak wood-burning brick oven. (In fact, world-renowned Chez Panisse in Berkeley used this oven as a model for their own oven, which then began producing a trend-setting gourmet mini pizza.) Movie director Francis Ford Coppola has been seen dashing in from his nearby office—sometimes to chow down from the menu, other times to whip up his own creations in the kitchen. Seating in the cheery cellar consists of both a large community dining table and smaller tables in semi-private compartments separated by wooden partitions. Wall murals dating to 1935 depict scenes of Naples and the Amalfi Coast. Any of the marinated salads—broccoli, string beans, or roasted peppers—make a good starter, and the crusty bread is excellent for soaking up excess marinade. The menu offers almost 20 kinds of pizza featuring a superb thin, crisp-yet-chewy crust and several calzones (a sort of pizza turnover), plus pasta, seafood (baked coo-coo clams are a specialty), veal, and chicken entrees. Desserts include cannoli, spumoni ice cream, and housemade tiramisu.

Ton Kiang

5821 Geary Blvd./22nd Ave., Outer Richmond District, (415) 752-4440, (415) 387-8273; www.tonkiang.net. Dim sum daily 10-10; $. No reservations.

Operating on two floors, this attractive spot specializes in Hakka-style cuisine. The exemplary dim sum (see page 17) items are considered the very best in San Francisco and include deep-fried taro croquettes, puffy deep-fried stuffed crab claws, ethereal chive-shrimp dumplings, exquisite steamed pea shoots, miniature egg-custard tarts, and crisp walnut cookies filled with lotus paste.

Tosca Cafe

242 Columbus Ave./Broadway, North Beach, (415) 986-9651. Tu-Sun 5pm-2am; $. No reservations. No cards.

Opened in 1919, this popular bar is a hangout for actors and writers, and it positively roars with excitement. The jukebox is said to have great selections—if only it were possible to *hear* them—and the 60-foot-long carved mahogany bar is San Francisco's longest. More seating is at an uninspired collection of tables

surrounded by comfy, wall-hugging red leather banquettes. Though the city's first cappuccino machines were introduced here in 1921, the house drink is a Tosca cappuccino—a yummy brandy-laced Ghirardelli hot chocolate.

Town Hall

342 Howard St./Fremont St., South of Market, (415) 908-3900; www.townhallsf.com. L M-F, D daily; $$$. Reservations advised.

Sitting in the wide-open, high-ceilinged main dining room here is the best, but when the place is jammin', a communal table near the bar is a good alternative to a long wait. The historic brick building it is within is the former Marine Electric warehouse, built just after the 1906 quake. Floors are stained the color of dark chocolate, and handmade wooden tables and chairs and original brick walls add to the inviting mood. Starter specialties include seafood chowder with housemade sourdough crackers, and steamed mussels in Old Bay tomato broth. Should scrumptious wild mushroom lasagna be among the choices on the ever-changing, mostly American menu, don't hesitate. Desserts are homey and special—warm pineapple upside down cake, pear-and-sour cherry crisp, butterscotch pot de crème—and the hot chocolate made with Parisian cocoa is like velvet.

Troya

349 Clement St./5th Ave., (415) 379-6000; www.troyasf.com. L F-Sun, D daily; $$. Reservations accepted.

Contemporary Turkish cuisine is served here in a light-filled room with a pleasing view of the street. Signature mezes, or starters, change regularly and include delicious delicacies such as borek (filo dough stuffed with fresh spinach and pine nuts), dolmas (grape leaves stuffed with braised lamb), and warm olives. A meal can be made from mezes alone, but it would be a shame not to try one of the entrees, perhaps a vegetarian moussaka or a satisfying manti (handmade ravioli). Turkish deserts include baklava and kunefe, which are even better with a cup of thick Turkish coffee or refreshing peppermint tea.

Before or after dining, duck into **Green Apple Books & Music** (*506 Clement St./6th Ave., (415) 387-2272; www.greenapplebooks.com. Daily 10-10:30.*) and **6th Ave Aquarium**

(425 Clement St., (415) 668-7190; www.6thave aquarium.net. M-F 11-10, Sat-Sun 10-10.) for an enjoyable browse.

XOX Truffles
754 Columbus Ave./Greenwich St., North Beach, (415) 421-4814; www.xoxtruffles.com. M-Sat 9-6; $.

San Francisco was the chocolate capital of the U.S. in 1870 due mainly to the fact that it was the only place in the country where the temperature was such that chocolate wouldn't melt. In this teeny, tiny cafe, the owner/chef can often be viewed hand-making the delectable petite-size chocolate truffles. Choose from an array of 27 flavors—including peanut butter, Earl Grey, and even vegan soy. (Chocolate truffles were named after the truffle fungus because of their physical resemblance.)

Yank Sing
101 Spear St./Mission St., in Rincon Center, South of Market, (415) 781-1111; www.yanksing.com. Dim sum M-F 11-3, Sat-Sun 10-4; $$. Reservations advised. Validated parking.

In 1957, when it opened in a previous location in Chinatown, this was the first Hong Kong-style dim sum (see page 17) parlor in the city. Compelling reasons to forsake tradition and visit this now more upscale restaurant at it location outside of Chinatown include that they take reservations and that the friendly servers will usually answer questions. Tablecloths, fabric napkins, and fresh flowers grace each table, and etched-glass partitions break up the windowless interior. Top items include cloud-soft rice noodles stuffed with a variety of meats, succulent stuffed black mushroom caps, deep-fried crab claws, sweet taro balls, Peking duck, flaky-crusted custard tarts, and especially for kids—wedges of orange peel filled with shimmering orange

Jell-O. It is a Cantonese custom to introduce a new baby to family and friends at a Red Egg and Ginger Party. Named for some of the food items included in the luncheon menu, these parties are catered here and set menus are available.

A branch is located at 49 Stevenson Street *(at 1st St., South of Market, (415) 541-4949. Daily 11-3.).*

Rincon Center's atrium is home to the intriguing "Rain Column" water sculpture and a plethora of fast-food dining options, and its lobby displays colorful W.P.A. murals depicting the history of Northern California.

Zarzuela
2000 Hyde St./Union St., Russian Hill, (415) 346-0800. L-D M-Sat; $$. No reservations.

With an open, yet cozy dining room warmed by butter-yellow Mediterranean walls and beamed ceilings, this gem serves tasty Spanish tapas. Each meal starts with bread and olive oil plus a complimentary plate of exquisite olives. For a terrific tapas dinner, begin with a small plate of salted almonds. Continue with grilled eggplant rolled around creamy goat cheese, crisp fried potatoes with garlic and sherry vinegar, and shrimps sautéed in garlic and olive oil. Make the meal more filling by adding a daily special such as fresh sardines, or a paella, or a larger plate—traditional Catalan seafood stew, grilled lamb chops, ox-tail stew—and wash it all down with some traditional sherry. Sponge cake stuffed with fruit and soaked in liqueur is a perfect ending.

After, jump on one of the cable cars passing by outside and take a refreshing ride.

Zazie
941 Cole St./Parnassus St., Haight-Ashbury, (415) 564-5332; www.zaziesf.com. B-L-D daily; $-$$. Reservations accepted for D only.

Situated in an appealing neighborhood and featuring a cozy ambiance, this small French Provençal-style restaurant has tall ceilings, brick walls, and a heated garden patio for sunny-day dining. Breakfast offers vast choices—some common, some less so: Irish oatmeal brûlée; gingerbread pancakes with roasted pears; French Toast Tahiti stuffed with caramelized bananas and walnuts; scrambled egg dishes (Fontainblue mixes several kinds of mushrooms with spinach and fontina; Mexico mixes chorizo with peppers and white cheddar); poached egg specialties (the colorful Valence features roasted eggplant, goat cheese, and a spicy tomato sauce). Eggs are from free-range chickens, and milk is organic. Lunch brings on delicious sandwiches and salads. A citron presse and chocolat chaud are reminiscent of Paris, as is the restaurant in general, but the blend of cranberry juice, fresh-squeezed orange juice, and bubbly water that is the Zazie spritzer is most definitely the drink of choice. A selection of memosas is also an option.

Should the wait to get in be ridiculous, many options are nearby: an Italian restaurant, a sushi bar, a crêperie, a burger shack, a coffee house, and a French bakery serving huge French-style cafes au lait.

Zuni Cafe
1658 Market St./Franklin St., Hayes Valley, (415) 552-2522; www.zunicafe.com. L-D Tu-Sun, SunBr; $$-$$$. Reservations advised. Valet parking.

It seems that all seats are good in this cheery warren of asymmetrically shaped spaces, where both the Market Street parade and chefs in the kitchen are part of the visual treat. The menu changes *twice* each day, and everything but the bread is housemade. A delightful brunch might consist of an antipasto plate spread with delicious Molinari salami and baked ricotta, followed by a pizza baked in the wood-burning brick oven and topped, perhaps, with artichoke hearts and capers. Other options might include eggs baked with tomato, fennel, and white beans and served in an oversize earthenware bowl, or the acclaimed house-ground hamburger on grilled rosemary focaccia bread (not available at dinner). The restaurant is known for its roasted chicken and Caesar salad, and they are always good choices. Do leave room for dessert, especially if the divine rhubarb tart is an option.

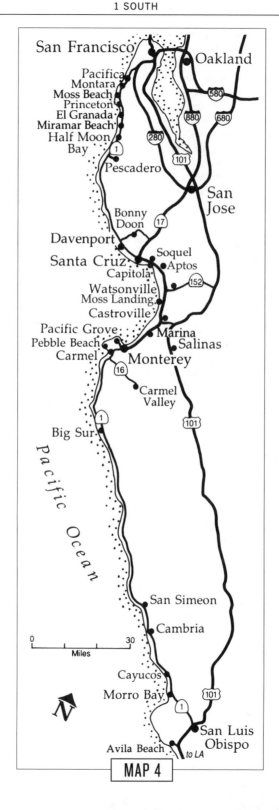

MAP 4

SOUTH

A LITTLE BACKGROUND

The trip down Highway 1 from San Francisco features a breathtaking, cliff-hugging ride along the Pacific Ocean.

After passing ridges of boxy houses in pastel tones (referred to as being made of "ticky-tacky" by folk singer Malvina Reynolds in her famous '60s song "Little Boxes") and the beach town of Pacifica, Highway 1 winds to the ocean through a eucalyptus-lined path in the coastal foothills. A stretch of this road known as Devil's Slide hugs cliffs dropping steeply into the sea. In fact, part of the road itself occasionally drops off, causing traffic congestion due to detours. Though many people make informal stops in the Devil's Slide area to take pictures, it is unsafe. Restraint is in order until finding an official parking area. Once passing this hilly area, the road moves inland and becomes more flat and straight.

When the Bay Area is blazing with sunshine, this area is often disappointingly socked in with fog. And vice versa. In fact, on many late summer and early fall days when San Francisco is covered with fog, this area is at its most beautiful. The area's spectacular unspoiled beaches are a popular destination anytime, but they are especially so then, when the weather is usually warm and clear.

Be careful, though, about going in the water, as tides can be dangerous. Always check with a ranger station or lifeguard before swimming.

PACIFICA

VISITOR INFORMATION

Pacifica Chamber of Commerce and Visitor Center
225 Rockaway Beach Ave. #1, (650) 355-4122; www.pacificachamber.com.

GETTING THERE

Located approximately 13 miles southeast of San Francisco. Take Highway 280 south to Highway 1.

ANNUAL EVENTS

Pacific Coast Fog Fest
September. (650) 355-8200; www.pacificcoastfogfest.com. Free.

This family-friendly event celebrates the cold fog that wraps this area in a cotton candy mist each fall.

WHAT TO DO

Sanchez Adobe Historic Site
*1000 Linda Mar Blvd., (650) 359-1462;
www.historysmc.org. Tu-Thur 10-4, Sat-Sun 1-5. Free.*

Actively used since prehistoric times, this site was once an Ohlone Indian village and then in 1786 became a support farm for Mission Dolores. The adobe house was built for a family of settlers in 1846 and later became a hotel, speakeasy, and artichoke storage shed. A video and a docent-led tour explain more details. An Indian refuse dump, known as a "shell midden," can be viewed in the yard.

WHERE TO STAY

Best Western Lighthouse Hotel
*105 Rockaway Beach Ave., (800) 832-4777,
(650) 355-6300; www.bestwesternlighthouse.com.
97 rooms; $$-$$$. Heated pool (open year round);
hot tub; sauna; fitness room. Room service;
restaurant.*

Eight rooms here have a full-on ocean view, while the rest have a range of partial views. Beach-front junior suites have a sliding door that opens to the sight and sound of the roaring ocean—no wimpy waves here. It's a thrill watching surfers while relaxing to nature's stereo performance. Time a visit well and luck might permit viewing passing whales, or maybe dolphins riding the waves like surfers, or even the great white shark that passes through twice a year. Several trails lead by the hotel: The Coastal Trail goes a mile north into the foothills, and the Linda Mar State Beach trail leads south to a popular surfing spot.

Operating on the hotel's second floor, romantic **Ristorante Portofino** *((650) 359-0303; www.ristorante-portofino.com. L-D daily; $$-$$$.)* is decorated to resemble the inside of a ship. Most tables have impressive oceanfront views and can hear the surf. Many comfortable half-moon booths are available, and as the evening progresses and the sun goes down, atmospheric penlight stars and a moon are turned on. Housemade pastas (including lobster ravioli and gnocchi), fresh seafood, and a tartufo limoncello gelato dessert are all exceptional. In the morning, breakfast can be dawdled over to that same incredible view.

Seabreeze Motel
*100 Rockaway Beach Ave., (650) 359-3903;
www.nicksrestaurant.net. 20 rooms; $. Continental
breakfast; restaurant. No pets.*

This is the place for a quick, inexpensive escape. Rooms are simple, but the beach and roaring sea are just a few steps away.

Nicks Seashore Restaurant *((650) 359-3900; www.nicksrestaurant.net. B-L-D daily; $-$$$. Reservations advised.)*, a merry steak and seafood house under the same ownership, offers comfy booths and an oceanfront view.

WHERE TO EAT

Taco Bell
*5200 Hwy. 1, (650) 355-4210; www.tacobell.com.
L-D daily; $. No reservations.*

Located inside an attractive redwood building, this fast-food restaurant's exceptional beachfront location on **Pacifica State Beach** *((650) 738-7381; www.parks.ca.gov.)* makes it worthy of a stop-in. The restaurant operates a special walk-up window for surfers, who provide diners free entertainment in the ocean just outside.

MONTARA

WHERE TO STAY

Point Montara Lighthouse Hostel
*On 16th St./Hwy. 1, (800) 909-4776 #153,
(650) 728-7177; www.pointmontarahostel.org. 45 beds;
5 private rooms.*

This restored 1875 lighthouse still operates from its cliff-side perch. Lodging is in a modern duplex that was formerly the light-keeper's quarters. Facilities include two kitchens, an espresso bar, a laundry, a private beach, and bicycle rentals. The lighthouse is not open for tours. See also page 468.

MOSS BEACH

WHAT TO DO

Fitzgerald Marine Reserve
*At end of California Ave., (650) 728-3584;
www.eparks.net. Daily 8am-sunset. Free. No pets.*

Tide pooling is excellent here. At least a few pools usually are accessible, with the occasional sea star or hermit crab stranded by the tide. And because visitors are not permitted to remove anything, the sand is rich with shells and interesting natural debris. Visiting when the tide is out assures seeing a large variety of specimens, and naturalist-led walks are scheduled then on weekends. Although the parking area can be deceptively warm and calm, the area by the ocean is usually windy and cold. Take wraps. Picnic tables are provided near the parking lot.

WHERE TO STAY

Seal Cove Inn

221 Cypress Ave., (800) 995-9987, (650) 728-4114; www.sealcoveinn.com. 10 rooms; $$$-$$$+. All wood-burning fireplaces. Evening snack; full breakfast. No pets.

Originally owned by Karen Brown, author and publisher of the popular *Karen Brown's Country Inns* series of guidebooks, this inn was built in 1991. Set way back from the road, it fronts a bank of mature cypress and offers access to secluded beaches and tide pools. Original oil paintings and botanical prints cozy up the interior, and comfortable public areas include a sitting room with a wood-burning fireplace and a patio with a view of the distant ocean. All rooms feature an European mattress, a private terrace or balcony, complimentary wine and soft drinks, a towel warmer, and fresh flowers. Breakfast can be taken either privately in-room or with other guests in the dining room.

WHERE TO EAT

Moss Beach Distillery

140 Beach Way/Ocean Blvd., (650) 728-5595; www.mossbeachdistillery.com. D daily, SunBr; $$$. Reservations advised.

Magnificently situated on a scenic bluff overlooking the unspoiled Fitzgerald Marine Reserve, this out-of-the-way surf-and-turf dinner house dates from the Prohibition era of the 1920s, when it was a notorious speakeasy. It is reputed to be haunted—it was featured on TV's *Unsolved Mysteries*—and is an official California State Historic Site. It is well worth seeking out

for a romantic repast, and do arrive before sundown to take in the incredible cliff-top view and to snuggle under one of the blankets thoughtfully provided on the ocean-side cocktail deck. Those who are lucky can sometimes snag a wooden bench swing, too. Tables in the cozy interior also offer a spectacular view.

PRINCETON-BY-THE-SEA

A LITTLE BACKGROUND

This scenic fishing village makes an inviting stop. A hotbed for bootlegging during Prohibition, it is known now for its surfers and seafood restaurants.

GETTING THERE

Located about 25 miles south of San Francisco.

WHAT TO DO

Surfer-watching: Mavericks
www.maverickssurf.com.

Named for a surfer's dog, this legendary surfing mecca is located just north of Pillar Point Harbor. Sporting killer waves—literally—in the winter, it was here on December 23, 1994 that world-famous big wave surfer Mark Foo died while surfing the world-class monster waves that break in this treacherous area. He had flown in from Honolulu that day especially to surf the unusually large waves, which have been known to reach up to 30 feet. Mavericks is rated one of the world's three best surfing spots (the others are Todos Santos Island off Ensenada in Baja California, Mexico, and Waimea Bay on the North Shore of Oahu in Hawaii).

Whale-watching:
Oceanic Society Expeditions
(800) 326-7491, (415) 474-3385; www.oceanic-society.org. Sat-Sun & some F; Dec-May. $45, 7-15 $40. Must be age 7+. Reservations required.

Each boat trip has a professional naturalist on board to educate participants about the whales and interpret their behavior. See also page 13.

WHERE TO STAY

Pillar Point Inn
380 Capistrano Rd., (800) 400-8281, (650) 728-7377; www.pillarpointinn.com. 11 rooms; $$-$$$. All gas fireplaces. Afternoon snack; full breakfast. No pets.

Facing a picturesque small boat harbor, this contemporary Cape Cod-style inn has spacious rooms that sport cloud-like feather beds and harbor views. A complimentary video library is available, and several good seafood restaurants and the busy harbor itself are just across the street.

WHERE TO EAT

Barbara's Fishtrap
281 Capistrano Rd., (650) 728-7049. L-D daily; $-$$. No reservations. No cards.

Perched on stilts over rocks and sea, this tiny roadside diner has a harbor view and casual atmosphere. It is a pleasant spot for a quick meal. In addition to a rustic interior room with fishnets hanging from the ceiling, it has an enclosed patio kept warm with heat lamps. Though usually there is a short wait for seating, fast service encourages a quick turnover. Lunch is served until 5 p.m. and includes an award-winning New England-style clam chowder, bouillabaisse, fish & chips, a killer crab sandwich, and deep-fried calamari as well as a hamburger. The dinner menu additionally offers scallops, prawns, and steak. The house specialty—rockfish fresh off the harbor fishing boats—is available either broiled or dipped in batter and deep-fried tempura-style.

Half Moon Bay Brewing Company
390 Capistrano Rd., (650) 728-BREW; www.hmb brewingco.com. L-D daily; $-$$. Reservations advised.

Featuring a dining room of cozy niches and a rustic decor of unfinished sandblasted wood, this brewpub has great harbor views and is ideal for a relaxing meal. Carpeting subdues the noise level, and children fit in well. The menu is the same all day, with well priced "pub grub" sandwiches and the de rigueur fish & chips. Soups, salads, and heartier entrees—fresh fish, ribs, steak—are also available. Desserts are rich and gooey: brownie a la mode, a root beer float, chocolate mousse cake. The full menu is also available in the bar (videos of surfing at nearby Mavericks are always running, and free live music is often scheduled) and out on a patio equipped with heaters and fire pits (well-behaved pets are welcome here); both areas have an ocean view. Beers—including Mavericks Amber Ale and Sandy Beach Blonde (a hefeweizen)—are brewed on the premises. A short tour of the brewing facility is available.

MIRAMAR BEACH

A LITTLE BACKGROUND

A few miles north of Half Moon Bay, a turn toward the sea on Magellan Avenue leads to peaceful Miramar Beach. Off the beaten path, it provides a chance to view the area in the way some lucky local residents do. Brown pelicans and scurrying sandpipers are easily observed from the beach, which is reached by climbing down a breakfront constructed of large boulders.

WHAT TO DO

Bach Dancing and Dynamite Society
307 Mirada Rd., (650) 726-4143; www.bachddsoc.org. Most Sun aft. at 4:30. $30, under 21 $25. No reservations.

Live jazz and classical music are performed at this beach house. Count Bassie, Duke Ellington, and Etta James have all played here. Arrive at 3 p.m. to claim a seat. A buffet with a wine and juice bar is available, but picnics and wine are permitted outside.

Dayle Dunn Gallery
337 Mirada Rd./Medio Ave., (650) 726-7667; www.dayledunn.com. W-M 10-6.

Situated in a contemporary redwood building just across the street from the ocean, this sophisticated gallery showcases an array of mostly three-dimensional art from American artisans.

WHERE TO STAY

Cypress Inn on Miramar Beach
407 Mirada Rd./Medio Ave., (800) 83-BEACH, (650) 726-6002; www.cypressinn.com. 18 rooms; $$$-$$$+. All fireplaces. Afternoon snack; full breakfast. No pets.

Located on a quiet frontage road across the street from the ocean, this inn is decorated with bright accents of Mexican folk art. Each room in the main building has a private balcony and faces the ocean, allowing guests always to hear the soothing sound of the ocean. To experience a bit of heaven, reserve the third-floor Las Nubes room. Its name meaning literally "the clouds," this penthouse room has a luxurious tiled bathroom with an oversize whirlpool tub, plus a bank of windows overlooking the ocean. Occupants want to stay forever. Four rooms are located in a newly added beach house behind the main inn. The afternoon snack features exquisite hors d'oeuvres.

WHERE TO EAT

Miramar Beach Restaurant & Bar
131 Mirada Rd., (650) 726-9053; www.beachfront dining.com. L M-Sat, D daily, SunBr; $$-$$$+. Reservations advised.

Situated off the beaten path and across the street from the ocean, this casual spot offers expansive views and is especially nice at lunch and Sunday brunch. The lunch menu has salads, hot sandwiches, hamburgers, omelettes, and housemade chowder with garlic bread. Pricier dinners include seafood, steak, and pasta. After dining, visit the beach behind a rocky breakfront to take a walk, build a sand castle, or maybe observe a flock of brown pelicans bobbing on the surf and diving for food.

HALF MOON BAY

A LITTLE BACKGROUND

First called San Benito, then Spanishtown after an influx of Spaniards in 1860, Half Moon Bay was ultimately named for the crescent-shaped bay north of town. The oldest of the coastal towns in this area, it has an old-fashioned Main Street. Uncutesied, it looks much as it always has, and boasts the state's first steel-reinforced concrete bridge—circa 1900 and spanning Pilarcitos Creek at the north end of town. The area is known for its fresh flowers and produce, and a colorful **flower market** is held downtown on the third Saturday of each month (except October).

VISITOR INFORMATION

Half Moon Bay Coastside Chamber of Commerce & Visitors Bureau
235 Main St., downtown, (650) 726-8380; www.halfmoonbaychamber.org, www.visithalf moonbay.org.

Harvest Trails
765 Main St., downtown, Half Moon Bay 94019, (650) 726-4485; www.sanmateo.cfbf.com.

For a free map to the area's farms, send a self-addressed, stamped, legal-size envelope.

GETTING THERE

Located approximately 25 miles south of San Francisco.

ANNUAL EVENTS

Pacific Coast Dream Machines
April. At Half Moon Bay Airport; (650) 726-2328; www.miramarevents.com. $20, 65+ & 11-17 $10.

See a century's worth of motorized mechanical marvels, including classic, vintage, exotic, and custom automobiles, trucks, motorcycles, and aircraft—plus early 20th-century farm equipment and one-of-a-kind gas and steam engines. Rides are available in vintage helicopters and airplanes.

Chamarita
May or June. (650) 712-1733; www.visithalfmoon bay.org. Free.

Held here for more than 100 years, this Portuguese festival takes place six weekends after Easter and includes a barbecue, parade, and carnival.

Half Moon Bay Art & Pumpkin Festival
October. (650) 726-9652; www.miramarevents.com. Free.

Children are invited to wear costumes and participate in the Great Pumpkin Parade celebrating the year's biggest pumpkin. Pumpkin-carving and pie-eating contests, a variety of pumpkin foods, and on-going entertainment are part of the fun. Farmer Mike, known as "the Picasso of pumpkin carvers," is usually busy making creative faces on gargantuan gourds, and craft booths run for blocks. A pumpkin weigh-off is held earlier in the week (the record

is held by a 2007 Oregon pumpkin that
weighed 1,524 pounds). The Half Moon Bay
Beautification Committee, which sponsors the
festival, pays the winning farmer $6 per pound.
Pumpkin patches, brightly colored with their
seasonal loot, are open nearby for picking.

WHAT TO DO

Half Moon Bay Nursery

*11691 San Mateo Rd. (Hwy. 92), 3 mi. E of town,
(650) 726-5392. Daily 9-5.*

In business for almost a half-century, this
nursery provides a fabulous plant browse and is
the perfect place to select blooming seasonal
plants to spiff up a home garden. When
Pavarotti is playing in the background, some
people think they've died and gone to heaven.

La Nebbia Winery

*12341 San Mateo Rd. (Hwy. 92), 2 mi. E of town,
(650) 726-9463; www.nebbiawinery.com. Tasting daily
10-5.*

Though the tasting room inside this rustic
building is tiny, a spacious picnic area with
tables and bocce ball courts is available out
back. A non-alcoholic grape juice varietal, such
as Gewurztraminer or Pinot Noir, usually is
served to kids while their parents taste the real
thing. On Bottle Your Own days, customers can
bring in bottles to fill directly from the barrel.

Picnic

Put one together by visiting the **Half
Moon Bay Bakery** *(514 Main St., (650) 726-
4841. Tu-Sun 6-6.),* which is still using its original brick ovens. It is known for its Portuguese

sweet and French breads and its great donuts,
and sandwiches are available to go.

While picking up supplies, allow some
time for poking around in some of the shops
on Main Street. Don't miss **Half Moon Bay
Feed & Fuel** *(331 Main St., (650) 726-4814;
www.halfmoonbayfeedandfuel.com. M-F 8:30-6,
Sat 9-5, Sun 10-4.),* an old-time farm supply
store established in 1911. It sells farm, pet, and
garden supplies to locals and has plenty of
chicks, ducklings, bunnies, and other small farm
animals to pet and purchase.

The area's spectacular beaches are popular
picnic destinations summer through fall, when
the weather tends to be warm and clear.
Dunes Beach *(At end of Young Ave.),* which is
part of **Half Moon Bay State Beach** *(At end of
Kelley Ave., (650) 726-8819; www.parks.ca.gov.
$6/vehicle. Campsites available.),* is prime.

Sea Horse Ranch and
Friendly Acres Horse Ranch

*1 mi. N of town, (650) 726-2362; www.horse
rentals.com/seahorse.html. Daily 8-6. $35+. Must be
age 5+.*

Ride on your own or hire a guide
(required for beach rides).

WHERE TO STAY

Beach House Hotel Half Moon Bay

*4100 Hwy. 1, (800) 315-9366, (650) 712-0220;
www.beach-house.com. 54 rooms; $$-$$$+. All mini-
kitchens & wood-burning fireplaces. Heated pool; hot
tub; fitness room. Continental breakfast. No pets.*

Those who are particularly lucky arrive
here at dusk on a night when the fog clings
above the water on a fluffy cloud, setting off a
continuous bleat from a nearby foghorn. The
contemporary-style suites are all privately
owned. All have private balconies and most
have views of the ocean beyond the harbor,
permitting the occasional sighting of an egret
or brown pelican. Beds are made with comfortable cotton blankets and feather duvets and face
the peaceful fishing harbor. Breakfast can be
taken to the room to enjoy at leisure. Order
ahead for a scrumptious box lunch to enjoy on
the beach.

A 6-mile coastal trail runs adjacent,
leading into nearby Princeton-by-the-Sea—
the perfect destination for dinner.

Half Moon Bay Lodge

2400 S. Cabrillo Hwy. (Hwy. 1), (800) 710-0778,
(650) 726-9000; www.halfmoonbaylodge.com.
80 rooms; $$-$$$. Some wood-burning fireplaces.
Heated pool; hot tub; sauna; fitness room. Continental
breakfast; dinner room service. No pets.

Located at the quiet southern end of town, this modern hacienda-style lodging overlooks the fourth fairway of the **Half Moon Bay Golf Links**—designed by Arnold Palmer and top-rated in the Bay Area. An oversize hot tub is within a semi-enclosed room. Special amenities for children include beach and pool toys that they can keep and kid-sized robes for use during their stay.

Mill Rose Inn

615 Mill St., downtown, (800) 900-ROSE,
(650) 726-8750; www.millroseinn.com. 6 rooms;
$$-$$$+. Some fireplaces. Hot tub. Afternoon snack;
full breakfast.
No pets.

Located just 2 easy blocks from Main Street, this B&B was San Mateo County's first. Guests are greeted by a magnificent English country-style garden filled with hundreds of varieties of roses and other blooms. All rooms in the 1902 house have European antiques, fluffy comforters, and private entrances. Some also have brass beds and clawfoot tubs. Breakfast and a newspaper are delivered to the room. A secluded hot tub inside a locked garden gazebo is available by reservation.

Old Thyme Inn

779 Main St., downtown, (800) 720-4277,
(650) 726-1616; www.oldthymeinn.com. 7 rooms.
Some fireplaces. Evening snack; full breakfast.
No pets.

Built in 1899, this charming Princess Anne Victorian has a small English-style garden filled with fragrant herbs and flowers. Each room is named for an herb, and produce from the garden seasons breakfast. Rooms have fluffy beds with featherbeds, down duvets, and crisp ironed sheets, and some have two-person whirlpool tubs.

The Ritz-Carlton

One Miramontes Point Rd., (800) 241-3333, (650)
712-7000; www.ritzcarlton.com. 6 stories; 261 rooms;
$$$+. Most gas fireplaces. Hot tub; full-service spa;
fitness room; 6 lighted tennis courts; 2 18-hole golf
courses. 2 restaurants; room service. Resort fee $25;
valet parking $45.

Located on a treeless bluff overlooking the sea, this classy resort is designed to resemble a 19th-century grand seaside lodge and is reminiscent of sites seen in Scotland. But never fear, this is not your parents' Ritz-Carlton—there is no dress code. Most rooms have a view of the ocean that can cause a maid to lean out a window mid-clean for a wistful gaze. All rooms feature white marble bathrooms with deep soaking tubs, silky Frette linens, goose down pillows, and featherbeds and duvets. The Club Level offers the added amenity of snacks all day long. "It is my pleasure" rolls off the lips of employees, who seem genuinely to enjoy attending to details. Facilities include a coastal walking path leading to a secluded beach and to picnic spots at scenic overlooks, an outdoor fire circle where guests can enjoy a s'mores basket from the bar, and a bluff-top hot tub. A bagpiper often plays ocean-side at sunset. The full-service spa has a central co-ed Roman mineral bath, plus a sauna and steam room. Treatments include a pumpkin body peel and both a four-hands and a maternity massage, and there is a massage room just for couples. The Ritz Kids program operates during busy times.

Gourmet **Navio** restaurant *((650) 712-7040. B-L-D daily, SunBr; $$$. Valet parking.),* whose name means "ship" in Portuguese, is a nod to the area's nautical heritage. It features a barrel ceiling resembling the lower deck of a vintage wooden sailing ship. On one side floor-to-ceiling windows provide ocean views, and on the other an open display kitchen provides further diversion. The kitchen creates a captivating menu of coastal cuisine using fresh local ingredients. A multi-course tasting menu with matched wines is sometimes available.

San Benito House

356 Main St., downtown, (650) 726-3425;
www.sanbenitohouse.com. 12 rooms; $-$$. Unsuitable
for children under 10. No TVs; some shared baths.
Sauna. Full breakfast; restaurant. No pets.

From its beginning in 1905, this lodging has offered well-priced rooms. Upstairs, guest rooms feature high ceilings, bathrooms with old-fashioned clawfoot tubs, and vividly colored, solid walls. They are decorated with

European antiques, contemporary paintings, and historical photographs. Guests can stroll in the formal English garden or play a round on the croquet lawn.

Downstairs, the cozy **restaurant** (D Thur-Sun; $$-$$$. Reservations advised.) invites romantic dining. The Mediterranean-style cuisine makes use of fresh local produce and seafood, and the soups and French pastries are particularly delicious. Make reservations when booking a room, as this cozy dining room is popular with locals. A **deli** (Daily 11-3; $.) dispenses inexpensive salads and sandwiches made with house-baked bread, and a lively Western-style **saloon** (Daily from 4pm.) is the perfect spot for a nightcap.

WHERE TO EAT

Cameron's Pub

1410 S. Cabrillo Hwy. (Hwy. 1), (650) 726-5705; www.cameronsinn.com. L Tu-Sun, D daily; $.

Home to the world's only double-decker smoking bus and maybe to the world's only double-decker video game bus, not to mention a beer can collection that numbers 3,000, this family-friendly neighborhood pub fills a warren of rooms. The extensive menu includes baked potatoes, housemade soups, sandwiches, pizza, and burgers, plus housemade pies, a full soda fountain with sundaes and shakes, and 26 beers on tap. Pub-style games include shuffleboard, darts, pinball, chess, and pool, and authentic English telephone booths are positioned both inside and out. Live entertainment is scheduled regularly. Celebrities sometimes stop in (Pierce Brosnan and family are patrons), but everyone is welcome—even babies and great-grandmums. A replica English village grocery sells imported English food staples and goods.

Want to stay the night? Three **guest rooms** are just upstairs. Two rooms share a bath but surprisingly, since this is billed as a B&B, **breakfast** is *not* included but a check-in **beverage**—a pint, a milkshake—is.

Pasta Moon

315 Main St., downtown, (650) 726-5125; www.pastamoon.com. L M-F, D daily, Sat-SunBr; $$-$$$. Reservations advised.

A favorite with locals, this is a simple but elegant space with large windows and white tablecloths. Breads are exceptional, and the housemade pasta is a must—perhaps a fabulous dish of wide pappardelle noodles mixed with house-cured pancetta, garlic, pine nuts, wild mushrooms, and a tomato cream sauce. Fresh fish and pizza are also winners on the lengthy menu. Affogato—white chocolate gelato with espresso and candied orange peel—is sublime for dessert.

Sam's Chowder House

4210 N. Cabrillo Hwy. (Hwy. 1), (650) 712-0245; www.samschowderhouse.com. L-D daily; $$$. Reservations taken.

This New England-style seafood house boasts excellent views of the Pacific Ocean from almost every table. Outdoor seating is also an option. Specialties include fresh fish, live lobsters and crabs, and a raw bar. Choose from New England (white) or Manhattan (red) clam chowders, and count on the award-winning lobster roll sandwich as always a good choice. Drinks are creative and fun—anyone for a Strawjito?—and Sam's is family-friendly, too.

A **seafood market** (W-F 4-8, Sat-Sun 12-8.) sells locally caught fresh fish, specialty seafood items, and side dishes, plus picnics-to-go—the all-inclusive lobster clambake pot is an easy way to entertain right on the beach but requires 48-hours notice.

Sushi Main Street

696 Mill St./Main St., downtown, (650) 726-6336; www.sushimainst.com. L M-Sat, D daily; $$. Reservations advised.

Serving everything Japanese and some things not, this cave-like spot is decorated with Asian artifacts that include Balinese carvings and ancient temple bells. Seating is at rough-hewn stone tables or a sushi bar. Hot and cold sake, plum wine, edamame (soy beans), kelp salad, gyoza (Japanese pot stickers), mochi-wrapped ice cream, and banana tempura are on the menu along with traditional tempuras, teriyakis, noodles, clay pot dishes, and sushi (the Half Moon Bay roll features artichoke hearts, avocado, and radish sprouts). At lunch, the bento box special is hard to beat.

PESCADERO

A LITTLE BACKGROUND

Named for the town creek that once was filled
with trout ("pescadero" means literally "fishing
place"), this tiny burg was settled by Portuguese
farmers. Now this peaceful place is known best
for its agricultural products—straw flowers and
artichokes—and Duarte's Tavern.

Do take a walk. Of special note are the colorful fields of straw flowers, the old-fashioned
general store, and a picturesque 130-year-old
church.

For a lovely ride through the backcountry,
follow the quiet, winding road that begins in
front of the restaurant (Stage Road) 7 miles
north to San Gregorio. Here, the **San
Gregorio General Store** *((650) 726-0565;
www.sangregoriostore.com. Daily 9-6.)*, an old-
fashioned country emporium that has been
serving area residents since 1889, makes an
interesting stop for picnic supplies or a snack.
Live music is scheduled every Saturday and
Sunday.

After stocking up, for a picturesque picnic
spot head to nearby **San Gregorio State Beach**
*((650) 879-2170; www.parks.ca.gov. Daily 8am-
sunset. $6/vehicle. No pets.)*, which often has sun
when none is to be found elsewhere along this
stretch of coast. Note that about a mile north of
here is a popular clothing-optional beach.

GETTING THERE

Located 50 miles south of San Francisco, and
about 15 miles south of Half Moon Bay. The
town is located about 1 mile inland from
Highway 1.

WHAT TO DO

Año Nuevo State Reserve
*On Hwy. 1, (650) 879-0227, reservations (800) 444-
4445; www.parks.ca.gov. Dec-March: reservations
required & can be made up to 8 wks. in advance; $5.
Apr-Nov 8:30-3, wildlife protection area open by free
permit. Park open daily 8-sunset; $6/vehicle. Closed
Dec 1-14. No pets.*

Huge elephant seals return to this beach
each year to mate and bear their young. It is the
largest elephant seal rookery on the U.S. main-

land (two others are at Pierdras Blancas by San
Simeon and at Point Reyes). Docent-guided
tours, lasting 2½ hours and covering 3 miles,
take visitors close enough to observe the seals
basking in the sun or sleeping. Usually that is
the extent of the activity seen, but occasionally
one of the weighty bulls (some weigh almost
8,000 pounds!) roars into battle with a challenging male. When picking a tour date note
that the adults arrive in December—when most
of the battles occur—and the babies are born in
January. Mating usually happens in February,
when the population is at its peak. Then the
adult seals begin to leave, and the weaned pups
are left alone until April, when the adult females
return to molt. Note that no food service is
available at the reserve, and no drinking water
is available along the tour trail.

Depending on the season, pick-your-own
olallieberries (June), pumpkins (October), kiwi
fruit (November), or Christmas trees are waiting across the street at 476-acre, usually sunny
Coastways Ranch *(640 Cabrillo Hwy. (Hwy. 1),
(831) 469-8804; www.swantonberryfarm.com.
June-July daily 9-5, Oct-Dec 10-4; closed Jan-
May & Aug-Sept.)*. This little piece of paradise
has been farmed by the Hudson family since
1917. It has twisting dirt trails, picnic tables,
and a snack bar. Call ahead for current information on crops, and bring along throwaway
surgical gloves to protect hands.

Harley Farms
*205 North St., (800) 394-2939, (650) 879-0480;
www.harleyfarms.com. Tours Sat-Sun at 11 & 1, by
reservation. $20, 6-10 $10.*

This 9-acre dairy goat farmstead (a term that indicates cheese here is made only from milk produced on this farm) offers a 2-hour behind-the-scenes tour that includes meeting some of the 200-plus curious American Alpine goats, milking one, and learning how to make goat cheese. Cheese tasting occurs in a rustic hayloft. Spring is kidding season. Guide Ryan Andrus says, "Sheep are dumb. Goats are smarter—noticeably smarter."

Pescadero State Beach

New Year's Creek Rd., (650) 879-2170; www.parks.ca.gov. 8am-sunset. $6/vehicle. No pets.

Sand dunes at the north end invite sliding, a creek invites wading, and tide pools invite exploring. Tide pool explorations are scheduled when the tides are right.

The adjoining 210-acre **Pescadero Marsh Natural Preserve** is a refuge for waterfowl and wildlife; it teems with migrating birds and native plants. It features marked hiking trails, and docent-led nature walks occur on weekends.

Phipps Country Store and Farm

2700 Pescadero Rd./Hwy. 1, 1 mi. E of town, (650) 879-0787; www.phippscountry.com. Daily 10-5; Apr-Oct 10-6. Farm: $3, 60+ & under 4 free.

Plants, fresh produce, herbs and spices, and 60 varieties of dried heirloom beans are for sale at this country store. Fresh goose eggs are often available from January through July (geese do not lay eggs year round). The 50-acre farm offers pick-your-own strawberries and blackberries in season, and visitors can view domestic farm animals—pigs, goats, and chickens—as well as exotic birds and a songbird aviary. Picnic facilities are available.

WHERE TO STAY

Costanoa Coastal Lodge & Camp

2001 Rossi Rd., (877) 262-7848, (650) 879-1100; www.costanoa.com. 40 rooms, 12 cabins, 135 tent cabins; $-$$$. No TVs. Hot tub; sauna; steam room. Breakfast voucher included with some lodging; restaurant. No pets.

Situated on a bluff on the up side of Highway 1, this "boutique campground" offers an upscale camping experience. Guests can stay in a tent and bring their own sleeping bag, stay in a canvas cabin equipped with bedding that includes a heated mattress pad and down comforter, or stay in a comfortable conventional cabin with a fireplace, an expansive pastoral view, and a private deck with porch swing. Any choice brings with it the adventure of trekking through chilly local air to communal "comfort stations." The upscale part means that the restrooms look attractive, smell nice, and have heated floors; some have private outdoor showers. (Regulations governing use of this prime coastal land limit the number of toilets.) Alternatively, lodge rooms with bathrooms en suite are also available, as are traditional campsites for tents and RVs. Prices reflect the level of pampering. Simple deli items are available in the General Store, and the property abuts four state parks and offers easy access to their hiking trails. Facilities include mountain bike rentals, year-round horseback riding, a children's mega-sandbox, and massage rooms. Costanoa Kids Camp for ages 5 through 12 is offered in summer and by request.

Pigeon Point Lighthouse Hostel

210 Pigeon Point Rd., (800) 909-4776 #73, (650) 879-0633; www.pigeonpointhostel.org. 52 beds; 4 private rooms. Hot tub $7/person.

Named after the first big ship that crashed on the rocks here—the *Carrier Pigeon*—this scenic lighthouse was built in 1872 and is the second-tallest freestanding lighthouse in the U.S. Guest beds are in adjacent bungalows, and a cliff-top hot tub is open in the evening by reservation. See also page 468.

Due to damage, lighthouse tours at **Pigeon Point Light Station State Historic Park** *((650) 879-2120; www.parks.ca.gov. Daily 7:30-sunset. Grounds tours: F-Sun 10-4. No pets.)* are no longer available. However, the grounds remain

open, and excellent tide pools are located just to the north.

WHERE TO EAT

Duarte's Tavern
202 Stage Rd., (650) 879-0464;
www.duartes tavern.com. B-L-D daily; $-$$.
Reservations advised for D.

Diners have been coming here since 1894 to enjoy drinks in the old-time bar, and since 1936 for a home-style meal in the cozy, casual coffee shop. (The name is pronounced "dew-arts.") Breakfast is served until 1 p.m. on weekdays and features giant buttermilk pancakes and outstanding omelettes—especially the sautéed garlic-artichoke and the linguica (a spicy Portuguese sausage) versions—as well as more common items. At lunch or dinner try the delicious creamy artichoke heart or green chili soups, giant boiled artichokes with garlic mayo dip, fried oysters, homemade pie, and fresh applesauce. (Artichoke items are made with 'chokes picked fresh in nearby fields.) Grilled fresh fish is available at dinner, and a popular fixed-price cioppino feed occurs on Friday, Saturday, and Sunday nights by reservation.

Norm's Market
287 Stage Rd., (650) 879-0147; www.norms market.com. Daily 10-6.

Family-owned and -run since 1929, this is the best stop in the area for picnic supplies. A deli in back makes sandwiches to go. Do try the delicious local goat cheese and the artichoke salsa, and be sure to pick up extra of the super artichoke-garlic and artichoke-pesto breads to finish baking at home—*and* don't forget some garlic-herb croutons and olallieberry muffins!

DAVENPORT

A LITTLE BACKGROUND

Once a well-known whaling town, this tiny village was wiped out by a fire in 1915. All that remains from those days is the town jail.

GETTING THERE

Located 70 miles south of San Francisco, and 9 miles north of Santa Cruz.

WHAT TO DO

Bonny Doon Vineyard Tasting Room
10 Pine Flat Rd., in Bonny Doon (1 mi. S of town, then 5 mi. up the hill), (866) 666-3396, (831) 425-4518; www.bonnydoonvineyard.com. Tasting daily 11-5.

The pleasant side trip to this winery follows a meandering country road to the tiny mountain town of Bonny Doon. (Not actually a town or city, but instead a community of landowners, this area once grew more grapes than Napa or Sonoma.) Winery specialties include exotic French and Italian varietals. Picnic tables are provided in a redwood grove complete with a gurgling creek.

Davenport Jail Museum
2 Davenport Ave./Ocean Ave., (831) 429-1964; www.santacruzmah.org. Sat-Sun 10-2. Free.

Due to the generally peaceful nature of the area's residents, this two-cell jail built in 1914 was used only twice. In 1987, it was transformed into a small museum with exhibits on the history of Santa Cruz county's north coast.

Rancho del Oso Nature and History Center

3600 Hwy. 1, 7 mi. N of town, (831) 427-2288;
www.parks.ca.gov. Park: daily 8am-sunset; guided
nature walk on 2nd Sat of month. History center:
Sat-Sun 12-4. Free. No pets.

Located on Waddell Creek and part of
Big Basin Redwoods State Park (see page 394),
this bucolic spot has a marked nature trail
leading through one of the few remaining
native Monterey pine forests. Former president
Herbert Hoover's brother, Theodore, settled this
valley in 1914, and his former family home is
now the museum. After viewing vintage photos
and checking out the logging artifacts and the
wildlife exhibit, consider a picnic either in the
sheltered courtyard or on the deck overlooking
the preserve.

Just across the street, where fresh water
Waddell Creek enters the ocean, **Waddell Beach**
is a popular spot for windsurfing and hang-
gliding.

WHERE TO STAY/EAT

Davenport Roadhouse at the Cash Store

1 Davenport Ave./Hwy. 1, (800) 870-1817,
(831) 426-8801; www.davenportroadhouse.com.
12 rooms; $$-$$$. Continental breakfast; restaurant.
No pets.

Some of the eco-friendly rooms here have
skylights and ocean views.

The comfortable **restaurant** *(B-L daily, D*
Tu-Sun; $-$$.) is one large open room—built
on the site of an old-time cash store that was
destroyed by fire in 1953. Fresh seafood and
housemade bread and pastries are menu
hallmarks.

SANTA CRUZ

A LITTLE BACKGROUND

Close enough to San Francisco to visit just for
the day, Santa Cruz has long been a popular
summer destination. Weather is reliably clear
and sunny, and the beach features fine sand and
a gentle surf. In fact, it is a Very Southern
California-style beach town. It's not unusual to
see tanned bodies with zinc-covered noses and
surfboards hanging out of cars, and to hear the
Beach Boys providing background sounds. And
even the police officers here wear shorts!

The 1989 Loma Prieta earthquake wreaked
havoc here. The damage was severe along popular Pacific Avenue, which is now rebuilt and
better than ever.

Beware! Don't drive here without a good
map. The street layout is not always logical.

VISITOR INFORMATION

Santa Cruz County Conference and Visitors Council

1211 Ocean St., (800) 833-3494, (831) 425-1234;
www.santacruzca.org.

GETTING THERE

Located approximately 65 miles south of San
Francisco. Take either Highway 101 or the more
scenic Highway 280 to Highway 17; or take
magnificently scenic Highway 1 all the way.

ANNUAL EVENTS

Cabrillo Festival of Contemporary Music

August. (831) 426-6966; www.cabrillomusic.org.
Free-$35.

This is said to be one of the country's best
small music festivals. The program includes a
variety of contemporary orchestral works,
including world premieres, and some events
occur at Mission San Juan Bautista.

WHAT TO DO

Beach & Boardwalk

400 Beach St., (831) 423-5590; www.beach
boardwalk.com. Open daily mid-Apr-Aug, weekends &
holidays Sept-Mar; closed Dec 1-25. Admission to
Boardwalk free; rides $2.25-$4.50, all-day ticket
$29.95.

Fortunately, this is one beach boardwalk
that has not degenerated over the years. Built in
1907, it is now the only boardwalk left on the
West Coast and the oldest amusement park in
California. It offers a variety of arcade games,
fast-food stands, and souvenir shops—plus 23
major rides and 11 kiddie rides. Don't miss the
salt water taffy—pulled and wrapped with
antique machines—and the caramel apples at
Marini's *((866) MARINIS, (831) 423-7258;*
www.mariniscandies.com.), where four generations of the family have made candy since 1915.
The half-mile-long concrete boardwalk parallels

a clean, gorgeous beach (a city ordinance permits no alcohol on beaches). Thrill rides include the **Giant Dipper**, a rickety wooden roller coaster built in 1924 and rated by *The New York Times* as one of the ten best in the country, and Logger's Revenge, a refreshing water flume ride. An old-fashioned **carousel** built in New Jersey by Charles Looff in 1911 is the largest of the four remaining classic merry-go-rounds in Northern California. It features 70 hand-carved horses (all with authentic horse-hair tails) and two chariots as well as its rare, original 1894 342-pipe Ruth Und Sohn band organ, and a ring toss—one of the few left in the world. All this plus free band concerts on Friday nights in summer and a 2-story indoor miniature golf course, too!

The Museum of Art and History

705 Front St./Cooper St., downtown, (831) 429-1964; www.santacruzmah.org. Tu-Sun 11-5. $5, 62+ $3, 12-17 $2; free 1st Fri of month.

The permanent collection exhibited here focuses on the social history of Santa Cruz County. Contemporary works by local artists are also displayed.

The Mystery Spot

465 Mystery Spot Rd., 3 mi. N of town (call for directions; finding it can be a bit of a mystery, too), (831) 423-8897; www.mysteryspot.com. Daily 9-5; in summer to 7. $5, under 3 free; parking $5.

Located in a grove of redwoods, this small, quiet, cool spot measures only about 150 feet in diameter. During the guided tour gravitational forces appear to be defied, and everyone leaves with a souvenir bumper sticker.

Natural Bridges State Beach

2531 West Cliff Dr., at N end, (831) 423-4609; www.parks.ca.gov. Daily 8am-sunset. $6/vehicle.

Enjoy a picnic in the sun on the sandy beach, or in the shade at sturdy tables. All but one of the mudstone arches—after which the beach is named—have collapsed, but there are still plenty of tide pools to explore. Swimming in the ocean is recommended only when a lifeguard is on duty, but sometimes a lagoon forms where small children can wade safely.

From October through February, large numbers of **monarch butterflies** make their winter home here. A short nature trail leads to good viewing points where they are seen hanging in clusters on mature eucalyptus trees, and guided walks are scheduled on weekends then. During monarch season, the Visitor Center *(Daily 10-4.)* displays informative exhibits.

Pacific Avenue/Downtown Santa Cruz

Betw. Water St. & Cathcart St., (831) 429-8433; www.downtownsantacruz.com.

These five landscaped blocks comprise downtown Santa Cruz. Once the park-like setting was home to a variety of boutiques, art galleries, and restaurants operating from within restored historic buildings. But the 1989 Loma Prieta earthquake turned the area into a disaster zone of destruction, which was followed by new construction. Now things are hopping again.

Spend some time browsing the impressive **Bookshop Santa Cruz** *(1520 Pacific Ave., (831) 423-0900; www.bookshopsantacruz.com. Daily 9am-10pm.)*, which is now in a grand new building.

Santa Cruz City Museum of Natural History

1305 East Cliff Dr., (831) 420-6115; www.santacruz museums.org. Tu-Sun 10-5. $2.50, 60+ $1.50, under 18 free.

Located across the street from wonderful Seabright Beach and operating within a vintage 1917 Carnegie library building, this museum displays the county's natural treasures. Exhibits include Native American artifacts, fossils, local wildlife specimens, an operating beehive, and a "touch tank" of live sea animals. Kids love the large grassy area outside and the life-size, 50-foot-long female grey whale sculpture that begs to be climbed on. Parking can be difficult.

Santa Cruz Mission State Historic Park
144 School St., (831) 425-5849; www.parks.ca.gov. Thur-Sun 10-4. Free.

A restored adobe building is all that remains of the original mission complex and is now the only remaining example of mission Indian housing in California. Exhibits include a furnished living quarters for Native American families. Tours are available. A large Victorian garden gone wild, with several tall redwoods and a giant avocado tree that is one of the oldest in the state, invites leisurely picnicking. Living History Day, when docents in period dress oversee a variety of crafts activities, occurs each month.

Mission Santa Cruz (*126 High St./Emmet St., (831) 426-5686; www.geocities.com/ missionbell. Tu-Sat 10-4, Sun 10-2; call to verify schedule. By donation.*) is a block away. It is 12th in the chain of missions. Built in 1794 and destroyed in an earthquake in 1857, the mission was rebuilt in 1931 as this half-size replica. It now houses a small museum displaying original statues, candlesticks, and paintings, as well as ornate vestments and a baptismal font.

Santa Cruz Surfing Museum
701 West Cliff Dr., at Lighthouse Point, (831) 420-6289; www.santacruzsurfingmuseum.org. Thur-M 12-4; in summer, W-M 10-5. Free.

The first place ever surfed outside of Hawaii, Santa Cruz is an appropriate spot for an homage to surfing. This tiny one-room museum displays vintage surfboards (don't miss the 10-foot redwood long board from the 1930s, or the contemporary polyurethane board sporting shark bites) and the world's first wetsuit (made in Santa Cruz). It is housed within the small brick **Mark Abbott Memorial Lighthouse**, which was funded by Chuck and Esther Abbott in memory of their 18-year-old son who drowned in a 1965 surfing accident near Pleasure Point.

Seal Rock, home to a herd of sea lions, and **Steamer Lane**, where surfers do their thing,

are visible off shore, and a scenic 3-mile bike and pedestrian pathway begins here.

Santa Cruz Municipal Wharf
Near the Boardwalk, (831) 420-5270; www.santacruzwharf.com. Daily 5am-2am. Parking: 30 min. free, then $1-$3/hr.

Visitors can walk, bike, or drive to the end of this ½-mile-long pier. Anglers fish from the side (licenses are not required), and sea lions are usually spotted around fishing holes at the south end. Seafood restaurants, snack stands, and benches are scattered along its length. Deep-sea fishing trips, boat tours, and kayak excursions originate at concessions here.

Seymour Marine Discovery Center
W end of Delaware Ave., (831) 459-3800; http://seymourcenter.ucsc.edu. Tu-Sat 10-5, Sun 12-5; tour at 1, 2, 3. $6, 64+ & 4-16 $4; free 1st Tu of month.

Part of a marine research station for U.C. Santa Cruz, this center provides impressive views of the Monterey Bay National Marine Sanctuary. It features exhibit galleries, aquariums stocked with local sea life, and a touching pool with hermit crabs, sea stars, and sea anemones. Research is conducted on marine mammal behavior, fish diseases, and coral genetics. Guided tours include viewing the sea lion tanks and the skeleton of an 86-foot-long blue whale that washed ashore up the coast on Pescadero Beach in 1979.

Surfing schools
Surfers have been riding the waves in Santa Cruz since the early 1920s. Part of *Endless Summer* was shot here, and *Surfer Magazine* named Santa Cruz one of the top ten surf towns in the country. Why even The Beach Boys sing a song about surfing here!

• Richard Schmidt Surf School
849 Almar Ave., (831) 423-0928; www.richard schmidt.com. Lessons year-round; camp June-Aug. Group lesson $80/2 hrs.; camp $1,000/wk.

This sage instructor gives a "stand-up guarantee" that promises a free ride (refund) to anyone who doesn't stand up in their first class. Camp attendees bring their own sleeping bags and share tents. Amenities include a pool, hot tub, and hammocks, plus inspirational surfing videos and a midweek massage. Educational excursions take participants to a surf museum and a surfboard factory.

• Club Ed International Surf School

2350 Paul Minnie Ave., (800) 287-SURF, (831) 464-0177; www.club-ed.com. Group lesson $85/2 hrs.; camp $1,090/wk.

Easy-going Ed is known as the Professor of Surfing at UCSC. His school is similar to Schmidt's, but the camp is more upscale and includes gourmet meals and a professional massage.

Tea House Spa

112 Elm St./Pacific Ave., downtown, (831) 426-9700; www.teahousespa.com. Daily 11am-midnight. Tubs: $12-$18/person/hr.

Private rooms with whirlpool hot tubs overlook a mature bamboo garden planted in the late 1940s. Two of the four rooms have cedar-lined saunas. Tea is prepared and left to be enjoyed at leisure, and fragrant Bonny Doon Farms lavender soap and shampoo are provided and can be purchased to go. Massage is available.

University of California, Santa Cruz Campus

1156 High St., (831) 459-0111; www.ucsc.edu. Parking: $5.

Located high in the hills above town, the buildings of this spectacularly beautiful campus are hidden among a forest of old-growth redwoods. Gorgeous views of the Monterey Bay are seen from many locations.

Pick up a map at the Public Information Office *((831) 459-2495)* and take a self-guided walking tour. **Guided tours** *((831) 459-4008. M-F at 10, 1, 3. Free. Reservations required.)* are also available, and free shuttle buses loop the campus daily.

The **Arboretum** *((831) 427-2998; http://arboretum.ucsc.edu. Daily 9-5. Free.)* has an extensive collection of plants from Australia and New Zealand and of South African proteas.

Bay Tree Bookstore *((831) 459-4544; http://slugstore.ucsc.edu. M-F 8:30-5:30, Sat 10-4.)* dispenses student books and supplies as well as the now-famous "U C Santa Cruz Banana Slugs" t-shirt worn by John Travolta in *Pulp Fiction*.

Wilder Ranch State Park

1401 Old Coast Rd., off Hwy. 1, 2 mi. N of town; www.parks.ca.gov. Park: (831) 423-9703; sunrise-sunset. Visitor Center: (831) 426-0505; Thur-Sun 10-4, closed Thur Dec-Feb. Tour: Sat-Sun at 1. $6/vehicle. No pets.

The perfect spot to spend a lazy day in the country, this 4,505-acre turn-of-the-19th-century ranch complex invites bringing a picnic. Formerly a dairy, it is built in an arroyo, or valley, that protects it from whipping coastal winds. When the Visitor Center is open, docents dressed in old-fashioned garb bring life to the old buildings, and visitors can inspect a large Queen Anne Victorian home, an 1854 Gothic farmhouse, an even older adobe, a bunk house, several barns, a chicken coop, and miscellaneous other structures. Domesticated animals—horses, cows, goats, and chickens—also add atmosphere. The Old Cove Landing Trail provides a 4-mile nature walk or mountain bike ride from which cormorants and harbor seals are often sighted; a fern grotto is also seen. A self-guiding brochure is available at the trailhead.

WHERE TO STAY

Babbling Brook Inn

1025 Laurel St., (800) 866-1131, (831) 427-2437; www.babblingbrookinn.com. 13 rooms; $$-$$$. Some wood-burning & gas fireplaces. Afternoon & evening snack; full breakfast. No pets.

Shaded by tall redwoods, this secluded hillside inn was built as a log cabin in 1909. Rooms have been added through the years, and it is now the oldest and largest B&B in the area. Most guest rooms are named after impressionist painters and decorated in the artist's favorite themes and colors. And the inn delivers what its name promises: a babbling brook runs through the property, plus there are even a few cascading waterfalls. An acre of beautifully landscaped grounds surrounding the inn has paths, a covered footbridge, an 18th-century water wheel, and a lacy wrought-iron gazebo.

Casablanca Inn

101 Main St., (800) 644-1570, (831) 423-1570; www.casablanca-santacruz.com. 39 rooms; $$-$$$+. Some kitchens; some wood-burning & gas fireplaces. Restaurant; limited room service. No pets.

Located across the street from the beach and Boardwalk, this converted 1918 mansion features spacious, pleasantly decorated rooms. Additional rooms with terraces are available in a 1950s annex.

The **Casablanca** restaurant (*(831) 426-9063. D daily, SunBr; $$-$$$. Reservations advised.*) has the largest wine cellar in the county and features a sophisticated menu of seafood, pastas, and meats.

Ocean Echo Inn & Beach Cottages
401 Johans Beach Dr., (831) 462-4192; www.oceanecho.com. 15 units; $-$$$+. Some kitchens. Continental breakfast.

Tucked in a quiet beach cove just a few miles south of the Boardwalk, these attractive rooms and cottages are on a private beach within sound of the surf. Many have ocean views and sundecks.

Pleasure Point Inn
2-3665 East Cliff Dr./37th Ave., (877) 557-2567, (831) 475-4657; www.pleasurepointinn.com. 4 rooms; $$$. All gas fireplaces. Hot tub. Continental breakfast. No pets.

Situated ocean front, on a scenic corner amid an eclectic mix of grand homes and modest surfer shacks in Santa Cruz's Pleasure Point area, this small inn blends in so well that it can be difficult to find. It was remodeled from a '70s beach house into a streamlined retro '30s inn with a curved exterior reminiscent of a cruise ship. Rooms are spacious and have a relaxing seaside decor accented with smooth blue marble and knotty pine. Each is equipped with a comforter-topped bed, gas fireplace, heated bathroom floor, and whirlpool bathtub. An expansive buffet breakfast is served in an ocean-view dining room. A hot tub gurgles continuously on a rooftop sundeck overlooking a popular surfing site, and a bluff-top trail in front of the inn is primo for walking, biking, and running.

Santa Cruz Dream Inn
175 West Cliff Dr., (800) 663-1144, (831) 426-4330; jdvhotels.com. 10 stories; 165 rooms; $$$-$$$+. Heated pool; child wading pool; hot tub. Restaurant; room service. No pets.

This hotel is located right on the beach within an easy walk of the Boardwalk. Each

room has a private balcony or patio overlooking Cowell's Beach and Monterey Bay. The pool and hot tub are one story up from the sand and enjoy the same view.

The **Mainsail** restaurant has a fantastic beach and ocean view, and its windows are usually open to the sounds of waves breaking on the shore.

Santa Cruz Hostel
321 Main St., (831) 423-8304; www.santacruz hostel.org. 40 beds; 5 private rooms.

Located on Beach Hill within the restored 1870s Carmelita Cottages, this hostel is just 2 blocks from the Boardwalk action.

Sea & Sand Inn
201 West Cliff Dr., (831) 427-3400; www.santacruzmotels.com/sea_and_sand.html. 20 rooms; $-$$$+. Afternoon snack; continental breakfast. No pets.

Perched on a cliff high above the beach, all rooms here have views of the ocean and Boardwalk, and some suites have private patio hot tubs. The soothing sound of the surf breaking on the shore below is continuous, and an extensive grassy area between the rooms and the ocean is bordered with colorful plants and flowers and furnished with tables and chairs, inviting repose. Though there is no direct beach access, it is just a short walk to the beach and Boardwalk.

West Cliff Inn
174 West Cliff Dr., (800) 979-0910, (831) 457-2200; www.westcliffinn.com. 9 rooms; $$$-$$$+. All gas fireplaces. Afternoon snack; full breakfast.

Built as a private home in 1877, this 3-story Italianate Victorian is now a historic landmark. It boasts a view of the beach and Boardwalk from some rooms and from its two porches. But it's not your grandma's Victorian. Inside, it features clean-lined, contemporary finishes and accents throughout. One room has a private outdoor hot tub, and breakfast is served in bed for a small fee. The inn is well positioned for an easy walk or ride (the inn has bicycles for loan) to the Wharf, beach, and Boardwalk.

Motel Row

Many motels are located in the area surrounding the Boardwalk, including some inexpensive ones dating from the 1930s. Rooms are usually available at the last minute.

WHERE TO EAT

Crow's Nest

2218 East Cliff Dr., (831) 476-4560;
www.crowsnest- santacruz.com. L-D daily, SunBr; $$.
Reservations advised in summer.

Fresh local seafood at reasonable prices is the specialty here, but steaks, pastas, and salads are also on the menu. Children get a color-in menu and a goodie from the treasure chest. Protected by a glass windbreaker, outdoor diners enjoy ocean views and can watch vessels come and go from the Santa Cruz Yacht Harbor.

The less formal **Upstairs Breakwater Bar & Grill** is open throughout the day and regularly schedules live entertainment and dancing.

Donnelly Fine Chocolates

1509 Mission St./Bay St., (888) 685-1871,
(831) 458-4214; www.donnellychocolates.com. M-F
10:30-6, Sat 12-5; call to confirm.

Located in the middle of a muddle of unimpressive storefronts, this shop resembles not in the least a trendy European chocolate *shoppe*. Yet, stuffed in the back of a teeny, tiny shop, surfer-chef Richard Donnelly and his troupe make ultra-fine, European-style chocolates the old-fashioned way—by hand. And every visitor gets a sample. Though Donnelly chocolates are known for their unusual spice and herb fillings—including ginseng and lavender—the classics continue to sell best. They can *almost* be considered diet chocolates . . . because they cost $65 per pound—enough to make anyone think twice before popping more than one in their mouth. Made with the best ingredients, they rate four yums on the yum scale. Yum, yum, yum, and yum! Chocolates are dispensed in sophisticated boxes wrapped in gorgeous handmade Japanese papers and tied up with smooth fabric ribbons. The package is *almost* as delicious as its contents. A selection of these award-winning chocolates makes a very special gift. Not in the mood for chocolate? Donnelly sells ice cream, too.

El Palomar

1336 Pacific Ave., downtown, (831) 425-7575;
www.elpalomarrestaurant.com. L-D daily, SunBr; $-$$.
No reservations.

Housed in the cool back room of a 1930s hotel, with ornately decorated high ceilings and colorful mural-adorned walls, this restaurant serves well-prepared, authentic Michoacan-style Mexican dishes and seafood. Tortillas are made by hand each day, and there is a large selection of Mexican beers. In addition to the expected staples, the menu includes the more unusual: pozole (pork and hominy stew), sopes (puffy tortillas with fillings), and occasionally menudo (tripe soup). The bar has a retractable ceiling that is opened in good weather, and the restaurant's inexpensive taco bar adjoins.

CAPITOLA

A LITTLE BACKGROUND

Dating back to 1861, when it was a tent village, this artsy-craftsy beach town was the state's first seaside resort. In those days, ladies would wear heavy wool swim suits and walk out into the surf holding on to a steadying rope to "sea bathe." The lovely mile-long beach is sheltered between two bluffs and offers both swimming in calm ocean waters and wading in the fresh water of Soquel Creek. Be cautious, however, as sometimes that creek water isn't so pristine.

Fronting the beach, **The Esplanade** is lined with coffeehouses and restaurants serving everything from hamburgers to lobster. Many have outdoor patios overlooking the beach.

In summer, free shuttle buses take visitors from parking lots on Bay Avenue to the beach. Some shuttle bikes are also available for loan.

VISITOR INFORMATION

Capitola-Soquel Chamber of Commerce

716-G Capitola Ave., (800) 474-6522, (831) 475-6522;
www.capitolasoquelchamber.com.

GETTING THERE

Located approximately 5 miles south of Santa Cruz.

ANNUAL EVENTS

Begonia Festival

September; on Labor Day weekend. (831) 476-3566;
www.begoniafestival.com. Free.

Begun years ago as a way to make use of
the beautiful blooms discarded by local begonia
growers interested only in the bulbs, this popular festival includes a sand sculpture contest,
fishing derby, and nautical parade of flower-
covered floats down Soquel Creek. (The world's
only other begonia festival is held in Ballarat,
Australia.)

WHAT TO DO

Bargetto Winery

3535 N. Main St., in Soquel, (800) 4BARGETTO,
(831) 475-2258; www.bargetto.com. Tasting daily 12-5;
tour by appt.

This family-run winery is one of the
largest in the area and is known both for its
premium dessert fruit wines made from hand-
picked fruit—including olallieberry and raspberry—and its excellent homemade wine vinegars. It also produces a popular Pinot Grigio
and an authentic Mead made from honey. A
patio tasting bar is open on weekends.
Sparkling grape juice is poured for kids and
non-drinkers. Bring a picnic to enjoy on the
outdoor patio overlooking gurgling Soquel
Creek.

Capitola Historical Museum

410 Capitola Ave., (831) 464-0322; www.capitola
museum.org. W, F-Sun 12-4. Free.

Situated near the town railroad trestle, this
tiny museum operates within an historical little
red house. Historical walking tours are scheduled regularly, and participants learn that many
of the streets are named for places the residents
came from and that in the Jewel Box area
streets are named after jewels.

WHERE TO STAY

Capitola Venetian Hotel

1500 Wharf Rd., (800) 332-2780, (831) 476-6471;
www.capitolavenetian.com. 20 units; $-$$$. All
kitchens; some fireplaces. No pets.

Built in the 1920s, this mini-village of
charming stucco apartments in ice cream colors
is located right on the beach. It was California's
first condominium complex. Some units have
balconies and ocean views, and one spectacular
unit has both a panoramic ocean view and a
fireplace in the bedroom.

Harbor Lights Motel

5000 Cliff Dr., (831) 476-0505; www.harborlights
motel.biz. 4 stories; 10 rooms; $-$$$. Some kitchens;
1 fireplace. No pets.

This ordinary motel boasts an extraordinary location just across from the beach. Some

Capitola Venetian Hotel

rooms have views of Monterey Bay, the village, and the beach.

WHERE TO EAT

Dharma's Natural Foods
4250 Capitola Rd./42nd Ave., (831) 462-1717; www.dharmaland.com. B-L-D daily; $. No reservations.

Legend has it that this vegetarian and vegan haven—it is the oldest completely vegetarian restaurant in the U.S.—once suffered a "Big Mac attack" by McDonald's, who sued over its original name of McDharma's. Formerly just a food stand by the beach in Santa Cruz, it has settled into a pleasant, spacious spot in a suburban shopping center. Items on the extensive menu include several vegetarian burgers, a variety of Mexican dishes, sautés, salads, pastas, and soups; at breakfast it's tofu scrambles. Ingredients are organic when available.

Gayle's Bakery & Rosticceria
504 Bay Ave./Capitola Ave., (831) 462-1200; www.gaylesbakery.com. Daily 6:30am-8:30pm; $. No reservations.

The talent behind it all here is Gayle, who once worked at Berkeley's Chez Panisse, and her husband Joe, who once was a house painter and musician. Their story is of the little bakery that grew and grew, expanding from a tiny storefront operation to occupying the entire building. It is an unpretentious bakery extraordinaire, featuring cases laden with a plethora of soul-satisfying, made-from-scratch choices that sometimes make a person dissolve into an abyss of indecision. What to put on the lunch tray? The red-potato salad? Yes. Christie's coleslaw made with fresh ginger, cilantro, and peanuts? But of course. The albacore sandwich prepared with housemade mayo and on an herb-cheese roll? Most definitely. But leave room for a dessert—perhaps the moist German chocolate cake, or maybe an éclair, a pecan crocodile bar, or some other decadent delight. Sidle up to the coffee bar for a drink, and then settle down either indoors at one of the French mosaic "earthquake tables" made from crockery broken in that infamous 1980s quake, or outdoors at a cheery table on the heated brick patio. A take-home order can be prepared for pick-up after dining; don't forget to include a loaf or two of

European-style bread, a bag of the melt-in-your mouth crostini, and maybe one of the dome-shaped lavender marzipan-frosted princess cakes, too. Oh, and don't forget the soups, or the spit-roasted meats prepared in a brick roasting oven imported from Italy, or . . .

Shadowbrook
1750 Wharf Rd., (800) 975-1511, (831) 475-1511; www.shadowbrook-capitola.com. D daily, SunBr; $$-$$$. Reservations advised.

At the heart of this popular venue, located on the banks of Soquel Creek, is a log cabin originally built as a summer home in the 1920s. Diners descend to the restaurant either by riding a bright red, self-operated funicular cable car down a flower-laden hill from the street above, or by strolling down an adjacent serpentine step-path through manicured gardens with fountains and koi-stocked ponds. Most tables offer a view of the creek, often with the added entertainment of ducks and geese cavorting in the water. The menu features prime rib and fresh fish as well as a generous assortment of other entrees. Scampi prepared with succulent giant prawns is a house specialty, as is a delicious creamy artichoke soup and a custard-filled dessert crêpe topped with caramel sauce. Though children are welcome, this restaurant exudes a romantic atmosphere.

Live entertainment is scheduled in the **Rock Room Lounge** on weekends.

APTOS

A LITTLE BACKGROUND

Located just a few miles south of the well-known coastal towns of Capitola and Santa Cruz, this tiny, less frenetic burg often gets lost in the shuffle. But that's all the more reason to head here for a restorative getaway.

First inhabited by the Ohlone Indians, the town was then settled by Rafael Castro when he received it in 1833 as a 6,000-acre land grant for raising cattle. The property started breaking up in 1872, when sugar millionaire Claus Spreckles bought 2,400 acres from Castro. He built a summer home and a deer park, which he stocked with deer, elk, and other game. Most of the village was constructed between 1850 and

1900—when it was a busy logging town—and at one time it bustled with 13 saloons and 2 railroad stations.

Because Aptos (pronounced "Ap-toss") is a very confusing town to navigate, it's smart to carry a good map (the chamber of commerce will send one free). Otherwise, it is possible to just go round and round in scenic circles. The town has three basic areas: Aptos Village, Seacliff State Beach, and Rio Del Mar. Tiny Aptos Village is sprinkled for 2 blocks along Soquel Drive just northeast of Highway 1, and it is home to several restaurants, an assortment of shops, and an historic inn.

Be particularly careful in late afternoon at the poorly marked intersection of Spreckles and Soquel drives, which seems designed especially to snag out-of-towners. Making a left-hand turn here can leave even a careful driver with an unwanted souvenir ticket.

VISITOR INFORMATION

Aptos Chamber of Commerce
7605-A Old Dominion Ct., (831) 688-1467; www.aptoschamber.com.

ANNUAL EVENTS

Fourth of July Parade
July. (831) 688-1467; www.aptoschamber.com.
This is billed as "the world's shortest parade."

WHAT TO DO

The Forest of Nisene Marks State Park
On Aptos Creek Rd., behind Aptos Village, (831) 763-7062; www.parks.ca.gov. Sunrise-sunset. $6/vehicle.
Aptos Creek Road meanders back among tall, dense redwood groves and into this scenic 10,000-acre park. An easy trail leads to the epicenter of the devastating 1989 Loma Prieta earthquake, which flattened buildings as far away as 80 miles north in San Francisco.

Seacliff State Beach
201 State Park Dr., (831) 685-6442; www.parks.ca.gov. Sunrise-sunset. $6/vehicle.
Aimlessly following the area's winding roads often eventually leads to this locally popular beach. From the parking area, it is a short, scenic walk to view the *Palo Alto*. This former

tanker was converted into a nightclub in 1930 and cracked up in a storm soon after. Its current incarnation is as an unusual fishing pier. Campsites are available.

WHERE TO STAY

Rio Sands Motel
116 Aptos Beach Dr., (800) 826-2077, (831) 688-3207; www.riosands.com. 50 rooms; $-$$. Some kitchens. Heated pool; hot tub. Continental breakfast. No pets.
Located just 1 block from the beach, this 1950s-era traditional motel offers the bonus of a nice garden-pool area with barbecue facilities.

Seascape Resort
One Seascape Resort Dr., Rio Del Mar area, (800) 929-7727, (831) 688-6800; www.seascaperesort.com. 285 rooms; $$$-$$$$+. All kitchens & fireplaces. 3 heated pools; hot tub. Restaurant; room service. No pets.
This cliff-top resort offers spacious contemporary condominium units with expansive ocean views. Guests have access to both an adjacent 18-hole golf course and a sports club with 9 tennis courts and a fully equipped fitness center. Facilities for families include a playground and an inexpensive summer children's program for ages 5 through 13. A small shopping center and full-service day spa are just across the street.

In the mood for a marshmallow roast on the beach? A bellman is available to take guests down to the beach in a golf cart, build a fire, and leave them with the makings for s'mores. For those in search of a more refined menu, **Sanderlings** (*(831) 662-7120. B-L-D daily; $$-$$$.*) offers a creative menu in an elegant, yet relaxed, setting.

WHERE TO EAT

Bittersweet Bistro
787 Rio Del Mar Blvd., in Deer Park Shopping Center, Rio Del Mar area, (831) 662-9799; www.bittersweetbistro.com. D daily; $$-$$$. Reservations advised.
Though situated at the edge of a shopping center, this restaurant does not disappoint. Operating inside a beautifully remodeled historical building that once sat right smack in the middle of Highway 1, it has original art decorating the walls and manages to be both simple and elegant in atmosphere as well as cuisine.

The chef uses high quality local ingredients whenever possible. One dinner here started with a shared pear-and-blood orange salad accented with Roquefort cheese. Entrees were a delicious Mediterranean angel hair pasta with tomatoes, pine nuts, and Feta cheese, and a delicate grilled fresh mahi-mahi served atop garlic mashed potatoes and sautéed fresh spinach. Portions are large, but some people manage to make room for Death by Chocolate—a giant platter showcasing some of the outrageous made-from-scratch chocolate desserts the restaurant is justly famous for, including a heavenly chocolate mousse and a devilishly refined chocolate bread pudding.

Britannia Arms

8017 Soquel Dr., in Aptos Village, (831) 688-1233. L-D daily; $.

This informal spot serves up imported draft beers, authentic pub fare like bangers and mash, and American favorites like baby back ribs. It has an authentic pub atmosphere and features satellite TV, darts, and pool.

Palapas Restaurant y Cantina

21 Seascape Village, Rio Del Mar area, (831) 662-9000; www.palapasrestaurant.com. L-D daily; $$. Reservations advised.

Featuring a Mexican-style thatched roof and boasting both comfortable half-moon booths and expansive ocean views, this popular restaurant specializes in fresh seafood. Among the temptations are grilled sand dabs served with tomatillo sauce, a spicy scampi, and crabmeat enchiladas. Vegetarian selections include a delicious enchilada filled with marinated tofu and topped with guacamole. All this and fabulously crisp complimentary tortilla chips with just-right dipping salsa, too, not to overlook handmade tortillas, housemade sauces, mango margaritas made with fresh Mexican fruit, and more than 35 tequilas.

WATSONVILLE

VISITOR INFORMATION

Pajaro Valley Chamber of Commerce

449 Union St., (831) 724-3900; www.pajarovalleychamber.com.

ANNUAL EVENTS

Watsonville Fly-In & Air Show

May; Memorial Day weekend. (831) 763-5600; www.watsonvilleflyin.org. $5-$15; F-Sun parking $5. No pets.

This is one of the largest antique fly-in and air shows on the West Coast. It features an assortment of vintage and classic airplanes, a car show, and fireworks.

Roses of Yesterday and Today

May & June. 803 Brown's Valley Rd. (call for directions); (831) 728-1901; www.rosesofyesterday.com. Daily 9-4. Free; catalog $5.

Tucked into a redwood canyon, this demonstration garden for a mail-order nursery is an extraordinary sight when its approximately 450 varieties of old-fashioned roses bloom in unison. Picnic tables are available.

WHAT TO DO

Bamboo Giant Nursery

5601 Freedom Blvd., (831) 687-0100; www.bamboogiant.com. M-F 9-4, Sat-Sun 10-4; in summer to 5. Free.

Situated in an old rock quarry, this 20-acre grove is home to 60 varieties of nonnative bamboo. A map guides visitors through the winding paths that pass a koi pond and Oriental gong. Benches are provided, and picnicking is permitted.

Gizdich Ranch

55 Peckham Rd., (take Riverside Dr./Hwy. 129 exit off Hwy. 1), (831) 722-1056; www.gizdich-ranch.com. Daily 9-5, Apr-Dec; Sat-Sun, Jan-Mar.

Folks come to this small, family-owned farm to U-pick strawberries May through July, olallieberries in June, raspberries in July, and apples from September through December. Hayrides are an option in November and December. Bring containers (they can also be purchased inexpensively). A barn cafe sells housemade pies, and a barn gift shop sells freshly picked fruit and the farm's own jams, including olallieberry and strawberry. Another barn is filled with antiques for sale. A picnic area has a playground, sandbox, and climbable vintage 1937 tractor for kids.

WHERE TO STAY

KOA Kampground
1186 San Andreas Rd., in La Selva Beach,
(800) KOA-7701, (831) 722-0551; www.koa.com.

Located 1 mile from the beach, this posh campground has a heated pool, hot tub, sauna, and playground, plus mini golf (fee) and bike rentals. See also page 467.

Pajaro Dunes
2661 Beach Rd., (800) 564-1771, (831) 728-7400;
www.pajarodunes.com. 120 units; $$$+. All kitchens
& wood-burning fireplaces. 19 tennis courts. No pets.

Situated in the shoreline dunes, this secluded compound consists of condominiums, townhouses, and homes; all are privately owned. Hiking and biking trails, jogging paths, and volleyball and basketball courts round out the recreational facilities. Bike rentals are also available.

MOSS LANDING AND AREA

A LITTLE BACKGROUND

There is enough to see and do in this commercial fishing port to fill a weekend itinerary. This small town is home to more than a dozen antiques shops, most on quiet Moss Landing Road. Among the most interesting are artistically arranged **Hamlin's Antiques,** which has many big pieces, and **Camelot By the Sea,** which has an eclectic collection displayed in several cozy rooms. Another shop operates out of a recycled train caboose. Hours are casual, but most are open Wednesday through Sunday from 11 a.m. to 4 p.m. A tiny post office acts as the town's unofficial museum and is also on Moss Landing Road. It displays historical photos of Moss Landing's past as a shipping port, a whaling station and cannery, and then a fishing village.

Fishing boats often are seen unloading their catch by the docks. **Tom's Sportfishing** *((831) 633-2564; www.tomssportfishing.com. $45-$60/person. Departs daily at 6am.)* takes visitors out deep-sea fishing on the *Kahuna*.

This area also is prime for bird-watching. Pelicans, cormorants, gulls, terns, herons, and egrets are drawn here to feast on the rich marine life. Rarer birds often show up during migrations.

VISITOR INFORMATION

Moss Landing Chamber of Commerce
8071 Moss Landing Rd., (831) 633-4501;
www.mosslandingchamber.com.

Marina Chamber of Commerce
3170 Vista Del Camino #C, (831) 384-9155;
www.marinachamber.com.

GETTING THERE

Located 8 miles north of the Monterey Peninsula, and 8 miles west of Salinas. Turn off Highway 1 just before reaching the two landmark smokestacks on the east side of the highway, and before the **PotStop at Little Baja** shop and its Mexican pottery on the west side.

ANNUAL EVENTS

Castroville Artichoke Festival
May. In Castroville; (831) 633-CHOK; www.artichoke-festival.org. $8, under 13 $4.

Starlet Named Artichoke Queen

Artichokes are cooked every which way at this old-time agricultural festivals. It was at this event in 1947 that then-starlet Marilyn Monroe became the very first California Artichoke Queen.

WHAT TO DO

Elkhorn Slough Safari
(831) 633-5555; www.elkhornslough.com. Schedule varies. $26, 65+ $24, 3-14 $19; unsuitable for children under 3. Reservations required.

The best way to see great numbers of birds up close in their natural habitat is to take this tour in a stable open-air pontoon boat. Tours last 2 hours and travel through Elkhorn Slough. (Wondering what a "slough"—pronounced "slew"—is? Simply "a wet, muddy place.") One of the state's largest wetlands, it winds inland for 7 miles and provides an important feeding and resting place for a variety of wildlife. A naturalist is aboard to point out unusual specimens, and participants are encouraged to help count various kinds of birds for an on-going research project. Sea otters are also usually spotted, and sometimes a "raft" of them is seen holding onto each other while floating. Bring binoculars and a camera.

Fort Ord
In Marina.

The expansive sand dune area that was formerly the Fort Ord military base is just a few miles south of Moss Landing. Now operated by the Bureau of Land Management, the fort is slowly metamorphosing into recreational use. Hiking and mountain bike trails snake through its 8,000 acres.

A skydiving facility is based here. (Afraid of skydiving? Here's some food for thought: At **Skydive Monterey Bay** *((888) BAY-JUMP, (831) 384-3483; www.skydivemontereybay.com. $138+/person. Reservations advised.)* it is claimed that "skydivers aren't afraid of dying, they're afraid of not living.")

For those who prefer to check out the skies from the ground, the **Monterey Institute for Research in Astronomy (MIRA)** *(200 Eighth St., (831) 883-1000; www.mira.org.)* schedules Star Parties regularly at its **Weaver Student Observatory**. Participants can look through a 14-inch telescope.

The largest art foundry on the West Coast, the **Monterey Sculpture Center** *(711 Neeson Rd., (831) 384-2100. Free tour; reservations advised.)* conducts informal tours that permit seeing sculptures manufactured from beginning to end. Participants view wax being taken from molds, molten metal being poured into molds, bronze castings being welded and ground, and patina colors being applied to the finished product.

Monterey Bay Kayaks
2390 Hwy. 1, (800) 649-5357; www.montereykayaks.com.

For description, see page 114.

WHERE TO STAY

Best Western Beach Dunes Inn
3290 Dunes Dr., in Marina, (800) 780-7234, (831) 883-0300. 84 rooms; $. Hot tub. Continental breakfast. No pets.

This bargain lodging is situated amid the dunes just a short walk from **Marina State Beach**. The beach has a boardwalk trail over the sand dunes, where the endangered Smith's Blue Butterfly makes its home, and pods of dolphins are sometimes spotted looping through the surf. The beach also provides a spectacular spot to watch the sun set.

Monterey Dunes Co.
(800) 55-DUNES, (831) 633-4883; www.montereydunes.com. 120 units; $$-$$$+. All kitchens & wood-burning fireplaces. Pool; hot tub; saunas; 6 tennis courts.

These beachfront vacation homes are nestled on 125 acres of sand dunes. All have a spectacular view, some have private hot tubs, and shared facilities include a sand volleyball court and a basketball court.

WHERE TO EAT

Giant Artichoke
11261 Merritt St., off Hwy. 1, in Castroville, (831) 633-3501. B-L-D daily; $. No reservations.

Located in "the artichoke capital of the world," where three-quarters of the nation's artichokes are grown, this novelty restaurant makes a good rest stop. To find it, just look for a giant artichoke. Artichoke specialties include

French-fried artichokes with mayonnaise dip, artichoke soup, artichoke salad, artichoke quiche, artichoke cake, and even an artichoke milkshake. Other more standard short-order items are also on the menu.

Phil's Fish Market & Eatery

7600 Sandholdt Rd., (831) 633-2152; www.phils fishmarket.com. L-D daily; $. No reservations.

Begun as a fish market in 1982, when owner Phil was a commercial fisherman, this humble spot has evolved into a wildly popular restaurant. That's because Phil, a warm and kind man, takes his Italian grandmother's peasant recipes and marries them to great effect with the freshest seafood and rock-bottom prices. Diners eat heartily on steamed Sicilian stuffed artichokes (with a bread crumb-garlic-mozzarella filling), fresh Manhattan chowder, and blackened salmon with sun-dried tomato sauce. Monterey Bay spot prawns (sautéed in white wine, capers, and roma tomatoes with a lemon-caper butter sauce), a seafood quesadilla, seafood salad, fish & chips, and even a burger are also on the extensive menu. California's First Family, the Schwarzeneggers—Arnold, Maria, and the kids—has eaten here.

The Whole Enchilada

Hwy. 1/Moss Landing Rd., (831) 633-3038; www.wenchilada.com. L-D daily; $-$$. Reservations advised.

This roadside cantina serves a slew of margaritas, including cucumber and prickly pear flavors, and also lines up some unusual suspects on its menu: seafood flautas, oyster shooters, an Oaxacan tamale wrapped in banana leaves. And because Castroville—the "artichoke capital of the world"—is just a few miles east of town, it also offers a humungous steamed artichoke appetizer.

MONTEREY PENINSULA

A LITTLE BACKGROUND

Popular for years because of its proximity to San Francisco, this area (Monterey, Pacific Grove, Pebble Beach, Carmel, and Carmel Valley) features a vast variety of overnight accommodations and restaurants. Due to the

area's immense popularity, there is no off-season and reservations are essential for both lodging and the more popular restaurants. Look on menus for fresh local delicacies such as sand dabs, Monterey Bay shrimp, and calamari.

The **Monterey Bay National Marine Sanctuary** *((831) 647-4201; www.mbnms. nos.noaa.gov.)* is the nation's largest protected marine area. It covers more than 300 miles—from the Farallon Islands near San Francisco in the north to Cambria in the south. Protected resources include the nation's most expansive kelp forests, one of North America's largest underwater canyons, and a deep ocean environment that is the closest to shore in the continental U.S. The Monterey Bay Aquarium acts as the sanctuary's interpretive center.

GETTING THERE

Located approximately 115 miles south of San Francisco, and 40 miles south of Santa Cruz.

MONTEREY

A LITTLE BACKGROUND

Settled before the Declaration of Independence was signed, Monterey was Spain's first headquarters in Alta California. A variety of historical museums bring the past to life, and the town currently has 32 noteworthy wood-frame buildings and adobes.

VISITOR INFORMATION

Monterey County Convention & Visitors Bureau

765 Wave St., (800) 555-6290, (831) 657-6400; www.montereyinfo.org. M-F 8:30-5.

Monterey Visitors Center

Franklin St./Camino El Estero, by Lake El Estero. No phone. Schedule varies.

ANNUAL EVENTS

Monterey Scottish Games & Celtic Festival

July. In Toro County Park; (831) 633-4444; www.montereyscotgames.com. $12-$15, 65+ & 13-18 $10-$12, 5-12 $5-$6.

Celebrating everything Scottish, this event is described as being like a Celtic three-ring circus. One ring features piping (as in bagpipes) and drumming contests, with massive pipe bands competing against each other. Another ring features unusual athletic events such as the Caber Toss (in which a huge pole is tossed end-over-end for accuracy) and Putting the Stone (in which a heavy stone is tossed). And another presents the Highland Dancing Championships, which in current times is participated in predominantly by females. Events, including several sheepdog demonstrations, run continuously.

Monterey Jazz Festival

September. At Monterey Fairgrounds; (831) 373-3366, tickets (925) 275-9255; www.montereyjazzfestival.org. $35+.

The oldest continuously presented jazz festival in the country, this well-known event offers three days of nonstop entertainment.

Christmas in the Adobes

December. (831) 649-7118; www.parks.ca.gov. $17-$20, 6-17 $2.

Each year a group of historic adobes are festively decked with period decorations and illuminated by candlelight. Docents and staff dress in era costumes, and luminarias guide visitors along walkways into the cozy, warm interiors, where they can shed the chill of the night with musical entertainment and fragrant refreshments such as Mexican hot chocolate and wassail. At the Stevenson House, former resident Robert Louis Stevenson is portrayed by an actor, and Scottish music and bagpipes provide enchanting entertainment. Entry is available to a few adobes that are usually closed to the public, including the Casa Amesti, which is now a private men's club. Purchase tickets early, as this event often sells out.

WHAT TO DO

Cannery Row

(831) 649-6690; www.canneryrow.org.

Once booming with sardine canneries, Cannery Row became a ghost town in 1945 when the sardines mysteriously disappeared from the area's ocean. In *Cannery Row*, John Steinbeck described it as "a poem, a stink, a grating noise, a quality of light, a tone, a habit, a nostalgia, a dream." Now this mile-long road houses restaurants, art galleries, shops, a **Bargetto Winery Tasting Room** *(#700, (831) 373-4053; www.bargetto.com. Tasting daily 10:30-6.),* **Steinbeck's Spirit of Monterey Wax Museum** *(#700, (831) 375-3770; www.wax-museum.com. Open daily, schedule varies. $8.95, 60+ $6.95, 13-17 $5.95, 6-12 $4.95.),* and the **Monterey Bay Aquarium** *(see page 114).*

A Taste of Monterey *(#700, (888) 646-5446, (831) 646-5446; www.tastemonterey.com. Tasting daily 11-6.)* provides samplings from a room with a spectacular 180-degree view of the bay, and a theater presents wine-related videos.

Reading John Steinbeck's *Cannery Row* provides background for visiting this historic street. Lee Chong's Heavenly Flower Grocery, mentioned in Steinbeck's novel, is now **Wing Chong Market**—a souvenir shop *(#835),* and La Ida's Cafe is now **Kalisa's** sandwich shop *(#851).* Doc's lab *(#800)* is currently owned by the city.

Just a block north of the aquarium, the **American Tin Cannery Premium Outlet** *(125 Ocean View Blvd., in Pacific Grove, (831) 372-1442; www.americantincannery.com. Daily 10-6.)* and its attractive industrial interior is worth a detour. **First Awakenings** *((831) 372-1125; www.firstawakenings.net. B-L daily; $. No reservations.)* has a pleasant outdoor patio here and sometimes provides soothing live guitar music. At breakfast it's fresh fruit crêpes and a variety of omelettes; at lunch look for salads and sandwiches.

Bay Bikes *(585 Cannery Row, (831) 646-9090; www.baybikes.com. Daily 9-6. $6+/hr., $20+/day.)* rents both 21-speed mountain bikes and multi-passenger Italian surrey bikes that are fun to ride on the spectacular waterfront bike trail—part of the **Monterey Bay Coastal Trail** *(www.monterey.org/rec/coastaltrail.html)*—hugging the bay from Fisherman's Wharf to Lover's Point. Children's bikes and jogging strollers are also available. Safety equipment is included with rentals.

El Estero Park

Del Monte Ave./Camino El Estero/Fremont Blvd., (831) 646-3866; www.monterey.org/rec/locations. html. Daily 10-dusk, Sept-May closed Tu. Free.

Hiking and bike trails and a lake filled with hungry ducks await here. Paddleboats and canoes can be rented, and children may fish from boats. Located by the lake on Pearl Street, **Dennis the Menace Playground** features colorful play equipment designed by former area resident and creator of the *Dennis the Menace* comic strip, Hank Ketchum. Notable are a hedge maze with a corkscrew slide in its center, a long suspension bridge, and an authentic Southern Pacific steam train engine to climb on. Picnic tables and a snack concession are available.

Jacks Peak County Park

25020 Jacks Peak Park Rd., off Hwy. 68 to Salinas, (888) 588-2267, (831) 755-4895; www.co.monterey.ca.us/parks. Schedule varies. $3-$4/vehicle.

This 525-acre park is in a Monterey pine forest with 8 miles of trails and a variety of picnic areas. Follow the .3-mile Jacks Peak Trail to the summit for a great view of Monterey Bay, Carmel Bay, and the valley.

Monterey Bay Aquarium

886 Cannery Row, (831) 648-4800; www.monterey bayaquarium.org. Daily 10-6, in summer 9:30-6. $24.95, 65+ & 13-17 $22.95, 3-12 $15.95. Tickets: At website, no fee; (800) 756-3737, $3/order.

Built on the site of what was once the row's largest sardine cannery, this spectacular facility is one of the nation's largest seawater aquariums. It is operated by a non-profit organization whose mission is to inspire conservation of the oceans. Well-arranged and architecturally interesting, the aquarium provides a close-up

view of the underwater habitats and creatures of Monterey Bay—an area known for its spectacular and varied marine life. Among the more than 200 galleries and exhibits is a tank that displays a 3-story-high kelp forest and another that is home to some of the area's playful sea otters. More than 30,000 fish, mammal, bird, invertebrate, and plant specimens are on display, and almost all are native to Monterey Bay. Don't miss the walk-through aviary of shorebirds or the bat ray petting pool. Children especially enjoy the Touch Pool, where they can handle a variety of sea stars and other tide pool life, and the fabulous Splash Zone, where kids under 12 can view a wall of comical moray eels and see magnificent weedy and leafy sea dragons. The 1-million-gallon Outer Bay exhibit features one of the world's largest acrylic windows and permits peeking into a simulated ocean where sharks, ocean sunfish, green sea turtles, and schools of yellowfin and giant bluefin tuna (the Maseratis of the ocean) swim in more than a million gallons of water. This area also has a fascinating display of sea jellies, including the largest jelly tank anywhere—a don't-miss psychedelic tank filled with orange sea nettles shown against a vibrant blue background.

Both a fast-food cafeteria and a pricier restaurant are available inside; picnic tables are available outside. Or get a hand-stamp for re-entry, and dine somewhere nearby.

Monterey Bay Kayaks

693 Del Monte Ave., (800) 649-5357, (831) 373-KELP; www.montereykayaks.com. Daily 9-6, in summer 9-8. $60/3-hr. tour.

Observe sea lions, harbor seals, and otters up close near Fisherman's Wharf and along Cannery Row. Tours are led by marine biologists and include a half-hour of safety instruction; no experience is necessary. Tour kayaks hold two people. Children must be at least 4½ feet tall; smaller children can be accommodated in a triple kayak with two adults.

Monterey Maritime & History Museum

5 Custom House Plaza, (831) 372-2608; www.montereyhistory.org. Tu-Sun 10-5. By donation.

Beginning with the history of Spanish ships that anchored in the area 4 centuries ago, this museum celebrates California's seafaring and fishing heritage. Learn about the area's naval history, and see ship models, bells, compasses, and the impressive 2-story-tall, 10,000-pound 1889 Fresnel lens once used at the Point Sur Lighthouse.

Monterey Movie Tours
Departs from downtown, (800) 343-6437, (831) 372-6278; www.montereymovietours.com. Daily; reservations required. $49, 65+ $45, under 15 $35.

This 3-hour bus tour visits movie sites in Monterey, Pacific Grove, Pebble Beach, and Carmel and includes the 17-Mile Drive. Narration is live, and appropriate movie clips are projected on overhead monitors.

Monterey Museum of Art
559 Pacific St., (831) 372-5477; www.montereyart.org. W-Sat 11-5, Sun 1-4. $5, under 13 free.

Located downtown, this museum is dubbed "the best small town museum in the United States." Indeed, it provides the delight of a well-displayed small collection of regional art and photography. Important artists of the Monterey Peninsula, including Ansel Adams and Edward Weston, are represented. A strong graphics collection includes works by Rembrandt, Manet, and Picasso.

An extension of the museum, the historic **La Mirada adobe** *(720 Via Mirada, (831) 372-3689.)* is located several miles away. (It is open the same hours, and a ticket bought in either location permits admission to the other on that day or a different day.) The adobe is one of the first built during the Mexican occupation of Monterey, and antique furnishings and early California art are displayed beautifully within it. (It is interesting to know that this was once a California governor's mansion and that for a while Liz and Dick called it home.) Works by contemporary regional artists are shown in a dramatic modern addition. Tours that include the galleries and also the house are sometimes scheduled. Additionally, spectacular gardens are planted with more than 100 varieties of rose and 300 varieties of rhododendron.

Monterey State Historic Park
office: 20 Custom Plaza, (831) 649-7118; www.parks.ca.gov/mshp. Daily 10-4, in summer 10-5; tours daily, schedule varies. Free.

Downtown Monterey holds one of the largest collections of historic buildings west of

Williamsburg. Historic sites include the **Stevenson House** *(530 Houston St.)*, once the boarding house of author Robert Louis Stevenson and now a museum of his personal belongings; the **Cooper-Molera Adobe** *(525 Polk St./Alvarado St./Munras St.)*, a 2.4-acre complex with chickens, sheep, and a visitor center; the **Larkin House** *(510 Calle Principal/ Jefferson St.)*; and the **Casa Soberanes** *(336 Pacific St./Del Monte Ave.)*. More buildings include: the **Old Whaling Station**, with one of the nation's last remaining whalebone sidewalks; the **Pacific House Museum**, home of the **Monterey Museum of the American Indian**; and the **Custom House**, California Historic Landmark #1 and the oldest government building in the state. **Historic Garden Tours** are given May through September *((831) 649-3364; www.historicgardenleague.org. Tu & Sat at 12. $5 donation.)*.

The Path of History, a self-guided walking tour following gold-colored tiles embedded in the sidewalk, leads past 55 historic buildings, sites, and gardens.

Old Fisherman's Wharf
(831) 649-6544; www.montereywharf.com.

Lined with restaurants and shops, the wharf also offers entertainment from sea lions that hang out around the pilings and often put on a free show. Whale-watching, sailing, and deep-sea fishing excursions leave from here.

Ventana Vineyards Tasting Room
2999 Monterey-Salinas Hwy. (Hwy. 68), 3 mi. from downtown, (800) BEST-VIN, (831) 372-7415; www.ventanawines.com. Tasting daily 11-5; no tours.

Said to have the most award winning single vineyard in the U.S., this winery's tasting room is in the historic, atmospheric Old Stone House. A flower-laden deck surrounded by tall pines is available for picnicking. It is interesting to note that the only existing French oak trees in the U.S. grow on a nearby bluff. Planted in 1978, they will be harvested eventually and turned into wine barrels. This winery is known for its white wines, particularly Chardonnays and Rieslings.

WHERE TO STAY

Casa Munras Garden Hotel

700 Munras Ave, (800) 222-2446, (831) 375-2411; www.hotelcasamunras.com. 166 rooms; $$-$$$. Some gas fireplaces. Heated pool; fitness room; full-service spa. Restaurant.

One of the first residences built outside the walls of the old Presidio in 1824, the original Casa is built of individual adobe bricks made by hand from native materials. Parts of the original dining room and porch remain. Converted into a hotel in 1941, its grounds are spacious, attractive, and peaceful. Rooms are spread among 11 buildings.

Clarion Hotel

1046 Munras Ave., (800) 821-0805, (831) 373-1337; www.clarionhotelmonterey.com. 52 rooms; $-$$$. Some kitchens & gas fireplaces. Indoor heated pool & hot tub; sauna. Continental breakfast. No pets.

Though the architecture of this motel is simple, its facilities are noteworthy.

Hotel Pacific

300 Pacific St., (800) 554-5542, (831) 373-5700; www.hotelpacific.com. 105 rooms; $$$-$$$+. All gas fireplaces. 2 hot tubs. Afternoon snack; continental breakfast. No pets.

Situated near the Wharf, this lodging melds the amenities of a B&B with the convenience of a hotel. It features adobe-style architecture and attractive gardens with fountains. All rooms are spacious suites equipped with down comforters and featherbeds, and nightly turn-down service is included.

Hyatt Regency Monterey

1 Old Golf Course Rd., (800) 228-9000, (831) 372-1234; www.monterey.hyatt.com. 4 stories; 550 rooms; $$-$$$. 2 heated pools; 2 hot tubs; fitness room; 6 tennis courts (some night lights). 3 restaurants; room service.

Located away from town, adjacent to the scenic **Del Monte Golf Course** *(1300 Sylvan Rd., (831) 373-2700; www.delmontegolf.com.)*— the oldest golf course west of the Mississippi.

Knuckles Historical Sports Bar has a casual, peanut shells-on-the-floor atmosphere with 18 flat-screen TVs tuned to the action.

InterContinental The Clement Monterey

750 Cannery Row, (831) 375-4500; www.intercontinental.com/montereyic. 4 stories; 208 rooms; $$$-$$$+. Some gas fireplaces. Heated lap pool; hot tub; full-service spa. Restaurant; room service. Self-parking $17, valet $20.

This brand new, sleek, luxurious hotel is now the closest lodging to the aquarium. Indeed, it is an easy walk to all the row's sights and restaurants of interest, and it is adjacent to Doc's weather-beaten lab made famous in Steinbeck's novel. The hotel consists of two buildings attached by an enclosed overpass over Cannery Row. Rooms are spacious, with a spare, clean design and basically grey decor— sort of mimicking the foggy mornings this area often sees—and 110 have an ocean view. A children's center operates for ages 4 through 13.

Monterey Bay Inn

242 Cannery Row, (800) 424-6242, (831) 373-6242; www.montereybayinn.com. 4 stories; 49 rooms; $$-$$$+. 2 hot tubs; sauna. Afternoon snack; continental breakfast; room service.

Located a short walk from the aquarium, all rooms in this waterfront lodging have private balconies and sleeper sofas. Most rooms also have spectacular bay views, and all guests have access to a rooftop hot tub with a breath-taking view of the bay. Breakfast is brought to the room.

Monterey Hostel

778 Hawthorne St./Irving Ave., (831) 649-0375; www.montereyhostel.org. 45 beds; 3 private rooms; $. No pets.

Located 4 blocks from Cannery Row, this comfortable hostel is in the renovated historic Carpenters Union Hall. Water-saving appliances are used throughout.

Monterey Marriott

350 Calle Principal, (800) 228-9290, (831) 649-4234; www.marriott.com. 10 stories; 341 rooms; $$-$$$+. Heated pool; hot tub; full-service spa. 2 restaurants; room service. No pets. Valet parking $19.

Located downtown near the Wharf, this attractive hotel is built on the former site of the grand old Hotel San Carlos. It is the tallest building in town and offers spectacular views and quiet, tastefully appointed rooms.

Monterey Plaza Hotel & Spa

400 Cannery Row, (800) 334-3999, (800) 368-2468, (831) 646-1700; www.montereyplazahotel.com. 290 rooms; $$-$$$+. 2 hot tubs; 2 saunas; fitness center; full-service spa. Restaurant; room service. Resort fee $25, includes valet parking.

Built partially over the bay, with rooms on both sides of the street, this well-situated luxury hotel features comfortably appointed, attractively decorated rooms with marble bathrooms. Some have private balconies and expansive bay views.

Dinner at a bayside window table in the **Duck Club** *(B-L-D daily; $$-$$$. Valet parking.)* is a delight, and, of course, duck is on the menu: crisp-roasted with Valencia orange sauce or wood-roasted with green peppercorn mustard sauce.

Old Monterey Inn

500 Martin St., (800) 350-2344, (831) 375-8284; www.oldmontereyinn.com. 10 rooms; $$$-$$$+. Unsuitable for children. All fireplaces. Evening snack; full breakfast. No pets.

Built in 1929, this magnificent half-timbered, Tudor-style inn resembles an elegant English country house. It is on an acre of tended flower gardens surrounded by massive Monterey pines, in a quiet residential neighborhood near enough to downtown to permit walking. Though any of the unique and tastefully decorated rooms should please, a few are quite special. The private Garden Cottage has a cozy fireplace and two-person whirlpool tub, while the Library has book-lined walls and a large stone fireplace. All have a fluffy bed made with a soft featherbed over the mattress and topped with a down comforter. Thoughtful touches make guests feel well cared for—small chocolates in an antique silver dish, candles by the bathtub, terry-lined silk robes, a CD player equipped with a soothing classical disc, and an enjoyable collection of books. Some sort of snack is always available in the communal area. In the morning, coffee is delivered to the room. Breakfast is served later at an enormous, beautifully set table in a dining room graced by plank floors, a huge copper fireplace, and a hand-plastered ceiling. Alternatively, breakfast can be served in bed.

Spindrift Inn

652 Cannery Row, (800) 841-1879, (831) 646-8900; www.spindriftinn.com. 4 stories; 42 rooms; $$$-$$$+. All wood-burning fireplaces. Afternoon snack; continental breakfast; room service. Valet parking $16. No pets.

Located in the heart of Cannery Row, just 2 blocks from the aquarium, this tasteful lodging has a 4-story atrium lobby. Some rooms have faux canopy beds and many have bay views that permit occupants to greet a foggy morning as Steinbeck described in *The Grapes of Wrath* journal, "I remember how grey and doleful Monday morning was. I could lie and look at it from my bed . . ." Breakfast is brought to the room on a silver tray, along with a newspaper. A good view is available from a rooftop garden, and the inn's backyard is tiny McAbee Beach, where ruins of concrete sardine holding tanks await exploration.

Motel Row

Modern motels abound along Munras Avenue. North Fremont Street and Del Monte Avenue in Seaside are also good places to look.

WHERE TO EAT

Abalonetti Seafood Trattoria

57 Fisherman's Wharf, (831) 373-1851; www.abalonettimonterey.com. L-D daily; $-$$. Reservations advised.

This small, unpretentious restaurant is named for a famous dish in which calamari (squid) is pounded until tender, then breaded and sautéed in butter. Over half the menu is devoted to squid dishes—the house specialty. Other seafood and Italian items, including pizza, are also available, and the dining room provides a good view of Monterey Bay.

Britannia Arms

444 Alvarado St./Bonafacio Plaza, (831) 656-9543. L-D daily; $.

For description, see page 109.

Bubba Gump Shrimp Co.

720 Cannery Row, (831) 373-1884; www.bubbagump.com. L-D daily; $. No reservations.

Based on the movie *Forrest Gump*, which won six Oscars, this is the first in a chain of seafood restaurants revolving around memorabilia from the movie—script pages, storyboards, costumes, photos, scrawled Gumpisms on tabletops. The movie plays continuously on video monitors. By the way, the men's room is Bubba's, the women's room Jenny's. For more description, see page 63.

Cafe Fina
47 Fisherman's Wharf, (800) THE-FINA, (831) 372-5200; www.cafefina.com. L-D daily; $$. Reservations advised.

Most tables in this narrow, deep, 2-story venue have excellent bay views. Any wait is pleasantly passed watching seabirds and seals. The menu offers roasted garlic, a cold steamed artichoke, pizza made in a wood-burning brick oven from Milan, fresh seafood (including spectacular sautéed local sand dabs), and pastas (the fettuccine, linguine, and ravioli are all housemade and topped with fresh herb sauces).

Fresh Cream
99 Pacific St., 100-C Heritage Harbor, (831) 375-9798; www.freshcream.com. D daily; $$$. Reservations advised.

Situated on the second story of a building across from the Wharf, this serene restaurant offers a great harbor view along with excellent classical French cuisine. Appetizers include housemade lobster raviolis with a rich lobster butter sauce and a sprinkling of both black and gold caviars. Entrees include fresh local fish and veal, a flawless rack of lamb Dijonnaise, and a filet mignon with truffle Madeira and Bearnaise sauces. Desserts are spectacular: a Grand Marnier soufflé and an incredible edible chocolate box containing a mocha milkshake.

Ghirardelli Soda Fountain & Chocolate Shop
660 Cannery Row, (831) 373-0997; www.ghirardelli.com. Sun-Thur 10-8, F 10-9, Sat 10-10.

This is a much smaller version of the flagship fountain in San Francisco. For more description, see page 71.

Hula's Island Grill and Tiki Room
622 Lighthouse Ave., (831) 655-HULA; www.hulastiki.com. L Tu-Sat, D daily; $-$$. Reservations advised.

Atmospheric, with a kitschy island decor and surf videos playing continuously, this casual restaurant serves a menu of island favorites.

Fresh fish is prepared in a variety of ways—pan-fried or encrusted with coconut, lemongrass, or macadamia nuts—and plate items include slow-roasted pulled pork in a super-tasty sauce. Ribs, fish tacos, and several burgers are also options. Sweet potato fries and tangy island slaw are popular sides. Better than dessert is an island drink to mellow things out.

Montrio Bistro
414 Calle Principal/Franklin St., (831) 648-8880; www.montrio.com. D daily; $$-$$$. Reservations advised.

Operating within a dramatically remodeled 1910 firehouse, with tall ceilings and contemporary lighting, this popular spot is always buzzing. If full, opt for a seat in the bar and order there. Small plates and salads are on the innovative menu. Favorites include crispy crab cakes, artichoke risotto, and juicy rotisserie chicken with mashed potatoes.

The Sardine Factory
701 Wave St., (831) 373-3775; www.sardinefactory.com. D daily; $$$-$$$+. Reservations advised. Valet parking.

This building, which once housed a canteen patronized by cannery workers, is home now to an elegant, award-winning restaurant with five very different dining rooms and a cellar with more than 30,000 bottles of wine. The kitchen is known for its fresh seafood—including abalone and Australian lobster tail—and aged beef. Appetizers include an acclaimed abalone cream bisque created for President Reagan's inaugural, as well as fresh clams, mussels, oysters, and Dungeness crab in season. But no sardines. A knock-out dessert features a spectacular foot-high lighted ice swan bearing a scoop of sorbet.

Stokes Restaurant & Bar
500 Hartnell St., (831) 373-1110; www.stokesrestaurant.com. D daily; $$-$$$. Reservations advised.

One of the oldest buildings in Monterey, the historic 1833 Stokes Adobe has been updated with a comfortable, airy, rustic-modern interior. The focus is on local ingredients, and the refined soups are particularly delicious.

Whaling Station

763 Wave St., (831) 373-3778;
www.whalingstationmonterey.com. D daily; $$$-$$$+.
Reservations advised. Valet parking.

Situated inside a building that dates from 1929 and once housed a Chinese grocery store, this restaurant produces creative and delicious dishes. Seafood selections have included barbecued Monterey Bay prawns—the fresh, sweet, firm-fleshed kind that are so hard to find—and blackened fresh salmon, and entrees come with a house salad consisting of Cajun-spiced walnuts on a bed of Belgian endive, spinach, and baby lettuce dressed in a sweet dressing fragrant with sesame oil. Grilled quail, rack of lamb, and prime steaks are among the non-seafood options. Be forewarned, the housemade desserts are irresistible.

PACIFIC GROVE

A LITTLE BACKGROUND

Originally settled as a Chinese fishing village, Pacific Grove was established in 1875 as a Methodist Episcopal Church summer camp. Some modest summer cottages and distinctive Victorian-style homes remain today. Due to ordinances in those early days, Pacific Grove was the last dry city in California and it wasn't until 1969 that a liquor store opened within the town limits. Still old-fashioned, the low-key main shopping street has free diagonal parking plus an additional row of parking in the street's center.

VISITOR INFORMATION

Pacific Grove Chamber of Commerce

584 Central Ave., (800) 656-6650, (831) 373-3304;
www.pacificgrove.org.

ANNUAL EVENTS

Historic Home Tour

October; (800) 656-6650, (831) 373-3304;
www.pacificgrove.org. $20.

This tour includes Victorian and historic homes, B&Bs, and churches.

Monarch Butterflies

October. Free.

Each year hundreds of thousands of stunning orange-and-black monarch butterflies return to Pacific Grove to winter on the needles of favored local pine trees. They migrate all the way from western Canada and Alaska and stay until March, when they again fly north.

Somewhat of a mystery is how they find their way here each year since, with a lifespan of less than a year, no butterfly makes the trip twice. It is, in fact, the great-grandchildren of the prior year's butterfly visitors that return. Somehow the monarchs program a genetic message into their progeny, which then return to these same trees the following fall and repeat the cycle.

Reacting to the weather somewhat as does a golden poppy, monarchs prefer to flutter about on sunny days between the hours of 10 a.m. and 4 p.m. In fact, they can't fly when temperatures drop below 55 degrees. So on cold and foggy days, which are quite common in this area, they huddle together with closed wings and are often overlooked as dull pieces of bark or dead leaves. On cold days observers must be careful where they step: Monarchs that have dropped to the ground to sip dew off the grass might be resting there, having found it too cold to fly back to their perch.

During early March the butterflies can be observed mating. Watch for females chasing males in a spiral flight. (Males are recognized by a characteristic black dot on their wings.) When a female finds a male she likes, they drop to the ground to mate. Literally standing on his head at one point, the male, while still mating, then lifts the female back to a perch in a tree, where they continue mating for almost an entire day!

Butterfly nets should be left at home. To discourage visitors from bothering these fragile creatures, Pacific Grove has made molesting a butterfly a misdemeanor crime carrying a $1,000 fine.

To celebrate the annual return of the butterflies, the town of Pacific Grove, also known as Butterfly Town U.S.A., has hosted a **Butterfly Parade** every October since 1938. Completely non-commercial, this delightful parade provides the low-key pleasure of viewing local grade school children marching down the street dressed as butterflies. Traditional bands and majorette corps from local schools also participate. Weather always cooperates: This parade has *never* been rained on.

WHAT TO DO

Lover's Point
626 Ocean View Blvd.
Located at the southern tip of Monterey Bay, this park holds a chunky granite statue honoring the monarch butterfly. It offers a pleasant beach for sunbathing and wading, and a grassy picnic area with barbecue pits.

Monarch Grove Sanctuary
1073 Lighthouse Ave./Ridge Rd., (831) 648-5716; www.ci.pg.ca.us/monarchs/default.htm. Daily dawn-dusk, Oct-Mar. Free.
The densest clusters of monarchs congregate in this pine and eucalyptus grove located behind the Butterfly Grove Inn. Guided tours are available from mid-October through mid-February; reservations advised.

Pacific Grove Museum of Natural History
165 Forest Ave./Central Ave., (831) 648-5716; www.pgmuseum.org. Tu-Sat 10-5. Free.
Opened in 1882, this museum is dedicated to telling the natural history of Monterey County through exhibits of marine and bird life, native plants, shells, and Native American artifacts. Notable exhibits include a large jade-stone that visitors rub upon entering, mollusks, stuffed seabirds, and fluorescent minerals. An informative 10-minute video tells about the monarch butterfly, and the butterfly's life history is portrayed in drawings. In summer

larvae are often on view, and milkweed—the only plant on which the female monarch will lay her eggs—attracts butterflies to a native plant garden outside the museum. Also outside, a full-size Sandy the Gray Whale invites kids to climb aboard.

Each year during the third weekend in April, a **Wildflower Show** displays as many as 600 central coast varieties.

Point Pinos Lighthouse
On Asilomar Blvd., about 2 blks. N of end of Lighthouse Ave., (831) 648-5716 x13; www.pg museum.org. Thur-M 1-4. By donation: $2, youths $1.
Docents dressed in period costume give informal tours of this oldest continuously operating Pacific Coast lighthouse, built in 1855 out of granite quarried nearby. The area surrounding the lighthouse is a good spot to walk, picnic, and observe sea otters; note that this is the site of Doc's Great Tide Pool in Steinbeck's *Cannery Row*.

Poor man's 17-Mile Drive
It costs nothing to take this scenic 4.2-mile drive past rugged seascapes and impressive homes. Begin at Ocean View Boulevard and 3rd Street. At Point Piños, turn left on Sunset Drive. Tide pooling is good in several spots, and from April to August beautiful lavender ice plant cascades in full bloom over the rocky beach front.

Special Shops
• **Antique Clock Shop**
489 Lighthouse Ave., (831) 372-6435. M-Sat 10-5.
Operating within a charming converted Victorian house, this unsual shop holds a constantly changing inventory of clocks. Be there on the hour for a chiming treat.

• **The Works**
667 Lighthouse Ave., (831) 372-2242; www.theworkspg.com. Daily 10-6.
This coffeehouse/bookstore offers free wireless internet and schedules free live entertainment.

WHERE TO STAY

Andril Cottages
569 Asilomar Blvd., (831) 375-0994; www.andril cottages.com. 21 units; $$-$$$+; 5-night min. in summer. All kitchens & wood-burning fireplaces. Hot tub.

These woodsy, pine-paneled cottages are especially comfortable for families and for longer stays. Situated around a tree-shaded courtyard furnished with picnic tables, they are just a block from the ocean.

Asilomar Conference Grounds

800 Asilomar Blvd., (888) 733-9005, (831) 372-8016; www.visitasilomar.com. 313 units; $$. No TVs; some kitchens, & wood-burning fireplaces. Heated pool. Full breakfast; dining room. No pets.

Founded as a YWCA camp in 1913 and boasting eight buildings designed by architect Julia Morgan, this 107-acre facility is used now mainly as a conference grounds. It is part of the California State Parks system. Rooms have neither phones nor TVs and are divided among 28 lodge buildings, including four historic ones. Leisure reservations (for those who are not part of a group or conference) can be made up to 180 days in advance, and last-minute accommodations are often available. It is the perfect place to try during holidays, when other lodgings in the area are full and conferences generally are not in session, and it is ideal for a family reunion. In Spanish the word "asilomar" means "refuge by the sea," and, indeed, the grounds are located among forest and sand dunes just a short walk from the ocean. Black-tailed deer and raccoon, and sometimes red foxes, are spotted on the grounds.

Both guests and non-guests are welcome to dine on set-menu meals that are served family-style in the **Crocker Dining Complex** *(B 7:30-9, L 12-1, D 6-7; $. Reservations not necessary; purchase dining tickets at registration desk.).* A sample breakfast consists of cream of wheat, orange juice, coffeecake, scrambled eggs, potato fries, sausage, and dry cereal; a sample lunch includes a mango lassi, barley soup, chicken curry salad, cabbage slaw, and fresh papaya. Each menu offers a vegetarian option.

Beachcomber Inn

1996 Sunset Dr., (800) 634-4769, (831) 373-4769; www.montereypeninsulainns.com. 26 rooms; $-$$. Heated pool; sauna. Continental breakfast; restaurant. No pets.

Factors rendering this typical motel special include its ocean-side location, a 90-degree pool, and free bikes and safety helmets for the use of guests.

The Fishwife *(1996½ Sunset Dr., (831) 375-7107; www.fishwife.com. L-D daily; $-$$.)* is located adjacent and justly popular with locals. A large variety of fresh seafood and pastas is featured, not to mention soups and flautas.

Butterfly Grove Inn

1073 Lighthouse Ave., (800) 337-9244, (831) 373-4921; www.butterflygroveinn.com. 29 rooms; $-$$$. Some kitchens & fireplaces. Heated pool; hot tub.

This attractive complex offers a choice of either two-bedroom family suites in a Victorian house or spacious rooms in a newly built motel. Located on a quiet side street, it is adjacent to the Monarch Grove Sanctuary.

Centrella Bed & Breakfast Inn

612 Central Ave., (800) 233-3372, (831) 372-3372; www.centrellainn.com. 26 rooms; $$-$$$. Some TVs & wood-burning & gas fireplaces. Afternoon snack; full breakfast. No pets.

This restored turn-of-the-century Victorian has won awards for its interior decor. Rooms are furnished with antiques and feature floral wallpapers and fabrics, and some bathrooms have clawfoot tubs. Suites on the third floor are particularly nice. Families with children under 12 are accommodated only in the cottage suites, each of which has a fireplace and private garden.

Gosby House Inn

643 Lighthouse Ave., (800) 527-8828, (831) 375-1287; www.gosbyhouseinn.com. 22 rooms; $$-$$$. Some TVs & gas fireplaces. Afternoon snack; full breakfast. No pets.

Located in the heart of the town's shopping area, this Queen Anne Victorian features a charming rounded corner tower and many bay windows. It was built in 1887 by a cobbler from Nova Scotia and is now an historic landmark. Noteworthy features include attractive wallpapers, a well-tended garden, and an assortment of stuffed bears that welcome guests throughout the inn (all are available for purchase).

The Martine Inn

255 Oceanview Blvd., (800) 852-5588, (831) 373-3388; www.martineinn.com. 19 rooms; $$-$$$+. Unsuitable for children under 16. No TVs; some wood-burning fireplaces. Indoor hot tub. Afternoon & evening snack; full breakfast. No pets.

Perched across the street from Monterey Bay, this 1899 Victorian inn is filled with American Victorian antiques put to good use. A game room holds an 1890s billiard table, and an intriguing 1870s steam box sits in the conservatory with the hot tub. The Edith Head room is furnished with a bedroom set the movie stylist once owned; another room holds an Eastlake suite from the estate of newspaper mogul C. K. McClatchy; and other rooms feature more lovely bedroom suites—all enhanced with white bedding. The evening hors d'oeuvres and sit-down three-course breakfast are served in the ocean-view dining room and feature antique silver, crystal and lace (being offered a *heated* coffee spoon from a unusual silver piece that holds them in hot water is a highlight), and complimentary fresh fruit always is available in a silver wedding basket. Oil paintings of early California landscapes and gorgeous wallpapers are part of the decor, and a large library in the parlor awaits browsing. Additionally, the owner displays his vintage MG car collection out back along with gas pumps and auto posters.

Seven Gables Inn

555 Ocean View Blvd., (831) 372-4341; www.pginns.com. 14 rooms; $$-$$$+. Unsuitable for children under 12. No TVs. Afternoon snack; full breakfast. No pets.

Located across the street from the ocean, this elegant yellow Victorian mansion was built in 1886. Rooms and cottages all have ocean views and are furnished with fine European and American antiques.

Motel Row

Numerous motels are located at the west end of Lighthouse Avenue and along Asilomar Boulevard.

WHERE TO EAT

Fandango

223 17th St./Lighthouse Ave., (831) 372-3456; www.fandangorestaurant.com. L M-Sat, D daily, SunBr; $$-$$$. Reservations advised.

In a converted house with a warren of small rooms, this chic, casual spot serves an eclectic menu of delicious continental-style cuisine: crisp duck a l'orange, mesquite-grilled seafood and meats, Mediterranean couscous,

paella, and pastas. Decadent housemade desserts include a frozen Grand Marnier soufflé big enough for two. Patio seating is available.

Holly's Lighthouse Cafe

602 Lighthouse Ave., (831) 372-7006. B-L daily; $.

This impossibly cheery little corner cafe is decorated with lace curtains and blue-and-white checked tablecloths. Its specialties are fluffy omelettes, char-broiled chicken and hamburgers, and housemade soups, and breakfast is served all day.

Peppers MexiCali Cafe

170 Forest Ave., (831) 373-6892; www.peppersmexicalicafe.com. L M&W-Sat, D W-M; $. Reservations advised.

This place is hot in more ways than one: popularity, atmosphere, and salsas. Pepper art in various formats, including hand-painted peppers above the doorway, enhance the rustic, comfy worn-wood floor decor. Portions are large, and seafood items, nightly specials, and really good chicken mole enchiladas are available in addition to Mexican standards. Unblended margaritas are poured with top tequilas.

Petra

477 Lighthouse Ave./13th St., (831) 649-2530. L-D M-Sat; $. Reservations accepted.

Situated in a converted house, this modest family-run restaurant serves a delicious Jordanian Middle Eastern menu. Best choices are the traditional dishes, and a great way to sample them is the combination platter of hummus, baba ghannouj, tabuli, stuffed grape leaves, and falafel. Kebabs are also available. Dessert is baklava, halva, or Turkish delight— a jelly-nut confection.

Red House Cafe

662 Lighthouse Ave., (831) 643-1060; www.redhousecafe.com. B Sat-Sun, L-D Tu-Sun; $. No reservations.

Sandwiches and salads are attractive and tasty, and soups sublime, in this cute little cottage converted into a charming cafe. Drinks include made-from-scratch lemonade and unfiltered apple juice, and desserts are devastatingly delicious.

Tucked around back is **Miss Trawick's Garden Shop** *(664 Lighthouse Ave., (831) 375-4605; www.misstrawicks.com. Daily 10-5.).*

Thai Bistro II
159 Central Ave./Dewey Ave., (408) 372-8700. L-D daily; $. Reservations advised.

Operating within a converted small white house with blue trim, this cozy spot offers delicious laab-gai (chopped chicken salad) and tom kha gai soup (chicken in coconut milk). An extensive vegetarian menu is available, and the housemade French desserts include a "floating island."

CARMEL-BY-THE-SEA

A LITTLE BACKGROUND

They had take the direct country road across the hills from Monterey, instead of the Seventeen Mile Drive around by the coast so that Carmel Bay came upon them without any fore-glimmering of its beauty. Dropping down throgent pines, they passed woods-embowered cottages, quaint and rustic, of artists and writers, and went on across wind-blown rolling sand hills held to place by sturdy lupines and nodding with pale California poppies. Saxon screamed in sudden wonder of delight, then caught her breath and gazed at the amazing peacock-blue of a breaker, shot through with golden sunlight, over-falling in a mile-long sweep and thundering into white ruin of foam on a crescent beach of scarcely less white.

— Jack London,
from *Valley of the Moon*, 1913

A well-established getaway destination, Carmel is best known for its abundant shops, cozy lodgings, and picturesque white sand beach. Exclusive Pebble Beach, located adjacent, is known for its famous golf courses.

It is also known for the things it doesn't have. No street signs, streetlights, electric or neon signs, jukeboxes, parking meters, or buildings over 2 stories high are allowed in town. No sidewalks, curbs, or house numbers are found in the residential sections. These absent items help Carmel keep its village ambiance.

Do be careful. Eccentric laws in the town make it illegal to wear high heels on the sidewalks, throw a ball in the park, play a musical instrument in a bar, or dig in the sand at the beach other than when making a sand castle.

It seems that almost every weekend some special event is scheduled in the area, making available lodging perpetually scarce. Book accommodations far in advance, especially for the quainter venues, and consider taking advantage of the special rates often available for midweek stays.

VISITOR INFORMATION

Carmel California Visitor & Information Center
San Carlos/5th St., (800) 550-4333, (831) 624-2522; www.carmelcalifornia.org.

GETTING THERE

Located 120 miles south of San Francisco, and 70 miles south of San Jose.

ANNUAL EVENTS

AT&T Pebble Beach National Pro-Am
February. In Pebble Beach; (800) 541-9091, (831) 649-1533; www.attpbgolf.com. $50, under 12 free.

This high profile event was formerly known as the Bing Crosby Golf Tournament. Top professionals and celebrity amateurs compete on three of the world's most famous golf courses—Pebble Beach, Spyglass Hill, and Poppy Hills.

Carmel Art Festival
May. (831) 642-2503; www.carmelartfestival.org. Free.

Events include the Plein Air Painting Competition and Sculpture in the Park events, plus an auction of festival paintings.

Carmel Bach Festival
July & August. (831) 624-2046; www.bachfestival.org. $20-$60.

Held annually since 1935 (except for two years off during World War II), this baroque music festival varies its highlights from year to year. Candlelight concerts are usually presented in the town's picturesque mission, and a children's concert is always scheduled.

Pebble Beach Concours d'Elegance™

August. In Pebble Beach; (831) 622-1700; www.pebblebeachconcours.net. $150-$175.

Car buffs don their dressiest summer attire for a stroll on the vast 18th fairway at the Pebble Beach Golf Links, where this elegant affair is held. Classic vintage and antique automobiles are displayed. This is considered America's premiere event of its kind.

WHAT TO DO

Art galleries

• **Carmel Art Association**

Dolores St./5th Ave., (831) 624-6176; www.carmelart.org. Daily 10-5.

This gallery is Carmel's oldest and the nation's second-oldest artist cooperative (the oldest is in Rockport, Massachusetts). It has showcased California's best artists since 1927.

• **Galerie Pleine Aire**

Dolores St., 5th St., (831) 625-5686; www.galeriepleinaire.com. Thur-M 11-5.

This gallery displays original works of art from a group of Monterey Bay plein air painters. Known as Informalists, these artists interpret natural landscapes in impressionistic and expressionistic styles.

• **New Masters Gallery**

Dolores St./Ocean Ave., (800) 336-4014, (831) 625-1511; www.newmastersgallery.com. M-Sat 10-5:30, Sun 10:30-5:30.

The work of accomplished contemporary artists is shown here.

• **Rodrigue Studio**

6th Ave./Dolores St., (831) 626-4444; www.georgerodrigue.com. M-Sat 10-5, Sun 12-5.

This gallery is devoted entirely to Cajun artist George Rodrigue's pop art blue dog.

Beaches

• **Carmel Beach**

At foot of Ocean Ave., (831) 626-2522.

Known for its white powdery sand and spectacular sunsets, this world-famous beach is a choice spot for a refreshing walk, a picnic, or flying a kite. Swimming is unsafe.

The **Great Sand Castle Contest** *((800) 550-4333; www.carmelcalifornia.org. Free.)* is held here each September or October, depending on the tides. Contestants are encouraged to bribe judges with food and drink.

• **Carmel River State Beach**

At end of Scenic Rd./Carmelo St., (831) 649-2836; www.parks.ca.gov. Daily 9-dusk. Free.

Very popular with families and divers, this beach features a fresh-water lagoon that is safe for wading and has an adjoining bird sanctuary. It is located behind the Carmel Mission, where the Carmel River flows into Carmel Bay, and offers beautiful views of Point Lobos. Locals refer to it as Oliver's Cove; the southern end is known as Monastery Beach. Swimming is dangerous. Picnic facilities are available.

Forest Theater

Mountain View/Santa Rita, (831) 626-1681; www.foresttheaterguild.org. Live performances Thur-Sun, June- mid-Oct. $15-$36; reduced rates for 60+ & 6-12; under 6 free. Film series Tu & W June-July. $5.

The oldest outdoor theater west of the Rockies, this venue opened in 1910. Renovations were made by the WPA in the 1930s. The small outdoor bowl boasts ideal acoustics. Seating in is on long wood benches, and two stone fireplaces on either side of the stage are lit for evening performances. Dress warmly, come early, and bring a picnic dinner to enjoy under the stars.

Mission San Carlos Borromeo del Rio Carmelo

3080 Rio Rd., 1 mi. S of town off Hwy. 1, (831) 624-3600; www.carmelmission.org. M-Sat 9:30-5, Sun 10:30-5; services on Sun. $5, seniors $4, 6-17 $1.

Father Junipero Serra, who established this mission in 1770 and used it as his headquarters for managing the entire chain of missions, is buried here at the foot of the altar. It is also known as the Carmel Mission. An intriguing star window graces the rough sandstone walls and Moorish bell tower of the façade, and a museum displays Native American artifacts, mission tools, and re-creations of both the original mission kitchen and California's first library. The quadrangle courtyard garden features a restful fountain stocked with colorful koi, and close by is a cemetery where more than 3,000 mission Indians are buried.

A **fiesta** is held each year on the last Sunday in September.

Across the street, 35-acre **Mission Trail Nature Preserve** *((831) 620-2070; www.ci.carmel.ca.us. Daily dawn-dusk. Free.)* has several hiking trails. The broad ¾-mile Serra Trail is an easy uphill hike. Doolittle Trail leads farther on for great views of Carmel Bay and a stop at the 1929 Tudor **Flanders Mansion** *(www.flandersfoundation.org)*, where it is possible to tour the grounds and stroll through the **Lester Rowntree Arboretum**.

Pacific Repertory Theatre

Monte Verde St./8th Ave., in Golden Bough Playhouse, (831) 622-0700; www.pacrep.org. Performances Mar-Dec. $7-$38.

In a building reconstructed on the site of a playhouse that has burned to the ground twice (each time after performances of *By Candlelight!*), this ambitious company presents varied fare in an intimate venue. The 99-seat Circle Theatre is located downstairs and is the venue for intimate theater-in-the-round stagings.

Pebble Beach Equestrian Center

Portola Rd./Alva Ln., in Pebble Beach, (831) 624-2756; www.ridepebblebeach.com. Group rides daily at 10, 12, 2, 3:30; reservations required. $65/person; must be age 12+.

Escorted rides follow the extensive bridle trails that wind through scenic Del Monte Forest, around the legendary Spyglass Hill Golf Course, down to the beach, and over the sand dunes. Family rides for ages 7 and older and pony rides for ages 3 through 6 are also available. Lessons are available.

Point Lobos State Reserve

3 mi. S of town off Hwy. 1, (831) 624-4909; www.parks.ca.gov. Daily 8-sunset; museum 11-3. $10/vehicle.

Described by Robert Louis Stevenson as "the greatest meeting of land and water in the world," Point Lobos provides the opportunity to see the rustic, undeveloped beauty of the Monterey Peninsula. Flat-topped, gnarled-limbed Monterey cypress trees are native to just the 4-mile stretch between here and Pebble Beach, and sea otters are often spotted in the 1,250-acre reserve's protected waters. Self-guiding trails are available, and guided ranger walks are scheduled daily in summer. Dress warmly,

and bring binoculars, a camera, and maybe a picnic, too.

The **Whalers Cabin Museum** interpretive center is inside a restored whaler's cabin built in 1851 by a Chinese fisherman. Artifacts and photographs tell about the area's history and one display highlights the location's various incarnations in movies.

17-Mile Drive

At Pebble Beach exit off Hwy. 1, betw. Carmel & Monterey, (800) 654-9300, (831) 647-7500; www.pebblebeach.com/17miledrive.html. Daily sunrise-sunset. $8.50/vehicle; no motorcycles.

A toll has been collected for this world-famous drive since 1901, when it was 25 cents, and the scenery—a combination of showplace homes, prestigious golf courses, and raw seascapes—is well worth the price of admission. Sights include the Restless Sea, where several ocean crosscurrents meet; Seal and Bird Rock, where herds of sea lions and flocks of shoreline birds congregate; the Pebble Beach Golf Links, one of three used during the annual AT&T Pebble Beach National Pro-Am tournament; and the landmark Lone Cypress, which clings to a jagged, barren rock base. Picnic facilities and short trails are also available.

Shopping complexes

• The Barnyard Shopping Village

Hwy. 1/Carmel Valley Rd., (831) 624-8886;
www.thebarnyard.com. M-Sat 10-6, Sun 11-5;
restaurants 8am-10pm.

The collection of shops here is worth a
leisurely browse.

• Carmel Plaza

Ocean Ave./Mission St., (831) 624-1385;
www.carmelplaza.com. M-Sat 10-6, Sun 11-5.

This noteworthy collection of upscale
shops surrounds a courtyard dotted with
flowers. The property's Concierge Center helps
visitors plan their trip in advance and provides
a complimentary itinerary.

Tor House

26304 Ocean View Ave., (831) 624-1813; www.tor
house.org. Tours F-Sat 10-3, on the hr.; reservations
required. $7; students $2-$4; must be age 12+.

Poet Robinson Jeffers built this medieval-
style house and tower retreat out of huge granite rocks hauled up from the beach below. He
did much of the work himself. He was of the
opinion that manual labor cleared his mind and
that his "fingers had the art to make stone love
stone." All of his major works and most of his
poetry were written while he lived with his wife
and twin sons on this craggy knoll overlooking
Carmel Bay.

WHERE TO STAY

Carmel River Inn

Hwy. 1/Oliver Rd., at N end of bridge, 1 mi.
from town, (800) 882-8142, (831) 624-1575;
www.carmelriverinn.com. 43 units; $-$$$. Some
kitchens & gas & wood-burning fireplaces. Heated
pool.

Located on the outskirts of town on the
banks of the Carmel River and here since the
1930s, this lodging complex recently updated
with flat screen TVs, flick-on gas fireplaces/
heaters, and whirlpool tubs. It stretches over
10 acres of gardens, forest, and meadow.
Guests may choose either a motel room or an
individual one- or two-bedroom cottage that
is especially comfortable with kids. Coveys of
quail are spotted regularly, and the Carmel
Mission is just a short, easy walk away.

Cobblestone Inn

Junipero St./8th Ave., (800) 833-8836,
(831) 625-5222; www.cobblestoneinncarmel.com.
24 rooms; $$-$$$+. All gas fireplaces. Afternoon
snack; full breakfast. No pets.

Located just 2 blocks from the main shop-
ping street, this charming inn features spacious
guest rooms furnished with country-style pine
pieces and iron-frame beds. Shutters provide
privacy, fireplaces constructed with large river
rocks provide atmosphere and warmth, and
mini-fridges provide complimentary cold
drinks. In the morning, a newspaper appears at
the door, and on warm days breakfast can be
enjoyed outside on a sunny slate-and-brick-
paved courtyard filled with flowers blooming in
stone containers. Bicycles are available for
guests to borrow.

Cypress Inn

Lincoln St./7th Ave., (800) 443-7443, (831) 624-3871;
www.cypress-inn.com. 33 rooms; $$-$$$+. Some gas
fireplaces. Evening snack; continental breakfast.

Featuring a Moorish Mediterranean style
of architecture, this inn dates from 1929 and is
located right in town. Owned now by actress
Doris Day along with several partners, its rooms
are distinctively decorated and comfortable and
a few have ocean views. All guest rooms have
fresh flowers and are stocked with a decanter of
cream sherry and a fruit basket. Pets are partic-
ularly welcome, and the inn offers pet sitting
services and recommendations for pet-friendly
dining.

A full **afternoon tea** *(Daily 1-4; $18.*
Reservations required.) includes sandwiches,
scones, and cookies and is open to non-guests.
Cozy **Terry's Lounge** *(daily 5-9:30pm, bar until*
11) serves appetizers and drinks as well as a
hamburger.

Green Lantern Inn Bed & Breakfast

7th Ave./Casanova St., (888) 414-4392, (831) 624-
4392; www.greenlanterninn.com. 18 rooms; $-$$$.
Some gas fireplaces. Afternoon snack; full breakfast.
No pets.

Operating as an inn since 1926, this
pleasant group of rustic multi-unit cottages is
located on a quiet side street just a few blocks
from the village and 4 blocks from the beach.

Highlands Inn, A Hyatt Hotel

120 Highlands Dr., off Hwy. 1, 4 mi. S of town, (800) 682-4811, (831) 620-1234; www.highlands inn.hyatt.com. 48 rooms; $$$-$$$+. Some kitchens & wood-burning fireplaces. Heated pool; 3 hot tubs; fitness room. 2 restaurants; room service. No pets.

Located in a fragrant pine forest in the scenic Carmel Highlands, up a hill just past the town gas station with its old-time pump and two authentic red English phone booths, this inn was built on its spectacular cliff-side setting in 1916. Through the years it has been host to many famous guests, including the Beatles and two presidents—Kennedy and Ford. Luxurious contemporary-style guest rooms are designed for privacy, making it possible to just hole up and listen to the birds tweeting and the sounds of the not-too-distant surf. All have ocean views and are equipped with robes and even binoculars. Complimentary bikes are available to guests, and upon check-in children are given an amenities bag filled with goodies.

A buffet breakfast and simple lunch menu are available in the casual **California Market** *(B-L-D daily; $-$$.)*, where diners enjoy a view of the rugged coastline from both the inside dining room and the outside balcony. The celebrated and elegant **Pacific's Edge** restaurant *((831) 622-5445; www.pacificsedge.com. D daily; $$$. Reservations advised. Valet parking.)* also features a stunning view (plan to dine during daylight).

Lamp Lighter Inn

Ocean Ave./Camino Real, (831) 624-7372; www.carmellamplighter.com. 9 units; $$-$$$+. Some kitchens; 1 wood-burning fireplace. Continental breakfast.

Conveniently located between the village and the ocean, this enclave has both charming rooms and gingerbread-style cottages that very well might fulfill a guest's fairy tale fantasies. Several of the cozy, comfortable cottages accommodate families, and the Hansel and Gretel has a sleeping loft for kids. The Blue Bird Room has a patinaed redwood cathedral ceiling and a picture window looking into a large oak tree. Children especially enjoy finding all 17 elves in the Elves Garden. Accommodations in an annex, located 1 block closer to the beach, are a little less expensive and a lot less interesting; however, several have ocean views.

La Playa Hotel & Cottages-by-the-Sea

Camino Real/8th Ave., (800) 582-8900, (831) 624-6476; www.laplayahotel.com. 80 units; $$-$$$+. Some kitchens & gas fireplaces. Heated pool. Restaurant; room service. No pets.

This luxury Mediterranean-style hotel is conveniently located just 2 blocks from the beach and 4 blocks from town. Remains of the mansion it began as in 1904—a home for landscape painter Christian Jorgensen—can be viewed in the lobby, and one of his original Yosemite paintings hangs casually near the check-in desk. Vintage photographs and other memorabilia decorate hallways throughout. Taking up an entire square block, this is the largest hotel in Carmel. Guest room beds have rustic carved headboards sporting the hotel's mermaid motif, and the beautifully maintained gardens are abloom with colorful flowers year-round. A group of charming cottages situated a block closer to the ocean is also available.

The casual **Terrace Grill** *(B-L-D daily; $$-$$$.)* features an elaborate Sunday brunch with a buffet of fresh fruits and pastries, Belgian waffles, and made-to-order omelettes. The restaurant's namesake terrace has both ocean and garden views and is covered overhead and heated, so al fresco dining can be enjoyed regardless of the weather. The bar makes a perfect spicy Bloody Mary.

Lincoln Green Inn

Carmelo St./15th Ave., (800) 262-1262, (831) 624-7738; www.lincolngreeninn.com. 4 units; $$$-$$$+. Some kitchens; all gas fireplaces. Afternoon snack; continental breakfast.

Located on the outskirts of town, just a few blocks from where the Carmel River flows into the ocean, this cluster of comfortable English housekeeping cottages features living rooms with cathedral-beamed ceilings and stone fireplaces. Each is named for a character from the Robin Hood tale, and a lush English country garden includes flowers, lawns, and ancient trees. Afternoon wine and cheese is served in the garden, and breakfast is brought to the cottage.

Mission Ranch

26270 Dolores St./Rio Rd., (800) 538-8221, (831) 624-6436; www.missionranchcarmel.com. 31 rooms; $$-$$$. Some gas fireplaces. Fitness room; 6 clay

tennis courts. *Continental breakfast; restaurant.
No pets.*

Owned by actor/director Clint Eastwood, who has invested a fistful of dollars in furnishings, this former dairy farm has operated as a lodging facility since 1937. It is located near the Carmel Mission. Accommodation choices include roomy cottages that work well for families, the 1857 Victorian-style Martin Family Farmhouse with B&B-style rooms, and the 1852 Bunkhouse cottage; simpler rooms are also available. Eastwood fans take note: The 19th-century pot-belly stove that appeared in *Unforgiven* resides in the inn's restaurant, which is situated in the ranch's former creamery.

Normandy Inn
Ocean Ave./Monte Verde St., (800) 343-3825, (831) 624-3825; www.normandyinncarmel.com. 48 units; $-$$$+. Some kitchens & wood-burning fireplaces. Heated pool (seasonal). Afternoon sherry; continental breakfast. No pets.

Conveniently located on the town's main shopping street and just 4 blocks from the ocean, this inn features an attractive half-beamed, Normandy-style architecture and has several large cottages. The comfortably appointed rooms are decorated in French country style and have featherbeds, and the pool is invitingly secluded.

Pine Inn
Ocean Ave./Monte Verde St., (800) 228-3851, (831) 624-3851; www.pine-inn.com. 49 rooms; $$-$$$+. 1 gas fireplace. Restaurant; room service. No pets.

This inn, which opened in 1889, is the oldest in town. It is decorated in elegant Victorian style and conveniently located in the center of town.

Il Fornaio restaurant *((831) 622-5100; www.ilfornaio.com.)* operates in a semi-subterranean space off a courtyard in back.

San Antonio House
San Antonio St./7th Ave., (800) 313-7770, (831) 624-6926; www.carmelgardencourtinn.com. 5 rooms; $$-$$$. Unsuitable for children under 12. All gas fireplaces. Continental breakfast. No pets.

This attractive guesthouse offers large rooms, a lovely garden, and a location in a quiet residential area just 1 block from the beach. One room has a private patio, another its own

doll house, and a breakfast tray is brought to each room in the morning.

Sea View Inn
Camino Real/12th Ave., (831) 624-8778; www.seaviewinncarmel.com. 8 rooms; $$. Unsuitable for children under 12. No TVs; some shared baths. Afternoon & evening snack; continental breakfast. No pets.

Located 3 blocks from the beach, this converted Victorian home offers pleasantly appointed rooms. The most requested guest room features a cozy canopy bed.

Stonehouse Inn
8th Ave./Monte Verde St., (800) 748-6618, (831) 624-4569; www.carmelstonehouse.com. 6 rooms; $$-$$$. Unsuitable for children under 12. Some shared baths. Afternoon snack; full breakfast. No pets.

Built by local Indians in 1906, this rustic stone country house is close to the village. The original owner often entertained well-known artists and writers, and the antique-furnished rooms are now named in honor of some of those guests.

Vagabond's House Inn Bed and Breakfast
4th Ave./Dolores St., (800) 262-1262, (831) 624-7738; www.vagabondshouseinn.com. 11 rooms; $$-$$$+. Unsuitable for children under 12. Some kitchens & wood-burning & gas fireplaces. Continental breakfast.

This rustic English Tudor-style building features cozily furnished rooms that open off a quiet, flower-bedecked courtyard.

WHERE TO EAT

Caffe Cardinale
Off Ocean Ave./betw. Dolores St. & San Carlos St., (800) 595-2090, (831) 626-2095; www.carmelcoffee.com. Daily from 7am.

Reached via a narrow passageway, this charming spot has an in-house coffee roaster and features outside seating in a 1920s Mediterranean-style courtyard. Water is put out for dogs, and pods of fresh coffee are sold for hotel coffee makers.

Carmel Bakery
Ocean Ave./Lincoln St., (831) 626-8885; www.carmelbakery.com. Sun-Thur 6:30am-7pm, F-Sat to 9.

Apricot log pastries, wild blueberry scones, focaccia with spicy pepper topping, and caramel apples are just a few of the delicacies available at this popular bakery.

Cottage of Sweets
Ocean Ave./Lincoln St., (831) 624-5170; www.cottageofsweets.com. M-Thur 10-7, F-Sun 10-8.

Among the sweet surprises in this charming candy cottage are imported chocolates, diet candy, gourmet jelly beans, taffy, and more than 55 kinds of licorice.

Em Le's
Dolores St./5th Ave., (831) 625-6780; www.em-les.com. B-L-D daily; $.

Football broadcaster John Madden is part owner of this cozy, casual spot touted as the town's only vintage soda fountain. Among the extensive breakfast items are buttermilk waffles—in a choice of light or dark bake—and wild blueberry pancakes. The basic all-American cuisine includes fried chicken, meatloaf, mashed potatoes, and apple pie. Pleasant views of sidewalk traffic and counter seating add to the low-key Carmel charm.

The Forge in the Forest
5th Ave./Junipero St., (831) 624-2233; www.forgeintheforest.com. L-D daily, SunBr; $-$$. Reservations advised.

This popular spot operates in a warren of spaces that include a heated outdoor patio. Its name is that of the blacksmith shop that once operated in this same space. The menu is eclectic—fresh seafood, pasta, pizza, salads, sandwiches—and the hours are late, making it popular with night owls.

Jack London's Bar & Grill
Dolores St./5th Ave., (831) 624-2336; www.jacklondonsgrill.com. L-D daily, SunBr; $-$$.

Even locals come here to enjoy the excellent bar drinks and cozy bistro atmosphere. Kids are welcome and can order fancy non-alcoholic drinks, and food is served until midnight. American and Mexican fare include pizzas, hamburgers, steaks, salads, soups, and fajitas. A "secret" breakfast menu is usually available, but only by request.

Patisserie Boissiere Cafe & Restaurant
Mission St./Ocean Ave., (831) 624-5008; www.patisserieboissiere.com. L M-F, D W-Sun, Sat-SunBr; $-$$. Reservations advised at D.

The menu at this elegant little gem offers housemade soups, sandwiches, more substantial entrees, and freshly baked pastries and desserts. Picnics can be ordered for pick up.

Piatti
6th Ave./Junipero St., (831) 625-1766; www.piatti.com. L-D daily.

For description, see page 221.

Rocky Point Restaurant
On Hwy. 1, 12 mi. S of town, (831) 624-2933; www.rocky-point.com. B-L-D daily; $$-$$$. Reservations advised.

Take a scenic drive down the coast to Big Sur, stopping here to enjoy the spectacular view along with a multi-course charcoal-broiled steak or fresh seafood dinner. Sandwiches and hamburgers are on the lunch menu, making it a relative bargain.

The Tuck Box
Dolores St./Ocean Ave., (831) 624-6365; www.tuckbox.com. B-L-afternoon tea daily; $. No reservations. No cards.

Featuring fairy-tale architecture and verily reeking of quaintness, this tiny English-style tearoom can be quite difficult to get seated in. If ever it is without a long line in front, go! Additional seating is available on a tiny outdoor patio. The breakfast menu offers egg items and hot oats as well as delightful fresh scones and English muffins served with a choice of homemade olallieberry preserves or orange marmalade. At lunch, sandwiches, salads, and

omelettes are available along with Welsh rarebit. Afternoon tea features scones, pies, and, of course, plenty of hot English tea.

Across the street, tiny **Picadilly Park** invites relaxing contemplation with its benches, flower garden, and goldfish pond.

Village Corner
Dolores St./6th Ave., (831) 624-3588; www.carmels best.com. B-L-D daily; $-$$. Reservations advised.

The large patio here is heated year-round and provides the chance to relax and watch the rest of the town stroll by. The Mediterranean bistro menu offers bruschetta and deep-fried local calamari for appetizers. Entrees include several pastas as well as a dramatic paella for two. Local wines pair perfectly.

CARMEL VALLEY

A LITTLE BACKGROUND

Reliably sunny and peaceful, with horse farms and flower nurseries lining its main road, Carmel Valley is often overlooked by visitors to the Monterey Peninsula. That's a shame, because it is a wonderful place to relax and is only a few miles inland from Carmel. Before World War II, this area was popular with the rich and famous, who came here to hunt boar and play polo. Now lodgings, restaurants, and shops dot Highway 16/Carmel Valley Road along its 15-mile stretch east into the hub of town.

VISITOR INFORMATION

Carmel Valley Chamber of Commerce
13 W. Carmel Valley Rd., (831) 659-4000; www.carmelvalleychamber.com.

WHAT TO DO

Garland Ranch Regional Park
On Carmel Valley Rd., 8.6 mi. from Hwy. 1, (831) 659-4488; www.mprpd.org/parks/garland.htm. Daily sunrise-sunset. Free.

Running along the banks of the Carmel River, this 4,500-acre park is home to the very spot where the boys caught frogs in Steinbeck's *Cannery Row*. Though frog collecting is not permitted, listening to them is. The 1.4-mile

Lupine Loop Trail provides an easy nature walk; more self-guided hiking trails lead up into the mountains. A Visitors Center provides orientation and maps.

WINERIES

Bernardus Winery
5 W. Carmel Valley Rd., 10 mi. from Hwy. 1, (800) 223-2533, (831) 659-1900; www.bernardus.com. Tasting daily 11-5.

The father of owner Ben (Bernardus) Pon is the designer of the Volkswagen bus and was the person who first exported the Beetle to the U.S. Ben himself has been a professional race car driver for Porsche and represented Holland in skeet shooting at the 1972 Olympics. With such an accomplished background, it isn't surprising that he would operate a successful winery. The winery makes wines in the old French Bordeaux and Burgundian styles and is known for its Chardonnay and Sauvignon Blanc.

Château Julien Wine Estate
8940 Carmel Valley Rd., 5 mi. from Hwy. 1, (831) 624-2600; www.chateaujulien.com. Tasting M-F 8-5, Sat-Sun 11-5; tours by appt. M-F at 10:30 & 2:30, Sat-Sun 12:30 & 2:30.

Styled after an actual château located on the French-Swiss border, this castle-like structure has no formal tasting bar. Tasters gather informally around a large table in the middle of a high-ceilinged room. Children are provided juice and crackers while their parents taste Chardonnays and Merlots—the two varietals this winery is noted for. A garden patio invites picnicking.

Heller Estate
69 W. Carmel Valley Rd., 11 mi. from Hwy. 1, (800) 625-8466, (831) 659-6220; www.hellerestate.com. Tasting M-Thur 11-5:30, F-Sun 11-6.

Promising "magical wines that dance on your palate," this winery uses only certified organically grown grapes. A Sculpture Garden, with pieces by Toby Heller, is equipped with picnic tables.

WHERE TO STAY

Bernardus Lodge
415 Carmel Valley Rd., 10 mi. from Hwy. 1, (888) 648-9463, (831) 658-3400; www.bernardus.com.

57 rooms; $$$+. All gas fireplaces. Heated pool; hot tub; full-service spa; 2 tennis courts. 2 restaurants. No pets.

Guests enter this luxury Tuscan village-style property through rolling vineyards and are greeted with a complimentary glass of wine at check-in. More complimentary wine and snacks await in each room. Amenities include a croquet lawn, and all rooms have private decks, a soft featherbed, and a bathtub big enough for two.

Carmel Valley Ranch Resort

One Old Ranch Rd., 6 mi. from Hwy. 1, (866) 282-4745, (831) 625-9500; www.carmelvalleyranch.com. 144 rooms; $$-$$$+. All wood-burning fireplaces. 2 heated pools; hot tub; sauna; fitness room; 12 tennis courts (2 clay); 18-hole golf course. 3 restaurants; room service. No pets.

Built in an elegant ranch-style architecture that features local stone and oak, this luxurious all-suite resort is situated on 400 scenic acres surrounded by rolling hills. It is the only resort on the Monterey Peninsula with a guarded gate. Each suite features cathedral ceilings and has a large private deck and two TVs; some have decks with private outdoor hot tubs.

The **Citronelle by Michel Richard** restaurant (D Tu-Sat. Reservations advised.) has a stunning view of the valley.

Quail Lodge Resort & Golf Club

8205 Valley Greens Dr., 3 mi. from Hwy. 1, (888) 828-8787, (831) 624-2888; www.quaillodge.com. 97 units; $$$+. Some gas fireplaces. 2 heated pools; hot tub; full-service spa; 4 tennis courts; 18-hole golf course. Continental breakfast; 2 restaurants; room service.

These luxurious guest rooms and suites are situated on 850 acres of golf fairways, meadows, and lakes. Guests can access hiking trails and visit 11 lakes that are also wildlife sanctuaries. Attracting a classy crowd, the resort's parking lot has been seen holding a DeLorean and several Ferraris at the same time.

Dressy **Covey Restaurant** (D Tu-Sun; $$$. Reservations advised.) overlooks a lake and offers California country cuisine.

The annual **Carmel TomatoFest** (September. (831) 625-6041; www.tomato fest.com. $85+, under 12 free.) features a tasting of hundreds of varieties plus a buffet of tomato dishes.

Tassajara Zen Mountain Center

39171 Tassajara Rd., 40 mi. from Hwy. 1. Reservations: (415) 865-1899 (M-F 9-12:30 & 1:30-4); www.sfzc.org/tassajara. 29 units; $$-$$$+; includes 3 vegetarian meals. Closed Sept-Apr. Child rates; number of children permitted is controlled. No TVs; some fireplaces; some shared baths. Hot springs pool; steam rooms. Day use: (831) 659-2229; $25, children $12; reservations essential; lunch by reservation. No pets.

Owned by the San Francisco Zen Center, this traditional Soto Zen Buddhist monastery is the oldest one outside of Asia. Located deep in the Ventana Wilderness in the Los Padres National Forest, it is home to 50 male and female monks. Getting there requires a 14-mile drive down a steep dirt road (a four-wheel-drive or stick shift is strongly advised), but overnight guests have the option of arranging a ride in on a four-wheel-drive "stage." The famous hot mineral springs are semi-enclosed in a Japanese-style bathhouse. Men's and women's baths and steam rooms are separate, and swimsuits are optional; mixed bathing is permitted after dinner. More activities include hiking, river wading, and picnicking. Guests stay in simple wood or stone cabins with no electricity. Kerosene lamps provide lighting, and everyone shares one phone. This is *not* a place to sleep in—bells go off at 5:30 a.m. to announce meditation time for any guests who want to participate. Getting a reservation can be difficult; call early. Reservations open on April 3 for overnight stays and on April 25 for day visits. Day guests must bring their own towels and food.

WHERE TO EAT

Corkscrew Restaurant

55 W. Carmel Valley Rd., in Carmel Valley Village, 11 mi. from Hwy. 1, (831) 659-8888; www.corkscrewcafe.com. L daily, D F-Sat; $$.

The interior of this color-washed bistro is a delight, and its outdoor garden, with tables covered in colorful Provençal tablecloths, is heavenly on a sunny day. Lunch choices might include a Niman Ranch cheeseburger or a California BLT with avocado. Save room for dessert, especially if fresh pear crisp with lavender ice cream is an option. Drinks include raspberry lemonade or a flight of wines from adjacent Georis Winery.

After dining, it is just a few steps through the garden to the **Georis Winery** tasting room *(4 Pilot Rd., (831) 659-1050; www.georis wine.com.)*, which features a small corkscrew display and an excellent collection of Mexican folk art in its rustic gift shop.

Wagon Wheel
7156 Carmel Valley Rd., in Valley Hills Shopping Center, 3 mi. from Hwy. 1, (831) 624-8878. B-L daily; $. No reservations. No cards.

This place is extremely popular with locals and is usually packed. Tables are tiny, but portions are generous. Breakfast is the busiest meal and is served until the 2 p.m. closing time. The menu includes omelettes, eggs Benedict, oatmeal, assorted styles of pancakes (don't miss the owner's favorite—raspberry), and fresh-squeezed orange juice. A late breakfast permits chowing-down more than enough grub to satisfy a tummy until dinner. The hamburgers, french fries, and homemade beans are also reputed to be very good.

BIG SUR

A LITTLE BACKGROUND

Whoever settles here hopes that he will be the last invader.
    — Henry Miller, from *Big Sur and the Oranges of Hieronymus Bosch*

Big Sur is such a special place that many people who have visited don't feel generous about sharing it. However, facilities are so limited that it's hard to imagine the area getting overrun with tourists. Except, perhaps, in the thick of summer.

The town of Big Sur seems to have no center. Located at the southern end of the coast redwoods range, it stretches along Highway 1 for 6 miles offering a string of amenities. Then, continuing south, the highway begins an isolated 90-mile stretch of some of the most spectacular scenery in the U.S.

Note that the river's bottom here is rocky. Bring along waterproof shoes for wading.

VISITOR INFORMATION

Big Sur Chamber of Commerce
P.O. Box 87, Big Sur 93920, (831) 667-2100; www.bigsurcalifornia.org.

Monterey County Convention & Visitors Bureau
See page 112.

GETTING THERE

Located approximately 25 miles south of the Monterey Peninsula.

WHAT TO DO

Big Sur is so non-commercial that there is little to list in this section. Visitors can look forward to relaxing, swimming in the river, picnicking on the beach, or taking a hike through the woods. Look out for poison oak, and bring along a good book.

Andrew Molera State Park
On Hwy. 1, (831) 667-2315; www.parks.ca.gov. Daily sunrise-sunset. $8/vehicle.

Located at the north end of town, near the photogenic Bixby Bridge, this beach park has plenty of hiking trails. Several are short and easy: The flat, 2-mile-round-trip Bluffs Trail follows the ocean to a promontory, and the more challenging 5-mile-round-trip Bobcat Trail follows the Big Sur River through dense redwoods. Walk-in campsites are available.

Operating within the park, **Molera Horseback Tours** *((800) 942-5486, (831) 625-5486; www.molerahorsebacktours.com. Schedule varies; closed Dec-Mar. $25+. Must be 6 or older. Reservations advised.)* takes riders to the beach.

Esalen Institute
55000 Hwy. 1, (831) 667-3000; www.esalen.org. No pets.

Located on a breathtaking crest above the ocean, this legendary educational facility offers lodging and dining in conjunction with its workshops. Self-exploration workshops include meditation, yoga, vision improvement, massage, and more. Nude bathing is de rigueur in the swimming pool and mineral spring-fed hot tubs in the 2-story cliff-top bathhouse. Non-guests can access the pools only from 1 to 3 a.m. *($20. Reservations required.)*—unless a massage is booked, in which case use of the baths is included.

Hawthorne Gallery

48485 Hwy. 1, (831) 667-3200; www.hawthornegallery.com. Daily 10-6.

Located across the street from Nepenthe restaurant, this exceptional art gallery is within a distinctive building featuring stunning architecture. It presents an impressive collection of garden sculpture and glasswork.

Henry Miller Library

On Hwy. 1, just S of Nepenthe restaurant, (831) 667-2574; www.henrymiller.org. Thur-Sun 11-6; also M & W in summer. Free.

Henry Miller lived in Big Sur for 18 years. The former home of his good friend, Emil White, is now a shrine honoring the late artist and author. It is filled with memorabilia, photos, and letters, and the bathroom features erotic tiles by Ephraim Doner. The library also serves as a community art center and bookstore, and picnicking on the redwood-sheltered lawn is encouraged. Special events are often scheduled on weekends.

Pfeiffer Beach

At end of Sycamore Canyon Rd., (831) 667-2315. Daily 9-8. $5/vehicle.

Watch for unmarked Sycamore Canyon Road on the west side of Highway 1. This narrow road begins about 1.7 miles south of Fernwood Resort and winds for 2 lovely miles to a beach parking lot. The only easily accessible public beach in the area, it features striking rock formations and arches carved out by the rough surf. Visitors can wade in a stream that meanders through the sandy beach but should stay out of the turbulent ocean. If it all looks vaguely familiar, it might be because this is where Elizabeth Taylor and Richard Burton acted out some memorable love scenes in *The Sandpiper*.

Pfeiffer Big Sur State Park

On Hwy. 1, (831) 667-2315; www.parks.ca.gov. Daily sunrise-sunset. $8/vehicle.

Activities at this 821-acre park include hiking (among the many trails is a ½-mile nature trail), river swimming, and ranger-led nature

walks and campfires, and an open meadow is perfect for playing baseball or throwing a Frisbee. Facilities include picnic tables, a restaurant, and a store. Campsites are available.

Point Sur State Historic Park

Off Hwy. 1, 19 mi. S of Carmel, (831) 625-4419; www.parks.ca.gov. Tour: schedule varies; $8, 6-17 $4. No pets.

Built in 1889, the **Point Sur Lightstation** is the center of this park. The strenuous 3-hour guided tours include a ½-mile hike and a 300-foot climb; they are not recommended for small children. Parking is limited to the first 40 vehicles to arrive. No strollers or picnicking permitted.

WHERE TO STAY

Big Sur Lodge

47225 Hwy. 1, (800) 4-BIG-SUR, (831) 667-3100; www.bigsurlodge.com. 62 rooms; $$-$$$. No TVs; some kitchens & fireplaces. Heated pool (seasonal). Restaurant. No pets.

Situated within Pfeiffer Big Sur State Park (guests have complimentary access), this complex has many spacious two-bedroom motel units. Each has a private deck or porch. Rooms are distributed throughout the spacious, grassy grounds, where deer are often seen grazing; those close to the pleasant pool area seem most desirable. In season, a casual, moderately priced restaurant serves meals all day.

Big Sur River Inn & Restaurant

Hwy. 1/Pheneger Creek, (800) 548-3610, (831)-667-2700; www.bigsurriverinn.com. 20 rooms; $$-$$$. Heated pool. Restaurant. No pets.

This is the first place seen when entering Big Sur from the north. Rooms are simple, but those on the river side of the road are two-room suites that open onto decks overlooking an expansive lawn and the Big Sur River, where bentwood chairs await in the water.

The **restaurant** *(B-L-D daily; $-$$.)* overlooks the river and has both a large, open inside room with a huge stone fireplace and an outside deck with sheltering multi-colored umbrellas. An eclectic schedule of live music is scheduled on summer Sunday afternoons. The **Habanero Burrito Bar** in the General Store serves made-to-order burritos *(Daily 11-7; $.).*

New Camaldoli Hermitage
62475 Hwy. 1, 25 mi. S of town, in Lucia, 2 mi. off
Hwy. 1, (831) 667-2456; www.contemplation.com.
9 rooms; $70-$80 donation/person. No TVs. Includes
3 simple vegetarian meals.

Founded in 1958 by three Benedictine
monks from Camaldoli, Italy, this quiet 800-
acre wildlife and wilderness preserve allows
guests to meditate, read, rest, and pray. Solitary,
silent, non-directed retreats in the Catholic
tradition of the Benedictine order are open to
people of all faiths. Chapel services are available
for those who wish to participate, and each of
the modest single-occupancy rooms has a
private garden overlooking the ocean. Five
remote trailers are also an option.

A **gift shop** *((800) 826-3740. Daily 8:30-11*
& 1:15-5.) sells pottery and religious items as
well as brandy-dipped fruitcake and date-nut
cake made by the 22 resident Camaldolese
monks.

Ripplewood Resort
On Hwy. 1, (831) 667-2242; www.ripplewood
resort.com. 17 cabins; $-$$. No TVs; some kitchens &
wood-burning fireplaces. Restaurant. No pets.

Rustic, pleasantly decorated redwood
cabins are located both above and below the
highway. The ones below are in a dense grove of
redwoods just a stone's throw from the Big Sur
River. A cafe serves breakfast and lunch.

Ventana Inn & Spa
On Hwy. 1, (800) 628-6500, (831) 667-2331;
www.ventanainn.com. 59 rooms; $$$+. Unsuitable for
children under 18. Most wood-burning fireplaces.
2 heated pools; hot tub; sauna; full-service spa; fit-
ness room. Afternoon snack; continental breakfast;
restaurant. No pets.

Built in 1975 by Larry Spector, with
money he made as a producer of *Easy Rider*,
this serene resort has a striking, clean-lined,
award-winning architecture that seems to fit in
perfectly with its spectacular, secluded hilltop
location back among the redwoods—1,200 feet
above the ocean. It is a choice spot for a restive,
revitalizing, and hedonistic retreat. Rooms lined
in unfinished redwood are distributed among
12 buildings. All have either a private balcony
or patio and either an ocean or mountain view;
some have private hot tubs. Clothing is optional
in one of the two Japanese hot baths and on the
sun decks.

Known for its accomplished California-
style cuisine, **Cielo** *((831) 667-4242. L-D daily;*
$$-$$$.) has seating both in a cedar-paneled
dining room with mountain and ocean views
and out on an expansive terrace with a
panoramic ocean view. A Nicoise salad and a
Bloody Mary out on the terrace at a table edg-
ing up against fragrant rosemary and lavender
hedging—while watching a circling hawk going
higher and higher or a hummingbird doing
dive-bombing maneuvers—is sublime.

WHERE TO EAT

Deetjen's Big Sur Inn
48865 Hwy. 1, (831) 667-2377; www.deetjens.com.
B-D daily; $-$$$. Reservations advised for D.

For aesthetic pleasure it's hard to beat
lingering over a hearty breakfast in this
Norwegian-style inn, especially when it's raining
outside and the table is positioned in front of
the fireplace. The mellow, rustic, and informal
setting provides a complementary background
to the fresh, simple, and wholesome foods
produced by its kitchen. Dinner by candlelight
is more expensive and sedate, and children
don't fit in as well then.

Rustic, casual **lodging** *(20 units; $-$$.*
No TVs; some wood-burning fireplaces & stoves;
some shared baths. No pets.) is available in

rooms and cabins built of local redwood and situated comfortably amid a forest of redwoods and firs. They usually book up far in advance.

Nepenthe
On Hwy. 1, (831) 667-2345; www.nepenthebigsur.com. L-D daily; $$. No reservations.

Located at the top of a cliff 808 feet above the ocean and offering a breathtaking view of the coastline, this famous restaurant was designed by a student of Frank Lloyd Wright. It is an elaboration of a cabin that Orson Welles originally built as a retreat for Rita Hayworth and himself. When the weather is mild, dining is available outside on a casual terrace. The menu features simple foods that include a steak, fresh seafood, roasted chicken, housemade soup, and a very good hamburger. The bar is a great place to stop in for a drink. Overall, this restaurant seems to be living up to the promise of its name, which refers to a mythical Egyptian drug that induced forgetfulness and the surcease of sorrow.

Café Kevah *((831) 667-2345. Closed Jan-Feb.)*, located downstairs, serves moderately priced brunch and lunch items on a patio with the same striking view. On a warm afternoon, it is a choice spot to enjoy a refreshing cold drink and tasty pastry.

The classy **Phoenix** gift shop *((831) 667-2347. Daily 10:30-7.)* provides pleasant browsing before or after dining.

SAN SIMEON

A LITTLE BACKGROUND

The world-famous Hearst Castle is located in the small town of San Simeon on the windblown coast south of Big Sur.

VISITOR INFORMATION

San Simeon Chamber of Commerce
250 San Simeon Dr. #3A, (800) 342-5613, (805) 927-3500; www.sansimeonsbest.com.

GETTING THERE

Located approximately 75 miles south of Big Sur.

For a more leisurely trip, try the train package offered by **Key Holidays** *((800) 783-0783, (925) 945-8938; www.keyholidays.com.).* Via rail is the way guests traveled to the castle in its heyday. Invitations then always included train tickets. Today travelers can still relax and enjoy the scenery while Amtrak's Coast Starlight transports them to Paso Robles. From there, after seeing the local sights, this package includes a minibus tour of the coast and an overnight in Paso Robles. The next day participants are bused to the famed castle for a guided tour, then down scenic Highway 1 for a stop in the village of Cambria, and then back to Paso Robles for the return train ride. The package does not include meals. Rates vary, and discounts are available for children.

WHAT TO DO

Elephant seals
On Hwy. 1, 5.5 mi. N of San Simeon, just S of Piedras Blancas Light Station, (805) 924-1628; www.elephantseal.org. Free.

This is a sort of mini Año Nuevo (see page 97.)

Hearst Castle®
On Hwy. 1, (800) 444-4445; www.hearstcastle.org. $20-24, 6-17 $10-$12; evening tour $30/$15. Reservations advised; if not sold out in advance, tickets can also be purchased at the Visitor Center after 8am on day of tour.

Perched atop La Cuesta Encantada (The Enchanted Hill®), this spectacular mansion designed by architect Julia Morgan is filled with art treasures and antiques from all over the world gathered by newspaper czar William Randolph Hearst mostly from auctions in the early part of the century. The castle took 28 years to build. Though unfinished, the estate contains 56 bedrooms, 102 bathrooms, 19 sitting rooms, a kitchen, a movie theater, 2 libraries, a billiard room, a dining hall, and an assembly hall! Colorful vines and plants grace the lovely gardens, and wild zebras, tahr goats, and sambar deer graze the hillsides—remnants of the private zoo that once included lions, monkeys, and a polar bear. Before 1958, visitors could get no closer than was permitted by a coin-operated telescope located on the road below. Now owned and operated by the State of

California Department of Parks and Recreation as an Historical Monument, the castle is open to the public. Five tours are available; all include a scenic bus ride up to the castle.

• **Tour 1** is suggested for a first visit and includes gardens, pools, a guesthouse, and the ground floor of the main house—Casa Grande—as well as admission to the visitor center movie.

• **Tour 2** covers the upper floors of the main house, including Mr. Hearst's private suite, the libraries, a guest duplex, the kitchen, and the pools.

• **Tour 3** covers the 36-room guest wing and includes the pools and a guesthouse.

• **Tour 4** stresses the gardens. It includes the elegant 19-room Casa del Mar guesthouse, the wine cellar, and the pools. This tour is given only April through October.

• **Tour 5** takes place in the evening and combines highlights of the daytime tours. Additionally, volunteers in period dress bring the magnificent surroundings to life. It is given

only on Friday and Saturday evenings in spring and fall.

During the entire month of December, the castle and guesthouses are decorated for the Christmas holidays—just as they were when Mr. Hearst lived here. Though all tours see some of the decorations, the daytime Tour 1 and evening Tour 5 both see the main rooms decorated full-on with Christmas trees, wrapped gifts, garlands, and wreaths. Rooms are dimly lit in daytime to protect the art, so lighted decorations are seen well then, too.

Children under 6 are free only if they sit on their parent's lap during the bus ride. Tours require walking about ½ mile and climbing approximately 150 to 400 steps; comfortable shoes are advised. Baby strollers are not permitted on the tours. Tours take approximately 2 to 3 hours. Picnic tables and a snack bar are available near the Visitor Center.

Piedras Blancas Light Station
6 mi. N of San Simeon, (888) 804-8608, (805) 927-6811; www.piedrasblancas.org. Tours: Tu & Thur at 10am ((805) 927-7361), by donation; & 3rd Sat at 10 & 1, $15.

This light station was originally built in 1875. The Saturday tour features guides dressed in period costume.

W.R. Hearst Memorial Beach
On Hwy. 1, across from Hearst Castle, (805) 927-2010; www.parks.ca.gov. Daily dawn-dusk. Free.

In addition to providing a very nice swimming beach, this park has picnic tables, barbecue grills, and an 801-foot-long fishing pier (no license is required to fish from the pier).

The **Coastal Discovery Center at San Simeon Bay** *((805) 927-6575; www.coastal discoverycenter.org. F-Sun, 10-4 in fall/winter, 11-5 in spring/summer. Free.)* is operated by the Monterey Bay National Marine Sanctuary and exhibits live rainbow trout, a talking tide pool sculpture, and video voyages to the deep sea.

WHERE TO STAY

Best Western Cavalier Oceanfront Resort
9415 Hearst Dr., (800) 826-8168, (805) 927-4688; www.cavalierresort.com. 90 rooms; $$-$$$+. Some wood-burning fireplaces. 2 heated pools; hot tub; fitness room. Restaurant; room service.

This contemporary-style resort motel has over 900 feet of ocean frontage. Many rooms have expansive ocean views, and some also have private patios. Each night at sunset fire pits are lit on the beach, and chairs are provided for guests to relax in.

Motel Row

Motels line both sides of Highway 1.

CAMBRIA

A LITTLE BACKGROUND

In this town filled with rose-covered cottages and Victorian storefronts, many residents are Brits. This is reflected in street names like Cornwall, Canterbury, and Cambridge. Note that the preferred pronunciation of Cambria is with a short "a," as in "Camelot.")

VISITOR INFORMATION

Cambria Chamber of Commerce
767 Main St., (805) 927-3624; www.cambria chamber.org.

GETTING THERE

Located 5 miles south of San Simeon, and 35 miles north of San Luis Obispo via Highway 1.

WHAT TO DO

Nitt Witt Ridge
881 Hillcrest Dr., above Main St. (hard to find), in west village, (805) 927-2690; www.moonstonehotels.com/ Nittwittridge.htm. Tour $10, kids $5; reservations required.

This three-level home was built over 40 years by its reclusive owner a piece at a time, using stones and seashells as well as beer cans and car parts. It is held together by cement, flour, and baking soda. Though it is a State Historic Landmark, it is the polar opposite of Hearst Castle.

The Pewter Plough Playhouse
824 Main St., (805) 927-3877; www.pewterplough playhouse.org. Performances F-Sat at 7:30, some Sun at 3. $19, 60+ $16. Reservations advised.

Stage plays are presented year-round in this intimate theater. Free dramatic readings occur on select Wednesday evenings, and jazz is sometimes presented in the lounge on Sunday evening.

WHERE TO STAY

Bluebird Inn
1880 Main St., (800) 552-5434, (805) 927-4634; www.bluebirdmotel.com. 37 rooms; $-$$. Some gas fireplaces. No pets.

Situated by Santa Rosa Creek and within easy walking distance of the village, this attractive motel surrounds a landmark mansion dating from 1880. Many rooms are creek-side, with private balconies or patios, and one spacious two-bedroom family suite is available.

Cambria Pines Lodge
2905 Burton Dr., (800) 445-6868, (805) 927-4200; www.cambriapineslodge.com. 152 rooms; $-$$$$+. Some wood-burning & gas fireplaces. Heated pool & hot tub. Full breakfast; restaurant.

Located on a pine-covered hill above town, this spacious 26-acre facility has 5 acres of themed gardens, both rustic cabins and newer Craftsman-style bungalows, and a sand volleyball court. The lodge was originally built in 1927 by an eccentric European baroness who wanted to live in opulent style near the Hearst Castle. A nature trail leads down into the village.

Recently updated, the Main Lodge now houses a moderately priced restaurant and the woodsy, casual **Fireside Lounge**, where live entertainment is scheduled every night in front of its large stone fireplace.

Cambria Nursery and Florist, under the same ownership and located just across the street, offers an array of unusual plants and succulents, a demonstration "sea coast tolerant garden," and a koi pond.

The J. Patrick House
2990 Burton Dr., (800) 341-5258, (805) 927-3812; www.jpatrickhouse.com. 8 rooms; $$-$$$. Unsuitable for children under 13. No TVs; all wood-burning fireplaces or stove. Evening snacks; full breakfast. No pets.

Situated in the woods above the East Village, this authentic log cabin holds one guest room; seven more are in an adjacent Carriage

House. All beds are topped with duvets and handmade quilts. Evening wine and hors d'oeuvres and bedtime chocolate chip cookies and milk are included. An all-vegetarian breakfast is served in the sunroom.

The Pickford House Bed & Breakfast

2555 MacLeod Way, (888) 270-8470, (805) 927-8619; www.thepickfordhouse.com. 8 rooms; $$-$$$. Some gas fireplaces. Evening snacks; full breakfast. No pets.

Though built in 1983, this inn is far from modern in feeling. All rooms bear the names and personalities of silent film stars and are outfitted with fresh roses and clawfoot bathtubs. Notable among them is the Valentino Room, which is furnished with dark-wood antiques and has a great view. Evening hors d'oeuvres are served at a massive inlaid mahogany bar dating from 1860, and everyone gets a bedtime cocktail or sweet. Breakfast features the traditional Danish pancake fritters known as aebleskivers.

The Squibb House

4063 Burton Dr., (866) 927-9600, (805) 927-9600; www.squibbhouse.net. 5 rooms; $$. Afternoon tea; evening snack; continental breakfast. No pets.

Built in 1877, this converted Victorian country home is well situated in the heart of the village and surrounded by a lovely garden. Rooms are decorated with custom-built furniture and old-fashioned handmade quilts. Breakfast includes baked goods and homemade plum jam prepared with fruit grown on site.

The **Shop Next Door** *(Daily 10-9.)* purveys handmade furniture, ceramic and glass pieces, antiques, Amish items, and contemporary metalwork.

Motel Row

Numerous motels are located along scenic oceanfront Moonstone Beach Drive. Several are described below. This popular beach's bluff-top boardwalk is popular for strolling.

• The Blue Whale Inn

6736 Moonstone Beach Dr., (800) 753-9000, (805) 927-4647; www.bluewhaleinn.com. 7 rooms; $$$+. All gas fireplaces. Evening snack; full breakfast.

This luxurious inn boasts ocean-view mini-suites with canopy beds and private outdoor entrances. Guests have access to a communal sitting area with a panoramic ocean view,

and breakfast is served in an adjacent room with a similar view.

• FogCatcher Inn

6400 Moonstone Beach Dr., (800) 425-4121, (805) 927-1400; www.fogcatcherinn.com. 60 rooms; $$-$$$+. All mini-kitchens & gas fireplaces. Heated pool; hot tub. Continental breakfast.

This English Tudor-style inn has a big two-bedroom suite for families and another ocean-view suite for honeymooners. Many rooms have ocean views.

• White Water Inn

6790 Moonstone Beach Dr., (800) 995-1715, (805) 927-1066; www.whitewaterinn.com. 17 rooms; $$-$$$. All gas fireplaces. Continental breakfast. No pets.

This contemporary motel court has two mini-suites with a private patio and ocean-view hot tub, plus six rooms with oversize whirlpool bathtubs. Breakfast is delivered to the room.

WHERE TO EAT

Linn's Main Bin Restaurant

2277 Main St., (805) 927-0371; www.linnsfruitbin.com. B-L-D daily, SunBr; $. No reservations.

Known for delicious breakfasts and a large selection of desserts and pies (don't miss the famous olallieberry), this pleasant dining spot's varied menu also includes a delectable chicken pot pie, sandwiches and wraps, and even meatloaf. Everything is made from scratch.

• Linn's Easy as Pie Cafe *(4251 Bridge St., (805) 924-3050. L-D; $.)* offers a lighter menu.

• Linn's Gourmet Goods *(4241 Bridge St., (805) 924-1064.)* sells all of Linn's own products—including fresh and frozen pies and baked goods—plus gourmet foods and gifts; a mail-order catalogue is available.

• Linn's Fruit Bin Original Farmstore *(On Santa Rosa Creek Rd., 5 mi. E of town, (805) 927-8134. Daily 10-5.)* is famous for fruit pies—especially olallieberry—and also sells preserves, packaged specialty foods, and gifts.

Robin's Restaurant

4095 Burton Dr., (805) 927-5007; www.robinsrestaurant.com. L-D daily; $-$$. Reservations advised.

Operating within a converted house surrounded by a cottage garden, this pleasant spot uses homegrown herbs in full-flavored ethnic and vegetarian dishes. The salmon bisque is a must, as are tasty curries prepared to order. Salads, sandwiches, pastas, seafood, and tofu dishes are also on the menu. Housemade desserts include a bread pudding and hot fudge sundae. One very special table is in an alcove with arched stained-glass windows and a privacy curtain, and patio seating is available.

The Tea Cozy

4286 Bridge St., (805) 927-8765; www.teacozy.com. Tea W-Sun 10-5. No reservations.

In England it is customary to conclude a visit to a stately home with a stop at a local tearoom, and the English proprietors here are attempting to interest Americans in this tradition. Situated within a modest 1890s schoolteacher's house, this cozy tearoom offers light meals and pastries along with a nice cup of tea (or coffee). The extensive Royal Tea and smaller Cream Tea are served all day. Imported English foods and an appealing collection of antique china are available for purchase.

MORRO BAY

A LITTLE BACKGROUND

Named "El Morro" in 1542 by explorer Juan Rodriguez Cabrillo because it reminded him of a turbaned Moor, the huge volcanic rock here is visible from just about everywhere in town. The area is also referred to as the "Gibraltar of the Pacific." Morro Rock stands 576 feet high and is now a State Monument. Peregrine falcons—said to be the fastest moving animal in the world and an endangered species—nest at the top.

Because the area's wide variety of landscapes offer myriad nesting sites for some of California's most interesting birds, bird-watching is particularly good here.

Commercial fishing is this small, picturesque town's main industry. Albacore and abalone are the local specialties, and they frequently show up on restaurant menus.

VISITOR INFORMATION

Morro Bay Visitors Center & Chamber of Commerce

845 Embarcadero Rd., (800) 231-0592, (805) 772-4467; www.morrobay.org.

GETTING THERE

Located approximately 30 miles south of San Simeon.

ANNUAL EVENTS

Morro Bay Winter Bird Festival

January. (866) 464-5105, (805) 275-4143; www.morrobaybirdfestival.org. $25-$65, under 13 free.

A prime birding destination, Morro Bay is one of just a few remaining estuaries on the Pacific flyway. Audubon Christmas Bird Counts have passed the 200 species mark, and festival bird lists have totaled more than 220 species. Among the events for all levels of birders are tours, kayaking excursions, and workshops.

Morro Bay Harbor Festival

October. (800) 366-6043, (805) 772-1155; www.mbhf.com. $8, under 13 free; free parking. No pets.

General merriment includes a sand sculpture spectacular, a Hawaiian shirt contest, and ship tours, plus live entertainment and plenty of seafood and wine tasting. Proceeds benefit community nonprofit organizations.

WHAT TO DO

Coleman Beach Park

Embarcadero Rd./Coleman Dr., E of Morro Rock.

Children are sure to enjoy this idyllic playground in the sand.

Fishing

The pier is a prime spot for fishing. Chartered fishing boats are also available.

Giant Chess Board

Embarcadero Rd./Front St., in Centennial Park, (805) 772-6278; www.morro-bay.ca.us/recreation.html. M-F 8-5. Reservations required.

At the base of a 44-step stairway is one of the two largest chessboards in the U.S. (The other is in New York City's Central Park.) The redwood chess pieces stand 2- and 3-feet high and weigh from 18 to 40 pounds, making a game here physical as well as mental exercise. From noon to 5 p.m. each Saturday the Morro Bay Chess Club sponsors games on the giant 16- by 16-foot concrete board, and non-members are welcome to challenge.

Morro Bay Aquarium & Marine Rehabilitation
595 Embarcadero Rd., (805) 772-7647. Daily 9:30-5. $2, 5-11 $1.

This tiny non-profit aquarium is a draw for the gift shop located in front. However, the price is right, and over 300 live marine specimens are displayed. All are injured and distressed animals that can't be returned to the wild. Some preserved specimens are also exhibited, and very noisy seals beg to be fed.

Morro Bay State Park
On State Park Rd., at S end of town, (805) 772-2560; www.parks.ca.gov. Campsites available.

• Bird Sanctuary
This is the third largest bird sanctuary in the world. A trail through the marsh and hills allows the possibility of sighting more than 250 bird species.

• Heron and Cormorant Rookery
At Fairbank Point, off State Park Rd.

No one is allowed inside the rookery—one of the last where the Great Blue Heron is found—but herons can be viewed from an observation area.

• Museum of Natural History
At White Point, (805) 772-2694; www.ccnha.org/museum.html. Daily 10-5. $2, under 17 free.

Situated on a scenic perch over the bay, this small museum has large windows that provide excellent views of the estuary. A telescope permits up-close viewing of wildlife. In winter, guided walks visit the monarch butterflies that congregate at **Pismo State Beach**—home to the largest overwintering colony of monarchs in the United States.

The Shell Shop
590 Embarcadero Rd., (805) 772-8014; www.theshellshop.net. Daily 9:30-7, in winter 9:30-5:30.

The perfect souvenir stop, this shop has the largest selection of seashells on the Central Coast and offers them at bargain prices.

WHAT TO DO NEARBY

Avila Beach
20 mi. S of town off Hwy. 101.

This tiny, old-fashioned beach community is a great place for watching surfers and for swimming in usually mild surf. As one of the California Coast's two south-facing beaches, it is sheltered and has warmer water. A playground in the sand is popular with children.

Cayucos
6 mi. N of town on Hwy. 1, (800) 563-1200; www.cayucoschamber.com.

This quiet little beach town has a string of inexpensive motels. It also boasts both a fine beach with gentle surf and a 400-foot-long fishing pier where equipment rentals are available.

WHERE TO STAY

Blue Sail Inn
*851 Market Ave., (888) 337-0707, (805) 772-2766;
www.bluesailinn.com. 48 rooms; $-$$$. Some gas
fireplaces. Hot tub. No pets.*

This streamline moderne motel is centrally
located, allowing an easy walk to restaurants.
The hot tub area has a view of Morro Rock, as
do most of the rooms.

Embarcadero Inn
*456 Embarcadero Rd., (888) 223-5777, (805) 772-
2700; www.embarcaderoinn.com. 32 rooms; $$-$$$+.
Some gas fireplaces. 2 indoor hot tubs. Continental
breakfast. No pets.*

Situated in a quiet spot at the south end of
the busy Embarcadero strip, this attractive
modern motel has a weathered-wood exterior.
All rooms have bay views, and most have
balconies.

The Inn at Morro Bay
*60 State Park Rd., (800) 321-9566, (805) 772-5651;
www.innatmorrobay.com. 98 rooms; $-$$$+.
Some fireplaces. Heated pool; full-service spa.
2 restaurants; room service. No pets.*

Located at the southern end of town in
Morro Bay State Park, this small resort is sheltered by a strand of old eucalyptus and provides
a restful spot to spend the night. Choice rooms
have gorgeous views of the estuary, and some
have private decks and hot tubs. Complimentary mountain bikes are available to guests,
and an 18-hole public golf course is just across
the street. A heron rookery located in an adjacent grove of eucalyptus often treats guests to
the raucous ranting of its occupants.

The **Orchid** restaurant *(D daily, SunBr;
$$.)* offers diners a mesmerizing panoramic
view of the estuary and sand spit, and wildlife-
watching from here is very good. Depending on
the time of year, diners see herons carrying
nesting materials or sea otters basking on their
backs. Kayaks and sailboats come and go as
well.

Motel Row
Though there doesn't seem to be one
official motel row, the town has a plethora of
lodgings. Just drive around.

WHERE TO EAT

Abba's Pacific Cafe
*571 Embarcadero Rd., (805) 772-2965. L-D daily;
$-$$. Reservations advised.*

This very popular spot offers a great view
along with great food. At dinner, the perfect
starter is the house special scampi fra Diavala
(perfect prawns in a tasty red sauce suitable for
bread dunking). Entrees are listed on a chalk
board and sometimes include a salmon Lilliano
(poached, wrapped around spinach, and topped
with a light red sauce) and snapper Griglia
(grilled and topped with a light white-wine
sauce). All meals end with a complimentary
liqueur, but don't miss a dessert of marinated
fresh strawberries, fresh peach cobbler, or
housemade vanilla ice cream. Lunch is a less
expensive selection of salads, sandwiches, and
hamburgers.

Dorn's Original Breakers Cafe
*801 Market Ave., (805) 772-4415; www.dornscafe.com.
B-L-D daily; $-$$. Reservations advised.*

This casual restaurant features a great bay
view and is especially pleasant at breakfast.,
when the menu offers a choice of hearty breakfasts as well as novelty items such as chocolate-
chip pancakes with chocolate syrup. The extensive dinner menu features fresh local fish and
an award-winning Boston clam chowder.

The Great American Fish Company
*1185 Embarcadero Rd., (805) 772-4407;
www.greatamericanfishcompany.com. L-D daily; $$.
No reservations.*

Located a short, scenic stroll from the
center of town, this restaurant provides a
comfortable, casual atmosphere and good views
of the rock. The extensive menu includes
mesquite-grilled fresh fish as well as deep-fried
fresh local prawns and Monterey squid. A steak
and hamburger are also available.

Hofbrau der Albatross
*901 Embarcadero Rd., (805) 772-5166;
www.hofbraurestaurant.com. L-D daily; $.
No reservations.*

This casual spot features cafeteria-style
service. The fish & chips are superb, and a very
good French dip sandwich and hamburger are
also available.

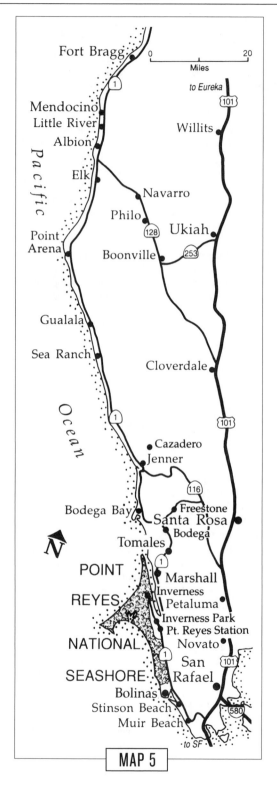

MAP 5

I NORTH

Point Arena Lighthouse

A LITTLE BACKGROUND

Highway 1 north from San Francisco allows an escape into a quieter, less-populated area. The two-lane road leading to Stinson Beach winds through fragrant eucalyptus groves, then rustic countryside that is rife with wildflowers in spring. It hugs ocean-side cliffs for long stretches, riding like a roller coaster and providing breathtaking views. The inland route known as Panoramic Highway is steep, with many blind curves. One of its nicknames is Kamikaze Alley, bestowed because of accidents that occur regularly in the fog. On sunny summer days, both roads become congested when everyone heads to the beach to soak up some of the famous California sunshine that is so elusive in the northern part of the state.

A word of warning: The rocky cliffs and beaches along the coast are scenic and beautiful, and people sometimes forget that they are also dangerous. Though it is tempting to stand at the edge, where the surf is pounding, people have been washed out to sea doing just that. Don't be one of them. Be careful. Stay on trails. Obey posted signs. And take special care not to let children run loose.

VISITOR INFORMATION

Redwood Empire Association
At PIER 39, in San Francisco. (800) 619-2125, (415) 292-5527; www.redwoodempire.com.

Information on the coastal counties north of San Francisco is available here.

West Marin Chamber of Commerce
P.O. Box 1045, Point Reyes Station 94956, (415) 663-9232; www.pointreyes.org.

143

MUIR BEACH

A LITTLE BACKGROUND

It was in this area (the exact spot is still in dispute) more than 400 years ago that Sir Francis Drake beached the *Golden Hinde*, formerly known as the *Pelican*, and claimed California for Queen Elizabeth I.

GETTING THERE

Located approximately 10 miles north of San Francisco. Take Highway 101 north to Highway 1.

WHAT TO DO

Green Gulch Farm
1601 Shoreline Hwy., just S of town, (415) 383-3134; www.sfzc.org.

Reached via a sharp downhill turnoff, this retreat is operated by the San Francisco Zen Center. Public meditation programs are scheduled daily, and a longer program on Sundays includes a dharma talk. Retreats, workshops, and children's programs are also scheduled. Visitors are welcome to take informal afternoon walks in the organic garden, which supplies the herbs and vegetables for Greens restaurant in San Francisco; plants are available for purchase from the nursery.

Overnight lodging is available in the peaceful, Japanese-style **Lindisfarne Guest House** *(12 rooms, 1 cottage; $-$$. No TVs; all shared baths. Vegetarian meals included.)*, which is constructed without nails. A separate cottage is available for families with children, and guests may take their meals at communal tables with the permanent residents.

Mount Tamalpais State Park
3801 Panoramic Hwy., in Mill Valley, (415) 388-2070; www.parks.ca.gov. Daily 7am-sunset; Summit visitor schedule varies; free guided hikes Sat-Sun at 9:30am. $6/vehicle.

From some locations, Mt. Tam—as the mountain is affectionately nicknamed—resembles the resting figure the local Native Americans called "The Sleeping Maiden," who they believed safeguarded the area. This 6,300-acre park offers 50 miles of hiking trails (and

connects to another 200-mile-long trail system), and the view from its 2,571-foot peak is spectacular (the Verna Dunshee Trail at East Peak is an easy ¾-mile loop near the summit). It is interesting to note that the mountain bike was first developed here for use on this park's hills, and it is said to be "the best spot on Earth to shoot a car commercial." Campsites are available.

Since 1904, the **Dipsea Race** has been run on the first Sunday of each June, when hordes of runners tromp the difficult 7.1-mile trail that leads from the center of Mill Valley to Stinson Beach.

The **Mountain Play** *(May-June. (415) 383-1100; www.mountainplay.org. $33-$37, 65+ & 4-17 $17-$26.)* has been presented in the natural outdoor amphitheater atop the mountain annually since 1913 and is always a well-known Broadway musical. In the old days people came on burros, by stagecoach, or on the now extinct Mount Tamalpais Scenic Railway, also known as the "Crookedest Railroad in the World" because along its 8¼-mile route it had 281 curves—including a five-fold switchback known as the Double Bow Knot. Now, many audience members ride the free shuttle buses up the mountain and, after the performance, hike 4 miles down, then board a shuttle bus for the rest of the journey back to the parking area.

Muir Beach

Off Pacific Way, (415) 388-2596;
www.nps.gov/goga/muir-beach.htm. Daily 9-sunset.
Free.

Reached by turning onto a leafy,
blackberry-lined lane located just south of the
Pelican Inn, this popular beach is unsafe for
swimming. However, it is excellent for sunbathing and people-watching, and picnic tables
and beach fire rings are available.

Muir Beach Overlook

www.nps.gov/goga/muir-beach.htm. Free.

Panoramic coastline views make this a
great picnic spot. In winter, it is a good perch
from which to watch the whale migration.

Muir Woods National Monument

Off Hwy. 1, on Panoramic Hwy., (415) 388-2595;
www.nps.gov/muwo. Daily 8-sunset. $5, under 16 free.

Located just off Highway 1 and enveloping
560 acres, this magnificent, fragrant old-growth
redwood forest has 2 miles of level walking
trails. The easy paved Main Trail has interpretive exhibits, and seven more-challenging,
unpaved trails lead away from the crowds.
Naturalist John Muir, for whom the forest was
named, said of it, "This is the best tree lover's
monument that could be found in all the
forests of the world." The largest tree here
measures 240 feet high by 16 feet wide. Because
nearly 1 million people come here each year,
only a visit early or late in the day (before
10 a.m. or after 4 p.m.) provides the hope of
some solitude; rainy days are also quiet. And no
matter what time of year it is, visitors are
advised to bring along warm wraps. The dense
forest lets in very little sunlight, and the weather
is usually damp, foggy, and cold. Children ages
6 through 12 can sign up for a free Junior
Ranger program (see also page 468) at the
Visitors Center when they arrive and receive a
sticker badge and workbook that helps them
explore nature. Picnicking is not permitted, but
a snack bar dispenses simple foods.

Slide Ranch

2025 Shoreline Hwy., (415) 381-6155;
www.slideranch.org. Program schedule varies;
grounds open daily sunrise-sunset. $20, under 2 free.
Reservations advised.

Perched dramatically on the ocean side of
Highway 1 near Muir Beach, this ranch offers
the city slicker a chance to get back to the land
. . . a chance to learn about a self-sustaining
rural lifestyle through exposure to frontier arts
. . . a chance to slow the pace. During Farm Day
programs, adults and children learn together
about things such as cheese making, compost-
ing, and papermaking. Though the program
varies according to the season and age of participants, a typical day begins with smiling staff
members greeting visitors in a fragrant grove of
cypress. A visit to the sheep and goat pen usually follows, giving everyone the chance to "pet a
four-legged sweater" and milk a goat. More
activities include collecting eggs, feeding chickens, carding and spinning sheep wool, making
bread and cheese, helping in the organic garden,
tide pooling, and hiking along one of the
coastal wild land trails.

WHERE TO STAY AND EAT

Mountain Home Inn

810 Panoramic Hwy., in Mill Valley, (415) 381-9000;
www.mtnhomeinn.com. 10 rooms; $$-$$$+.
Unsuitable for children under 14. No TVs; some wood-
burning fireplaces. Full breakfast; restaurant. No pets.

Built atop Mount Tamalpais in West Marin
in 1912 by a Swiss-German couple homesick for
the Alps, this inn was accessible then only by
train. It is a literal landmark in that it is on
maps as a trail head for the area, and also a literary landmark in that long ago Jack London
was a frequent overnight guest. Rebuilt in the
original footprint in 1985, the inn now features
multi-angled rooms, stained-glass windows,
and whole redwood tree trunks as interior support beams. A self-contained evening here
requires no driving. Guests have only to walk
upstairs from their room to enjoy a romantic
dinner, then walk back down the stairs to their
room for the night. They fall asleep to the delicious sounds of silence in the deep, dark nights
and awaken to squawking jays and chirping
chickadees. Some rooms have a deck with a
view overlooking treetops to Richardson Bay
and permit seeing the occasional hawk glide by,
and some have large oval tubs—water pressure
is satisfyingly vigorous—with a louver-covered
opening looking through the bedroom to the
view. On fair days, the full breakfast—maybe

Bolinas farm eggs with crispy bacon or a vegetable omelet and a cuppa Peet's—can be taken
on the expansive deck.

The inn's **restaurant** *(B Sat-Sun, L-D W-
Sun; $$. Reservations advised.)* is the oldest con-
tinuously operating restaurant in Marin County
and is open to non-guests. Three-course menu
options might include an appetizer of chilled
white corn and vine-ripened tomato soup; a
main course of grain-fed top sirloin with
German butterball potatoes, or a crisp confit of
Bolinas-raised rabbit leg with toasted faro; and
a chocolate ganache cake or blueberry tart for
dessert. A picnic lunch can be packed up for
guests by request.

Options to fill a day include:
• Hiking the popular, mostly shady and flat,
Matt Davis Trail, where yellow finches and
lizards abound. Going all the way to the **West
Point Inn** *((415) 388-9955; www.westpoint
inn.com. Tu-Sun 11-6, Nov-Apr to 5.)* takes
about 3 hours round-trip. Built in 1904 by the
railroad as a restaurant and stopover for passen-
gers, it still accepts hike-in overnight guests
today. The inn isn't open on Mondays, but
picnic tables and the spectacular panoramic
view may be enjoyed at any time.
• Mountain biking one of the mountain's trails
(Mt. Tam is credited as the "birthplace of
mountain biking"). Those in super shape might
consider the Railroad Grade Trail, which begins
across the road. It is almost 8 miles long, with a
7% grade and 2,000-foot gain.

The Pelican Inn
*10 Pacific Way, (866) 383-6005, (415) 383-6000;
www.pelicaninn.com. 7 rooms; $$$. Unsuitable for
young children. No TVs. Full breakfast; restaurant.
No pets.*

Sheltered by towering pines and alders,
this authentic reconstruction of an actual 16th-
century English Tudor inn was built in 1979.
The snug rooms are furnished with English
antiques, oriental carpets, and canopied beds,
and each has a private water closet.

The lunch menu in the **pub restaurant**
*(L-D daily; $-$$; reservations accepted. High tea
daily at 3:30; $14.95; by 48-hr. advance reserva-
tion.)* features housemade traditional English
pub fare such as bangers and mash, shepherd's
pie, and the ever-popular ploughman's plate.
Dinner brings on prime rib, beef Wellington,

and lamb chops, and complementary British
ales and beers are on tap. Diners can sit outside
on an enclosed patio or inside in a rustic can-
dle-lit dining room with several long communal
tables plus a few private tables for couples. On
cold, foggy days, a fireplace warms the interior.

STINSON BEACH

A LITTLE BACKGROUND

This town has no gas station. According to a
local resident, "It disappeared one night and
didn't come back." For more information, see
www.stinsonbeachonline.com.

WHAT TO DO

Audubon Canyon Ranch/
Bolinas Lagoon Preserve
*4900 Hwy. 1, 3.5 mi. N of town, (415) 868-9244;
www.egret.org. Sat-Sun 10-4; mid-March-mid-July. By
donation. No pets.*

Situated on picturesque Bolinas Lagoon
just north of town, this preserve is open only
during breeding season. Then, pairs of Great
Blue Herons (measuring 4 to 5 feet tall and
with a wingspan of nearly 6 feet), Snowy Egrets,
and Great Egrets nest noisily in the tall redwood
trees located in the ranch's Schwarz Grove.

Approximately 60 other bird species also make their home here, making this a bird-watcher's paradise. Nests contain an average of two to five eggs, which incubate for about 28 days. Once hatched, baby birds covered in fluffy down waddle about their nests while waiting for their parents to return from gathering a meal of fish and crustaceans in nearby Bolinas Lagoon. (Baby egrets fly at 7 weeks, herons at 9 weeks.) Several scenic trails of varying length and challenge, including a self-guided nature trail, lead to an overlook where telescopes are available and a ranch guide is on hand to interpret and assist. Visitors can rest on benches and observe these graceful birds as they court, establish a pecking order, build their nests, and begin rearing their young.

Exhibits in the Display Hall museum, a converted milking barn left from the days when the ranch was a dairy, give visitors detailed information about the birds as well as about the geology and natural history of the area. Nearby, a stream-side, sod-roofed Bird Hide is designed so people can see out, but birds can't see in. Its feeders attract a variety of unsuspecting birds, including many colorful hummingbirds. A picnic area, from which the nesting site is visible, provides a scenic spot to relax and enjoy a leisurely lunch in peaceful surroundings.

A **Mother's Day Barbecue** is held annually.

Stinson Beach

Off Hwy. 1, (415) 868-0942; www.nps.gov/muwo/stbe. Daily 9-sunset. Free.

This magnificent beach offers a small taste of the Southern California beach scene. Conditions often permit swimming here, though the water is cold and lifeguards are on duty usually only in summer. Since the weather here is often different from everywhere else in the Bay Area, it is wise to call and check conditions before setting out *((415) 868-1922)*. Beachcombing is excellent at the north end of the beach and beyond, especially during low tides. A word of caution: the waters off this stretch of coast known as the Red Triangle have suffered more shark attacks than anywhere else in the world.

WHERE TO STAY

Steep Ravine Cabins

On Hwy. 1, 1 mi. S of town, (800) 444-7275, (415) 388-2070; www.reserveamerica.com. 10 cabins; $. No TVs; all wood-burning stoves.

Perched on a rocky bluff overlooking the ocean and located within Mount Tamalpais State Park, each of these primitive cabins dating from the 1930s sleeps up to five people. Each has a picnic table and benches, a sleeping platform, and an outdoor barbecue. They do not have running water, electricity, or shower facilities. Primitive toilets, water faucets, and firewood are nearby. Guests must provide their own bedding, cooking equipment, and light source. Paths lead down to the beach, where seven primitive campsites are also available.

WHERE TO EAT

Stinson Beach Grill

3465 Hwy. 1, (415) 868-2002. L-D daily, Sat-SunBr; $-$$. Reservations advised.

This informal grill has an eclectic menu offering everything from hamburgers to osso bucco. In between are a Greek salad, an impeccably fresh salmon with tomato-basil sauce, and a spicy blackened snapper. A large selection of complementary beers from microbreweries are also available.

BOLINAS

A LITTLE BACKGROUND

So shy of visitors is this tiny ocean-side hamlet that maverick residents spirit away directional signs as soon as they are posted. All visitors are hereby warned that the reception in town can be chilly.

POINT REYES AREA

GETTING THERE

Located about 60 miles north of San Francisco. Take either Highway 1, or Sir Francis Drake Boulevard from Larkspur off Highway 101.

WHERE TO STAY

Reservations services

For information on the area's B&Bs call:

• Inns of Marin
(800) 887-2880, (415) 663-2000;
www.innsofmarin.com.

• Point Reyes Lodging
(800) 539-1872, (415) 663-1872; www.ptreyes.com.

OLEMA

WHAT TO DO

Point Reyes National Seashore

Park Headquarters on Bear Valley Rd., W of town,
(415) 464-5137; www.nps.gov/pore. Park: daily sun-
rise-sunset. Bear Valley Visitor Center: M-F 9-5, Sat-
Sun 8-5. Free.

Known for its beaches and hiking trails,
this 71,000-acre refuge has plenty of other
interesting things for visitors to do. Many activities cluster around the Park Headquarters. The
Bear Valley Visitor Center houses a working
seismograph and a variety of nature displays.
The **Morgan Horse Ranch**, where pack and trail
animals are trained, is adjacent. (The Morgan
was the first American horse breed.) A short
walk away, a Coast Miwok Indian village, **Kule
Loklo**, has been replicated using the same types
of tools and materials as the Native Americans
themselves originally used.

Trails beginning near the headquarters
include the .5-mile self-guided Woodpecker
Nature Trail; the .6-mile-long self-guided Earthquake Trail, which follows the San Andreas
fault and passes a spot where the Pacific plate
moved 16 feet north in about 45 seconds
during the 1906 earthquake; and the popular
4.1-mile Bear Valley Trail, which winds through
meadows, fern grottos, and forests before
ending at the ocean. The area has 147 miles of
hiking trails, most of which are open to horses.
Mountain bikes are permitted on some trails,
and walk-in backpacking campsites are available
by reservation for a fee *((415) 663-8054).*

Guided trail rides, buggy rides, hayrides,
and overnight pack trips are available at nearby
Five Brooks Stables *(80001 State Route #1,*
(415) 663-1570; www.fivebrooks.com.).

Away from the headquarters, in the
Inverness area, is the 1870 **Point Reyes
Lighthouse** *((415) 669-1534. Thur-M 10-4:30.*
Free.). Winds have been recorded blowing here
at 133 miles per hour—the highest rate in the
continental U.S. The bottom line is that it can
get mighty windy, cold, and wet at this scenic
spot. The lighthouse is reached by maneuvering
300 steps down the side of a steep, rocky cliff. It
is a popular spot in winter for viewing migrating gray whales. **Shuttle buses** *(Sat-Sun 9-5,*
weather permitting; Jan-April. $5, under 16 free.)
depart regularly then from the Drake's Beach
visitor center.

Drake's Beach offers easy beach access and
has a great little short-order cafe. The **Ken
Patrick Visitor Center** *((415) 669-1250. Sat-Sun
10-5.)* here has maritime history displays and a
250-gallon salt water aquarium.

A herd of approximately 450 elk is often
seen grazing in the **Tule Elk Reserve** on
Tomales Point. Found only in California and
once hunted almost to extinction, these elk are
descended from a group of 10 brought here in
1978. Late summer is rutting season, when the
males "bugle" to attract females. The Historic
Pierce Point Ranch is open for a self-guided
tour of its buildings, including a barn,
bunkhouse, and blacksmith shop. This area is

dotted with historic ranches that were once part of a Mexican land grant and that now are leased from the park. Cows are plentiful, and it is refreshing to see them out here in the wide-open green spaces instead of stuffed into a stinky dirt feedlot.

The Point Reyes National Seashore Association offers seminars and classes in natural history, environmental education, photography, and art. To request a free catalog, call (415) 663-1200.

Samuel P. Taylor State Park

On Sir Francis Drake Blvd., 5 mi. E of town, in Lagunitas, (415) 488-9897; www.parks.ca.gov. $6/vehicle.

This 2,700-acre park features redwood groves and open grassland. The most common animal in the park is the black-tailed deer, and silver salmon and steelhead trout are sometimes seen migrating up Papermill Creek to spawn. A 3-mile paved bike trail runs through the park, and a network of hiking trails and fire roads leads to the top of Mount Barnabe. Devil's Gulch is perfect for a picnic, and a nearly level trail beginning there follows the old Northwest Pacific Railroad right-of-way. The park is named after gold miner and lumber baron Samuel Penfield Taylor, who came to California from Boston in 1849.

WHERE TO STAY AND EAT

Olema Farm House Restaurant & Bar

10005 Hwy. 1/Sir Francis Drake Blvd., (415) 663-1264; www.olemafarmhouse.com. L-D daily, Sat-SunBr; $-$$. Reservations taken for D.

This building was the town's first and has been here for more than a century, since 1845. Stagecoaches stopped here on the way to San Francisco. Now it holds a full deli, a bar, and a casual restaurant that serves up barbecued oysters, steamed clams, and fish & chips as well as prime rib and lamb. A collection of more than 950 antique liquor bottles is displayed throughout.

Olema Inn & Restaurant

10000 Sir Francis Drake Blvd./Hwy. 1, (415) 663-9559; www.theolemainn.com. 6 rooms; $$. Continental breakfast; restaurant.

Built in 1876 as a saloon, this beautifully restored inn is furnished with lovely antiques. Upstairs, guest rooms are outfitted with luxurious new Scandinavian beds topped with fluffy comforters.

Downstairs, the stylish **restaurant** *(L W-Sun, D daily; $$-$$$. Reservations advised.)* has the pleasant feel of an updated farmhouse. It operates in a dining room with high ceilings, multi-paned windows, and a wood floor salvaged from a 19th-century tobacco warehouse in West Virginia. The kitchen uses organic ingredients and vegetables from their own garden whenever possible, and the meats are from the esteemed local Niman Ranch. Menu items have included soup prepared with local wild mushrooms, a pork chop with a crispy corn cake, and a poached pear upside-down cake.

POINT REYES STATION

A LITTLE BACKGROUND

This hamlet is an area crossroads. Small cafes and intriguing one-of-a-kind shops predominate.

WHERE TO STAY

Holly Tree Inn & Cottages

3 Silverhills Rd., (415) 663-1554; www.hollytreeinn.com. 4 rooms, 3 cabins; $$-$$$. No TVs; some kitchens & wood-burning fireplaces & stoves. Hot tub. Afternoon snack; full breakfast.

Tucked away in its very own valley just beneath the Inverness Ridge, this rustic B&B offers four attractive rooms. A spacious cottage is equipped with a wood-burning stove and a clawfoot tub. A stream runs picturesquely through the property, and there is an authentic bocce ball court. Another rustic cottage is perched on stilts over Tomales Bay and features a solarium with a hot tub.

Point Reyes Hostel

1390 Limantour Spit Rd., (415) 663-8811; www.pointreyeshostel.org. 44 beds; 1 private room.

Nestled in a secluded valley, this former ranch house offers both a kitchen and an outdoor barbecue for preparing meals. Two cozy common rooms with wood-burning stoves are also available to guests. See also page 468.

WHERE TO EAT

Picnic Pick-Ups

• Cowgirl Creamery
80 4th St., in Tomales Bay Foods, (415) 663-9335; www.cowgirlcreamery.com. W-Sun 10-6. Tours F at 11:30; reservations required.

Fresh organic cheeses can be viewed being made here—including cottage cheese and their signature Red Hawk cheese, whose orange rind comes from a native area bacteria—and can be purchased along with other local and imported cheeses.

The Station House Cafe
11180 Hwy. 1, (415) 663-1515; www.stationhousecafe.com. B-L-D daily; $-$$. Reservations advised Sat-Sun.

Menu choices in this casual, popular spot include sandwiches, light entrees, and specials that often feature fresh fish and local shellfish. Hamburgers are prepared with Niman Ranch ground beef from cattle raised without hormones or antibiotics and in chemical-free pastures. Old-fashioned desserts include berry pie, chocolate cake, bread pudding, butterscotch pudding, and local organic ice cream. Indeed, all stages of hunger can be satisfied here at the same table. Service is fast and unpretentious, and a spacious patio is delightful on sunny days. Live entertainment is scheduled Thursday and Sunday evenings.

INVERNESS

WHAT TO DO

Drakes Bay Oyster Company
17171 Sir Francis Drake Blvd., (415) 669-1149; www.drakesbayoyster.com. Daily 8-4.

A visit to this scenically situated enterprise allows viewing the various stages of the oyster-farming process. A Japanese technique of growing oysters on suspended ropes is used here, promising a sweeter meat. Oysters are available for purchase.

Tomales Bay State Park
Star Route, (415) 669-1140; www.parks.ca.gov. Daily 8-sunset. $6/vehicle.

Access to warm bay waters for swimming and wading is available at popular **Heart's Desire Beach.** The easy self-guided Indian Trail begins here and leads to a Miwok garden, where native plants used for food and medicine are labeled. It then climbs a slope that skirts the bay and ends at Indian Beach.

WHERE TO STAY

Cottages on the Beach
(415) 663-9696; www.ptreyescountryinn.com. 2 cabins; $$. No TVs. Continental breakfast.

Located down a steep driveway (directions are provided upon booking), Walt's Cabin fulfills inflated expectations. The couch, breakfast table, and white comforter-covered bed all face a spectacular view of Tomales Bay. Allow time for gazing out at an amazing array of passing birds that includes hawks and small white egrets. A well-stocked pantry and fridge permit indulging in an afternoon snack of hot chocolate and preparing dinner in-house. Breakfast supplies are there, too, and usually include locally produced Straus organic butter and Clover half-and-half. Outside, a bevy of quail hang out in the bushes, and a walk along the beach permits examining a wrecked fishing boat.

WHERE TO EAT

Priscilla's Pizza & Café
12781 Sir Francis Drake Blvd., (415) 669-1244; www.priscillas-cafe.com. L-D W-M.

Pretty much the only game in town, this small cafe serves up huge salads and delicious pizzas. The "Greek"—topped with feta, artichoke hearts, and red peppers—is a favorite. Sandwiches, pastas, tempting desserts, and organic coffees are also options.

MARSHALL

A LITTLE BACKGROUND

A former railroad stop, tiny Marshall (its population is 394) was the site of the first wireless communications system on the West Coast. Also once a dairy center, it is now home to the first organic dairy ranch in the West. It is also home to more than half of California's commercial oyster growers and additionally is known for its clams and mussels.

WHERE TO EAT

Hog Island Oyster Company
20215 Hwy 1, (415) 663-9218; www.hogislandoysters.com. Daily 9-5. Reservations required for picnic; Sat-Sun $5/person.

The clean water here permits growing top-notch oysters and clams. Live farm-raised oysters and clams are for sale to take home or to eat on site. Bring a picnic, purchase some oysters, and rent a package that includes shucking knives, a shucking glove, and a waterfront picnic table.

Tony's Seafood
18863 Hwy. 1, (415) 663-1107. L-D F-Sun; $. No reservations. No cards.

Relaxing views of Tomales Bay are enjoyed here from inside the wood-paneled dining room perched atop stilts over the bay. Many restaurants in the area offer oyster items made with the fresh local supply. The house specialty is oysters barbecued in the shell, but deep-fried oysters, fresh local fish, and a hamburger are also available. Beer, which pairs especially well with oysters, is available from the bar.

BODEGA BAY

A LITTLE BACKGROUND

Claimed for England in 1579 by Sir Francis Drake and later discovered by Don Juan del la Bodega of Spain, this area was settled in the early 1800s when Russian explorers arrived to trap sea otters. It is the second largest salmon port on the Pacific coast and the busiest commercial fishing port between San Francisco and Eureka, but it is probably best known as the location for the 1962 Alfred Hitchcock film *The Birds*. Now a private residence, the old Potter School featured in the movie still stands in the tiny inland town of Bodega, as does **St. Theresa's Church**, a picturesque building dating from 1859 that is Sonoma County's oldest continuously active Catholic church and a state historical landmark.

VISITOR INFORMATION

Bodega Bay Area Chamber of Commerce
575 Hwy. 1, (707) 875-3866; www.bodegabay.com.

GETTING THERE

Located approximately 75 miles north of San Francisco via Highway 1, or via Highway 101 to Highway 116 west to Highway 12 west.

ANNUAL EVENTS

Fisherman's Festival
April. (707) 875-3866; www.bbfishfest.com. $8, seniors $4, under 13 free.

Held each year at the beginning of the commercial salmon season, this festival's highlights are a traditional parade of colorfully decorated commercial fishing boats and a Blessing of the Fleet, but bathtub races, stunt kite demonstrations, and a juried art show are also part of the fun. All proceeds benefit local non-profit organizations.

WHAT TO DO

Bodega Marine Laboratory
2099 Westside Rd., (707) 875-2211; www.bml.uc davis.edu. F 2-4. By donation, adults $5, students $2.

Sitting on a 365-acre marine reserve near Bodega Head, this laboratory complex has a variety of aquariums, a lobster nursery where the babies are just 3 inches long, and a touch tank where a variety of tide pool dwellers may be handled. Tours led by graduate students begin every 15 minutes.

Chanslor Guest Ranch & Stables
2660 Hwy. 1; www.chanslorranch.com. (707) 875-3333. Daily 9-5. Horses $30+/hr., must be age 8+; ponies $10/10 min., for kids under 8.

Guided trail rides through a wetlands preserve and beach rides across sand dunes are offered at this 378-acre working guest ranch.

Lodging *((707) 875-2721. 6 rooms; $$-$$$.)* is available.

Osmosis Day Spa Sanctuary

209 Bohemian Hwy., in Freestone, 5 mi. E of town, (707) 823-8231; www.osmosis.com. Daily 9-9. Enzyme bath with blanket wrap $75-$80, with massage $155-$170. Unsuitable for children. Reservations required.

Long popular in Japan, an enzyme bath is similar to a mud bath—only lighter, more fragrant, and *dry*. It improves circulation, breaks down body toxins, and relieves stress, and this is the only place in the U.S. where it is available. The experience begins in a tranquil tea garden with a soothing cup of enzyme tea to aid digestion. Then bathers, either nude or in a swimsuit, submerge for 20 minutes in a hot mixture of Hinoki cedar fiber, rice bran, and more than 600 active plant enzymes that naturally generate heat. A blanket wrap, 75-minute massage, or aromatherapy facial follows. Private massages are given in serene outdoor Japanese pagodas nestled in a wooded area near Salmon Creek, and a Zen-inspired meditation garden is available to relax in following a treatment.

Sonoma Coast State Park

(707) 875-3483; www.parks.ca.gov. Daily 8-sunset. $6/vehicle.

Actually a series of beaches separated by rocky bluffs, this state park extends for 18 miles from Bodega Head to Meyers Gulch, which is just south of Fort Ross State Historic Park. It is accessible from more than a dozen points along Highway 1, and campsites are available.

• Goat Rock Beach

Off Hwy. 1, 4 mi. S of Jenner, (707) 865-2391. No pets.

Located where the Russian River flows into the ocean, this beach is a hangout for harbor seals. March is the beginning of pupping season, when Seal Watch volunteers are on hand to interpret and answer questions for visitors. Seeing the baby seals, many people are tempted to get closer, but visitors should stay at least 50 yards away. When pups are born, they depend on the mother's milk for the first 48 hours. During that critical period, the mother will often go out to feed and leave newborn pups by themselves. If a mother finds humans around her pup when she returns, she will abandon it. Seals remain in this area in large numbers through July. Then the population thins out until the following March. Driftwood collecting is encouraged, because pile-ups of wood debris are a potential fire hazard to the town. Note that swimming in the ocean is hazardous due to sleeper waves and riptides.

WHERE TO STAY

Bodega Bay Lodge & Spa

103 Coast Hwy. 1, (888) 875-3525, (707) 875-3525; www.bodegabaylodge.com. 48 rooms; $$$-$$$+. Most wood-burning fireplaces. Heated pool; hot tub; sauna; fitness room; full-service spa. Afternoon wine; restaurant. No pets.

Situated at the southern end of town, overlooking the scenic wetlands marsh and sand dunes of **Doran Regional Park** (*(707) 875-3540; www.sonoma-county.org/parks/pk_doran.htm. $5/vehicle. Campsites available.*) and the ocean beyond, this rustically attractive property features contemporary rooms with stunning views.

An exceptional whirlpool hot tub is sheltered from the elements by glass walls, but its ceiling is open to the possibility of a light mist or rain providing a cooling touch. An 18-hole golf course adjoins.

The **Duck Club** (*B&D daily; $$. Reservations advised.*) serves regional coastal cuisine made with fresh local ingredients, including Tomales Bay oysters, Petaluma escargot, and rack of Sonoma lamb. Breakfast is excellent here, and the ocean view is often at its best then. Delectable box lunches are also available for guests.

The Inn at the Tides

800 Hwy. 1, (800) 541-7788, (707) 875-2751; www.innatthetides.com. 86 rooms; $$-$$$. Some wood-burning fireplaces. Heated indoor-outdoor pool; hot tub; sauna; fitness room. Continental breakfast; 2 restaurants; limited room service. No pets.

This comfortable inn provides attractive contemporary rooms with bay views. At a monthly Dinner with the Winemaker, a gut-busting five-course meal is paired with wines from a guest winery.

WHERE TO EAT

The Tides Wharf & Restaurant

835 Hwy. 1, (707) 875-3652; www.innatthetides.com. B-L-D daily; $-$$. No reservations.

This busy spot offers a well-priced breakfast until 11 a.m. Lunch and dinner menus are a pricier selection of seafood entrees. A Dungeness crab cocktail, though sometimes made with frozen crab, is always delicious. Complete dinners come with a starter of either potato-rich New England clam chowder, seafood chowder, or a green salad with shrimp garnish, plus a vegetable, starch, and sourdough bread. The tasty tartar sauce is housemade, and several vegetarian items, fried chicken, and steak are options. In addition to fish & chips, the children's menu offers a hamburger, hot dog, and grilled cheese sandwich. (One kid was overheard here saying, "It's a really good hamburger for a *nice* restaurant.") Because most tables afford sweeping views of Bodega Bay, try to dine before sunset.

An inexpensive **snack bar** is also open for lunch.

JENNER

WHAT TO DO

Fort Ross State Historic Park

19005 Hwy. 1, 11 mi. N of town, (707) 847-3286; www.parks.ca.gov. Daily 10-4:30. $6/vehicle.

Built by Russian and Alaskan hunters in 1812 as a trading outpost, this authentically restored historic fort compound consists of two blockhouses equipped with cannons, a small Russian Orthodox chapel, a manacor's house, and a barracks. An architecturally striking Visitors Center and picnic tables are also available. Outside the gates, a picturesque bluff at the edge of the ocean has a path leading down to the beach.

Held annually on the last Saturday in July, **Living History Day** allows visitors to step back in time to the 1800s. Costumed staff and volunteers perform musket drills and fire cannons, craftspeople demonstrate their skills, and a blacksmith pounds at his forge.

Kruse Rhododendron State Reserve

On Kruse Ranch Rd. (road to Plantation), 22 mi. N of town, at marker 42.7, (707) 847-3221; www.parks.ca.gov. Daily sunrise-sunset. Free.

Best known for its spring floral display in April and May, depending on the weather, this 317-acre park has 5 miles of hiking trails that lead visitors over picturesque bridges and through fern-filled canyons. An easy short trail begins just above the parking area located about ¼-mile down a gravel road.

Salt Point State Park

25050 Hwy. 1, 18 mi. N of town, (707) 847-3221; www.parks.ca.gov. Daily sunrise-sunset. Visitor Center: Sat-Sun 10-3, Apr-Oct. $6/vehicle.

A popular spot with skin divers because of its underwater park, this spot is also choice for a walk along the beach. Stump Cove has a short, easy trail down to its scenic beach. Campsites are available.

WHERE TO STAY

Fort Ross Lodge

20705 Hwy. 1, 12 mi. N of town, (800) 968-4537, (707) 847-3333; www.fortrosslodge.com. 23 units; $$-$$$. Most wood-burning fireplaces. Hot tub; sauna. No pets.

This collection of comfortable rustic-modern cabins is on a large, open, grassy bluff on the ocean side of the highway. Some units have ocean views; all have a small refrigerator, a coffee maker, a microwave oven, and a barbecue on a private patio. A beach access trail is available to guests.

Jenner Inn & Cottages

10400 Hwy. 1, (800) 732-2377, (707) 865-2377; www.jennerinn.com. 23 units; $$-$$$+. No TVs; some kitchens; some wood-burning fireplaces & stoves. Afternoon snack; continental breakfast; restaurant.

Tucked into a curve in the highway at the point where the Russian River runs into the Pacific Ocean, this inn offers a choice of lodge rooms, cottages, and private homes. Three rooms in the River House have unobstructed views of the estuary and share a hot tub. A cozy communal lounge has an antique wood-burning stove and a library of books and games.

Salt Point Lodge

23255 Hwy. 1, 17 mi. N of town, (800) 956-3437, (707) 847-3234; www.saltpointlodgebarandgrill.com. 16 rooms; $-$$. Some wood-burning stoves. Hot tub. Restaurant (seasonal). No pets.

Located across the street from the Pacific Ocean, this motel's large expanse of lawn is dotted with a swing set and a giant sculpted slide designed and built by local artist Bruce Johnson. Family rooms have a queen bed and two twin bunk beds, and two rooms for couples have an ocean view and a private deck and hot tub.

Timber Cove Inn

21780 Hwy. 1, 14 mi. N of town, (800) 987-8319, (707) 847-3231; www.timbercoveinn.com. 47 rooms; $-$$$+. Unsuitable for children. No TVs; some fireplaces. Restaurant. No pets.

Perched on a rocky seaside cliff, this inn offers many rooms with magnificent ocean views and some with sunken tubs and private hot tubs. A tall Bufano sculpture juts above the lodge, acting as a landmark, and the lobby, bar, and restaurant feature a dramatic Japanese-modern style architecture and spectacular ocean views.

THE SEA RANCH

WHERE TO STAY

House rentals

Rams Head Realty & Rentals, 1000 Annapolis Rd., (800) 785-3455, (707) 785-2427; www.ramshead.com. 100+ units; $$-$$$+. All kitchens; some fireplaces. Some hot tubs.

Stunningly beautiful wind-swept coastal scenery is the backdrop for the vacation homes in this development. A spectacular example is the oceanfront Monette House, which has three bedrooms and a very special hot tub in an enclosed room with sliding glass doors opening to the ocean. Rustic hike-in cabins are also available. Guests have access to three recreation centers with swimming pools, a children's playground, and hiking and jogging trails. An 18-hole golf course, designed in the Scottish manner by Robert Muir Graves, is available on site at extra charge.

Sea Ranch Lodge

60 Sea Walk Dr., (800) SEARANCH, (707) 785-2371; www.searanchlodge.com. 20 rooms; $$-$$$+. Some TVs; some wood-burning fireplaces & stoves. Full breakfast; restaurant.

In this rustic contemporary facility, each room has an ocean view. Two rooms have private courtyards with hot tubs.

GUALALA

A LITTLE BACKGROUND

Named for an Indian word that is pronounced "wha-LA-la" and means "water coming down place," this town is located in a banana belt of regularly warm weather. The area's many celebrity property owners are rumored to include singer Kris Kristofferson and comedian Robin Williams.

VISITOR INFORMATION

Redwood Coast Chamber of Commerce

P.O. Box 199, Gualala 95445, (800) 778-LALA, (707) 884-1080; www.redwoodcoastchamber.com.

WHERE TO STAY

Mar Vista Cottages

*35101 Hwy. 1, 5 mi. N of town, (877) 855-3522,
(707) 884-3522; www.marvistamendocino.com.
12 cottages; $$-$$$. No TVs; all kitchens; some
wood-burning fireplaces & stoves. Hot tub.*

Most of these no-frills, one and two-bed-room cottages dating from the '30s have ocean views; all are just a short walk from a sandy beach with a gentle surf. Recent spiffing has enlarged windows for better views and topped beds with down comforters. A Japanese-style soaking tub that makes use of water from an adjacent creek is ensconced in a meadow. Guests can pick and use produce from a large organic vegetable garden and fruit orchard and also collect fresh eggs from a flock of hens.

Serenisea

*36100 Hwy. 1, 3 mi. N of town, (800) 331-3836,
(707) 884-3836; www.serenisea.com. 23 units; $-$$$.
Some TVs; all kitchens; some wood-burning fireplaces
& stoves.*

Most of these housekeeping cabins and vacation homes are spread over a scenic ocean bluff with a trail leading down to the beach. Some have private hot tubs, and one has a private sauna.

St. Orres

*36601 Hwy. 1, 2 mi. N of town, (707) 884-3303;
www.saintorres.com. 8 rooms, 13 cottages; $$-$$$+.
No TVs; some wood-burning fireplaces; some shared
baths. Hot tub; sauna. Full breakfast; restaurant.*

This inn has a weathered wood exterior and a Russian style of architecture featuring onion-domed turrets. Detached cabins are set in a redwood forest.

A striking **dining room** *((707) 884-3335.
D daily; $$$. Reservations advised.)* features a 3-story-high ceiling and large windows with ocean views. Menu items often make use of locally foraged ingredients and wild game such as boar and venison, and a fixed-price, three-course dinner is an option.

Whale Watch Inn

*35100 Hwy. 1, 5 mi. N of town, (800) WHALE-42,
(707) 884-3667; www.whalewatchinn.com. 18 rooms;
$$-$$$. No TVs; some kitchens; all wood-burning*
*fireplaces. Sauna. Full breakfast; limited room service.
No pets.*

Perched on an ocean-side cliff, this dramatic contemporary-style inn offers plenty of peace and quiet. Rooms are spread among five buildings; all have private decks and ocean views, and eight have two-person whirlpool bathtubs. The Bath Suite features a spiral staircase leading to a whirlpool bathtub for two that is positioned under a skylight and features an ocean view. The Crystal Sea offers a mesmerizing view of an ocean cove—from the couch, the bed, and another of those whirlpool tubs for two. In the morning, a delicious breakfast is brought to the room in a willow basket. Guests can relax in the communal Whale Watch Room equipped with a cozy circular fireplace, panoramic view of the ocean, and telescope for whale-watching. Guests also have access to a half-mile stretch of private beach.

POINT ARENA

WHAT TO DO

Point Arena Lighthouse

*45500 Lighthouse Rd., 2 mi. off Hwy. 1, (877) 725-4448, (707) 882-2777; www.pointarenalighthouse.com.
Daily 10-3:30 Oct-Mar; 10-4:30 Apr-Sept. $5,
under 12 $1.*

Originally built in 1870, this lighthouse was destroyed in the '06 quake and then rebuilt. It was automated in 1976. A museum in the former foghorn house displays historical photos and features a whale-watching room. Then it's a 145-step climb (equivalent to 6 stories) up the 115-foot-tall light for a guided tour of the tower.

Bargain three-bedroom, two-bath light-keeper's **homes** *(4 units; $-$$. All kitchens & wood-burning stoves.)* are located adjacent and can be rented for the night.

MANCHESTER

A LITTLE BACKGROUND

This picturesque area, with the ocean to its west and redwood and Douglas fir forests to its east, is in the heart of Mendocino County's dairy country. In winter, the rare whistling tundra swan flies in from Siberia.

GETTING THERE

Located 5 miles north of Point Arena and 30 miles south of Mendocino.

WHAT TO DO

Manchester State Park
(707) 882-2463; www.parks.ca.gov. Free.
Located where the San Andreas Fault meets the sea, this 760-acre park is the closest spot in North America to Hawaii. Campsites are available.

WHERE TO STAY

KOA Kampground
(800) KOA-4188, (707) 882-2375;
www.manchesterbeachkoa.com.
Situated within a thick grove of pine and cypress, this campground has Kamping Kottages and boasts a heated pool, a hot tub, a game room, a large dog park, and beach access. For more description, see page 467.

ELK

A LITTLE BACKGROUND

Measuring less than a mile from south to north, this tiny town consists of a general store, a garage (no gasoline), two restaurants, and five small inns. Much of the town is perched precariously on bluffs overlooking the Pacific. Once a logging town, it now is home to a clutch of B&Bs with access to its secluded rocky beaches.

GETTING THERE

Located 14 miles south of Mendocino.

WHERE TO STAY

Harbor House Inn
5600 S. Hwy. 1, (800) 720-7474, (707) 877-3203;
www.theharborhouseinn.com. 6 rooms, 4 cabins;
$$$+. Unsuitable for children under 16. No TVs; all
gas fireplaces. Dinner & full breakfast included.
No pets.

This Craftsman-style building was constructed entirely of redwood in 1916 as a lodge for lumber company executives. Throughout, traditional furnishings are mixed with antiques and accented by modern luxuries. A path leads to a private beach where guests can sun, explore tide pools, and gather driftwood, and Adirondack chairs dotting the gardens invite lounging. Meals are served in a beautifully appointed dining room with a spectacular ocean view, where it is a delight watching the sky fade to black. A sample four-course dinner menu might include pasta with Italian sausage and spinach, arugula salad with marinated fresh beets, a tender osso bucco alla Milanese, and a strawberry tart. Breakfast entree choices might include eggs and apple sausage, French toast with white chocolate garni, and oatmeal with dried cranberries and toasted hazelnuts and coconut. A few tables in the restaurant are available to non-guests by reservation.

MENDOCINO

A LITTLE BACKGROUND

Mendocino provides a rejuvenating, quiet escape from the hectic pace of city life. A designated historic district since 1971, this remote village features a pastel Cape Cod-style of architecture and exudes the feeling that it

belongs to a time past. In the early 1800s, it was a center for redwood mills and the main shipping port for sending lumber to San Francisco. In the late 19th century, it was known as "The Town of the Water Towers." Today, some of these picturesque wooden towers have been converted into lodgings, and the town is better known for its unique shops and art galleries. Visitors can slow down their systems by leaving their cars parked for the duration of a visit. Anywhere in town is reached easily via a short walk.

The nightlife here is of the early-to-bed, early-to-rise variety. Consider this itinerary: dinner out, a stroll through town, a nightcap at the Mendocino Hotel, and then off to bed. Be advised that Mendocino's volunteer fire department alarm sometimes goes off in the middle of the night. Resembling the scream of an air-raid siren, it can be quite startling, even when a person is aware of what it is. Interestingly, sounding the alarm has become a tradition, because nowadays all the firefighters have beepers.

Make lodging reservations as far in advance as possible; in-town lodging is limited and popular.

VISITOR INFORMATION

Mendocino Coast Chamber of Commerce and Visitor Center
332 N. Main St, in Fort Bragg, (800) 726-2780, (707) 961-6300; www.mendocinocoast.com.

Mendocino County Promotional Alliance
(800) 877-6864, (707) 462-7414; www.goMendo.com.

GETTING THERE

Located approximately 150 miles north of San Francisco. Take Highway 101 to Highway 1, or Highway 101 to Highway 128 to Highway 1.

ANNUAL EVENTS

Mendocino Coast Whale Festival
March. In Mendocino & Fort Bragg; (800) 726-2780; www.mendowhale.com.

In Mendocino, the fun includes wine tasting, seafood chowder tasting, and a classic rock concert. In Fort Bragg, it takes the form of a microbrewery beer tasting and a classic car show, and whale-watching cruises are available.

Mendocino Music Festival
July. (707) 937-2044; www.mendocinomusic.com. $16-$48+; under 18 $15.

A variety of music styles—including orchestra, chamber music, opera, and jazz—are presented in an ocean-side tent in Mendocino Headlands State Park.

WHAT TO DO

Beachcombing
Follow down to the beach the little path behind the landmark **Mendocino Presbyterian Church** on Main Street. (Built in 1868 from local redwood, this American Gothic church is considered a masterpiece and is California's oldest continuously-used Presbyterian church.) Make a kelp horn by cutting the bulb off the end of a long, thin piece of fresh bull kelp. Rinse out the tube in the ocean so that it is hollow. Then wrap it over one shoulder and blow through the small end. The longer the tube, the greater the resonance.

Catch A Canoe & Bicycles Too
On Comptche-Ukiah Rd., (800) 331-8884, (707) 937-0273; www.stanfordinn.com. Daily 9:30-5:30. $12+/hr., 2-hr. min.

Drifting down calm Big River affords the opportunity to picnic in the wilderness, go for a dip in a secluded swimming hole, and observe a variety of wildlife. Canoe rentals include paddles and life jackets. Bicycle rentals are also available.

Ford House Museum and Visitor Center
735 Main St., (707) 937-5397. Daily 11-4. $2 donation, $5/family.

Inside this historic 1854 home, an interpretive center focuses on the cultural and natural history of the area. A popular exhibit is a scale model of Mendocino as it was in 1890. During whale-watching season, visitors can view a related short orientation film and get information on interpretive programs at nearby **Mendocino Headlands State Park**. (From December through April, whales migrate close to shore and, from the headlands, can sometimes easily be seen "breaching," or jumping out of the water.) Picnic tables in the backyard offer a spectacular ocean view.

Kelley House Historical Museum
45007 Albion St., (707) 937-5791;
www.mendocinohistory.org. F-M 1-4; Thur-Tu in
summer. $2.

This house was built by William H. Kelley (Daisy MacCallum's father) in 1861. Unfortunately, the gigantic cypress tree that grew in the front yard was knocked down by a storm, but the gardens and pond remain. The restored first floor displays a collection of photos from the 1800s as well as changing exhibits of local artifacts and private collections.

Mendocino Art Center
45200 Little Lake St., (800) 653-3328,
(707) 937-5818; www.mendocinoartcenter.org.
Daily 10-5. Free.

Four galleries display art here, and fine arts workshops are scheduled year-round. Cookies and coffee are sometimes available in the lobby, and an inviting garden and tiled courtyard are the perfect place to enjoy them.

The **Mendocino Theatre Company** *((707) 937-4477; www.mendocinotheatre.org. $10-$25, under 16 half-price.)* stages productions in the center's theater.

Russian Gulch State Park
On Hwy. 1, 2 mi. N of town, (707) 937-5804;
www.parks.ca.gov. Daily dawn-dusk. $6/vehicle.

A protected beach, a 36-foot-high water-fall, and a blowhole known as the Devil's Punch Bowl are among this rustic park's features. Picnic tables overlook an ocean cove, and campsites are available.

Shopping
A plethora of unique boutiques makes shopping in this town a pleasure. The following rectangular route hits most of the best shops. Start on Main Street at the **Golden Goose** (luxurious housewares) near the Mendocino Hotel, then continue west to **Ocean Quilts** and on down to the tiny, utterly charming shoppe known as **Mendocino Jams and Preserves**. Make a jog north/right over to Albion Street and turn east/right and continue on to **Sticks** (antique binoculars and home accessories). At Lansing Street, make a jog north/left to **Sallie Mac** (all things French).

Van Damme State Park
8125 Hwy. 1, in Little River, 2 mi. S of town,
(707) 937-5804; www.parks.ca.gov. Daily dawn-dusk.
Visitor Center: Daily 10-4. $6/vehicle.

Among the interesting features in this 1,831-acre park is a canyon wall covered with ferns and a ⅓-mile Bog Trail leading to a large area of skunk cabbage. Picnic facilities and campsites are available.

An unusual **Pygmy Forest,** where stunted trees grow in leached soil, is nearby. It has a "short" boardwalk trail, and a brochure describing the various types of trees is available at the trailhead. To reach the forest, follow Little River Airport Road approximately 3 miles inland.

WHERE TO STAY IN TOWN

Blair House Inn
45110 Little Lake St., (800) 699-9296,
(707) 937-1800; www.blairhouse.com. 4 rooms,
1 cottage; $$-$$$. Unsuitable for children under 6.
Continental breakfast.

Famous as the exterior for Jessica Fletcher's house in the TV series *Murder, She Wrote*, this delightful 1888 Victorian is constructed of now absurdly expensive virgin clearheart redwood. All the rooms are decorated with antiques and hand-crafted quilts, and the Angela Suite has a Victorian pivoting dip sink and a clawfoot tub. The exterior of the house looks much as it did when originally built and is surrounded by a picket fence and a cottage garden.

Hill House Inn

10701 Palette Dr., (800) 422-0554, (707) 937-0554; www.hillhouseinn.com. 44 rooms; $$-$$$. Some wood-burning fireplaces. Restaurant; room service.

Located on a 2-acre knoll above the village, this attractive lodging dates only from 1978. It was the setting for many of the early episodes of the TV series *Murder, She Wrote*, and the Bette Davis Suite is where the namesake star lodged for 6 weeks while filming her final movie. Because of this Hollywood connection, it attracts many stars as patrons. Rooms are spacious and appointed with brass beds and lace curtains.

John Dougherty House

571 Ukiah St., (800) 486-2104, (707) 937-5266; www.jdhouse.com. 8 units; $$-$$$. Unsuitable for children under 12. Some wood-burning stoves. Full breakfast. No pets.

Situated on a quiet back street, this salt box-style house, built in 1867, is one of the oldest in town. An adjacent water tower now serves as a charming two-room suite with an 18-foot-high beamed ceiling and fireplace, and two cottages are situated in an English garden. Most of the cozy rooms have great ocean views.

Joshua Grindle Inn

44800 Little Lake Rd., (800) GRINDLE, (707) 937-4143; www.joshgrin.com. 10 rooms; $$$-$$$+. Unsuitable for children. Some TVs; some wood-burning fireplaces & stoves. Afternoon snack; full breakfast.

Situated on a 2-acre knoll at the edge of town, this Victorian farmhouse was built in 1879 by the town banker. It has a New England country atmosphere, with Early American antiques furnishing each room. Guest rooms are in the main house, a cottage, a water tower, a nearby historic home, and two rental houses.

MacCallum House Inn & Restaurant

45020 Albion St., (800) 609-0492, (707) 937-0289; www.maccallumhouse.com. 19 rooms; $$-$$$+. 1 kitchen; some wood-burning fireplaces & stoves. Hot tub. Full breakfast; restaurant.

Built in 1882 by William H. Kelley for his newlywed daughter, Daisy MacCallum, this converted Victorian home was one of the first B&Bs in the area. The attractively decorated rooms are furnished with antiques, many of

which belonged to the original owner. A water tower suite is fitted with a bed on the first floor, a bathroom with an ocean view on the second, and another bed with an ocean view on the third. (The water tower has a working redwood tank on the very top, and the original 50-foot-deep hand-dug well below still produces water.) Accommodations are also available in newer cottages adjacent to the house. Some rooms have private hot tubs, and bicycles are available to rent. Non-guests can purchase a gourmet organic breakfast, which is served in the restaurant or, in good weather, outdoors.

The **restaurant** *(D daily; $$$. Closed Jan-mid-Feb. Reservations advised.)* serves elegant seafood and game dinners in the house's magnificent dining rooms. On cold nights, guests are warmed by crackling fires in two fireplaces built of smooth river stone. Light dinners and snacks are available across the hall in the cozy **Grey Whale Bar**, also operated by the restaurant. Drinks include a classic 19th-century cocktail menu and fresh organic fruit margaritas and daiquiris.

Mendocino Hotel & Garden Suites

45080 Main St., (800) 548-0513, (707) 937-0511; www.mendocinohotel.com. 51 rooms; $-$$$. Some TVs & fireplaces; some shared baths. 2 restaurants; room service.

Built in 1878, this authentic Victorian hotel dates back to when the town was a booming port for the logging trade. Its small rooms combine 19th-century elegance with modern convenience. Contemporary cottages, located behind the hotel amidst almost an acre of well-tended gardens, have luxurious suites featuring canopied beds and marble bathrooms. Antiques are scattered throughout the hotel, and one of the most interesting is the registration desk—an ornate teller's cage from a Kansas bank.

The casual ocean-view **Garden Room Cafe**, built around living ficus trees established in the ground below, is open for breakfast and lunch. The eggs Benedict is perfect, and the unusual potato cake wedges are delicious. Dinner is served in the more formal **Victorian Dining Room** *($$$. Reservations advised.)* furnished in vintage oak. Starters include French onion soup and a very good Caesar salad, entrees are fresh seafood and meats, and the dessert tray always includes the house specialty—deep-dish olallieberry pie with homemade ice cream. A Victorian lady ghost is said to haunt tables six and eight. The hotel's **lobby bar** features a stained-glass dome that is believed to be a Tiffany and is a good setting for enjoying a fancy drink among antique oriental carpets and more beautiful specimens of stained glass.

Mendocino Village Inn
44860 Main St., (800) 882-7029, (707) 937-0246; www.maccallumhouse.com. 12 rooms; $$-$$$+. Unsuitable for children under 10. No TVs; some wood-burning fireplaces & stoves; some shared baths. Afternoon snack; full breakfast.

Built in 1882, this Queen Anne Victorian is known as "the house of the doctors" because it was originally built by a doctor, then was bought in turn by three more doctors. All the cozy rooms are decorated with a mix of antiques and contemporary art. A suite with a private deck and ocean view is inside a converted 2-story water tower.

Sea Gull Inn
44960 Albion St., (888) 937-5204, (707) 937-5204; www.seagullbb.com. 9 rooms; $-$$. 1 TV. Continental breakfast. No pets.

Built in 1883 as a town house, this simple inn has a casual, friendly atmosphere. A mature garden with giant fuchsias and a century-old rosemary bush surrounds it. The organic breakfast is brought to the room.

Whitegate Inn
499 Howard St., (800) 531-7282, (707) 937-4892; www.whitegateinn.com. 6 rooms, 1 cottage; $$-$$$+. All wood-burning or gas fireplaces. Evening snack; full breakfast.

This 1883 Victorian has a view of the ocean and town and is surrounded by a garden and white picket fence. Tastefully furnished with French and Victorian antiques, its rooms feature lace-edged sheets and lofty down comforters. One bathroom has a clawfoot tub. Homemade cookies are always available, chocolates arrive at bedtime, and a lavish breakfast is served on antique china and sterling silver.

WHERE TO STAY NEARBY

Brewery Gulch Inn
9401 Hwy. 1 N., 1 mi. S of town, (800) 578-4454, (707) 937-4752; www.brewerygulchinn.com. 10 rooms;

$$-$$$+. Unsuitable for children under 12. All gas fireplaces. Afternoon snack; full breakfast. No pets.

A rural drive leads past a 2-acre woodland garden of native plants, up to an open meadow and forest where this luxurious contemporary inn is situated. Wooden Pomo Indian tepees await exploration on the state park land adjoining, which also has picnic tables. Check-in occurs at a handcrafted redwood desk topped with granite in a reception area paneled with eco-salvaged redwood. The public area beyond, known as the Great Room, has 35-foot-high ceilings and a dramatic, oversized steel-and-glass-paneled wood-burning fireplace. It is the perfect place to relax with a good book, and it is where guests gather for the wine hour. Breakfast is eaten at one of several massive dining tables at one end of the Great Room, where diners enjoy a spectacular view and choose from a menu that includes housemade granola, brioche French toast, and caramelized banana-and-praline pecan pancakes. Simple bacon and eggs are prepared exquisitely with eggs just laid by organically fed chickens. All this and 100% pure, sweet well water comes out of the taps, too! Upper floor guest rooms have an ocean view filtered through tall pines. The story of how former owner Dr. Arky Ciancutti built the inn is fascinating. As luck would have it, he overheard some locals talking about "bottom cuts" one night in a local bar. The term refers to giant virgin redwood logs up to 16 feet in diameter that sank in Big River sludge back in the 1800s. He decided personally to salvage as many as possible. To make a long story short—and it is quite a lengthy, fascinating tale wrapped around a lot of hard work—he used this magnificent wood to build this gorgeous inn.

Fensalden Inn
33810 Navarro Ridge Rd., in Albion, 7 mi. S of town, (800) 959-3850, (707) 937-4042; www.fensalden.com. 8 rooms; $$-$$$. Unsuitable for children under 12. No TVs; some kitchens; all wood-burning or gas fireplaces. Evening snack; full breakfast.

Originally a Wells Fargo stagecoach way station in the 1860s, this restful B&B sits atop several tree-lined acres of headlands meadow offering quiet respite. Among the options in the large main house is an upstairs two-room suite with a sweeping ocean view over a pasture lined with cypress trees. Another 2-story suite is built around an 1890s water tower, and a private bungalow with an unobstructed ocean view is situated at the head of the pasture. Antique furnishings are scattered throughout.

Glendeven Inn
8205 N. Hwy. 1, in Little River, 1½ mi. S of town, (800) 822-4536, (707) 937-0083; www.glend even.com. 10 rooms; $$-$$$+. Most fireplaces. Afternoon & evening snack; full breakfast. No pets.

Built in 1867, this attractive New England-style farmhouse is set back from the highway on 2½ quiet acres overlooking the headland meadows and bay at Little River. Rooms are in a farmhouse as well as in a restored hay barn, water tower, and well-designed addition. All are decorated tastefully and eclectically with antiques and contemporary art. Handmade quilts cover beds and walls, and peaceful views are viewed from every window. Favorites include charming Eastlin, hidden behind a bookcase door in the main house, and Briar Rose, featuring a view from its bed of both the ocean *and* a fireplace. By request, breakfast is delivered to the room.

Heritage House
5200 N. Hwy. 1, in Little River, 4 mi. S of town, (800) 235-5885, (707) 937-5885; www.heritage houseinn.com. 41 rooms; $$-$$$+. Some wood-burning fireplaces. Full-service spa. Afternoon tea; restaurant.

Located on a craggy stretch of coast with magnificent ocean views and spread over 37 roomy acres of well-tended gardens, this luxurious inn offers rooms and cottages furnished either with antiques or in contemporary style. Most have ocean views and decks. If it all looks familiar, it could be because it's been seen before in the movie *Same Time Next Year*, which was filmed here. The cabin the movie was filmed in has been divided into a unit called "Same Time" and another called "Next Year."

Fine dining is available in an ocean-view **restaurant** *(B M-F, D daily, Sat-SunBr; $$$. Reservations advised for D.),* and non-guests are welcome.

Little River Inn
7751 Hwy. 1, in Little River, 2 mi. S of town, (888) INN-LOVE, (707) 937-5942; www.littleriverinn.com.

65 units; $$-$$$+. Some wood-burning fireplaces & stoves. Full-service spa; 2 tennis courts (with night lights); 9-hole golf course. Restaurant; room service.

Built on this spectacular location in 1853 by an ancestor of the current owner, this gingerbread Victorian house became an inn in 1939 and now offers a choice of cozy attic rooms, cottages, and standard motel units. Most have expansive ocean views. On the ocean side of Highway 1, new rooms have both an indoor whirlpool tub and a private outdoor hot tub. The beach and hiking trails of Van Damme State Park are adjacent.

A lovely garden-view **restaurant** *(B M-F, D daily, Sat-SunBr.)* and ocean-view **bar** are open to non-guests. James Dean once hung out here and was tossed out of the dining room when he put his feet on the table.

Mendocino Coast Reservations
45084 Little Lake St., (800) 262-7801, (707) 937-5033; www.mendocinovacations.com. 40 units; $$$-$$$+. All kitchens; some fireplaces.

This service arranges vacation home rentals in privately owned houses located on the Mendocino coast. Some units are oceanfront, some have ocean views, and some have hot tubs.

Stanford Inn by the Sea
On Comptche-Ukiah Rd., in Mendocino, (800) 331-8884, (707) 937-5615; www.stanfordinn.com. 33 rooms; $$$-$$$+. Some kitchens; all wood-burning fireplaces. Indoor heated pool & hot tub; sauna; fitness room. Afternoon tea; evening snack; full breakfast.

Located on the outskirts of town, upon a bluff above a scenic llama farm and duck pond that is home to black swans, these luxurious yet cozy pineand redwood-paneled contemporary rooms are decorated with antiques, fresh flowers, and the work of local artists. Many have views overlooking the gardens to the ocean beyond. Operating as a self-sufficient ecosystem, this unique property has a certified organic garden, nursery, and working farm spread over 10 acres. The greenhouse-enclosed pool and hot tub are like a tropical retreat, and mountain bikes are available for guests to borrow at no charge. Dogs get VIP treatment with special bedding, bones, biscuits, and water dishes.

The inn's exceptional, *totally* vegetarian restaurant, **The Ravens** (*B&D daily; $$. Reservations advised.*), offers exciting, refined cuisine using only the freshest ingredients. In addition to serving complex dishes such as wild mushroom galette and blackened tofu Creole, this elegant, creative gourmet venue also offers pizza, polenta, and a portabella burger.

WHERE TO EAT

Ledford House

3000 N. Hwy. 1, in Albion, 7 mi. S of town, (707) 937-0282; www.ledfordhouse.com. D W-Sun; $$$. Reservations advised.

Situated near the edge of a bluff overlooking the ocean, this inviting restaurant offers delicious views from most tables and schedules live jazz nightly. In addition to an intriguing lavender lemonade, the menu lists bistro dishes such as the house specialty white bean-and-mixed meats cassoulet, vegetarian dishes such as eggplant Wellington, and also more substantial entrees incorporating steak, duckling, and prawns. Allow time to take a walk on the property as the sun falls into the ocean, and listen to the sounds of a stream sloshing beside the path and of frogs singing in the pond.

Mendocino Bakery & Pizzeria

10483 Lansing St., (707) 937-0836. Daily 8-7; $.

The perfect spot for a light lunch, this super bakery dispenses tasty housemade soup and pizza warm from the oven. A hunk of fragrant, moist gingerbread makes a memorable dessert, as do chewy cinnamon twists and oatmeal-chocolate chip Cowboy Cookies. The bakery also makes an assortment of breads and breakfast pastries without mixes or preservatives. Everything is exceptional.

Behind the bakery, tiny **Mendo Burgers** (*(707) 937-1111. Thur-Tu 11-6, later in summer; $.*) dishes up the obvious in a variety of delicious renditions—beef, chicken, turkey, veggie, fish, kid-size—plus hot dogs, fresh fish & chips, housemade soups, salads, and fresh-cut fries. Sitting outdoors at roomy picnic tables is sublime on a sunny day.

The Moosse Café

390 Kasten St./Albion St., (707) 937-4323; www.the moosse.com. L-D daily; $-$$. D reservations advised.

This sparely decorated restaurant operates inside a reconstructed house. The original structure burned to the ground in 1994 and was completely rebuilt in 1995 in the footprint and as close to the original as possible. It features a brick fireplace in the main dining room, blond wood floors throughout, and numerous dining nooks and crannies. A few choice tables sit in front of a window overlooking a flower garden and the ocean beyond. This cafe has fed Julia Roberts, Sean Penn, and Angela Lansbury, who ate dinner here regularly during the shooting of *Murder She Wrote.* In fact, the house starred as the travel agency depicted in that TV series. These celebrities and everyone else probably choose to eat here because everything is so innovative and tasty. The lunch menu might offer a delicious electric-orange puréed yam soup; a lip-smacking-good bowtie pasta salad mixed with chicken breast, asparagus, fennel, green beans, sweet peppers, and celery tossed with a buttermilk-tarragon dressing; or a hot linguini prepared with rock shrimp, shitake and porcini mushrooms, sweet peppers, and tomatoes and tossed with an unusual, colorful butternut squash sauce. Dinners are more substantial, with cioppino, boneless roasted crispy chicken, and osso bucco among the choices. Desserts include an old-fashioned creamy chocolate pudding, a light lemon mousse, and a warm bread pudding.

The Blue Heron Inn (*www.theblue heron.com. 3 rooms; $$. Unsuitable for children under 12. Continental breakfast. No pets.*) operates upstairs. It features the same spare, unfussy, simple decor and is furnished with tasteful antiques and puffy comforters.

955 Ukiah Street

955 Ukiah St., (707) 937-1955; www.955restaurant.com. D Thur-Sun; $$. Reservations advised.

After walking down a narrow, flower-edged path, diners are seated in a room with large windows and a view of some of the town's famous water towers. Perhaps in tribute to its former life as an artist's loft, the knotty-pine walls of the massive open room now hold local artwork and all of it is for sale. The restaurant is known for its seafood dishes but has an eclectic menu offering everything from a garden salad to a giant ravioli stuffed with spinach, red chard, and five cheeses. Pastas, meats, and a signature bread pudding topped with local blackberry or huckleberry compote round out the menu.

FORT BRAGG

A LITTLE BACKGROUND

The largest city on the Mendocino coast, Fort Bragg also has the largest working seaport between San Francisco and Eureka. Known as Noyo Harbor, the port is home to busy seafood restaurants serving fresh fish from the daily catch. The city's cheaper rents are attracting many businesses here from tonier Mendocino.

GETTING THERE

Located 10 miles north of Mendocino.

ANNUAL EVENTS

John Druecker Memorial Rhododendron Show
May. (800) 726-2780, (707) 964-4435. Free.

One of the largest such shows in the West, this is hosted by the Noyo chapter of the American Rhododendron Society. An enormous exhibit includes everything from alpine dwarf species to huge trusses of hybrids.

World's Largest Salmon Barbeque
July. (800) 726-2780, (707) 964-1228; www.salmonrestoration.com. $20, under 12 $10.

In addition to feasting on king salmon, participants can look forward to music, danc-ing, a variety of educational salmon displays, and a fireworks show over the ocean. Proceeds benefit the non-profit Salmon Restoration Association and assist them in restocking Northern California salmon runs.

WHAT TO DO

Glass Beach
On N side of town, across from Noyo Bowl at 900 N. Main St.

Ask for precise directions when in town, then park in the dirt lot and walk down the path to the beach. Many years ago this was a dump, but now it is the source of great joy for kids and adults alike as they scoop up bits of pottery and glass that have been smoothed by the ocean into jewels. Local artists make jewelry from their finds, but anyone can easily put them in a clear glass full of water at home for a fabulous free souvenir.

Guest House Museum
343 N. Main St., (707) 964-4251. Irregular schedule. $2 donation.

Get a sense of this area's history by view-ing the old logging photos and artifacts on display inside this beautifully restored 1892 mansion constructed entirely of redwood.

Jug Handle State Reserve
On Hwy. 1, 3 mi. S of town, (707) 937-5804; www.parks.ca.gov. Daily dawn-dusk. Free.

A unique self-guided nature trail takes hikers through an ecological staircase consisting of five wave-cut terraces that demonstrate how plants and soils affect one another. During the 5-mile walk (allow 3 hours), the terrain changes from grass-covered headlands, to a pine and redwood forest, to a pygmy forest filled with full-grown trees measuring only 1 or 2 feet tall. Wear sturdy shoes, and bring water and a lunch.

Mendocino Coast Botanical Gardens
18220 N. Hwy. 1, 2 mi. S of town, (707) 964-4352; www.gardenbythesea.org. Daily 9-5; Nov-Feb 9-4. $10, 60+ $7.50, 13-17 $4, 6-12 $2.

A self-guided tour leads through 47 acres of flowering plants. Known for its rhododen-drons, fuchsias, and heathers, this garden also boasts a major collection of succulents, camellias, and old heritage roses. The nursery sells unusual perennials, and picnic tables are available.

Ricochet Ridge Ranch
24201 Hwy. 1, 2 mi. N of town, across from MacKerricher State Park, (888)873-5777, (707) 964-7669; www.horse-vacation.com. Daily trail rides at 10, 12, 2, 4. $45+. Must be age 6+. Reservations required

Equestrian excursions vary from by-the-hour guided rides on the beach to week-long, all-inclusive treks with nightly stops at inns. Ride venues include Fort Bragg's Ten Mile Beach, cattle ranches overlooking the ocean, and Mendocino's majestic redwood forests. Catered trips and private tours can also be arranged.

Shopping

A walk along North Main Street allows a look at some of the town's most interesting shops.

• Carol Hall's Hot Pepper Jelly Company
330 N. Main St., (866) 737-7379, (707) 961-1899; www.hotpepperjelly.com. Daily 10-5:30.

Pick up some souvenir jars of delicious pepper jelly and many other local food products here.

• Mendocino Chocolate Company
232 N. Main St., (800) 722-1107, (707) 964-8800. www.mendocino-chocolate.com. Daily 10-5:30.

Stop in for hand-dipped chocolates and truffles.

• Northcoast Artists Gallery
362 N. Main St., (707) 964-8266. Daily 10-6.

This gallery displays and sells the works of local artists.

• Roundman's Smoke House
412 N. Main St., (800) 545-2935, (707) 964-5954; www.roundmans.com. M-F 9-5:30, Sat 10-5:30, Sun 10-3.

Stop in for smoked meat, fish, cheese, and an assortment of jerkys.

Skunk Train
Foot of Laurel St., (866) 45-SKUNK, (707) 964-6371; www.skunktrain.com. Daily; schedule varies. $47, 3-11 $20. Reservations advised.

This train gets its name from the fact that the original logging trains emitted unpleasant odors from their gasoline engines. Loggers said they "could smell 'em before they could see 'em." Today, a few vintage motorcars are still used in winter, but most trains are pulled by steam or diesel engines as they travel through dense redwood forest, through deep mountain tunnels, and over many bridges and trestles.

WHERE TO STAY

DeHaven Valley Inn
39247 N. Hwy. 1, in Westport, 17 mi. N of town, (707) 961-1660; www.dehavenvalleyinn.com. 6 rooms, 3 cabins; $-$$$. Some TVs; some wood-burning fireplaces & stoves; some shared baths. Hot tub. Full breakfast; restaurant.

Romance and family fun are both possible on this 20-acre property. For romance, request the cozy Valley View room and enjoy its private bathroom, unusual corner fireplace, and view of the valley. The spacious Eagle's Nest, with its Franklin stove and expansive windows overlooking the valley, is another winner. With kids in tow, opt for one of the large cottages. One teenager who stayed here actually uttered, "Mom, you did right. This place is great!" A cozy communal living room in the traditional Victorian farmhouse invites mingling with other guests, and a hilltop hot tub offers a view of the valley and spectacular nighttime stargazing.

Guests and non-guests alike can make reservations for dinner in the intimate **dining room**.

The tide pools of **Westport-Union Landing Beach** *((707) 937-5804; www.parks.ca.gov.)* await just across the highway.

The Grey Whale Inn
615 N. Main St., (800) 382-7244, (707) 964-0640; www.greywhaleinn.com. 13 rooms; $$. Some kitchenettes; some wood-burning & gas fireplaces. Full breakfast. No pets.

Originally built as a hospital, this stately redwood building was converted into an especially spacious inn in 1976. Some of the pleasantly decorated rooms have a private deck. Others have ocean views that permit viewing the whale migration, and one has a whirlpool bathtub for two. A large communal guest area is equipped with a fireplace, pool table, and plenty of board games. A relaxing stay here can be just what the doctor ordered.

Pine Beach Inn
16801 N. Hwy. 1, 4 mi. S of town, (888) 987-8388, (707) 964-5603; www.pinebeachinn.com. 51 rooms; $-$$. 2 tennis courts. Restaurant.

This motel complex is located on 11 acres of private land. Facilities include a private beach and cove.

Motel Row
Two traditional motels at the north end of town offer good value and an extraordinary beachfront location.

• Beachcomber Motel
1111 N. Main St., (800) 400-SURF, (707) 964-2402; www.thebeachcombermotel.com. 45 rooms; $-$$$. Some kitchens & fireplaces. Fitness room. Continental breakfast.

Two rooms have private hot tubs.

• Ocean View Lodge
1141 N. Main St., (800) 643-5482, (707) 964-1951; www.oceanviewlodging.com. 30 rooms; $$-$$$. Some fireplaces. No pets.

All rooms have ocean views.

WHERE TO EAT

Cap'n Flint's
32250 N. Harbor Dr., (707) 964-9447. L-D daily; $. No reservations. No cards.

Popular with locals, the menu here offers various kinds of fish & chips, clam chowder, and the house specialty—deep-fried shrimp won tons made with a tasty cream cheese filling. Hamburgers, hot dogs, sandwiches, and wine-based drinks are also available. Though the decor consists of well-worn, mismatched furniture, the view of picturesque Noyo Harbor is excellent.

Egghead's Restaurant
326 N. Main St., (707) 964-5005; www.eggheadsrestaurant.com. B-L Thur-Tu; $. No reservations.

Decorated with movie photos from *The Wizard of Oz* and related knickknacks, this cheerful, popular, and tiny diner serves 40-plus varieties of crêpes and *big* omelettes. Other breakfast items and an assortment of sandwiches are also available. Families will appreciate the privacy afforded by the high-back wooden booths.

Laurel Deli
401 N. Main St., (707) 964-7812. Daily 7-4:30; $.

This informal spot dishes up freshly made soups and sandwiches as well as gigantic blackberry muffins and delicious housemade pies.

Old Coast Hotel Bar & Grill
101 N. Franklin St./Oak, (888) 468-3550, (707) 961-4488; www.oldcoasthotel.com. L-D Thur-M; $$.

Extensively renovated and restored to its 1892 glory, this historic building features s pectacular original pressed-tin walls. The airy, open dining room has an attractive bar area and features beautiful original wood floors throughout. Dinner appetizers include onion rings, popcorn shrimp, and roasted mussels. Entrees consist of seafood, pasta, and an assortment of sandwiches and salads.

Hotel rooms *(15 rooms; $-$$$. Some fireplaces. Continental breakfast.)* are simple but comfortable.

The Restaurant
418 N. Main St., (707) 964-9800; www.therestaurantfortbragg.com. D Thur-M; $$. Reservations advised.

An ad for this restaurant reads, "If you like to eat, you'd probably like to eat at a place where people who like to eat, eat what they like—and like it!" It's an unusual ad—just like the restaurant, which, in completely unpretentious surroundings, serves interesting food at reasonable prices. The eclectic menu changes regularly, but the emphasis is on fresh local seafood and vegetarian items. A sample dinner menu offers Thai-style shrimp in green curry sauce, Denver lamb riblets with sweet & sour glaze, and chicken breast Amalfi topped with lemony arugula. Desserts are a chocolate shortcake with fresh berries and cream, a housemade ice cream, and a lemon tart.

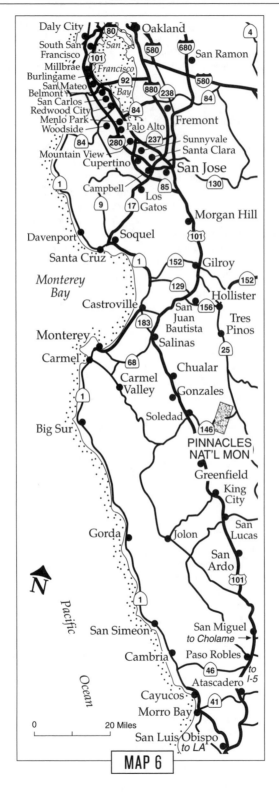

MAP 6

Mission San Juan Bautista

BRISBANE

VISITOR INFORMATION

Brisbane Chamber of Commerce
50 Park Pl., (415) 467-7283;
www.brisbanechamber.com.

WHERE TO STAY

Radisson Hotel San Francisco Airport at Sierra Point
5000 Sierra Point Pkwy., 2 mi. N of airport, (800) 333-3333, (415) 467-4400; www.radisson.com/ brisbaneca_airport. 8 stories; 210 rooms; $$-$$$. Indoor pool & hot tub; fitness room. Restaurant; room service. No pets.

This comfortable business hotel features large rooms, many with two queen beds and some with a view of the bay and airport traffic. Complimentary shuttle service is provided to and from San Francisco Airport.

Colorful, trendy **Xebec** restaurant and bar features California-Mediterranean fusion dishes and a sushi bar.

MILLBRAE

VISITOR INFORMATION

Millbrae Chamber of Commerce
50 Victoria Ave. #103, (650) 697-7324;
www.millbrae.com.

WHAT TO DO

San Francisco International Airport (SFO)
800-IFLYSFO, (650) 821-8211; www.flysfo.com, www.sfoarts.org.

SFO offers an ever-changing set of art exhibits to entertain waiting passengers. In fact, it is the only airport in the U.S. accredited as a museum by the American Association of Museums, and each terminal has exhibits.

The **Louis A. Turpen Aviation Museum** *(Level 3, International Terminal, before security checkpoint for Boarding Area A, (650) 821-9900. Sun-F 10-4:30. Free.)* is modeled on the 1937 San Francisco Airport passenger waiting room.

WHERE TO EAT

Fook Yuen Seafood Restaurant
195 El Camino Real/Millbrae Ave., (650) 692-8600. L-D daily; $. Reservations accepted.

A branch of a chain found also in Hong Kong, Singapore, and Australia, this popular spot stands out on this Chinese restaurant row. It serves delicious, distinctive food, including dim sum at lunch and a Cantonese menu at dinner. Specialties include tank-fresh seafood, pork with pickled plums, and crispy chicken.

Hong Kong Flower Lounge
51 Millbrae Ave./El Camino Real, (650) 692-6666; www.flowerlounge.net. L-D daily; $$. Reservations advised.

Authentic Hong Kong-style fresh seafood dishes, superior dim sum, and the restaurant's signature Peking duck are served in a cavernous, yet stylish, room that seats 400.

Shanghai Dumpling Shop
455 Broadway, 1 blk. W of El Camino Real, (650) 697-0682. L-D daily; $. No reservations.

Some people who visit this small cafe manage to snag one of the booths, which are particularly comfortable after the usual wait to get in. The specialty dumplings are made fresh in the small kitchen and include Shanghai steamed pork dumplings and Beijing-style boiled chives dumplings. Rice rolls, an assortment of rice and noodle dishes, and typical Chinese dishes round out the extensive menu.

A few doors down, **Dean's Produce** *(461 Broadway, (650) 692-1042.)* displays colorful produce outside and offers plenty more inside along with exotic imported goods. More shops line the street.

BURLINGAME

VISITOR INFORMATION

San Mateo County Convention & Visitors Bureau
111 Anza Blvd. #410, (800) 288-4748, (650) 348-7600; www.sanmateocountycvb.com.

Burlingame Chamber of Commerce
290 California Dr., (650) 344-1735; www.burlingamechamber.org.

WHAT TO DO

Burlingame Museum of Pez Memorabilia
214 California Dr./Howard Ave., (650) 347-2301;

www.burlingamepezmuseum.com. Tu-Sat 10-6. $3, 65+ & 4-12 $1; free on 1st Thur of month.

Operating in the front of a computer store, this homespun exhibition includes some interactive exhibits. It displays all of the more than 600 styles of plastic Pez candy dispensers that have been produced from the 1950s to the present. The rarest is a 1972 Make-a-Face. Snoopy, Bugs Bunny, and Fred Flintstone are all on display, along with Tweety Bird, who starred in a *Seinfeld* episode. (The Pez mint was invented in Austria in 1927. It was introduced to the U.S. in fruit flavors and offered in a head dispenser in 1952.) A large selection of contemporary and collectible Pez dispensers and candy refills are for sale. A collection of classic toys—including Lincoln Logs, Tinker Toys, Lego, and Mr. Potato Head—are also displayed.

WHERE TO STAY

Embassy Suites Hotel San Francisco-Airport
150 Anza Blvd., (800) EMBASSY, (650) 342-4600; www.sfoburlingame.embassysuites.com. 9 stories; 340 suites; $$-$$$. Indoor pool & hot tub; fitness room. Evening reception; full breakfast; restaurant.

Located on the bay 2 miles south of the airport and far enough from the freeway to be restive, this bay front hotel has a 9-story tropical atrium. A free shuttle is provided to the airport. For more description, see page 445.

Hyatt Regency San Francisco Airport
1333 Bayshore Hwy., (800) 233-1234, (650) 347-1234; www.sanfranciscoairport.hyatt.com. 10 stories; 815 rooms; $$. Heated pool; hot tub; fitness room. 3 restaurants.

The fabulous atrium here is filled with greenery and cascading waterfalls, objects de art, and plenty of revitalizing natural light. Amenities include a complimentary 24-hour airport shuttle.

Knuckles Historical Sports Bar *(L-D daily.)* has more than 20 beers on tap, 27 TV monitors plus a large screen, and pool tables.

WHERE TO EAT

Benihana
1496 Old Bayshore Hwy./Broadway, (650) 342-5202; www.benihana.com. L M-F, D daily; $$. Reservations advised. Valet parking.

The sushi bar here has a spectacular bay view. For more description, see page 62.

Copenhagen Bakery & Cafe

1216 Burlingame Ave./Lorton Ave., (650) 342-1357; www.copenhagenbakery.com. B-L daily, D W-Sun; $.

This combination Danish bakery and restaurant produces great six-grain and sweet French breads as well as exquisite European-style pastries. The extensive breakfast menu includes omelettes and pancakes as well as bacon and eggs and is served until 2:30 on weekends. For lunch try a delicious German bologna on sweet French bread with a side of tasty potato salad and, of course, a dessert pastry. Or get the Royal Lunch, a collection of far-from-dainty open face sandwiches—each is an ice cream scoop of salad atop a tiny piece of pumpernickel. Specialty coffee drinks and ice cream treats are also available. Order at the counter, then find a seat in the cheery open dining rooms with sidewalk views.

After, spend some time shopping the stores lining this avenue.

Il Fornaio

327 Lorton Ave./Burlingame Ave., (650) 375-8000; www.ilfornaio.com. B Sat-Sun, L M-F, D daily; $$.

For description, see page 73.

Isobune Burlingame

1451 Burlingame Ave./El Camino Real, (650) 344-8433; www.isobuneburlingame.com. L-D daily; $.

For description, see page 73.

Nectar Wine Lounge & Restaurant

270 Lorton Ave./Burlingame Ave., (650) 558-9200; www.nectarwinelounge.com. L-D daily; $$$. Reservations advised.

Diners are seated in a warren of spaces, under tall ceilings with skylights, and treated to a rotating display of contemporary artwork and to peeks into the very large wine cellar. And then there is the food. One perfect parade of shared small plates began with a rocket salad tossed with toasted hazelnuts; followed by a sumptuous housemade chicken-artichoke-lemon sausage with Bloomsdale spinach; then by a barbecued pork biscuit that was just too, too cute and tasty; and then by a larger plate of Hawaiian walu fish served with roasted whole baby potatoes and asparagus; and concluding with a dessert of silky milk chocolate panna cotta accompanied by a trio of housemade cookies. Diners can choose from a flight of three wines— "bad-assed reds" is one option— or order either a glass or a half-glass "taste." Most diners leave with a pleasurably exhausted palate.

SAN MATEO

GETTING THERE

Located approximately 20 miles south of San Francisco.

ANNUAL EVENTS

San Mateo County Fair

August. (650) 574-3247; www.sanmateocountyfair.com. $9, 62+ & 6-12 $7.

WHAT TO DO

Coyote Point Recreation Area

1701 Coyote Point Dr., (650) 573-2593; www.sanmateo countyparks.com. Daily 8-sunset. $5/vehicle.

This 670-acre park is equipped with a barbecue area, several playgrounds, inviting grassy expanses, an 18-hole golf course, a rifle range, and a swimming beach with bathhouse. It is one of the best windsurfing sites in the U.S. and considered prime for beginners. As if all this isn't enough, it's also located on the descent route for the San Francisco International Airport, making it a great place to just sit and watch planes land.

Bay-side and surrounded by an aromatic grove of eucalyptus trees, the architecturally impressive **Coyote Point Museum** *(1651 Coyote Point Dr., (650) 342-7755; www.coyotept museum.org. Tu-Sat 10-5, Sun 12-5. $6, 62+ & 13-17 $4, 3-12 $2; free on 1st W of month.)* aims to educate visitors about local ecology and the environment with numerous hands-on and multi-media displays. Exhibits inside include live colonies of termites and bees. Exhibits in the impressive outdoor Wildlife Habitats area include non-releasable live native animals (burrowing owls, a porcupine, a banana slug), a walk-through aviary of native Bay Area birds, and a colorful demonstration garden composed of plants that attract hummingbirds and butterflies. The foxes are fed daily at 11:30, and the otters at 12:30. Nature's Marketplace shows how Native Americans used plants, shrubs, and trees in everyday life. Bring a lunch to enjoy in the inviting picnic area.

Central Park

El Camino Real/5th Ave., downtown, (650) 522-7434; www.ci.sanmateo.ca.us/dept/parks. Free.

Dating from 1922, this is the oldest municipal park in the county. Facilities include a **kiddie train** *((650) 340-1520. Schedule varies. $1.)*—a miniature version of the long-gone Southern Pacific Coast Daylight—plus a botanical garden, tennis courts, and a playground.

The park's tidy **Japanese Garden** *(5th Ave. M-F 10-4, Sat-Sun 11-4. Free.)* was designed by Nagao Sakurai, a former landscape architect at the Imperial Palace in Tokyo. Features include a teahouse (no tea service), a central pond divided by a narrow bridge (koi are usually fed at 11 a.m.), two waterfalls, a pagoda, and a shrine. Narrow pathways are designed to make visitors slow down and really look. Rare and unusual plants include a weeping beech and an umbrella pine.

WHERE TO EAT

Fernando's Mexican Restaurant

63 W. 37th Ave./Colgrove St., (650) 345-9042. L-D daily. No reservations.

This old-time family restaurant has a long bar on one side of the entry and an inviting open room filled with comfortable carved wood booths on the other. Order up one of the margaritas or "mocktails" (the virgin piña colada is primo) to sip while perusing the extensive menu. Choices include a la carte or traditional combination plates, fajitas, and house specialties—sopitos, mole enchiladas, and an assortment of seafood dishes. A three-piece mariachi band plays on Sundays from 5:30 to 8:30 p.m.

For dessert, it's just a few steps to **Romolo's Cannoli & Spumoni Factory** *(81 37th Ave., (650) 574-0625; www.romolosfactory.com. Tu-Sun 11-5:30.)* for Old World treats: ice cream creations, granita, tiramisu, Italian specialty cakes, and even cappuccino. Take it away or linger for a while seated on old-fashioned wire heart chairs.

Heidi Pies

1941 S. El Camino Real/20th Ave., (650) 574-0505. B-L-D daily; $. No reservations.

The selection of freshly baked pies is replenished constantly from this old-fashioned coffee shop's own kitchen. Choices include fruit (raisin and gooseberry in addition to more common varieties), meringue (black bottom, banana), and specialty (German chocolate, pecan, cream cheese). The house specialty is hot apple pie—served plain, a la mode, with hot cinnamon sauce, with whipped cream, or with either Cheddar or American cheese. A vast selection of short-order items, including a hamburger and grilled cheese sandwich, comprise the rest of the menu. This restaurant is open around the clock, and whole pies are available to go.

Joy Luck Place

88 E. 4th Ave./San Mateo Dr., downtown, (650) 343-6988. Dim sum M-F 11-2:30, Sat-Sun 10-2:30, D daily; $. Reservations advised.

Delicious dim sum includes many shrimp and vegetarian options. It is served from carts and trays in a spacious, high-ceilinged room with cheery yellow accents. Noticeably efficient service keeps the tea pot filled and dishes cleared.

Kaimuki Grill

104 S. El Camino Real/2nd Ave. & Crystal Springs Rd., (650) 548-9320. L M-F, D daily; $-$$. No reservations.

Japanese cuisine with California and Hawaiian accents is the specialty in this simple, yet atmospheric, venue. Choose from a menu that includes Chinese-style won ton-ramen noodle soup and a large variety of sushi. Housemade noodle dishes and small appetizer items—eggplant stuffed with ground chicken, shitakes stuffed with ground beef—are particularly tasty.

La Michoacana

251 S. B St./3rd Ave., downtown, (650) 558-0069. L-D daily; $. No reservations.

This tiny Mexican restaurant provides comfortable seating in its 2-story dining area. Everything is made fresh and is of exceptional taste, quality, and value, and a la carte and combination plates allow a satisfying meal whatever the stage of hunger. A selection of Salvadorean

dishes includes pupusas—handmade corn tortillas stuffed with delicious cheese and flavorful
seasoned pork. Horchata, Mexican hot chocolate, and wine margaritas are among the drink
choices, and flan is the single dessert.

Left Bank

*1100 Park Pl./Bay Meadows, (650) 345-2250;
www.leftbank.com. L-D daily; $$.*

For description, see page 225.

Little Sichuan Restaurant

*168 E. 4th Ave./Ellsworth St., downtown,
(650) 345-9168. L-D Tu-Sun; $. Reservations advised.*

A large selection of delicious hot and spicy
dishes is served here in light, airy rooms.
Seating is comfortable, and tablecloths provide
a nice touch. Dinners begin with a complimen-
tary appetizer of boiled peanuts in shell and a
kimchi-style cabbage dish. Hot-and-sour soup,
kung pao chicken, and house specialty dry-
cooked string beans are particularly good. Many
rice and noodle dishes—including wide chow
fun rice noodles—are on the menu, along with
a good selection of less spicy dishes.

The Noodle Shop

*164 W. 25th Ave./El Camino Real, (650) 345-1277.
L-D Thur-Tu; $. No reservations.*

A branch of Millbrae's Shanghai
Dumpling Shop (see page 168), this spot serves
popular xiao long bao (pork-filled steamed
soup dumplings) as well as pot stickers, deep-
fried turnip cakes, and spicy tofu buns. Small
plates and hand-pulled noodle dishes are also
available.

Picnic Pick-Ups

• Draeger's Market

*222 E. 4th Ave./B St., downtown, (650) 685-3700;
www.draegers.com. Daily 7am-10pm.*

This enormous market is the largest gour-
met food emporium in the U.S. More than a
grocery store, this European-style facility caters
to the educated palate with a sushi bar, wine
tasting room, smoothie bar, deli, and bakery as
well as a cooking school. It offers a vast selec-
tion of wines and beers, an expansive olive bar,
and exotic meats that include alligator, turtle,
and buffalo. A second-floor shop purveys an
expansive selection of cookbooks, housewares,
and gift items.

In a subdued, open, second-floor space
drenched with light, upscale **Viognier**
restaurant *((650) 685-3727; www.viognier
restaurant.com. L M-Sat, D daily, SunBr; $$-$$$.
Reservations advised.)* serves a rustic
Mediterranean menu of salads, pizzettas, grilled
and rotisseried meats, and pastas. An exhibition
kitchen and fireplace enhance the setting.
Desserts are a high point—look for a chocolate-
raspberry parfait dome that tastes as good as it
sounds. The namesake wine is featured on the
wine list.

Taxi's Hamburgers

*2700 S. El Camino Real, (650) 377-1947; www.taxis
hamburgers.com. L-D daily; $. No reservations.*

All kinds of burgers, sandwiches, salads,
and shakes—including a low-fat version—are
on the menu, as well as a "top your own baked
potato bar" with over 20 toppings. The decor
pays homage to taxicabs, and table-top
jukeboxes play oldies but goodies.

231 Ellsworth

*231 S. Ellsworth Ave./3rd Ave., downtown,
(650) 347-7231; www.231ellsworth.com. L M-F, D M-
Sat; $$$. Reservations advised. Valet parking at D.*

In the sophisticated atmosphere of a
darkened dining room with deep-brown walls,
a surprising deep-blue ceiling, and crispy white
napery, this stylish restaurant delivers a small
but palate-pleasing menu of California dishes.
The chef likes to make complex mixtures and
use unusual mushrooms. Appetizers might
include a delicate prawn-and-quail egg tempura
presented with a spicy green papaya salad and a
light, flavorful passion fruit dipping sauce, or
perhaps a warm frisée and endive salad topped
with goat cheese, hazelnuts, and sherry vinaigrette. Entrees have included a delicate sole with
fava beans and Hon Shemiji mushrooms, as
well as delicious, full-flavored lamb loin cutlets
with a ragout of black trumpets, olives, and
basil gnocchetti. A five- and seven-course tasting menu is also available, along with selected
wines. Desserts are divine, perhaps a milk
chocolate tart with caramel sauce and cashews
or a true-flavored pear sorbet with a delicate
Riesling gelée. Attentive service and unobtrusive
background music enhance this special-
occasion dining spot. A comfortable bar area in
front is worth a visit, and late-night dessert is
served there.

SAN CARLOS

VISITOR INFORMATION

San Carlos Chamber of Commerce
1500 Laurel St. #B, (650) 593-1068;
www.sancarloschamber.org.

WHAT TO DO

Hiller Aviation Museum
601 Skyway Rd., Holly St. exit off Hwy. 101, (650) 654-0200; www.hiller.org. Daily 10-5. $8, 65+ & 8-17 $5.

This huge museum at the San Carlos Airport is heaven for aviation buffs. Approximately 50 aircraft and 100 exhibits span the history of aviation in California. Many displays are interactive, and fascinating videotapes show some unusual aircraft in motion. Vertical take-off and landing craft, hypersonic craft, and various wing configurations are displayed, as is a Boeing Condor that can stay in the air for 4 days—it is the largest aircraft hanging in any museum in the world. A restoration workshop viewed through giant windows allows a glimpse of the latest acquisitions. Multi-media presentations and a library enhance the experience and educate about this area's powerful influence on aviation (for example, the first "aeroplane" with three-axis control flew in this very area in 1869—3 decades *before* Kitty Hawk). Kids love visiting the 747 cockpit outdoors and climbing into the Blue Angels cockpit indoors. From 11 a.m. to 1 p.m. on the third Saturday of each month, kids age 8 through 17 are eligible to register in the Young Eagles program and take a free ride in an airplane. Flight classes for kids are scheduled regularly. Also worth a gander, the gift shops stocks helicopter cookie cutters, pint-sized flight suits and bomber jackets, and astronaut-tested freeze-dried pizza and ice cream.

REDWOOD CITY

ANNUAL EVENTS

4th of July Parade
July. 650-365-1825; www.parade.org. Free.

This biggest of Bay Area Independence Day parades has been happening since 1939 and once included a rodeo. The parade begins at 10 a.m. and is followed by a festival. Evening fireworks conclude the event.

WHAT TO DO

Fox Theatre
2215 Broadway Ave., (650) FOX-4119;
www.foxdream.com. Schedule & fees vary.

Now completely refurbished and used for both movies and live performances, this grand old art deco theater has a Vaudeville stage, a pipe organ, and a state-of-the-art audio system.

Next door, the **Little Fox** theater presents live music and dancing in a 1920s-style cabaret atmosphere.

Malibu Grand Prix/Malibu Castle
Malibu Grand Prix: 340 Blomquist St./Seaport Blvd., (650) 366-6463. Malibu Castle: 320 Blomquist St., (650) 367-1906. www.malibugrandprix.com. Schedule & fees vary.

Young daredevils can race Indy-style cars here in a safe, fun environment. Oneand two-seat Virage cars may be driven by ages 18 and older with a valid driver's license (younger passengers are permitted in the two-seaters), and junior drivers measuring 4 feet 8 inches or taller can drive scaled-down F-50s. The adjacent Castle rounds out the fun with three 18-hole miniature golf courses, a video-game arcade, go-karts, and batting cages.

San Mateo County History Museum
2200 Broadway St., (650) 299-0104;
www.historysmc.org. Tu-Sun 10-4. $4, 65+ $2, under 5 free.

This former San Mateo County Courthouse building dates to 1910 and boasts the largest complete stained-glass dome on the West Coast. Exhibits portray life on the Peninsula from 250 years ago through today. They include a historic courtroom and a gallery displaying 18 scale-model ships.

WHERE TO STAY

Sofitel San Francisco Bay
223 Twin Dolphin Dr., 12 mi. from airport, (800) SOFITEL, (650) 598-9000; www.sofitel.com. 9 stories; 421 rooms; $$-$$$+. Heated pool; fitness room. 2 restaurants; room service.

Experience France without leaving the Bay Area. This link in the sleek French hotel chain is situated on Redwood Shores Lagoon among the glossy hi-rise headquarters of hi-tech companies that include the Oracle campus. (This quiet area of waterways is the long-ago home of Six Flags Discovery Kingdom.) French touches include the charming accents borne by many employees and the use of bath mitts instead of washcloths.

WHERE TO EAT

Amelia's
2042 Broadway St./Jefferson, downtown, (650) 368-1390. B-L-D daily; $. No cards.

This casual spot offers an extensive menu that includes unusual Salvadoran pupusas with more than a dozen fillings (several are vegetarian), plus more familiar Mexican tacos and burritos. Flautas, sopitos, and fajitas are also options. Agua fresca is a blending of fresh fruits topped with chopped fruit and a snippet of watercress. Order at the window in back, then keep hunger at bay with complimentary chips and delicious housemade salsas. Seating is in a large, pleasant interior space and also outside along the sidewalk.

Mandaloun
2021 Broadway St./Main St., (650) 367-7974; www.mandaloun.biz. L M-Sat, D daily; $$$.

The decor here—textured stone floor, high wood-plank ceiling, wrought iron fixtures—goes well with the seasonal Mediterranean menu. On a warm evening, seating in an open-air courtyard off the entrance is sublime, while in cooler weather, the open interior room featuring a view of the exhibition kitchen is more welcoming. Menu items include wood-fired pizzas and a pasta or two. Many items are flavored with Middle Eastern spices, including the excellent crispy calamari with harissa aioli and the Moroccan-spiced olives and peppers. Salads reflect the season—think baby beets with Sausalito cress or Frog Hollow Farms peaches with Serrano ham in the summer—and main plates might include wild salmon or rotisserie free-range chicken. Cocktails are interesting and pretty, and desserts might include churros with chocolate sauce or fresh fruits with warm zabaglione.

WOODSIDE

A LITTLE BACKGROUND

Though located just a few miles from bustling El Camino Real, Woodside feels very rural. It has been called the "horsiest community in the United States," and, indeed, it has more horses per capita than any other community in the county. Hitching posts found outside some of the town's restaurants back up the claim, and horses and wagons are often seen "parked" by them. With the recent heavy influx of people who have made their fortune in Silicon Valley, a millionaire here now is considered average—just a member of the middle class. Fortunately, the restaurant prices don't reflect this reality.

GETTING THERE

Located on Highway 84, approximately 5 miles west of Highway 101.

ANNUAL EVENTS

Kings Mountain Art Fair
August or September. (650) 851-2710; www.kingsmountainartfair.org. Free. No pets.

This juried art show takes place in a redwood forest. It begins with an 8 a.m. breakfast with the artists. Unlike many other art fairs, it has no loud rock music or wine tastings. It features top artists, the sound of the breeze in the trees, and perhaps some Celtic harp music. Hiking trails surround the site.

WHAT TO DO

Filoli
86 Cañada Rd., Edgewood Rd. exit off I-280, (650) 364-8300; www.filoli.org. Tu-Sat 10-3:30, Sun 11-3:30; tour by reservation; closed Nov-mid-Feb. $12, 5-17 $5. No pets.

Named for the family motto—"Fight for a just cause; Love your fellow man; and Live a full life"—this 654-acre country estate surrounds a 43-room modified Georgian mansion built for William Bowers Bourn II in 1917 by his hunting buddy, architect Willis Polk. Its ballroom is gilded with gold leaf extracted from Bourn's Empire Mine in Grass Valley. (The mansion is the setting for the 1978 film *Heaven Can Wait* and is seen as the exterior of the Carrington home shown at the beginning of TV's *Dynasty*.) Guided tours of the house and 16 landscaped acres of European-inspired formal gardens include such delights as two manicured English knot gardens, a garden designed to resemble a stained-glass window in Chartres cathedral in France, and a practical cutting garden used for mansion floral arrangements. Also special is a sunken garden replicated after one on the Ireland estate the Bourns bought for their daughter. (Note that self-guided tours are also an option.) The gardens are spectacular in April, when more than 70,000 tulips and 200,000 daffodils bloom, and in May, when the rose garden is at its peak. A garden shop and cafe are near the exit; picnicking is not permitted.

The Woodside Store

3300 Tripp Rd./off Woodside Rd. (Hwy. 84), (650) 851-7615; www.historysmc.org. Tu-Thur 10-4, Sat-Sun 12-4. Free.

Constructed of redwood in 1854, this was the first general store built between San Francisco and San Jose. It has also been a post office, a blacksmith shop, and a dental office. Meticulously restored, it now appears as it did in the 1880s.

WHERE TO EAT

Buck's

3062 Woodside Rd./Cañada Rd., (650) 851-8010; www.buckswoodside.com. B-L-D daily; $$. Reservations advised.

Especially popular in the morning, when local computer executives gather for power breakfasts of buckwheat pancakes and huevos rancheros, this attractive spot is filled with comfy booths and has lots of windows. It's sort of like an updated old-time coffee shop, but with a full bar. Breakfast is served until 2:30 on weekends and includes all the usual suspects plus an extensive selection of omelettes and pancakes. Lunch brings on soups, salads, sandwiches, burgers, and a popular chili. American-style entrees are added at dinner along with a few more frou-frou items such as lobster ravioli with red pesto sauce or baked local halibut with pineapple salsa. Dessert portions are large enough to satisfy two or three people—the

menu claims "all desserts have been tested by the American Trucking Association and found to be way too large"—and include a signature hot fudge sundae and delicious peach cobbler. Should boredom set in, just check out the mish-mash of curiosities lining the walls.

MENLO PARK

A LITTLE BACKGROUND

Developed in the 1800s by two Irishmen, this peaceful tree-filled suburb centers around its historic train station—the oldest passenger station in the state. Leland Stanford and Mark Hopkins, both rail tycoons in their time, once boarded the train here for the ride into San Francisco. Today the station is a shelter for CalTrain passengers.

VISITOR INFORMATION

Menlo Park Chamber of Commerce

1100 Merrill St., (650) 325-2818; www.menlopark chamber.com.

WHAT TO DO

Sunset Magazine Garden

80 Willow Rd./Middlefield Rd., (650) 321-3600; www.sunset.com. M-F 9-4:30. Free.

A self-guided walking tour leads visitors through 7 acres of landscaped gardens surrounding an impressive 1.3-acre lawn.

WHERE TO STAY

Stanford Park Hotel

100 El Camino Real, (800) 368-2468, (650) 322-1234; www.woodsidehotels.com. 4 stories; 163 rooms; $$-$$$+. Some fireplaces. Heated pool; hot tub; sauna; fitness room. Evening snack; restaurant; room service. No pets.

Located at the north end of town, this hotel offers spacious rooms furnished with custom-made English yew wood pieces. It was one of the first hotels in the U.S. to offer the innovative computer-operated "video on command" system.

WHERE TO EAT

Allied Arts Guild

*75 Arbor Rd./Cambridge Ave., (650) 322-2405;
www.alliedartsguild.org. Shops: M-Sat 10-5; Nov-Dec,
also Sun 12-5.*

Located in a quiet residential neighborhood and housed in a former weaving studio, the **Red Currant** cafe *(650-322-2626. B-L M-Sat; $-$$. Reservations advised.)* was opened by the Palo Alto Auxiliary of Children's Hospital at Stanford in 1932. In those days guild members prepared food in their homes and transported it to the premises for serving. Now a modern kitchen lets volunteers prepare three-course luncheons that include a soup, hot entree with vegetable or salad, freshly baked rolls, dessert, and choice of beverage. The menu is different each day, and all the recipes are for sale. In warm weather, a patio is available (request seating there when reserving). All profits and tips help support the Lucile Packard Children's Hospital.

Allow time to wander through the attractive Spanish Colonial-style estate, once part of the vast Rancho de las Pulgas Spanish land grant dating back to the late 1700s. An assortment of small shops invite browsing, and the peaceful 3.5-acre gardens—designed after the Alhambra Gardens in Granada, Spain—invite a leisurely stroll.

Left Bank

*635 Santa Cruz Ave./Doyle St., (650) 473-6543;
www.leftbank.com. L M-Sat, D daily, SunBr; $$.*

For description, see page 225.

Lisa's Tea Treasures

1175 Merrill St./Oak Grove St., across from train station, (650) 322-5544; www.lisastea.com. Tea Tu-Fr 11-4, Sat at 11 & 1:30, 4, Sun at 12 & 3; $$. Reservations advised.

For description, see page 198.

Picnic Pick-Ups

• **Draeger's Market**
1010 University Dr./near Santa Cruz Ave., (650) 324-7700; www.draegers.com. Daily 7am-10pm.

For description, see page 171.

PALO ALTO

A LITTLE BACKGROUND

With wide tree-lined streets and impressive mansions on its outlying boulevards, Palo Alto historically has been home to upper-class residents. It is famous as the home of Stanford University and, more recently, for being a part of that nebulous area known as Silicon Valley. The University Avenue exit off Highway 101 leads under a canopy of magnolias, then oaks, then, upon entering the Stanford campus, palms.

VISITOR INFORMATION

Palo Alto Chamber of Commerce

*122 Hamilton Ave., (650) 324-3121,
www.paloaltochamber.com.*

GETTING THERE

Located approximately 13 miles south of San Mateo, and 32 miles south of San Francisco.

WHAT TO DO

Elizabeth F. Gamble Garden

1431 Waverley St./Embarcadero Rd., (650) 329-1356; www.gamblegarden.org. House: M-F 9-noon. Garden: Daily dawn to dusk. Free.

Built in 1902, the Colonial Georgian Revival house here features enormous pieces of interior redwood paneling unmarred by knots. Today, volunteers maintain both the house and the manicured classic Edwardian gardens, which include small "rooms," an assortment of soothing fountains, and scattered benches for quiet reflection. Each month has its pleasures, but April's promise of a cascade of blossoms along a cherry allée might be the best. Picnicking is enjoyable at tables sheltered by an old oak, and the lawns next door at **Bowling Green Park** are also inviting.

HP Garage

*367 Addison Ave./Waverley St.;
www.hp.com/go/history.*

The product (an audio oscillator) and the company (Hewlett-Packard) that launched the high tech industry were developed in 1939 in this garage by Stanford graduates William Hewlett and David Packard. Beside the driveway, a monument to the birthplace of Silicon Valley tells the story.

Museum of American Heritage

351 Homer Ave./Waverly St., (650) 321-1004; www.moah.org. F-Sun 11-4. Free.

Situated inside a charming English country-style house that it rents from the city, this museum displays 19th- and 20th-century electrical and mechanical inventions. Among the 2,000-plus artifacts are obsolete typewriters, toasters, washing machines, and cameras—all arranged into themed settings such as The Kitchen, The Laundry, and The General Store. Volunteers are sometimes on hand to demonstrate a group of elevator models and the Linotype machine in The Print Shop set up in a garage out back. Special exhibits and a large garden also beckon.

Palo Alto Children's Theatre

1305 Middlefield Rd., (650) 463-4930; www.city.palo-alto.ca.us/theatre. Schedule varies. $8, under 18 $4.

Seasonal productions are performed by child actors ages 8 through 18 and appeal especially to children. Past shows have included such favorites as *The Tales of Beatrix Potter* and *Charlotte's Web*. Summer performances are usually staged outside, and picnics are encouraged.

Palo Alto Duck Pond

At E end of Embarcadero Rd. Daily sunrise-sunset. Free.

Located in a quiet, unpopulated area away from town, this pond is one of the Bay Area's best spots to see ducks, birds, and the occasional swans. In winter, unusual migrating birds are also seen. A nearby small airport provides plane-watching fun.

Also nearby, the **Lucy Evans Baylands Nature Interpretive Center** (*(650) 329-2506. Tu-F 2-5, Sat-Sun 1-5. Free.*) has exhibits that orient visitors to the area. During daylight hours, visitors can walk out over the 120-acre salt marsh on an 800-foot-long raised wooden walkway. Naturalist-led walks are scheduled on weekends.

Palo Alto Junior Museum & Zoo

1451 Middlefield Rd./Embarcadero, (650) 329-2111; www.pajmzfriends.org. Tu-Sat 10-5, Sun 1-4. Free.

Opened in 1934, this was the first children's museum on the West Coast. Inside exhibits are hands-on and include colorful play structures that are especially fun for children through age 10. A well-maintained outdoor mini-zoo houses local and exotic animals—raccoons, skinks, ducks, birds, bunnies, pythons—and puts windows at kid's-eye level.

Adjacent **Rinconada Park** has a large, colorful playground.

Stanford Shopping Center

On El Camino Real, just N of Stanford campus, (650) 617-8200; www.stanfordshop.com. M-F 10-9, Sat 10-7, Sun 11-6.

Beautifully designed, this is the only shopping center in the world owned by a university. Among the 150 fashionable stores are: California's first **Bloomingdale's**; **Gleim Jewelers**, where the world's largest emerald is sometimes on display; the only Northern California outlet for Dutch retailer **Oilily**; an unusual open-air **Polo/Ralph Lauren** shop; the world's first **Victoria's Secret**, which opened here in 1977. Department stores include **Macy's**, **Nordstrom**, and **Neiman Marcus**.

The Health Library, operated by Stanford University Hospital as a community service, provides an archive of medical information and helpful volunteer reference librarians.

Food outlets include a branch of the Wine Country's **Oakville Grocery** (see page 424), filled with esoteric foods, and a branch of Berkeley's **Andronico's Market** (see page 295). Among the restaurants attracting diners at all hours are branches of **Palo Alto Creamery Fountain & Grill** (see page 182) and **Piatti Ristorante** (see page 221).

In addition to being an environmentally conscious mall, with recycling receptacles throughout, it is a showcase for California artists. Look for David Gilhooley's "Merfrog Fountain," Larry Binkley's "Flying People," and John Pugh's 180-foot-long mural of an 18th-century Parisian street scene.

The Stanford Theatre

221 University Ave., (650) 324-3700; www.stanfordtheatre.org. $7, 65+ & under 18 $5.

This 1,175-seat movie palace has been meticulously restored to its 1925-era grandeur by former classics professor David Packard, Jr., son of the computer tycoon. Plush red mohair seats, elaborate ceiling paintings, and magnificent tile work in the lobby help take audiences back in time as they view pre-1950 Hollywood films. Some movies play here that can be seen nowhere else. Retrospectives are scheduled regularly, and an organist often accompanies silent films on the theater's Wurlitzer. Box office proceeds go to film restoration and preservation.

Stanford University Campus

Entrance at El Camino Real/University Ave., (650) 723-2560; www.stanford.edu. Facilities sometimes closed during academic breaks.

Founded by Leland Stanford in 1885 on what had been his family's horse farm, California's premier private university is dedicated to the memory of Stanford's son, who died of typhoid fever at the age of 15. It is fittingly nicknamed "The Farm" and is home to 13 Nobel Prize winners. The **Quadrangle**, which is the oldest part of the campus, features Mission-style architecture. Hour-long **campus tours** *((650) 723-2560. Daily at 11, 3:15. Free.)* leave from the front steps of Memorial Auditorium. Tours of the 2-mile-long **linear accelerator** are also available *(2575 Sand Hill Rd., in Menlo Park, (650) 926-2204; www.slac.stanford.edu. M-F at 10, 1. Free. Reservation required.).* East of the Quad is **Hoover Tower** *((650) 723-2053. Daily 10-4:30. $2, 65+ & under 13 $1.).* Stanford's shorter version of the University of California's campanile, it stands 285 feet tall and affords a panoramic view of the area from its observation platform. At the tower's base, a museum that is part of the **Hoover Institution on War, Revolution, and Peace** *(550 Serra Mall, (650) 723-3563;*

Stanford University chapel in the Quadrangle

www.hoover.org. Tu-Sat 11-4. Free.) honors Stanford graduate and former president Herbert Hoover. Nearby, the **Thomas Welton Stanford Art Gallery** is home to revolving exhibitions of works by international and regional artists.

Built in 1892, the neoclassical **Cantor Arts Center** *(Museum Way/Lomita Dr., (650) 723-4177; www.museum.stanford.edu. W-Sun 11-5, Thur to 8; docent tour W at 12, Sat-Sun at 1, family tour 2nd Sat at 3. Free.)* is the oldest museum west of the Mississippi, and the first building constructed of structurally reinforced concrete—quite a technical accomplishment at the time. Having suffered severe damage in the 1989 earthquake, it is repaired and once again showing its eclectic collection of extraordinary ancient Asian and Egyptian treasures, modern and contemporary art, Stanford family memorabilia, and California Native American objects (a noteworthy item in this latter collection is a canoe carved by Yurok Indians from a single redwood log). The gold spike that marked the meeting of the two sections of the Transcontinental Railroad in 1869 is also displayed. The adjacent 1-acre **Rodin Sculpture Garden** *((650) 723-3469. Daily dawn-dusk; tour W at 2, Sat at 11:30, Sun at 3. Free.)* holds 20 bronzes, including "The Gates of Hell." Together the museum and garden hold the world's second-largest collection of Rodin sculpture (the largest is in Paris). All this and the fabulous **Cool Cafe** *((650) 725-4758.)* providing organic fare and dramatic views of the sculpture garden, too!

Nearby, the **New Guinea Sculpture Garden** displays totem poles and other wood and stone sculptures made on the campus in 1994 by New Guinea master carvers.

Winter Lodge

3009 Middlefield Rd./Oregon Expressway, (650) 493-4566; www.winterlodge.com. Daily 3-5, other session times vary; closed May-Sept. $7, skate rental $3.

An *outdoor* ice skating rink in Palo Alto? Well, it's *not* on a frozen lake. Indeed, it is located in a nicely manicured residential section of town. But it *is* removed from traffic and surrounded by tall eucalyptus trees, and it's the *only* permanent outdoor rink west of the Sierra. Designed for families and children, the rink measures about two-thirds the size of an average indoor rink, making it too small for competitive skating.

WHERE TO STAY

Creekside Inn

3400 El Camino Real/Matadero Ave., ½-mi. S of Pagemill Rd., (800) 492-7335, (650) 493-2411; www.creekside-inn.com. 5 stories; 136 rooms. Heated pool; fitness room. Evening wine; 2 restaurants; room service.

All rooms have a patio or balcony, and gardens, a fountain, and a footbridge over the creek await exploration. A shady, secluded pool is surrounded by a privacy fence. Parking is motel-style just outside rooms in nine mostly 2-story structures scattered through the tranquil setting alongside Matadero Creek, and a complimentary town car shuttle provides transportation to locations within a 5-mile radius.

Cheery **Cibo Restaurant & Bar** *(B-L-D daily; $.)* has comfy booths lining two walls and big windows for viewing the street action outside. The extensive breakfast menu includes the usual as well as Belgian waffles, crepes, and frittatas. **Driftwood Market and Deli** acts as a combination fast-food stop, coffee bar, and gift shop.

Crowne Plaza Cabaña Palo Alto

4290 El Camino Real/San Antionio Rd., 4 mi. from downtown, (800) 2-CROWNE, (650) 857-0787; www.cppaloalto.crowneplaza.com. 8 stories; 194 rooms; $$-$$$. Heated pool; hot tub; fitness room. Restaurant; room service. Self-parking $10, valet $15.

This attractively renovated hotel has a curving entry hugged by 16 of its original Italian cypress trees planted in 1962. Once owned by Doris Day (and still reflecting that fact today with its pet-friendly policy) and co-owned by Jay J. Sarno (who designed and built Caesar's Palace in Las Vegas), it was popular with Rat Pack members Sammy Davis, Jr. and Frank Sinatra. It made another big splash in 1965 when the Beatles took over the eighth floor during a concert tour, and a suite on that floor now honors them. All guest rooms have refrigerators with complimentary cold drinks, and complimentary car service is available within a 5-mile radius.

4290 Bistro & Bar serves Mediterranean-inspired cuisine and offers heavenly outdoor seating in nice weather.

Dinah's Garden Hotel

4261 El Camino Real/W. Charleston Rd., (800) 227-8220, (415) 493-2844; www.dinahshotel.com. 145 rooms. Some gas fireplaces. 2 heated pools; sauna; fitness room. 2 restaurants.

An impressive collection of Asian art is on display throughout this unique property, including two life-size 19th-century Indian processional elephant statues by the entry and a

2nd-century Gandharan stone seated Buddha. Each room is individually decorated. One suite has antique embroidered panels on the wall, sophisticated Italian leather chairs, and a Lifecycle bike placed strategically between the dining table and the bed; a large window covered by motor-driven drapes looks out over a serene lagoon, populated with koi and ducks, and onto a stone Buddha. The property's quiet gardens are tended by three full-time gardeners. They feature the sounds of fountains and attract a white heron that sometimes can be observed fishing from one of the guest room porches. Themed suites include the Railroad Baron Suite, stocked with a whistle and engineer's cap and sporting a model train running on track mounted near the ceiling; the African Suite, outfitted with antique Jarred-wood furniture, an African Chief's armchair with carved lions, and an elephant dance mask; and the FDR Memorial Suite, which is wheelchair accessible, has an adjacent caretaker suite, and is equipped with an old-time radio that plays an authentic FDR fireside chat. Rooms are stocked with fresh fruit, and pillows are topped with a Ghirardelli chocolate at turndown. Parking is right in front of the room, and the *Wall Street Journal* is available in a distribution box by the lagoon.

The hotel restaurant, **Trader Vic's** *(4269 El Camino Real, (650) 849-9800; www.tradervics paloalto.com. D daily; $$$. Valet parking.)*, is rich with more Asian art: a pair of 19th-century Japanese bronze shi-shi lions, a raft of Oceanic/South Pacific art—mostly Paupa New Guinea, and an original Henry Moore tapestry. Don't miss having a tropical drink in the Mai Tai Lounge, along with some appetizers— perhaps a crab Rangoon and a cup of bongo bongo soup. Seating is also available on a veranda. For more description, see page 280. The **Poolside Grill Restaurant** *(B-L daily.)* serves breakfast.

Four Seasons Hotel Silicon Valley at East Palo Alto

2050 University Ave., just W of Hwy. 101, in East Palo Alto, (866) 556-4001, (650) 566-1200; www.fourseasons.com/siliconvalley. 10 stories; 200 rooms; $$$-$$$+. Heated pool; hot tub; fitness room; full-service spa. Restaurant; room service. Self-parking $12, valet $22.

Sleek and classy, this is the 70th Four Seasons hotel and the footprint for all of their future hotels. Original art decorates the hallways and guest rooms, which are done in a tasteful contemporary style and feature marble bathrooms with deep tubs. Amenities include a rooftop pool and whirlpool tub with a waterfall wall—all set amid a bank of cabanas and potted palms. A spa equipped with a large steam room offers serenity and a sublime package that includes a massage, wrap, and scalp treatment/massage.

Situated in a stunning room with high ceilings, a dramatic limestone wall, and floor-to-ceiling windows that bring the outdoors in, **Quattro** *((650) 470-2889; www.quattro restaurant.com. B-L-D daily; $$$+. Valet parking.)* features original art by masters Salvador Dali and Pablo Picasso as well as four life-size marble sculptures of human figures representing the four seasons done by contemporary South Korean artist Yong Deok Lee. Starters on the seasonally-changing, contemporary California-Italian menu might include a full-flavored artichoke-spinach salad with candied almonds or a quartet of varied bruschette. Pastas are a strong point; a stellar example is chestnut pappardelle with venison ragu, chard, and ricotta. Stellar desserts have included panettone bread pudding, chocolate lava cake, and cinnamon-and-sugar donuts with dips for two. Ingredients are local when possible, and service is attentive. The bar serves cocktails in artsy martini glasses and is a good choice for a small meal, and patio dining is available in good weather.

Garden Court Hotel

520 Cowper St./University Ave., (800) 824-9028, (650) 322-9000; www.gardencourt.com. 4 stories; 62 rooms; $$$+. Some wood-burning fireplaces. Fitness room. Restaurant; room service. Valet parking $15.

Located just off the main street, this attractive hotel offers posh comfort. A central courtyard with fountains and flowers conveys a far-away-from-it-all feeling. The staff strives to give personal service and claims never to forget a name. Tastefully appointed guest rooms have private terraces and four-poster beds with European-style down bedding. Amenities include local shuttle service.

On the ground floor, Il **Fornaio**
Restaurant *((650) 853-3888; www.ilfornaio.com.
B-L-D daily; $$. Reservations advised.)* serves up
rustic pizzas in an elegant interior space as well
as out on a sunny, peaceful courtyard. For more
description, see page 73.

Sheraton Palo Alto

*625 El Camino Real/University Ave., (800) 874-3516,
(650) 328-2800; www.sheraton.com/paloalto. 4 sto-
ries; 346 rooms; $$-$$$. Heated pool; fitness room.
Restaurant; room service. Self-parking $10, valet $15.*

Centrally located and offering the ameni-
ties typical of the chain, this comfortable
lodging has an attractively landscaped garden
area with a large koi pond.

Westin Palo Alto

*675 El Camino Real, (800) WESTIN-1, (650) 321-4422;
www.westin.com/paloalto. 5 stories; 184 rooms; $$-
$$$+. Heated pool; hot tub. Restaurant; room service.
Self-parking $10, valet $15.*

The Mediterranean design of this location
of the luxe chain features large Etruscan-style
vases in five courtyards. The expected upscale
features are all here, including spacious marble
bathrooms and trademark soft, down-topped
Heavenly Beds.

WHERE TO EAT

Andalé

*209 University Ave./Emerson St., (650) 323-2939;
www.andalemexican.com. L-D daily; $.*

Delicious Mexican menu items include
fresh fish tacos, vegetarian flautas, and seasonal
fresh-fruit agua fresca drinks. After placing an
order at the back counter, items are prepared to
specifications using fresh ingredients and no
lard. Meats sizzle continuously on the open
grills. On weekends from 11 to 2, brunch items
join the menu. In good weather, choice seating
is on the patio just in from the sidewalk, and
sometimes live music from a public square
across the street provides free entertainment.

Blue Chalk Cafe

*630 Ramona St./Hamilton St., (650) 326-1020;
www.bluechalkcafe.com. D M-Sat; $-$$. Reservations
accepted.*

Operating within a historical building
dating from 1927, this busy spot features an

inviting open-air front patio and an interior
equipped with pool tables. The kitchen dishes
up delicious down-home Southern cuisine.
Appetizers are exceptional and might include
roasted Blue Lake green beans, catfish chips, or
hoppin' john (blackeyed peas). Dinner is a
choice of salads (a blackened chicken Caesar, a
warm spinach with smoked chicken) and hefty
dinner plates (house-smoked pork chops, old-
fashioned meatloaf, barbecued short ribs).
Don't miss a side of roasted garlic mashed
potatoes or housemade buttermilk biscuits.
Servers can provide a complete description of
the original Southern folk art and photography
decorating the premises.

Buca di Beppo

*643 Emerson St./Forest St., (650) 329-0665;
www.bucadibeppo.com. L-D daily; $$.*

For description, see page 63.

The Cheesecake Factory

*375 University Ave., (650) 473-9622;
www.thecheesecakefactory.com. L M-Sat, D daily,
SunBr; $-$$. Valet parking at D.*

For description, see page 66.

Coupa Cafe

*538 Ramona St./University Ave., (650) 322-6872;
www.coupacafe.com. B-L-D daily; $.*

Located within a historic Spanish Colonial
building with a tile floor, a wood-beamed
ceiling, and a fireplace in the back room, this
casual spot is a branch of the original café in
Caracas, Venezuela. Order at the counter, then
select seating inside or out. The kitchen serves
up hot breakfasts, salads, soups, panini, pastas,
crepes, Caribbean-style empanadas, and
arepas—traditional Venezuelan white-cornmeal
griddle cakes with a variety of fillings. Picture-
perfect pastries and hand-made Venezuelan
chocolate bonbons perch invitingly in glass
cases, and drinks include coffees made with
patio-dried fair-trade Venezuelan beans and
a spicy hot chocolate—all available either
hot or iced.

Empire Grill & Tap Room

*651 Emerson St./Forest St., (650) 321-3030. L-D daily;
$-$$. Reservations advised.*

On warm days, dining in the lovely courtyard shaded with umbrellas and serene with the

sounds of a wall fountain is the way to go. Heaters make it a good choice even on cooler days and evenings. Inside, the upscale pub-style atmosphere includes a long bar with seating and a very long banquette. It seems to always be crowded, perhaps because of the menu featuring "American cuisine with French and Italian regional influences," which translates into pastas, salads, and grilled meats and fish, plus a good hamburger and club sandwich. Don't miss a side of the famous french fries, served with addictive garlic mayo and housemade ketchup dips. More than 15 beers are on draft.

Evvia

420 Emerson St./Lytton St., (650) 326-0983; www.evvia.net. L M-F, D daily; $$$. Reservations advised. Valet parking.

The welcoming open dining room of this very popular Greek restaurant features rustic beamed ceilings and an open kitchen. Seating in the back, where colored bottles decorating the wall glow like gemstones, is particularly comfortable. The menu includes classic dishes such as spanakotiropita (phyllo stuffed with a spinach-feta mixture), Greek salad, egg-lemon soup, and moussaka, as well as delicious mesquite-grilled whole striped bass and lamb chops. Because everything is made in-house, desserts are special, and the array of baklavas—chocolate, pistachio, walnut—rate as exquisite.

A sister restaurant, Kokkari, is in San Francisco (see page 75).

Gordon Biersch Brewery Restaurant

640 Emerson St./Forest St., (650) 323-7723; www.gordonbiersch.com. L-D daily; $$.

For description, see page 198.

Junnoon

150 University Ave./High St., (650) 329-9644; www.junnoon.com. L M-F, D M-Sat; $$$. Reservations advised.

Choose to sit either outdoors in a heated pavilion or inside beneath tall ceilings and amid a sexy, spice-colored decor featuring gauzy curtains and bead-fringed lampshades. Junnoon (pronounced "juh-noon") is the Hindi word for passion, energy, obsession, and the "modern" Indian cuisine here is executed with same. Dining with a group is ideal, as it permits trying a larger variety of dishes, but another good

idea is to over order and take the leftovers home for a follow-up feast. For appetizers, semolina shells filled with chickpeas and sweetened with tamarind chutney are divine; the more unusual sprouted mung bean salad is also good. Entrees include delicious tandoor-grilled tiger prawns in an unusual Bengali coconut-mustard sauce and a rich sliced tikka chicken in a fenugreek-seasoned, old Delhi-style tomato-onion sauce. And then there are the sides—roasted eggplant crush, snow peas poriyal, and several raitas and chutneys. The dessert of choice is saffron kulfi served in a crispy pistachio tuile bowl. A cocktail menu offers unique, cleverly named concoctions such as the Manic Masala Mary (an Indian Bloody Mary) and a Buddha Belly-ni (champagne, peach schnapps, guava nectar), plus a tasty non-alcoholic Bombay ginger ale made with freshly squeezed ginger juice, fresh pineapple, and raspberries.

MacArthur Park

27 University Ave./near El Camino Real, (650) 321-9990; www.macarthurparkpaloalto.com. L M-F, D daily, SunBr; $$-$$$. Reservations advised. Valet parking.

Situated just off the beaten path, this popular restaurant operates within a historical landmark originally designed for the U.S. War Department in 1918 by Hearst Castle architect Julia Morgan. The building is now divided into several dining areas, including two indoor balconies and a grand, barn-like room on the main floor. The kitchen is celebrated for its dry-aged steaks, California game, and baby back ribs cooked in an oak wood smoker.

Mango Caribbean Restaurant

435 Hamilton Ave./Waverley, (650) 324-9443; www.mangocaribbean.com. L-D daily; $. Reservations accepted.

Traditional Jamaican, Trinidad, and Tobago cuisines dominate the menu. Chicken roti from Trinidad is a combination of curried chicken, potatoes, and veggies wrapped up burrito-style. Jamaican beef and chicken patties have a flaky crust, and vegetarian Rasta Pea Cook-Up includes a variety of beans. Curried goat and the house specialty, spicy jerked chicken, are also available. The menu also offers a large selection of playful tropical smoothies, as well as a blend-your-own version—all served in humungous globe glasses with a big straw. Though the decor is simple, the dining room is comfortable and service is friendly and efficient.

Ming's
1700 Embarcadero Rd. (at Embarcadero East exit off Hwy. 101), (650) 856-7700; www.mings.com. Dim sum daily 11-2:30; L-D daily; $$-$$$. Reservations advised.

This popular restaurant has existed in Palo Alto since the 1950s, when it opened on El Camino Real. Ming's beef—a somewhat sweet dish prepared with wok-charred beef—and Chinese chicken salad were both this restaurant's invention. Made with shredded, deep-fried chicken, the salad is labor-intensive to make and in such heavy demand that one chef is employed to prepare just that. Every morning another chef prepares fresh dim sum delicacies, including steamed shark's fin dumplings, delicious fresh shrimp items, and an electric-bright mango pudding in strawberry sauce. Other noteworthy dishes include dramatic drunken prawns flambé and steamed fresh garlic lobster. A full vegetarian menu is also available.

Nola
535 Ramona St./University Ave., (650) 328-2722; www.nolas.com. L M-F, D daily; $$. Reservations advised.

Featuring ornate iron balconies, colorful tiles, and stone floors, this New Orleans-style spot has a warren of seating areas. In good weather, the outdoor patio and upstairs balcony are favorites with the fun-seeking clientele. Genre food includes jambalaya, gumbo, crawfish dumplings, po-boys, pecan pie, and a rum-laden Hurricane cocktail that packs a wallop.

Palo Alto Creamery Fountain & Grill
566 Emerson St./Hamilton St., (650) 323-3131; www.paloaltocreamery.com/. B-L-D daily; $. No reservations.

Opened by the Peninsula Dairy in 1923 and featuring red leatherette booths and an authentic soda fountain, this popular diner is known for serving tasty simple food—oatmeal and buttermilk pancakes in the morning, a variety of sandwiches and hamburgers (on housemade bread and buns) at lunch, and chicken pot pies and pork chops at dinner—

at reasonable prices. Fountain items are made by "authentic soda jerks" and include their famous hand-blended milk shakes. Other favorites include sour cherry pie, housemade soups, and cherry coke.

A branch is located at the Stanford Shopping Center.

Picnic Pick-Ups
• A. G. Ferrari Foods
200 Hamilton Ave./Emerson St., (650) 752-0900; www.agferrari.com. M-Sat 10-8, Sun 10-6.

For description, see page 295.

Saint Michael's Alley
806 Emerson St./Homer Ave., (650) 326-2530; www.stmikes.com. L-D Tu-Sat, Sat-SunBr; $$-$$$. Reservations advised.

With its slate floor, sponged gold walls, and oversize central skylight, this cheery spot is primo for weekend brunch. Egg dishes are served with perfectly herbed Yukon gold potatoes; they include a really good St. Mike's Omelet filled with smoked bacon, sautéed mushrooms, spinach, and both cheddar and cream cheeses. A Belgian waffle, Blue Monkey pancakes dotted with banana chunks and blueberries, and an assortment of salads and sandwiches are also options. The restaurant also has a reputation for romantic dinners. This venture began in 1959 on University Avenue, where The Grateful Dead and Joan Baez performed before they were famous. Plans are in the works to move nearby to 140 Homer Avenue.

Straits Cafe
3295 El Camino Real/Lambert Ave., (650) 494-7168; www.straitspaloalto.com. L M-F, D daily; $$-$$$. Reservations advised.

In warm weather, the tropical-style outside patio of this stylish restaurant is prime. Among the intriguing menu choices are Ikan Pangang, a delicious salmon filet spiced with fresh chili sauce and grilled in a banana leaf, and Mee Goreng, a spicy Indian-style noodle dish with tofu and prawns. Desserts are standouts, among them a silky banana pudding shaped like a cone. Live jazz is scheduled on Friday and Saturday nights.

Tamarine

546 University Ave./Cowper St., (650) 325-8500;
www.tamarinerestaurant.com. L M-F, D daily; $$.
Reservations advised.

The Vietnamese menu offers an array of delicious and dazzling small plates meant for sharing. Among the best are ginger-chicken salad (with cabbage, cashews, and caramelized onions), shaking beef (a toned-down version served on watercress salad), and delicate chili-lime aubergine (grilled white eggplants). Several kinds of flavor-infused rice are served attractively in a banana leaf wrapping. Do leave space for the chocolate-filled dessert won tons. This sophisticated restaurant displays the work of contemporary Vietnamese artists. Semi-annual auctions are scheduled, with profits donated to a Ho Chi Minh City orphanage.

Taxi's Hamburgers

403 University Ave., 650-322-TAXI;
www.taxishamburgers.com. L-D daily.

For description, see page 171.

Tea Time

542 Ramona St./Hamilton Ave., (650) 32T-CUPS;
www.tea-time.com. M-Sat 10:30-7, Sun 11-6.
Reservations accepted.

More than 100 kinds of bulk loose-leaf teas are stocked in this little shop for tea lovers, and the menu of teatime tidbits includes tea sandwiches, crumpets, and scones. Some patrons love the place so much that they leave their decorative china cup in a cupboard on the premises for use when they visit. In between, the cups are displayed nicely for all to enjoy. Antique cups and brand-new cozies galore are for sale along with an array of teapots, and tasting classes are scheduled regularly.

MOUNTAIN VIEW

WHAT TO DO

Computer History Museum

1401 N. Shoreline Blvd., just E of Hwy. 101,
(650) 810-1010; www.computerhistory.org. W & F 1-4
(tour at 1, 2:30), Sat 11-5 (tour at 11:30, 1, 2:30),
Sun 1-4 (tour times vary). Free.

Formerly part of The Computer Museum in Boston, this comprehensive collection of computer-related artifacts moved to the Bay Area in 1996 and opened here in 2002. Displaying 500 to 600 items (only 1% of the collection), it is the world's largest collection of computer artifacts. It exhibits hardware and software as well as photos and videos. Among the gems seen on docent-led tours are the first Apple computer (which sells now for more than it did when it went on the market), a WW II Enigma machine encrypter, and the 1975 Illiac IV (an earlier Illiac computer is said to have inspired director Stanley Kubrick for *2001*). A 1980 Japanese Sharp calculator with abacus (for those who didn't trust the calculator) and a 1969 Neiman Marcus "Kitchen Computer" that was priced at $10,000 (they didn't sell any) are also displayed.

NASA/Ames Research Center Visitor Center

Moffett Blvd./NASA Pkwy., off Hwy 101, (650) 604-
6497; www.arc.nasa.gov. Tu-F 10-4, Sat-Sun 12-4. Free.

Research in aeronautics, space technology, and more is conducted at this 430-acre facility.

WHERE TO STAY

Hotel Avante

860 E. El Camino Real/Crestview Dr., (800) 538-1600,
(650), 940-1000; www.hotelavante.com. 4 stories;
91 rooms; $$-$$$. Solar-heated pool; hot tub; fitness
room. Afternoon snack; evening wine M-F; continental
breakfast. No pets.

Decorated smartly in dark colors, this boutique hotel is fun to wander through. A literally *cool* air-conditioned hi-fi lounge invites a visit on the third floor, and CDs can be borrowed from the front desk. Room desks are stocked with toys: a Slinky, a mini Etch A Sketch, a Rubik's Cube, a deck of Bicycle cards, and a Duncan yo-yo.

WHERE TO EAT

Castro Street

The 100 through 300 blocks of this street are lined with exotic restaurants. Most are inexpensive Asian, but things are beginning to change and a few more upscale venues and fusion spots have joined the array. Among the most reliable old-timers are:

• Amarin Thai

174-176 Castro St./Villa, (650) 988-9323; www.amarinthaicuisine.com. L-D daily; $.

Amarin means "I shall live forever." Though that probably will not be the final result of a meal here, living well now will be. The extensive menu has many vegetarian and simulated-meat dishes, as well as the more expected items. Soft shell crab and assorted deep-fried fish with a variety of sauces are available along with more unusual roasted duck salad and hot and sizzling curry. Special ingredients are ordered in from Thailand, including teeny fresh pepper berries still on their tiny branches.

A branch is at 156 Castro St., (650) 938-8424.

• Godavari

216 Castro St., (650) 969-1112; www.godavari.us. L-D daily; $$.

This simple restaurant is named in honor of the River Godavari in Mumbai, India. The extensive menu includes dosas, a variety of spicy-hot vindaloos, complete thali meals, many tasty vegetarian selections, and a well-spiced coriander chicken specialty that arrives sizzling on an iron skillet. Portions are generous, and full dinners are served with pilau rice, nan bread, dal and raita. Adding to the visual interest, paintings by the late former owner and former namesake, Sue, hang on the wall.

• Pho Hoa

220 Castro St., (650) 969-5805; www.phohoa.com. L-D daily; $.

This always-busy cog in a world-wide chain provides a satisfying bowl of noodle soup. Rice plates and vermicelli bowls are also available. Feeling ready for whatever? Try an unusual iced white or red bean drink.

• Red Rock Coffee

201 Castro St./Villa St., (650) 967-4473; www.redrockcoffee.org. M-F 7-10, Sat 8-11, Sun 8-5; $.

Located within the oldest historical building in downtown Mountain View, this laid-back coffee house promises, "The music's good, the coffee is hot, the staff is friendly." And the tea comes in a tea pot with loose tea leaves. Live music is scheduled some evenings, and free access to two computers and free Wi-Fi are provided. Traditional coffee shop fare is available—pastries, cookies, desserts—plus sandwiches on weekdays. In early morning, the cheery red interior is inviting and mellow music plays softly—the perfect way to start a new day.

• Xanh

110 Castro St./W. Evelyn Ave., (650) 964-1888; www.xanhrestaurant.com. L M-F; D daily; $$. Reservations advised.

Portions of the Modern Vietnamese cuisine served here are large, and the presentations are spectacular. Signature dishes include the Deuce Roll (a mix of pork and shrimp), the Xanh Salad and Shaking Beef (dishes taste similar, but salad is huge and dramatic), Fighting Prawns, and any of the housemade noodle dishes. Desserts include a hazelnut mousse (delivered atop a charming tall, thin-stemmed glass plate with dome cover) and Menage a Trois (a delicious Vietnamese classic that mixes tapioca, sweet yellow mung beans, and coconut milk) desserts. Intriguing cocktails with catchy names seem to go particularly well with the cuisine. The restaurant is expansive, with three sleek interior dining rooms (one is a cool, very loud glass box punctuated with stainless-steel bead curtains), a street-side outdoor area in good weather, and a bar that sometimes has a DJ or live music (it also has a dramatic stone wall over which water cascades gently.

LOS ALTOS

WHERE TO STAY

Hidden Villa Hostel

26870 Moody Rd., 8 mi. from downtown, (650) 949-8648; www.hiddenvilla.org. 35 beds, 3 private cabins. Closed June-Aug.

Located on a 1,600-acre ranch in the foothills east of town, this privately owned hostel was built in 1937 and was the first on the Pacific Coast. It is now the oldest existing hostel in the U.S. The property includes a working farm, organic garden, and land preserve. See also page 468.

WHERE TO EAT

Chef Chu's

1067 N. San Antonio Rd./El Camino Real, (650) 948-2696; www.chefchu.com. L-D daily; $$. Reservations advised, 4+ only.

Chef Chu watches closely over his large kitchen staff and sees to it that excellence prevails in this well-appointed restaurant. Tasty dishes include crisp fried won tons, flavorful Szechwan beef, and hot-and-sour soup fragrant with sesame oil. Mu shu pork comes with unusual square pancakes for wrapping, and a beautifully presented lemon chicken consists of deep-fried whole chicken breasts—each glazed with lemon sauce and topped with a thin slice of lemon and a bright red maraschino cherry. A large window in the reception area provides views of the busy kitchen.

Picnic Pick-Ups

• A. G. Ferrari Foods

295 Main St., (650) 947-7930; www.agferrari.com. M-F 9:30-8, Sat 9-7, Sun 9:30-6.

For description, see page 295.

• Draeger's Market

342 First St., (650) 948-4425; www.draegers.com. Daily 7am-10pm.

For description, see page 171.

SUNNYVALE

VISITOR INFORMATION

Sunnyvale Chamber of Commerce

260 S. Sunnyvale Ave. #4, (408) 736-4971; www.svcoc.org.

WHAT TO DO

The Lace Museum

552 S. Murphy Ave./El Camino Real, (408) 730-4695; www.thelacemuseum.org. Tu-Sat 11-4. Free.

Located in a small strip mall, this tiny museum displays all manner of lace: knitted lace, bobbin lace, and nature's lace—a delicate spider web. Changing exhibits feature antique laces and related items. Lace-making materials

are for sale in the shop, as is an assortment of antique hat pins and silver pill boxes.

WHERE TO STAY

Wild Palms Hotel

910 E. Fremont Ave./Wolfe Rd., off El Camino Real, (800) 538-1600, (408) 738-0500; www.wildpalms hotel.com. 208 rooms; $$. Heated pool; hot tub; fitness room. Afternoon snack; continental breakfast. No pets.

Painted banana yellow and sporting a peachy beachy ambiance, this low-rise motel has been converted into a tropical confection. A Hawaiian-style open-air lobby greets guests, and exotic tropical flowers and colors are found throughout. Whimsy shines through in original murals painted on some guest room doors and in the occasional chartreuse stuffed toy snake slithering across the back of a couch. Rooms surround a nicely landscaped garden courtyard with a hot tub and pool sporting bright vinyl playthings and are set far enough back from traffic to be quiet.

WHERE TO EAT

Picnic Pick-Ups

• A. G. Ferrari Foods

304 W. El Camino Real/S. Mathilda Ave., (408) 524-4000; www.agferrari.com. M-Sat 10-9, Sun 10-8.

For description, see page 295.

• C.J. Olson Cherries

348 W. El Camino Real/Mathilda St., (800) 738-BING, (408) 736-3726; www.cjolsoncherries.com. Daily 10-6.

Owned by the Olson family and operated at this location since 1933, this old-time fruit stand is a blast from the past. It looks a lot like the overwhelmed, crowded-out dwelling in the children's classic storybook *The Little House.* Let's hope it can hold out amid the urban sprawl and construction occurring everywhere around it, because the 1899 farm that once stood where P.F. Chang's Chinese Bistro and a few other chain businesses stand now was leveled in 1999 as the heavens wept. Actually, this small stand might have a chance, because it too was torn down and completely rebuilt in 2002. Though not inexpensive, the finest fruit is found here—most especially the biggest, plumpest, juiciest cherries—and it all can be tasted before purchase. A few of the nine different types of cherries grown are available continuously May through August and in December and January. Most are farmed, along with apricots, on 13 acres the family now leases from the city. Additionally, cherry pies, chocolate-covered apricots, Medjool dates, and more are for sale.

South Murphy Avenue
100 block of Murphy Ave./betw. Evelyn Ave. & E. Washington Ave., near Macy's.

This historical downtown block is lined with vintage early-1900s buildings holding many restaurants and a few boutiques. Note that most restaurants are closed for Sunday dinner.

• Dishdash
190 S. Murphy Ave., (408) 774-1889; www.dishdash.net. L-D M-Sat; $. Reservations advised.

Named for a traditional article of Middle Eastern clothing that symbolizes warmth and comfort (an example is displayed), this popular restaurant offers a large and interesting contemporary Mediterranean menu. Meals begin with complimentary pita bread and zaatar—a dipping sauce of sumac, thyme, sesame seeds, and olive oil. Ordering the Mediterranean Maza sampler platter of appetizers is a good move. Especially delectable menu items include tabouli, hummus, kibbeh (seasoned ground lamb stuffed with pine nuts), and stuffed grape leaves. An assortment of salads, wraps, kebabs, and vegetarian items (the m'shakaleh is exceptional) are also available. In good weather, sidewalk tables augment the small, usually-crowded interior.

• Taverna Bistro
133 S. Murphy Ave., (408) 735-9971; www.tavernabistro.com. L-D daily; $$.

Appointed with many comfortable booths, this spacious restaurant specializes in Greek and Turkish cuisines. The mezza plate appetizer is a three-tiered extravaganza of all the tastiest dishes. It, along with one main course, makes a nice dinner for two people. Try the homey stuffed bell peppers, delicious mousakka with potatoes, or kebabs. Unusual simple casserole dishes are also interesting option. Bellydancing is scheduled on Saturdays.

Udupi Palace
976 E. El Camino Real/Dale Ave., (408) 830-9600; www.udupipalaceca.com. L-D daily; $. No cards.

For description, see page 297.

SANTA CLARA

GETTING THERE

Located off the San Tomas Expressway (G4), 2 miles west of Highway 101.

VISITOR INFORMATION

Santa Clara Chamber of Commerce & Convention-Visitors Bureau
1850 Warburton Ave., (800) 272-6822, (408) 244-9660; www.santaclara.org.

WHAT TO DO

California's Great America
On Great America Parkway, off Hwys. 101 & 237, (408) 988-1776; www.cagreatamerica.com. Schedule varies; closed Nov-Feb. Age 3-61 $51.99, 62+ $34.99, under 48" tall $34.99; parking $10.

There's no question about it. The thrill rides at Northern California's most elaborate theme park are spectacular, and the roller coasters are great shocking fun: The Vortex is the West's first stand-up roller coaster; the

Demon features two 360-degree loops and a double helix; and the Grizzly is a classic wooden coaster based on the extinct Coney Island Wildcat. The circa 1976 double-decker Carousel Columbia is the world's tallest, and the Drop Tower free-fall ride is Santa Clara's tallest structure. The Kidzville and Nickelodeon Central areas have colorful rides and attractions especially for children 12 and under, and the Boomerang Bay Beach Club water park and nine live shows round out the fun.

Intel Museum
2200 Mission College Blvd./Burton St., (408) 765-0503; www.intel.com/museum. M-F 9-6, Sat 10-5. Free.

Located at Intel Corporation's headquarters (Intel is the world's largest semiconductor company and the inventor of the Pentium processor), this technology museum shows how computer chips are made and how they are used in everyday life. A live video feed shows the company's chip-fabrication facility. Hands-on educational exhibits appeal to both children and adults and change regularly, and kids can try on "bunny suits" like those worn in actual computer chip factories.

Mission Santa Clara de Asis
500 El Camino Real, (408) 554-4023; www.scu.edu/ visitors/mission. Daily sunrise-sunset. Free.

The original Santa Clara mission, built on a site beside the Guadalupe River in 1777, was destroyed by a flood. Rebuilt in 1928, this replica of the eighth mission in the chain of California missions is on the immaculately groomed grounds of **Santa Clara University** *((408) 554-4000; www.scu.edu. Tours M-F.).* The university was built on the mission grounds in 1851 as California's first institution of higher learning and is the state's first coeducational Catholic university. Now a state historical landmark, the mission holds some interesting relics, including three bells that were a gift from the king of Spain and original artwork by professional artist Agustin Davila, who painted the original mission's interior. Extensive lush gardens showcase hundreds of roses—several are classified as antique varieties—and a wide variety of trees and plants. Some of the oldest cultivated plants in California are found here: olive trees planted by Franciscan friars in 1822,

a giant 123-year-old Jacaranda tree, and the oldest wisteria in Northern California. Full bloom occurs April through May.

Just across from the mission, the university's **de Saissat Museum** *((408) 554-4528; www.scu.edu/deSaisset. Tu-Sun 11-4. Free.)* hosts rotating exhibits from a permanent collection featuring the work of artists such as Goya, Bonnard, and Hogarth, and of photographers such as Ansel Adams, Imogen Cunningham, and Annie Leibovitz. It also features an extensive California history collection related to the area.

Triton Museum of Art
1505 Warburton Ave., across from City Hall, (408) 247-3754; www.tritonmuseum.org. Daily 11-5, Thur to 9. Free.

This small art museum is inside an award-winning building inspired by early California missions. It boasts a sculpture garden and is surrounded by 7 landscaped acres featuring several kinds of palm trees and a grove of redwoods. Exhibitions focus on works by Northern California artists that are aesthetically and historically significant to the region.

Inside the 1913 arts and crafts-style Headen-Inman House, a charming converted farmhouse located in the park adjacent to the Triton, the **Santa Clara History Museum** *((408) 248-ARTS. Sun 1-4. Free.)* displays photographs and artifacts relating to the city's history. Farther back in the park, the 1866 Jamison-Brown House is famous for its porch where Jack London wrote part of *The Call of the Wild.*

WHERE TO STAY

Embassy Suites Santa Clara—Silicon Valley
2885 Lakeside Dr., (800) EMBASSY, (408) 496-6400; www.santaclara.embsuites.com. 10 stories; 257 rooms; $-$$$. Indoor heated pool; hot tub; fitness room. Evening cocktails; full breakfast; room service. No pets.

All guests get a spacious two-room suite consisting of one bedroom plus a separate living room with sofa bed. Each is equipped with a microwave, refrigerator, and coffee maker. The hotel is just minutes from California's Great America theme park and has packages that include admission tickets. For more description, see page 445.

Hilton Santa Clara

*4949 Great America Pkwy., (800) HILTONS,
(408) 330-0001; www.santaclara.hilton.com.
8 stories; 280 rooms; $$-$$$. Heated pool; hot tub;
fitness room. Restaurant; room service.*

Well-situated just across the parking lot
from Great America, and across the street from
the Santa Clara Convention Center and a Light
Rail stop, this elegant, richly-appointed hotel
serves both the business and leisure traveler.
Rooms feature colorful golden granite vanities
and original artwork, and some have views of
Great America. Half the pool is shaded by an
overhang, a nice feature in summer.

Madison Street Inn

*1390 Madison St., (408) 249-5541;
www.madisonstreetinn.com. 6 rooms; $-$$. Some
shared baths. Pool; hot tub; sauna. Evening snack;
full breakfast.*

Located just 10 minutes from the San Jose
Airport, this comfy B&B is surrounded by
⅓ acre of landscaped gardens. The evening
snack is homemade chocolate chip cookies and
sherry, and breakfast includes fresh fruit juice,
muffins, and eggs Benedict.

Plaza Suites

*3100 Lakeside Dr., (800) 345-1554, (408) 748-9800;
www.theplazasuites.com. 7 stories; 219 rooms; $-$$$.
Heated pool; hot tub; fitness room. Evening cocktails;
full breakfast; restaurant.*

All units are spacious two-room suites, and
the pool area is nicely landscaped.

Santa Clara Marriott

*2700 Mission College Blvd., (800) 228-9290, (408)
988-1500; www.scmarriott.com. 15 stories; 759
rooms; $-$$$. Heated pool; hot tub; sauna; fitness
room; 4 tennis courts (with night lights). 2 restaurant;
room service. Self-parking $9, valet $18.*

The largest hotel in the area, this lodging
consists of one 10- and one 15-story tower, plus
a 2-story wing surrounding the pool. It is located adjacent to Great America.

Parcel 104 *((408) 970-6104; www.parcel
104.com. B daily, L M-F, D M-Sat. Valet parking.)* showcases American regional cuisine. It's
the kind of place where little forks and spoons
appear between courses holding an "amuse."
The accomplished kitchen produces perfectly
seasoned salads and soups, and main courses

might be a full-flavored housemade fettuccine
with spicy lamb sausage and broccoli or a
delicious rabbit dish seasoned with balsamic
vinegar. Dessert brings on fabulous double-
chocolate spoon bread, a banana Napoleon, and
homey tapioca pudding. Presentation is faultless, with each dish arranged on the perfect
accent plate, wines poured into their complementary oversize glass, and the table set with
classy Frette linens. *Yes!*

WHERE TO EAT

Pedro's Restaurant & Cantina

*3935 Freedom Cir., (408) 496-6777;
www.pedrosrestaurants.com. L-D daily; $$.*

For description, see page 391.

Piatti Ristorante & Bar

*3905 Rivermark Plaza, (408) 330-9212;
www.piatti.com. L M-F, D daily; $$.*

For description, see page 221.

Pizza & Pipes

*3581 Homestead Rd./Lawrence Expwy., (866) BEST-
PIZZA, (408) 248-5680; www.pizzaandpipes.com.
L-D daily; $.*

This pizza parlor has a separate game
room and kids' play area. In 1984, a Yamaha FX
20 electronic organ replaced the ailing antique
pipe organ, but the pizza is as good as ever.

Taxi's Hamburgers

*3139 Mission College Blvd., (408) 235-8877;
www.taxishamburgers.com. L-D daily; $.*

For description, see page 171.

SAN JOSE

A LITTLE BACKGROUND

Touted as the "capital of Silicon Valley" (a title
that seems valid considering that 24 of the
area's largest computer companies have headquarters or divisions here), San Jose—the country's 10th-largest city and California's 3rd-
largest and oldest city (it was founded as a
Spanish pueblo in 1777 and was the state
capital from 1849 to 1851)—receives relatively
little attention for its attractions. But that seems
to be changing as the city concentrates on

revitalizing its downtown area. Now, visitors to the city center can enjoy its many cultural offerings as well as a reliably mild climate—it boasts more than 300 days of sunshine annually. But be warned, the song "Do You Know the Way to San Jose" was written for a reason. Though downtown is easy to maneuver on foot, the city is gigantic and easy to get lost in. Secure a good map, and always allow extra time.

VISITOR INFORMATION

San Jose Convention & Visitors Bureau
408 Almaden Blvd., (800) SAN-JOSE, (408) 295-9600; www.sanjose.org.

ANNUAL EVENTS

Vietnamese Spring Festival and Parade
February. (408) 292-8283; www.vsfsanjose.com. Free.

This festive event reflects San Jose's enormous Vietnamese population—the largest outside Vietnam. It features Vietnamese arts and crafts, live performances by famous Vietnamese entertainers, martial art demonstrations, children's games and rides, a talent show, a colorful parade, and food booths showcasing authentic Vietnamese cuisine and other multicultural fare.

San Jose International Mariachi Festival
September. (800) 642-8482, (408) 928-5563; www.mhcviva.org. $5.

This 2-day outdoor festival includes concerts and a "feria."

Downtown Ice
Mid-November-mid-January. On Market St., in open plaza betw. San Jose Museum of Art & Fairmont Hotel, (408) 279-1775; www.sjdowntown.com. Daily; schedule varies. $12-$14; skate rental included.

Each winter, this small section of downtown San Jose is transformed into a winter wonderland.

GETTING THERE

Located approximately 50 miles south of San Francisco.

WHAT TO DO

Alum Rock Park
End of Alum Rock Ave. (E of Hwy. 101), (408) 259-5477; www.sjparks.org. Daily 8-sunset. Sat-Sun, parking $6. No pets.

Located in the foothills of the Diablo Range northeast of town, this serene 720-acre park was dedicated in 1872 and is California's very first city park. The city maintains it for hiking, horseback riding, bicycling, and picnicking. In some spots mineral water bubbles up from sulphur springs, a reminder of the park's past as a nationally known health spa in the early 1900s. Facilities include picnic tables, barbecue pits, and a children's playground.

The **Youth Science Institute** *(16260 Penitencia Creek Rd., (408) 258-4322; www.youthscience.org. Tu-Sun 12-4:30. $1, under 18 50¢.)* displays live birds of prey, including hawks and owls, as well as other native animals and a large taxidermy collection. Hands-on activities are available for children.

Cathedral Basilica of Saint Joseph
80 S. Market St., downtown, (408) 283-8100; www.stjosephcathedral.org. M-F 7-5, Sat-Sun 9-5:30. Free.

Designed by architect Bryan J. Clinch and constructed in 1877, when it was known as St. Joseph Cathedral, this is one of downtown's most architecturally stunning buildings. It replaced the Pueblo de San Jose's first small adobe church built in 1803. The cathedral features extraordinary stained glass and murals as well as a completely restored multi-domed edifice. A circa 1886 mechanical Odell organ in the choir loft is one of only four in the U.S. and the only one in original condition on the West Coast; evening concerts are sometimes scheduled.

Children's Discovery Museum of San Jose
180 Woz Way, in Guadalupe River Park, (408) 298-5437; www.cdm.org. Tu-Sat 10-5, Sun 12-5; in summer also M 10-5. $8, 60+ $7.

This striking lavender building designed by Mexico City architect Ricardo Legorreta houses the largest children's museum in the West. It is aimed at ages 1 through 10 and includes resting places for adults to sit and watch their high-energy kids have a great time doing everything

from making a corn husk doll, to blowing gigantic bubbles, to climbing on a full-size fire engine. A snack bar serves inexpensive things that kids like to eat: hot dogs, peanut butter & jelly sandwiches, pizza, chicken nuggets. The street the museum is located on is named for Steve Wozniak, of Apple Computer fame.

Emma Prusch Farm Park

647 S. King Rd., at Hwys. 680 & 280, (408) 926-5555; www.sjparks.org. Daily 8:30-sunset. Free.

One of the things discovered when visiting this old-time farm is that not all apples are computers. Deeded to the City of San Jose in 1962, this 47-acre dairy farm—surrounded now by the city—presents the opportunity to step back in time to San Jose's rural past. The restored original 19th-century white farmhouse is now the information center. The barn, which is the city's largest and the third-largest in California, is home to an assortment of domesticated farm animals that includes cows, sheep, and pigs—all thriving in spite of their closeness to the freeway. Don't miss the fruit orchard, where more than 100 kinds of rare fruits grow, among them limequat, pawpaw, gumi, and sapote as well as exotic varieties of cherries, guavas, persimmons, grapefruit and other citruses, and . . . apples.

Guadalupe River Park and Gardens

Spring & Taylor sts, betw. Hwy. 87 & Coleman Ave., (408) 298-7657; www.grpg.org. Daily dawn-dusk. Free.

This narrow, 3-mile-long park follows the river. It features a **Children's Carousel** *(525 W. Santa Clara St./Autumn St., (408) 999-6817. Schedule varies. $1; under 13 free on 2nd Tu of month)* with 33 fiberglass animals. The renowned **Heritage Rose Garden** *(Spring St./Taylor St., 2 mi. N of downtown; www.heritageroses.us.),* with more than 3,700 varieties of roses spread across 5 acres (it is one of the largest collections in the Western Hemisphere), is just south of the airport. Peak bloom occurs each May, though the show is good from April through November.

Japantown

N. 5th St./Jackson St., (408) 298-4303; www.japantownsanjose.org.

Dating back to the late 1800s, when bachelors from Japan migrated to the area, this historic neighborhood features streets lined with cherry trees that bloom spectacularly in the spring. One of only three remaining Japantowns in the U.S. (the others are in San Francisco and Los Angeles), it is just south of downtown and can be reached via the Light Rail line.

Historical sites of interest include the **San Jose Buddhist Church Betsuin** *(640 N. 5th St., (408) 293-9292; www.sjbetsuin.com.)*, which dates from 1937 and features a Japanese garden and tile roof; and the **Wesley United Methodist Church** *(566 N. 5th St., (408) 295-0367; www.wesleysj.net.)* built in 1941. A new **Japanese American Museum of San Jose** *(535 N. 5th St., (408) 294-3138; www.jamsj.org.)* will open soon.

Shops, galleries, and Japanese restaurants abound, and on Sunday mornings a bustling **Farmers' Market** unfolds. **Happi House** *(695 N. 5th St./Taylor St., (408) 295-5554. L-D daily; $.)* serves Japanese-style fast food. Diners order at the counter—noodle soups, tempura, teriyaki items—and then food is delivered to the table lickety-split.

Annual festivals celebrating the changing seasons include **Nikkei Matsuri** in May, the **Obon Festival** in July, and **Aki Matsuri** in September.

Kelley Park

Senter Rd./Story Rd., 3 mi. from downtown, (408) 27-PARKS; www.sjparks.org. Daily 8-sunset. Parking $6.

• Happy Hollow Park & Zoo

1300 Senter Rd./Keyes Rd., (408) 277-3000; www.hhpz.org. Daily 10-5. $6, 65+ $5.50, 75+ & under 2 free.

Children through age 10 love this mini amusement park. Spacious and shady, it offers a satisfying combination of kiddie rides and more than 150 zoo animals, including a family of endangered black-and-white ruffed lemurs. The small zoo also has a bird enclosure and a petting area, where for small change children can hand-feed animals. The zoo is known for actively breeding its lemurs. Five rides, daily puppet shows, and use of a concrete maze and playground equipment are included with admission. Single and double strollers can be rented, as can wagons, and picnic tables are available. At press time this attraction was scheduled to close for expansion and reopen in fall 2009.

• History Park

1650 Senter Rd., (408) 287-2291; www.historysanjose.org. Daily 11-4, May-Oct 12-5. Free; tours $6, 65+ $5, 6-17 $4.

This ever-growing 14-acre complex is laid out like a small town. It incorporates period San Jose buildings, including a replica Chinese temple from the mid-1800s and a gas station from the 1920s. Currently, more than 28 relocated or replicated historic houses and business buildings express the culture and history of San Jose and the Santa Clara Valley. Docent-led tours begin at the Pacific Hotel; a self-guided tour brochure is also available. Take time for a free trolley ride, and do to stop in for refreshments at the cafe at O'Brien's Candy Store—a replica of the first place west of Detroit to serve ice cream sodas. Many buildings are closed on weekdays.

• Japanese Friendship Garden

(408) 277-4192; www.sjparks.org. Daily 10-sunset. Free.

Patterned after the Korakuen Garden in San Jose's sister city of Okayama, this tranquil 6½-acre garden includes four heart-shaped ponds populated with rare koi. Walk on the Moon Bridge for good luck; cross the Zigzag Bridge to get rid of evil spirits.

Lick Observatory

On Mount Hamilton Rd., 23 mi. E of downtown, (831) 274-5061; www.ucolick.org. M-F 12:30-5, Sat-Sun 10-5. Free.

This observatory, built in 1887, is far from city lights at the top of 4,372-foot-high Mount Hamilton. Now a division of U.C. Santa Cruz, it is reached via the original carriage trail—a laborious 19-mile drive up a narrow, winding two-lane road with no less than 347 curves. But its view of San Jose and the Santa Clara Valley makes the effort worthwhile. A self-guided tour includes seeing through a glass window the world's second-largest reflecting telescope—the 120-inch Shane telescope, which has been in use for more than a century. Visitors also see the 36-inch Great Lick Refractor telescope, which has been here from the beginning and was the largest in the world when the observatory was built. Allow 90 minutes to reach the observatory, and be aware that no food or gas is available in the area.

Municipal Rose Garden

On Naglee Ave./Dana Ave., (408) 277-2757; www.sjparks.org. Daily 8-sunset. Free. No pets.

Located west of downtown and 2 blocks from the Egyptian Museum, this 5½-acre garden began as a prune orchard in 1931. It boasts 3,500 bushes representing 189 varieties of heritage, modern, and miniature roses. Hybrid-teas comprise 75% of the collection. The garden centers around a two-tiered fountain that is surrounded by green lawns and tree-shaded picnic tables. Other features include a reflection pool, a sundial, concrete benches, and a natural grass stage surrounded by redwood trees. The roses are at their showy peak in May and June but continue blooming through October.

Overfelt Gardens

2145 McKee Rd./Educational Park Dr. (betw. Hwys. 680 & 101), 3 mi. from downtown, (408) 277-2757; www.sjparks.org. Daily 10-sunset. Free.

Featuring expansive lawns, picnic tables, and a sometimes-gurgling stream, this peaceful 33-acre park is filled with native and exotic plants. Special features include a paved arboreal trail that meanders through the entire park, a California native plant and wildlife area, several natural wildlife sanctuaries, a fragrance garden, and three small percolation ponds that hold water for the Santa Clara Valley's water table.

A 5-acre **Chinese Cultural Garden** *(www.chineseculturalgarden.org)* holds impressive statuary that includes a 30-foot bronze-and-marble depiction of the ancient Chinese philosopher Confucius overlooking a reflecting pond. The Chinese garden has a massive white marble-and-ceramic Friendship Gate at the main entrance and displays a 15-ton piece of carved black marble that was presented by Taiwan to the citizens of San Jose.

Peralta Adobe & Fallon House Historic Site

175 W. St. John St./San Pedro St., downtown, (408) 287-2290; www.historysanjose.org. Tour on 3rd Sun; reservations required. $6, 62+ $5, under 13 free.

Both of these historic houses are surrounded now by modern high rises. Touring them provides a look into the daily life of two prominent early San Jose families. Built in 1797, the Peralta Adobe is San Jose's oldest structure remaining from when the city was El Pueblo de San Jose de Guadalupe and is a legacy to the city's Spanish influence. Named after Luis Peralta, who occupied the adobe from 1807 to 1851 and was one of the state's first million-

aires, it has two rooms outfitted in period style—a bedroom furnished as it would have appeared in 1777 and a living room furnished to reflect the 1830s—plus an outside working horno oven. Across the street, the lavish Victorian Fallon House mansion dates from 1855. Built for an early mayor, it has 15 furnished rooms decorated in the style of the 1860s. Though its kitchen was state of the art for the times, it has no bathrooms or indoor plumbing.

Raging Waters

2333 S. White Rd. (Capitol Expressway/Tully Rd.), in Lake Cunningham Regional Park, (408) 238-9900; www.rwsplash.com. Daily 10:30-6, June-Aug; Sat-Sun only May-Sept; closed Oct-Apr. $29.99, 55+ & under 48" $21.99; parking $6.

This water-oriented amusement park is the Bay Area's largest and claims to have the fastest waterslides this side of the Rockies. Sliders can reach speeds up to 25 miles per hour and can be dropped 6 stories into a catch pool below. An inner tube ride, a sled ride, a rope swing, and myriad other water activities round out the fun. Importantly, an army of 40 lifeguards watches over frolickers, and facilities include free changing rooms and showers plus inexpensive lockers. Where else can a family find such good clean fun? Note that food and beverages may not be brought into the park, but a picnic area is provided just outside the main gate. Food service is available inside.

Rosicrucian Egyptian Museum & Planetarium

1342 Naglee Ave./Park Ave., (408) 947-3600; www.egyptianmuseum.org. M-F 10-5, Sat-Sun 11-6; planetarium show daily at 2, also Sat-Sun at 3:30. $9, 55+ $7, 5-10 $5.

This museum houses the largest exhibit of Egyptian, Babylonian, and Assyrian artifacts in the western U.S. Highlights of the collection include mummies, fine jewelry, and a full-size reproduction of a 4,000-year-old rock tomb—the only such tomb in the United States. Mummies include four humans, several cats, a fish, a baboon, and the head of a sacred bull. The stunning surrounding park is adorned with exotic trees and flowers and Egyptian statuary. A show in a 1930s planetarium is included with admission.

San Jose Flea Market

1590 Berryessa Rd. (betw. Hwys. 680 & 101),
(800) BIG-FLEA, (408) 453-1110; www.sjfm.com.
W-Sun dawn-dusk. Free; parking W-F $2, Sat-Sun $6.

Said to be the largest outdoor flea market
in the world, bigger even than the famous Paris
marketplace that started the whole thing, this
was the first in the U.S. It features over 2,700
vendors spread out over 120 acres. Most everything can be found here, and at bargain prices.
In addition, there are more than 35 restaurants
and snack stands, and a ¼-mile-long section
that is California's largest outdoor produce
market. A variety of free entertainment is provided, and for a fee kids can play skee-ball and
ride on a pony, a merry-go-round, and go-carts.
Thursdays and Fridays are least crowded;
Wednesdays and weekends are usually quite
busy.

San Jose Improv

62 S. 2nd St., (408) 280-7475;
www.sanjoseimprov.com. Tu-Sun; show time varies.
Cover $10-$45+ 2-item min. Some age restrictions.

Performers and audience alike enjoy the
cozy ambiance of this beautifully renovated former classic movie house, built in 1904 and the
city's oldest theater. Top comedians are booked,
and the two-item minimum can be either food

or drink (the fruity vodka-based Sex on the
Stage is a satisfying number). Dinner reservations get priority seating; the menu includes
well-priced salads, pastas, and a burger. It is
interesting to know that The Smothers Brothers
comedy duo attended San Jose State and began
their career in the town's small clubs.

San Jose Museum of Art

110 S. Market St./San Fernando St., downtown,
(408) 271-6840; www.sanjosemuseumofart.org.
Tu-Sun 11-5. $8, seniors $5, under 6 free.

Holding a collection of primarily
contemporary American art, this unusual part-
1892 Romanesque sandstone/part-1991 stark
modern building is said to serve as a metaphor
for contemporary art's ties to tradition. A cafe is
located in the original wing, and baby strollers
can be borrowed at no charge.

San Jose Museum of Quilts & Textiles

520 S. 1st St., downtown, (408) 971-0323;
www.sjquiltmuseum.org. Tu-Sun 10-5, 1st F also 8-11.
$6.50, 65+ $5, under 13 free; free on 1st F of month.

This is the first museum in the United
States to focus exclusively on quilts and
textiles as an art form. Most of the exhibits are
of contemporary textile art.

San Jose Repertory Theatre
101 Paseo de San Antonio, downtown, (408) 367-7266; www.sjrep.com. Sept-July only. $15-$59.

Housed in a architecturally striking angular modern building colored deep blue, this residential theater company offers a wide variety of contemporary and classic plays.

Santana Row
Stevens Creek Blvd./S. Winchester Blvd. (at Hwys. 880 & 280), (408) 551-4611; www.santanarow.com.

The 3-block-long main drag here resembles a European shopping street, with fountains, flowers, and soft sounds encouraging slowing down and strolling. Nice touches include incorporating existing mature oak trees and using a 19th-century neo-Gothic chapel façade from Montpellier, France, as the entry to a shop. Both antiques and modern public art are placed throughout, and a peaceful park in the row's center offers comfortable seating and outdoor chess tables. This new complex combines high-end stores, branches of popular restaurants, a hotel, and apartments. Several day spas round out the offerings, and on Sundays a **farmer's market** operates from 10 to 3.

Rooms at sleek, sophisticated **Hotel Valencia** (*355 Santana Row, (866) 842-0100, (408) 551-0010; www.hotelvalencia.com. 7 stories; 213 rooms; $$$-$$$+. Heated pool; hot tub; fitness room; full-service spa. Continental breakfast; restaurant; room service. No pets. Self-parking free, valet $20.*) are appointed with a stainless steel bathroom sink, a faux fur bed cover, and stylish furnishings. Mattresses are among the most comfortable ever, and a pillow menu allows for personal fine-tuning. The ultra-hip **Vbar** sports a decor that includes metal-bead doorway curtains and is *the* place to be each evening when it serves up a Red Hot Mama (Bacardi silver, cranberry juice, club soda) that is especially delicious with salmon and caviar on corn blinis. The Indian-inspired **Ayoma LifeSpa** is colorful with rich Indian fabrics and antiques and offers pampering treatments (including traditional Indian Ayurveda treatments). Hand and foot treatments include pressure point massage that makes it possible to once again carry shopping bags and walk the row.

Restaurants are numerous. Most are open daily for lunch and dinner, and most have outdoor seating that takes advantage of the generally good weather. Among the choices are:

• Blowfish Sushi To Die For
#355, (408) 345-FUGU; www.blowfishsushi.com. L-D daily; $$.

A row of chefs is always busy here rolling out the sushi menu. The Ritsu, with two kinds of raw tuna, and the flash-fried Crunchy California are among the most popular versions. Tempura shrimp is exquisite, and sake is the best way to wash it all down. For dessert, try wasabe ice cream.

• Consuelo Mexican Bistro
#377, (408) 260-7082; www.consuelomexican bistro.com. L M-F, D daily, Sat-SunBr; $$.

Dishes here are not the usual Mexican items and are meant to be shared tapas-style. A crunchy jicama salad, a trio of tiny stuffed sopes, and a green pipian mole over chicken makes a satisfying meal. A full bar prepares an array of Latino drinks.

• Left Bank
#377, (408) 984-3500; www.leftbank.com. L M-F, D daily, Sat-SunBr; $$.

For description, see page 225.

• Maggiano's Little Italy
3055 Olin Ave., (408) 423-8973; www.maggianos.com. L M-Sat, D daily; $$.

With floors covered with tiny mosaic tiles and a large open room ringed with burgundy leather booths and filled with tables covered with red-and-white-checked cloths, this classic Italian restaurant looks like it's been here forever. Frank Sinatra convincingly sings away any doubts that might linger. Service is family-style and family-friendly, portions are large, and the menu is traditional.

• Straits Cafe
#333, (408) 246-6320; www.straitsrestaurants.com. L-D daily; $$.

For description, see page 182.

The Tech Museum of Innovation
201 S. Market St./Park Ave., downtown, (408) 294-TECH; www.thetech.org. Daily 10-5. $8.

Originally called "The Garage," in whimsical reference to the garages in which many Silicon Valley inventions had their humble beginnings (the most famous being the personal computer developed by Steve Jobs and Stephen

Wozniak in their garage), the nickname was dropped in favor of something more befitting the major science and technology museum it has become. Museum exhibits focus on how technology affects everyday life. Visitors see how silicon chips are produced and can design a roller coaster and pilot an ROV (remotely operated vehicle). Volunteers and staff are on hand to answer questions. Admission includes a show in the **IMAX Dome Theater**, where the audience is almost completely surrounded by a film projected onto an 82-foot-diameter screen—the largest dome IMAX in Northern California. When leaving this mango-colored building, be sure to see the whimsical, mesmerizing auto kinetic sculpture by George Rhoads located just outside the Park Street entrance.

Winchester Mystery House

525 S. Winchester Blvd./Stevens Creek Blvd., (408) 247-2101; www.winchestermysteryhouse.com. Tours daily from 9am; last tour varies by season. $23.95, 65+ $20.95, 6-12 $17.95.

The story goes that Sarah Winchester, heir to the $20 million Winchester rifle fortune, believed that to make amends for a past wrongdoing she had to build additions to her circa 1884 Victorian mansion continuously, 24 hours a day. Her eccentric ideas resulted in some unusual features: asymmetrical rooms, narrow passageways, zigzag stairwells, and doors opening into empty shafts. The tour of this city landmark takes in 110 of the 160 rooms, climbs more than 200 steps, and covers almost a mile. An add-on Behind the Scenes tour enters areas formerly not open to the public, including the stables, an unfinished ballroom, and the basement. Baby strollers not permitted on the tour.

The **Winchester Firearms Museum**, which holds one of the largest collections of Winchester rifles on the West Coast, and **Winchester Antique Products Museum** provide an interesting way to pass time while waiting for the tour to begin. A self-guided tour of 6 acres of Victorian gardens, sprinkled liberally with fountains and statues, is also included with admission. Food service and picnic tables are available.

Spooky nighttime **Flashlight Tours** are scheduled annually in October and every Friday the 13th.

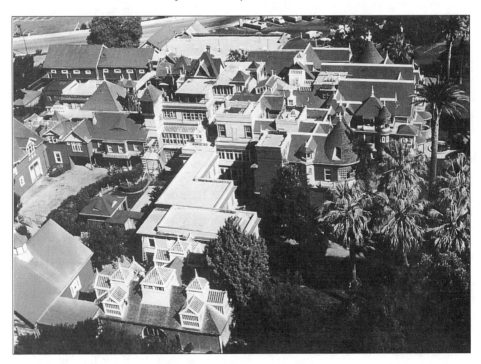

Wineries

• J. Lohr Vineyards & Wines
1000 Lenzen Ave., (408) 288-5057 x35; www.jlohr.com. Tasting daily 10-5; no tour.

Tucked into a residential part of the city near Highway 880, this premium winery operates on the site of a former beer brewery. All wine is made on the premises, but the grapes are grown on Lohr-owned vineyards scattered from Paso Robles to St. Helena.

• Ridge Vineyards
17100 Monte Bello Rd., in Cupertino, (408) 867-3233; www.ridgewine.com. Tasting Sat-Sun 11-4; no tour.

Started by three Stanford Research Institute engineers in 1959, this destination winery is positioned high on a limestone ridge way back in the Santa Cruz Mountains and is reached via a beautiful, curvy back road. On warm days, tasting sometimes occurs outdoors, and by reservation picnics can be enjoyed at vineyard-side tables offering a magnificent view of the bay below. On cooler days, tasting occurs in a room beside a 100-year-old barn. Known for its Cabernets and Zinfandels, Ridge has been called "the Château Latour of California," and the wines *are* good. So good, in fact, that a Zin brought to Paris as a gift to a native was personally witnessed being sniffed by that Parisian, who expressed surprise and then swallowed with absolute delight.

WHERE TO STAY

Campbell Inn
675 E. Campbell Ave., in Campbell, (800) 582-4449, (408) 374-4300; www.campbell-inn.com. 95 rooms; $$. Some fireplaces. Heated pool; hot tub; fitness room; 1 tennis court (with night lights). Full breakfast.

This B&B-style inn has one and two-bedroom suites. Facilities include an adjacent 16-mile jogging/bicycle/nature trail that passes through forests and alongside a stream and two lakes and that connects to a full-series par course, and the hotel provides complimentary use of 10-speed bikes. A lavish European-style hot breakfast is served in a poolside breakfast room. The inn is close to upscale shopping, and a complimentary airport shuttle is available.

Dolce Hayes Mansion
200 Edenvale Ave., 7 mi. from downtown, (800) 420-3200, (408) 226-3200; www.hayesmansion. dolce.com. 214 rooms; $$-$$$. Heated pool; hot tub; fitness room; full-service spa; tennis courts. 2 restaurants; room service. No pets.

Once the largest private home in Northern California, this fabulous mansion is located about 15 minutes from downtown. The spacious rooms in the original house are a particular delight, but the newer added rooms match the mansion's architectural style and feature contemporary comforts. Guests have access to volleyball courts and a jogging/walking trail running through a scenic park across the entry drive.

A meal in the exquisite dining room that houses **Orlo's** *(DTu-F. Reservations advised.)*, which is furnished with antiques and features a beautiful antique crystal goblet collection, is not to be missed. The cuisine matches the setting. The **Silver Creek Dining Room**'s expansive Sunday brunch is also exceptional.

The Fairmont San Jose
170 S. Market St., downtown, (800) 346-5550, (408) 998-1900; www.fairmont.com. 20 stories; 805 rooms; $$-$$$+. Heated pool; 2 saunas; 2 steam rooms; fitness room; full-service spa. 4 restaurants; room service. Valet parking $20.

Built on the site of what was California's capitol building from 1849 to 1851, this luxury high-rise hotel has three restaurants operating off the lobby: **The Grill on the Alley** features a clubby ambiance, with dark wood paneling and black leather-upholstered booths; **The Pagoda** has striking high ceilings and gorgeous flower arrangements in addition to a Chinese menu; **The Fountain** serves casual cafe meals and a lavish Sunday brunch. Additionally, **The Lobby Lounge** serves afternoon tea and cocktails and presents live music on weekends.

Hotel De Anza
233 W. Santa Clara St., downtown, (800) 843-3700, (408) 286-1000; www.hoteldeanza.com. 10 stories; 101 rooms; $$-$$$. Fitness room. Evening snack; restaurant; room service. Valet parking $20.

Referred to as the "Grand Lady of San Jose," this 1931 hotel is new again. Refurbished to its original art deco grandeur, it exudes a cozy feeling and features attractively appointed, spacious rooms and well-designed tile bathrooms equipped with a phone and TV. Amenities include a Raid Our Pantry nighttime snack buffet that permits bathrobe-clad guests to perch on the kitchen counter while gobbling up goodies such as chocolate chip cookies and salami cracker sandwiches. For a small additional fee, an extensive breakfast buffet is offered in a charming room that is cleverly painted to bring a cheery atmosphere into a windowless space. Celebrity guests include Eddie Murphy and Paul McCartney.

La Pastaia Restaurant *((408) 286-8686; www.lapastaia.com. L-D daily; $$-$$$. Reservations advised.)* serves acclaimed Italian cuisine, and the **Hedley Club Lounge** presents live jazz on Friday and Saturday evenings.

Hotel Montgomery

211 S. First St., downtown, (866) 823-0530, (408) 282-8800; www.hotelmontgomerysj.com. 4 stories; 86 rooms; $-$$$+. Fitness room. Restaurant; room service. No pets. Self-parking $20, valet $23.

This landmark Renaissance Revival hotel opened in 1911 and is San Jose's oldest. Moved in 2000 from its original location just 186 feet away at a cost of more than $30 million, it holds the Guinness World Record for the largest building ever moved in one piece. A decor theme throughout seems to be faux animal hide, as is seen in the lobby's plush faux fur-covered chairs. Though the hotel designer intended for the decor to be texture-driven and to heighten the sense of touch, the coincidental faux aspect continues in the contemporary-style guest rooms. Appointed with custom-made furniture, they feature faux leather walls, faux lattice-leather headboard, faux fur chair pillow, faux bark-covered drawers on desk and vanity, and faux leather trash cans. Rooms are equipped with both a high-top chair covered in Burberry plaid and a stylish bedside iPod docking station. Original artwork by San Francisco artist Rex Ray and an elegant deep red Cortina faux leather desk chair on rollers also enhance each room.

Dining in the ground-floor **Paragon Restaurant & Bar**, which serves everything from seared wild salmon to a burger, is popular with locals, and in good weather a large outdoor area screened with potted plants is packed.

A bocce ball court awaits use whenever the restaurant is open. For more description, see page 288.

Hotel Valencia

For description, see page 194.

PruneYard Plaza Hotel

1995 S. Bascom Ave., in Campbell, (800) 559-4344, (408) 559-4300; www.pruneyardplazahotel.com. 171 rooms; $$-$$$. Some fireplaces. Heated pool; hot tub; fitness room. Evening snack; continental breakfast. No pets.

One of only three hotels in the western U.S. that is located in a shopping center, this tastefully decorated lodging is adjacent to the attractive **PruneYard** shopping complex *((408) 371-4700; www.thepruneyard.com.)*. In spite of the location, it provides a secluded feeling.

The Sainte Claire

302 S. Market St., downtown, (866) 870-0726, (408) 295-2000; www.thesainteclaire.com. 6 stories; 170 rooms; $$-$$$. Fitness room. Restaurant; room service. No pets. Valet parking $21.

Designed in 1926 in Spanish Revival Renaissance style by the same architects who did the Mark Hopkins in San Francisco, this meticulously restored hotel is a national historic landmark. It boasts an elegant public sitting lounge with beautiful original hand-painted ceiling panels. Rooms are decorated rooms in an attractive contemporary style.

Tuscan-style **Il Fornaio** *((408) 271-3366; www.ilfornaio.com. B-L-D daily; $$.)* serves its celebrated fare in a spectacular open room with high, high ceilings. For more description, see page 73.

WHERE TO EAT

Arcadia

100 W. San Carlos St./Market St., in the San Jose Marriott, (408) 278-4555; www.sanjosemarriott.com/dining.html. B-L-D daily; $$$+. Reservations advised. Valet parking.

Overseen by well-known chef Michael Mina, this sophisticated spot is well removed from the hotel lobby and features a dramatic beige decor with black accents. The open kitchen adds drama. The cuisine is contemporary American with an emphasis on seafood—

the chef's forte—but also includes steaks and meats. Items such as a salad with a bevy of beets in pretty shades or foie gras sliders are also options, and, at lunch, wood-oven pizzas and toasted brioche sandwiches are on the menu. Signature dishes include a lobster corn dog and a whole fried chicken for two with truffled macaroni and cheese. Many dishes feature sauces that are poured on dramatically at the table, and all are served on oversize plates. A tasting menu with paired wines is available by request, and fun cocktails are made at the bar. Desserts might include a tangerine soufflé on a shortbread crust or a delicious mascarpone mini-cheesecake.

Benihana
2074 Vallco Fashion Park, in Cupertino, (408) 253-1221; www.benihana.com. L-D daily; $$-$$$.

For description, see page 62.

Buca di Beppo
925 Blossom Hill Rd., in Oakridge Mall, (408) 226-1444; www.bucadibeppo.com; also at 1875 S. Bascom Ave., in The PruneYard, in Campbell, (408) 377-7722. L-D daily; $-$$.

For description, see page 63.

E&O Trading Company
96 S. First St., downtown, (408) 938-4100; www.eotrading.com. L M-F, D daily; $$. Reservations advised.

This branch is housed in an 1800s building and features an open dining room with exposed brick walls and dramatic 20-foot-high ceilings. Authentic artifacts from throughout Southeast Asia are displayed. For more description, see page 68.

Emiles
545 S. Second St., downtown, (408) 289-1960; www.emilesrestaurant.com. D Tu-Sat; $$$. Reservations advised. Valet parking.

Owner-chef Emile Mooser grew up in the French part of Switzerland. He trained in the wine country of Lausanne, above Lake Geneva, and now produces a California-moderated synthesis of all that experience. In his long-lived, elegantly appointed restaurant, the menu changes with the season. Appetizers might include a vegetable ragoût with truffle oil, baked burgundy snails, or French onion soup. Entrees

include several styles of fresh fish, rack of lamb, and a seasonal game—perhaps a tender, mild moose or wild boar flavored with a classic game sauce. Prompted by the chef's need to cut butter from his own diet, lighter dishes that avoid fats—cuisine minceur—are always available. Desserts are seductive, and a signature soufflé for two, flavored perhaps with cappuccino or Grand Marnier, is definitely—excuse the expression—to die for. Adding to the overall tone of the experience, service is excellent, dishes arrive flamboyantly under silver warming domes, and chef Emile finds time to personally visit each table and chat amiably with diners.

Gordon Biersch Brewery Restaurant
33 E. San Fernando St./First St., downtown, (408) 294-6785; www.gordonbiersch.com. L-D daily; $-$$. Reservations advised.

Seating choices include both a pleasant patio and a spacious, airy dining room overlooking stainless steel brew tanks. The eclectic menu changes regularly and features salads, sandwiches, and individual pizzas as well as more serious entrees and desserts. In addition to three styles of housemade beer, the menu offers wines and coffees. Live jazz is sometimes scheduled outdoors on Sunday afternoon and inside in the evening. Brewmaster Dan Gordon is the only American in more than 40 years to graduate from the rigorous 5-year brewing program at the Technical University of Munich in Weihenstephan, Germany.

La Taqueria
15 S. First St./Santa Clara Ave., downtown, (408) 287-1542. L M-Sat, D F-Sat; $.

For description, see page 75.

Lisa's Tea Treasures
1875 S. Bascom Ave., in The PruneYard, in Campbell, (408) 371-7377; www.lisastea.com. Tea M-F 11-4, Sat at 11, 1:30, & 4, Sun at 12 & 3; $$.

Tea is served in three intimate tearooms here at tables dressed in linen and set with fussy china and silver. Servers dressed in Victorian costume are summoned by ringing a small bell. Tea-related items are for sale in a small gift shop.

This is the perfect place to stop in for refreshment after a visit to **Trudys** *((408) 377-1987; www.trudysspecialoccasions.com)* to select a wedding dress or, perhaps even more daunting, a mother-of-the-bride orgroom dress.

The Old Spaghetti Factory

51 N. San Pedro St./St. John St., downtown, (408) 288-7488; www.osf.com. L M-F, D daily; $. No reservations.

Oodles of noodle selections await spaghetti connoisseurs here. Choose regular marinara sauce, mushroom sauce, white clam sauce, or meat sauce. For those who can't make up their minds, a sampler of sauces is an option. Meatballs, spinach tortellini, and baked chicken are also available. Complete dinners come with bread, soup or salad, drink, and ice cream. The restaurant is in what was once the warehouse for the *San Jose Mercury News*. It features bordello decor and a variety of unusual seating options: an antique barber's chair in the bar, within a restored streetcar, on a brass bed converted into a booth.

Peggy Sue's

183 Park Ave./Market St., downtown, (408) 294-0252; www.peggysues.com. B-L daily; $.

Located just across the street from The Tech, this '50s diner grinds chuck daily for what it claims is "just possibly the best hamburger in the world." Hot dogs, sandwiches, and salads are also available, as are smoothies, shakes, and sundaes. Breakfast is a choice of egg dishes—including a really good spinach and avocado omelette—and pancakes. Diners order at the counter, then settle into one of the cheery cherry-red booths or chrome tables and check out the room-full of nostalgia that includes autographed rock and sports memorabilia adorning the walls and even an old-time gas pump. And all the while, those oldies but goodies play in the background.

Teske's Germania Restaurant and Bar

255 N. First St./Divine St., (408) 292-0291; www.teskes-germania.com. L Tu-F, D Tu-Sat; $$. Reservations accepted.

Situated in a historical building, this family-run German restaurant is entered through swinging saloon doors. After passing through an atmospheric dark bar, diners enter two large dining rooms. The one is front has a slightly cozier feel, while the back room features tall ceilings and a giant moose head. In good weather, a brick patio with a big wall fountain becomes a festive beer garden where nothing can be finer than sipping a big stein of Spaten amber lager. The menu offers a plethora of good German dishes—crisp potato pancakes, schnitzels, sauerbraten, and wursts—plus German beers and schnapps galore. Many entrees include housemade spatzle noodles, and all dinners include bread and butter, soup, salad, and apple strudel.

Special events include **Sommerfest** in summer, **Oktoberfest** in September and October, and *Seinfeld*-inspired **Festivus** in November.

MORGAN HILL

A LITTLE BACKGROUND

Situated at the southern tip of Silicon Valley, about 20 miles south of San Jose, Morgan Hill emanates the image of an all-American home town. Maybe that's why artist Thomas Kinkade—who counts among his famous paintings "Morgan Hill: An All-American Town"—selected it for his world headquarters.

But most people just whiz by on Highway 101, on their way to or from somewhere else. That's a shame, since slowing down permits enjoying a variety of family-friendly pleasures, and most are just a few blocks off the freeway.

GETTING THERE

Located approximately 20 miles south of San Jose via Highway 101.

VISITOR INFORMATION

Morgan Hill Chamber of Commerce

90 E. Second St., (408) 779-9444; www.morganhill.org.

ANNUAL EVENTS

Pumpkin Farms

October.

• San Martin Pumpkin Patch

13865 Monterey Rd., in San Martin Country Park, (408) 778-5436; www.sanmartincountrypark.com. Daily 9-8. Free admission; train ride $3.

At this family farm you'll find train rides, pony rides, a barnyard zoo, an ivy maze, and a giant water fountain. Barbecue tri-tip sandwiches can be purchased on weekends, and plenty of shady lawn invites an impromptu picnic. Many visitors come back in December to cut down a Christmas tree.

• Uesugi Farms Pumpkin Patch
14485 Monterey Hwy., (408) 778-7225; www.uesugifarms.com. Free admission; train ride & carousel $3; maze $1; Mutant Creek hayride F-Sun, 7pm-midnight, $20.

Two small trains chug through a tunnel and past fields containing scarecrows and blooming sunflowers and marigolds. A video shows how a pumpkin grows from seed to harvest, and an area filled with giant hay bales invites kids to jump freely. And then there is the photo op in front of a 4,000-pumpkin pyramid. All this, plus live entertainment and more than 50 varieties of pumpkin.

WHAT TO DO

Andy's Orchard
1615 Half Rd., (408) 782-7600; www.andysorchard.com. In summer & Nov-Dec M-F 10-5, Sat-Sun 10-4; call ahead rest of year. Orchard tasting/tour $15, under 11 free; unsuitable for children under 8.

One of the area's few remaining family farms, this spot lets visitors taste and purchase unusual varieties of delicious tree-ripened heirloom stone fruit—cherries (40 varieties), peaches (20 kinds), and apricots (only 1, the magnificent Blenheim), plus nectarines, plums, and pluots in season. Favorites include the old-fashioned yellow peach known as a Baby Crawford and the heavenly White Nectarine. All are for sale inside a rustic country store, where the walls are made from old drying trays and weathered barn wood. In season, visitors can pick-ur-own or take an educational tour. Andy says, "We're not Disneyland. We're a working farm." But he does keep a rusting 1920s tractor out front for kids of all ages to admire.

Clos LaChance Winery
1 Hummingbird Ln., in San Martin, (800) ITS-WINE, (408) 686-1050; www.closlachance.com. Tasting daily 11-5; tours by appt. No pets.

Built in the style of a Tuscan villa, this premium winery offers breathtaking vineyard views, plenty of picnic tables, and a bocce ball court.

Guglielmo Winery
1480 E. Main Ave., (408) 779-2145; www.guglielmowinery.com. Tasting daily 10-5; no tour.

Located in the state's oldest commercial wine region, this rural family winery set amid 100 acres of vines also produces wine vinegar made from Grandpa Guglielmo's (pronounced "Gool-yell-mo") original "mother."

Periodic **Cork Equity Days** reintroduce the popular 1930s tradition of filling customer's own bottles with red wine.

Henry W. Coe State Park
At end of E. Dunne Ave., 14 mi. E of town, (408) 779-2728; www.parks.ca.gov. Park open 24 hours; visitor center Sat-Sun 8-4. $5/vehicle.

Reached via a scenic, curvy back road, this park invites spending a few hours or an entire day of exploring. At 87,000 acres it is Northern California's largest state park and has more than 250 miles of trails through a terrain of steep hills, lush meadows, and cool creeks. Guided nature hikes are scheduled, and a hike-in primitive wilderness campground is available. A small museum in the visitor center displays local flora and fauna, and a gift shop sells area hiking maps. Campsites are available.

Thomas Kinkade Co.
900 Lightpost Way, (800) 366-3733; www.thomaskinkade.com. Tour by reservation. Free.

Kinkade is known as the "Painter of Light tm" and is the most collected living artist in the U.S. Visitors to this world headquarters can view a gallery of his works, see canvas and paper reproductions being manufactured, and watch "master highlighters" apply extra "pop" to some of the works. An autopen that signs some of the paintings has Kinkade's DNA in the ink (extracted from his hair).

Wings of History Air Museum
12777 Murphy Ave., in San Martin, (408) 683-2290; www.wingsofhistory.org. Tu & Thur 10-3, Sat-Sun 11-4. By donation; $5, 5-12 $3.

Within the two display hangars here are a 1928 American Eagle, a full-scale replica of the

1903 Wright Flyer, and a P-51—the most famous World War II fighter plane and the last propeller-driven American fighter. Model planes that once circulated on a recycled cleaner's rack at the now-closed Flying Lady restaurant across the street are displayed once again, as is the cockpit of a 1956 Vickers Viscount formerly used by Ray Charles. A restoration hangar doubles as a gift shop. The staff is all volunteer, and tours are enthusiastically given upon request.

During the annual **Open House** in May, children ages 8 through 17 can take a free airplane ride as part of the Young Eagles program. A pancake breakfast and displays of antique cars and farm equipment also enter the fun formula then.

WHERE TO STAY

CordeValle, A Rosewood Resort
One CordeValle Club Dr., in San Martin, (888) ROSE-WOOD, (408) 695-4500; www.cordevalle.com. 44 rooms; $$$+. All gas fireplaces. Heated pool; fitness room; full-service spa; 2 tennis courts; 18-hole golf course. 3 restaurants.

This secluded private golf club costs $185,000 to join, but non-members can enjoy the idyllic property for the price of an overnight stay. The luxurious lodging complex overlooks

rolling, tree-covered hills and sprawling meadowlands. All units are spacious and spoiling, and four ultra-luxurious bungalow rooms have a private hot tub and outdoor shower. A majestic entry to the reception building welcomes guests with tall open-beamed ceilings and a crackling fire. Cars are parked away from lodgings, and bell boys transport guests around the property in golf carts. Adding to a carefree atmosphere, tipping is included in the room price. Though pronounced as if it is French, CordeValle is actually derived from the Spanish phrase "'El Corazon del Valle,' or "Heart of the Valley."

Clos LaChance Winery (see page 220) is located on the 6th green.

Motel Row
Many chain lodgings are located on Condit Road between the Dunne & Tennant exits.

WHERE TO EAT

Rosy's at the Beach
17320 Monterey Rd., downtown, (408) 778-0551; www.rosysatthebeach.com. L-D daily; $. Reservations advised.

The name (as in "Where's Rosy? Rosy's at the beach.") for this super-popular cafe comes from the fact that the owner was previously a beach volleyball pro and wanted to bring a bit of surf and sand to Morgan Hill—thus the decor of colorful umbrellas and other beach paraphernalia. The menu favors fresh seafood—fish & chips, a salmon Caesar, and albacore melt—but also has a burger, several pastas, and soup. Its most popular items are a classic lettuce wedge salad and a soup-spoon sundae. Kids' items come with soda or milk, a soup-spoon sundae, and *no* veggies.

Scrambl'z
775 E. Dunne Ave., (408) 779-0779. B-L-D daily; $. No reservations.

A great day begins with breakfast in this cheery diner. Most everything is BIG and made in the kitchen from scratch—including superb, gigantic buttermilk biscuits and an especially delicious California Scramble. Kids' eyes grow round as saucers when they find out they get to select a *giant* lollipop as a good-bye treat after their meal. A playful decor of black-and-white tablecloths, bright yellow chairs, and a host of oversize wall decorations add to the fun.

GILROY

A LITTLE BACKGROUND

Though little garlic is grown here anymore, Gilroy is still famous as "the garlic capital of the world."

GETTING THERE

Located 80 miles south of San Francisco.

VISITOR INFORMATION

Gilroy Visitors Bureau
7780 Monterey St., (408) 842-6436; www.gilroyvisitor.org.

ANNUAL EVENTS

Gilroy Garlic Festival
July. (408) 842-1625; www.gilroygarlicfestival.com. $12, 60+ & 6-12 $6.

Gilroy turns into a giant open-air kitchen for this celebration of "the stinking rose." Bring a healthy appetite for all things garlic— including ice cream! Cooking demonstrations, live music, and children's activities round things out. Dress in shorts, wear a visor, and bring plenty of sunscreen.

Northern California Renaissance Faire
September & October. At Casa de Fruta, in Hollister; (408) 847-FAIR; www.norcalrenfaire.com. $25, 5-12 $10. No pets.

Formerly known as the Renaissance Pleasure Faire, this event morphed into its new name in 2004. Regarded internationally as the most historically correct Renaissance-period event of its kind in the U.S., this faire is an authentic re-creation of an Elizabethan village as it would have appeared more than 400 years ago during a harvest festival. More than 1,000 actors, musicians, jesters, jugglers, acrobats, dancers, puppeteers, and mimes dressed in traditional Elizabethan attire are on hand to provide authentic period entertainment and mingle with visitors. Exotic food and drink, quality crafts, and era-appropriate diversions are purveyed throughout. Visitors are encouraged to dress in Renaissance costume. Indeed, this fair has been described as "the largest costume party in the world."

WHAT TO DO

Gilroy Gardens Family Theme Park
3050 Hecker Pass Hwy. (Hwy. 152), 3 mi. W of Hwy. 101, (408) 840-7100; www.gilroygardens.org. Schedule varies; closed Nov-Feb. $41.99, 65+ & 3-6 $31.99; parking $7.

An undulating hedge leads the way into this unique, horticulturally-inspired amusement park aimed at children 10 and under. The theme is trees, but amazingly the park has only one indigenous tree (located by the Artichoke Dip ride). All the rest are transplanted! The park's 19 "circus trees" date from the 1920s and were displayed at the Tree Circus in Scotts Valley in the 1940s and '50s. They are grafted into extraordinary shapes and are spread evenly throughout the park, providing great photo ops.

Four themed gardens are also found here and there. Rides are low-key and old-fashioned but fun, with the Quicksilver Mine Coaster being the fastest while the tamer Timber Twister coaster provides thrills for the little ones in its tucked-away location. Don't misses include riding the ornate 1927 M.C. Illions Supreme Carousel and driving a Chevy Corvette or a Model T-style roadster through a tree tunnel of Italian cypresses. Dining options are reasonably priced and include barbecue, tacos, pasta, deep-fried artichokes, orange freezes, and plenty more. Though teens will probably enjoy it here with their younger siblings, this kinder, gentler theme park is a primo experience for grade-schoolers and their parents and for senior citizens. All proceeds go back into the park and into local beautification projects.

Mt. Madonna County Park

7850 Pole Line Rd./Hwy. 152, 10 mi. W of Gilroy, (408) 842-2341; www.parkhere.org. Daily 8am-sunset. $6/vehicle.

This 3,688-acre park offers stunning views of Monterey Bay and the Santa Clara Valley from its 20 miles of trails. A 1-mile self-guided nature trail winds around the crumbling ruins of cattle baron Henry Miller's summer home. White fallow deer, descendants of a pair donated by William Randolph Hearst in 1932, are displayed in an enclosed pen. A visitor center highlights the park's natural history, geology, and cultural history. On Saturday evenings in summer, live music and slide shows are presented in an amphitheater. Campsites are available.

SAN JUAN BAUTISTA

A LITTLE BACKGROUND

Once the largest city in central California, this town is now just a sleepy remnant of that time. It's hard to believe that at one time seven stage lines operated out of the town and that there were numerous busy hotels and saloons. Now the town holds just a few Mexican restaurants, boutiques, and antiques shops.

VISITOR INFORMATION

San Juan Bautista Chamber of Commerce
209 Third St., (831) 623-2454; www.sjbchamber.com.

GETTING THERE

Located approximately 85 miles south of San Francisco, and 35 miles south of San Jose. Take Highway 101 south, then Highway 156 east.

ANNUAL EVENTS

Early Days at San Juan Bautista
June. (831) 623-4881. $2, under 17 free.

Visitors to the state historic park on these days witness re-enactments of 19th-century townspeople performing everyday tasks. Volunteers in period dress demonstrate cooking, blacksmithing, and carpentry, and the saloon is open for card games and drinking sodas.

El Teatro Campesino
December. (831) 623-2444; www.elteatro campesino.com. $22, seniors $18, under 13 $14.

Each year this local acting company presents a seasonal Christmas production in the town mission. Throughout the year, they perform other productions in the new El Teatro Campesino Playhouse at 705 Fourth Street.

WHAT TO DO

Fremont Peak State Park
At end of San Juan Canyon Rd., 11 mi. from town, (831) 623-4255; www.parks.ca.gov. Daily 8-sunset. $4/vehicle. Observatory: (831) 623-2465; www.fpoa.net; Apr-Oct only.

A popular destination for picnickers and hikers, this park's summit is an easy 15-minute climb from the parking area. An observatory with a 30-inch reflecting telescope is open to the public twice each month. Campsites are available.

Mission San Juan Bautista
402 S. Second St., (831) 623-4528; www.oldmissionsjb.org. Daily 9:30-5. By donation.

Founded in 1797, this is 15th in the chain of 21 California missions. It is owned by the Catholic Church and has the largest church of all the missions. Thomas Doak, the first American settler in California, painted its bright red and blue reredos and altar. If everything looks familiar, it could be because this park was a major location in the Hitchcock movie *Vertigo*.

San Juan Bautista State Historic Park
2nd St., (831) 623-4881; www.parks.ca.gov. Daily 10-4:30. $2, under 17 free.

The restored buildings here show visitors what life was like in this area in the early 1800s. See a video introduction to the mission complex in The Plaza Hotel, and consider picnicking in the yard of the picturesque Castro-Breen Adobe. Living History days occur on the first Saturday of each month.

WHERE TO STAY

Posada de San Juan Hotel
310 Fourth, (831) 623-4030. 34 rooms; $-$$. All gas fireplaces. Continental breakfast.

This attractive mission-style inn makes lavish use of tiles. Situated just 2 blocks from the mission, it is connected by a breezeway to the town's main street.

WHERE TO EAT

Jardines de San Juan
115 Third St., (831) 623-4466; www.jardines restaurant.com. L-D daily; $. Reservations accepted.

What a wonderful fair-weather experience it is to sit outside under a sheltering umbrella on the brick courtyard here. Among the profusely flowering gardens, with autumn-colored roosters sometimes running loose, diners peruse the menu while sipping icy-cold margaritas and dipping tortilla chips in tasty salsa. Flautas consist of shredded beef rolled in a deep-fried tortilla and topped with guacamole. Tacos, enchiladas, and deliciously spicy tamales are options, as are plenty of a la carte items and veggie dishes. On weekends after 5 p.m., regional specialties join the menu. Red snapper a La Alicia is available on Fridays, shrimp fajitas on Saturdays, and pollos borrachos (drunken chicken) on Sundays. Limited amounts of these specialties are prepared, so diners are wise to call and reserve their portion. All fried items are prepared in trans fat-free oil. Live music is scheduled on the outdoor patio each Saturday and Sunday from noon to 3:30.

San Juan Bakery
319 Third St., (831) 623-4570. Daily 7-5.

Situated inside an historic building, this old-fashioned bakery makes 35 kinds of breads—including fabulous sourdough French and down-soft buttermilk—and an assortment of delicious pastries. The sugar cookies are particularly good and make a great car snack. Picnic supplies are also available.

SALINAS

A LITTLE BACKGROUND

Known as "the salad bowl of the nation," Salinas is one of the biggest cities in the Salinas Valley. This valley is where author John Steinbeck spent his formative years, and many of his novels are set here. In fact, the first working title for *East of Eden* was "Salinas Valley." Agriculturally, it is an unusual and valuable area because of its ability to grow winter vegetables—broccoli, cauliflower, head lettuce—during the summer.

VISITOR INFORMATION

Salinas Valley Chamber of Commerce
119 E. Alisal St., (831) 424-7611; www.salinaschamber.com.

GETTING THERE

Located approximately 90 miles south of San Francisco, and approximately 10 miles south of San Juan Bautista.

It is also possible to take Amtrak *(800-USA-RAIL; www.amtrak.com.)* from Oakland or San Jose and return the same day.

ANNUAL EVENTS

California Rodeo Salinas
July. (800) 549-4989, (831) 775-3100; www.carodeo.com. $12-$19, under 12 $7.

First presented in 1911, this outdoor rodeo is California's largest and ranked one of the top ten in the world. It is especially noted for its great clowns and thoroughbred races. Prize money totals more than $250,000, attracting the best of the cowboys and cowgirls to the competitions.

Steinbeck Festival™

August. (831) 775-4721; www.steinbeck.org. $17-$75.

Each year one of Steinbeck's many novels is emphasized at this intellectual festival honoring the town's native son. Bus and walking tours, films, lectures, and panel discussions are all part of the festivities.

WHAT TO DO

Mazda Raceway Laguna Seca

1021 Monterey-Salinas Hwy., (800) 327-SECA, (831) 648-5111; www.laguna-seca.com.

Standard Grand Prix-style races are scheduled here as well the **Monterey Historic Automobile Races** *(www.montereyhistoric.com. August. $45-$65, under 13 free.)*, which demonstrate the abilities of a broad range of vintage sports and racing cars.

National Steinbeck Center

One Main St., (831) 796-3833; www.steinbeck.org. Daily 10-5. $10.95, 62+ $8.95, 13-17 $7.95, 6-12 $5.95.

A visit here begins with a 10-minute introductory film detailing highlights of Steinbeck's life. Then six galleries of interactive exhibits illustrate famous scenes from his books and his life, enhanced by selected quotes and film clips. *East of Eden* is represented by a full-size boxcar filled with faux iced lettuce and clips from the movie featuring James Dean. *The Red Pony*, which Steinbeck wrote while living in his boyhood home a few blocks away, features a corral with a replica pony that kids can mount. But the premiere exhibit is the original "Rocinante"—the custom-built pick-up camper that Steinbeck drove when he traveled around the country writing *Travels with Charley*.

Wild Things

400 River Rd., at Vision Quest Ranch, (800) 228-7382, (831) 455-1902; www.wildthingsinc.com. Tour daily at 1, in summer also at 3; reservations not necessary. $10, under 14 $8; private tour $18/$12.

This facility trains animals for film, TV, and stage productions. The 1-hour tour introduces Josef—the MGM lion used by Disney animators as the model for *The Lion King*—and Elvis the kangaroo, as well as elephants, alligators, and bears, and shows how they are trained.

John Steinbeck and his sister Mary on Jill—the inspiration for The Red Pony

Vision Quest Bed & Breakfast *(4 rooms; $$-$$$. Unsuitable for children under 14. Continental breakfast.)* has four themed, high-end South African tent-cabins, including Zebra Zone and Pachyderm Palace. Breakfast is delivered to the room, sometimes with an animal's assistance. Rooms overlook a 5-acre sunken elephant playpen and have a view of Salinas Valley. Overnight guests get a discounted rate on tours.

WHERE TO STAY

Motel Row

On the east side of the freeway, the whole of North Main Street offers inexpensive generic lodging.

WHERE TO EAT

Fast-food heaven

1300 block of N. Main St.

First Awakenings

171 Main St., (831) 784-1125; www.firstawakenings.net. B-L daily; $.

For description, see page 113.

The Steinbeck House

132 Central Ave., (831) 424-2735; www.steinbeckhouse.com. L Tu-Sat; $. Closed 2 wks. in Dec. Reservations advised.

John Steinbeck was born in 1902 in the front bedroom of this beautifully renovated 1897 Victorian house. In *East of Eden* he described it as ". . . an immaculate and friendly house, grand enough but not pretentious . . . inside its white fence surrounded by its clipped lawn and roses . . ." A volunteer group now owns the house and operates a gourmet luncheon restaurant within. The menu changes weekly and includes items such as crunchy, cool gazpacho soup and tasty chicken-walnut salad—all made using seasonal produce grown in the Salinas Valley. Though the dining rooms are elegantly decorated, and Steinbeck memorabilia covers the walls, the atmosphere is casual. Comfortable travel attire is acceptable, and children are welcome.

After lunch, a well-priced cellar gift shop invites browsing and perhaps selecting a souvenir book by Steinbeck. Guided house tours operate on summer Sundays.

SOLEDAD

WHAT TO DO

Mission Nuestra Señora de la Soledad

36641 Fort Romie Rd., off Paraiso Springs Rd., 3 mi. W of Hwy. 101, (831) 678-2586. Daily10-4. By donation.

This isolated mission was 13th in the chain and named for the Spanish word for solitude. Built in 1791, it was abandoned in 1835 and then crumbled into ruin. In 1935, volunteers rebuilt the living quarters and the chapel, which retains its original tile floor. Now it sits next to the Salinas River among peaceful green pastures and rolling hills.

Pinnacles National Monument

12 mi. SE of town, take Hwy. 146 E, (831) 389-4485; www.nps.gov/pinn. Park: Daily 7:30-8. Visitor centers: Daily 9-5. $5/vehicle.

Formed by ancient volcanic activity, this 26,000-plus-acre scenic area is home to craggy pinnacles and spires that are surprising to come across in an area that is otherwise flat. Spring and fall are good times for hiking and camping, spring being particularly popular because of the stunning display of wildflowers. At other times, the temperature can be uncomfortable. A variety of raptors—prairie falcons, red-shouldered hawks, turkey vultures, and golden eagles—are sometimes sighted (some nest in the rocks), and 410 bee species make their home here—more than are found anywhere else in North America. The more developed east side of the park is reached by taking Highway 25 south to Highway 146. There, Pinnacles Visitor Center offers orientation. Campsites are available.

KING CITY

VISITOR INFORMATION

King City Chamber of Commerce

200 Broadway #40, (831) 385-3814; www.kingcitychamber.com.

ANNUAL EVENTS

Eagle tours at Lake San Antonio
January & February. In Bradley, (888) 588-2267, (831) 755-4899; www.co.monterey.ca.us/parks. $10-$12; reservations required.

This lake is one of the largest habitats for golden and bald eagles in central California, and these 2-hour boat tours are one of the best ways to view them. Call in December for the Eagle Watch schedule.

Wildflower Triathlons Festival
May; at Lake San Antonio, in Bradley. www.tricalifornia.com.

This has emerged as the largest triathlon event in the world and attracts more than 9,000 athletes and 35,000 spectators. Live music, camping, and more make it fun for people of all ages and interests. Benefits The Challenged Athlete Foundation and The Leukemia Lymphoma Society's Team in Training Program.

WHAT TO DO

Mission San Antonio de Padua
Exit at Jolon Rd. (G14) just before King City, 23 mi. SW of Hwy. 101 via Jolon Rd., in Fort Hunter Liggett, (831) 385-4478. Daily 10-4, in summer 8:30-6. By donation.

Founded in 1771 by Father Serra as the third mission and known as the "Jewel of the Santa Lucias," this is one of the largest restored and rebuilt missions. Original remains at the remote, picturesque site include the well, gristmill, tannery, and parts of the aqueduct system. The imposing façade of its church is known for both the campanile located in front and its archway bells. Both the church and the quadrangle are restored to an authentic approximation of their original luster. A museum exhibits Native American artifacts.

The site is especially beautiful in the spring, when the surrounding grasslands are ablaze with a profusion of wildflowers, and an annual **fiesta** occurs the second weekend in June.

SAN MIGUEL

GETTING THERE

Located approximately 65 miles south of Soledad.

WHAT TO DO

Mission San Miguel Arcangel
775 Mission St., (805) 467-3256; www.mission sanmiguel.org. Daily 9:30-4:30. By donation.

Founded in 1797, this is 16th in the chain of California's 21 missions. The present mission building was constructed in 1816. Though the outside architecture is simple, the delicate original and unretouched neoclassical frescoes inside and the rustic wooden All-Seeing Eye of Gare are especially noteworthy. They were painted by parish Indians under the direction of professional artist Esteban Munras. The reredos feature marble pillars with intricate geometric patterns displaying a dazzling array of colors. Windows are covered by their original sheepskin drapes, and beehive ovens and olive presses are displayed in fragrant gardens. Shaded picnic tables are provided. Unfortunately, much of the mission is inaccessible due to earthquake damage in 2003.

A **fiesta** occurs each September on the third Sunday.

The 1846 **Rios Caledonia Adobe** *(700 S. Main St., (805) 467-3357; www.rios-caledonia adobe.org. F-Sun 11-4.)* is located nearby. Once part of the mission estate, this 2-story adobe has served as a hotel, stagecoach office, school, and family home. It is restored and furnished to reflect the past.

PASO ROBLES

A LITTLE BACKGROUND

Originally a hot springs resort in the 1800s, this "pass of the oaks" (as its name translates) is fast becoming known for its award-winning wineries. This is the largest and most diverse wine region in California, with distinct soils and microclimates, and it has nearly 170 bonded wineries. Downtown, which borders the grassy

City Park town square, was devastated by an earthquake in 2003 but is now almost fully recovered. Restaurants, boutiques, and a plethora of winery tasting rooms populate the street surrounding the square.

VISITOR INFORMATION

Paso Robles Visitors & Conference Bureau
1225 Park St., (800) 406-4040, (805) 238-0506; www.pasorobleschamber.com.

GETTING THERE

Located approximately 5 miles south of San Miguel.

WHAT TO DO

James Dean Memorial
On Hwy. 46, 25 mi. E of town, in Cholame (pronounced "show-LAMB"); www.jamesdeanmemorialjunction.com.

Depending on a person's mood, this can be either an interesting or a bizarre side trip. It was here that legendary actor James Dean crashed his racing-model Porsche 550 Spyder roadster and died in 1955 (at the intersection of Highways 46 and 41). A concrete-and-stainless steel shrine to Dean's memory stands just 900 yards from the actual death site. Constructed and maintained by a Japanese national who comes to pay homage twice a year, it is located in the parking lot of the Jack Ranch Cafe, which is now a convenience store.

WINERIES

Paso Robles Wine Country Alliance
530 10th St., (800) 549-WINE, (805) 239-VINE; www.pasowine.com.

Request a free map and brochure to this area's many wineries.

Back-roads wine-tasting tour

• West Side
Begin on Spring Street, turning west on 24th Street. Use a local map to chart a course.

This scenic area of bucolic, oak-studded farmland has limestone soil similar to that found in Provence in the south of France, and it produces flavorful grapes. The long, hot sum-

mers turn them into fodder for ripe, robust Merlots and Zinfandels.

• Adelaida Cellars
5805 Adelaida Rd., (800) 676-1232, (805) 239-8980; www.adelaida.com. Tasting daily 10-5; no tour.

This scenically situated winery specializes in producing small quantities of low-tech premium wines fermented with natural yeast. Of special interest is an expansive walnut orchard, the bountiful fruit of which is sold in the tasting room.

• Carmody McKnight Estate Wines
11240 Chimney Rock Rd., (800) 282-0730, (805) 238-9392; www.carmodymcknight.com. Tasting daily 10-5; no tour.

Owner Gary Carmody Conway first saw this winery property when his helicopter crash-landed on the site. He emerged unhurt, and as an artist was thinking, "I've never seen light like this," so he told his real estate broker, "I'll take it!" The historic pioneer farmhouse tasting room looks out at a lake that sometimes blooms with lily and lotus blossoms. It is also a gallery for Gary's brightly colored paintings, which appears on his estate winery's bottle labels. As complex as his wines, Gary had a former career as an actor and starred in the TV series *Land of the Giants* and *Burke's Law*. The winery also produces refined Tuscan olive oil from the property's olive groves. A picnic area is available.

• Pasolivo
8530 Vineyard Dr., (805) 227-0186; www.pasolivo.com. Thur & M 11-4, F-Sun 11-5.

This family-run olive farm grows around a dozen mostly Tuscan varietals. A visit permits tasting award-winning olive oils and learning how olive oil is made. Tasting terminology, it turns out, is much like that for wines ("baby vomit" is one descriptor for "bad"). Ask to see the state-of-the-art Italian crusher, and allow time for tasting **Jack Creek Cellars** *(F-Sat 12-4:30.)* wines as well.

• East Side

• Eberle Winery
On Hwy. 46 East, 3.5 mi. E of Hwy. 101, (805) 238-9607; www.eberlewinery.com. Tasting daily 10-5, in summer to 6; tour: Sat-Sun on half-hr., M-F by request.

Taste the winery's excellent reds in a room filled with medals and awards from competitions. Picnic tables are provided on a sheltered patio.

• Tobin James Cellars
8950 Union Rd., off Hwy. 46, 9 mi. E of Hwy. 101, (805) 239-2204; www.tobinjames.com. Tasting daily 10-6; no tour.

Built on the site of an old stagecoach stop, the tasting room here has an Old West saloon ambiance and plays toe-tapping country and rock music to taste by. Kids are entertained by free video games. Wine is poured—including some spectacular Zinfandels—on an antique 1860s Brunswick mahogany bar from Blue Eye, Missouri. A picnic area is provided in a grotto.

WHERE TO STAY

Hotel Cheval
1021 Pine St., downtown, (805) 226-9995; www.hotelcheval.com. 16 rooms; $$-$$$+. Some gas fireplaces. Continental breakfast M-F, full breakfast Sat-Sun. No pets.

In keeping with the hotel's equestrian theme, each room is named after a famous racehorse. The contemporary-style rooms are spacious and appointed with original art and plenty of hardcover books. Some have window seats and patios. Beds are high California kings and are so soft and fluffy that getting into them is like climbing into a cloud. On weekdays, a breakfast basket is delivered to the door along with the local newspaper; it consists of fresh fruit and a delicious pastry from a local bakery, and guests make coffee in the room. On Saturday and Sunday, a hot breakfast buffet is served in the Pony Club. Picnic lunches can be arranged with 24 hours notice, and rooms are

equipped with complimentary bottled water and freshly made cookies.

On Friday and Saturday nights, guests get a complimentary ride to their restaurant in a carriage pulled by Chester, the hotel's 18-hands-tall Red Belgian draft horse.

The Pony Club bar *(Daily 3-10.)* serves wine and beer plus small plates that include cheeses, olives, and artisan breads for dipping in various olive oils. Seating is both at a horseshoe-shaped zinc bar and in an outside courtyard with a wood-burning fireplace.

Paso Robles Inn
1103 Spring St., (800) 676-1713, (805) 238-2660; www.pasoroblesinn.com. 100 rooms; $$-$$$+. Some gas fireplaces. Heated pool; hot tub. 2 restaurants. No pets.

Built in 1891, the original inn here was a fashionable resort popular with the wealthy and famous. It burned to the ground in 1940. (Like the Titanic was touted "unsinkable," this hotel was hailed as "absolutely fireproof.") The lobby and much of the original brick were saved and are incorporated into the inn's bungalows. Then, in this area's chic heyday, Marilyn Monroe and Joe DiMaggio honeymooned here. And if it's good enough for them . . . In fact, guests today can do something Marilyn and Joe couldn't—book a room with a private whirlpool hot tub that fills with hot, hot water direct from the thermal springs that are found 800 feet down under most of the town. The inn has spacious grounds with well-tended gardens, a koi pond, and convenient parking spaces right outside the door. But the main attraction is 30 comfortable, spacious spa rooms—each with a private patio with a chocolate-brown tub and privacy curtain. The tub fills in about a half-hour with the 124-degree, stinky, rotten-egg-smelling—but-healthy-for-what-ails-you—sulphur water that is reputed to help with skin problems, arthritis, and aching muscles and joints. Recommended soak time is 30 minutes or more. Do bring along favorite fruits and drinks to store in the room's refrigerator for after-soaking snacking. Note that the communal pool and hot tub are filled with regular water.

The inn has a popular bar, a vintage '40s coffee shop featuring a 50-foot circular counter with swivel stools, and a steakhouse with oversize ¾-moon booths that is famous for its

Sunday brunch. It is conveniently located just across the street from the town park and a downtown area filled with shops, restaurants, and a multi-plex cinema.

Motel Row

Best Western, Holiday Inn, Motel 6, and Travelodge are all represented along Spring Street.

WHERE TO EAT

Artisan

1401 Park St./14th St., downtown, (805) 237-8084; www.artisanpasorobles.com. L M-F, D daily, SunBr; $$$. Reservations advised.

A favorite gathering spot of local wine makers, this vibrant venue offers contemporary American cuisine that makes use of locally grown products and complements the area's wines. The open kitchen is visible from the dining room. A nice feature is the option to order a flight of wines instead of a glass or bottle, and eight taps dispense seasonal ales and micro-brews. Fresh scallops and Kobe beef are on the menu, soups are spectacular, and desserts include a flight of West Coast artisan cheeses and sometimes banana cream pie. An unusual "sniffing tray" of loose-leaf teas is offered to tea drinkers.

Brothers and co-owners Michael Kobayashi (general manager) and Chris Kobayashi (executive chef)

Cider Creek

3760 Hwy. 46 West, (805) 238-4144. Daily 8-5.

This tiny barn-like, apple-green building with apple-red awnings purveys a collection of apple foods and provides tastes of an assort-ment of apple juice blends made especially for them in Davis. Perhaps the best of the lot are the cold bottles to go, the red plastic apple "sip-pers" for kids, and the freshly baked pastries.

Panolivo French Bistro

1344 Park St./14th St., downtown, (805) 239-3366; www.panolivo.com. B-L daily, D F-Sat; $.

Though the bakery here seems to be the focus (the exquisite chocolate croissant is to die for), accomplished meals are also served in the spacious dining area. Breakfast is particularly popular, and at lunch housemade sandwiches, quiches, soups, salads, and french fries join the menu.

ATASCADERO

VISITOR INFORMATION

Atascadero Chamber of Commerce

6550 El Camino Real, (805) 466-2044; www.atascaderochamber.org.

WHAT TO DO

Charles Paddock Zoo

9305 Pismo Ave., off Hwy. 41, 1 mi. W of Hwy. 101, (805) 461-5080; www.charlespaddockzoo.org. Daily 10-4; Apr-Oct 10-5. $5, 65+ $4.25, 3-11 $4.

Though small, this 5-acre zoo takes good care of its diverse population. An adjacent park has shady picnic tables and a lake with paddle-boat rentals.

SAN LUIS OBISPO

VISITOR INFORMATION

San Luis Obispo Chamber of Commerce

1039 Chorro St., (805) 781-2777; www.visitslo.com.

San Luis Obispo County Visitors & Conference Bureau

811 El Capitan Way #200, (800) 634-1414, (805) 541-8000; www.sanluisobispocounty.com.

GETTING THERE

Located approximately 200 miles south of San Francisco (it is the halfway point between San Francisco and Los Angeles) and 30 miles south of Paso Robles via Highway 101, and approximately 45 miles south of San Simeon via Highway 1. It is also possible to take Amtrak ((800) 872-7245).

WHAT TO DO

California Polytechnic State University (Cal Poly)
On Grand Ave., (805) 756-1111; www.calpoly.edu. Tour: (805) 756-5734; M-F at 11; free.

Guided walking tours of this attractive campus begin in the University Union.

Gum Alley
Next to 733 Higuera St., downtown.

For several decades, gum-chewers have been depositing their product on these brick walls. Some have even taken the time to make designs. A vulgar, tacky eyesore to many, it is a cheap thrill for gum aficionados and most children. So don't get stuck here without a stick. Stock up on different colors of gum before arriving, and note that Double Bubble reputedly sticks best.

Hot springs

• Avila Valley Hot Springs
250 Avila Beach Dr., (800) 332-2359, (805) 595-2359; www.avilahotsprings.com. Daily 8:30am-8pm, in summer to 9. $9, 55+ & 2-14 $7.

At this family-friendly spot, facilities include a large freshwater pool and a smaller 105-degree mineral pool. Campsites are available.

• Sycamore Mineral Springs Resort
1215 Avila Beach Dr., (800) 234-5831, (805) 595-7302; www.sycamoresprings.com. 74 rooms; $$-$$$+. Some kitchens & fireplaces. Heated pool; 23 public hot tubs, $12.50+/hr.; full-service spa. Restaurant.

Situated on a back road leading to the coast, each guest room at this inn has a private hot tub. Outdoor mineral spring hot tubs can be rented by the hour by non-guests. The springs' history dates to 1897, when two men drilling for oil were disappointed to find sulfur-based mineral water instead. First called the "oil wells," the springs became popular in the 1920s when W. C. Fields and other celebrities who stayed at Hearst Castle stopped in.

Mission San Luis Obispo de Tolosa
782 Monterey St., downtown, (805) 543-6850; www.missionsanluisobispo.org. Daily 9-4; in summer to 5. By donation.

Founded in 1772, this is the fifth mission in the California chain. It was the first mission to introduce the red clay roof tile, which successfully repelled flaming arrows used in attacks by Native Americans. The extensively restored complex includes a fragrant rose garden and a museum exhibiting rare early California photos. Its charming chapel has a simple façade with a belfry and vestibule (unique among the state's missions) and is still used for services. An adjacent plaza and park provide shady trees, large grassy areas, stream-hugging paths, and inviting open-air cafes.

The nearby **San Luis Obispo County Historical Museum** (*696 Monterey St., (805) 543-0638; www.slochs.org. W-Sun 10-4. Free.*) is housed in a former Carnegie Library building and features historical exhibits that highlight the history and culture of the county.

San Luis Obispo Children's Museum

1010 Nipomo St., downtown, (805) 544-KIDS;
www.slocm.org. Tu-Sat 9:30-5, Sun 10:30-5. $8,
under 2 free.

This museum is especially for kids and
holds numerous hands-on exhibits that entice
them to explore and interact. They can play in
a child-sized town and climb 17 feet up in the
air to see above treetops. Baby strollers are not
permitted.

WHERE TO STAY

Embassy Suites Hotel

333 Madonna Rd., (800) 864-6000, (800) EMBASSY,
(805) 549-0800; www.embassysuitesslo.com.
4 stories; 196 suites; $-$$$. Indoor heated pool &
hot tub; fitness room. Full breakfast; restaurant;
room service.

This branch of the all-suites hotel chain is
located adjacent to a beautifully landscaped,
open-air shopping mall. For more description,
see page 445.

Garden Street Inn

1212 Garden St./Marsh St., downtown,
(800) 488-2045, (805) 545-9802;
www.garden streetinn.com. 13 rooms; $$-$$$.
Unsuitable for children under 16. Some fireplaces.
Hot tub. Evening snack; full breakfast. No pets.

This enormous 1887 Italianate/Queen
Anne-style mansion is beautifully restored.
Fragrant old citrus trees greet guests at the front
gate, and a communal parlor area features an
interesting browsing library.

Hostel Obispo

1617 Santa Rosa St., (805) 544-4678;
www.hostel obispo.com. 20 beds; some private
rooms.

Located just 1 block from the Amtrak
station and within walking distance of down-
town, this hostel in a converted Victorian has a
B&B atmosphere. Bicycles are available for
rental, and complimentary pancakes are served
each morning. See also page 468.

KOA Kampground

4765 Santa Margarita Lake Rd., in Santa Margarita,
10 mi. from town, (800) KOA-5619, (805) 438-5618;
www.koa.com. Pool.

For description, see page 467.

Madonna Inn

100 Madonna Rd., (800) 543-9666, (805) 543-3000;
www.madonnainn.com. 109 rooms; $$-$$$+.
Some fireplaces. Pool; 2 hot tubs; fitness room.
2 restaurants. No pets.

Begun in 1958 with just 12 rooms, this
sprawling pink motel now has more than
100 guest rooms. All are uniquely decorated,
some more uniquely than others—like the Cave
Man Room, with its stone walls, ceilings, and
floors plus cascading waterfall shower; and the
Barrel of Fun Room, in which all the furniture
is made from barrels.

For those not spending the night, a
meal in either the flamboyant **Copper Café**
(B-L-D daily; $$.)—where sitting on red
leather-upholstered swivel stools at an elabo-
rately carved, horseshoe-shaped coffee bar is an
option—or dinner in the more formal **Alex
Madonna's Gold Rush Steakhouse** *(D daily;*
$$$. Reservations advised.)—where the menu is
surf and turf and all the supporting courses are
included—is a must. Also, a bakery dispenses
goodies such as French cream puffs, cinnamon
pull-aparts, and an assortment of pies. And
don't miss the restrooms—especially the men's
room featuring a stone waterfall urinal.

Motel Inn

2223 Monterey St.

Opened on December 12, 1925 as the
Milestone Inn, this Spanish Mission-style
structure is the world's very first motel. It is
currently closed.

Motel Row

A vast array of motels lines the north end
of Monterey Street.

WHERE TO EAT

Farmers' Market and Street Faire

600 & 700 blks. of Higuera St., downtown,
(805) 541-0286; www.downtownslo.com. Thur 6-9pm.
Free.

Shoppers can buy dinner fully prepared
or pick up the fixings. This market is known
for its delicious barbecued items and live
entertainment.

Pepe Delgado's

1601 Monterey St., (805) 544-6660. L-D Tu-Sun; $.
No reservations.

Comfortable booths and large, solid tables make this popular Mexican spot an especially good choice for families. The hacienda-style building features tile floors, velvet paintings, and papier-mâché parrots on perches hanging from the ceiling. Potent fruit margaritas and daiquiris come in small, medium, and large to help diners get festive. A large variety of traditional Mexican items is on the menu, and many are available in small portions. Fajitas are particularly fun to order because they arrive sizzling on raised platters and are kept warm on the table by candles.

Picnic Pick-Ups

Enjoy a riverside picnic in downtown's Mission Plaza park.

• Muzio's Grocery Deli

870 Monterey St., downtown, ½ block to park, (805) 543-0800. M-Sat 9-6.

This atmospheric old shop has worn wooden floors. Mouth-watering sandwiches are made to order in the back, and a few tables are provided in front. Call ahead to have your order ready for pick-up when you arrive.

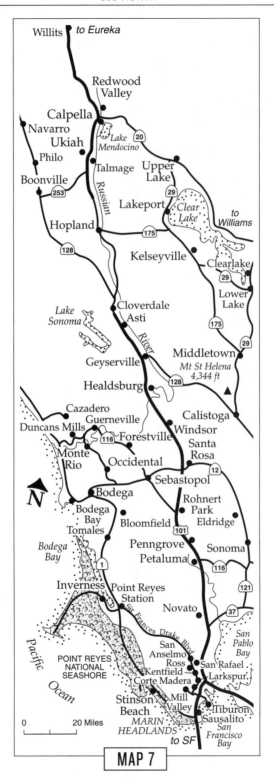

MAP 7

101 NORTH

A LITTLE BACKGROUND

Just across the Golden Gate Bridge from San Francisco, spectacularly scenic Marin County comprises a number of prosperous bedroom communities. It is home to numerous rock stars and celebrities, including *Star Wars* filmmaker George Lucas, who built his studios in the hilly backcountry.

Books and films have poked fun at the generally upscale residents, presenting them as flaky New Agers with an easygoing, laid-back approach to life, who seek nothing more than to tickle each other with peacock feathers while soaking in a hot tub. The reality is, of course, something else.

Consistently fair weather makes Marin County a popular destination with Bay Area residents, especially when other areas are covered by fog.

VISITOR INFORMATION

Marin Convention & Visitors Bureau
1 Mitchell Blvd. #B, San Rafael, (866) 925-2060, (415) 925-2060; www.visitmarin.org.

MARIN HEADLANDS

A LITTLE BACKGROUND

Converted from military to recreational use in 1972, this 12,000-acre park is part of the Golden Gate National Recreation Area. It consists of three areas: Forts Baker, Barry, and Cronkhite and is part of the city of Sausalito.

VISITOR INFORMATION

Visitor Center
(415) 331-1540; www.nps.gov/goga/marin-headlands.htm. Daily 9:30-4:30. Free.
This information center is located inside Fort Barry's old chapel.

GETTING THERE

Take the first exit (Alexander Avenue) off Highway 101 after crossing the Golden Gate Bridge.

WHAT TO DO

• Take a soul-soothing walk along **Rodeo Beach**.

• Hike up the Coastal Trail for ocean views and to see the innards of **Battery Townsley** *(1st Sun of month, 12-4.)*, a once-secret World War II installation carved into the hills.

• Drive along Conzelman Road, which leads past some of the old **bunkers and gun batteries** that attest to the area's military past.

• Visit the volunteer-restored **Nike Missile Site** *((415) 331-1453. Tours W-F & 1st Sat of month, 12-3:30.)*, built to protect the Bay Area against the Soviet threat during the 1950s through '70s.

• See **Hawk Hill** at Battery 129. It is considered the best site on the West Coast to view birds of prey. More than 36,000 hawks and other raptors migrate over this area each year.

• Drive along the northern edge, where several twists in the road offer magnificent views of the Golden Gate Bridge, and behind it, San Francisco. A picture taken here makes the subject look as if they are standing on the edge of the earth.

Bay Area Discovery Museum
557 McReynolds Rd., in East Fort Baker, (415) 339-3900; www.baykidsmuseum.org. Tu-F 9-4, Sat-Sun 10-5. $10, 62+ & 1-17 $8; free on 2nd Sat of month 1-5.

This activity-oriented, hands-on museum designed especially for infants to 10-year-olds is especially nice as a rainy day outing. Themes include the bay environment, art, nature, and architecture. Related activities are spread among eight buildings and include constructing a model suspension bridge and playing in a tide pool. The excitement is contagious, and parents find themselves being pulled along from one activity to another by their eager children. Visitors can also explore the outdoor area immediately surrounding the museum. For those caught picnic-less, a cafe serves kid-friendly fare, and outdoor picnic tables afford a magnificent close-up view of the Golden Gate Bridge.

The Marine Mammal Center
1065 Fort Cronkhite, (415) 289-SEAL; www.tmmc.org. Daily 10-4. Free.

Staffed by volunteers, this is one of the largest wild animal hospitals in the world. Injured, sick, and orphaned marine mammals (seals, dolphins, porpoises, whales) are brought here to be nursed back to health. When ready, they are released back into their natural habitat. Docent-led tours are available on weekends, self-guided tours during the week.

Point Bonita Lighthouse
(415) 331-1540; www.nps.gov/goga/pobo.htm. Trail open Sat-Mon 12:30-3:30; tour schedule varies. Free.

This lovely old light was the last on the Pacific Coast to be automated. The mostly dirt, ½-mile trail can be scary; participants must walk through a tunnel and cross a 120-foot suspension bridge. Full moon tours are sometimes scheduled.

WHERE TO STAY

Marin Headlands Hostel
Bldg. 941 at Fort Barry, (415) 331-2777; www.marinhostel.org. 104 beds; 8 private rooms.

On the National Historic Register, this spacious, homey hostel operates in two charming turn-of-the-century buildings. See also page 468.

SAUSALITO

A LITTLE BACKGROUND

People come from all over the world to stroll Bridgeway, the main street in this warm and sunny town. A former fishing village, Sausalito is often referred to as California's Riviera and is now a magnet for both artists and tourists and remains a pleasure for both. Restaurants and boutiques abound, and the view across the bay to Tiburon and San Francisco is stellar. Take time to climb some of the intriguing hillside stairways found throughout town. And do be careful—the largest source of income for the city is parking fines. It is interesting to note that Jack London wrote the opening chapters of *The Sea Wolf* here.

VISITOR INFORMATION

Sausalito Chamber of Commerce
10 Liberty Ship Way, Bay 2 #250, (415) 331-7262; www.sausalito.org.

This office is located in the Schoonmaker Building, where the huge Liberty ships of World War II were built. Now it is filled with art studios. Check the board by the entry to determine which artists have their studios open to visitors.

Visitor Center and Historical Exhibit
780 Bridgeway, (415) 332-0505. Tu-Sun 11:30-4. Free.

The Sausalito Historical Society operates a small museum inside this former icehouse originally located on Caledonia Street. Exhibits include photos of the building of World War II's Liberty ships.

GETTING THERE

Take the first exit (Alexander Avenue) off Highway 101 after crossing the Golden Gate Bridge. Another exit marked "Sausalito" is 3 miles farther north. Sausalito can also be reached from San Francisco via ferry.

ANNUAL EVENTS

Floating Homes Tour
Date varies. (415) 332-1916; www.floatinghomes.org. $30.

Approximately 10 houseboats open their doors for tours during this exciting event at Kappas Marina. A portion of the proceeds benefits a local non-profit organization.

Spring Open Studios *May.*
Winter Open Studios *December.*
Industrial Center Building, 480 Gate Five Rd., (415) 332-0730; www.icbbuilding.com. Free.

Known locally as the "ICB Building"—some people also refer to it as the "Tribeca of Sausalito"—this is the workspace for many local artists and is not open to the public. These events present the opportunity to wander in and out of studios where more than 100 painters, sculptors, fabric artists, jewelers, photographers, multimedia producers, and other artists create their work.

Sausalito Art Festival
September, on Labor Day weekend. (415) 332-3555; www.sausalitoartfestival.org. $20, 62+ $10, 6-12 $5; parking $5-$10.

This juried exhibit of more than 250 artists—all of whom attend in person—includes live music, good food and fine wine, and a waterfront setting with magnificent bay views. It is the top-rated non-profit fine arts festival in the U.S.

WHAT TO DO

Bay Model Visitor Center
2100 Bridgeway, (415) 332-3870; www.spn.usace.army.mil/bmvc. Tu-Sat 9-4; in summer Tu-F 9-4, Sat-Sun 10-5. Free.

Located on the outskirts of town on the site of a shipyard that produced World War II Liberty ships and tankers, this is a working hydraulic scale model of the Bay Area and Delta estuary systems. As big as two football fields, it is designed to simulate bay water conditions for research. Interpretive displays help make this complex scientific project understandable to the layman. The model operates irregularly; call for upcoming dates. A small museum tells about shipbuilding here during World War II.

The non-profit **Schooner Seaward** (*(800) 401-7835, (415) 331-3214; www.callofthesea.org. $20-$50.*), an 82-foot steel staysail schooner, is berthed here and schedules public sailings.

Heath Ceramics

400 Gate 5 Rd., (415) 332-3732;
www.heathceramics.com. Thur-Sat 10-6, Sun-W 10-5.

A store adjoining this ceramics factory sells seconds of its well-known tiles and classically simple, contemporary ceramic dinnerware. The line is used in many upscale restaurants, including Chez Panisse in Berkeley, and is in the permanent collection of the Museum of Modern Art in NYC.

Sea Trek Ocean Kayaking Center

85 Liberty Ship Way, (415) 488-1000;
www.seatrek.com. Guided trips $65-$95, under 13 $30-$50.

Take a 3-hour or full-day guided trip, or rent a kayak for just an hour or the entire day. Trips set out on a calm lagoon and include paddling the "streets" of the town's houseboat community. A customized Take the Kids Sea Kayaking program includes wet suits for the whole family.

Waldo Point

At north end of town; www.waldopoint.net.

This private houseboat colony contains both the funky and the exquisite. Visitors are not particularly welcomed by residents but are

legally permitted to view the area if they respect posted no-trespassing signs. It is said that in 1967 singer Otis Redding rented a houseboat on the main dock here, which was the inspiration for his well-known song titled "(Sittin' On) The Dock of the Bay."

WHERE TO STAY

Casa Madrona Hotel

801 Bridgeway, (800) 567-9524, (415) 332-0502; www.casamadrona.com. 63 rooms; $$$-$$$+. Some kitchens & fireplaces. Full service spa. Evening snack; full breakfast; restaurant. No pets. Valet parking $20.

Nestled against a picturesque hill above Bridgeway, this hotel offers lodging in either a converted 1885 Victorian house in back (the oldest structure in Sausalito) or in newer, tastefully decorated contemporary rooms sprinkled down the hillside amid fragrant, blooming gardens and featuring water views. Some rooms are themed. One of the most popular is the uniquely decorated Artist's Loft, but the Fireside Suite, with its clawfoot tub for two and canopy bed with harbor view, is also in heavy demand.

Breakfast is served to guests in the hotel's elegant restaurant, **Poggio Trattoria** *(777 Bridgeway, (415) 332-7771; www.poggio trattoria.com. B-L-D daily; $$. Reservations advised. Valet parking.)*, which specializes in classic northern Italian fare. Diners feast on delectable items such as crostini topped with Tuscan chicken liver, twice-cooked Tuscan vegetable-and-bread soup, and delicate wood-roasted whole fish with fennel. Rustic pastas and grilled chicken are also very good.

Hotel Sausalito

16 El Portal/Bridgeway, (888) 442-0700, (415) 332-0700; www.hotelsausalito.com. 16 rooms; $$-$$$. Continental breakfast. No pets. Self-parking $10.

Well-located next to the ferry landing, this small European-style boutique hotel was built in 1915 in Mission Revival style. It was once a bordello. In his heyday, Baby Face Nelson was a regular hotel guest, and writer Sterling Hayden once lived here. Now renovated into a bit of the French Riviera, it has a sunny decor. Colorful commissioned art decorates the halls, and handmade furniture and accents are found throughout. Most of the rooms retain their original stained-glass windows and overlook either Bridgeway or tiny **Vina del Mar Park**, where the charming elephant light posts and ornate fountain date back to the 1917 World Exposition (this park is named for Sausalito's sister city in Chile).

Across the street, the steep Excelsior Stairs lead up to the world-famous **Sausalito Presbyterian Church.**

The Inn Above Tide

30 El Portal, (800) 893-8433, (415) 332-9535; www.innabovetide.com. 29 rooms; $$$+. Most gas fireplaces. Evening snack; continental breakfast. No pets. Valet parking $18.

At the only hotel *on* San Francisco Bay—all rooms are built out over the water—all rooms have spectacular views of San Francisco and of a continuous parade of vessels. Most have private decks with glass walls for even better, unobstructed gazing. Amenities include robes and binoculars, and all rooms are equipped with comfy San Francisco-made McRoskey Airflex mattresses. Evening wine and breakfast are served in the parlor but are delivered to guest rooms upon request. The ferry from San Francisco docks immediately adjacent.

WHERE TO EAT

Caffe Trieste

1000 Bridgeway, (415) 332-7660; www.caffetrieste.com. M-Thur 6:30-10, F-Sat 6:30-midnight, Sun 7-11.

This is a branch of the famous North Beach coffeehouse. Pizza, pastas, sandwiches, and salads are available. For description, see page 65.

No Name Bar

757 Bridgeway/El Portal, (415) 332-1392. Daily 10am-2am; $. Must be age 21+. No dogs.

Famous for its low profile, this casual spot is inside the second-oldest building in town. Stop here and relax over a pitcher of Ramos fizzes in the garden-like back room. Live Dixieland jazz is performed every Sunday afternoon, and live jazz and blues are scheduled most evenings. Chess games happen on Friday afternoons.

MILL VALLEY

A LITTLE BACKGROUND

Thought of by many as the quintessential Marin, this tiny town originated as an enclave of vacation cabins built by San Franciscans eager to escape the city's notoriously cool summers. It is said more professionals per capita live here than in any other community in the country. The town rests at the base of Mount Tamalpais, the county's principal landmark.

The unofficial center of town seems to be **The Depot Bookstore and Cafe** (*87 Throckmorton Ave., (415) 383-2665; www.depotbookstore.com. Daily 7-7.*). Once the town's Northwestern Pacific Railroad depot, it offers both indoor and outdoor seating and a plethora of reading material.

VISITOR INFORMATION

Mill Valley Chamber of Commerce

85 Throckmorton Ave., (415) 388-9700; www.millvalley.org.

GETTING THERE

Located approximately 5 miles north of Sausalito. Take exit off Highway 101 and follow signs to intersection of Miller and Throckmorton avenues.

ANNUAL EVENTS

Mill Valley Film Festival

October. (415) 383-5256; www.mvff.org. Screenings $12.

Running for 11 days, this well-established festival offers screenings of both American independent cinema and foreign films, major film premières, and tributes to top filmmakers and industry leaders. Seminars are scheduled for both aspiring filmmakers and the layman in search of enlightenment. A **Children's FilmFest**, with special screenings and workshops, occurs at the same time.

WHAT TO DO

Old Mill Park

On Throckmorton Ave./Old Mill Rd., (415) 383-1370. Free.

Holding the town's namesake 1834 sawmill, this park is sheltered by an old-growth redwood grove and offers idyllic streamside picnicking. A rustic sun-speckled playground area has picnic tables, some of which are inside a circle of giant redwoods.

WHERE TO STAY

Mill Valley Inn
165 Throckmorton Ave., (800) 595-2100, (415) 389-6608; www.millvalleyinn.com. 25 rooms; $$-$$$+. Some wood-burning fireplaces. Afternoon wine; continental breakfast; limited room service. No pets.

Conveniently situated downtown, this lodging is tucked against a redwood-covered hill and consists of a turn-of-the-19th-century Victorian, a newer building, and two cabins. Rooms are furnished stylishly with attractive handcrafted pieces made by Northern California artists. Some have a balcony with views of redwoods and Mount Tamalpais, and two cottages offer privacy in a creek-side forest setting. Breakfast is taken on the Sun Terrace and includes an espresso bar.

WHERE TO EAT

Avatar's Punjabi Burritos
15 Madrona Ave., (415) 381-8293. L-D M-Sat; $.

The whole family helps out in the kitchen and behind the counter at this small spot. About ten combinations are available, either as rice plates with nan on the side or as burritos with the filling wrapped in nan. Tasty options include curried sweet potato and lamb, smoked eggplant and chicken, and curried garbanzo beans and potatoes. Soup, a few salads, and a fresh mango lassi are also available. Order at the counter, then sit at one of the few tables available indoors and out, or better yet carry it away to the park.

Buckeye Roadhouse
15 Shoreline Hwy., at Mill Valley/Stinson Beach exit off Hwy. 101, (415) 331-2600; www.buckeye roadhouse.com. L M-Sat, D daily, SunBr; $$-$$$. Reservations advised. Valet parking.

Situated inside an updated 1937 Bavarian-style chalet, this restaurant features generous portions of tasty all-American food at reasonable prices. The main dining room has high peaked ceilings and a large stone fireplace, and some tables have a pleasant view over the freeway to Strawberry Point. Mixed drinks on the menu include a deliciously spicy Bloody Mary, but don't overlook the cold draft beers. Among the particularly tasty items at lunch are a well-seasoned coleslaw, an ahi sandwich served with pesto mayo, a tangy pulled-pork sandwich, crisp housemade potato chips, and great onion rings—sliced very thin and served with housemade ketchup. Dinner entrees include steaks, chops, and fresh seafood. If the dining room is crowded, a comfy half-moon booth in the pubby bar is a good alternative and permits ordering from the same menu.

Champagne French Bakery Cafe
41 Throckmorton Ave., (415) 380-0410; www.champagnebakery.com. B-L daily; $.

It can be difficult to make a decision when choosing from among the items in the fabulous pastry case here. Pastries are crispy-light and reminiscent of France's best, and cookies and tarts vie for attention. However, the almond croissant is a sure thing. Soups, sandwiches, and quiches are also available

Gira Polli
590 E. Blithedale Ave./Camino Alto, (415) 383-6040. D daily.

Eat in, or take it away. In a flash, the "special" is ready to go—a fragrant rotisserie-roasted chicken prepared in a wood-fired oven and packed with sides of potatoes, fresh vegetables, and rolls. Soups and salads, pastas and risottos, and housemade desserts such as cannoli, lemon-flavored cheesecake, biscotti, and tiramisu are also on the menu.

La Ginestra
127 Throckmorton Ave./Miller Ave., (415) 388-0224. D Tu-Sun; $$. Closed 2 wks. in summer. No reservations.

Named for the Scotch Broom flower that is native to both Mount Tamalpais and Sorrento, Italy, this popular, casual spot specializes in Neapolitan cuisine. The ample menu includes a large selection of pastas, pizzas, and veal dishes as well as minestrone soup made with fresh vegetables and an excellent eggplant Parmesan. Fried or sautéed fresh squid is always on the menu along with potato gnocchi, saltimbocca, and housemade ravioli. Desserts include a rich housemade cannoli and a frothy white-wine zabaglione.

Maria Maria
651 E. Blithedale Ave./Camino Alto, in Blithedale Plaza, (415) 381-1070; www.mariamariarestaurants.com. L M-Sat, D daily, SunBr; $$$. Reservations advised.

It is not unusual in Marin County to find a very good restaurant located in a shopping center, as this one is. It is co-owned by musician Carlos Santana and is named for one of his popular tunes. Menu selections are extensive and include items such as rolled duck tacos and steak fajitas, and bar drinks feature hand-squeezed juices.

Piatti Ristorante
625 Redwood Hwy., at Seminary exit, (415) 380-2525; www.piatti.com. L-D daily; $$. Reservations advised.

Rustic terra cotta tile floors, an open kitchen that allows viewing the cooks in action, and big windows overlooking Shelter Bay and Mt. Tamalpais beyond combine to make this a comfortable venue. A new menu is created daily featuring fresh local ingredients and house-prepared pastas. Meals begin with warm house-baked bread and a mouth-watering dipping oil. A memorable dinner might include an antipasta of arancini—risotto cakes that are crispy on the outside, creamy on the inside; a chopped salad, perhaps with Pt. Reyes Blue cheese vinaigrette; the specialty saffron pappardelle with prawns and arugula; a hearty plate of long-braised beef short ribs with polenta; and a dessert of profiteroles filled with hazelnut ice cream. Sharing allows tasting more items and is highly recommended. Children especially favor the wood-fired pizzas and can make their own on Monday evenings. Live jazz entertains during Thursday dinner.

Piazza D'Angelo
22 Miller Ave., (415) 388-2000; www.piazza dangelo.com. L-D daily; $-$$. Reservations advised.

Designed to resemble an Italian town square, this comfortable restaurant has a retractable skylight over its main dining room and an Italian villa-style garden cafe for al fresco dining. Terra cotta floors, original modern art, and contemporary Italian music combine to set the mood. Rotisserie-grilled meats are excellent, as are the antipastos, pastas, risotti, and innovative pizzas baked in a wood-burning oven. A rich tiramisu dessert, served in an oversize stemmed glass, is ample for two.

Picnic Pick-Ups
• Mill Valley Market
12 Corte Madera Ave./Throckmorton Ave., (415) 388-3222; www.millvalleymarket.com. M-Sat 7-7:30, Sun 9-7.

Family-owned since 1929, this small but well-stocked grocery sells everything required for a fabulous picnic. An extensive selection of honeys, mustards, green olives, vinegars, salad dressings, and jams are on the shelves, and a deli/bakery tucked in the back dispenses prepared salads and baked goods.

TIBURON

A LITTLE BACKGROUND

Smaller and less well known than Sausalito, Tiburon has a tiny Main Street lined with boutiques, galleries, and restaurants.

Nearby **Belvedere**, which is Italian for "beautiful view," is Marin's smallest and most exclusive community, and its narrow, hilly roads are lined with expensive homes.

VISITOR INFORMATION

Tiburon Peninsula Chamber of Commerce
96 Main St., (415) 435-5633; www.tiburonchamber.org.

GETTING THERE

Located 20 miles north of San Francisco. Take the Tiburon Boulevard exit off Highway 101. Follow Tiburon Boulevard 4 miles east into town.

WHAT TO DO

Angel Island State Park
(415) 435-1915; www.angelisland.org. No dogs.

A ferry leaves from a dock behind Main Street's restaurants. For description, see page 30.

Ark Row
West end of Main St.

In times past, this street was a lagoon lined with arks and houseboats. Now boutiques fill land-bound houseboats, or "arks," that are more than 100 years old.

The **Windsor Vineyards tasting room** *(72 Main St., (800) 214-9463, (415) 435-3113; www.windsorvineyards.com. Tasting Sun-Thur 10-6, F-Sat 10-7.)* dispenses samplings of wines available for purchase only here and also sells their wines with custom messages on the labels.

Blackie's Pasture
On Greenwood Beach Rd., off Tiburon Blvd.; www.tiburonpeninsulafoundation.org/blackie.htm.

Blackie was a legendary local horse that grazed here from 1938 to 1966. He was beloved by children in the area, who fed him goodies from their lunch bags on the way to school. His former pasture is paved over now and is a parking lot. Thankfully, his charming gravesite surrounded by a white picket fence was spared and can be visited at the edge of the lot, and a metal statue of his likeness now stands here.

A short walk away is **McKegney Green**, an expanse of grass overlooking the bay that is perfect for picnicking and kite-flying. The paved 2-mile Tiburon Historical Trail, formerly a railroad grade, starts at Strawberry Point and continues into town.

Old St. Hilary's
201 Esperanza St./Mar West St., (415) 435-1853; www.landmarks-society.org. Church: W & Sun 1-4, Apr-Oct. Preserve: daily dawn-dusk. Free.

Two rare wildflowers grow in the fields surrounding this also-rare white Carpenter Gothic church dating from 1888. The Black Jewel and the Tiburon Paintbrush are found nowhere else in the world. When spring wildflowers are blooming, this church displays these two and others from the 217 species protected here as needlepoint pew cushions. Wildflower identification cards are also available.

Paradise Beach Park
On Paradise Dr., 1 mi. from town, (415) 499-6387. Daily 10-sunset. $5-7/vehicle.

This sheltered, 19-acre bay-front park has a large lawn area and barbecues. The small, quiet beach is nice for wading, and license-free fishing is permitted from the pier. On warm days, the small parking lot fills early.

Richardson Bay Audubon Center & Sanctuary
376 Greenwood Beach Rd./Tiburon Blvd., (415) 388-2524; http://richardsonbay.audubon.org. M-Sat 9-5, Apr-Oct only. Free.

The 11 acres of upland and 900 acres of bay that comprise this National Audubon Society wildlife sanctuary reflect grassland, coastal scrub, freshwater pond, and marsh habitats. A self-guided nature trail leads to a rocky beach and to a lookout spot with sweeping views of Richardson Bay and San Francisco.

Also on the property, the yellow 1876 **Lyford House** is the first and oldest Victorian home in Marin County. Once part of a dairy farm, it was barged across Richardson Bay to this location. It now displays some of John James Audubon's artwork. Call ahead for guided nature walks or house tours.

SS *China* Cabin
52 Beach Rd./Tiburon Blvd., in Belvedere, (415) 435-1853; www.landmarks-society.org. W & Sun 1-4, Apr-Oct. Free.

This exquisitely restored Victorian social saloon is from the side-wheel steamer SS *China*, which provided transpacific mail and passenger service between 1866 and 1886. It features 22-karat gold-leaf trim, cut-glass accents, walnut woodwork, and oil-burning crystal-and-brass chandeliers.

WHERE TO STAY

The Lodge at Tiburon
1651 Tiburon Blvd., (800) TIBURON, (800) 762-7770, (415) 435-3133; www.thelodgeattiburon.com. 102 rooms; $$-$$$+. Some kitchens. Heated pool; hot tub. Restaurant; room service.

Located just 1 block from Main Street, this 3-story California Craftsman Design building features exposed wood, beamed ceilings, river rock, and slate and is set among 3 acres of landscaped gardens.

Three Degrees Restaurant *((415) 435-5996; www.threedegreesrestaurant.com. B-L-D daily; $$$.)* gives a nod to the area's history as a railroad town with its bar constructed from salvaged railroad ties.

Waters Edge Hotel
25 Main St., (877) 789-5999, (415) 789-5999; www.marinhotels.com. 23 rooms; $$-$$$+. All fireplaces. Evening wine; continental breakfast. No pets.

This contemporary-style hotel takes full advantage of its location on an historic dock jutting into the heart of a picturesque marina by providing almost every room with a private balcony. Comfortable chaises and cloud-soft beds with fluffy white cotton duvets beg to be plopped on for a long rest under a cozy throw. Many rooms have high-ceilings and are decorated with dark Asian-style furnishings and vintage botanical prints. Breakfast is brought to the room.

WHERE TO EAT

Guaymas
5 Main St., (415) 435-6300; www.guaymasrestaurant.com. L-D daily, SunBr; $$-$$$. Reservations advised.

Authentic regional Mexican fare is the specialty at this always-bustling spot. In pleasant surroundings of bleached-wood furnishings and adobe-style decor, diners enjoy a sweeping view of San Francisco. On warm days, two outdoor decks are also opened. Three styles of margarita and a variety of Mexican beers are on the menu along with approximately 30 different tequilas—each comes with a complimentary sangrita chaser (a blend of tomato and orange juices spiked with chilies). The drinks go well with the delicious complimentary house salsas and tortillas. Though a light meal can be made of just the appetizer platter, save room for the imaginative menu offering a large selection of tantalizing seafood items, three kinds of tamale, and the kitchen's forte—spit-roasted meats. Everything is made in-house from scratch.

Picnic Pick-Ups
• **Foodniks**
1 Blackfield Dr./Tiburon Blvd., in Cove Shopping Center, (415) 383-FOOD; www.foodniks.com. M-F 10-7, Sat 10-6, Sun 10-4.

Choose from a continuously changing menu of delicious salads—perhaps wild rice with smoked cheese and grapes, or flavorful Mexican chicken sprinkled generously with cilantro. Sandwiches are made to order, and a delicious "panhandle pastry" is sometimes available.

• **Sweet Things**
(415) 388-8583; www.sweetthings.com. M-F 7:30-6, Sat 8:30-6, Sun 9:30-5.

A few doors away, this spot specializes in great desserts that include a weighty carrot cake, a variety of interesting cookies, and the intriguingly named Fallen Angel Torte and Black Magic Layer Cake. Whole-wheat Bowser Biscuits for dogs are also available.

Sam's Anchor Cafe
27 Main St., (415) 435-4527; www.samscafe.com. L M-F, D daily, Sat-SunBr; $-$$. No reservations on deck.

When the sun is shining, watching the boats and sea gulls while sitting outside on the deck here can be sublime. Dress is casual, and a typical weekend morning finds the rich and famous dining happily right alongside everyday people. Singles make their connections here at brunch, while parents relax with Sam's famous Ramos gin fizz. Cranky sounds from children don't travel far, but seem instead to magically vanish in the air. The brunch menu offers a variety of egg dishes, sandwiches, and salads as well as a good burger and fries. Unfortunately, the wait to get in can be long. This is the oldest continuously operating restaurant in town.

Sweden House Bakery & Cafe
35 Main St., (415) 435-9767. B-L daily; $. No reservations.

This bakery cafe is a good choice for a casual breakfast or lunch enjoyed either in the cozy interior or out on a small deck with a great bay view. For lunch, open-face sandwiches are made with a choice of either German six-grain bread or Swedish Limpa—a rye bread made with molasses and grated orange peel. Soups and salads are also available. Walk-away goodies can be selected from a tantalizing housemade array that includes chocolate tortes, fruit tarts, raspberry shortbread, and chocolate chip cookies.

CORTE MADERA

VISITOR INFORMATION

Corte Madera Chamber of Commerce
129 Corte Madera Town Center, (415) 924-0441; www.cortemadera.org.

WHAT TO DO

Book Passage
51 Tamal Vista Blvd., (800) 999-7909, (415) 927-0960; www.bookpassage.com. Daily 9-9.

This bookstore has the best collection of travel books and mysteries around and is a joy to browse. A cafe serves coffees and simple foods, and author events are scheduled regularly.

WHERE TO EAT

Picnic Pick-Ups
• A. G. Ferrari Foods
107 Corte Madera Town Center, (415) 927-4347; www.agferrari.com. M-Sat 10-8, Sun 10-6:30.

For description, see page 295.

World Wrapps
208 Corte Madera Town Center, (415) 927-3663; www.worldwrapps.com.

Tasty, wholesome, made-to-order meals include an international array of stuffed tortillas as well as some "unwrapped" rice bowls and soups. Signature mixtures include salmon and asparagus, portobello mushroom and goat cheese, and Thai chicken. They all go particularly well with an assortment of smoothies. The decor is colorful, and the seating is especially pleasant for solitary diners. Take-out orders can be placed online.

LARKSPUR

A LITTLE BACKGROUND

The downtown area of charming Larkspur is listed on the National Register of Historic Places.

VISITOR INFORMATION

Larkspur Chamber of Commerce
P.O. Box 998, Larkspur 94977, (415) 686-2062; www.larkspurchamber.org.

GETTING THERE

Take the Paradise exit off Highway 101. Follow Tamalpais Drive west until it becomes Magnolia Avenue, then follow Magnolia north.

WHERE TO EAT

E&O Trading Co.
2231 Larkspur Landing Circle, (415) 925-0303; www.eotrading.com. L-D daily; $$. Reservations advised.

The lofty-ceilinged main dining room here is augmented by two outdoor patios that are perfect for the area's often warm weather. Drinks are particularly alluring and include exotic housemade cocktail elixirs—a classic Singapore Sling, a Lanai Cocktail made with fresh pineapple aged in glass for three days—as well as draft beers and housemade sodas. Spicing of the Southeast Asian cuisine is mild. Signature dishes include whole-kernel corn fritters and banana spring rolls; pad Thai, braised eggplant, and roti paratha bread are personal favorites. Don't miss a trip to the restroom, if just to see the heavy, metal-bead entry curtain and the startling uni-sex wash-up area. For more description, see page 68.

Emporio Rulli
464 Magnolia Ave./Cane St., (888) 88-RULLI, (415) 924-7478; www.rulli.com. Daily 7:30-5:30; $.

Offering what must be the most mouth-watering selection of sweets found this side of Milan, and displaying them in gleaming mahogany-and-glass cases worthy of jewels, this authentic Italian pasty shop is a treasure trove of exquisite confections. Among them are an enormous selection of imported chocolates and candies and ten kinds of gelato, plus Italian cakes and pastries and seasonal specialties. It is possible to select and indulge on site, along with an espresso or other beverage, and an extensive hot panini (sandwich) menu is also available.

Lark Creek Inn

234 Magnolia Ave., (415) 924-7766; www.larkcreek.com. D daily, SunBr; $$$+. Reservations advised. Valet parking.

Situated within a landmark 1888 Victorian house beneath a cluster of tall redwoods, this destination restaurant is known for its seasonal farm-fresh American fare created by owner-chef Bradley Ogden. Seating is in an airy main dining room, in a smaller upstairs room, and on a brick patio—the venue of choice in warm weather. One dinner enjoyed on the patio here, out under the stars on a night of perfect temperature, started with a salad of heirloom tomatoes and local goat cheese. An oak-grilled salmon entree with a variety of baby vegetables followed, and the memorable conclusion was housemade coconut cake with blackberry-swirl ice cream. Ingredients are secured from local sources when possible.

Left Bank

507 Magnolia Ave./Ward St., (415) 927-3331; www.leftbank.com. L-D daily; $$. Reservations advised. Valet parking F-Sat D.

The vintage 1895 building this atmospheric Parisian-style brasserie is located within—known as the Blue Rock Inn—is in this small town's Historic District. A restaurant has operated on its ground floor since the early 1900s. The name is derived from the blue rock façade, which was quarried from the base of Mount Tamalpais. Today's airy restaurant retains the original pressed-tin ceiling and often greets diners with a welcoming fire in its massive stone fireplace. Theater posters enliven the walls, and clocks above the bar tell time locally as well as in Tahiti, Montreal, and Lyon (the chef's hometown). In good weather, outdoor dining on the veranda fronting the town's quiet main street is an option. The menu is rustic, unfussy cuisine grand-mère, or "grandma's cooking," and portions are big. Lunch is sandwiches, a hamburger Américain, salads, and a

few entrees. Dinner brings on signature dishes: bouillabaisse, rotisserie chicken, steak frites. Cocktails include a Pamplemousse (grapefruit vodka with 7-Up) and 12 kinds of pastis. Apple tarte tatin, Bing cherry clafouti, and molten chocolate cake are among the scrumptious endings. Special events are often scheduled.

Yankee Pier

286 Magnolia Ave., (415) 924-7676; www.yankee pier.com. L-D daily; $$. Reservations advised.

Though it isn't anywhere near water, this casual spot serves up a large selection of delicious fresh seafood. New England clam chowder, a shrimp Louis, and a bargain beer-battered snapper fish 'n' chips with housemade tartar sauce are among the choices. A burger, steak, and pasta are also options. Their popular butterscotch pudding is *the* dessert, and the bill arrives with a saltwater taffy from Marini's in Santa Cruz. Tablecloths add panache, and an open galley kitchen with porthole swinging doors adds atmosphere. A casual covered front porch and open-air back porch, both with picnic tables, are inviting in good weather.

SAN ANSELMO

A LITTLE BACKGROUND

With more than 130 antiques dealers, this sunny town is Northern California's antiques capital. But best of all, it has *no* parking meters on its main streets.

VISITOR INFORMATION

San Anselmo Chamber of Commerce
P.O. Box 2844, San Anselmo 94979-2844, (415) 454-2510; www.sananselmochamber.org.

GETTING THERE

Located approximately 20 miles north of San Francisco. Take San Anselmo/Sir Francis Drake Boulevard exit off Highway 101 and continue west for approximately 5 miles.

ANNUAL EVENTS

San Anselmo Antiques Faire
May. (415) 459-2002 or (415) 460-0400. Free.

WHAT TO DO

Marin Art and Garden Center

*30 Sir Frances Drake Blvd., in Ross, (415) 455-5260;
www.magc.org. Free.*

Operated by local volunteers, this historical 11-acre facility is planted with birch, laurel,
holly, and rhododendrons and is also home to a
rare dawn redwood, an unusual domed sequoia,
and a spectacular magnolia ring. Theatrical and
special events are often scheduled.

Laurel House Antiques *((415) 454-8472.
M & Thur 10-3; Tu-W, F-Sat 11-4.)* sells con-
signment antiques; proceeds benefit the center.
Also, the **Marin Society of Artists' Gallery**
((415) 454-9561. M-Thur 11-4, Sat-Sun 1-4.)
shows, sells, and rents art.

WHERE TO EAT

Bubba's Diner

*566 San Anselmo Ave./Tunstead Ave.,
(415) 459-6862; www.bubbas-diner.net. B-L-D
W-Sun; $. No reservations.*

Choose a comfy red-vinyl booth or a
swivel-stool at the long counter. Breakfast is
served all day and includes a large selection of
waffles, pancakes, and omelettes, plus acclaimed
housemade biscuits and gravy. Lunch brings on
a hamburger made with fresh house-ground
chuck, sandwiches, and salads, and dinner selections include meatloaf and rib-eye steak. Soda
fountain items are also available, including an
egg cream, a sherbet freeze, and their specialty
old-fashioned ice cream sodas. With food this
good, prices this low, and space this tight, there
is usually a wait to get in.

Cucina Restaurant & Wine Bar

*510 San Anselmo Ave./Tunstead Ave., (415) 454-2942;
www.cucinarestaurantandwinebar.com. D Tu-Sun; $$.*

For description, see "Jackson Fillmore"
on page 74. The menus are different, and this
location has a wood-fired oven.

Insalata's

*120 Sir Francis Drake Blvd./Barber Ave.,
(415) 457-7700; www.insalatas.com. L-D daily;
$$-$$$. Reservations advised.*

The airy, open interior here is filled with
tables and a few secluded booths, and walls are
decorated with large French oil pastels of fruits

done by San Francisco artist Laura Parker.
Mediterranean fare dominates the menu and
has included a Tunisian seven-vegetable tagine
with preserved lemons, a Syrian chicken
Fattoush salad tossed with toasted pita and
lemon-herb vinaigrette, and delicious Spanish-
style short ribs flavored with chocolate, sherry,
and orange. All breads and desserts are made
in-house. By the way, Insalata is chef-owner
Heidi Krahling's maiden name.

The neighborhood's prime antiques shops
make for great after-dining browsing.

Taco Jane's

*21 Tamalpais Ave./San Anselmo Ave., (415) 454-6562;
www.tacojanes.com. L-D daily; $-$$. No reservations.*

Mexican classics—tacos, enchiladas,
burritos, plus mole items and fish tacos—are
served in a colorful converted house with a
sunshine yellow walls. Outdoor deck seating is
equally cheery, with tables covered in floral
cloths. The cafe is famous for its black gold
salsa and large portions, and agua fresca and
margaritas are the drinks of choice.

Taqueria Mexican Grill

*1001 Sir Francis Drake Blvd./College Ave., in Kentfield,
(415) 453-5811. L-D daily; $. No reservations.*

Nestled under tall redwoods, this fast-food
spot has massive wooden benches and tables, a
jukebox playing Mexican tunes, and plenty of
piñatas. All help set the mood for the burritos,
chimichangas, and tacos that are the menu
mainstays. A hamburger is also available.

SAN RAFAEL

A LITTLE BACKGROUND

The oldest and largest city in Marin, San Rafael
also has the best weather. It is located in Marin
County's sunbelt and is an enchanting place to
dine outdoors on a warm summer evening.
Many artists and performers hide away here.
A further claim to fame is that many old silent
films were shot here, and 4th Street was the
setting for director George Lucas's *American
Graffiti*. For a walking tour of the historic
downtown area, get a guide from the chamber
of commerce and follow the plaque markers
embedded in the sidewalk across the street from
each site.

VISITOR INFORMATION

San Rafael Chamber of Commerce
817 Mission Ave., (800) 454-4163, (415) 454-4163; www.sanrafael.org.

ANNUAL EVENTS

Italian Street Painting Festival
June. 5th Ave./A St.; (415) 457-4878; www.youth inarts.org. Free.

Using chalk as a medium, hundreds of artists transform a downtown block into a huge canvas in homage to an Italian tradition that has survived since the 16th century. Proceeds benefit Youth in Arts.

Marin County Fair
July. Civic Center Fairgrounds; (415) 499-6400; www.marinfair.org. $14, 65+& 4-12 $12; parking $6.

Five days of fun include barnyard animal events, crafts competitions, and short film screenings, plus performances by big name entertainers and a low-level fireworks display over the lake. All this plus carnival rides are included in the admission fee. Highly regarded for its innovation and creativity, this mellow fair is a lot of fun.

Marin Shakespeare Company
July-Sept. Forest Meadows Amphitheatre, Dominican University of California; (415) 499-4488; www.marinshakespeare.org. $30, under 19 $15.

This summer-long festival is presented in an intimate 600-seat outdoor theater.

WHAT TO DO

Art Works Downtown
1337 4th St./C St., (415) 451-8119; www.artworksdowntown.org. Tu-Sat 10-5.

Housed in the town's 1870 opera house, which features lovely natural brick walls, this art gallery also houses active studios where visitors may view artists at work.

China Camp State Park
Take Civic Center exit off Hwy. 101, follow N. San Pedro Rd. E for 5 mi., (415) 456-0766; www.parks.ca.gov. Daily 8-sunset. Museum: Daily 10-5. $5/vehicle.

Once the largest fishing settlement along this shore, this spot was home to hundreds of Chinese fishermen in the late 1800s. Now all that's left is the rustic, weathered remains of the pier and buildings. A visitor center/museum displays period photographs and artifacts documenting the shrimping and fishing that occurred here until a 1911 ordinance outlawed the camp's primitive shrimp-trapping method. A small beach invites sunbathing and picnicking, and on weekends an old-time snack bar with a counter and swivel stools dispenses fast fare—including a delicious shrimp-and-cucumber sandwich (local musicians Huey Lewis and the News shot the cover for their 1980s *Sports* album inside). In addition to the village, this 1,640-acre park has hiking trails through the hills (the Turtle Nature Trail is an easy ¾-mile loop), and campsites are available.

The Christopher B. Smith Rafael Film Center
1118 4th St./B St., (415) 454-1222; www.cafilm.org. $10, 60+ & under 13 $6.50.

Built in 1938, this vintage film palace was renovated into a three-screen theater featuring first-run, independent, and period films. Each theater is equipped with the very best in sound and image projection (THX and Dolby sound systems are used), and each has its own personality. The lobby and richly colored main theater reflect the original art deco style, with blue velvet drapes and marvelous period chandeliers. On the second floor, theater Two has the posh feel of the '20s, while the more streamlined decor of theater Three has a futuristic sense. Everything used in construction is non-toxic, so patrons needn't fear the headaches and other health problems associated with off-gassing in most new construction.

Falkirk Cultural Center
1408 Mission Ave./E St., (415) 485-3328; www.falkirkculturalcenter.org. M-F 1-5, Sat 10-1. Free.

Built in 1888 atop a hill just a few blocks from town and named for the lumber baron-owner's birthplace in Scotland, this 17-room Queen Anne Victorian mansion features original coffered ceilings, rich redwood paneling, decorative fireplaces, and stunning floor-to-ceiling stained-glass windows. Upstairs galleries display contemporary art, and 11 acres of formal gardens surround the house. Special events include an Alice-in-Wonderland egg hunt at Easter, a haunted house in October, and a Victorian holiday program.

Guide Dogs for the Blind

350 Los Ranchitos Rd., (800) 295-4050, (415) 499-4000; www.guidedogs.com. Tour M-Sat at 10:30, 2. Free.

Formed to help servicemen blinded in World War II, this is the largest accredited school for guide dogs in the U.S. New graduates are presented to their visually impaired partners at a monthly graduation ceremony that is open to the public. Tours include the kennels, dorms, and 11-acre campus. New foster homes are always needed to raise puppies and care for dogs in transition.

Marin County Civic Center

N. San Pedro Rd./Civic Center exit off Hwy. 101, (415) 499-7009; www.co.marin.ca.us/visitorservices. Self-guided tour: M-F 9-6; free. Guided tour: W at 10:30am; $5; reservation required.

The last building designed by Frank Lloyd Wright before he died, this "bridge between two hills" is a national and state historic landmark. It also is where local resident George Lucas filmed his first big movie in 1971—*THX11380*—and houses various city offices and a performing arts and convention center. A 14-acre lagoon is surrounded by grassy areas perfect for picnicking and strolling.

Marin History Museum

1125 B St., in Boyd Memorial Park, (415) 454-8538; www.marinhistory.org. Tu-Thur 11-4, also 2nd & 3rd Sat of month. Free.

Situated within the Victorian Gothic Boyd Gate House, built in 1879, this museum puts on local history exhibitions.

McNears Beach County Park

201 Cantera Rd., (415) 499-6387; www.co.marin.ca.us/depts/PK/Main/pos/pdmnbch.cfm. Daily 7am-8pm in summer; off-season schedule varies. $4; parking $8.

A former country club, this very popular recreation area has a seasonal heated swimming pool, a concession stand, a fishing pier, a picnic area with barbecue pits and tables, and two tennis courts. A terrific sandy wading beach fronts San Pablo Bay.

Mission San Rafael Archangel

1104 5th Ave./A St., (415) 456-3016; www.saintraphael.com. Museum daily 11-4. Free.

Founded in 1817, this is the 20th mission. Replicated in 1949 on the approximate site of the original mission, it embodies some of that structure's characteristics—star windows modeled after those at the Carmel Mission and a bell hung from cross beams. Visitors can take a self-guided tour. A tiny adjoining museum displays vintage photos of its reconstruction and original furniture.

WildCare: Terwilliger Nature Education and Wildlife Rehabilitation

76 Albert Park Ln./B St., (415) 453-1000; www.wildcarebayarea. Daily 9-5. Free.

This wildlife rehabilitation hospital nurses ill and orphaned native animals back to health, then returns them to their natural habitat. Visitors can view non-releasable animals in an open-air courtyard and handle a display of taxidermied animals in the education center. This organization also operates the Living with Wildlife Hotline, which provides tips on how to persuade various wild animals to take up residence elsewhere.

WHERE TO STAY

Embassy Suites Hotel

101 McInnis Pkwy., (800) EMBASSY, (415) 499-9222; www.sanrafael.embassysuites.com. 5 stories; 235 rooms; $$-$$$. Heated indoor pool; hot tub; fitness room. Evening snack; full breakfast; restaurant; room service.

Situated just a footbridge away from the Marin Civic Center, this hotel usually offers a special package for the Marin County Fair. For more description, see page 445.

WHERE TO EAT

Casa Mañana

711 D St./2nd St., (415) 456-7345. B-L-D daily; $. No reservations.

Tucked away in the unlikely interior of a small medical complex, this tiny Salvadoran/Mexican cafe serves an extensive menu of tasty, housemade classic fare—pupusas, tamales, crab enchiladas verde, flautas stuffed with mashed potatos, chalupas—as well as mussels and hamburgers and plenty of vegetarian options.

Portions are large and delicious, and breakfast is served all day.

Las Camelias
912 Lincoln Ave./4th St., (415) 453-5850; www.lascameliasrestaurant.com. L M-Sat, D daily; $-$$. No reservations.

This homey spot has hardwood floors and oak furnishings. Mexican dishes are adapted from family recipes and include a variety of fish items, chicken in mole sauce, and fajitas. Generous combination plates come with the usual enchiladas and tacos, but more unusual chiles encuerados (roasted poblano peppers stuffed with caramelized onions and vegetables) and zincronizadas (flour tortilla stuffed with cheese, avocado, and veggies) are also options.

Mayflower Inne
1533 4th St./E St., (415) 456-1011. L-D daily; $-$$. Reservations advised.

This place offers the chance to experience the cozy ambiance of an English pub without crossing the pond. Waitresses sometimes even greet customers with a cheery "Hello, lovies" when presenting the menu. Among the traditional bland-but-hearty English items: steak and kidney pie, Cornish pasties (beef stew wrapped in a crescent pie pastry), bangers (English sausages), and fish & chips. Appetizers include a sausage roll (sausage baked in a pastry) and a Scotch egg (hard-boiled egg rolled in sausage meat and breadcrumbs and then deep-fried). English ales and beers are on tap, and dessert is a choice of fresh rhubarb pie, sherry trifle (a pudding), or chocolate cake. It is possible to relax in the English manner by indulging in a friendly game of darts or Ping-Pong.

Panama Hotel Restaurant & Inn
4 Bayview St., (800) 899-3993, (415) 457-3993; www.panamahotel.com. L M-F, D Tu-Sun, SunBr; $$-$$$. Reservations advised.

A former owner thought every town should have a Panama Hotel, and so this rambling structure, consisting of two 1910 homes connected by a patio, became San Rafael's.

The charming dining room, with color-washed walls and eclectic decor, serves delicious, full-flavored renditions of Mexican-, Italian-, and Asian-influenced cuisines. Don't miss the stuffed pepper appetizer or the Tuscan toast with relish. Fresh seafood and pastas are primo. Jazz is on the menu Tuesday and Thursday nights, and a tropical garden patio, reminiscent of something found in Central America, is the place to sit in warm weather.

Guest rooms *(15 rooms; $$. Some kitchens; some shared baths. Continental breakfast; room service.)* are also available. Some rooms have clawfoot tubs, others have canopy beds, and yet others have vine-covered private balconies. A well-known local rock musician is rumored to have kept a girlfriend lodged here for months and months.

NOVATO

VISITOR INFORMATION

Novato Chamber of Commerce
807 DeLong Ave., (800) 897-1164, (415) 897-1164; www.tourism.novato.org.

WHAT TO DO

Marin Museum of the American Indian
2200 Novato Blvd., in Miwok Park, (415) 897-4064; www.marinindian.com. Tu-F 12-5, Sat-Sun 12-4. $5; 65+ & 6-18 $3.

Marin County's earliest residents, the Miwok and Pomo Indians, are honored at this interactive museum. Artifacts displayed include tools, baskets, boats, and animal skins. Visitors can learn traditional Native American games, grind acorns with an authentic mortar, and visit a native plant garden. The adjoining 35-acre park has hiking trails, playing fields, and picnic facilities.

Novato History Museum
815 DeLong Ave., (415) 897-4320; www.ci.novato.ca.us/prcs/museum.cfm. W, Thur, Sat 12-4. Free.

Built in 1850, the Victorian house this museum operates within is now home to a collection of antique dolls, toy trains, and pioneer tools that reflect the town's history.

PETALUMA

A LITTLE BACKGROUND

Located less than an hour's drive north of San Francisco, Petaluma offers an old-fashioned small town atmosphere. Perhaps this is why it was selected as the filming location for both *American Graffiti* and *Peggy Sue Got Married*. In fact, director Francis Ford Coppola is quoted as saying, "You can find any decade you want somewhere in Petaluma."

Once known as the "World's Egg Basket," this area still produces plenty of eggs but is currently better known as a dairy center.

It's pleasant to spend a day here, just walking around the downtown area. Noteworthy among the numerous shops are the architecturally magnificent **Vintage Bank Antiques** *(101 Petaluma Blvd. N., (707) 769-3097. Daily 10:30-5.)*, located inside a former Wells Fargo bank, and **Monarch Interiors & Oriental Rugs** *(199 Petaluma Blvd. N., (707) 769-3092; www.monarchinteriors.com.)*, located inside the old Sonoma County National Bank. Another gem is the old-time barbershop with a swirling pole at 152 Kentucky Street. The residential area is also worth checking out for its large collection of Victorian homes.

VISITOR INFORMATION

Petaluma Visitor Center
210 Lakeville St./Hwy. 116, (877)-2-PETALUMA, (707) 769-0429; www.visitpetaluma.com. M-F 9-5, Sat-Sun 10-6; Nov-May, M-F 9-5, Sat-Sun 10-4; Jan, M-F 9-5, closed Sat-Sun.

Located inside the renovated 1914 Historic Depot Building, this center is a treat to visit in person.

GETTING THERE

Located approximately 50 miles north of San Francisco.

ANNUAL EVENTS

Butter & Egg Days
April. (707) 762-9348; www.butterandeggdays.com. Free.

Celebrating this area's past as a dairy and poultry center, this festival kicks off with a hometown parade populated with giant papier-mâché cows, huge dairy trucks converted into floats, and flocks of children dressed as chickens. Other events have included an Egg Toss, a Team Butter-Churning Contest, and the Cutest Little Chick in Town Contest—when the imaginative costumes of those marching chickens, limited to ages 1 through 8, are judged.

The **Downtown Antique Faire** takes place the next day on a street blocked off to traffic.

World's Ugliest Dog Contest
June. (707) 283-FAIR; www.sonoma-marinfair.org. Fair: $14, 65+ & 4-12 $9, free to those who enter a dog; parking $3.

Just one of the many events scheduled at the annual **Sonoma-Marin Fair**, this good-spirited contest has three divisions: Pedigree Class, Mutt Class, and Ring of Champions.

Petaluma Summer Music Festival
July-August. (707) 763-8920; www.cinnabartheater.org. $20-$22.

This festival features diverse musical events that appeal to all ages. Events are scheduled in the Cinnabar Theater-which is inside a mission-style former schoolhouse—and in other locations of historical interest.

WHAT TO DO

Garden Valley Ranch

*498 Pepper Rd., 3 mi. N of town, (707) 795-0919;
www.gardenvalley.com. W-Sun 10-4. $5, under 12 free;
docent tour $10, reservation required. No pets.*

This 8-acre ranch is the largest commercial grower of garden roses in the U.S. Among their well-known customers are the late Jacqueline Onassis (for daughter Caroline's wedding), Elizabeth Taylor, Whitney Huston, Barbra Streisand, and Martha Stewart. In one garden, more than 10,000 rosebushes are cultivated for cut flowers. In another garden, plants are grown for their perfume (some are used for potpourri). The best time for viewing is May through October, when the roses are in full bloom. The admission fee includes a self-guided tour brochure. When a private party is scheduled, the gardens are closed to the public, but the nursery and test garden remain open; call ahead to verify.

The Great Petaluma Desert

*5010 Bodega Ave., (707) 778-8278;
www.gpdesert.com. F-Sun 10-4. Free.*

Featuring one of the largest selections of rare and exotic cacti and succulents in the country, this dramatic back-road nursery boasts nine greenhouses. A few of the greenhouses are off-limits except to collectors who call ahead, but those that are accessible will satisfy most people. Nearly all of the stock is propagated on site. Among the most popular plants are tillandsia, also known as "air plants" because they require no soil.

Mrs. Grossman's Paper Company

*3810 Cypress Dr., (800) 429-4549, (707) 763-1700;
www.mrsgrossmans.com. Tours M-F at 9:30, 11, 1,
2:30; in summer, on the hr. 9-3. $3, under 3 free.
Reservations advised.*

The oldest and largest decorative sticker manufacturer in the U.S., Mrs. Grossman's prints 15,000 miles of stickers each year—enough to circle half the globe! Find out what all the fuss is about with a guided walk-through of this bright and happy printing plant. The tour begins with a video show narrated by the owner's dog, Angus, and concludes with a sticker art project and a gift bag of stickers. A shop sells the company's 700 sticker

designs—which include everything from the original simple red heart that launched the business to a delicate 12-inch-long laser-cut roller coaster—plus cards and kits. Space is provided for children's birthday parties.

After, take a walk in nearby **Shollenberger Park** *(South McDowell Blvd., (707) 778-4380; www.petalumawetlands.org. Daily sunrise-sunset. Free.).* A 2¼-mile walking path hugs the Petaluma River, and spotting at least a few of the more than 100 species of bird found here is almost a sure thing.

Petaluma Adobe State Historic Park

*3325 Adobe Rd., 5 mi. E of town, (707) 762-4871;
www.petalumaadobe.com. Daily 10-5. $2, under
18 free.*

The boundaries of General Vallejo's vast 66,000-acre land grant once stretched from the Petaluma River on the west, to San Pablo Bay on the south, to Sonoma on the east, to Cotati and Glen Ellen on the North. This rancho, which was part of the estate, is restored to reflect life as it was here in 1840. Sheep roam freely, and the living quarters, a weaving room, and a blacksmith's forge display authentic furnishings. Shaded picnic tables are available beside Adobe Creek.

The most interesting time to visit is for an annual event, including **Sheep Shearing** in April and **Living History Day** in May—with demonstrations of early California crafts and the chance for visitors to weave baskets and make hand-dipped candles.

Petaluma Historical Library & Museum

*20 4th St., (707) 778-4398;
www.petaluma.net/historicalmuseum. Thur-Sat 10-4,
Sun 12-3. Free.*

On the National Register of Historic Places, this lovely 1903 Carnegie Library building is now in use as the town's history museum. Its interior features the original woodwork and a rare freestanding stained-glass dome. Exhibits include a Victorian dollhouse and a chicken coop.

Tours of the Historic Downtown *(Sat-Sun at 10:30; May-Oct. Free.)* are led by docents attired elegantly in Victorian dress and include seeing the only full block of still-standing iron front buildings west of the Mississippi (in the first block of Western Avenue).

WHERE TO STAY

KOA Kampground
20 Rainsville Rd., (800) 992-2267, (800) KOA-1233, (707) 763-1492; www.petalumakoa.com. Heated pool (seasonal); hot tub.

This branch is set on a 60-acre rural farm. Amenities include a playground, petting farm, and summer entertainment program. For more description, see page 467.

Quality Inn
5100 Montero Way, (800) 228-5151, (707) 664-1155; www.winecountryqi.com. 109 rooms; $-$$. Heated pool (seasonal); hot tub; sauna. Continental breakfast.

Located on the outskirts of town, this is a link in a chain known for its attractive Cape Cod-style of architecture and comfortable modern rooms. A generous buffet breakfast is served in the lobby.

WHERE TO EAT

Dempsey's Restaurant & Brewery
50 E. Washington St., (707) 765-9694; www.dempseys.com. L-D daily; $-$$. No reservations.

The oldest brewery in Sonoma County, this comfortable, atmospheric brewpub serves the usual grub—cheeseburger, fries, wood-fired pizza—but also offers more sophisticated fare—magnificent flat bread with beer-spiked olives, a carnitas sandwich with tangy avocado spread, Shaken Beef served with lettuce wrappers. Full dinner entrees include roasted chicken and a pork chop. Leave room for dessert, perhaps an extraordinary fig tart with rich caramel. A beer sampler is a good way to try the wares, but Petaluma Pale Ale and Ugly Dog Stout are sure things. The housemade root beer is also very good. Organic produce used in the restaurant is grown by the chef and picked fresh every day.

Hallie's Diner
125 Keller St./Western Ave., (707) 773-1143. B-L daily; $. No reservations.

This simple cafe uses organic dairy products and has an expansive breakfast menu that includes the unusual—eggs with fried plantains and black beans; fried plantain rum soufflé; Cajun sausage and corncakes with eggs—as well as lattes and Mickey Mouse pancakes for kids. Lunch brings on hot and cold sandwiches. So

grab a seat in one of the vinyl booths or on a round swivel stool at the long counter and chow down.

McNear's Saloon & Dining House
23 Petaluma Blvd. N., (707) 765-2121; www.mcnears.com. L-D daily, Sat-SunBr; $-$$. Reservations must be made 1 day in advance.

Located inside the historic 1886 iron-front McNear Building, this casual restaurant and sports bar serves an extensive eclectic menu. It is particularly popular with young adults and serves good well drinks. Diners can get great bar food, such as spicy buffalo wings and beer-batter deep-fried mushrooms, as well as house-made soups, salads, sandwiches, hamburgers, barbecued chicken and ribs, pastas, and steaks. On fair weather days, windows are opened wide in the front dining area near the sidewalk, allowing for pleasant people watching.

The attached **McNear's Mystic Theatre** presents live music on Friday and Saturday nights. It was in the adjacent parking lot that the cop in *American Graffiti* lost his axel.

Picnic Pick-Ups
• Marin French Cheese Company
7500 Red Hill Rd. (also known as Petaluma-Point Reyes Rd.), (800) 292-6001, (707) 762-6001; www.marinfrenchcheese.com. Daily 8:30-5

Located way out in the country, this cheese factory has been operating since 1865. By now, they have perfected the art of making Camembert cheese, and they also make good Brie, schloss, and breakfast cheeses—all from milk produced by a local herd of Jersey cows. Cheeses may be sampled and purchased, and picnic supplies are available. Two expansive grassy areas—one with a large pond—beckon, and some picnic tables are available.

SANTA ROSA

A LITTLE BACKGROUND

Believe it or not!, Robert Ripley was born, raised, and buried in Santa Rosa! Unfortunately, the museum that once honored him here has been dismantled.

VISITOR INFORMATION

Santa Rosa Convention & Visitor's Bureau
9 4th St., at Railroad Square, (800) 404-ROSE, (707) 577-8674; www.visitsantarosa.com.

The **California Welcome Center** *(www.visitcalifornia.com.)* is also at this address. Both organizations operate within the Historic Railroad Depot.

Sonoma County Tourism Bureau
420 Aviation Blvd. #106, (800) 5-SONOMA, (707) 522-5800; www.sonomacounty.com.

Sonoma County Farm Trails
(800) 207-9464, (707) 571-8288; www.farmtrails.org.

Call for a free map of area farms that sell directly to the consumer. The map pinpoints the location of u-pick farms as well as of farms selling more unusual items such as pheasants, herbs, and mushrooms—even feather pillows and earthworms.

GETTING THERE

Located approximately 10 miles north of Petaluma, and 60 miles north of San Francisco.

ANNUAL EVENTS

Luther Burbank Rose Parade Festival
May. (707) 542-7673; www.roseparadefestival.com. Free.

Begun in 1894 as a Rose Carnival, this celebration has morphed into a parade.

WHAT TO DO

Howarth Memorial Park
On Summerfield Rd., access from Sonoma Ave. & Montgomery Dr., (707) 543-3282; www.howarthpark.com. Free. Rides & boat rental: in summer, Tu-Sun 11-5; in spring & fall, Sat-Sun only; closed Nov-Jan.

There is something for everyone in this scenic park. Children especially enjoy the free playground (with water feature "spouts" in summer) but, of course, also love the attractions with an admission fee: miniature train, animal barn, pony rides, carousel, and jump house. Paddleboat, canoe, kayak, rowboat, and sailboat rentals are available at Lake Ralphine,

and hiking trails, tennis courts, and a softball field round out the facilities.

Luther Burbank Home & Gardens
Santa Rosa Ave./Sonoma Ave., (707) 524-5445; www.lutherburbank.org. Gardens: Daily 8-dusk; free; cell phone audio tour, $5, 65+ $4. House tour: Tu-Sun 10-3:30; Apr-Oct only; $5, 65+ & 12-18 $4. Museum: Tu-Sun 10-4; free.

During his 50-year horticultural career, Luther Burbank developed more than 800 new plants. This memorial garden displays many of his achievements, including a Santa Rosa plum and a plumcot tree, the ornamental Shasta daisy, and a warren of spineless cacti. (He also developed elephant garlic.) Burbank is buried here in an unmarked grave. Guided tours of his charming greenhouse and modified Greek Revival-style home, which retains many of its original furnishings, last 40 minutes.

The adjacent **Carriage House Museum** offers annual exhibits related to Burbank's life and work.

Railroad Square
4th St./Davis St., (707) 578-8478; ww.railroadsquare.net.

Now a national historic district, this area is home to antique stores, restaurants, and specialty shops.

Safari West
3115 Porter Creek Rd., 7 mi. NE of town, (800) 616-2695, (707) 579-2551; www.safariwest.com. Tour: Daily at 9, 1, 4 (in winter at 10, 2); $65, 3-12 $30, 1-2 $10; reservations required. Tents: $$$; no TVs; continental breakfast; no pets. Restaurant: L at 12 (1 in winter), $15, 4-12 $12; D at 6:30 (5:30 in winter), $25, 4-12 $15; reservations required.

A visit here saves thousands of dollars in airfare and packager fees and also allows avoiding the jet lag that accompanies such a journey to Africa. This unique enterprise is run by Nancy Lang, a former curator at the San Francisco Zoo, and her husband Peter Lang, whose father Otto Lang helped make the film *The Snows of Kilimanjaro*. The Langs devote their lives to preserving African species. Their 400-acre compound now holds more than 500 rare and endangered African animals and birds, including zebras, wildebeest, and curved-horn aoudads, but no man-eating lions or body-

flattening elephants to cause concern. Some, like the addax antelope and scimitar-horned Oryx, are actually extinct now in the wild. Most amazing is the herd of enormous, impressively horned Watusi cattle. (Africa's Maasai people rarely sacrifice a live cow. Instead, as their primary source of protein they prepare a "Maasai cocktail" composed of the blood, milk, and urine of these cattle.) Part of the compound tour is in an authentic safari jeep, and part is on foot—including a visit to a large aviary holding rare and endangered birds, plus the opportunity to get up close to giraffes, lemurs, and cheetahs. Tour fees help pay the expenses incurred in maintaining the menagerie (the monthly feed bill runs more than $11,000). Nancy and Peter tend to sick and injured animals as lovingly as if they were their own offspring. True to Safari West's goal of propagating endangered species, eventually most of the animals move on to zoos where they help promote healthy breeding.

Consider staying the night in an authentic African **safari tent-cabin**. Delightfully simple in design, tents have hardwood floors, a thoroughly civilized bathroom with slate floors, a canvas ceiling, and mesh sides that let air in and keep insects out. The bed frames are constructed of whole logs, and other furniture is handcrafted from local woods. Mesh "windows" permit viewing the animals and being lulled to sleep by a cacophony of crickets and the intermittent grunt from an unknown wild beast. An optional buffet barbecue dinner is taken in a vast, rustic dining room cooled by ceiling fans and furnished with massive wood-slab tables and comfy canvas chairs.

Snoopy's Home Ice/ Redwood Empire Ice Arena

1667 W. Steele Ln., (707) 546-7147; www.snoopyshomeice.com. Open daily; schedule varies. $7, under 12 $5.50, skate rental $2.

Opened in 1969 by the late cartoonist Charles Schulz, this ice-skating rink with an Alpine decor has been called "the most beautiful ice arena in the world." The Zamboni resurfacing machine—made familiar to many through Schulz's "Peanuts" cartoon strip—is painted with a "Peanuts" winter skating theme. **The Warm Puppy Coffee Shop** has a few stained-glass windows depicting Snoopy and is where Schulz once ate every day (an English muffin with grape jelly for breakfast, a tuna salad sandwich for lunch).

Located adjacent, **Snoopy's Gallery and Gift Shop** *(1665 W. Steele Ln., (800) 959-3385, (707) 546-3385; www.snoopygift.com. Daily 10-6.)* purveys the largest selection of "Peanuts" merchandise in the world, and cuddly Snoopys are available in many sizes.

Across the street, the spacious **Charles M. Schulz Museum** *(2301 Hardies Ln., (707) 579-4452; www.charlesmschulzmuseum.org. M & W-F 12-5, Sat-Sun 10-5; in summer to 5:30. $8, 62+ & 4-18 $5.)* is dedicated to exhibiting thousands of original Schulz sketches. A highlight is an 8- by 12-foot wall extracted from the cartoonist's Colorado home; it was decorated by him in 1951. Take time to relax and watch some animated cartoons or documentaries.

Sonoma County Museum

425 7th St., (707) 579-1500; www.sonomacounty museum.org. W-Sun 11-5. $5, 65+ & 13-19 $2.

Located inside the city's beautifully restored 1910 post office building, this museum exhibits material relating to the county's history.

Victorian homes

Lovely Victorian mansions line MacDonald Avenue in the older part of town.

WINERIES

Kendall-Jackson Wine Center

5007 Fulton Rd., N of town, in Fulton, (866) 287-9818, (707) 571-8100; www.kj.com. Tasting daily 10-5; garden tour at 11, 1, 3.

Set amidst a mature walnut orchard and surrounded by 120 acres of vineyards, this château-like tasting room features new releases often not yet available in retail outlets. The four International Gardens are planted with herbs and vegetables representing Asia, South America, France, and Italy. They demonstrate the diversity as well as the similarities of these cultures. The unique Wine Sensory Gardens permit visitors to wander, wine glass in hand, sniffing and tasting the various vegetables, herbs, fruits, and flowers that compose wine-tasting descriptors, and a Viticulture Exhibit permits a self-guided tour of a 1-acre vineyard identifying 26 distinct types of grapes and illus-trating the 19 grapevine trellising systems most commonly used in California.

Matanzas Creek Winery

6097 Bennett Valley Rd., 5 mi. E of Hwy. 101, (800) 590-6464, (707) 528-6464; www.matanzas creek.com. Tasting & tours daily 10-4:30.

Located off the beaten track, back amid some rolling foothills far away from other enterprise, this winery is known for its Chardonnays, Merlots, and Sauvignons. It also grows fields of lavender—both the Provence variety (for cooking) and the Grosso variety (for scenting soaps and oils). Peak bloom is in June, and an assortment of products made with the bounty, including handmade soaps and sachets, are sold in the gift shop. A picnic area is available.

WHERE TO STAY

Flamingo Resort Hotel & Conference Center

2777 Fourth St./Hwy. 12, (800) 848-8300, (707) 545-8530; www.flamingoresort.com. 170 rooms; $$-$$$. Heated pool; children's wading pool; hot tub; fitness room; full-service spa; 5 tennis courts. Restaurant; room service.

When this spacious, unpretentious resort was originally built in the 1950s, it was way out in the country. Now, due to urban sprawl, it is right in town. It gives guests all the comforts of a full-service resort but also provides the con-venience of a motel—parking just outside the room; not having to walk through a lobby—and the amenities of a hotel—a piano bar with live entertainment and dancing; a full-service restaurant with poolside dining. Facilities include a children's playground, shuffleboard, Ping-Pong, and a lighted jogging path. The spa features racquetball and basketball courts, and childcare is also available. Stars love it too—everyone from Jayne Mansfield to Ted Danson has stayed here.

Fountaingrove Inn

101 Fountaingrove Pkwy., (800) 222-6101, (707) 578-6101; www.fountaingroveinn.com. 124 rooms; $-$$$. Heated pool (seasonal); hot tub. Restaurant; room service. No pets.

This sophisticated lodging features striking contemporary architecture and decor, with an equestrian theme throughout.

The hotel's piano lounge is an inviting spot to while away some time. **Equus Restaurant** *((707) 578-0149. L M-F, D daily; $$. Reservations advised.)* offers bistro-style dining.

Gables Wine Country Inn

4257 Petaluma Hill Rd., (800) 422-5376, (707) 585-7777; www.thegablesinn.com. 7 rooms, 1 cottage; $$-$$$. Unsuitable for children under 12. No TVs (except cottage); 1 kitchen; some wood-burning & gas fireplaces. Afternoon snack; full breakfast. No pets.

Named for the 15 gables that crown this 1877 High Victorian Gothic Revival house, this inn's spacious rooms are furnished with antiques and sport clawfoot tubs. Unusual fea-tures include three Italian marble fireplaces that were shipped around the Horn, a steep mahogany spiral staircase, keyhole-shaped win-dows, and 12-foot ceilings. In the horse-and-buggy days, governors and legislators stopped their wagons here for country hospitality. More house history is found in the parlor, where his-torical photos of the house and a copy of a the-sis written about it by a Sonoma State professor are available for perusal, and where quilt pieces made by the original owner are displayed as wall decorations. The house is set on 3½ acres in a rural area reminiscent of the south of France. The original outhouse and a 150-year-old barn remain, and a bucolic deck invites sun worship. All this and one of Northern California's best inn breakfasts, too!

Hilton Sonoma Wine Country

3555 Round Barn Blvd., (800) HILTONS,
(707) 523-7555; www.winecountryhilton.com.
250 rooms; $$-$$$. Heated pool; hot tub; fitness
room. Restaurant; room service.

Sprawled across one of the few hills in
town, this comfortable contemporary lodging
offers guests a 7.5-mile jogging trail as well as
access to golf and tennis facilities at a nearby
country club.

Hotel La Rose

308 Wilson St., at Railroad Square, (800) LAROSE-8,
(707) 579-3200; www.hotellarose.com. 4 stories;
49 rooms; $$-$$$. Hot tub. Continental breakfast;
restaurant; room service. Free valet parking. No pets.

This well-located, European-style small
hotel was built in 1907 of cut stone quarried
from the nearby area now known as Annadel
State Park. On the National Register of Historic
Places, it combines turn-of-the-century charm
with modern conveniences. Rooms are stylishly
decorated and furnished with English country
antiques and reproductions, and they feature
nice touches such as shiny marble floors and
floral wallpapers. Many on the top floor have
pitched ceilings, and some have private
balconies. Twenty of the rooms are in a more
modern annex across the street from the main
hotel. A communal sun deck equipped with a
hot tub is available for relaxation, and a continental breakfast is served each morning in a
cheery, high-ceilinged room but can also be
delivered to the room. All this and a handmade
candy on the pillow at turndown each night,
too!

Cozy **Josef's Restaurant** *((707) 571-8664;*
www.josefsrestaurant.com. L Tu-F, D daily.
Reservations advised.) serves elegant French continental cuisine.

Hyatt Vineyard Creek Hotel & Spa

170 Railroad St., at Railroad Square, (800) 233-1234,
(707) 284-1234; www.vineyardcreek.hyatt.com.
155 rooms; $$-$$$+. Heated pool; full service spa;
fitness room. Restaurant; room service. No pets.

A low-rise Mediterranean-style building
surrounds two large courtyards here. The back
courtyard accesses a riverside walkway and has
a "water wall" feature that serves the dual
purpose of deadening freeway noise. Rooms are
large and feature a bed topped by a semi-

canopy and made with cotton sheets and down
comforters, and bathrooms have granite
counters.

The **Brasserie** *((707) 636-7388. B-L-D*
daily; $$.) showcases the local bounty with a
Wine Country flair. It has an exhibition kitchen,
high ceilings, and a prominent bar that serves
only hand-mixed drinks made without a
blender.

Vintners Inn

4350 Barnes Rd., (800) 421-2584, (707) 575-7350;
www.vintnersinn.com. 44 rooms; $$-$$$+. Some
wood-burning fireplaces. Hot tub; fitness room.
Continental breakfast; restaurant; room service.
No pets.

The rooms in this elegant country inn are
furnished with European furnishings, and each
has a private patio or balcony. They are spread
through three separate buildings and cozily
surrounded by a 92-acre working vineyard.
Amenities include feather bedding and Italian
toiletries, a jogging path through the vineyards,
and a complimentary bottle of wine at
check-in.

The inn's highly acclaimed restaurant,
John Ash & Co. *(4330 Barnes Rd., (707) 527-*
7687; D daily; $$$. Reservations advised.), fea-
tures vineyard views, a wood-burning fireplace,
and dishes highlighting local products. Menu
choices include creative soups and salads, fresh
seafood and local poultry, and exceptional
desserts made by the in-house pastry chef.
(Note that founding chef John Ash no longer
owns the restaurant or cooks here, but current
chef, Jeffrey Madura, was well trained by him.)

WHERE TO EAT

Santa Rosa is where John A. McDougall, author
of *The McDougall Plan for Super Health and
Life-Long Weight Loss* and promoter of heart-
healthy eating, makes his home. It is interesting
to note his influence on this area. Most, if not
all, of the restaurants have at least one heart-
healthy item on the menu. Many have more.
Surprisingly, even small fast-food spots such
as the **Sonoma Taco Shop** *(57 Montgomery Dr./*
2nd St., in Creekside Center, (707) 525-8585. L-D
daily; $.), can be counted on to satisfy this need.
It offers an impressive 33 heart-healthy options,
and a complete nutrient breakdown of each
item is available.

Don Taylor's Omelette Express
112 4th St., at Railroad Square, (707) 525-1690; www.omelette.com. B-L daily; $. No reservations.

Diners sit on pressed-back chairs at old-fashioned oak tables in this popular spot. All omelettes are available with egg whites only, and hamburgers, sandwiches, and a variety of salads are also on the menu.

Flying Goat Coffee
10 4th St., at Railroad Square, (800) 675-3599, (707) 575-1202; www.flyinggoatcoffee.com. Daily 7-6; $.

Fresh-roasted specialty coffees can be sipped either inside, in the laid-back atmosphere of a high-ceilinged shop, or outside, where the sport is train-watching. Housemade pastries are also available.

Maria Maria
500 4th St., in Courthouse Square, (707) 523-3663; mariamariarestaurants.com. L-D daily.

For description, see page 221.

Picnic Pick-Ups
• **Traverso's**
106 B St./3rd St., downtown, (707) 542-2530; www.traversos.com. M-Sat 9:30-5:30; $.

Here since 1922, this Old World deli has been run by the same family for four generations. Choose from more than 101 varieties of cheese plus boutique wines and gourmet foods—including Italian cold cuts. Sandwiches and housemade ravioli are available for take-out.

Santa Rosa Downtown Market
On 4th St. & B St., (707) 524-2123; www.srdowntown market.com. W 5-8; June-Aug. only. Free.

At this festive event, local restaurants serve up inexpensive portions of barbecued turkey legs, sausage, kebobs, burgers, and oysters along with salads, calzone, chili, and burritos. Farmers are on hand with fresh produce, arts-and-crafts artists display their wares, and plenty of street entertainers do their thing.

Syrah
205 5th St./Davis St., at Railroad Square, (707) 568-4002; www.syrahbistro.com. L Tu-Sat, D daily; $$. Reservations advised.

This California-French bistro serves flavorful dishes and features a cozy dining room as well as an overflow area in a quirky but interesting industrial space in back (it was a car showroom in the 1940s). A recent dinner here included meaty crab cakes with sherry-cayenne mayo; a mega-size, fall-off-the-bone-tender lamb shank; and a magnificent Meyer lemon angel food cake enhanced by a pot of three-mint loose leaf herbal tea.

Willie Bird's Restaurant
1150 Santa Rosa Ave./Barham Ave., (707) 542-0861; www.williebirdsrestaurant.com. B-L-D daily; $-$$. Reservations accepted.

This casual, old-time restaurant celebrates Thanksgiving every day by serving their own natural brand of tasty turkey in varied forms. Try the Willie Bird Special—a traditional turkey feast with giblet gravy and celery-onion bread stuffing—or something more unusual, such as turkey scallopini or turkey sausage. The motto here is "Turkey always and turkey all ways." Children's portions include a turkey hamburger and turkey hot dog. Plenty of non-turkey items are also available.

Willi's Wine Bar
4404 Old Redwood Hwy., (707) 526-3096; www.williswinebar.net. L W-Sat, D W-M; $$.

Located on a twisty road north of town, this roadhouse is well worth the trip. Portions are small and meant to be shared tapas-style, and it's hard to go wrong in ordering. Creative concoctions include Dungeness crab tacos, bacon-wrapped scallops with sun choke purée, filet mignon sliders, Moroccan-style lamb chops, surprisingly spectacular baked macaroni and cheese with cauliflower, and delectable Tunisian roasted carrots.

GUERNEVILLE AND RUSSIAN RIVER AREA

A LITTLE BACKGROUND

Once upon a time, in 1809, a party of Russians and Aleuts from the Russian-American Fur Company in Sitka, Alaska, landed at the mouth of what is now the Russian River. They named it "Slavianka," or "little beauty." In recognition of the Russian influence in the area, it became referred to as the "Russian" River.

Originally used as a summer camp by the native Pomo Indians, in the '20s and '30s the area became a summer resort favored by wealthy San Franciscans who traveled here by ferry and train to see the ancient redwood forests. A little later they flocked here to dance halls where live entertainment included Ozzie Nelson and Bennie Goodman. Then the area faded in popularity and became a pleasant and uncrowded retreat. Today, slowly recovering from a state of decay, it is regaining some of its former popularity and is known nationally for its resorts catering to gays. The atmosphere is easygoing, and it is acceptable to dine anywhere in casual clothing.

Guerneville, the hub of the Russian River resort area, is surrounded by many smaller towns. The area is nestled in towering redwoods and has numerous public beaches, even more privately-owned ones, and also some unofficial nude beaches. Inquire in town about how to find, or avoid, them. The town also has a delightful selection of one-of-a-kind shops.

VISITOR INFORMATION

Russian River Chamber of Commerce Visitor Center
16209 First St., (877) 644-9001, (707) 869-9000; www.russianriver.com.

GETTING THERE

Located approximately 75 miles north of San Francisco. Exit Highway 101 at Highway 12 west, following it to Highway 116. For a more scenic route, take the River Road exit just north of Santa Rosa and follow it west. Located approximately 15 miles west of Santa Rosa.

ANNUAL EVENTS

Russian River Wine Road Barrel Tasting
March. (800) 723-6336, (707) 433-4335; www.wineroad.com. $5 purchases a glass good at all wineries. Must be age 21+. No pets.

Participants are permitted to get behind the scenes in wine making and sample special wines that aren't usually available for tasting. Wineries provide tastes of wines still in the barrel as well as of some new vintages and old library treasures.

Apple Blossom Festival
April. In Sebastopol; (877) 828-4748, (707) 823-3032; www.sebastopolappleblossom.org. $7, 62+ & 11-17 $5. No pets.

Scheduled each year to occur when the area's plentiful apple orchards are snowy-white with blossoms, this festival includes a parade down Main Street and plenty of booths purveying apple-related crafts and foods.

Bohemian Grove
Last 2 wks. of July.

Many of the world's most powerful political, military, and corporate leaders have been getting together at this 2,700-acre private resort since 1873. The public is not invited.

Gravenstein Apple Fair
August. In Sebastopol; (800) 207-9464, (707) 824-1765; www.farmtrails.org. $10, 65+ $8, 6-12 $5. No pets.

Held on and off since the turn of the century, this old-time country fair is staged amid the shady oak trees and rolling hills of Ragle Ranch Park. The fair specifically celebrates the flavorful, crisp, early-ripening Gravenstein apple—an old German variety dating from 1790 that is indigenous to the area and well known for making the best juices and pies. In fact, this area is known as the world's Gravenstein capital. Fun at the fair is of the down-home variety, with opportunities to taste apple delicacies, observe beekeepers in action, and pet a variety of farm animals. Apples and related foods and products are available for purchase directly from farmers—don't leave for home without a pie. Proceeds fund the printing of the Sonoma County Farm Trails map.

Jazz on the River
September. (707) 869-1595; www.russianriverfestivals.com/jazz. $40+, under 11 free. No pets.

Music festivals don't get much more casual than this one. Audience members can actually float in the placid river on an inner tube while listening to a range of jazz. It's a good idea to pack an ice chest and picnic basket, but food and drink are available for sale. Note that bottles and cans are not permitted.

WHAT TO DO

Armstrong Redwoods State Reserve
17000 Armstrong Woods Rd., (707) 869-2015; www.parks.ca.gov. Daily 8am-sunset. $6/vehicle.

A Visitor Center *((707) 869-2958. Daily 11-3.)* orients hikers to the trail system within this 700-plus-acre park of thousand-year-old redwood groves. A free parking lot is located just outside the tollgate, and no admission fee is charged for parking there and walking in.

The **Armstrong Woods Pack Station** *((707) 887-2939; www.redwoodhorses.com. Schedule varies. $70+. Reservations required. Must be age 10+ or have guide's permission.)* offers trail rides and full-day lunch rides among the mammoth trees found here. Overnight rides and longer pack trips are available May through October.

Almost 4 miles farther, at the end of a narrow, steep, winding road, **Austin Creek State Recreation Area** *((707) 869-2015; www.parks. sonoma.net/austin.html.)* offers 20 miles of hiking trails, plus rustic camping facilities and four hike-in campsites.

Duncans Mills
On Hwy. 116, 10 mi. W of Guerneville, (707) 865-2024.

Once a lumber village, this tiny rustic town—population 85 in 2006—is now home to a collection of eclectic shops, a general store with a deli, a restaurant, and a riverside campground with private beach. Cattle graze on the peaceful adjacent hillside, and benches invite relaxing for a stretch, especially on a sunny day.

Kozlowski Farms
5566 Hwy. 116 N. (Gravenstein Hwy.), in Forestville, (800) 4-R-FARMS, (707) 887-1587; www.kozlowskifarms.com. Daily 9-5.

This scenic farm is planted with acres of grapes and apple trees. The family-owned and -operated business produces housemade juices, berry vinegars, wine jellies, and berry jams and fruit butters made without sugar. Most are available for sampling and sold year-round in the farm's original barn along with housemade baked goods. A mail-order catalogue is available.

Pegasus Theater Company
20347 Hwy. 116, in Monte Rio, (707) 522-9043; www.pegasustheater.com. $18, 62+ $15, pay-what-you-can Thursdays.

Known for its elaborate sets, this company presents live theatre in an intimate setting.

River swimming

Almost anywhere along the banks of the Russian River is a nice place to lay a blanket. A prime spot is under the Monte Rio bridge, where parking and beach access are free. Another choice spot is Johnson's Beach (see page 240). Canoe and paddleboat rentals and snack stands are available at both. The riverbed and beaches are covered with pebbles, so water-proof shoes are advised.

A good game to play with children here is "Find the Siamese Twin Clam Shells." Be prepared with a special prize for the kid who finds the largest number of intact pairs.

WINERIES

Korbel Champagne Cellars
13250 River Rd., (707) 824-7000; www.korbel.com. Tasting daily 10-4; tours daily 10-3, on the hr.; more frequent tours in summer. Rose garden tour: Tu-Sun at 11, 1, 3; Apr-Oct only; free.

The nation's oldest producer of méthode champenoise champagne, this century-old winery also produces brandy and wine. Several varieties of champagne can be tasted, and chilled splits can be purchased for impromptu picnics. A deli provides an array of tasty salads and picnic foods and offers seating on a deck out under some redwoods.

The grounds are landscaped with beautifully maintained flower gardens. An **Antique Rose Garden**, faithfully restored to its turn-of-the-century beauty, is filled with old-time flowers such as coral bells, primroses, and violets, as well as more unusual plants. Among the more than 250 varieties of rose are rare specimens such as the original Burbank Tea, the Double Musk celebrated in Shakespeare's plays, and the True Ambassador, which was once thought to be extinct.

WHERE TO STAY

Applewood Inn & Restaurant

*13555 Hwy. 116, (800) 555-8509, (707) 869-9093;
www.applewoodinn.com. 19 rooms; $$-$$$+.
Unsuitable for children under 21. Some gas fireplaces.
Heated pool (seasonal); hot tub. Full breakfast;
restaurant.*

Built in 1922 as a private home, the
Mission Revival-style mansion is now a county
historical landmark. Two newer Mediterranean-
style villas are part of the 6-acre complex featuring an idyllic pool area surrounded by tall
redwood trees. The hot tub is wonderful at
night, especially when all the stars are out.
Public tennis courts, located adjacent to the
property, are a short walk away through a valley
still populated with apple trees that once comprised an orchard. The inn's decor is tasteful
and unfussy, with aesthetically pleasing touches.
Rooms are spacious and comfortable, and some
have private patios or balconies overlooking the
redwoods and peaceful pastures beyond.
Breakfast is simple, yet special—perhaps a sec-
tioned grapefruit topped with a perfect red
maraschino cherry, followed by beautifully presented eggs Florentine prepared with tender
baby spinach fresh from the inn's own garden.

Enticing, sophisticated California-
Provençale dinners are served in the **restaurant**
(D Tu-Sat; $$$. Reservations advised.). Designed
to resemble a French Barn, the dining room has
two river rock fireplaces, lofty beamed ceilings,
and windows looking out over tall redwoods.

Creekside Inn & Resort

*16180 Neeley Rd., (800) 776-6586, (707) 869-3623;
www.creeksideinn.com. 6 rooms, 22 cabins; $-$$$.
Some kitchens, & wood-burning fireplaces;
some shared baths. Unheated pool (seasonal).
Full breakfast (B&B rooms only).*

Located a short stroll from town, just
across the historical bridge, this quiet resort
dates back to the '30s. Guests have a choice of
lodgings. The main house operates as a B&B,
with four rooms sharing two bathrooms and
two suites having private baths. Modernized
housekeeping cottages all feature attractive half-
timbered exteriors; a favorite is the Tree
House—named for the fact that trees can be
observed from every window. New eco-friendly
cottages have private decks and full kitchens.

Facilities include a large outdoor pool area with
a barbecue, pool table, Ping-Pong table, croquet
lawn, and lending library. When rains are
normal, Pocket Canyon Creek provides the
soothing sound of running water as it meanders
through the property.

Fern Grove Cottages

*16650 Hwy. 116, (888) 243-2674, (707) 869-8105;
www.ferngrove.com. 20 cabins; $-$$$. Some
wood-burning fireplaces & gas stoves; some kitchens.
Heated pool. Continental breakfast.*

These cozy, 1920s knotty pine-paneled
cottages are tucked amid blooming gardens
under tall redwoods. Most rooms have a
theme—"cowboy," "flamingo." Town is an easy
stroll away, and one of the area's best beaches is
just across the street.

The Inn at Occidental

*3657 Church St., in Occidental, (800) 522-6324,
(707) 874-1047; www.innatoccidental.com. 16 rooms,
1 cabin; $$-$$$+. Some fireplaces. Evening snack;
full breakfast.*

Not your average B&B, this exquisite, yet
cozy, inn presents guests with the very best in
food and hospitality. A restored Victorian and
the town's oldest residential structure, it sits
tucked among tall redwoods on a hillside just
above town. Outside, covered porches are
furnished with wicker and the garden features
a fountain and walled courtyard. Inside, high-
lights include fir floors, wainscoted hallways,
and themed guest rooms—one with a private
hot tub. The inn is furnished delightfully
with the owner's vast and ever-growing collec-
tions of antiques and art.

Johnson's Beach & Resort

*16241 First St., (707) 869-2022;
www.johnsonsbeach.com. 10 rooms; $.
Closed Nov-Apr. Some kitchens. No pets.*

These bargain old-time hotel rooms are
adjacent to the river. Only weeklong rentals are
reservable; shorter stays are first-come, first-
served. Facilities include two rustic wooden
swings, a large-tire sandbox, pool and Ping-
Pong tables, and access to a beach with a snack
bar and both boat and beach paraphernalia
rentals. Campsites are also available.

Rio Villa Beach Resort

20292 Hwy. 116, in Monte Rio, (877) 746-8455, (707) 865-1143; www.riovilla.com. 12 rooms, 2 cabins; $$. Some kitchens & wood-burning fireplaces. Continental breakfast on weekends. No pets.

Some of the rooms in this peaceful spot have private balconies with river views. Guests can relax both on a large deck surrounded by manicured grounds overlooking the river and on a private beach.

Riverlane Resort

16320 1st St., (800) 201-2324, (707) 869-2323; www.riverlaneresort.com. 12 cabins; $-$$$. All kitchens; some wood-burning fireplaces & stoves. Heated pool (seasonal); hot tub. No pets.

Located by the river, this pleasant enclave of housekeeping cabins offers river access.

Sonoma Orchid Inn

12850 River Rd., (888) 877-4466, (707) 887-1033; www.sonomaorchidinn.com. 8 rooms; $$-$$$. Some TVs; 1 gas fireplace & 1 wood-burning stove. Hot tub. Afternoon snack; full breakfast.

Built of redwood in 1906, this canary-yellow 1906 farmhouse was constructed by the first settlers in the area. Two rooms are in an adjacent cottage dating from 1934, and all rooms are decorated eclectically with a mix of antiques and contemporary furnishings. Recreational facilities include a hot tub situated pleasantly beneath sheltering trees, a badminton area, and a bocce ball lawn. Across the highway, secluded beaches are reached via a short walk down a blackberry-lined lane. A favorite breakfast dish is decadent French toast soufflé, perhaps served with ham steaks and a fresh fruit salad. When the inn's hens are laying, a dish made with freshly collected eggs is a delicious possibility. Fresh cookies are always out in the guest kitchen, and shelves in the poshly decorated front room are well equipped with board games and reading matter as well as a selection of blooming orchids from the inn's greenhouse.

Village Inn & Restaurant

20822 River Blvd., in Monte Rio, (800) 303-2303, (707) 865-2304; www.villageinn-ca.com. 10 rooms; $-$$$. Continental breakfast; restaurant; room service.

Built as a summer home in 1906, this cozy rustic structure was turned into a hotel in 1908 and has remained one ever since. A worthy claim to fame is that *Holiday Inn*, starring Bing Crosby, was filmed here. Some rooms have a garden view, others a riverfront deck, and all are equipped with a refrigerator and microwave.

In summer, the **restaurant** *(D W-Sun; $$. Reservations advised.)* serves a popular Sunday live jazz barbecue outdoors on a pleasant deck overlooking the river.

House rentals

Contact the Visitors Bureau for the names of realty companies that rent private homes to vacationers.

WHERE TO EAT

Ace-In-The-Hole Cider Pub

3100 Hwy. 116 N. (Gravenstein Hwy.), in Sebastopol, (707) 829-1ACE; www.acecider.com. L-D daily; $.

Taste refreshing hard ciders made from local ingredients at America's very first cider pub. They're made from fermented apple juice (5% alcohol), are said to be an "exhilarating" alternative to the heaviness of beer and the high alcohol content of wine, and come in five flavors, including apple, pear, and berry. Can't decide? Try a sampler. A hamburger, fish & chips, and pizza are on the menu. The large, open interior is welcoming on dreary days, while the ample patio is prime in sunny weather. A tours of the cider mill behind the pub is available upon request, and live music is scheduled nightly.

CazSonoma Inn

1000 Kidd Creek Rd., in Cazadero, 3 mi. W of town, (707) 632-5255. D daily, SunBr; $$. Closed Dec-Apr. Reservations advised.

Nestled between two creeks in a protected valley, this 1926 lodge is reached via a 1-mile-long dirt road. The dining room serves California cuisine and offers great views of the tranquil forest setting. In warm weather, a large deck under the redwoods is irresistible. Live music is usually scheduled on weekends.

Cabins and lodge rooms *(4 rooms, 2 cabins; $$. No TVs; some kitchens & wood-burning fireplaces. Unheated pool (seasonal). Evening snack; continental breakfast.)* are also available. A man-made waterfall and 2 miles of hiking trails are among the features found on the 147-acre site.

Mom's Apple Pie
4550 Hwy. 116 N./near Hwy. 12, in Sebastopol, (707) 823-8330; www.momsapplepieusa.com. Daily 10-6; $.

Located beside an 8-acre apple orchard, this cheery bakery is always worth a stop. Pies are made by hand and include not just the famous apple but banana cream, peach, raspberry, pecan and more—all available in several sizes to take home as well. Tasty soup and sandwiches are also available.

The Occidental Two
In Occidental.

Both of these restaurants serve bountiful multi-course, family-style Italian dinners. Prices are moderate, they have a reasonable plate charge for small children, and inexpensive ravioli and spaghetti dinners with fewer side dishes also are available. Reservations are advised at prime dining times during the summer, and on weekends and holidays year-round. People come to these restaurants to eat BIG. Picking a favorite can prove fattening.

• Negri's
3700 Main St., (707) 823-5301; www.negrisrestaurant.com. L-D daily.

Meals here start with a steaming bowl of minestrone soup, rounds of moist salami, and a hunk of crusty Italian bread. Then come more plates bearing pickled vegetables, marinated bean salad, creamy large-curd cottage cheese, and a salad tossed with Thousand Island dressing. Just as tummies begin to fill, the ravioli arrives—stuffed with spinach and topped with an excellent tomato-meat sauce—followed by the entrée—a choice of crispy, moist fried chicken, saucy duck, or grilled porterhouse steak (seafood entrees are available on weeknights)—and a side of thick french fries and heavy zucchini pancakes. Then come the doggie bags. For those with space, apple fritters are available at additional charge.

• Union Hotel
3731 Main St., (707) 874-3444; www.unionhotel.com. L-D daily.

In operation since 1876, this restaurant seats 400 people in three enormous dining rooms and on an outdoor patio. The choice is expansive, and side dishes include an antipasto plate, minestrone soup, a salad, and bread and butter. Dessert—apple fritters, spumoni ice cream, or apple pie—and coffee are extra. A bakery, pizzeria, and cafe adjoin.

Pat's Restaurant & Bar
16236 Main St., (707) 869-9904. B-L daily; $.

This is a simple spot with booths and counter seating. Pastries and pies are housemade. A mural map of Russian River fishing holes decorates the wall, providing food for thought.

River Inn Grill
16141 Main St., (707) 869-0481; www.riverinngrill.com. B-L daily, D Tu-Sat; shorter schedule in winter; $-$$. No reservations.

The breakfast menu includes crisp waffles, thin Swedish pancakes, perfect French toast, omelettes, oatmeal, and fresh fruit. At lunch and dinner, seafood is the star.

Stella's at Russian River Vineyards
5700 Hwy. 116 N., in Forestville, (707) 887-2300; www.russianrivervineyards.com. L-D daily in summer, SunBr; closed M-Tu rest of year; $$. Reservations advised.

In good weather, diners are seated outdoors and shaded by grape arbors and umbrellas. In colder weather, seating is inside the century-old farmhouse that is now the restaurant. Greek dishes are the specialty, but a hamburger is on the lunch menu and the eclectic menu changes every 2 weeks. Extensive use is made of local products as well as of fresh organic herbs and vegetables grown on site. House-smoked items and vegan items are usually available, and a large selection of the winery's own vintages are poured by the glass. This is the only family-owned and -operated winery/restaurant in the state.

Organically-grown wines can be sampled in the adjacent **Russian River Vineyards** tasting room *(707) 887-3344; www.russianrivervine-yards.com. Tasting daily 11-5; tours by appt.).* The winery is known for its late harvest Pinot Noirs and Merlots, and the complex Petite Sirahs are also noteworthy.

HEALDSBURG

A LITTLE BACKGROUND

Small town America is alive and well in Northern California. When visitors arrive in this charming old-fashioned town, they sometimes are shocked to find cars stopping *willingly* as they wait in a crosswalk to cross the street. Even the cars in the far lane sometimes wait! And parking places are usually easy to find, and free, even around the popular town square. All this plus the weather is generally sunny.

Healdsburg was incorporated in 1867 and then slowly rose around a central Spanish-style plaza. It is one of the few examples remaining of a planned early California town. The plaza's original owner gave it to the town as a gift with the provision that it be used forever as a "pleasure ground" free from public buildings. Nowadays, a free **Summer Sunday Concert Series** is scheduled on the plaza June through August. Historic homes and buildings are sprinkled around the square and throughout the surrounding neighborhood, adding greatly to the town's turn-of-the century flavor.

Once known as "the buckle of the prune belt," the surrounding area has replanted the fruit orchards with grapes. It is now home to more than 50 premium wineries, a few of which have tasting rooms in town. Visitors can spend the day driving or biking the back roads, happily hopping from winery to winery, or opt to just stay in town antiquing and shopping.

VISITOR INFORMATION

Healdsburg Chamber of Commerce & Visitors Bureau
217 Healdsburg Ave., (800) 648-9922, (707) 433-6935; www.healdsburg.org.

Russian River Wine Road
(800) 723-6336, (707) 433-4335; www.wineroad.com.

This free brochure provides a map and details on wineries and lodgings stretching from Forestville to Cloverdale.

GETTING THERE

Located 75 miles north of San Francisco, and 12 miles north of Santa Rosa.

WHAT TO DO

Hand Fan Museum of Healdsburg
327 Healdsburg Ave., in Hotel Healdsburg complex, (707) 431-2500; www.handfanmuseum.com. W-Sun 11-4. Free.

The first museum in the U.S. dedicated to hand fans, this teeny, tiny spot has a permanent collection of almost 3,000 fans from around the world (the oldest is French and dates from 1680). Unlike the fixed fan, which seems to have been around forever, the folding fan was invented in Japan in the 6th century. Legend has it that a Buddhist monk developed it after observing a bird's wing action on a hot day. More than 75 fans are displayed in this happy place—even guys like it—and both antique and new fans are for sale.

Healdsburg Museum
221 Matheson St./First St., (707) 431-3325; www.healdsburgmuseum.org. Thur-Sun 11-4. Free.

Located inside a Carnegie Library building and dedicated to the preservation and exhibition of northern Sonoma County history, this small museum displays Pomo Indian baskets, tools (including a gigantic bear trap), weapons, and crafts.

Healdsburg Veterans Memorial Beach

13839 Old Redwood Hwy., (707) 433-1625;
www.sonoma-county.org/parks/pk_hvet.htm.
Daily sunrise-sunset; swimming June-Sept only.
$5-$6/vehicle.

This is a choice spot to swim in the warm
Russian River, which in summer has an average
water temperature of 70 to 75 degrees. A lifeguard is on duty from 10 a.m., and canoe and
inner tube rentals are available. Facilities
include a diving board, a children's wading area,
a picnic area with barbecues, and a snack bar.
Sunbathers have a choice of a large sandy beach
or a shady lawn area.

River's Edge Kayak & Canoe Trips

13840 Healdsburg Ave., (707) 433-7247;
www.riversedgekayakandcanoe.com. $60/canoe/half
day, $85/full day. Must be age 5+. Reservations
advised.

The canoe fee for these unguided trips
includes life jackets, paddles, and canoe transport. An after-canoeing barbecue is an option
each weekend at additional cost, and a 2-day
trip is also available. River's Edge has five other
rental sites along the river. This long-time
business formerly was known as W.C. "Bob"
Trowbridge Canoe Trips.

WINERIES

Dry Creek Vineyard

3770 Lambert Bridge Rd., 3 mi. W of Hwy. 101,
(800) 864-WINE, (707) 433-1000; www.drycreek
vineyard.com. Tasting daily 10:30-4:30; no tour.

Known for its Fumé Blancs and Chenin
Blancs, this winery has a cool, shady picnic area
under a canopy of old pine and maple trees.

An annual November **Open House** (*$15*)
celebrates the season with live music, wine tasting, and plenty of good food.

Ferrari-Carano Vineyards & Winery

8761 Dry Creek Rd., (800) 831-0381, (707) 433-6700;
www.ferrari-carano.com. Tasting daily 10-5;
tour M-Sat at 10, reservation required.

Designed like an elegant Italianate villa,
the visitor center is surrounded by flower
gardens that spread over 5 acres, include several
cork oak trees, and are enhanced by bridges,
brooks, and gazebos. In spring, 18,000 tulips
burst into bloom. A drooling brass boar at the
entrance is believed to bring good luck to
those who pet it. The winery is known for its
Fume Blancs, Chardonnays, and Cabernet
Sauvignons.

Foppiano Vineyards

12707 Old Redwood Hwy., (707) 433-7272;
www.foppiano.com. Tasting daily 10-4:30;
self-guided tour.

Established in 1896, this family-owned
winery offers a self-guided tour through its
Chardonnay, Cabernet Sauvignon, and Petite
Sirah vineyards. It takes about 30 minutes, and
a free explanatory brochure is available in the
tasting room.

Hop Kiln Winery

6050 Westside Rd., (707) 433-6491;
www.hopkilnwinery.com. Tasting daily 10-5; no tour.

Known for its Pinots and Chardonnays,
this unique winery is reached by taking a quiet
back road through miles of scenic vineyards.
Tasting occurs inside a landmark 1905 hops-
drying barn built by Italian stonemasons (it
once supplied San Francisco breweries). The
winery provides two appealing picnic areas: one
overlooks a duck pond and vineyards; the other
is in a well-shaded rose garden.

J Wine Company

11447 Old Redwood Hwy., (888) J WINE CO, (707) 431-5400; www.jwine.com. Tasting daily 11-5; tour by appt.

The lines of this elegant, ultra-modern winery are softened with attractive landscaping and a lily pond moat. It produces an array of sparkling wines as well as Pinot Noirs. In a bar area enhanced by a massive metal-and-glass sculpture backlit in fiber optics (it is symbolic of diamonds and champagne bubbles and certain to provoke discussion), tasters can try wines by the glass or sample an entire flight accompanied by foods designed to complement them.

A stop here allows killing the proverbial two birds with one stone. Park once, taste twice: Rodney Strong Vineyards is located just across the way. And speaking of birds, blue herons—as well as otters—are sometimes seen in the pond.

Preston of Dry Creek

9282 W. Dry Creek Rd., (800) 305-9707, (707) 433-3372; www.prestonvineyards.com. Tasting daily 11-4:30; no tour.

This small family-owned winery produces terrific Rhone-style wines and good Fumé Blancs. Outside the tasting room, a shaded brick patio holds comfy wicker chairs and numerous resident cats. Call ahead to find out what Lou, the winery owner, is baking in the Italian-style forno oven and when it's available for sale. Picnic tables are shaded by an old walnut tree, and courts for Italian bocce ball and French petanque are available. On the way in or out, an inviting roadside creek invites frolicking.

Rodney Strong Vineyards

11455 Old Redwood Hwy., (800) 678-4763, (707) 431-1533; www.rodneystrong.com. Tasting daily 10-5; tour daily at 11, 3.

A self-guided tour circles the tasting room, where the winery's delicious Chardonnays and Cabernet Sauvignons can be sampled. Picnic tables are available, and special events are scheduled regularly in summer.

Seghesio Vineyards & Winery

14730 Grove St./Dry Creek Rd., (866) 734-4374, (707) 433-3579; www.seghesio.com. Tasting daily 10-5; no tour.

Founded in 1895, this small winery continues to be operated by family members from the third, fourth, and fifth generations. Its tasting bar overlooks the barrel room. Mature trees shade a spacious picnic area, and an expansive rose garden is particularly lovely in summer. The winery is best known for its Italian varietals and Zinfandels (more than half of their vineyards grow Zinfandel grapes). It has the oldest planting of Sangiovese grapes in California, dating back 1910, and produces an unusual big Aglianico varietal red that dates to the 7th century.

Simi Winery

16275 Healdsburg Ave., (800) 746-4880, (707) 473-3232; www.simiwinery.com. Tasting daily 10-5; tour daily at 11, 2.

Opened in 1890, this friendly winery pours samples of reserve wines. An inviting redwood-shaded picnic area is available.

WHERE TO STAY

Best Western Dry Creek Inn

198 Dry Creek Rd., (800) 222-5784, (707) 433-0300; www.drycreekinn.com. 102 rooms; $$. Heated pool (seasonal); hot tub; fitness room. Continental breakfast; restaurant.

At this attractive contemporary motel, all guests are greeted with a complimentary bottle of wine in their room.

Camellia Inn

211 North St., (800) 727-8182, (707) 433-8182; www.camelliainn.com. 9 rooms; $$-$$$. No TVs; some gas fireplaces. Heated pool (seasonal). Afternoon snack; evening snack; full breakfast.

Situated just 2 blocks from the town square, this 1869 Italianate Victorian townhouse is a quiet retreat. The surrounding grounds are planted with more than 50 varieties of camellias, some of which were given to the original owner by Luther Burbank. In keeping with the theme, each room is named for a camellia variety. The tastefully furnished, high-ceilinged Royalty Room—originally the home's dining room—boasts an antique Scottish high bed with a step stool and a ceiling-hung canopy, as well as an unusual, ornate antique-brass sink fitting. Several rooms have whirlpool bathtubs for two. An afternoon spent out in the oak-shaded, villa-style pool area is incredibly relaxing. The early evening snack includes the inn's own **Camellia Cellars** wines *(a tasting room is at 57 Front St., (888) 404-WINE, (707) 433-1290; www.camelliacellars.com. Daily 11-6.).* Breakfast is served buffet-style in the dining room, where guests are seated at a large claw-foot mahogany table.

Healdsburg Inn on the Plaza

112 Matheson St., (800) 431-8663, (707) 433-6991; www.healdsburginn.com. 12 rooms; $$$-$$$+. All gas fireplaces. Afternoon snack; full breakfast. No pets.

Located right on the town square, this 1901 Victorian was once a stagecoach stop. Rooms—situated mostly on the second floor and reached via either a grand staircase or modern elevator—are furnished in tasteful contemporary style and have generously-sized bathrooms. The Early Light Room was the town's first photography studio and features a spectacular skylight. It just can't get any cozier than being in the peach-colored Sonnet Room on a rainy morning, with the fireplace flickering and the church bells across the plaza ringing out the hour. Breakfast is taken in a second-floor solarium overlooking a row of trees fronting the town plaza. A bottomless jar of cookies and a fridge full of cold drinks are always available. The work of local artists decorates each room and is for sale in a small shop operating in the hotel lobby.

Honor Mansion

14891 Grove St., (800) 554-4667, (707) 433-4277; www.honormansion.com. 13 units; $$$-$$$+. Some gas fireplaces. Solar-heated pool; 1 tennis court. Afternoon & evening snack; full breakfast; room service.

Sporting an ancient magnolia tree in an expansive grassy front yard surrounded by a white picket fence, this Italianate Victorian built in 1883 was a family home for 108 years before it was restored and converted into a B&B. A well-treated staff of 14 keeps things humming, and their attention to detail delights guests in the form of dishes filled with candies and jars filled with cookies. Many rooms have fireplaces requiring just the flip of a switch to deliver a full-blown blaze, and some rooms have clawfoot tubs with mommy and baby rubber duckies ready to float. Room choices include a two-story converted water tower suite, a detached cottage furnished with an oak buffet fitted with a small refrigerator and a wet bar, and several suites with a private patio and Jacuzzi. Recreational facilities include a six-hole putting green, a ¼-mile jogging trail, two bocce courts, a half-basketball court, and a competition croquet lawn. After a swim in the pool or a nap atop a fluffy bed or a long soak in a deep tub with copy of *Millionaire* and *Billionaire* magazines to dream over, it's time for the evening hors d'oeuvres and wine service designed to keep guests from feeling any twinge of hunger. In the morning, indulge in a sobering espresso or frothy cappucino from the automatic maker that is available to guests around the clock, or arrange for delivery of a pot of coffee or tea right to the room. A sumptuous buffet breakfast served in the dining room includes fresh fruit, a hot entree—perhaps Grand Marnier French Toast or Honor Mansion Eggs Benedict—and plenty of fresh scones. And do take time to hand-feed the colorful, hungry koi in the "kissing koi pond" just outside the dining room.

Hotel Healdsburg

25 Matheson St., (800) 889-7188, (707) 431-2800; www.hotelhealdsburg.com. 55 rooms; $$$-$$$+. Heated pool; full-service spa; fitness room. Full breakfast; restaurant; room service.

Featuring a stylish minimalist decor and with a collection of Tibetan rugs accenting its polished wood floors, this luxurious hotel fronts on the plaza. Subdued guest rooms are appointed with the best linens and oversize soaking tubs, and breakfast is served in the lobby. A wine-and-honey wrap is among the many relaxing spa options.

The **lobby bar** serves refreshments fireside or on a screened porch, weather permitting, with live jazz on Friday and Saturday nights, and the casual **Café Newsstand** dispenses espresso, panini, and housemade gelato. Celebrity chef Charlie Palmer's **Dry Creek Kitchen** *(317 Healdsburg Ave./Matheson St., (707) 431-0330; www.charliepalmer.com. L-D daily; $$$+. Reservations advised.)* uses the best local ingredients for its innovative menu, which changes daily. Past items have included the delicious likes of baby beet salad with goat cheese, tortellini stuffed with roasted cauliflower in a browned butter-Cabernet sauce, and duck with pomegranate-molasses glaze. A tasting menu is also available. Seating in the sophisticated dining room is comfortable, and diners get a glimpse of the busy kitchen through a frosted glass wall.

Madrona Manor
1001 Westside Rd., (800) 258-4003, (707) 433-4231; www.madronamanor.com. 22 rooms; $$$-$$$+. Unsuitable for children under 12. No TVs; some wood-burning & gas fireplaces. Heated pool (seasonal). Full breakfast; restaurant.

Featuring an unusual mansard roof, this majestic mansion was built in 1881 as a country retreat and is now on the National Historic Register. It is located on an 8-acre estate off a side road running through rural vineyards, and an imposing archway frames a long driveway leading up it. Five rooms on the second floor feature furniture original to the house, and they also variously feature fireplaces with hand-painted tiles, 12-foot ceilings, and clawfoot tubs. Four outer structures, including an 1881 Carriage House and a 2002 Schoolhouse, hold more rooms. Breakfast is reminiscent of a typical European morning spread, with fresh-squeezed orange juice, coffee, breakfast breads, jams, seasonal fruits, meats and cheeses, hard-boiled eggs (in a chicken-shaped basket), vegetable frittata or quiche, and housemade granola among the choices.

For dinner, guests need only enter the elegant **restaurant** *(D W-Sun; $$$. Reservations advised.)*, where items often feature produce from the estate's own gardens and orchards. Both tasting menus and an a la carte menu are offered. One dinner enjoyed here featured a delicious soft-shell crab tempura and a peachy-keen dessert sampler of peach shortcake, peach crisp, and peach ice cream. The wine list features local Sonoma vintages. Outside seating is available on a heated terrace.

WHERE TO EAT

Barndiva
231 Center St./Matheson, (707) 431-0100; www.barndiva.com. L Thur-F, D daily, Sat-SunBr; $$. No reservations.

Designed to resemble a big red barn, this bar-restaurant has very high ceilings and a sleek, spare contemporary decor. Fair weather

dining occurs on an expansive patio in the back, where a large fountain provides soothing sounds and twinkling lights adorn the trees. The short menu is generally tasty, but savory pies, deep-fried items, and salads are particularly good. Do try bartender Dave's award winning All Dave All Night cocktail—a refreshing citrussy, orangey concoction that is also quite beautiful and garnished with orange segments. Call ahead; the restaurant often closes for private events. The owners live upstairs, and an enticing related home decor store operates next door.

Bear Republic Brewing Co.
345 Healdsburg Ave., (707) 433-BEER; www.bearrepublic.com. L-D daily; $. No reservations.

Though the dining room is wide-open so diners can view the brewing vats, this warehouse-like spot still manages to feel cozy. Or perhaps it just seems that way because of the warm greeting provided by its owner. Get acquainted with the house brews—including the award-winning Red Rocket Ale—with a sampler, or try a delicious house-brewed root beer or cream soda. Burgers, sandwiches, and salads are all choice, but more substantial entrees and smaller appetizer plates—including addictive garlic-chili fries—are on the menu as well.

Flying Goat Coffee
324 Center St., (707) 433-3599, M-Sat 7-6; & 419 Center St., (707) 433-8003, M-F 6-1, Sat 7-1; www.flyinggoatcoffee.com.

For description, see page 237.

Picnic Pick-Ups
• **Costeaux French Bakery & Cafe**
417 Healdsburg Ave., (888) 355-0217, (707) 433-1913; www.costeaux.com. B-L Tu-Sun; $. No reservations.

Family-owned andoperated since 1923, this spot is choice for picking up picnic supplies or a pre-ordered ribbon-tied box lunch. Sit-down service includes sandwiches on house-made breads, delicious French onion soup, and selections from the awe-inspiring pastry case: caramel-macadamia nut tart, cheesecake, fresh fruit tart, French pastries. The bakery is famous for its round sourdough pull-a-part bread and once baked the world's largest pumpkin pie in its oven. Breakfast is served all day. Seating is either in the airy, high-ceilinged interior or outside on a pleasant sidewalk-side patio.

• Downtown Bakery and Creamery
308-A Center St., (707) 431-2719; www.downtown bakery.net. M-F 6am-5:30, Sat 7-5:30, Sun 7-4. No cards.

Co-owner Lindsey Shere did time in the kitchen at Berkeley's renowned Chez Panisse. She also wrote the best-selling cookbook *Chez Panisse Desserts*. So the exceptional hand-shaped, slow-rise breads and the pastries and ice creams produced in her kitchen here are not a complete surprise. When available, the focaccia, sticky buns, and fruit turnovers are a must. On warm Wine Country days, it is a refreshing pleasure to indulge in one of the shop's old-fashioned milkshakes or sundaes, and it's always a good idea to purchase frozen cookie dough to bake at home. Organically grown, freshly milled flours are used, and produce and dairy products are organic and locally produced whenever possible.

• Dry Creek General Store
3495 Dry Creek Rd., (707) 433-4171; www.dcgstore.com. Daily 6-5:30, in summer to 7.

Opened in 1881, this old-fashioned general store/deli is now a state historical landmark. Claiming to be "the best deli by a dam site!," it *is* located by the Warm Springs Dam and it sure *does* dispense good picnic fare! Sandwiches are made to order, and plenty of housemade salads and garnishes are available.

• Jimtown Store
6706 Hwy. 128, (707) 433-1212; www.jimtown.com. M-F 7-5, Sat-Sun 7:30-5; closed 2 wks. in Jan.

Dating back to the late 1800s, this landmark country store and café specializes in preparing seasonal foods and great boxed picnic lunches to enjoy right on their colorful back patio—perhaps with a latte—or to take along to a winery. Order boxes 24 hours in advance. Among the eclectic gourmet sandwiches are Brie with chopped olives and house-roasted turkey with chickpea chipotle, but chicken salad and peanut butter & jelly are also available. Suggestions are provided about where to find the perfect picnic spot. Antiques, folk art, and local products are also for sale.

Next door, **Hawkes Winery** *(6734 Hwy. 128, (707) 433-HAWK; www.hawkeswine.com. Tasting daily 10-5.)* is known for its delicious

Cabernet Sauvignons and Merlots. Its tasting room is in the airy, white-painted interior of a former barn, and the tasting bar overlooks a vast vineyard. An extensive collection of teapots is displayed, and a pot of tea is offered to designated drivers.

• Oakville Grocery
124 Matheson St., (707) 433-3200; www.oakvillegrocery.com. Daily 8-6.

For description, see page 424.

Restaurant Charcuterie
335 Healdsburg Ave., (707) 431-7213. L-D daily; $-$$. Reservations accepted for D.

The light, French-influenced menu at this casual spot is perfect for a quick meal. Particularly tasty salads—the item of choice in this generally warm area—include one with strips of blackened chicken breast served over a lightly dressed Caesar salad, and another with toasted walnuts, cubes of apple, golden raisins, and Gorgonzola over baby greens with poppy seed dressing. Sandwiches and pastas are available at lunch, and more substantial entrees—such as baked chicken and rabbit fricassée—are added at dinner.

Zin
344 Center St., (707) 473-0946; www.zinrestaurant.com. L-D daily; $$. Reservations advised.

Located just a few blocks from the Plaza, this stylish yet casual restaurant has an open dining room with an industrial-style decor featuring cement walls and open rafters. Natural wood trim and paintings of rural scenes add to the warm and cozy feeling. The classic American cooking with a Southern influence is designed to pair with hearty, all-American Zinfandels. The slow-braised lamb shank is a hands-down winner, but in addition to the expected Zin-friendly meats, lighter fish items and roasted chicken are also on the menu. For a starter the deep-fried beer-battered green beans with mango salsa is choice, and for dessert the coffee ice cream with Kahlua chocolate sauce should not be passed up. The wine list, but of course, is dominated with Zins.

GEYSERVILLE

VISITOR INFORMATION

Geyserville Chamber of Commerce
P.O. Box 276, Geyserville 95441, (707) 857-3745; www.geyservillecc.com.

GETTING THERE

Located approximately 8 miles north of Healdsburg.

ANNUAL EVENTS

Geyserville Fall Colors Festival & Vintage Car Show
October. (707) 857-3745; www.geyservillecc.com. Free.

The whole town celebrates the end of the grape harvest with this festival.

WHAT TO DO

Lake Sonoma
3333 Skaggs Springs Rd., (707) 433-9483; www.parks.sonoma.net/laktrls.html. Free.

This scenic spot hosts all manner of water activities—fishing, boating, water-skiing, swimming. Everything from a canoe to a patio boat or houseboat can be rented from the **Lake Sonoma Resort** *(Stewarts Point Rd., (707) 433-2200.)*.

The **Milt Brandt Visitors Center** *((707) 431-4533.)* displays the area's wildlife and provides a self-guided tour through the **Congressman Don Clausen Fish Hatchery.** When the steelhead trout and salmon run here, usually from November through April, they can be observed using a man-made fish ladder.

WINERIES

Francis Ford Coppola Presents Rosso & Bianco
300 Via Archimedes, at Independence Lane exit off Hwy. 101, (877) ROSSOBIANCO, (707) 857-1400; www.rossobianco.com. Tasting daily 11-5; tour daily.

Tucked into a vineyard-covered hill and featuring distinctive towers reminiscent of the area's once-common hop kilns, this was formerly the Château Souverain winery. The winery is currently undergoing renovation and will eventually reopen the cafe. Tasting consists of a flight of three of the same varietal served with complementary food bites.

Geyser Peak Winery
22281 Chianti Rd., 1 mi. N of town at Canyon Rd. exit off Hwy. 101, (800) 255-WINE, (707) 891-5400; www.geyserpeakwinery.com. Tasting daily 10-5; no tour.

Shaded patio picnic tables here overlook Alexander Valley.

Locals Tasting Room
21023 Geyserville Ave., (707) 857-4900; www.tastelocalwines.com. W-M 11-6. Free.

Taste a flight of delicious wines from ten small-production wineries that are not distributed through retail outlets or restaurants.

Trentadue Winery
19170 Geyserville Ave., (888) 332-3032, (707) 433-3104; www.trentadue.com. Tasting daily 10-5; no tour.

Known for its spicy red Carignane and Sengoviese, this small family enterprise also sells picnic supplies in its tasting room and provides a picnic area in the welcoming shade of a grape arbor. Children get soft drinks, cookies, and candy to keep them happy while their parents taste.

WHERE TO STAY

The Hope-Bosworth Bed & Breakfast Inn
The Hope-Merrill Bed & Breakfast Inn
21253 Geyserville Ave., (800) 825-4233, (707) 857-3356; www.hope-inns.com. 12 rooms; $$-$$$. Some TVs; some gas fireplaces. Heated pool (seasonal). Full breakfast. No pets.

The solid redwood 1870 Eastlake Stick Victorian Hope-Merrill house is restored exquisitely to that period with antique Eastlake furnishings and authentic Bradbury & Bradbury silk-screened wallpapers. In fact, the owner's restoration efforts won a first place award from the National Trust for Historic Preservation. Should this lovely inn be booked, opt for the charming Queen Anne Victorian Hope-Bosworth house located across the street. Under the same ownership, these two houses share communal facilities. When the temperature permits, a dip in the attractively situated pool is sublime, and in the morning a full breakfast is served around one large table in the formal dining room. Guests at either house can order a gourmet picnic lunch for two featuring local foods. A two-part "Pick and Press" package is offered for wannabe winemakers. Participants check in at harvest time in September for a round of grape picking and pressing, plus, of course, some tasting and dining. They return in spring for a bottling and labeling session, plus, of course, more tasting and dining, and then depart with two cases of their own wine sporting personalized labels.

ANDERSON VALLEY

A LITTLE BACKGROUND

Once famous for apple orchards, this area is now best known for its grapes and wines. In Boonville, a town that has yet to install a stop sign or traffic light, the townspeople speak an unusual 19th-century slang known as "Boontling." Here public telephones are labeled "Buckey Walter" and quail are called—after the sound they make—"rookie-to."

VISITOR INFORMATION

Anderson Valley Chamber of Commerce
P.O. Box 275, Boonville 95415, (707) 895-2379;
www.andersonvalleychamber.com.

Anderson Valley Winegrowers Association
P.O. Box 63, Philo 95466, (707) 895-WINE;
www.avwines.com.
    This organization provides free information on the valley's wineries.

GETTING THERE

Take Highway 128 north. Boonville, the valley's largest town, is about 50 miles north of Geyserville and 115 miles north of San Francisco. This spectacular winding route is a rural two-lane back road that follows the Navarro River through oak-wooded hills dotted with sheep peacefully grazing in meadows. After Philo, it enters the Navarro River Redwoods and passes through an 11-mile corridor of tall trees known as the "tunnel to the sea." Gas up before heading out, and avoid this route after dusk.

ANNUAL EVENTS

California Wine Tasting Championships
July. (707) 895-2002. Free for spectators.
    Held at **Greenwood Ridge Vineyards** (5501 Hwy. 128, in Philo; www.greenwood ridge.com. Tasting daily 10-5; no tour.), this unique and festive event includes good food, chocolate- and cheese-tasting contests, and novice, amateur, and professional wine-tasting competitions.

Mendo-Lake Woolgrowers BBQ and Sheep Dog Trials
July. In Boonville, at Mendocino County Fairgrounds; (707) 895-3011; www.mendocountyfair.com. Free.
    In addition to the sheep dog trials, visitors see sheep-shearing, wool spun into yarn, and related crafts. A barbecued lamb feast and a sheep weight-guessing contest are also part of the fun.

WHAT TO DO

Anderson Valley Historical Museum
Hwy. 128/Anderson Valley Way, in Boonville, (707) 895-3207; www.andersonvalleymuseum.org. F-Sun 1-4; in summer from 11; closed Dec-Feb. Free.
    This old-fashioned, one-room red schoolhouse is located just west of town and worth a stop.

The Apple Farm
18501 Greenwood Rd., in Philo, (707) 895-2461; www.philoapplefarm.com. Fruit stand: Daily 9-5; later in summer & fall.
    One part of this enterprise is a 30-acre certified organic farm with more than 80 varieties of apples ripening at different times from August through October. The bounty and related products are sold at the farm's **fruit stand**.
    The other part is a **cooking school** operated by the original proprietors of the highly acclaimed French Laundry restaurant in Yountville. The school strives to simplify everyday cooking and to get participants back in their kitchens preparing daily meals and enjoying it. On Farm Weekends everyone gets hands-on experience, preparing and consuming Friday dinner, Saturday lunch and dinner, and Sunday brunch. According to owner Sally Schmitt, it is

"like a house party with some cooking lessons thrown in." Students learn to use what is already in their garden and panty and also learn to use the best ingredients while doing the least possible to them. Participants get 3 hours off on Saturday afternoon to hike, bike, or visit local wineries on their own. One guest room and three cabins are available on the premises.

Hendy Woods State Park

On Greenwood Rd., just off Hwy. 128, 8 mi. NW of Boonville, (707) 895-3141; www.parks.ca.gov. $6/vehicle.

Situated along the Navarro River, this 850-acre park holds two groves of old-growth redwoods, a riverside picnic area with tables under a grove of sprawling walnuts, and a 1-mile self-guided nature Loop Trail. Campsites and five cabins with wood-burning stoves are available.

WINERIES

Husch Vineyards

4400 Hwy. 128, in Philo, (800) 55-HUSCH, (707) 895-3216; www.huschvineyards.com. Tasting daily 10-5, in summer to 6; tour by appt.

The tasting room here is inside a charming 19th-century pony barn covered with roses. Don't miss tasting the delicious Carignane and Muscat Canelli. Picnic tables under a vine-sheltered arbor invite lingering.

Navarro Vineyards

5601 Hwy. 128, in Philo, (800) 537-WINE, (707) 895-3686; www.navarrowine.com. Tasting daily 10-5, in summer to 6; tour by appt.

Known for its Pinot Noir and Gewurztraminer varietal grape juices—which children get to sample—and its Alsatian wines, including a variety of Gewurztraminers, this winery is situated within a striking Craftsman-style redwood building. Its wines are available only at the winery. Attractive picnic areas are provided on a deck overlooking the vineyard and under a trellis amid the grapevines.

Roederer Estate

4501 Hwy. 128, in Philo, (707) 895-2288; www.roedererestate.net. Tasting daily 11-5; tour by appt.

Boasting state-of-the-art méthode champenoise wine-making facilities, this winery has a tasting room with beautiful valley views. It produces all of its own grapes, which are pressed gently and then aged elegantly in carved French oak barrels. Louis Roederer Cristal, priced at around $200, is the wine celebrity rappers like to celebrate with.

WHERE TO STAY

Highland Ranch

18941 Philo-Greenwood Rd., in Philo, (707) 895-3600; www.highlandranch.com. 11 cabins; $$$+. No TVs; all wood-burning fireplaces. Solar-heated pool (seasonal); 2 tennis courts. All meals included.

Stays at this secluded guest ranch—reached via a 2-mile drive over gravel road—include the rural pleasures of fishing, swimming, and boating in three ponds, plus mountain biking, hiking, and, of course, horseback riding. Clay pigeon shooting, riding lessons, and massage and yoga are at an additional fee. Lodging is in modern redwood cabins.

Wellspring Renewal Center

18450 Ray's Rd./Hwy. 138, in Philo, (707) 895-3893; www.wellspringrenewal.org. 9 cabins; $+. No TVs; some kitchens & wood-burning stoves; some shared baths.

Founded in 1979 as an interfaith center, this 50-acre facility located adjacent to Hendy Woods State Park offers programs focused on deepening spirituality and engendering creativity. Regularly scheduled programs include planting and harvesting weekends, meditation and healing retreats, an arts and crafts week, and storytelling workshops. A variety of lodging is available: lodge rooms; both rustic and improved cabins; a campground at which guests can either pitch their own tent or rent a tent cabin. All guests are asked, but not required, to donate 1 hour of their time each day to a needed chore, and guests must bring their own towels and bedding. Individuals, families, and groups are welcome.

WHERE TO EAT

Boonville Hotel

14050 Hwy. 128/Lambert Ln., in Boonville, (707) 895-2210; www.boonvillehotel.com. Closed 1st 2 wks. in Jan. D Thur-M. Reservations advised.

Owner-chef Johnny Schmitt did his internship at his parent's former restaurant, the French Laundry in Yountville, and he displays his expertise in every dish. Here he uses local bounty for salads, soups, upscale pizza, hearty entrees, and wonderful desserts, and he features Anderson Valley wines. All-inclusive regional dinners are scheduled regularly and worth going out of the way for.

Lodging *(12 rooms; $$-$$$. No TVs. Continental breakfast.)* is also available. Eight light, airy rooms and two bungalows have a clean-lined contemporary style, with light woods and sumptuous tiled bathrooms, and are furnished with simple pieces handmade by local craftspeople (many items are available for purchase). Beds are made with all-cotton sheets and boldly-striped down comforters, and unusual, attractive floral arrangements—perhaps white hydrangea balls mixed with wispy blue forget-me-nots—add a touch of whimsy.

Picnic Pick-Ups

• Boont Berry Farm
13981 Hwy. 128, in Boonville, (707) 895-3576. Daily 9-6.

This tiny health food store has a cozy, old-fashioned atmosphere and is well-stocked with deli items, locally-grown organic produce, pastries, breads (including the town's famous Bruce Bread), and homemade ice cream.

HOPLAND

A LITTLE BACKGROUND

Tiny Hopland is easy to overlook as a getaway destination. Located just 1½ hours from the Bay Area and about 45 minutes north of Santa Rosa, this 3-block-long slow-down in the road seems too soon to stop for the night. But it is well equipped to provide a satisfying weekend escape.

Prior to the arrival of white settlers in the mid-1800s, this area was home to Pomo Indians, who were accomplished basket weavers. Hopland was named after the hops that still grow wild here, and which have been cultivated since 1860 for brewing beer. Though hops were once the area's primary crop, they were displaced in the 1940s by fruits, and now by wine

grapes. And while this low-key area is slowly transforming from a farming community into a recreational destination, it has a long way to go.

GETTING THERE

Located approximately 25 miles north of Geyserville, and 110 miles north of San Francisco.

ANNUAL EVENTS

Redwood Run
June. (707) 247-3424; www.redwoodrun.com.

Hopland's answer to the Rose Parade, this event finds thousands of motorcycles and their riders making the run from the Bay Area to the Garberville-Piercy area on the Eel River and back again. Most seem to stopover mid-way, mid-day in Hopland, making for quite a sight. The group has a reputation for not causing trouble and is certainly an exciting mass to witness.

WHAT TO DO

Sho-Ka-Wah Casino
13101 Nokomis Rd., (888) 746-5292, (707) 744-1395; www.shokawah.com. Open 24 hours.

Offering a bit of nightlife, this Native American-run casino operates in a magical rural area just a few miles east of Highway 101.

Solar Living Center

*13771 S. Hwy. 101, (707) 744-2017;
www.solarliving.org. M-Sat 10-6, Sun 10-5. Guided
tour: F-Sun at 11, 3; by donation, $5.*

Pick up a self-guided tour brochure at the
entrance to this surprising, impressive 12½-acre
complex, or time your visit for a guided tour.
An especially refreshing stop on a hot day (it
can soar to 110 degrees around here in summer,
and the town claims 300 days of sunshine every
year), this small oasis has an Agave Cooling
Tower that dispenses a refreshing mist, and a
Children's Play Area with an optional pipe-tun-
nel entrance, a sandbox, and a water pump. A
solar-powered carousel *(Daily 12-4, on the hr.
(seasonal). $1.)* designed by Bill Dentzel—a
descendant of the famous carousel maker—
features salmon, skunk, and mountain lion
mounts. The symbolic center of the site is
formed by the Central Oasis—a sort of a mini-
Yellowstone fountain of dancing geysers—and
the Solar Calendar—a sort of mini-Stonehenge
designed to reconnect visitors to the changing
seasons. Once inside the cool shop (double-
entendre intended), browse the useful merchandise and check out a wall cutaway showing the
building's unusual straw-bale construction. On
the way out, a sign urges, "Turn inspiration into
action."

WINERIES

The town has five tasting rooms within easy
walking distance of each other.

Brutocao Cellars Tasting Room

*13500 S. Hwy. 101, (800) 433-3689, (707) 744-1664;
www.brutocaoschoolhouseplaza.com. Tasting Sun-Thur
10-5, F-Sat to 6; tour at winery (2 mi. away).*

This tasting room operates inside a historic building that formerly served as the town's
high school. An adjacent garden with 5,000
roses forming a rainbow, some bocce ball
courts, a concert area, and several shops are also
part of the package.

WHERE TO STAY

Hopland Inn

*13401 S. Hwy. 101, (800) 266-1891, (707) 744-1890;
www.hoplandinn.com. 21 rooms; $$. Unsuitable for
children. Unheated pool (seasonal). Continental
breakfast. No pets.*

Around since 1890, this inn is the oldest
building in town and on the discerning
National Historic Register. It is authentically
restored, down to the original exterior colors
and period furnishings sprinkled throughout.
Large, high-ceilinged guest rooms feature coor-
dinated wallpapers and bedspreads. Each is
named for a local pioneer family and decorated
with fascinating historical black-and-white
photos of the family. Though situated right on
Highway 101, its back rooms are quiet, but as
evening descends or as the sun rises, the crow-
ing of a crazed rural rooster might be heard.
Staying here permits walking just about any-
where in town. In warm weather, breakfast is
served on an outdoor patio under an enormous
500-year-old oak.

WHERE TO EAT

Bluebird Cafe

*13340 S. Hwy. 101, (707) 744-1633. B-L daily,
D F-Sun; $$.*

It's cool and comfortable inside this
restored 1870s commercial building decorated
with lace curtains and featuring original light
fixtures. Choose from five types of grape juice
and five types of burger—ostrich, salmon,
turkey, garden, or regular—as well as stir-frys,
pastas, and salads. Attractive paintings—all
for sale—and a stuffed moose head hang on
the walls.

CLEAR LAKE AREA

A LITTLE BACKGROUND

Believed to be the oldest lake in North America,
spring-fed Clear Lake is the largest natural
fresh-water lake that is totally within California
(Lake Tahoe is partially in Nevada). It measures
19 miles by 8 miles. The 90-mile drive around
the perimeter takes 2½ to 3 hours.

Clear Lake is situated on volcanic terrain,
giving it an unusual physical appearance and a
profusion of hot springs. According to a
Pomo Indian legend, when there is no snow on
4,200-foot Mount Konocti in April, the volcano
will erupt. Those who heed legends should
check the April snowfall before making vacation
plans.

From the 1870s into the early 1900s, this area was world-famous for its health spas and huge luxury resort hotels. Then, for various reasons, it fell into a state of disrepair and slowly lost its acclaim. Now it is a reasonably priced family resort area.

Lake County is also noted for its high elevation wines, and some wineries and vineyards offer spectacular views. Grapes were planted here extensively before Prohibition, when they were taken out and replaced with plum, pear, and walnut trees. Now the trees are losing their hold, and the grapes are coming back.

And North America's only eagle species— bald eagles and golden eagles—come to Lake County to nest each year.

Lake County's first traffic light was installed in 1982. There are now seven, but it still has no parking meters.

VISITOR INFORMATION

Lake County Visitor Information Center
6110 E. Hwy. 20, in Lucerne, north lake, (800) LAKE-SIDE, (707) 274-5652; www.lakecounty.com.

GETTING THERE

Located approximately 19 miles east of Hopland via curvy Highway 175, and 110 miles north of San Francisco.

An alternate route follows Highway 29 north from St. Helena. This scenic route goes through the heart of the Wine Country. The rolling hills are strewn with blooming wild flowers in spring and with brilliantly colored foliage in fall. Make the drive during daylight; this winding two-lane road is tedious to drive at night, and, of course, the lovely scenery cannot be enjoyed then.

ANNUAL EVENTS

Heron Festival
April. In Kelseyville, in Clear Lake State Park, west lake, (800) 525-3743; www.heronfestival.org. Free-$15.

This major event includes nature walks, children's activities, and pontoon boat rides and kayak tours to view heron rookeries.

Summer Concert Series
June-August. In Lakeport, in Library Park, west lake; www.kxbx.com/articles/Concerts.shtml. Free.

A little bit of everything is on the program at this casual event. In the past, the mostly California bands have included Joe Louis Walker and Country Joe and the Fish.

Clearlake International Worm Races
June or July. In Clearlake, in Austin Park, east lake, (707) 994-3600. Free.

Begun in 1966 by C.C. Schoenberger, a relative of Mark Twain, this event includes a parade and festival. Rental worms are available.

Lake County Rodeo
July. In Lakeport, west lake, (707) 263-1845; www.lakecountyrodeo.com. $9-$13, 60+ $6-$10, 7-12 $4-$6. No pets.

Among the typical rodeo events are an all-horse parade and a junior horsemen drill team performance.

Kelseyville Pear Festival
September. In Kelseyville, on Main Street, west lake; (707) 279-9022; www.kelseyvillepearfestival.com. Free.

Old-time fun includes a parade, some contests, and pear-related food and displays.

WHAT TO DO

Fishing, swimming, boating, rock hunting, golfing, wine tasting, and wake boarding are the big activities here. Fishing is the biggest. The lake is reputed to be the best bass-fishing spot in the West—maybe even the best in the entire country. The lake's nutrient-rich waters are credited with producing plenty of 10-pounders, and the lake record is a 17.52-pounder! A favorite rock to find is a semi-precious "Lake County diamond," also known as a "moon tear."

Anderson Marsh State Historic Park
8825 Hwy. 53, betw. Lower Lake & Clearlake, south lake, (707) 279-2267; www.parks.ca.gov. Tu-Sun 10-5. $2/vehicle. No pets.

This 1,065-acre park contains an additional 470 acres of tule marsh. An 1855 ranch house is open to visitors during special events, and tree-shaded picnic tables are provided.

Clear Lake State Park
5300 Soda Bay Rd., in Kelseyville, 3.5 mi. NE of town, west lake, (707) 279-4293; www.parks.ca.gov. Daily sunrise-sunset. $5/vehicle.

Located on the shores of the lake, this park offers swimming, fishing, a boat-launching ramp, picnic facilities, campsites, and miles of hiking trails—including the ¼-mile Indian Nature Trail and 3-mile Dorn Nature Trail. A Visitor Center provides a slide show introduction to the area and a Touch Corner for children. Displays include local wildlife dioramas, a native fish aquarium, an erupting volcano, and exhibits on the area's Pomo Indian history.

Lake County Historic Courthouse Museum
255 N. Main St., in Lakeport, west lake, (707) 263-4555; www.lakecounty.com/things/museums.html. W-Sat 10-4, Sun 12-4. Free.

Formerly a courthouse, this 1871 brick building now reveals "The Mystery and History of Clear Lake" through its renowned collection of Pomo Indian baskets, stone arrowheads, and tools, plus historical records, a restored courtroom, and a hunting and gun exhibit.

Lower Lake Historical Schoolhouse Museum
16435 Morgan Valley Rd., in Lower Lake, south lake, (707) 995-3565; www.lakecounty.com/things/museums.html. W-Sat 11-4. Free.

The restored Lower Lake Grammar School houses a reconstructed turn-of-the-century classroom. Museum exhibits include an extensive geological display, a scale model of the dam on Cache Creek, and collections from pioneer families.

WINERIES

Lake County Winery Association
PO Box 1917, Lakeport 95453, west lake, (707) 279-2927; www.lakecountywineries.org.

Ceago del Lago
5115 E. Hwy. 20, in Nice, north lake, 707-274-1462; www.ceago.com. Tasting daily 10-5; tour by appt.

This spectacular property is right on the lake and is the only winery in North American accessible by boat and seaplane. Though anytime is a good time to view the good-for-you biodynamic farming they practice here, June and July permit seeing the vast, fragrant lavender fields in bloom. That is also when the sheep are shorn. And don't miss seeing the vineyard chickens that live in mobile chicken coops. Bring a picnic and enjoy the views.

Langtry Estate
21000 Butts Canyon Rd., in Middletown, 707-987-2385; www.langtryestate.com. Tasting daily 10-5; tour Tu-Sat at 11 & 1, reservations required.

In the late 1800s, this picturesque property was purchased by British actress Lillie Langtry. According to winemaker Paul Brasset, "She was the Madonna of her time. She was outrageous in many ways and one of the first famous women to capitalize on her image." Now named for her, it is a vast 22,000-acre (that's 37 square miles) estate—the biggest winery in Lake County—and produces a Petite Sirah that has won more gold medals than any other in the world. Getting here via the mandatory back roads is half the fun; the other half is tasting that Sirah and taking the Tephra Vineyard Lunch Tour, during which participants picnic at a table overlooking the Guenoc Valley and sit within the very vineyard that produced the grapes for the wine served with lunch. Their Guenoc label is known for delicious, well-priced wines.

Shannon Ridge tasting room

12599 E. Hwy. 20, Clearlake Oaks, east lake, (707) 998-9656; www.shannonridge.com. Tasting daily 10:30-5; no tour.

This tasting room is inside a cozy 100-year-old one-room schoolhouse that retains its original ceiling and floor. The landscaped yard is loaded with picnic tables, and a deli is right next door. One of the bigger growers in the area, the winery grows 90% of their own grapes at their nearby vineyards and makes a lightly oaked, buttery Chardonnay and a tasty Wrangler Red.

Wildhurst Vineyards tasting room

3855 Main St., Kelseyville, west lake, (800) 595-WINE, (707) 279-4302; www.wildhurst.com. Daily 10-5; no tour.

This winery uses only Lake County grapes and is celebrated for its Sauvignon Blanc and Syrah. It is one of the few area wineries that grows Chardonnay grapes.

WHERE TO STAY

Konocti Harbor Resort & Spa

8727 Soda Bay Rd., in Kelseyville, west lake, (800) 660-LAKE, (707) 279-4281; www.konoctiharbor.com. 250 rooms; $-$$$+. Some kitchens. 2 heated pools; 2 children's wading pools; fitness room; full-service spa; 8 clay tennis courts (with night lights). Restaurant. No pets.

Nestled in the shadow of Mount Konocti on the rim of the lake, this beautifully land-scaped 100-acre luxury resort enjoys a superb setting. The list of facilities and services is extensive: a children's playground, a recreation room, a jogging trail, a bar with live music in the evenings, a miniature golf course, and a marina that rents fishing boats, water-skiing equipment, and pedal boats. Babysitting can be arranged, and tennis, spa, concert, and fishing packages are available. The spa and fitness center offer an additional indoor pool and hot tub, a sauna and steam room, a gym, and a variety of pampering treatments.

The **Classic Rock Cafe** offers fun and innovative American meals in a rock museum setting. A **Classic Concerts by the Lake** series, which has both dinner and cocktail seatings, brings in big name entertainment year-round. In good weather, shows are held in an outdoor amphitheater.

Lakeport English Inn

675 N. Main St., in Lakeport, west lake, (707) 263-4317; www.lakeportenglishinn.com. 10 rooms; $$-$$$. Full breakfast.

The innkeepers here raised their children in this 1875 Carpenter Victorian, which was a county hospital from 1926 to 1946. It is unpretentious, unfussy, yet satisfying in an English-style B&B way. Guest rooms are furnished with high beds fitted with Frette sheets, and most of the large bathrooms have a whirlpool tub for two. Sometimes Myrtle Hobbs, the nice resident ghost, is encountered. The back garden is enclosed by a very tall Italian cypress wall, and a teeny pub (for guests only) opens on weekends for "a bit."

A full-on proper **high tea** served on bone china is scheduled during holidays and is open to non-guests.

Sea Breeze Resort

9595 Harbor Dr., in Glenhaven, east lake, (707) 998-3327; www.seabreeze-resort.com. 7 cabins; $-$$. All kitchens. No pets.

This white-washed waterside lodging has a private beach and pier, a rose garden, and barbecue facilities. Some cottages open to a grassy area and are perfect for children; others have lake views.

Skylark Shores Resort Motel

1120 N. Main St., in Lakeport, west lake, (800) 675-6151, (707) 263-6151; www.skylarkshoresresort.com. 40 rooms, 5 cabins; $-$$. Some kitchens. Pool (seasonal).

These modern motel rooms and cabins are located lakefront. The spacious, well-maintained grounds feature an expansive lawn, swings, and a wading area in the lake, plus amenities include three docks and a boat ramp.

Soda Bay Inn

3397 Live Oak Ln., in Kelseyville, west lake, (707) 279-4722; www.sodabayinn.com. 7 suites; $$. All kitchens; some wood-burning stoves. No pets.

Located lakefront, back in a peaceful residential area, this appealing property has knotty pine cabin-style rooms in a bungalow. Some have lake views. Facilities include a barbeque area and private pier, and boat rentals are available on site.

Tallman Hotel

9550 Main St., in Upper Lake, north lake, (866) 708-5253, (707) 275-2244; www.tallmanhotel.com. 17 rooms; $$-$$$. Heated pool, hot tub. Continental breakfast, restaurant.

Built in 1895, this beautifully restored hotel combines rustic and chic in a delightful manner. The original hotel has 4 high-ceilinged guest rooms that are decorator-adorned in a

soothing mix of subdued colors in a fashionable mix of patterns and styles. Should a guest fall in love with any fabric or color, a resource book is kept at the desk to advise of brands and numbers. One of the most interesting features is the highly functional antique bathroom plumbing, which is so old it's new again. Room #1 has both an oversize clawfoot tub with center drain and a tall shower enclosure with a wrap-around chrome fixture sporting all kinds of porcelain knobs and levers that control a giant sunflower head and side sprayers. Lodging is available in several other buildings, and some new-construction garden rooms have a Japanese ofuro soaking tub on a private patio with outdoor shower.

The complex's **Blue Wing Saloon & Cafe** *(9520 Main St., (707) 275-2233; www.blue wingsaloon.com. L-D daily; $-$$.)* serves a well-priced eclectic menu. Specialties include barbecued tri tip, agave citrus salmon, and portobello mushroom ravioli. Local wines are featured, and beers and sarsaparilla are on tap. Diners can sit in the cozy interior or, in good weather, outside in a delightful garden patio sheltered by umbrellas and plane trees. It is hard to believe the saloon is all new construction; do take time to admire the long, seamless, straight-grained black walnut bar made from one piece of wood.

Upper Lake is a tad larger than a one-horse town. Once the end of the stage line from Cloverdale, it now holds a wine tasting bar and several antiques shops—including one right across the street from the hotel where the owner leads an eccentric tour of his homage to the old west (it includes western art, a stage coach, and guns galore).

Motel Row

Just drive around the lake. Lakeshore Drive in Clearlake is particularly laden with possibility.

WHERE TO STAY NEARBY

Wilbur Hot Springs

3375 Wilbur Springs Rd., near intersection of Hwys. 16 & 20, 25 mi. E of lake, 22 mi. W of Williams, in Wilbur Springs, (530) 473-2306; www.wilburhot springs.com. 17 rooms; $$-$$$. Unsuitable for children under 3. No TVs; all shared baths. Unheated pool (seasonal); 4 "flumes." No pets. Day use: $45; reservations required.

Soaking in one of the four "flumes" (hot tubs) filled with hot sulfurous spring water and then plunging into the cool water of the outdoor pool is the main activity at this historic spa. The roofed but open-sided Fluminarium (a bathhouse) is located creek side, and clothing is optional in pool and tub areas only. The ambitious can take walks in the surrounding 1,800-acre nature preserve. A 1915 inn with wraparound veranda provides both private rooms and dormitory-style shared rooms; campsites are also available. Rooms have no electrical outlets, so solar-powered lamps light the night. A "great room" holds a pool table and piano for amusement, and a large communal kitchen is provided for guests to prepare their own meals in (the nearest restaurant is 20 miles away). Children age 4 and older are welcome but have some restrictions.

WHERE TO EAT

Molly Brennans
175 N. Main St., in Lakeport, west lake, (707) 262-1600; www.mollybrennans.com. L-D W-M; $-$$.

Operating inside a vintage brick building with a high, pressed-tin ceiling and featuring furniture handcrafted from a 100-year-old wine vat, this traditional Irish pub has many comfy booths and serves up a menu featuring tasty renditions of Guinness Irish stew, shepherd's pie, and rock cod fish & chips. Brews are on tap. In good weather, drinks only are served in a beer garden out back.

Park Place
50 3rd St., in Lakeport, west lake, (707) 263-0444. L-D daily; $-$$. Reservations advised.

Located lakefront and across the street from Library Park, this cafe offers great views from its outdoor rooftop dining area. For starters, don't miss the magnificent bruchetta—a baguette topped with pesto and sun-dried tomatoes and then grilled. The menu has a large selection of fresh pastas, including several kinds of tortellini and raviolis, plus fresh fish, steaks, and hamburgers.

Studebaker's Coffee House and Delicatessen
3990 Main St., in Kelseyville, west lake, 707-279-8871. B-L daily.

Enjoy their signature dark roast coffee, some fresh-baked pastries, or a "build-your-own" deli sandwich in either the informal interior or out on the sidewalk patio.

UKIAH

VISITOR INFORMATION

Greater Ukiah Chamber of Commerce
200 S. School St., (707) 462-4705; www.ukiahchamber.com.

Mendocino County Promotional Alliance
525 S. Main St., (866) 466-3636, (707) 462-7414; www.goMendo.com.

GETTING THERE

Located approximately 15 miles north of Hopland, and 110 miles north of San Francisco.

WHAT TO DO

Grace Hudson Museum and Sun House
431 S. Main St., (707) 467-2836; www.gracehudson museum.org. W-Sat 10-4:30, Sun 12-4:30; tour of house on the hr., 12-3. By donation: $2, $5/family.

Named for the prominent painter who specialized in doing portraits of the area's Pomo Indians, this museum displays Ms. Hudson's artwork and some of her personal paraphernalia, as well as a collection of Pomo Indian baskets. Her six-room home, the California Craftsman-style Sun House, is adjacent. Built of redwood in 1911, it still holds most of its original furnishings. Picnic facilities are available in a park within the 4½-acre complex.

WHERE TO STAY

Orr Hot Springs
13201 Orr Springs Rd., 13 mi. W of Hwy. 101, (707) 462-6277. 3 rooms, 14 cabins; $$. No TVs; some kitchens + communal kitchen; some wood-burning stoves; some shared baths. Unheated mineral water pool; 4 private & 2 communal hot tubs; sauna; steam room. Day use: $15-$22, under 18 half price.

In the 1850s, when this mineral springs resort was built, patrons reached it via stagecoach. Now they get here by driving a scenic, winding, two-lane road. A natural rock swimming pool built into the hillside is filled with cool mineral spring water, and several underground springs are tapped to fill—with body-temperature water—four porcelain Victorian tubs in an 1863 bathhouse. A gas-fired sauna features a stained-glass window and a clear skylight. Note that this is a clothing-optional establishment. Guests sleep in either dormitories, guest rooms, or cottages built in the 1940s from locally milled redwood, and must bring their own food. Campsites are also available.

Montgomery Redwoods State Park, which offers two loop trails for hiking, is just 1 mile down the road.

Vichy Springs Resort

2605 Vichy Springs Rd., 3 mi. E of Hwy. 101, (707) 462-9515; www.vichysprings.com. 18 rooms, 8 cabins; $$-$$$+. No TVs; some kitchens & gas fireplaces. Solar heated pool & natural hot springs pool; hot springs tubs. Full breakfast. No pets. Day use: $27-$45/person.

Founded in 1854, this 700-acre resort still has three renovated cottages that were built then—they are the oldest still-standing struc-tures in Mendocino County—and a hotel built of redwood in the 1860s. The resort has the only naturally carbonated warm mineral baths in North America and is named for the famous French springs, which have the same kind of alkaline waters and were discovered by Julius Caesar. In its heyday, the resort attracted guests from San Francisco who endured a day's journey to get here—by ferry across the bay, by train to Cloverdale, then by stagecoach to the resort. They came in search of curative powers attributed to the waters. Among the famous guests were writers Mark Twain, Jack London, and Robert Louis Stevenson, and presidents Ulysses S. Grant, Benjamin Harrison, and Teddy Roosevelt. The resort's 148-year-old concrete "champagne" tubs are filled with 90-degree, tingling, naturally carbonated water and situated in a shady area overlooking a creek. Swimsuits are required. Guests can swim in an unchlorinated Olympic-size pool, schedule a treatment in the massage cottage, or get in some more rigorous activity with a hike to a 40-foot-high waterfall or a mountain bike ride over dirt roads. Picnic lunches can be arranged, and the resort's own Vichy Springs Mineral Water is available bottled for drinking.

Mark Twain taking the waters

WILLITS

A LITTLE BACKGROUND

The old-time sign above Main Street, welcoming visitors to the "Gateway to the Redwoods," is Reno's second arch recycled. It topped Virginia Street in Reno, Nevada from 1964 through 1987 and has been here since 1990. (Reno retains its first and third arches.) The famous race horse Seabiscuit was stabled nearby.

VISITOR INFORMATION

Willits Chamber of Commerce
239 S. Main St., (707) 459-7910; www.willits.org.

GETTING THERE

Located approximately 25 miles north of Ukiah, and 140 miles north of San Francisco. Heading north after here, the terrain begins getting mountainous and scenic.

WHERE TO STAY

Emandal Farm
16500 Hearst Rd., 16 mi. NE of town, (707) 459-5439; www.emandal.com. Open for 1-wk. stays during Aug; weekends in spring & fall. 19 cabins; rates vary according to age & include 3 meals per day. No TVs; all shared bathrooms.

On weekend visits to this 1,000-acre working farm, guests arrive for Friday night dinner. Families are assigned a table for their stay and then spend some blissful hours there chowing down superb home cooking prepared with the farm's own organically grown produce. Days are filled with leisurely activities—perhaps a short hike down to a sandy beach on the magnificent Eel River for a swim, or maybe a hike up the steep hill behind the barn to Rainbow Lake. Some folks just doze in the hammocks outside each of the rustic one-room redwood cabins dating from 1916. Others get involved with farm chores: milking goats, collecting eggs, feeding pigs.

KOA Kampground
1600 Hwy. 20, (800) KOA-8542, (707) 459-6179; www.koa.com.

Set amid rolling hills and trees, this campground has an Old West theme. Facilities include a swimming pool, fishing pond, petting zoo, mini golf, playground, arcade, rental bikes, and more. In summer, special activities include hayrides and ice cream socials. For more description, see page 467.

WHERE TO EAT

Fast food
It's all here. Families with small children will favor **Burger King**, **Fosters Freeze**, and **McDonald's**—all of which have colorful playgrounds attached to their dining areas.

Loose Caboose Cafe
10 Wood St./Hwy. 101, (707) 459-1434. M-Sat 10-4; $. Reservations advised. No cards.

Folks sometimes get loose as a goose relaxing at this simple old-time cafe filled with locals. A collection of train memorabilia is displayed throughout. Seating is either indoors at tables and in tall-back wood booths or outside on an entrance patio. Service is casual—in Styrofoam cups and on paper plates—and food is simple—hot New York- and Kansas City-style subs made to order, dogs, salads, pizza, soup and chili, and milkshakes.

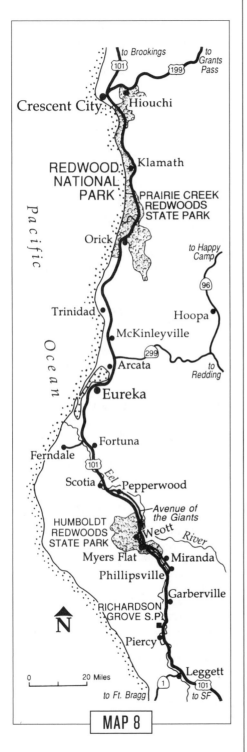

MAP 8

THE AVENUE OF THE GIANTS

A LITTLE BACKGROUND

The redwoods, once seen, leave a mark or create a vision that stays with you always . . . It's not their stature nor the color that seems to shift and vary under your eyes; no, they are not like any other trees we know, they are ambassadors from another time.
— John Steinbeck, 1962

This spectacularly scenic drive officially begins at Phillipsville, though the scenery begins farther south around Leggett. Actually the old Highway 101, The Avenue of the Giants parallels the freeway and Eel River and is a breathtaking route that winds through grove after grove of huge sequoia sempervirens redwoods. In fact, this route is home to 60 percent of the tallest trees in the world. It continues for 32 miles to Pepperwood, where it rejoins the busier new Highway 101. Unusual sights along this unique stretch of road are numerous. In spots, it juxtaposes nature's best and most majestic with humankind's most kitchy and trite. Fortunately, the number of shops displaying chainsaw-carved redwood souvenirs is small, with plenty of long stretches of uninterrupted tall trees in between.

Millions of years ago, when dinosaurs roamed the earth, forests of gigantic redwoods were plentiful. After the Ice Age, the redwood—which has a life span of 400 to 800 years but sometimes lives beyond 2,000 years—survived only in a narrow 540-mile-long by 40-mile-wide strip along the northern coast of California. Before the logging days on the north coast, it is estimated this area contained 2½ million acres of redwoods. Now only 100,000 acres of ancient old-growth redwoods remain—most preserved in the state and national park systems. Approximately half of these huge old trees are found in Humboldt Redwoods State Park.

GETTING THERE

Phillipsville is 78 miles north of Willits, and 214 miles north of San Francisco.

WHAT TO DO

Confusion Hill
75001 N. Hwy. 101, in Piercy, (707) 925-6456;
www.confusionhill.com. Daily 9-5, in summer 9-6.
House: $5, 4-12 $4. Train (summer only): $7, 4-12 $5.

In the Gravity House here, water runs uphill—appearing to defy gravity. A miniature train takes passengers through a tree tunnel to the crest of a hill in the redwoods. This is also home to the world's tallest redwood chainsaw carving.

Drive-through trees

• Drive-Thru Tree Park
67402 Drive-Thru Tree Rd., in Leggett, (707) 925-6363;
www.drivethrutree.com. Daily 8:30-dusk. $5/car.

Most average-size cars can squeeze through the hole in this 315-foot-high, 21-foot-diameter, 2,400-year-old giant redwood known as the Chandelier Tree. Bring a camera. Nature trails and lakeside picnic tables are available.

• Shrine Drive-Thru Tree
13078 Avenue of the Giants, in Myers Flat,
(707) 943-1658. $2, under 7 free.

This 275-foot-tall, still-living tree has a circumference of approximately 64 feet. A natural fire cavity has been widened to accommodate cars, providing the opportunity to take an unusual picture. The site also has a drive-on log and a children's walk-through stump and 2-story tree house, plus each car gets a free postcard.

Humboldt Redwoods State Park
In Weott; www.parks.ca.gov. Daily dawn-dusk.
$6/vehicle. Visitor Center: 2 mi. S of town, next to
Burlington Campground, (707) 946-2409; daily 10-4,
in summer 9-5.

This 51,222-acre park straddles the two-lane road, and parts are so dense with trees that sunlight barely filters through. Campsites are available.

The 10,000-acre **Rockefeller Forest** *(Near Weott; accessed from Mattole Rd., (707) 946-2311.)* is the world's largest grove of old-growth virgin redwoods. The entire forest has never been cut, a rarity in these parts. Also referred to as "the world's finest forest," it features hiking trails leading to the Flatiron Tree (shaped like an old-fashioned flat iron), the Giant Tree (which—based on a combination of height, circumference, and crown size—is considered the champion redwood by the American Forestry Association), and the 356-foot-high Tall Tree. In fact, believe it or not!, 10 of the 16 tallest trees in the world stand in this single grove. Easy, baby stroller-friendly trails include Founders Grove Loop and Giant Tree Loop.

The **Children's Forest**, a 1,120-acre memorial to children, is located across the south fork of the Eel River. It is reached by a moderate 2.4-mile round-trip trail beginning at Williams Grove. **Williams Grove** features picturesque picnic and swimming sites on the river.

Richardson Grove State Park
1600 Hwy. 101, 8 mi. S of Garberville, (707) 247-3318;
www.parks.ca.gov. $6/vehicle.

This park holds the ninth-tallest coast redwood and a walk-through tree, both of which are easily accessible. Campsites are available.

WHERE TO STAY

Benbow Hotel & Resort
445 Lake Benbow Dr., in Garberville, (800) 355-3301,
(707) 923-2124; www.benbowinn.com. 55 rooms;
$$-$$$+. Some TVs & wood-burning fireplaces.
Afternoon tea; evening snack; restaurant. No pets.

This magnificent English Tudor inn, which opened to the public in 1926, offers a variety of rooms—all furnished with antiques. Some have lake views and private patios; all are equipped with a basket of mystery novels and a carafe of sherry. A majestic communal lounge with fireplace and library invites socializing, and game tables are set with chessboards and jigsaw puzzles. Interesting art prints decorate the walls throughout. This spot enjoys perfect summer temperatures. Outside pleasures that make the most of it include colorful English gardens with grassy expanses, a small private beach and lake, a putting green, lawn games, and complimentary use of bicycles. Off premises, a 9-hole golf course and heated swimming pool are within walking distance. A complimentary tea is served each afternoon at 3 p.m. (non-guests may partake for a small charge). Special events are often scheduled, and holiday festivities occur throughout December.

The elegant **restaurant** *(B&D daily, also L in summer; $-$$$. Reservations advised.)* has an expansive menu, with both simple dishes and more sophisticated fare. In fair weather, diners may sit outdoors on a large terrace overlooking the lake. Additionally, a cozy taproom bar dispenses good cheer—and live entertainment on some evenings—and guests can order picnic lunches.

Miranda Gardens Resort
6766 Avenue of the Giants, in Miranda, (707) 943-3011; www.mirandagardens.com. 16 units; $-$$$. Some kitchens & fireplaces. Heated pool (seasonal). Continental breakfast in summer.

Lodging here is in a collection of cottages. A children's playground and plenty of outdoor games—croquet, shuffleboard, horseshoes—are available out under the redwoods.

FERNDALE

A LITTLE BACKGROUND

Composed of well-preserved and restored Victorian buildings, this tiny village was founded in 1852 and is now a state historical landmark. It remains largely unchanged since the 1890s—except that then it had nine churches and nine saloons and now it has six churches and three saloons. Of special note are the many "butterfat palaces," a local nickname for the elaborate Victorian homes paid for by the area's rich dairy industry.

Now, in addition to the dairy farming, the town prospers as an artists' colony and is filled with galleries and antique shops. Shops of particular interest include the old-time **Ferndale Meat Company** at 376 Main Street, which uses old-fashioned curing and smoking techniques

and sells deli items, and the **Golden Gait Mercantile** department store at 421 Main Street, which has creaky floorboards and sells penny candy and other vintage items associated with the good old days.

The scenic pioneer cemetery on a hill behind the old Methodist church is also interesting to visit, and don't miss seeing the circa 1860 gumdrop-shaped coast cypress trees on Ocean Avenue.

In 1994, the whole town starred in the film *Outbreak*, and in 2001 *The Majestic* was filmed here.

VISITOR INFORMATION

Ferndale Chamber of Commerce
P.O. Box 325, Ferndale 95536, (707) 786-4477; www.victorianferndale.org/chamber.

Fortuna Chamber of Commerce
735 14th St., (707) 725-3959; www.sunnyfortuna.com.

GETTING THERE

Located approximately 265 miles north of San Francisco, 15 miles south of Eureka, and 5 miles west of Highway 101. The exit that leads through Fernbridge permits crossing the Eel River over an historic 1911 bridge that is the oldest reinforced concrete bridge still in existence.

ANNUAL EVENTS

Cross Country Kinetic Sculpture Race
May; on Memorial Day Weekend. (707) 499-0643; www.kineticgrandchampionship.com. Free.

In this unusual competition, bizarre and artistic people-powered sculptures race 38 miles over dunes and rivers from Arcata to Ferndale. Cheating is encouraged, and the prizes are questionable. Founder Hobart Brown created this event to promote "adults having fun so kids want to grow up."

Fortuna Rodeo
July. In Fortuna; (707) 725-3959; www.fortunarodeo.com. $7, under 12 $3.

The oldest professional rodeo in the West, this event includes a chili cook-off, street games, a parade, a carnival, and more.

Humboldt County Fair

August. (707) 786-9511; www.humboldtcountyfair.org.
$6, 62+ $3, 6-12 $2; parking $2.

The oldest uninterrupted county fair in California, this event has happened annually since 1897 and includes carnival rides, horseracing, a goat-calling contest, and more.

Lighting of America's Tallest Living Christmas Tree

December. (707) 786-4477;
www.victorianferndale.org/chamber/events.htm.

Heralding the beginning of the holidays, volunteer firemen in this village deck this 125-foot Sitka spruce with colored lights. Then the whole town turns out for the lighting ceremony, a tradition since 1934.

Lighted Tractor Parade

December. (800) 346-3482, (707) 786-4477;
www.victorianferndale.org/chamber/events.htm.

Area farmers decorate their antique and modern tractors, trailers, and wagons with Christmas lights and holiday scenes.

WHAT TO DO

Ferndale Kinetic Sculpture Museum

580 Main St./Shaw Ave., (707) 499-0643. Daily 9-5.
By donation.

Human-powered vehicles designed to travel over roadway, mud, sand, and water are displayed in this quirky museum.

Ferndale Museum

515 Shaw Ave., (707) 786-4466;
www.ferndale-museum.org. W-Sat 11-4, Sun 1-4;
also Tu in summer; closed Jan. $1, children 50¢,
under 6 free.

Exhibits here include Victorian room settings, a crosscut of a 1,237-year-old redwood, and a working century-old seismograph. An annex displays farming, logging, and dairy equipment.

Loleta Cheese Factory

252 Loleta Dr., in Loleta, (800) 995-0453,
(707) 733-5470; www.loletacheese.com. Daily 9-5.

Known for their Monterey Jacks and smoked salmon Cheddar, this factory has big windows through which the cheese-making process can be observed. Arrive before noon to

assure seeing some action. Cheeses are made from the rich milk of cows grazed on the grass and clover pastures of the Eel River Valley, and more than 24 kinds can be tasted, including white cheddars. A note of interest is that part of *Halloween II* was filmed across the street in the Familiar Foods building.

Lost Coast

www.sheltercove-lostcoast.com.

The wildly scenic area of Cape Mendocino—the westernmost point in the continental U.S.—is called "the lost coast" because of its remoteness. Beginning just south of town, it is reached via steep Wildcat Road. Dating back to the 1870s, Wildcat begins off Ocean Avenue 1 block west of Main Street, then twists and turns for 30 scenic miles to the treacherous waters of the ocean. Look for the sign to "Cape Town—Petrolia." Not many redwoods grow here, as they are repelled by the salt air, but dense Douglas fir forests and unspoiled farmlands make up for that. Make a day of it by traveling all the way to Petrolia, which was the home of California's first oil well in 1865 and where there are campsites and a few inns; then on to Honeydew, to the Rockefeller Forest, and to Highway 101 to return to Ferndale. Pack in food, a good map, and a full tank of gas, as there are few, if any, concessions along the way.

WHERE TO STAY

Gingerbread Mansion Inn

400 Berding St., (800) 952-4136, (707) 786-4000;
www.gingerbread-mansion.com. 11 rooms; $$-$$$+.
Unsuitable for children under 12. Some TVs; some
wood-burning, gas, & electric fireplaces. Afternoon
high tea; full breakfast.

Built in 1899 as a doctor's home, this carefully restored, cheery peach-and-yellow Queen Anne-Eastlake Victorian mansion boasts gables and turrets and elaborate gingerbread trim. Rooms are furnished with Victorian antiques, and each has its own charm. The Gingerbread Suite features antique "his" and "hers" clawfoot tubs perched toe to toe right in the bedroom, with framed art depicting bathing babies hanging on the wall above. Several other rooms have spectacular spacious bathrooms equipped with wood-burning fireplaces or twin clawfoot tubs placed side by side. The third-floor attic is the opulent Empire Suite, with a dramatic 12-foot ceiling and marble floor. Guests are pampered: with bathrobes and bubble bath; with breakfast served in the grand dining room and enhanced by use of the owner's collection of Depression glass; and with a proper Victorian high tea served in the house's formal tea parlor. All food is prepared on premises. Guests can stroll or sit in the formal English garden and marvel at its unusual topiaries, 2-story-high camellia bushes, and variety of fuchsias; they can also sit on the second-floor porch and watch the very limited street action. Reproduction 1950s-style fat wheel bicycles are available for guests to borrow.

Shaw House Inn

703 Main St., (800) 557-SHAW, (707) 786-9958; www.shawhouse.com. 8 rooms; $$-$$$. Some wood-burning & electric fireplaces. Afternoon tea; full breakfast.

Built in 1854 by the town founder, this white-and-blue gabled Carpenter Gothic Victorian farmhouse, set on park-like grounds way back from the street behind a white picket fence, is the oldest house in town. It is so old that it predates the town of Ferndale. In fact, its original name was Ferndale. Made entirely of redwood, and with unusual paneled ceilings, it is listed on the National Register of Historic Places. Public spaces include a library, three parlors, a dining room, and balconies, and antique furnishings are used throughout. The expansive garden surrounding the house includes vintage wildflowers, old roses, and fragrant wisterias.

Victorian Inn

400 Ocean Ave., (888) 589-1808, (707) 786-4949; www.a-victorian-inn.com. 12 rooms; $$-$$$. Some wood-burning & electric fireplaces. Full breakfast; restaurant.

Built in 1890 of local redwood, this massive, high-ceilinged hotel features beautifully appointed rooms with vintage fixtures and furnishings. Some rooms have clawfoot tubs and window alcoves overlooking Main Street.

Comfortable **Curley's Grill** *((707) 786-9696; www.curleysgrill.com. L-D daily, SunBr; $-$$. Reservations advised.)* serves generous portions of consistently good food at fair prices and is extremely popular with locals. The atmosphere is bright and cheery, with a collection of vintage salt-and-pepper shakers adding a touch of whimsy to each table. Highly touted dishes include a tortilla-and-onion cake and a Caesar salad. More sure things include the housemade soups and the delicate fresh snapper sautéed with lemon and white wine. In addition to full dinners, a hamburger, a vegetarian burger, and several sandwiches and salads are available.

WHERE TO EAT

Ferndale Pizza Company

607 Main St., (707) 786-4345. L-D Tu-Sun; $. Reservations accepted.

Operating out of a converted vintage gas station, this modest, cozy spot serves up delicious hand-thrown pizza and sandwiches prepared with housemade rolls. The owner grinds his meats and hand-forms the meatballs.

EUREKA

A LITTLE BACKGROUND

Eureka was founded in 1850 as a gold rush supply base for inland mines. By 1865 it had shifted into harvesting lumber for shipbuilding and housing. Over time, ambitious logging activity has changed the scenery here quite a bit. The best of the remaining virgin redwoods are in this area's state parks, all of which were established in the 1920s.

A small town with a welcoming attitude and atmosphere, Eureka is known as "the

coolest city in the nation." The average temperature in July ranges from 52 to 60 degrees. In January, it drops to between 41 and 53 degrees. In fact, the highest temperature ever recorded in Eureka was 87 degrees on October 26, 1993. The average annual rainfall is 37 inches, and fog is sometimes heavy even in summer.

The winter off-season is an uncrowded time to visit the north coast redwood country around Humboldt Bay. Visitors then should pack warm clothing, kiss the sunshine good-bye, and prepare to enjoy the stunning beauty of this quiet, often misty area. But keep in mind that the parks and beaches are generally uncrowded year round, and fall brings the best weather.

Eureka and nearby Arcata are both known for their brightly painted, well-preserved Victorian houses. In fact, Eureka has more Victorian buildings than any other city in the U.S. See an interesting selection by driving down Hillsdale Street between E and C streets.

Be warned that gas is expensive here. That's because it is brought in by barge.

VISITOR INFORMATION

Humboldt County Convention & Visitors Bureau
1034 2nd St., (800) 346-3482, (707) 443-5097; www.redwoods.info.

The Greater Eureka Chamber of Commerce
2112 Broadway, (800) 356-6381, (707) 442-3738; www.eurekachamber.com.

GETTING THERE

Located approximately 130 miles north of Willits, and approximately 280 miles north of San Francisco.

ANNUAL EVENTS

4th of July Festival & Fireworks in Eureka
July. (707) 442-9054; www.redwoods.info. Free.

For this old-fashioned celebration, a street festival takes over four city blocks with live entertainment, train rides, and children's activities. It culminates with a fireworks extravaganza over Humboldt Bay.

Truckers Christmas Convoy
December. (707) 442-5744; www.redwoods.info. Free.

Each year more than 150 18-wheel big rigs—decorated with thousands of twinkling lights and loaded with "candy cane" logs—are seen truckin' through town in a slow procession. A crane carries the manger scene, carolers sing from a hay hauler, and cows pull Santa's sled.

WHAT TO DO

Blue Ox Millworks
Foot of X St., 3 blks. N of 4th St., (800) 248-4259, (707) 444-3437; www.blueoxmill.com. Tours M-Sat 9-4. $7.50, 65+ $6.50, 6-12 $3.50.

On the self-guided tour of this working museum, visitors see dozens of antique woodworking machines. The oldest dates back to 1860, the newest to 1948. Many Victorian-era machines are pedal-powered and currently used to reproduce gingerbread trim for renovated Victorian homes. Of special interest are several cabins built on sleds, or "skids," so they could be pulled through the snow to new logging sites. Kids particularly enjoy meeting the assortment of farm animals, including two resident blue oxen weighing in at 2,000 pounds each.

Carson Mansion
143 M St./2nd St.; www.eurekaheritage.org/ the_carson_mansion.htm.

Built between 1884 and 1886, this is said to be the most photographed Victorian house in the world and is the "queen" of Victorian architecture. It is a mixture of several building styles—including Queen Anne, Italianate, and Stick-Eastlake—and took 100 men more than

2 years to build. Pioneer lumber baron William Carson, a failed gold miner, privately financed it in order to avoid laying off his best men during a depression. It now houses a private club and can be viewed only from the exterior.

Clarke Historical Museum
240 E St./3rd St., in Old Town, (707) 443-1947; www.clarkemuseum.org. Tu-Sat 11-4. Free.

An important collection of local Indian baskets and ceremonial regalia is on display here along with an extensive collection of 19th-century regional artifacts and pioneer relics. The palatial 1912 building is also the backdrop for displays of antique weapons and Victorian furniture and decorative arts.

Covered bridges
Take Hwy. 101 S to Elk River Rd., then follow Elk River Rd. to either Bertas Rd. (2 mi.) or Zanes Rd. (3 mi.).

These two all-wood covered bridges were constructed of redwood in 1936. **Berta's Ranch bridge** is the most westerly covered bridge in the U.S. **Zane's Ranch bridge** is the second-most westerly covered bridge in the U.S. Both are 52 feet long.

Discovery Museum
Corner of 3rd St./F St., in Old Town, (707) 443-9694; www.discovery-museum.org. Tu-Sat 10-4, Sun 12-4. $4, under 2 free.

Filled with hands-on activities for kids through age 11, this children's museum is fun anytime but really buzzes on rainy days. Stairs lead through a lighthouse to a boat with life vests and captain's hats to don, a periscope to look through, and a slide to exit by. A real hospital incubator and a mini grocery store with a moving check-out belt are the most popular exhibits, but crawlers favor the baby room where toys are disinfected every day. Though one parent must remain with children, it is possible for the other to leave and take in the sights and shops of Old Town child-free.

Fort Humboldt State Historic Park
3431 Fort Ave., at S end of town, (707) 445-6567; www.parks.ca.gov. Daily 8-5. Free.

U.S. Grant was posted here in 1854. The hospital, which dates to 1863, is restored and now used as a museum. Exhibits within the park include some locomotives, a restored

Dolbur steam donkey

logger's cabin, and displays of pioneer logging methods. An excellent view of Humboldt Bay makes this a nice spot for a picnic. The Junior Ranger Program operates in summer (see page 468).

At the annual **Dolbeer Donkey Days**, held in April, antique equipment is put into action. Steam donkeys are operated, and logging techniques are demonstrated. Train rides are part of the fun.

Humboldt Bay Harbor Cruise

Departs from foot of F St., (707) 445-1910; www.humboldtbaymaritimemuseum.com/ madaketcruises.html. Schedule varies; closed Nov-Apr. $15, 55+ $13, 5-12 $7.50; additional charge for cocktail cruise.

The 75-minute cruise aboard the tiny 40-passenger *M/V Madaket*—which once ferried workers to the lumber mills across the bay in Samoa—allows a view of the bustling activity and native wildlife of the bay. Built in 1910 in nearby Fairhaven, it is the oldest operating passenger vessel in the U.S. and has the smallest licensed bar in the state.

Morris Graves Museum of Art

636 F St./7th St., (707) 442-0278; www.humboldtarts.org. W-Sun 12-5. By donation.

Located within the town's historic Carnegie Library building, which in 1904 was the state's first free public library, this museum features beautifully restored woodwork and a magnificent tile floor. It has an outdoor sculpture garden, a small performance space, and a children's gallery.

Old Town

1st St./2nd St./3rd St., from C St. to G St., (707) 443-5097.

This waterfront area consists of restored commercial and residential Victorian buildings. Many restaurants, boutiques, and antique shops are located here, including the original **Restoration Hardware** *(417 2nd St., (707) 443-3152.)*. The **Romano Gabriel Sculpture Garden**—a folk art garden constructed from vegetable crates by the late artist Romano Gabriel—can be viewed at 315 2nd Street. A new Boardwalk along the waterfront stretches for 4 blocks and is a great place to stroll, sit, and just watch people and wildlife.

Sequoia Park Zoo

*3414 W St./Glatt St., (707) 442-6552; www.sequoia
parkzoo.net. Tu-Sun 10-5; May-Sept to 7. Free.*

The backdrop for this combination
zoo/playground/picnic area is a 77-acre forest of
old-growth redwoods. Local black bears are
among the animals displayed, and a petting zoo
is popular with children. The forest has hiking
trails, formal flower gardens, and a duck pond.

WHERE TO STAY

Abigail's "Elegant Victorian Mansion"

*1406 C St., (707) 444-3144;
www.eureka-california.com. 3 rooms; $$. Unsuitable
for children. Sauna. No pets.*

A National Historic Landmark, this spec-
tacular 1888 Queen Anne-influenced Eastlake
Victorian was built originally for the town
mayor. It is located in a residential neighbor-
hood overlooking Humboldt Bay. Opulently
decorated with many of the innkeeper's family
heirlooms, its public spaces include two parlors,
a library, and a sitting room. Guests are enter-
tained by such nostalgic pleasures as listening to
the Victrola and watching silent movies. Each
guest room is unique, but the Van Gogh Room
is exceptional in that it displays an original
watercolor by the artist as well as several origi-
nal works by Dali. The house is set on a tran-
quil, park-like estate complete with manicured
Victorian flower gardens and a croquet lawn,
and bicycles can be borrowed. Perfectly accent-
ing the inn's splendor is the spirited innkeepers'
enthusiasm for sharing information about any-
thing that might intrigue a guest. Town tours
from the rumble seat of a lovingly restored
1928 Ford Model A can be arranged, with the
dramatic innkeeper/driver dressed in charming
era garb and donning a straw hat. A visit here
offers a step back in time to a more gracious
era; it is a sort of Victorian living history expe-
rience.

Carter House Inns

*(800) 404-1390, (707) 444-8062;
www.carterhouse.com. $$-$$$+. Afternoon & evening
snack; full breakfast; restaurant; room service.*

Looking like it has been here forever, the
weather-darkened redwood inn that is the
Carter House *(1033 3rd St./L St. 4 stories; 6*

rooms. Unsuitable for toddlers. 1 fireplace.) was
actually built by owner Mark Carter in 1982. It
is a replica of an 1884 Eastlake Victorian design
of two San Francisco architects, one of whom
designed Eureka's famous Carson Mansion.
(The original house stood on the corner of
Bush and Jones streets in San Francisco and was
destroyed in the fire following the 1906 earth-
quake.) Rooms are all oversize and elegantly
furnished.

Across the street, the **Hotel Carter**
(301 L St. 24 rooms. Some gas fireplaces.) was
built in 1984 to replicate a long gone Victorian
inn originally in the area. It provides casual,
tasteful lodging amenable to families. Some
large suites have showers for two and in-room
hot tubs large enough for a family of four. An
impressive **wine shop** operates off the lobby.

Bell Cottage *(1023 3rd St. 3 rooms. Shared
kitchen; some wood-burning & gas fireplaces.)* is
adjacent to the Carter House. The romantic
Victorian **Carter Cottage** *(1027 3rd St. 1 room.
Kitchen; 2 gas fireplaces.)* features a deep marble
spa tub and fireplaces in both the sleeping and
living areas.

The owner's substantial collection of origi-
nal local art is displayed throughout the lodg-
ings. In the evening complimentary wine and
hors d'oeuvres are served, and at bedtime cook-
ies and tea appear. Interested guests may visit
the herb and vegetable garden that supplies the
restaurant. It is the most extensive inn kitchen
garden on the West Coast.

Restaurant 301 *(In Hotel Carter. B-D daily.
Reservations advised.)* offers an elegant dinner
menu showcasing the region's finest seasonal
delicacies, including Kumamoto oysters and
Pacific salmon. Designed to please both the eye
and the palate, entrees are arranged artistically
on oversize plates and garnished with such
delights as fresh flowers and herb sprigs. Past
menu selections have included flavorful squash
cakes, chicken cacciatora with creamy polenta,
and grilled pork loin with both housemade
chutney and applesauce. A well-priced five-
course, fixed price dinner is available with
optional selected wine pairings. Bar drinks are
available as well as a several thousand wines,
including vintages from Envy Wines, the pro-
prietor's winery in Calistoga. Breakfast for the
inns is provided here and includes a pastry
buffet and a hot egg dish served to the table.

The Daly Inn

1125 H St., (800) 321-9656, (707) 445-3638;
www.dalyinn.com. 5 rooms; $$. Unsuitable for
children under 12. Evening snack; full breakfast.
No pets.

Built in 1905, this elegantly restored
Colonial Revival mansion is furnished with
interesting antiques and decorated with an
array of exquisite wallpaper patterns. Public
spaces include a sun porch and TV room.

KOA Kampground

4050 N. Hwy 101, 4 mi. N of town, (800) KOA-3136,
(707) 822-4243; www.koa.com. Heated pool & hot tub
(seasonal); sauna.

For description, see page 467.

Motel Row

Last-minute accommodations can usually
be found along both 4th and 5th streets and
Broadway.

WHERE TO EAT

Bon Boniere

215 F St., in Old Town, (707) 268-0122;
www.bonboniere.biz. M-F 11-9, Sat-Sun to 11; $.

The most kid-friendly place around, this
old-fashioned ice cream parlor operates inside
an atmospheric brick-walled room with high
ceilings, marble-topped tables, and a long
counter topped with jars of sweets. It's been
serving up goodies since 1898. The best lunch
just might be a hot dog with all the trimmings
and a black cherry milkshake prepared with
housemade ice cream. Before leaving, stock up
on golf ball-size jawbreakers and long red
licorice whips. Cones and frozen bananas to go
are also an option.

Café Waterfront

102 F St., in Old Town, (707) 443-9190. B-L-D daily;
$-$$. Reservations advised.

Operating within a Queen Anne Victorian,
this restaurant is one cozy room with a very
high ceiling and a tall bar that provides additional seating. The menu offers tasty fresh
seafood dishes as well as simple soups, salads,
and burgers.

Two beautifully decorated **guest rooms** are
available upstairs.

Los Bagels

403 2nd St., in Old Town, (707) 442-8525;
www.losbagels.com. B-L W-M; $. No reservations.

This attractive, high-ceilinged space is the
place to go for a quick snack or meal of bagels
and other freshly baked goods. Eggs, Mexican
hot chocolate, and espresso are also on the
limited menu.

Lost Coast Brewery & Cafe

617 4th St., in Old Town, (707) 445-4480; www.lost
coast.com. L-D daily; $. Reservations accepted.

Situated within a historic building, this
is the first brewery in the U.S. founded and
operated by women. Among the several kinds
of handcrafted microbrews, the hands-down
favorites seems to be Great White beer and
Downtown Brown ale. Pub fare is on the
menu—some prepared with house beers as
an ingredient—and goes well with a pint.

Samoa Cookhouse

Off Cookhouse Rd. (call for directions),
(707) 442-1659; www.samoacookhouse.net. B-L-D
daily; $. No reservations.

Originally built in the 1890s by the
Georgia-Pacific Corporation to feed its loggers,
this is the last surviving cookhouse in the West.
There is no menu. Just sit down at one of the
long, boarding house-style tables and a hearty,
delicious, family-style meal starts arriving.
Though the menu changes daily, a typical
breakfast consists of biscuits and gravy, fluffy
scrambled eggs, pancakes, sausage, and coffee or
tea. Lunch might be a marinated three-bean
salad, long-simmered and flavorful Florentine
tomato soup, fresh-baked bread with butter and
assorted jams, green salad with ranch dressing
and croutons, rice pilaf, lemon-pepper chicken,
saucy beans, peas, chocolate cake with chocolate
pudding frosting and whipped cream topping,
and coffee or tea. A fantastic value! Most dishes
are prepared from scratch with fresh ingredients. The only items not included in the fixed
price are milk and sodas.

After dining, wander through the free
Historic Logging Museum of artifacts and historical photos.

Work up an appetite before, or work off
some calories after, with a walk along the area's
driftwood-strewn beaches. To find them, follow
any of the unmarked turnoffs from Samoa
Boulevard.

ARCATA

A LITTLE BACKGROUND

Home to Humboldt State University, this small
city is centered around an old-fashioned town
square lined with bookstores, coffeehouses, and
inexpensive restaurants. It is a birder's paradise;
enthusiasts can call (707) 822-LOON for a
rundown on the current rare-bird sightings in
the area.

VISITOR INFORMATION

Arcata Chamber of Commerce
1635 Heindon Rd., (707) 822-3619;
www.arcatachamber.com.
     This is also the location of a **California
Welcome Center**.

GETTING THERE

Located 5 miles north of Eureka.

ANNUAL EVENTS

Godwit Days
April. (800) 908-WING, (707) 826-7050;
www.godwitdays.com. Free-$40.
     Named for the Marbled Godwit—a large
brown shorebird with a long, slightly upturned
bill—this fair celebrates the spring bird migration with seminars and exhibits.

Arcata Bay Oyster Festival
June. (707) 822-4500; www.oysterfestival.net.
     Humboldt Bay produces 90% of
California's oysters. Most local restaurants
feature them on their menus, and this annual
festival celebrates the bounty.

WHAT TO DO

Arcata Marsh and Wildlife Sanctuary
600 S. G St., (707) 826-2359;
*www.humboldt.edu/~ere_dept/marsh. Interpretive
center: Daily 9-5; tour Sat at 8:30am. Free.*
     Home and temporary refuge to more than
200 species of bird, this is a breeding area for
ducks and other waterfowl and a feeding area
for fish-eating birds such as osprey, herons,
grebes, and egrets. At low tide, people flock here

Marbled Godwit

to view the thousands of shore birds foraging
on the mud flats of Humboldt Bay. Though
birds are here year-round, the largest variety is
seen during the fall and spring migrations.
Facilities include 4½ miles of trails, observation
blinds, an interpretive center, and a picnic area.
After that description, it is amazing to learn
that this thriving, scenic wetlands preserve is
positioned over the former city dump and currently treats and recycles the city's wastewater
and sewage.

WHERE TO EAT

Jacoby's Storehouse
791 8th St., on the plaza, (707) 822-4500;
www.jacobystorehouse.com.
     Built in 1857, this fireproof stone store-
house once supplied the mule trains headed to
the gold mines. It is the oldest masonry building in Humboldt County. Interesting features
include pressed-tin ceilings and unusual
stained-glass light fixtures.
     On the first floor, **Abruzzi** *((707) 826-
2345; www.abruzziarcata.com. D daily; $$-$$$.
Reservations advised.)* is a popular spot to celebrate a special occasion. With crisp white nap-
pery and a romantic atmosphere, the restaurant

specializes in housemade breads and pastas and serves fine Italian cuisine.

On the second floor, amid a pathway of interesting boutiques, the **Bon Boniere** ice cream parlor *((707) 822-6388. Daily 10-10.)*, dishes up everything cold and creamy. For more description, see page 270.

On the third floor, the casual **Plaza Grill** *((707) 826-0860; www.plazagrillarcata.com. D daily; $. Reservations advised.)* is a good spot with kids. A barkeep mixes up cocktails, and the menu offers sandwiches, salads, and grilled fresh fish and steaks. The fireplace here came from actor Humphrey Bogart's house in Los Angeles, and beautiful etched glass-and-grill-work windows hail from the Plaza Hotel in New York City.

Los Bagels
1061 I St., (707) 822-3150; www.losbagels.com.
For description, see page 270.

TRINIDAD

A LITTLE BACKGROUND

Older than Eureka by about 4 months, this scenic fishing village was a supply port for gold miners in the 1850s and later became a whaling port. The town's circa 1860 lighthouse still operates, and it boasts a very nice beach.

VISITOR INFORMATION

Greater Trinidad Chamber of Commerce
P.O. Box 356, Trinidad 95570, (707) 677-1610; www.trinidadcalif.com.

GETTING THERE

Located 23 miles north of Eureka.

WHAT TO DO

Humboldt State University Marine Laboratory
570 Ewing St., (707) 826-3671; www.humboldt.edu/~marinelb. Hour vary. Free.

This research facility has a small aquarium exhibit and a touch tank that are open to the public.

Patrick's Point State Park
4150 Patrick's Point Dr., 6 mi. N of town, (707) 677-3570; www.parks.ca.gov. $6/vehicle. No pets.

Whale-watching and weddings are both prime at Wedding Rock. In fact, some grey whales have become year-round residents off shore. A few years ago, stargazing was part of the scene, too, literally, when *The Lost World* was filmed here. Agate Beach Trail leads to its namesake beach via a steep, winding trail with lots of stairs, and Octopus Trees Trail passes by Sitka spruces, whose odd roots cause them to resemble octopuses. This 632-acre park is also home to an authentically re-created Yurok Indian village, and a Visitor Center has relevant displays. Campsites are available.

WHERE TO STAY

Bishop Pine Lodge
1481 Patrick's Point Dr., (707) 677-3314; www.bishoppinelodge.com. 12 cabins; $$. Some kitchens. Fitness room.

These cozy one-room and two-bedroom cabins are tucked among redwoods. Built in the 1920s, they are renovated and feature modern amenities. Charming shutters with pine tree cutouts frame the multi-paned windows on the rustic exteriors, while knotty-pine paneling warms up interiors. A few swings and a basketball area are available for children on the spacious, well-maintained grounds, and one unit has a semi-private sunken hot tub on its redwood deck.

The Emerald Forest
753 Patrick's Point Dr., (888) 677-3800, (707) 677-3554; www.cabinsintheredwoods.com. 12 cabins; $$-$$$.

Set back in a deep, dark forest of tall trees, this spacious old-time property has a campground as well as rustic cabins. A three-bedroom, two-bath family cabin that sleeps eight is available, or parents of older children can rent one cabin for themselves and a separate, smaller one nearby equipped with bunk beds for the kids. Facilities include a children's playground with wooden structures, a rec room, and a small general store.

The Lost Whale Inn
3452 Patrick's Point Dr., (800) 677-7859, (707) 677-3425; www.lostwhaleinn.com. 8 rooms, 3 houses; $$-$$$+. No TVs. Hot tub. Afternoon & evening snack; full breakfast. No pets.

Set back on a bluff above the ocean, this contemporary Cape Cod-style farmhouse inn features spacious rooms—five with spectacular ocean views. Guests often wake up to the sound of sea lions barking out on Turtle Rock, and migrating whales are sometimes spotted from the dining room or deck while eating breakfast. A steep, scenic wooded trail leads to the inn's private beach, and Patrick's Point State Park is just down the road. Children are especially welcomed and well cared for here and can look forward to picking berries, fantasizing in a playhouse, frolicking on a playground, and feeding the inn's ducks and goats. Two suites have special sleeping lofts for kids.

WHERE TO EAT

Seascape Restaurant
1 Bay St., (707) 677-3762. B-L-D daily; $$. No reservations.

Owned and operated by the Cher-Ae Heights Indian Community of the Trinidad Rancheria, this casual spot at the base of the pier has rustic stone walls, comfy booths, and big windows with views of the scenic cliff-edged bay. Breakfast is served until 4 p.m. The menu stresses fresh seafood, and lunches are a particular bargain. Don't miss the blackberry pie.

KLAMATH

VISITOR INFORMATION

Klamath Chamber of Commerce
P.O. Box 476, Klamath 95548, (800) 200-2335, (707) 482-7165; www.klamathcc.org.

GETTING THERE

Located approximately 60 miles north of Eureka, and approximately 40 miles south of the Oregon border.

WHAT TO DO

Klamath River Jet Boat Tours
On Hwy. 101 S., (800) 887-JETS, (707) 482-5822; www.jetboattours.com. Schedule varies; May-Sept only. $38, seniors $34, 4-11 $19.

This invigorating journey begins at the Klamath estuary called "Rekwoi"—the Native American word for where fresh water meets the Pacific Ocean. From there, the boat turns upriver for a closer look at the area's wildlife. With flat bottoms and no rudder or propeller, jet boats provide a smooth and safe, yet fast and exciting, ride. Some trips include an optional barbecue dinner, and overnighting at a remote wilderness lodge can be arranged.

Prairie Creek Redwoods State Park
On Hwy. 101, 6 mi. N of Orick, (707) 465-7347; www.parks.ca.gov. Daily 9:30-5. $6/vehicle.

The 8-mile unpaved gravel road to Gold Bluffs Beach—where gold was once found among the sand—passes through a beautiful forest into Fern Canyon. A short, easy 1¾-mile loop trail leads through this scenic area of vertical cliff walls carpeted with ferns and mosses. Steven Spielberg filmed part of *The Lost World: Jurassic Park II* here. This 14,000-acre park is a refuge for one of the few remaining herds of native Roosevelt elk, which are the largest mammals in California and the largest subspecies of North American elk. Viewing is prime from mid-September to mid-October at the Elk Prairie section on Newton Drury Scenic Parkway. Campsites are available.

Trees of Mystery

15500 Hwy. 101 N., (800) 638-3389, (707) 482-2251;
www.treesofmystery.net. Daily 9-5, in summer 8-7.
$13.50, 60+ $10, 4-10 $6.50.

As visitors approach this privately owned
grove of redwoods, they are greeted by a 50-
foot-tall Paul Bunyan and a 32-foot-tall Babe.
This is fun for kids, and they can pose free for a
picture on Paul's boot without entering the
park. The 8/10-mile trail inside, which is steep
in parts, passes through a tunnel made from a
hollowed-out log and continues on past a well-
maintained group of unusual trees. In a setting
at times reminiscent of Disney meets Ripley's
Believe It or Not!, visitors see the Candelabra
Tree with new trees growing off its fallen trunk,
the famous Cathedral Tree with nine trees
growing from one root structure, and similar
natural wonders. One section displays intricate
redwood carvings that tell the tale of Paul
Bunyan along with a recorded narration.
A silent ¼-mile SkyTrail aerial gondola ride
through the redwood forest canopy lets riders
get off at the top to view the panorama through
binoculars provided on an observation deck.

The world's largest private collection of
Native American artifacts is displayed in the
back of the gift shop in the **End of the Trail
Native American Museum**; admission is free.
Displays include colorful beaded-leather clothing, arrowheads, dolls, and baskets. Two snack
bars and picnic facilities are available.

WHERE TO STAY

Historic Requa Inn
451 Requa Rd., (866) 800-8777, (707) 482-1425;
www.requainn.com. 10 rooms; $-$$. Closed Dec-Feb.
Unsuitable for young children. No TVs. Full breakfast.
No pets.

This restored historic hotel dating from
1885 has comfortable, pleasantly decorated
rooms. Dinner is available to guests. Fishermen
particularly favor this location at the scenic
mouth of the Klamath River in the center of
Redwood National Park.

Redwood National Park Hostel
14480 Hwy. 101 N., 7 mi. N of town, (800) 295-1805,
(707) 482-8265; www.redwoodhostel.org. 30 beds;
2 private rooms. Open weekends only Nov-Feb.

This northernmost link in the California
coast hostel chain is located within national
park boundaries. Operating within the circa
1890s pioneer DeMartin House, it has a full
kitchen and spectacular ocean views. See also
page 468.

CRESCENT CITY

A LITTLE BACKGROUND

This often-foggy, isolated, somewhat desolate
stretch of coast suffered a 21-foot-high tsunami
in 1964 that killed 11 people and destroyed
most of the town center, then a typhoon in
1972. The area is home to the pristine Smith
River, where you can still see through the water
to the bottom, and maximum-security Pelican
Bay State Prison is just outside of town. Bring
cash—many restaurants here are living in
pre-credit card times.

VISITOR INFORMATION

Crescent City/Del Norte County
Chamber of Commerce
1001 Front St., (800) 343-8300, (707) 464-3174;
www.exploredelnorte.com.

GETTING THERE

Crescent City is located 85 miles north of Eureka over a winding road, and 20 miles south of the Oregon border.

WHAT TO DO

Battery Point Lighthouse

Foot of A St., (707) 464-3089; www.delnortehistory.org. Tours W-Sun 10-4, tides permitting; April-Oct only. $3, under 13 $1.

The tide has to be out in order to walk over to the island that holds this charming little gem of a Cape Cod-style lighthouse, which is separated from the shore when the tide is in. Getting there is half the fun, requiring as it does a walk over a gravel bed leading past tide pools and the occasional wild iris or magenta ice plant. The light's bluff-top location provides a stunning view of the sea and of flocks of sea birds, including pelicans. Picnic tables are available. The first light keeper came out with James Marshall (who discovered gold elsewhere). The current light keeper has cable and internet and got the job by luckily being on a tour on the last day of the previous keeper's stay. On the

tour participants climb up a spiral staircase to view the modern automated light, see the original fourth-order Fresnel lens displayed in the gift shop, see and hear an intriguing demonstration of an antique Victrola, and view the living quarters of the current keepers that is decorated with lace curtains, rag rugs, and antiques galore (it is one of the longest continually lived in lighthouse on the West Coast). At least one kid on a tour has screamed, "Wow!" Folks might also wonder if that is a whale they see out there . . . or just a whale of a rock.

Brother Jonathan Park

9th St./Pebble Beach.

This open expanse holds several graves and provides a viewpoint of the largest shipwreck—in terms of life and money—ever to occur off the coast of California.

Del Norte County Historical Society Museum

577 H St./6th St., (707) 464-3922; www.delnortehistory.org. M-Sat 10-4; May-Sept only. $3, under 12 $1.

Housed in a warren of rooms in the building that once served as the town's Hall of Records and jail, this museum devotes two rooms to local Tolowa and Yurok Native American artifacts. Other exhibits include antique musical instruments, vintage needlework, and a stage coach, and an annex houses the magnificent 5,000-pound, 18-foot-high, first-order Fresnel lens from the **Point Saint George Reef Lighthouse** located 6 miles off shore.

Northcoast Marine Mammal Center

424 Howe Ave., adjacent to Front Street Park, (707) 465-MAML; www.northcoastmmc.org. Gift shop open daily 12-4; feedings at 8am, 12, 4, 8pm.

This hospital is dedicated to the rescue and rehabilitation of stranded, sick or injured seals, sea lions, dolphins, porpoises, and whales. Patients are often viewable through a chain fence around the perimeter, and volunteers are sometimes available to answer questions.

Picnic tables and a small cove and beach are just across the street.

Ocean World

304 Hwy. 101 S., (707) 464-3522;
www.oceanworldonline.com. Guided tours 8am-9pm in
summer; 9-6 in winter. $9.95, 4-11 $5.95.

Visitors can pick up starfish and sea
anemones and pet live sharks. A sea lion show
is part of the fun.

Redwood National and State Parks

Visitor Centers in Orick, Crescent City, & Hiouchi,
(707) 464-6101; www.nps.gov/redw. Daily 9-5. Free.

This magnificent, sprawling national park
encompasses more than 130,000 acres. It has
numerous entrances, so stop at a visitor center
to get oriented and inquire about borrowing
Family Adventure Packs to use with children.
Ranger-led interpretive programs are scheduled
daily June through August. **Ladybird Johnson
Grove** *(On Bald Hills Rd., off Hwy. 101.)* is an
easy, level 1-mile loop. Permits are required
(free at the Orick Visitor Center) for visiting the
Tall Trees Grove, which contains some of the
world's tallest trees (over 360 feet). The walk
takes about 4 hours and covers 3.2 miles.

Roosevelt elk are often seen in the Elk Meadow
section of the park on Davison Road, south of
Prairie Creek Redwoods State Park.

WHERE TO STAY

Crescent Beach Motel

1455 Hwy. 101 S., 2 mi. S of town, (707) 464-5436;
www.crescentbeachmotel.com. 27 rooms; $-$$.
Afternoon hot drinks; instant breakfast. No pets.

The city's only beachfront lodging, this
splendidly located motel is on South Beach.
It is simple but nicely maintained, and all but
two of the rooms have a large window
facing the ocean. Most new arrivals sit for a
spell on the beach chairs provided outside each
room, releasing the tensions of the drive. The
beach is just beyond a protective row of boulders, and the grey ocean is alive with diving
pelicans and bobbing surfers. Windows are
operable so it is possible to keep them open
to the soothing sounds of the rolling waves and
bleating fog horn. Breakfast is simple—hot
drinks and instant oatmeal.

View from Crescent Beach Motel

KOA Kampground

4241 N. Hwy. 101, 5 mi. N of town, (800) KOA-5754, (707) 464-5744; www.crescentcitykoa.com.

This 21-acre campground features 10 acres of redwoods. For description, see page 467.

WHERE TO EAT

Ambrosia Grill

1270 Front St., (707) 464-2400. D M-Sat, SunBr; $$. Reservations accepted.

A favorite with locals, the kitchen here prepares tasty fish (perhaps a horseradish-crusted wild salmon with mashed potatoes, asparagus, and a Caesar salad) and rich desserts.

Beachcomber Restaurant

1400 Hwy. 101, 2 mi. S of town, (707) 464-2205. D Thur-Tu; $-$$; closed Dec-Jan & part of Feb. Reservations advised.

The nautical decor of rough-cut planks and fishnets is nice, and the comfortable booths are cozy, but the ocean view is the big event. Fresh fish—often locally caught and usually grilled over madrone-wood barbecue pits—is very good, and the fish & chips-coleslaw-curly fries basket is primo.

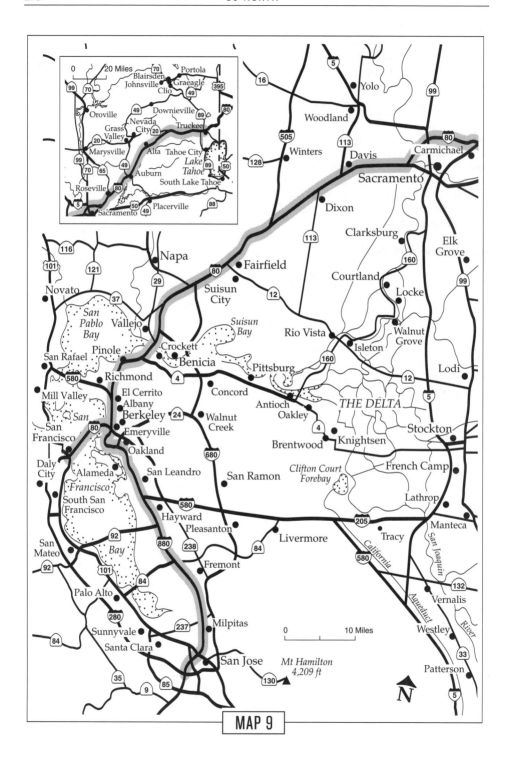

MAP 9

80 NORTH

EMERYVILLE

A LITTLE BACKGROUND

This industrial city is home to **Pixar Studios**, famous for animation movies such as *Toy Story* and *Finding Nemo*.

GETTING THERE

Located 14 miles west of San Francisco. Cross the Bay Bridge, and follow the signs to I-80 north.

WHAT TO DO

Bay Street Emeryville
Bay St./Christie Ave., (510) 655-4002; www.baystreetemeryville.com. Most shops: M-W 10-8, Thur-Sat 10-9, Sun 11-6. Parking $1/4 hrs.

Built above a large Indian burial ground, this shopping center has shops and restaurants galore plus a 16-screen AMC movie complex.

WHERE TO EAT

Emeryville Public Market
5959 Shellmound St./Powell St., (510) 652-9300; www.emerymarket.com. B-L-D daily.

In this cavernous building's food court, just about every ethnic cuisine imaginable is purveyed at bargain prices. Middle Eastern items from **Sara Deli** *((510) 923-1588)* and both Chinese items and fish & chips from **The Crispy Fry** *((510) 655-9955)*, which uses no MSG, are especially delicious. People-watching is prime, and a Borders bookstore and a movie multi-plex are adjacent.

Hong Kong East Ocean Seafood Restaurant
3199 Powell St., (510) 655-3388; www.hongkongeast ocean.com. Dim sum M-F 11-2:30, Sat-Sun 10-2:30; D daily; $-$$. Reservations accepted for D.

This out-of-the-way restaurant, reached via a scenic waterfront drive, serves superb dim sum. Items are not brought around on carts or trays. Instead, diners mark selections on a menu form. The deep-fried taro balls and jumbo shrimp dumplings are simply the best. Light Cantonese seafood and vegetable dishes are also available. A gorgeous bay view is part of the package, and a trail alongside the bay is perfect for an after-meal stroll.

Townhouse Bar & Grill
5862 Doyle St./59th St., (510) 652-6151; www.townhousebarandgrill.com. L M-F, D M-Sat. Reservations advised. Valet parking at L.

A speakeasy when it opened in 1926, then transformed into a western honky-tonk joint in the 1970s, this spot retains its rustic charm and sense of history but has morphed now into a comfortable, uptown-style dining destination. Diners are seated in one big room, with a deck option in warm weather. Starters include delicious grilled gulf shrimp with chipotle aioli that is so good some diners wipe the plate clean with bread. The daily soup and hefty Caesar salad are also winners. Entrees include pastas and fish, but meats seem the way to go—succulent roasted baby-back pork ribs or a juicy flat-iron steak, both served with crisp French-style frites. The hamburger is also a favorite. Bar drinks are colorful and tasty and made without mixes (try the Whiskey Sour), and desserts sometimes includes a fresh peach-blueberry crisp. Live jazz entertains on Wednesday and Thursday nights from 7 to 10 p.m.

Trader Vic's
9 Anchor Dr./Powell St., (510) 653-3400; www.tradervics.com. L M-Sat, D daily, SunBr; $$. Reservations advised.

The original Trader Vic's opened in Oakland in 1934 and is said to be where the Mai Tai was invented in 1944 (the name of the drink is coined from the Tahitian phrase "Mai Tai, Roa Ae," which translates to "Out of this world, the best"). That location closed and then reopened in this new incarnation. Now it is a link in the world-wide chain of Polynesian bars and restaurants. Famous dishes include bongo bongo soup and Calcutta curry. For more description, see page 179.

BERKELEY

A LITTLE BACKGROUND

The always-fascinating community of Berkeley is a study in contrasts. Visitors arrive with a variety of expectations. Some seek the intellectual climate associated with a community built around the University of California, the state's most prestigious public university. Others expect to see weird people and hippie communes. Those who know their food come seeking the acclaimed restaurants, and those who know one of the town's nicknames, Berserkley,

expect to see a bit of that. Then there is the well-known ultra-liberal political climate, in which someone who would be thought a liberal elsewhere is here considered a conservative, which explains another nickname—the People's Republic of Berkeley. In reality, Berkeley is all these things, and, making any stereotype impossible, it is also the place where the word "yuppie" was coined. Berkeley has also pioneered many frontiers. It was the first city in the nation with a public health department, the first to have a lie-detector machine, the first with curb cuts for wheelchairs, the first with a dog park, the first to ban Styrofoam, and the first to rename Columbus Day the more politically correct "Indigenous Peoples Day" (it's listed that way under "holidays" on parking meters). And it is the place where plutonium and berkelium—the 97th element—were discovered.

VISITOR INFORMATION

Berkeley Convention & Visitors Bureau
2015 Center St., (800) 847-4823, (510) 549-7040; www.visitberkeley.com.

Berkeley Chamber of Commerce
1834 University Ave., (510) 549-7000; www.berkeleychamber.com.

GETTING THERE

The central Berkeley exit is University Avenue.

ANNUAL EVENTS

Spring House Tour
April. (510) 841-2242; www.berkeleyheritage.com. $25-$35.

Sponsored by the Berkeley Architectural Heritage Association, this tour provides access to some of the city's many architecturally interesting homes. Related talks are usually scheduled.

Live Oak Park Fair
June. (510) 898-3282; www.liveoakparkfair.com. Free.

This fair has evolved into a first-rate juried crafts and fine art show, with live entertainment and some food booths. The park itself—with its mature shade trees, rolling lawns, and meandering creek—is inviting to visit any time.

Berkeley Kite Festival & West Coast Kite Championships

July. In Cesar E. Chavez Park at Berkeley Marina. (510) 235-KITE; www.highlinekites.com/Berkeley_Kite_Festival. Free.

Tell someone to "go fly a kite" at this exhilarating event. Or better yet, tag along and see kites galore, plus Japanese-style Rokkaku kite battles and taiko drummers.

How Berkeley Can You Be? Parade

September. Along University Ave., (510) 654-6346; www.howberkeleycanyoube.com. Free.

This zany parade includes puppets, floats, and art cars, as well as bizarre marching groups wearing their Berkeleyest costumes. A festival in Martin Luther King Park follows.

Solano Stroll

September. (510) 527-5358; www.solanostroll.org. Free.

This mile-long block party is the oldest and largest free street festival in the East Bay. Strollers can browse and munch their way from one end to the other.

International Taiko Festival

November. At U.C. Berkeley, Zellerbach Hall. (415) 928-2456; www.taikodojo.org. $36-$48.

It's hard to imagine something more exhilarating than witnessing one muscle-bound taiko drummer after another beating out an intoxicating primal rhythm. Dating back 2,000 years, the thunderous sound of these drums was once used to stimulate rain and then, later, to signal Japanese armies into battle. It is said to be the heartbeat of the Japanese people. San Francisco's internationally acclaimed Taiko Dojo usually performs on a 1-ton, 12-foot-high drum—the largest in the western hemisphere.

Berkeley Artisans Holiday Open Studios

November & December. (510) 845-2612; www.berkeleyartisans.com. Free.

This self-guided tour allows participants to meet the artists in their studios and to purchase quality gifts.

WHAT TO DO

Adventure Playground

160 University Ave., in Shorebird Park, (510) 981-6720; ww.ci.berkeley.ca.us/parks. Sat-Sun 11-4; in summer M-F 9-5, Sat-Sun 11-5. Free for age 7+ accompanied by adult, or $7/3 hrs.

The story goes that in Europe after World War II a designer built a series of modern playgrounds. But the children continued, indeed *preferred*, to play in bombed-out buildings and to construct their own play equipment from the plentiful rubble and debris. Taking that cue, he designed the first adventure playground. This U.S. version offers a storage shed full of tools and recycled wood that children can use to build forts and clubhouses and other things, and then leave them up or tear them down when they are done. The playground also has a tire swing, climbing net, and fast-moving trolley hanging from a pulley. A more traditional play area is just outside the fence.

Next door, **Shorebird Park Nature Center** *((510) 981-6720; www.ci.berkeley.ca.us/marina. Tu-Sat 1-5. Free.)* has a 100-gallon aquarium in the classroom and a 50-gallon tank in the new green Strawbale Visitor Center.

Nearby, at the bay end of University Avenue where the Berkeley Pier begins, is a sculpture depicting a bow-and-arrow-wielding Native American astride his horse. Artist Fred Fierstein is said to have placed it here himself in 1985 when he got tired of waiting for Berkeley politicians to decide to do it for him. He had offered "The Guardian" to the city at no cost, but after long deliberation it was rejected as too aggressive—not to mention that the animal appears to urinate when it rains. Berkeley residents then voted to keep it here, but their decision might not be final. See it *now*.

Berkeley Rose Garden
1200 Euclid Ave./Bayview Pl., (510) 981-5150; www.ci.berkeley.ca.us/parks. Daily sunrise-sunset. Free.

Planted at the turn of the century, this terraced garden was originally conceived as a classical Green arboretum. It is a particular delight in late spring and summer, when the 250 varieties of rose are in full bloom. Benches sheltered by arbors covered with climbing roses make for pleasant picnicking and provide gorgeous views of the bay and San Francisco. Tennis courts adjoin. The garden is a popular spot for weddings, and a knot of people is found at the top most evenings watching the sun set.

Across the street, **Codornices Park** is equipped with a playground, a basketball court, and a long, exciting, and potentially dangerous (be careful!) concrete slide. Trails follow the creek and pass the oldest grove of dawn redwoods found outside of China.

Blake Garden
70 Rincon Rd./Arlington Ave., in Kensington, (510) 524-2449; www-laep.ced.berkeley.edu/laep/ blakegarden. M-F 8-4:30. Free.

Surrounding the residence of the president of the University of California, this enormously varied 10½-acre hillside garden was designed in the 1920s by Anita Blake—one of the first students in the landscape architecture department at U.C. Berkeley—and her sister Mabel Symmes. The garden is used by both U.C. and other area educational institutions as an outdoor laboratory and educational facility. It divides more than 1,000 plant species into several areas: a formal Italianate garden with reflecting pool; a redwood canyon with under plantings of ferns, gingers, and other woodland exotic species; a drought-tolerant garden; a flower cutting garden; a vegetable garden; and an undeveloped Australian Hollow. Benches positioned throughout invite quiet reflection, and picnic tables are available.

A Carmelite Monastery is adjacent on what was once part of the original lot.

Downtown Arts District
Addison St. betw. Shattuck Ave. & Milvia St.

Works by local artists are displayed here, and 127 cast-iron panels imprinted with poetry are embedded in the sidewalk (they were selected by Kensington resident Robert Hass, former U.S. Poet Laureate).

• Aurora Theatre
2081 Addison St./Shattuck Ave., (510) 843-4822; www.auroratheatre.org. $28-$40.

In this intimate venue, no seat is more than 4 rows from the stage.

• Berkeley Repertory Theatre
2025 Addison St./Shattuck Ave., (510) 647-2949; www.berkeleyrep.org. $10-$55. Must be age 10+. No performances in Aug.

This Tony Award-winning company has established a national reputation for ambitious programming and dynamic productions. It is well known for presenting important new dramatic voices and fresh adaptations of seldom-seen classics. Multi-talented Rita Moreno, now a local resident, appears in some productions. Performances are held in two spaces: the 400-seat Thrust Stage, and the 600-seat Roda Theatre.

Fourth Street
1800 block, (510) 644-3002; www.fourthstreet.com. Shop schedules vary.

For a city of the size and income level of Berkeley, it is surprising that it has no department stores or traditional shopping malls. This trendy block featuring a 1920s industrial style of architecture is as close to one as the city comes. It is a shopping mall done Berkeley-style. Designed, built, and owned by a Berkeley developer/architectural firm, the street's buildings are kept at 2 stories. The owner controls leasing of the entire block and hand picks the unusual stores. A variety of restaurants offers delicious fare and spectacular people-watching.

• Builders Booksource
#1817, (800) 843-2028, (510) 845-6874; www.builders booksource.com.

Stocks books on architecture and design as well as "nesting" books on interior design and gardening.

• East Bay Vivarium

1827 5th St., 1 blk. E, (510) 841-1400;
www.eastbayvivarium.com.

This is the oldest retail herpetological store
in the nation. A pet shop, it has the largest
selection of reptiles in the country. Rumor has
it actor Nicolas Cage shops here for giant moni-
tor lizards and ball player Jose Canseco checks
out the tortoises. Others come to purchase
Mexican red-legged tarantulas, mouse-sized
Madagascar hissing cockroaches, and Burmese
pythons. Yet others view it as a sort of living
museum.

• The Gardener

#1836, (510) 548-4545; www.thegardener.com.

Specializes in elegant accessories for the
garden and home.

• George

#1844, (877) 322-3232, (510) 644-1033;
www.georgesf.com.

Everything tempting for cats and dogs,
including fresh-baked treats, is found here.

• Lighting Studio

#1808, (510) 843-3468;
www.lightingstudioberkeley.com.

Displays the very best and latest in lighting
fixtures.

• Miki's Paper

#1801, (510) 845-9530.

An impressive selection of handmade
Japanese papers is purveyed here.

• The Pasta Shop

#1786, (510) 528-1786.

This is a spacious branch of the mother
ship in Oakland (see page 321).

• Sur La Table

#1806, (510) 849-2252; www.surlatable.com.

Purveys fine kitchen equipment at fair
prices.

The Judah L. Magnes Museum

2911 Russell St./College Ave., (510) 549-6950;
www.magnes.org. Sun-W 11-4, Thur 11-8. By donation:
$4, seniors $3, under 12 free.

The first Jewish museum established in the
western U.S., the Magnes focuses on the art and
history of the Jewish experience. It is housed in
a converted 1908 mansion, the gardens for
which were landscaped by John McLaren,
designer of San Francisco's Golden Gate Park.

Ohlone Dog Park

Hearst St./Grant St., in Ohlone Park, (510) 981-6700;
www.ci.berkeley.ca.us/parks. M-F 6am-10pm, Sat-Sun
9am-10pm. Free.

Established as an experiment in 1979, this
was the first leash-free dog park in the nation.
It has 4-foot-high fences that foil even the most
gifted jumpers. A concrete walkway is equipped
with seating areas alongside, and a lawn with
wood chips is on either side of the walkway.
Water taps are provided at both ends of the
park. Because it is partially paved, the park is a
particularly good choice in wet weather, and
dogs like to run here. Owners must clean up
after their dogs, and plastic bags are provided.

Scharffen Berger Chocolate Maker factory tour

914 Heinz Ave./7th St., (510) 981-4066;
www.scharffenberger.com. Schedule varies;
reservations required. Free. Must be age 8+.

Operating inside a 1906 brick warehouse,
this small factory turns out small batches of
high-grade chocolate using cacao beans from
Venezuela, Madagascar, and Papua New Guinea.
The tour includes an informative lecture
enhanced with chocolate tasting, a stroll
through the factory, and a visit to the themed
gift shop.

In an interior intoxicatingly fragrant with
chocolate, **Café Cacao** *((510) 843-6000;*
www.cafecacao.biz. B M-F, L daily, D F, Sat-
SunBr; $-$$. No reservations.) serves up choco-
late drinks and desserts galore (hot cocoa,
scones studded with bittersweet chocolate and
cherries, lofty bittersweet chocolate bread pudding) and some main courses (chocolate
noodles with beef ragu, a chocolate sandwich).
Plenty of conventional salads and entrees are
also options. An outdoor patio is open in good
weather.

Takara Sake USA Tasting Room and Sake Museum

708 Addison St./4th St., (800) 4-TAKARA,
(510) 540-8250; www.takarasake.com. Tasting daily
12-6; closed last week in Dec. Free.

Sample several kinds of sake and plum
wine in the spacious tasting room of this
nation's largest sake brewery. A raised tatami
room invites removing shoes and relaxing for a
bit. Upon request, an informative video can be

viewed that tells about the history and making of sake. The country's only sake museum displays artifacts related to this subtle beverage.

Telegraph Avenue
4 blks. betw. Bancroft Way & Dwight Way, S of campus; www.telegraphave.org.

Fondly referred to as "the Ave" or "Tele" by locals, this famous, or perhaps infamous, avenue is probably best known for its role as a gathering spot and point of confrontation during the 1960s Free Speech Movement. It has now slipped into a more peaceful state, but still appears stalled in the '60s. On weekdays rushing students crowd the sidewalks, and on weekends shoppers crowd its many small shops. A stroll here passes a street bazaar of crafts stalls selling souvenirs such as colorful tie-dyed t-shirts and peace symbol jewelry. Thoroughly modern chain stores are also well represented.

• People's Park
Bounded by Telegraph Ave., Haste St., Hillegass Ave., & Dwight Way.

This was the rallying place for some of the anti-war and free speech protests in the '60s and '70s.

• Annapurna
#2416, (510) 841-6187; www.annapurnaberkeley.com.

This is a psychedelic "head shop" left over from the turbulent 1960s.

• Bookstores in the 2400 block include:
• Moe's Books
#2476, (510) 849-2087; www.moesbooks.com.

This is said to be the biggest used bookstore west of the Hudson; and

• Shakespeare & Co.
#2499, (510) 841-8916.

This beloved institution sells unusual used editions.

Tilden Nature Area
www.ebparks.org/parks/vc/tna.

This 740-acre preserve is located just north of Tilden Regional Park. It has more than 10 miles of hiking trails, including both the self-guided boardwalk trail to Jewel Lake and the vigorous climb up 1,211-foot Wildcat Peak for panoramic San Francisco Bay view.

• Environmental Education Center
(510) 525-2233. Tu-Sun 10-5. Free.

This is a good place to get oriented and obtain current information about park attrac-

tions. Exhibits stress local natural history. Educational programs and naturalist-guided walks, many designed especially for families and children, are scheduled regularly.

• Little Farm
(510) 525-2233. Daily 8:30-3:30. Free.

Built in 1955, this brightly painted, well-maintained farm is home to cows, sheep, chickens, goats, rabbits, pigs, and assorted other barnyard animals. Several heritage breeds are preserved here, including Milking Shorthorn Cattle. Visitors may bring lettuce or celery (but nothing else) to feed the animals.

Tilden Regional Park
Off Grizzly Peak, along Wildcat Canyon Rd., (510) 843-2137; www.ebparks.org/parks/tilden. Daily 5am-10pm. Free.

This beautiful, well-developed 2,079-acre park has 35 miles of hiking trails as well as numerous picnic spots, many with tables and barbecues.

• Golf Course
(510) 848-7373. Daily sunrise-sunset. M-Thur $34, F $39, Sat-Sun $57; reduced twilight rates.

This scenic 18-hole course has all types of holes permitting all types of shots.

• Lake Anza
(510) 843-2137. Daily 11-6, May-Sept only. $3.50, 62+ & 1-15 $2.50.

This low-key swimming area has lifeguards on duty, and a snack bar is available.

• Merry-Go-Round
(510) 524-6773. Sat-Sun 11-5; daily in summer. $2.

One of only four classic four-row carousels remaining in Northern California, this restored antique gem is located in the center of the park. Built in 1911 by the Herschel-Spillman firm in New York, it spent time before it settled here at Urbita Springs Park in San Bernardino, at Ocean Beach in San Diego, and at Griffith Park in Los Angeles. In addition to horses, it sports an assortment of colorful animals, including a stork, a dragon, and a frog. Its large band organ operates like a player piano and is regarded as one of the finest examples of its kind.

• Regional Parks Botanic Garden
(510) 841-8732; www.nativeplants.org. Daily 8:30-5; tours Sat-Sun at 2. Free.

Located across from the carousel, this 10-acre garden was begun in 1940. It offers the opportunity for a leisurely, quiet walk. Over 3,000 drought-resistant species and subspecies are displayed, and native plants are also featured.

• Steam Train/Redwood Valley Railway
Grizzly Peak Blvd./Lomas Cantadas, (510) 548-6100; www.redwoodvalleyrailway.com. Sat-Sun 11-6, weather permitting; in summer, daily 11-5. $2.

Started in 1952 by the late Erich Thomsen, a career railroad man, and now operated by his daughter Ellen, this miniature train concession is described as "a hobby that got out of hand." The replica 15-inch gauge, 5-inch scale narrow-gauge, oil-burning miniature steam train (whew!) follows a scenic route that includes one tunnel and two trestles. The ride covers 1¼ mile and lasts 12 minutes.

University of California
Telegraph Ave./Bancroft Way, (510) 642-6000; www.berkeley.edu.

The foremost attraction here is, of course, higher learning. Known for academic excellence, U.C. Berkeley boasts a faculty distinguished by 17 Nobel Prize winners. Many noteworthy facilities on this 1,232-acre campus are open to the public.

• Berkeley Art Museum
2626 Bancroft Way/College Ave., (510) 642-0808; www.bampfa.berkeley.edu. W-Sun 11-5. $8, 65+ & 13-17 $5; free 1st Thur of month.

Many visitors think that this building itself is as interesting and unusual as its contents. Built in a Modernist style of architecture, it is strikingly reminiscent of New York's Guggenheim—except that it is angular instead of circular. The permanent collection stresses modern and Asian art and includes a large collection of paintings by Abstract Expressionist Hans Hofmann.

On the basement level, **Café Muse** (*2625 Durant Ave., (510) 548-4366; www.bampfa. berkeley.edu/visit/cafemuse. L daily; $.*) opens to a courtyard and grassy sculpture garden. The specialty is raw cuisine, but some sandwiches and cooked dishes are also on the menu.

The **Pacific Film Archive** (*2575 Bancroft Way/College Ave., (510) 642-1124; www.bampfa. berkeley.edu. Daily programs. $9.50, 65+ & under 18 $6.50.*) is one of five world-class public archival film collections in the U.S. It has the largest collection of Japanese titles outside of Japan and one of the world's largest collections

of silent and early films from the former Soviet Union and pre-1960 Eastern Europe, plus hundreds of experimental movies by West Coast filmmakers. Programs span world cinema from the silent era to the present. The theater is clean, the sound system excellent, and the audience well mannered. No snacks are available.

• Botanical Garden
200 Centennial Dr., (510) 643-2755; www.botanical garden.berkeley.edu. Daily 9-5; in summer also W-Sun to 8; closed on 1st Tu of month. $7, 65+ & 13-17 $5, 5-12 $2; free on 1st Thur; free tour Thur, Sat-Sun at 1:30; parking $1-$1.50/hr. No pets.

Located behind the campus in lush Strawberry Canyon, this "library of living plants" covers 34 acres and contains more than 13,000 different types of plants organized by continent of origin. Of special interest are the herb garden, rhododendron dell, redwood grove, California native plants area (which includes more than half of the state's native species), old rose garden, and Chinese medicinal herb garden featuring more than 90 rare plants. Children particularly enjoy the greenhouse filled with carnivorous plants and the lily pond stocked with colorful koi. Additionally, this peaceful spot has a lawn area that is perfect for picnicking, and several picnic tables are also scattered throughout.

• Cal Day Open House
Annually in April. (510) 642-2294; http://calday.berkeley.edu. Free.

Most of the university departments sponsor exhibits and events, and some campus museums are open to the public only at this event.

• Cal Performances
(510) 642-9988; www.calperfs.berkeley.edu. Free-$125.

Acclaimed internationally for presenting extraordinary talent, this series is famous for showcasing the latest works of established artists and the debuts of new talent.

• Campanile
In center of campus; www.berkeley.edu/visitors/ campanile.html. Elevator: M-F 10-4, Sat 10-5, Sun 10-1:30 & 3-5; $2, seniors & under 19 $1.

Modeled after the slightly taller campanile in St. Marks Square in Venice, this campus landmark stands 307 feet tall—the equivalent of 30 stories. When classes are in session, 10-minute mini-concerts are hand-played on its

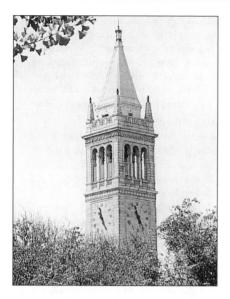

61-bell carillon three times each weekday at 7:50 a.m., noon, and 6 p.m. On Sundays, a 45-minute recital is performed at 2 p.m.— the perfect time to enjoy a picnic on the surrounding lawn. An elevator takes visitors up 200 feet to an observation platform for a 360-degree view of the area.

• Campus Tour

2200 University Ave./Oxford St., Visitors Center, 101 University Hall, (510) 642-5215; www.berkeley.edu/ visitors. M-Sat at 10, Sun at 1; confirm time and departure location. Free.

This guided tour is a good way to get an overview of the campus. A self-guiding tour brochure is also available.

• Lawrence Hall of Science

On Centennial Dr., below Grizzly Peak Blvd.,
(510) 642-5132; www.lawrencehallofscience.org. Daily 10-5. $11, 62+ & 7-18 $9, 3-6 $6; planetarium +$3, under 19 +$2.50; parking $1+/hr.

Located high in the hills behind the campus, this hands-on museum was established by the university in 1968 as a memorial to Ernest Orlando Lawrence, who developed the cyclotron and was the university's first Nobel laureate. Exhibits are of special interest to school-age children and include educational games, a seismic recorder, and the small Holt Planetarium. The hall's permanent exhibits include Math Rules—puzzles and mathematical challenges defy the popular notion that math isn't fun—and an outdoor science park. On weekends, a Biology Lab permits experimenting with animal mazes and learning about a variety of small animals. Outside on the entry plaza, kids can play on a life-size adolescent fin whale and a DNA molecule climbing structure.

The short-order **Bay View Cafe** provides a magnificent panoramic view of the bay and San Francisco.

• Museum of Paleontology

Near Oxford St./University Ave., 1101 Valley Life Sciences Bldg., (510) 642-1821; www.ucmp. berkeley.edu. M-F 9-5, F 8-5, Sat 10-5, Sun 1-10. Free.

Initiated in the 1860s, this is a research museum with limited public exhibits. Its collection of fossils is one of the largest and oldest in North America, and displays include a complete Tyrannosaurus rex skeleton and the largest Triceratops skull ever found.

In the same building, the **Museum of Vertebrate Zoology** *(rm. 3101; (510) 642-3567; http://mvz.berkeley.edu. M-F 8-12 & 1-5. Free.)* holds one of the largest and most important collections of vertebrates in the world.

DNA Model at Lawrence Hall of Science

The Claremont Resort

• Phoebe A. Hearst Museum of Anthropology
Bancroft Way/College Ave., 102 Kroeber Hall,
(510) 643-7648; http://hearstmuseum.berkeley.edu.
W-Sat 10-4:30, Sun 12-4. Free.

Part of the campus since 1901, this
museum houses the largest anthropological
research collection (more than 4 million
artifacts) in the western U.S.

WHERE TO STAY

Bancroft Hotel
2680 Bancroft Way/College Ave., (800) 549-1002,
(510) 549-1000; www.bancrofthotel.com. 22 rooms;
$$. Continental breakfast. No pets. Self-parking $12.

Located directly across from the campus,
this landmark 1928 arts and crafts-style hotel
was designed by Walter T. Steilberg, an associate
of Julia Morgan. It offers peaceful, airy rooms
with sweeping views of San Francisco Bay
and the Berkeley hills. Many also have large
balconies or decks.

Berkeley City Club
2315 Durant Ave./Dana St., (510) 848-7800;
www.berkeleycityclub.com. 6 stories; 36 rooms; $$-
$$$. No TVs. Indoor heated pool. Continental break-
fast; restaurant. No pets. Self-parking $12.

Opened in 1930 as the Berkeley Women's
City Club, this magnificent historical landmark

building was designed by Julia Morgan—the
well-known architect who designed Hearst
Castle. Featuring Moorish and Italian Gothic
elements, it is decorated with oriental rugs and
tasteful vintage furniture that enhance the Old
World beauty of its lead-paned windows and
aged redwood trim. Free **tours** are given on the
fourth Sunday of each month. Rooms are com-
fortably furnished, and all have views of either
the San Francisco Bay or the campus and hills.
A bar and restaurant are available to guests
only, and a beauty salon operates on site. An
intimate theater venue often schedules perform-
ances that are open to the public.

Claremont Resort & Spa
41 Tunnel Rd., at Ashby Ave./Domingo Ave., (800)
551-7266, (510) 843-3000; www.claremontresort.com.
6 stories; 279 rooms; $$$+. 2 heated pools; hot tub;
4 saunas; 2 steam rooms; full-service spa; fitness
room; 10 tennis courts (fee; 6 with night lights).
2 restaurants; room service. Self-parking or valet
$17.50.

Built originally by a Kansas farmer who
struck it rich and wanted to fulfill his wife's
dream of living in a home resembling an
English castle, the first incarnation of this hotel
burned to the ground in 1901. The current
Victorian hotel, built in 1915, once charmed
architect Frank Lloyd Wright into describing it

as ". . . one of the few hotels in the world with warmth, character and charm." The hotel now provides all the amenities of a resort, but in an urban setting. Some rooms boast Jacuzzi tubs for two and views of San Francisco, others have charm from the past—a deep closet here, a vintage tub there. The hotel's two pools and hot tub are surrounded by several long rows of chaise lounges—looking like something out of sunny Southern California or Hawaii, but certainly *not* Berkeley. The spa features a hot tub with a view of San Francisco and the Golden Gate Bridge, 2 silent flotation tanks, a therapeutic "deluge" shower, and 32 treatment rooms. Additionally, a kids' activity center permits dropping them off for a few hours of fun and games.

In addition to fresh fish and meats, romantic **Jordan's** *((510) 549-8510. B-L-D daily, SunBr; $$$. Reservations advised. Valet parking.)* provides a menu of Lifestyle Cuisine— California fare with a touch of the Pacific Rim—and a fixed-price four-course tasting menu. Comfortable chairs invite sitting back and enjoying the spectacular bay view. Sunday brunch here is an extravagant buffet of salads, fresh fruit, seafood, and meats. It includes a design-your-own-omelette station and a dessert table laden with fine cakes, chocolate éclairs, chocolate fondue, and several flavors of mousse. Live music is scheduled on Sunday evenings.

Paragon Bar & Café *((510) 549-8585; www.paragonrestaurant.com. L-D daily; $$. Valet parking.)* is more casual, with a comfortable bar area providing entertainment Thursday through Sunday evenings. The bar makes specialty cocktails and pours more than 75 vodkas. The dining room has a transitional area of communal tables, with traditional unshared tables in the back—all with impressive bay views. The American brasserie menu has included a flavorful roasted beet salad and a tasty, satisfying orecchiette consisting of housemade fennel sausage, cauliflower, and cute little cap-shaped pasta. A burger is always on the menu and a reliably good choice, and a butter-pecan bread pudding is a favorite dessert.

Doubletree Hotel Berkeley Marina
200 Marina Blvd., (800) 222-TREE, (510) 548-7920; www.berkeleymarina.doubletree.com. 378 rooms; $$-$$$. 2 indoor heated pools & 2 hot tubs; sauna; fitness room. Restaurant; room service.

Featuring a tranquil setting on the marina, this comfortable low-rise lodging provides marina views and easy parking. All rooms have either a patio or balcony.

The French Hotel
1538 Shattuck Ave./Cedar St., (510) 548-9930. 18 rooms; $-$$. Cafe; room service. No pets.

In this European-modern hotel situated just across the street from Chez Panisse, all rooms have a private patio. Just off the lobby, the hotel's coffeehouse has sidewalk tables that are popular with locals.

Hotel Durant
2600 Durant Ave./Bowditch St., (800) 2-DURANT, (510) 845-8981; www.hoteldurant.com. 6 stories; 144 rooms; $$. Restaurant; room service. No pets. Self-parking or valet $10.

Particularly popular with parents in town to visit their children at the university, this atmospheric hotel is just 1 block from the university. Historic photographs of the campus hang in the hallways, and some of the attractively appointed rooms feature campanile views.

Henry's Publick House *((510) 809-4132; www.henrysberkeley.com. B-L-D daily; $-$$.)* features a cozy, comfortable pub atmosphere and authentic Tiffany lamp fixtures. Food is well prepared and includes a good hamburger, fresh fish items, and a variety of sandwiches and salads.

Rose Garden Inn
2740 Telegraph Ave./Ward St., (800) 992-9005, (510) 549-2145; www.rosegardeninn.com. 40 rooms; $$-$$$. Some wood-burning & gas fireplaces. Afternoon snack; full breakfast.

Situated 7 blocks from the university, this charming B&B includes two landmark Tudor-style mansions and three additional buildings that open onto a central garden oasis featuring fountains, patios, and hundreds of rose bushes. Rooms are attractively decorated and comfortable, and some have views of San Francisco. Families are accommodated comfortably in the larger junior suites.

WHERE TO EAT

Berkeley was the first city in the state to introduce legislation regulating smoking in public places. It was also the first city to require non-smoking sections in restaurants. Now California is the first state in the nation to require that all restaurants and bars in the state are 100% non-smoking. Smoking in workplaces is also prohibited.

Ajanta

1888 Solano Ave./The Alameda, (510) 526-4373; www.ajantarestaurant.com. L-D daily; $$. Reservations advised.

With an ever-changing menu of creative, complex regional Indian dishes, this popular, attractive restaurant is always a delight. Complete dinners are well priced, and presentation is part of the pleasure. Appetizers include papadam (a crisp lentil wafer served with dipping sauce) and alu tikki (deep-fried potato-and-pea patties). Complimentary condiments include mango chutney, housemade spicy carrots, and sour lime pickles. Entrees change regularly and include curries, tandoori meats (including signature lamb-rib chops) and fish, plus a selection of vegetarian and vegan dishes; all can be ordered in any degree of spiciness. Plates are attractively arranged with three scoops of saffron-laced rice anchored in the middle by a mound of spinach purée. A light mango mousse and liquidy kulfi rice pudding are especially delicious desserts. Use is made of local products, including Berkeley-brewed beers and Peet's coffee, and decaf chai—a rarity—is available. This restaurant is named for the site of ancient Buddhist cave temples that is a famous tourist attraction in western India. Reproductions of some of the cave paintings appear on wall murals that were painted in India.

Alborz

2142 Center St./Shattuck Ave., (510) 848-8877. L-D daily; $$.

Cocktails are available here made with soju (a distilled Asian spirit made from barley that is similar to vodka) mixed with fresh pomegranate juice or orange juice. For more description, see page 59.

Au Coquelet

2000 University Ave./Milvia St., (510) 845-0433. B-L-D daily; $. No reservations.

This spot is popular with students and night owls and is as Berkeley as you can get. It is a great spot for a coffee and pastry anytime, since it stays open until 1:30 a.m., and its regulars have been described as "defying description." Indeed, it attracts a cross-section. The cafe menu is simple—omelettes, cold and hot sandwiches, burgers, salads, soups—but the selection of housemade tortes and tarts and coffee drinks is outstanding.

Berkeley Thai House

2511 Channing Way/Telegraph Ave., (510) 843-7352; www.berkeleythaihouse.com. L M-Sat, D daily; $. Reservations advised at D.

In good weather, a table on the spacious wooden deck here is a choice spot to relax with a cooling, sweet Thai iced tea. On nippier days and in the evening, the cozy inside dining room decorated with Indonesian artifacts is an inviting option. Specials chalked on a board by the entrance are usually a good bet. Favorite dishes include spicy-hot basil chicken, full-flavored cashew nut chicken, moo-prik-khing (a superb stir-fry with pork and fresh green beans in a spicy sauce), panang neur (beef and sweet basil in a spicy red curry sauce with a coconut milk base), and pad thai (a sweet, orange-colored noodle dish accented with ground peanuts, bean sprouts, bean cake, and a few tiny shrimp).

Bette's Oceanview Diner

1807 Fourth St./Hearst Ave., (510) 644-3230; www.bettesdiner.com. B-L daily; $. No reservations.

It's fun to sit on a counter stool (a purse hook is provided underneath) and watch the cooks hustle in this casual, noisy diner featuring a 1950s truck-stop decor and a menu of traditional American food. A jukebox provides more entertainment with an eclectic mix of everything from '50s classics to reggae. Breakfast is served all day beginning at 6:30 a.m., and choices include spicy scrambled eggs, steak and eggs, omelettes, griddle cakes with real maple syrup, delicious French toast, and some combination plates—The New York (smoked salmon, bagel, cream cheese, red onion, and tomato) and The Philadelphia (scrapple, poached eggs, toast, and grilled tomato). Blintzes are sometimes also available. Lunch is a satisfying assortment of well-prepared classic sandwiches (the Reuben and meatloaf are particularly good), housemade soups, and homey items such as grilled bockwurst and potato pancakes. Thick old-fashioned milkshakes are on the menu, too, but oddly no hamburger or fries. By the way, about that ocean view. There is none. Oceanview is the name of the neighborhood in which the restaurant is located.

Next door, **Bette's To Go** *((510) 548-9494. M-F 6:30-5, Sat-Sun 8-5.)* dispenses take-out pastries, sandwiches, salads, pizza by the slice, and other goodies.

Blakes on Telegraph

2367 Telegraph Ave./Durant Ave., (510) 848-0886; www.blakesontelegraph.com. L-D daily; $. Reservations accepted.

A campus hangout since 1940, this restaurant serves a large variety of hamburgers and snacks. On weekdays, lunch is served both downstairs in the funky rathskeller, with its sawdust-covered floor and old wooden booths, and upstairs, where diners get excellent views of the sidewalk parade outside. A cover charge is levied on the live music scheduled most evenings.

Boran Thai

1892 Solano Ave./The Alameda, (510) 525-3625. L M-F, D daily; $. Reservations accepted.

Diners select seating either at regular tables or in an area where they remove their shoes and sit on floor cushions with feet dangling under the table. Once settled, complimentary shrimp chips and dipping sauce are brought for munching on while perusing the menu. Winners include delicate basil chicken, tasty cashew nut chicken, crispy-fried fresh red snapper glazed with a hot-and-sweet tamarind sauce, and flavorful Panang beef in peanut-curry sauce. A good selection of vegetarian options is available, and at lunch all entrees include cabbage soup, steamed rice, and fresh steamed vegetables.

Breads of India

2448 Sacramento St./Dwight Way, (510) 848-7684; www.breadsofindia.com. L-D daily; $. No reservations.

In spite of having few tables and little ambiance, this popular spot usually has a line waiting to get in. A sign-up sheet is posted outside. The teeny kitchen stuffed with cooks produces dishes such as jumbo prawns in a complexly spiced, tomato-based masala sauce, and organic Yukon gold potatoes in a mild fresh spinach purée. The garlic naan is exceptional, and additional delicious exotic bread options—all prepared with organic flour—include roomali roti (a thin unleavened bread prepared with a blend of white and wheat flours) and tawa daal paratha (stuffed with spicy chickpeas). Entrees are served on one American-style plate with trimmings of basmati rice and dahl. The kitchen uses the best ingredients, blends their own spices, and never freezes or microwaves anything (indeed, there doesn't seem to be any room for these appliances in the tiny kitchen). Only olive oil is used—none of that fattening Indian ghee. The menu, which changes daily, provided fascinating, detailed descriptions and always includes a tandoori-cooked meat item and two vegetarian dishes. With 700 recipes for entrees and 170 for breads, this restaurant aims to surprise.

Brennan's

720 University Ave./4th St., (510) 841-0960. L-D daily; $; closed part of July. No reservations.

Reminiscent of a shamrock, with its dark green exterior, this Berkeley institution's hall-like dining room is dominated by an enormous rectangular bar. Two large-screen TVs are tuned perpetually to sporting events. Always crowded and sometimes boisterous, it has a variety of beers and microbrews on tap and is furnished with decidedly untrendy Formica tables. The menu consists of generous portions of hofbrau-style meat and potatoes, and each night has its hot-plate special. Hot sandwiches come with made-from-scratch mashed potatoes smothered in gravy, and side dishes include tasty stuffing, macaroni salad, potato salad, and coleslaw. Service is cafeteria-style: pick a table, wait in line, chow down.

Bua Luang Thai

1166 Solano Ave./Cornell Ave., in Albany, (510) 527-8288. L-D daily; $. Reservations accepted.

Though this tiny dining room is a treat any time, it is especially delightful as a refuge on a warm afternoon or as a cozy retreat on a cool evening. Ingredients are fresh, spicing is simple, and portions are generous. Stars on the menu include deep-fried curry puffs, red Panang beef curry, and an unusual, tasty pumpkin curry. Dark brown rice and a large selection of seafood and vegetarian items are also available.

Cactus Taqueria

1881 Solano Ave./The Alameda, (510) 528-1881;
www.cactustaqueria.com. L-D daily; $. No reserva-
tions.

Mexican fast food at its best is served cafeteria-style in this popular taqueria. Burritos are
custom made, with a choice of several kinds of
flavored tortillas, black or pinto beans, and a
variety of well-seasoned fillings. Tacos and
tamales are also available. Tortillas are lard-free,
meats are the best, and tortilla chips are fried in
safflower oil. Housemade drinks include several
fresh fruit agua frescas and horchata (a sweet
rice drink), and several addictive salsas are
available. Seating is at colorfully-stained wood-
en tables, and an indoor water fountain provides restive background sound.

Café Fanny

1603 San Pablo Ave./Cedar St., (510) 524-5447;
www.cafefanny.com. B-L daily; $. No reservations.

Operated by the venerable Alice Waters,
this simple spot, named for her daughter (who
was named for the beautiful fishwife's daughter
in Marcel Pagnol's film trilogy about life on the
waterfront in Marseille), is an outpost of tonier
Chez Panisse. Bread and wine comes from next-
door neighbors—Acme Bread Company and
Kermit Lynch Wine Merchant. Breakfasts are
simple, but the boiled egg—perhaps a blue or

green Araucana—is perfect and the toast is, too.
Lunch is a selection of several sandwiches.
Limited seating is available outside with a view
of a noisy parking lot, but no one seems to
mind.

Before departing, stop in next door at the
famous, famous **Acme Bread Company** *(1601
San Pablo Ave., (510) 524-1327. M-Sat 8-6, Sun
8:30-3.)* for a take-away baguette fresh from the
oven.

Cafe Panini

2115 Allston Way/Shattuck Ave., in Trumpetvine Court,
(510) 849-0405; www.cafe-panini.com. L M-F; $.
No reservations.

Popular with university students and staff,
this tiny spot produces simple yet divine open-
face sandwiches. Diners order at the counter,
then select a seat either in the brick-walled interior or out in a sheltered courtyard—the top
choice on a sunny day. Panini are made with
magnificent Semifreddi Bakery sweet baguettes
and topped with enticing combinations, including a mushroom-pesto-sun dried tomato finished with melted mozzarella. As at Chez
Panisse—where this cafe's owner was once a
waitress and then a wine buyer—all ingredients
are fresh. Tuna is not from a can. Meats are
cooked in-house. Mayonnaise is made from
scratch. Herbs are fresh. A soup, a pasta salad,
and some delicious housemade desserts are also
available.

Cancun Taqueria

2134 Allston Way/Shattuck Ave., (510) 549-0964.
L-D daily; $. No reservations.

Meats here are broiled over open flames,
seafood is grilled, and there are plenty of vegetarian specials. Lard and MSG are not used, but
purified water is. Everything—soft and crispy
tacos, burritos, quesadillas, tostadas—is super
tasty, especially when tarted up with delicious
selections from the extensive complimentary
salsa bar.

César

1515 Shattuck Ave./Cedar St., (510) 883-0222;
www.barcesar.com. L-D daily; $-$$. No reservations.

Casual and cozy, this tapas bar is operated
by a group that includes Alice Waters' husband
and is located in the Gourmet Ghetto next door
to Chez Panisse. A true bar, its menu offers a

large selection of spirits and wines, and food is served until 11 p.m. The short menu changes daily but always includes some delicious options: a tiny plate of two tasty red piquillo peppers filled with melted cheese; a more substantial stack of flat, thin fried potatoes seasoned with rosemary and whole sage leaves; rock cod with a spicy red romesco sauce; a bocadillo (sandwich) of spicy tuna and egg. Chewy Catalan almond cookies and dessert wines provide fine finishes. The open room has a large communal table in the center made from floorboards brought in from an old London warehouse.

Cha-Am
1543 Shattuck Ave./Cedar St., (510) 848-9664. L-D daily; $. Reservations advised.

Still the leader in the informal ranking of this city's best Thai restaurants, this gem features a festive atmosphere, an attentive staff, and chefs who produce complex flavors and interesting combinations. Among the winners on its exciting menu are laap-gai (a chopped chicken salad tossed with fresh mint and coriander), pad-makua-yao (chicken sautéed with basil, chilies, and eggplant), and pad-ped-gung (prawns sautéed with sweet curry sauce, fresh Thai herbs, and green beans).

Chez Panisse
1517 Shattuck Ave./Cedar St.; www.chezpanisse.com. M-Sat. Cafe: L-D; $$-$$$; reservations advised; accepted up to 1 month in advance; (510) 548-5049. Restaurant: D; $$$+; reservations essential; accepted up to 1 month in advance; (510) 548-5525.

Opened in 1971 by U.C. graduate Alice Waters as a hangout for her friends, this fabulously famous **restaurant** inside a converted art deco-style house features the definitive California cuisine—simply prepared food made with the freshest ingredients. A different fixed-price menu is served each night in the legendary downstairs dining room. A less expensive upstairs **cafe** serves a seasonal menu of simple items such as baked goat cheese salad, Spanish-style grilled chicken with lentils, and almond cake with poached Bosc pears and sour cherries. Meals in both venues are usually a perfect 10. A 15% service charge is automatically added to the bill and divided by the entire staff, so no need to tip more unless service was above and beyond.

The area surrounding this restaurant is known as the "Gourmet Ghetto." Allow time to explore.

Dara Thai Lao Cuisine
1549 Shattuck Ave./Cedar St., (510) 841-2002. L-D daily; $. Reservations accepted.

In warm weather, the front patio here is a delight. Vines and exotic flowers mingle with weathered-wood tables, providing a mini jungle through which the filtered street-scene view is mesmerizing. Particularly good dishes include priking (sautéed chili string beans with shrimp), pad pet makeur (grilled eggplant sautéed in a spicy sauce), and spicy panang red curry with fried tofu and veggies. The deep-fried sweet potato appetizer and pad thai noodles are also very good, and a sweet Thai iced tea provides the perfect lift.

FatApple's
1346 Martin Luther King Jr. Way/Rose St., (510) 526-2260. B-L-D daily; $-$$. No reservations.

This popular restaurant's forte is good food made from scratch using basic ingredients: The lean ground chuck used for hamburgers is ground on the premises; soup is made fresh; blue cheese salad dressing is made with the real stuff; robust Peet's coffee is freshly ground and served with heavy whipping cream. The famous hamburger is served on a housemade wheat or white bun, and just-right milkshakes—the olallieberry is outstanding—are served in the metal mixing canister. For dessert, it's impossible to go wrong with a slice of the puffy apple pie the restaurant is named for, but the chocolate velvet and lemon meringue pies are also delicious. Breakfast features fresh-squeezed orange juice, crisp waffles served with pure Vermont maple syrup, omelettes, buckwheat or whole-wheat pancakes, and freshly baked pastries.

Inn Kensington
293 Arlington Ave./Amherst, in Kensington, (510) 527-5919. B daily, L M-F, D M-Sat; $. No reservations. No cards.

Situated amid a strip of shops, this popular spot has been here since 1981. Breakfast choices are extensive—dozens of omelettes and scrambles, excellent home fries, gigantic housemade buttermilk biscuits—and are available through lunch, when an enticing selection of tasty international dishes joins the menu. Lunch items might include a Santa Fe pita pizzetta, a Moroccan-style deep-fried lemon-ginger chicken breast with salsa, or East Indian curried chicken in filo dough. Desserts include housemade ice cream and a bargain oversize cookie.

Juan's Place
941 Carleton/9th St., (510) 845-6904. L M-F, D daily; $. Reservations advised.

Always bustling, this family-friendly spot is reminiscent of a Mexican roadhouse. All the usual traditional Mexican food suspects are on the menu: burritos, tacos, tostadas, quesadillas, tamales, fajitas, flautas. Enchiladas come stuffed with the usual, as well as with crab or shrimp, and are topped with a variety of sauces, including a deep, smoky mole. Heavier meat entrees and several chilis are also options, as is a horchata rice drink and a caramel flan dessert.

Kathmandu
1410 Solano Ave./Santa Fe Ave., in Albany, (510) 526-3222. D daily; $-$$. Reservations advised.

Tibetan and Napalese fare—a cross between Chinese and Indian cuisines—is served in this tiny space. A good selection of vegetarian items is available, and various kinds of sprouted beans add a pleasing crunch to many dishes. Lamb items are a specialty, and khashi ko chhwela—a spicy smoked-lamb stew served at room temperature—is choice. Though entree dishes come with condiments, rice, and bread, do also try chatmari—a soft rice-flour bread stuffed with curried chicken. Beer and either cinnamon or banana lassi yogurt drinks make good accompaniments, and a pot of chai (spiced tea served with milk) makes a nice ending.

King Tsin
1699 Solano Ave./Tulare Ave., (510) 525-9890. L-D daily; $$. Reservations advised.

The first Mandarin Chinese restaurant in town, this popular spot recently remodeled its dining room and now has hardwood floors and big windows looking out on the street. No MSG is used in preparing the tasty items that include hot-and-sour soup, juicy pot stickers, spiced prawns (coated with batter, deep-fried, and served in a spicy-sweet sauce), Mongolian beef (smothered in green onions and served on a bed of crisp rice noodles), vegetarian green beans, and dramatic sizzling meat and fish plates. Soft-shell crab and Peking duck are also on the menu. Dim sum is served all day, and mixed drinks are available from a full bar.

King Yen
2995 College Ave./Ashby Ave., (510) 845-1286. L-D daily; $-$$. Reservations accepted.

The high-ceilinged main dining room here, with its generous flower arrangements and potted plants, is as delightful as the cuisine. Dishes include Szechwan beef (batter-dipped meat is deep-fried, then stir-fried with a spicy-sweet sauce), General's chicken (lots of crunchy water chestnuts), and delicately seasoned mu shu pork. Exotic beggar's chicken and Peking duck are available by advance order. Good vegetarian items include crispy spring rolls, dry-cooked string beans, and bean curd with black bean sauce, and chow mein and hot-and-sour soup can be requested without meat. Both white and brown rice are available, and the kitchen uses no MSG.

Kirala
2100 Ward St./Shattuck Ave., (510) 549-3486; www.kiralaberkeley.com. L Tu-F, D daily; $$. No reservations.

Pass the inevitable wait here in the tiny bar, where a dish of edamame (soybeans) and a bottle of sake or Japanese beer speed it along. The Japanese fare includes appetizers (delicate seafood or pork gyoza (like pot stickers); light-as-air tempura), robata grill items (spicy sardines; baby lobster tail with tiny red caviar; silky shitake mushrooms), an array of sushi (fresh water or sea eel among them) and sashimi, and full meals with soup, salad, and rice. A la carte portions are delicious but small, so do order a side of rice.

Before or after, **Berkeley Bowl** (*2020 Oregon St., (510) 843-6929; www.berkeley bowl.com. M-Sat 9-8, Sun 10-6.*) is just a block away. This counter-culture grocery store is legendary for its produce section and also has a large take-out selection.

La Mediterranée
2936 College Ave./Ashby Ave., (510) 540-7773; www.cafelamed.com. B-L M-F, D daily, Sat-SunBr; $. No reservations.

Situated in the low-key Elmwood neighborhood, this spot has a pleasant, protected sidewalk-side patio. The Middle Eastern menu offers an outstanding cinnamony chicken Cilicia in phyllo dough and a succulent chicken pomegranate, as well as soups and salads for lighter appetites.

La Note Restaurant Provencal
2377 Shattuck Ave./Channing Way, (510) 843-1535; www.lanoterestaurant.com. B-L M-F, D Thur-Sat, Sat-SunBr; $-$$. Reservations for 4-5+.

Touching just the right culinary notes, this charming restaurant situated inside a vintage 1894 building delivers the Provence dining experience without the native negatives of small dogs and cigarette smoke. On the patio on a warm, sunny day, while sipping a cafe au lait from a big bowl, it's possible to fantasize about actually being in the south of France. Winning items on the breakfast menu include lemon-gingerbread pancakes with poached pears, fluffy scrambled eggs, and perfectly fried rosemary potatoes. Omelettes, hot cereals, and French toast made with cinnamon brioche soaked in orange water batter and drizzled with lavender honey are also available. Lunch brings on les salades, les soupes, and les sandwiches, and dinner les bagnats (traditional Provençale open-face sandwiches), les poissons (fish), and les viandes (meats). Bon appetit!

La Val's
1834 Euclid Ave./Hearst Ave., (510) 843-5617; www.lavals.com. L-D daily; $. No reservations.

Located on the quieter north side of the U.C. campus, this long-popular student hangout has good pizza, pastas, and brew—all at great prices. The super-casual seating inside is enhanced with overhead TVs broadcasting sporting events, but on warm afternoons sitting at a picnic table in the courtyard beer garden is hard to beat. Waiting time can be spent playing video games.

The Med (iterraneum Caffe)
2475 Telegraph Ave./Haste St., (510) 549-1128. Daily 7am-11:30pm; $. No reservations.

With a casual atmosphere and untidy decor, this coffeehouse seems to have been serving students forever. It catered the Free Speech Movement activists back in the '60s as they planned their moves, including Jerry "You can't trust anybody over 30" Rubin. But, as everyone knows, times change. Now it has an ATM on the premises and serves smoothies and ice cream cones. Try a Berliner—a sort of coffee-ice cream float—and the fabulous chocolate layer cake with rum custard filling. Short-order breakfast and lunch items are available.

O Chamé
1830 Fourth St./Hearst Ave., (510) 841-8783. L-D M-Sat; $$. Reservations advised for D.

Reminiscent of Chez Panisse in its simplicity and use of the freshest ingredients, this tranquil spot has a refined menu that changes weekly. Offerings are whimsical (a "tower" salad composed of stacked slices of daikon radish, smoked salmon, and mango) as well as more traditional (soup prepared with king salmon, mustard greens, fresh shitake mushrooms, and brown buckwheat soba noodles). The restaurant is known for its noodle dishes, one of the most popular being chunky white udon noodles with smoked trout. A variety of sakes and an extensive list of teas are also available. Simple but exquisite desserts might include fresh sweet cherries served chilling amid ice cubes. Beautiful bento box lunches are available to go.

Peet's Coffee & Tea
2112 Vine St./Cedar St., (510) 841-0564; www.peets.com. M-Sat 6am-8pm, Sun 6-7.

It was here in 1966 that now-retired owner Alfred Peet, a Dutch émigré, became the first in the U.S. trade to import specialty varieties of coffees and to dark-roast whole coffee beans—a radical move at the time that touched off a revolution among coffee drinkers. A Berkeley institution, this coffee boutique dispenses an impressive variety of coffees and teas and, though it has no place to sit down, is the gathering spot each morning for large numbers of coffee freaks. Holding their hot cups of java, they spill right into the street. Professionals in three-piece suits mingle here with blue-collar workers, all chatting happily. Sometimes it seems that almost everyone in this town, no matter what kind of work they do, has a curious, educated mind. Perhaps they would like to mull this over: Starbucks owned Peet's from 1984 to 1987. But Peet's is now an independent company once again, with a plethora of outlets throughout the Bay Area.

Picante

1328 6th St./Gilman St., (510) 525-3121;
www.picante.biz. L-D daily, Sat-SunBr; $.
No reservations.

Claiming to be the largest taqueria in the Bay Area, this casual spot has two indoor dining rooms and an outside area with a soothing wall fountain. Menu choices include the expected burritos, tamales, tacos (prepared with handmade corn tortillas), quesadillas, and tostadas. Especially good fillings include carnitas (slow-cooked pork), pollo asado (grilled chicken with fresh salsa), rajas (roasted Poblano chilies with sautéed onions and Mexican cheese), and chorizo y papas (spicy Mexican sausage and potatoes). Vegetarian and vegan items are also available. Among the drinks are aguas frescas (fresh fruit drinks), margaritas made with agave wine, and a large selection of Mexican beers.

Picnic Pick-Ups

• A. G. Ferrari Foods

2905 College Ave./Ashby Ave., (510) 849-2701;
www.agferrari.com. M-F 9:30-8, Sat 10-8, Sun 10-6:30. Also at 1843 Solano Ave., (510) 559-6860;
M-Sat 9:30-8:30, Sun 10-7.

Dine in or take away a picnic from this totally Italian deli. Housemade fresh pastas include a delectable pappardelle that is even better topped with either the housemade meat sauce or roasted red pepper sauce. An olive bar holds particularly good black olives with almonds, and the deli case always has an assortment of tempting salads and entrees.

• Andronico's Market

1550 Shattuck Ave./Cedar St., (510) 841-7942;
www.andronicos.com. Daily 7:30am-11pm.

This upscale supermarket carries delicious take-out fare and locally-made gourmet treats, and boxed lunches are available by 24-hour advance reservation. It is located within what was once the consumer-owned Co-op, a supermarket that operated here from 1938 to 1988 and was the country's largest urban cooperative.

• Campus food stalls

At the campus entrance, on Bancroft Way/Telegraph Ave. M-F 11-3, more or less; $. No cards.

These informal stands offer simple fast foods such as donuts, soft pretzels, fresh juices and smoothies, falafel (a Middle Eastern vegetarian sandwich made with pocket bread), and other ethnic dishes. Nearby benches, steps, and grassy areas offer impromptu picnic possibilities. And because this famous intersection attracts all kinds of entertainers—jugglers, musicians, revivalists, you-name-it—an amazing floor show is free.

• Grégoire

2109 Cedar St./Shattuck Ave., (510) 883-1893;
www.gregoirerestaurant.com. L-D daily.

This upscale hole-in-the-wall produces accomplished French take-out fare, and it *must* be good because California Cuisine guru Alice Waters is a customer. Chef Grégoire makes everything from scratch using fresh local ingredients. A few tables are available for dining, but it's more fun to fax in an order and pick it up dressed in delightful eight-sided corrugated boxes made of recycled material (this *is* Berkeley). The monthly menu is posted conveniently at the website with a downloadable, faxable order form. A recent dinner started with thick, tasty mushroom soup, moved on to falling-off-the-bone-tender braised lamb shank Provençal and crispy round potato puffs, and ended with a flaky housemade apple tarte tatin. Have merci!

• Monterey Market

1550 Hopkins St./Monterey Ave., (510) 526-6042;
www.montereymarket.com. M-F 9-7, Sat 8:30-6.

This low-key, much-heralded produce market caters to the sophisticated Berkeley palate with an impressive assortment of produce, including tender baby vegetables, exotic melons, and wild mushrooms. The market also supplies the area's fine restaurants, and prices are unexpectedly low.

• Noah's Bagels

1883 Solano Ave./The Alameda, (510) 525-4447;
www.noahs.com. M-F 6am-5pm, Sat-Sun 6:30-4.

The very first Noah's store opened in nearby Emeryville. This branch was among the first in what has now become a very large chain. Promising "a taste of old New York," this shop delivers a bagel that is described by the founder as "crusty outside, chewy inside, tasty and big." They come in many varieties, including "super onion" and "multi-grain," and a selection of freshly made cream cheese "shmears" make the perfect topping. Bagel sandwiches are made to order, and plenty of supporting items and cold drinks are available. Noah says, "Protect your bagels . . . put lox on them!"

• **The Pasta Shop**

For description, see page 283.

• **Whole Foods Market**

*3000 Telegraph Ave./Ashby Ave., (510) 649-1333;
www.wholefoodsmarket.com. Daily 8am-10pm.*

This Texas-based natural foods retailer purveys an amazing selection of good-for-you foods, and its bakery, deli, and coffee bar offer the makings for a great picnic. Alternatively, some seating is available inside, more at sheltered tables outside. Special child-size shopping carts are fun for kids. In 2002, this was the national's first major food retailer, and the first in the chain, to go solar.

Pyramid Alehouse, Brewery & Restaurant

*901 Gilman St./6th St., (510) 528-9880;
www.pyramidbrew.com. L-D daily; $-$$. Reservations accepted.*

Situated within one gargantuan room, this massive, very noisy operation can still feel cozy for diners seated in one of the comfy, private booths. And for those in the mood to mingle, tables and chairs and high bar-tables abound. Fifteen beers are on tap, all brewed on the premises in huge vats visible from the dining room. Try the popular traditional Amber Lager, the Hefeweizen wheat beer served with a lemon wedge, or the Weizen Berry—Hefeweizen flavored with raspberry. Can't decide? Get a sampler. Light drinkers will like that single 4-ounce sample sizes can be ordered individually, too. The expansive, eclectic menu offers snacks, soups, pizzas, sandwiches, burgers, and salads, as well as heftier entrees of fish & chips, ribs, and assorted steaks. For dessert, be daring and order up an Espresso Stout float.

Brewery tours are given Monday through Friday at 5:30 p.m., and Saturday and Sunday at 4 p.m. On Saturday nights in summer, **movies** are screened outdoors in the parking lot.

Rick & Ann's

*2922 Domingo Ave./Ashby Ave., (510) 649-8538;
www.rickandanns.com. B-L daily, D W-Sun; $.
Reservations accepted for D.*

The extensive breakfast menu at this cozy neighborhood spot is served until 2:30 p.m. and features both the usual and the unusual—gingerbread waffles, hash prepared with beets, lacy corn cakes, French toast made with challah dipped in orange-cardamom batter. Superb

home fries are prepared using fresh potatoes and served topped with sour cream and chopped green onions. At lunch, hamburgers, salads, and a variety of sandwiches join the menu, and dinner brings on American classics such as meatloaf and macaroni and cheese. Good pie is available anytime. Banquettes along the wall, Shaker-style chairs, and tables with hammered metal tops lend a solid feeling. Kids get a coloring place mat and a basket of crayons to keep them occupied.

Skates

*100 Seawall Dr., at foot of University Ave.,
(510) 549-1900; www.skatesonthebay.com. L M-Sat,
D daily, SunBr; $$-$$$. Reservations advised.*

Window tables take best advantage of the stunning three-bridge view here. The extensive lunch menu offers a variety of soups, salads, and pastas, and the dinner menu features fresh fish items. Desserts are traditional and include a hot fudge sundae, a burnt-cream custard, and, in season, a giant strawberry shortcake.

Spenger's Fresh Fish Grotto

*1919 Fourth St./University Ave., (888) 344-6861,
(510) 845-7771; www.spengers.com. L-D daily;
$$-$$$. Reservations advised.*

Begun in 1890 as a country store, Spenger's evolved into a fish market and then morphed again after Prohibition into a bar and restaurant. Now part of the McCormick & Schmick seafood restaurant chain, it serves the very freshest fish flown in from everywhere. The menu changes daily and includes favorite classics as well as more unusual items. The restaurant remains one of Berkeley's most popular. Seating includes spacious wood booths in a warren of rooms decorated with everything sea-related—it's a veritable maritime museum. Don't miss viewing the extensive collection of model ships or the massive 34-carat Star of Denmark canary diamond once owned by Hawaii's Queen Kapiolani and now displayed in the Diamond Bar. A well-stocked fish market adjoins.

Tacubaya

*1788 Fourth St., (510) 525-5160; www.tacubaya.net.
B-L daily, D W-M; $. No reservations.*

In this vibrant spot featuring a high tin ceiling and bright walls in shades of red, pink, and mango, diners step up to the counter to order Mexican-style fast food. Among the delicious options: a sope de chorizo y papas (a fat masa cake topped with spicy Mexican sausage and potatoes); a vegetarian tamal de verduras (a vegetarian tamale topped with tangy tomatillo sauce); a shredded pork tamale topped with a complex mole; a chile relleno stuffed with cheese; chilaquiles (tortilla chips topped with chili, scrambled eggs, and cheese); and a hearty sopa de tortilla. Side dishes include elote (grilled corn on the cob) and papas con crema (potato and cheese fritters in poblano cream sauce). Conclude with a trio of churros (long, thin Mexican doughnuts). Everything is made in house, including handmade corn tortillas, and Niman Ranch meats are used in beef and pork dishes.

Taiwan

2071 University Ave./Shattuck Ave., (510) 845-1456. L-D daily; $. No reservations.

Taiwanese specialties and representative dishes from most of the Chinese provinces are served here. Portions are generous, and a vegetarian menu is available. Favorites include kuo teh (pot stickers), spinach with garlic, dry-braised green beans, vegetable chow fun, General Tsao's chicken, spicy fish-flavored chicken, beef a la Shangtung (deep-fried pieces of battered beef in a tasty sauce), showy sizzling beef and sizzling chicken platters, Mongolian beef, and spicy prawns. Exotic items include Taiwan pickle cabbage with pork tripe soup, boneless duck web, and numerous squid dishes. Beggar's chicken and Peking duck are available when ordered a day in advance. On weekends, a Chinese breakfast is available. The fortune cookies here are unusually prophetic. The strip inside mine once read, "You would make an excellent critic."

Top Dog

#1: 2534 Durant Ave./Telegraph Ave., (510) 843-5967; #2: 2503 Hearst Ave./Euclid Ave., (510) 843-1241; www.topdoghotdogs.com. L-D daily; $. No reservations.

Hot dogs are the extent of the menu at this atmospheric hole-in-the-wall. Twelve different kinds are available, including a veggie version. The most popular dog is the namesake kosher Top Dog. Topped off with sauerkraut and hot mustard, it's one of the best dogs on the West Coast. To dine, grab a counter stool or just stomp and chomp.

Udupi Palace

1901 University Ave./Martin Luther King Blvd., (510) 843-6600; www.udupipalaceca.com. L-D daily; $. Reservations accepted. No cards.

A cog in a chain that stretches to Toronto, Canada, this all-vegetarian cafe serves up the pancakes and other dishes that comprise South Indian cuisine. Thin, rolled, rice-flour crêpes known as dosas are especially good. They include a gargantuan paper dosa that measures almost 2 feet long and is filled with yellow split peas, a triangular mysore masala dosa filled with spicy potatoes, and a lacy rava masala dosa made with two kinds of onion and filled with potatoes. Uthappam are smaller and fatter— more like Western pancakes—and topped with various mixtures. Rice dishes, curries, and a daily special ten-item thali plate flesh out the focused menu.

VIK's Chaat Corner

726 Allston Way/4th St., (510) 644-4432; www.vikschaatcorner.com. L Tu-Sun, D Sat-Sun; $. No reservations.

Operating within a wide-open former garage-warehouse, this casual Indian cafe is described as reminiscent of a New Delhi bazaar. Eager diners line up to order at the counter and then volley for space at the charmless tables, and food is served unceremoniously on disposable plates with plastic utensils. Favorites among the deliciously spiced chaat, which translates as "small snacks," include: dahi pakori (cold lentil dumplings with tamarind chutney), sev puri (cold potatoes and onions with garlic chutney), samosa cholle (deep-fried potato-stuffed pastries served with spicy garbanzo curry), and the dramatic bhatura cholle (a huge puffy puri, also called "balloon bread," served with spicy garbanzos and onion chutney). A dosa and both a meat and a vegetarian curry plate complete with rice and bread are also available; on weekends more delights join the options. Drinks include a delicious creamy mango lassi and a thick guava nectar, and for dessert Indian sweets can be selected from a glass case.

Next door, a related grocery sells exotic Indian cooking staples.

CROCKETT

A LITTLE BACKGROUND

Famous for its antiques shops, this small town is situated on a scenic knoll overlooking the Carquinez Bridge and bay.

VISITOR INFORMATION

Crockett Chamber of Commerce
1214 A Pomona St., (510) 787-1155; www.crockettca-chamber.org.

WHERE TO EAT

The Nantucket
At foot of Port St., (Pomona St. exit off I-80), (510) 787-2233. L-D daily; $$. Reservations advised.

Situated at the end of a twisting road under the Carquinez Bridge, on the other side of the tracks, this unpretentious restaurant specializes in New England-style fresh fish items. Most are available either charcoal-broiled or pan-fried. Favorites are lightly breaded shellfish, deep-fried Cape Cod-style. Shellfish cioppino, a house specialty, is prepared either old-fashioned style (in the shell) or lazy man's style (out of the shell). Lobster and steak comprise the higher-priced end of the menu. All dinners come with a choice of either creamy white clam chowder or a green salad, garlic French bread, a fresh vegetable, and a choice of baked potato, french fries, or seasoned rice. At lunch it's hard to beat the crab cake sandwich with housemade potato chips. All tables have a water view.

Should there be a wait, drinks and seafood appetizers can be ordered from the bar and enjoyed either indoors or out on the pier.

Crockett is the major center for sugar production on the West Coast. Driving back to the freeway, the large red brick building seen to the east is the circa 1906 C&H Sugar refinery.

BENICIA

A LITTLE BACKGROUND

Founded in 1847 by General Vallejo and named for his bride, this low-key town was the state capital for a short time in 1853. Situated on the Carquinez Strait, about 30 miles northeast of San Francisco, it was also a very busy port.

Now it is known for its many antiques shops (located along First Street) and the **Benicia Glass Studios** consortium of glass-blowing factories *(675 & 701 E. H St., (707) 745-2614; www.beniciaglassstudios.com. M-Sat 10-4, Sun 12-5. Free.).* Note that many town shops are closed on Mondays and Tuesdays.

VISITOR INFORMATION

Benicia Chamber of Commerce and Visitor's Center
601 First St., (800) 559-7377, (707) 745-2120; www.beniciachamber.com.

GETTING THERE

Located about 35 miles from San Francisco, and 7 miles east of Vallejo via I-780.

WHAT TO DO

Benicia Capitol State Historic Park
115 W. G St., (707) 745-3385; www.parks.ca.gov. Daily 10-5. $2, 6-12 $1.

Historic information, artifacts, and period furniture await visitors inside this restored 2-story, red brick Greek Revival building that served as the state capitol from February 4, 1853 to February 25, 1854.

Also in the park is the 1858 Federal-style Victorian **Fischer-Hanlon House,** a renovated Gold Rush hotel. It holds an impressive collection of period furniture, and tours are sometimes available.

WHERE TO STAY & EAT

The Union Hotel

401 First St., (866) 445-2323, (707) 746-0110;
www.unionhotelbenicia.com. 12 rooms; $$.
Full breakfast Sat-Sun; restaurant.

Located right on the main street, in the part of town reflecting the ambiance of a quieter era, this 1885 Victorian hotel offers individually decorated rooms furnished with period antiques.

For dinner, hotel guests need just catch the elevator down to the **restaurant** *((707) 746-7847. L-D daily, Sat-SunBr. Reservations advised.).* For a relaxing after-dinner drink, it's just a few steps over to a cozy **lounge** with an impressive 110-year-old mahogany bar and stained-glass windows.

VALLEJO

VISITOR INFORMATION

Vallejo Convention & Visitors Bureau

289 Mare Island Way, (800) 4-VALLEJO,
(707) 642-3653; www.visitvallejo.com.

This bureau also provides information on Benicia.

GETTING THERE

Located 30 miles northeast of San Francisco.

WHAT TO DO

Mare Island Historic Park

(707) 557-1538; www.mareislandhpf.org. Tour:
(707) 280-5742; by donation, $14, 6-12 $5;
reservations required.

Historic Mare Island, the West Coast's first Naval base and shipyard, was founded in 1854 to fend off pirates who were then roaming the local seas. Interestingly, it is named after a female horse that swam to the island. Over a period of 142 years, 513 ships were built here. The base also launched 17 nuclear submarines, and the movie *Sphere*—starring Sharon Stone—was filmed here. The 3-hour tour includes seeing world-famous **St. Peter's Chapel**, built in 1901 and featuring beautiful Tiffany stained-glass windows and an inverted-keel redwood ceiling (it was the Navy's first inter-denominational chapel); the historic cemetery (burial place of Anna Turner, daughter of Francis Scott Key); Officer's Row mansions and gardens; and an 1855 building and a World War II gunboat that both serve as museums. The tour also visits Alden Park, which is home to a cannon from the War of 1812, torpedoes from the Civil War, and a German Marder suicide submarine from 1944.

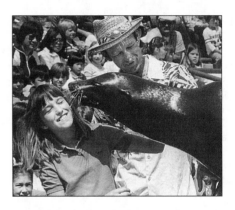

Six Flags Discovery Kingdom

1001 Fairgrounds Dr./Hwy. 37, (707) 643-6722;
www.sixflags.com/discoverykingdom. F-Sun spring &
fall, daily in summer, some weekends in winter; opens
at 10:30, closing time varies. $49.99, children 48" tall
& under $29.99; parking $15.

Just a few years ago, this theme park completely reinvented itself by adding rides to its world-famous collection of wildlife shows. It is now the nation's only combination wildlife park/oceanarium/theme park. The exciting animal shows feature a killer whale, dolphins, sea lions, tigers, and exotic birds. Visitors can walk through animal habitat areas to see African animals and ride an Asian elephant *($10)*. The Looney Tunes Acme Foam Factory—with slides and climbing structures and hundreds of orange foam balls for kids to toss or shoot from air cannons—is particularly popular with young children. The walk-through Butterfly Habitat is a free-flight butterfly enclosure, and the walk-in Lorikeet Aviary provides up-close observation of these brightly colored birds and the opportunity to feed them. Now adding thrills to the mix are eight roller coasters and an assortment of other wild rides.

Consider taking the ferry from San Francisco—the **Blue & Gold Fleet** *((415) 705-5555; www.blueandgoldfleet.com.)* departs from Pier 39—or **BART** *((415) 992-2278; www.bart.gov; runs M-Sat.).*

Vallejo Naval and Historical Museum
734 Marin St./Virginia St., (707) 643-0077; www.vallejomuseum.org. Tu-Sat 10-4:30. $3, seniors $2, under 12 free.

Operating inside the town's former City Hall, this museum's treasures include a working submarine periscope that pokes through the roof and provides a view of Mare Island.

FAIRFIELD

WHAT TO DO

Anheuser-Busch Brewery Tour
3101 Busch Dr., (707) 429-7595; www.budweisertours.com. Tu-Sat 10-4, on the hr., Sept-May; also M June-Aug. Free.

The tour here starts with a short video explaining how a Bud is made. Then visitors don plastic safety glasses and head out to see the beer bottled and capped—or canned—and then boxed. Back in the Hospitality Room everyone gets free samples and snacks. All ages are welcome.

Jelly Belly Candy Company
One Jelly Belly Lane, Abernathy Rd. east exit off I-80, (800) 953-5592, (707) 428-2838; www.jellybelly.com. Tour: Daily 9-4; free.

Family-run since 1898, this company has been making candy corn since around 1900 and the famous, flavorful Jelly Belly® jelly bean since 1976. After taking the 40-minute Candyland factory tour, everyone gets a souvenir bag of the company's jelly beans. No reservations are needed. Note that though tours are given daily, workers are off on weekends so the factory isn't operating. The gift shop sells Belly Flops (rejects) at bargain prices when available, and an exhibition candy kitchen lets visitors view the making of an array of sweets (the company makes more than 100 other kinds of candy). A cafe offers Jelly Belly-shaped pizzas and hamburgers, and a picnic area and dog walk are also available.

Western Railway Museum
5848 Hwy. 12, in Suisun City, betw.Fairfield & Rio Vista (exit Hwy. 80 at Hwy. 12, then drive 12 mi. E), (707) 374-2978; www.wrm.org. Sat-Sun 10:30-5; W-Sun in summer. $8, 65+ $7, 2-14 $5.

Located between two sheep pastures in the middle of a flat, arid no-man's land, this very

special museum displays and actually operates its collection of historic electric streetcars and interurban trains. Among the dozen or so operating electric cars are both a bright red car from the Peninsular Railway and an articulated car, which is hinged so it can go around corners and which ran on the Bay Bridge from 1939 to 1958. Several cars operate each weekend, running along a 10-mile stretch of track with overhead electric trolley wires. Cars are operated by the same volunteers who spent countless hours lovingly restoring them. Stationary cars awaiting repair can be viewed in several large barns. An oasis-like picnic and play area is available to visitors, and a bookstore offers a large collection of railroad books and paraphernalia. All fees collected are used to restore and maintain the streetcars. (It costs about $170,000 to restore a car and, because the labor is volunteer, it can take as long as 10 years!)

The museum also operates theme trains over the Sacramento Northern Railway, and Pumpkin Patch Trains run at Halloween.

SACRAMENTO

A LITTLE BACKGROUND

It is fiery summer always, and you can gather roses, and eat strawberries and ice-cream, and wear white linen clothes, and pant and perspire at eight or nine o'clock in the morning.

—Mark Twain

Gold was discovered in 1848 just 30 miles east of Sacramento, and the rest is history. As news of the discovery spread like wildfire around the globe, fortune hunters came here before setting out for the mining fields. Sacramento has been the state capital since 1854. In 1866, Mark Twain was a special news correspondent with the *Sacramento Union Newspaper*.

Most major historic attractions are concentrated in the downtown area. This flat, central part of the city was laid out in a grid of lettered and numbered streets by town founder John Sutter's son, John Sutter, Jr., making it easy to get around even now.

As in New York City, the streets here are almost empty on Sunday, and they are relatively quiet on Saturday. So, surprisingly, on weekends it is a great destination for avoiding crowds.

VISITOR INFORMATION

Sacramento Convention & Visitors Bureau
1608 I St., (800) 292-2334, (916) 808-7777; www.discovergold.org.

GETTING THERE

Located approximately 90 miles northeast of San Francisco.

Alternatively, take the scenic route via Highway 160 through the Delta (see page 399).

Also, **Amtrak Capitol Corridor trains** *((877) 974-3322; www.amtrakcapitols.com.)* leave for Sacramento daily from San Jose, San Francisco (via bus connection to Oakland), and Oakland. Family fares are available. Overnight train-hotel packages can be booked through **Amtrak Vacations** *((800) 268-7252; www.amtrakvacations.com.).*

ANNUAL EVENTS

Sacramento Jazz Jubilee
May; Memorial Day weekend. (916) 372-5277; www.sacjazz.com. $9-$40.

This is the world's largest traditional jazz festival. Styles include zydeco, blues, Latin jazz, Western swing, and gospel.

Raging Waters Sacramento
Mid-May to mid-September. 1600 Exposition Blvd., (916) 924-3747; www.ragingwaters.com. Daily 10:30-6. Over 4' tall $24.99, under 4' $19.99, 60+ $12.99, under age 2 free; parking $8.

Located adjacent to the state fair site, this attraction features the largest wave pool in Northern California, the highest waterslides in the West, and an assortment of other attractions.

California State Fair
August. 1600 Exposition Blvd.; (877) CAL-EXPO, (916) 263-FAIR; www.bigfun.org. $10, 62+ $8, 5-12 $6; parking $8.

There's something for everyone at the oldest state fair in the West, which is also the largest agricultural fair in the U.S. Pleasures include monorail and carnival rides, a free concert series, thoroughbred racing, educational exhibits, and live entertainment. Special for children are a petting farm, pony rides, and a livestock nursery where baby animals are born each day.

WHAT TO DO

American River Parkway
(916) 875-6672; www.sacparks.net. Daily sunrise-sunset. $5/vehicle.

This is 23 miles of water fun. Call for a free map and more information about facilities.

• Effie Yeaw Nature Center
Tarshes Dr./San Lorenzo Way, in Ancil Hoffman County Park, in Carmichael, (916) 489-4918; www.effieyeaw.org. Daily 9-5, Mar-Oct; 9:30-4, Nov-Feb. Free.

Displays and hands-on exhibits bring the area's natural and cultural history to life. The center includes a Maidu Indian Village and a 77-acre nature preserve with three self-guided nature trails.

• Fishing
The best month for salmon and steelhead is October. Favorite spots are the Nimbus Basin below the dam and Sailor Bar. A state license in required.

• Jedediah Smith National Recreation Trail
This 35-mile paved pathway runs along the American River from Old Sacramento to Folsom.

• Raft trips
Trips begin in the Upper Sunrise Recreation Area, located north of the Sunrise Boulevard exit off Highway 50. In summer, several companies rent rafts and provide shuttle bus return.

Bridges
Located near Old Sacramento, the Tower Bridge—a lift span drawbridge—sometimes can be observed going up. To the right of it, the I Street Bridge is one of the few remaining pedestrian bridges in the country; sometimes it can be observed turning.

The B Street Theatre
2711 B St./27th St., (916) 443-5300; www.bstreet theatre.org. Schedule varies. $17.50-$21.50.

Founded by actor Timothy Busfield—who starred in TV's memorable *Thirty-Something*—

Tower Bridge

and his brother Buck, this small non-profit professional theater company presents several world premieres each year. Everything is in place for a satisfying night of theater. The theater is small, and seating in the round means performances are in-your-face intimate. The audience is close enough to the actors to see their warts, wrinkles, and other human imperfections.

An offshoot, the **Street Theatre Family Series**, presents professional performances for family audiences.

California Museum for History, Women and the Arts
1020 O St./10th St., (916) 653-7524; www.californiamuseum.org. Tu-Sat 10-5, Sun 12-5. $7.50, 55+ $6, 6-13 $5.

This museum occupies the first two floors of the California State Archives building. Before leaving, visit the 6-story-tall interior courtyard sculpture known as "Constitution Wall."

California State Capitol tour
10th St./L St., (916) 324-0333; www.capitol museum.ca.gov. Tour on the hr., daily 9-4. Free.

Restored now to its turn-of-the-century decor and made earthquake-safe—a job that cost $68 million and was the largest restoration project in the history of the country—the Capitol is quite a showcase. Sign up for a tour upon arrival.

A short-order **cafeteria** operates in the basement, and a full-service **cafe** is open weekdays on the sixth floor.

The surrounding park is the largest **arboretum** west of the Mississippi and home to more than 300 varieties of trees and flowers from all over the world, as well as to one of the largest camellia groves in the world. The circular **California Vietnam Veteran's Memorial** *(15th St./Capitol Ave.)* is located by the rose garden at the park's east end. The 22 shiny black granite panels of this privately funded monument are engraved with the 5,822 names of California's dead and missing. The **International World Peace Rose Garden** *((800) 205-1223; www.worldpeacegardens.org.)* here displays more than 800 roses.

Crocker Art Museum
216 O St./3rd St., (916) 808-7000; www.crockerart museum.org. Tu-Sun 10-5, 1st & 3rd Thur to 9. $6, 65+ $4, 7-17 3.

Founded in 1885 and situated within a magnificent Italianate building dating from 1874, this is the oldest public art museum west of the Mississippi. Collection highlights include Master drawings, 19th-century American and European paintings, and contemporary Northern California art in all media. The California Gallery is hung Salon-style, with painting squeezed together, as the Victorian-era Crocker family originally hung their entire collection. Family activities occur every weekend, and Sunday afternoon concerts are often scheduled. The museum is scheduled to close in 2010 for new construction.

Picnic tables are available across the street in lovely **Crocker Park**.

Governor's Mansion State Historic Park
1526 H St./16th St., (916) 323-3047; www.parks. ca.gov. Tours: Daily 10-4, on the hr.; $4, 6-17 $2.

This 30-room 1877 Victorian mansion was purchased by the state in 1903 for $32,500. During the next 64 years, it was home to 13 governors and their families. It remains just as it was when vacated by its last tenant— Governor Ronald Reagan. Now serving the public as a museum, it displays 15 rooms of furnishings and personal items left behind by each family. Visitors see Governor George Pardee's 1902 Steinway piano, Earl Warren's hand-tied Persian carpets, and Hiram Johnson's plum velvet sofa and chairs. Among the interesting artifacts are marble fireplaces from Italy

and gold-framed mirrors from France. The official State of California china, selected by the wife of Goodwin Knight in the late 1950s, also is on display.

Old Sacramento Historic District
Situated along the Sacramento River, Old Sacramento was the kickoff point for the gold fields during the Gold Rush. It was the western terminus for both the Pony Express and the country's first long distance telegraph, and the country's first transcontinental railroad started here. Said to be the largest historic preservation project in the West, Old Sacramento is a 28-acre living museum of the Old West. Vintage buildings, wooden walkways, and cobblestone streets recall the period from 1850 to 1880. Restaurants, shops, and historic exhibits combine to make it both an entertaining and educational spot to visit.

Information on tours can be obtained at the **Visitor Information Center** *(1004 2nd St./ J St., (916) 442-7644; www.oldsacramento.com. Daily 10-5.).* **Horse-drawn carriages** can be hired for rides from Old Sacramento to the Capitol.

• California State Railroad Museum
111 I St./2nd St., (916) 445-6645; www.csrmf.org. Daily 10-5. $4, under 17 free; ticket good on same day for Central Pacific Passenger Depot.

This gigantic 3-story building holds the largest interpretive railroad museum in North America. Inside, 21 beautifully restored, full-size railroad locomotives and cars representing the 1860s through the 1960s are on display. Among them are an apartment-size, lushly furnished Georgia Northern private car complete with stained-glass windows, and a Canadian Pullman rigged to feel as if it is actually moving. A film, a 30-projector multi-image slide show, and assorted interpretive displays tell the history of American railroading. Docent-led tours are available, and well-trained, railroad-loving volunteers, wearing historically authentic railroad workers' garb, are always on hand to answer questions. Upstairs, great views of the trains below are afforded from an oversize catwalk. A large collection of toy trains—including a 1957 pastel pink Lionel train designed especially for little girls—is also displayed.

Nearby, the **Central Pacific Passenger Depot** *(930 Front St./J St. Free audio tour wand.)* displays nine more locomotives and cars. Visiting this reconstructed train depot provides the opportunity to step back in time to 1876—an era when riding the train was the chic way to travel. The **Sacramento Southern Railroad** excursion steam train departs from the depot for a 6-mile, 40-minute round-trip *(Sat-Sun 11-5, on the hr.; Apr-Sept only. $6, 6-12 $3.).*

• **Discovery Museum History Center**
101 I St., (916) 264-7057; www.thediscovery.org. Tu-Sun 10-5; daily July-Aug. $5, 60+ & 13-17 $4, 4-12 $3.

This 3-story brick building is a replica of Sacramento's first public building—the 1854 City Hall. The museum brings Sacramento's history and the 1849 Gold Rush to life with an extensive collection of gold specimens worth more than $1 million, historical photos, and historic farm equipment. Among the exhibits are a replica mineshaft and an antique poultry incubator.

The nearby **Discovery Museum Science & Space Center** *(3615 Auburn Blvd., just E of Watt Ave., (916) 575-3941. Tu-F 12-5, Sat-Sun 10-5; daily 10-5, July-Aug. $5, 60+ & 13-17 $4, 4-12 $3.)* has the area's only planetarium, plus live animals and a nature trail.

• **Eagle Theatre**
925 Front St./J St., (916) 323-6343; www.csrmf.org. Performances sometimes presented. Tour: Schedule varies; free.

A reconstruction of California's first theater building built in 1849, the Eagle now occasionally presents Gold Rush-era plays and musicals. Children's programs are also sometimes scheduled.

• **Old Sacramento Schoolhouse**
1200 Front St./L St., (916) 482-6675; www.oldsac schoolhouse.org. M-F 10-4, Sat-Sun 1-4. Free.

Now a museum, this 1800s one-room schoolhouse has a play yard with old-fashioned board swings that kids can still use.

State Indian Museum State Historic Park
2618 K St./26th St., (916) 324-0971; www.parks.ca. gov/indianmuseum. Daily 10-5. $2, 6-17 $1.

Established in 1940, this museum displays the basketry, beadwork, and dance regalia of various California Native American groups. Examples include everything from a 1-centimeter basket to an 18-foot redwood canoe. Picnicking is particularly pleasant beside a duck pond across from the museum.

Sutter's Fort State Historic Park
2701 L St./27th St., (916) 445-4422; www.parks.ca.gov. Daily 10-5. $4-$6, under 17 $2-$3; includes audio tour.

A reconstruction of the settlement founded in 1839 by Captain John A. Sutter—who originally arrived with 10 Hawaiians and lived in a grass hut built by them out native grasses—this is the first permanent interior settlement built in California and the oldest restored fort in the West. The central building is the original built by Sutter and Native Americans. Exhibits include carpenter, cooper, and blacksmith shops as well as prison and living quarters.

On Living History Days, demonstrators stay in character for 1846: The man portraying James Marshall, who was a carpenter before he discovered gold, might be working on wood projects and will look startled if asked about gold since it wasn't discovered in this part of California until 1848. Blacksmithing, musket and cannon demos, and military drills are also part of the show. For monthly Pioneer Demonstration Days, interpreters dress in character but recognize that it is 2002. Then, visitors can participate in some of the crafts, including rope-making, cornhusk doll-making, basketry, and baking. In summer, interpreters dress in period garb, demonstrate crafts, and give historical information daily. As part of the Environmental Living program, school groups take over the fort on Tuesday and Thursday from November through June, dressing in period clothing and doing demonstrations.

Towe Auto Museum
2200 Front St./V St., (916) 442-6802; www.towe automuseum.org. Daily 10-6. $7, 65+ $6, 5-18 $3.

This cavernous museum displays more than 160 vehicles that depict the history of the American automobile. In addition to the cars, the museum displays a Mighty Wurlitzer Theater Pipe Organ with more than 1,000 pipes (it was originally owned by director Cecile B. DeMille). Call for directions; this museum can be difficult to find.

Victorian houses
Elaborate Victorian homes are found between 7th and 16th streets, from E to I streets. Don't miss the Heilbron house at 740 O Street and the Stanford house at 800 N Street.

William Land Park
On Freeport Blvd. betw. 13th Ave. & Sutterville Rd., (916) 277-6060.

This 236-acre park has a playground, amphitheater, several ball fields, picnic areas,

gardens, a 9-hole golf course, and a fishing pond. It also incorporates:

• Fairytale Town
3901 Land Park Dr., (916) 264-5233; www.fairytale town.org. Schedule varies. $3.75-$4.50, under 3 free.

Nursery rhymes and fairy tales come to life in this 2½-acre amusement park.

• Funderland
1350 17th Ave., Sutterville Rd./S. Land Park Dr., (916) 456-0115; www.funderlandpark.com. Schedule varies; closed Dec-Jan. $1.50-$1.75/ride.

In operation since 1948, this old-fashioned amusement park for young children delights them with an assortment of rides. Pony rides are available adjacent.

• Sacramento Zoo
3930 W. Land Park Dr./Sutterville Rd., (916) 808-5888; www.saczoo.com. Daily 9-4; Nov-Jan 10-4. $8.50-$9, 3-12 $6.50.

Open since 1927, this small 15-acre zoo is home to more than 140 native, rare, and endangered species. It holds enough exhibits to keep visitors busy for a pleasant few hours, and safari wagons can be rented for toting children.

WHERE TO STAY

Motels abound. Call a favorite chain for reservations, or contact the Convention & Visitors Bureau for a list of lodgings.

Delta King
1000 Front St., in Old Sacramento, (800) 825-KING, (916) 444-KING; www.deltaking.com. 5 stories; 44 rooms; $$. Restaurant. No pets. Valet parking $12.

Launched in 1927, this flat-bottomed riverboat plied the waters between Sacramento and San Francisco in the late 1920s and '30s. After having spent 15 months partially submerged in the San Francisco Bay, she received years of restoration work costing $9.5 million and is now appropriately moored dockside in Old Sacramento. All guest rooms have private bathrooms with an old-fashioned pedestal sink and high-tank toilet with pull-chain, and a few have clawfoot tubs. The vessel's wheelhouse guest room has a private second-story observation deck.

An elegant dinner with a river view can be enjoyed in the **Pilothouse Restaurant** *((916) 441-4440. L M-Sat, D daily, SunBr. Reservations* *advised.)* on the Promenade Deck. Entrees include luxury items such as prawns, steak, and rack of lamb, and a well-executed Caesar salad is dramatically prepared tableside. A grand piano entertains most evenings in a cozy lounge-style bar adjoining the restaurant.

Live performances are scheduled Thursday through Sunday down on the Cargo Deck in the intimate **Delta King Theatre**.

Hyatt Regency Sacramento
1209 L St./12th St., (800) HYATT-CA, (916) 443-1234; www.sacramento.hyatt.com. 15 stories, 503 rooms; $$-$$$+. Heated pool; hot tub; fitness room. 2 restaurants; room service. No pets. Self-parking $15, valet $18.

Situated across the street from the Capitol and adjacent to both the convention center and the pedestrian K Street Mall, this well-located luxury hotel features a Mediterranean architectural style, an atrium lobby, and marble floors. A charming topiary hedge fence in the shape of people and animals defines its front entrance.

KOA Kampground
3951 Lake Rd., in West Sacramento, (800) KOA-2747, (916) 371-6771; www.koa.com.

For description, see page 467.

Radisson Hotel Sacramento
500 Leisure Ln., (800) 333-3333, (916) 922-2020; www.radisson.com/sacramentoca. 306 rooms; $-$$$. Unheated pool; hot tub; fitness room. Restaurant; room service.

Located on the outskirts of downtown, about 2 miles from the capitol, this low-rise hotel complex operates much like a vacation resort. Rooms are spacious and comfortable, and some overlook a natural spring-fed lake and koi pond. On weekends throughout the summer, jazz and rock performances are scheduled in the property's own amphitheater and are free to guests. Bicycle rentals are available for rides along the scenic Jedediah Smith bike trail, which runs along the American River Parkway adjacent to the hotel. A courtesy shuttle takes guests to the grand, indoor Arden Fair Shopping Mall located nearby.

Sacramento Hostel
925 H St./10th St., (800) 909-4776 #40, (916) 443-1691; www.sacramentohostel.org. 80 beds; 5 private rooms.

Operating within a restored 1885 Victorian mansion, this jewel is centrally located on Merchant's Row and convenient to major attractions. It features a drawing room, recreation room, wraparound porch, patio with barbecue, and gardens. See also page 468.

WHERE TO EAT

Buca di Beppo
1249 Howe Ave./Hurley Way, (916) 92-AMORE; www.bucadibeppo.com. L-D dailly.

For description, see page 63.

Fanny Ann's Saloon
1023 2nd St., in Old Sacramento, (916) 441-0505; www.fannyanns.com. L-D daily; $. No reservations.

This narrow, four-level restaurant has a raucous ambiance and funky decor that provide the makings for instant fun. Children and adults alike enjoy the casual atmosphere and American-style fare: good half-pound hamburgers, assorted styles of 9-inch hot dogs, curly french fries, and large bowls of housemade soup. A variety of sandwiches and salads are also available. After placing orders with the cook at the back window, diners can relax with a game of pinball or get a downright cheap drink at the old bar. When one mother inquired whether there were booster seats, the cheerful hostess replied, "I'll hold the kids on my lap."

Fat City Bar & Grill
1001 Front St., in Old Sacramento, (916) 446-6768; www.fatsrestaurants.com/fatcity. L M-F, D daily, Sat-SunBr; $$. No reservations.

This high-ceilinged brick building was constructed around 1849 by Samuel Brannan as a general merchandise store. It was the first store established after the City of Sacramento was laid out. Now it holds a popular restaurant featuring Tiffany-style lamps, stained-glass windows, and Victorian-style furnishings. Delicious specialty drinks are served at an ornate old mahogany bar, or with meals at dining tables overlooking sidewalk traffic. Appetizers such as Southern fried chicken strips and French onion soup are on the menu along with a variety of pasta dishes and hamburgers. Old-fashioned desserts such as strawberry shortcake and hot fudge sundaes wind things up.

Fox & Goose Public House

1001 R St./10th St., (916) 443-8825;
www.foxand goose.com. B daily, L M-F, D M-Sat; $.
No reservations.

Located within a 1913 building that was
once the Fuller Paint and Glass Company, this
English-style pub features high ceilings, rustic
unfinished floors, multi-paned windows, and
roomy booths. Breakfast doesn't get any better.
The menu then offers British-style grilled tomatoes, bangers, and crumpets, as well as
American standards and a large variety of
omelettes. Many items are prepared on the
premises—granola, scones, muffins—and free-
range chicken eggs are available. Lunch items
include Cornish pasties, Welsh rarebit, English
tea sandwiches, and a classic ploughman's plate,
plus desserts of rich burnt cream custard and
layered trifle. Live music is scheduled most
evenings, when pub grub is served until 9:30.
Over 15 English and Irish beers are on tap, and
a good selection of California wines is available.

Hard Rock Cafe

7th St./K St., #545 in Downtown Plaza,
(916) 441-5591; www.hardrock.com. L-D daily.

For description, see page 72.

The Old Spaghetti Factory

1910 J St., near Old Sacramento, (916) 443-2862;
www.osf.com. L M-F, D daily.

Located within a former Western Pacific
Depot outside the main tourist area, this is a
link in the popular noodle chain. For more
description, see page 199.

Pyramid Alehouse, Brewery & Restaurant

1029 K St., downtown, (916) 498-9800;
www.pyramidbrew.com. L-D daily.

For description, see page 296.

The Virgin Sturgeon

1577 Garden Hwy., (916) 921-2694. B Sat-Sun, L M-F,
D daily; $-$$. No reservations.

This funky, often raucous spot is reached
via a recycled San Francisco airport jetway. It's
popular with politicians and "river rats" (people
with boats). Situated atop a floating former
cargo barge, it has outdoor deck seating overlooking the placid Sacramento River—a great
idea in warm weather—as well as cozy interior
seating and is famous for serving great Cuban

black beans and rice, steamed clams, fresh fish,
barbecued pork ribs, and mushroom cheese-
burgers. Several other wildly popular river
restaurants are on this highway.

TRUCKEE

A LITTLE BACKGROUND

Much of the original architecture in this old
mining town is well preserved, and many shops
and restaurants on the main street operate
within interesting, sometimes beautifully
restored, historic buildings. The town's yellow
Victorian Southern Pacific Depot dates from
1896 and is now the Amtrak and Greyhound
station as well as the Visitors Center.

VISITOR INFORMATION

Truckee Donner Chamber of Commerce and Visitor Information Center

10065 Donner Pass Rd., in the train depot,
(530) 587-2757; www.truckee.com.

GETTING THERE

Located approximately 185 miles northeast of
San Francisco, and 100 miles northeast of
Sacramento. Located approximately 11 miles
northwest of North Lake Tahoe via
Highway 267.

WHAT TO DO

Donner Memorial State Park

12593 Donner Pass Rd., off Hwy. 40, 2 mi. W of town,
(530) 582-7892; www.parks.ca.gov. Daily 8-dusk.
$6/vehicle. Museum: Daily 9-4; $3, 6-16 $1.

Located on Donner Lake, this park is a
monument to the tragic Donner Party stranded
here by blizzards in 1846. Picnic facilities, lake
swimming, hiking trails, nature programs, and
campsites (June through September only) are
available.

The **Emigrant Trail Museum** features
exhibits on the area's history, including a video
telling the Donner Party story and also the very
Hawken rifle that William Eddy used in 1846 to
kill an 800-pound grizzly bear.

WHERE TO STAY

The Truckee Hotel

10007 Bridge St., (800) 659-6921, (530) 587-4444;
www.thetruckeehotel.com. 4 stories; 37 rooms; $-$$.
Some TVs; some shared baths. Continental breakfast.
No pets.

Originally built as a stagecoach stop in
1868, this beautifully renovated Victorian offers
stylish period lodging.

Moody's Bistro and Lounge *((530) 587-*
8688; www.moodysbistro.com. L-D daily, Sat-
SunBr; $$. Reservations advised.) is known for
good food, good music, and occasional great
surprises: In 2004, Paul McCartney stopped in
as a customer and sang a few tunes with the
jazz trio. Live jazz is scheduled Wednesday
through Saturday.

WHERE TO EAT

Squeeze In

10060 Donner Pass Rd., (530) 587-9814;
www.squeezein.com. B-L daily; $. No reservations.

At breakfast in this long, narrow cafe,
diners have a choice of 63 kinds of omelettes—
everything from peanut butter to chicken liver.
At lunch, the Squeezeburger is the best, though
some say the Squeeze with Cheese is even
better. A variety of other breakfast items and
sandwiches are also on the menu. Outside seat-
ing at picnic tables is available in good weather.

PLUMAS COUNTY

A LITTLE BACKGROUND

Boasting an abundance of national forest land,
this area is noted for its outdoor recreation.
Visitors can fish, ride horses, take pack trips,
hike, camp, ride bikes, white water raft, kayak,
and golf (on 11 courses, including Whitehawk
Ranch—the only course in the country that
permits players to wear jeans). Bird-watching is
prime on man-made Lake Davis, where camp-
sites are available, and wildlife spotting is
generally good throughout the area. The **Lakes
Basin Recreation Area**, a former gold mining
hideaway, now offers all the sports mentioned
above plus historic lodgings. More than
30 natural mountain lakes are hidden in this

remote, unspoiled terrain located within the
Plumas National Forest.

North of old-time **Wiggin's Trading Post**
(In Chilcoot, (530) 993-4721), where everything
from worms to Daniel Boone fur hats are for
sale, Frenchman Lake is reached via a scenic
drive through Little Last Chance Creek canyon
and its unique geological formations of volcanic
rock. The lake is known for giving up trophy
trout.

The main drag in the charming town of
Graeagle is lined with red cottages that were
once the homes of lumber mill workers and
now are converted into unique shops. It is one
of the area's larger towns and a convenient spot
to settle in for a visit. The town's Mill Pond has
paddleboat and kayak rentals.

VISITOR INFORMATION

Eastern Plumas Chamber of Commerce

8989 Hwy. 89, in Blairsden, (800) 995-6057,
(530) 836-6811; www.easternplumaschamber.com.

Plumas County Visitors Bureau

550 Crescent St., in Quincy, (800) 326-2247,
(530) 283-6345; www.plumascounty.org.

GETTING THERE

Follow Highway 89 north for 50 miles into
Graeagle. This route passes through the Sierra
Valley, which is the largest alpine valley in
North America and which has scenery varying
from conifer and aspen forests to pastures and
wildflowers. Alternatively, travel here via
Highway 5, to Highway 99, to Highway 70, fol-
lowing Highway 70 to north of Oroville and
then along the 130-mile Feather River National
Scenic Byway through the spectacular Feather
River Canyon, and on to Hallelujah Junction at
Highway 395, just east of Chilcoot. The route
crosses vintage railroad bridges and passes
through tunnels. This area is 240 miles north-
east of San Francisco.

ANNUAL EVENTS

Mohawk Valley Independence Day Celebration

July. In Graeagle; (800) 326-2247;
www.graeagle.com/events.

Festivities include a small parade with marching bands and bagpipers, fireworks over the town pond, a pancake breakfast, live music in the park, and dancing in the streets.

Railroad Days
August. In Portola; (800) 326-2247; www.portolarailroaddays.com.

This festive event celebrates the railroad, mining, and logging industries that shaped Portola's past. Train rides, music, arts and crafts, and kids' activities are part of the fun.

Fall Colors
October-November. (800) 326-2247; www.plumascounty.org.

Call for a free fall colors brochure, for best routes, and for daily peak color reports.

WHAT TO DO

Graeagle Stables/Reid Horse & Cattle Co.
On Hwy. 89, in Graeagle, (530) 836-0430; www.reidhorse.com. June-Oct only. $34/1 hr.

In addition to trail rides, pack trips can be arranged *((530) 283-1147)*. Stables are also located at Gold Lake and Bucks Lake.

Jim Beckwourth Museum
2180 Rocky Point Rd., E of Portola, (800) 326-2247. Sat-Sun 1-4, summer only. Free.

Also known as the Beckwourth Cabin, this refurbished 1850s log cabin was once a trading post and hotel. It now honors African-American frontiersman James P. Beckwourth, who discovered in 1851 the lowest pass through the Sierra Nevada. The trail named for him begins in Reno, runs through this area, and ends in Oroville.

Charming cottage shop in Graeagle

Plumas-Eureka State Park and Museum
310 Johnsville Rd., 5 mi. W of Graeagle, (530) 836-2380; www.parks.ca.gov. Daily 9-4, summer only. Free.

Situated on the site of one of the region's largest quartz-mining operations, the museum here is located in a former bunkhouse. It features an exhibit on longboard ski racing, which originated nearby, and displays a majestic stuffed golden eagle and a ceramic foot warmer. An outdoor complex includes a restored stamp mill, miner's home, blacksmith shop, and assayer's office. During summer, supervised gold-panning and a Junior Ranger Program (see page 468) are offered. Picnic tables, campsites, and ranger programs are available.

In July, **Gold Discovery Days** features costumed docents and hands-on pioneer activities.

Western Pacific Railroad Museum
700 Western Pacific Way, off Commercial St., in Portola, (530) 832-4131; www.wplives.org. Daily 10-5, Mar-Oct only. By donation. Train rides: Sat-Sun, June-Aug only; $5, under 12 $2, family $12. Run-A-Locomotive: (530) 832-4532; $150+.

Housed in a former Western Pacific diesel shop, this hands-on museum features one of the largest and most historic collections of diesel locomotives in the nation. It also has 95 freight and passenger cars, 12,000 feet of track, and displays assorted photos and artifacts. Visitors can climb aboard the cars outside, though a few rarer cars stored inside require a guided tour. A ride on a train of cabooses along a 1-mile balloon track is offered on summer weekends. This facility is world-famous for its unique Run-A-Locomotive program, allowing visitors to drive a diesel engine.

WHERE TO STAY

Gray Eagle Lodge
5000 Gold Lake Rd., in Lakes Basin Recreation Area,
5 mi. S of Graeagle, (800) 635-8778, (530) 836-2511;
www.grayeaglelodge.com. 18 cabins; $$$-$$$+;
closed mid-Oct-mid-May. No TVs. Unheated swimming
hole. Includes full breakfast & dinner; restaurant.

This rustic, remote, and very inviting
complex includes a massive log lodge with an
open, log-beam ceiling. Comfortably appointed
cabins with knotty pine interiors are spread
along Graeagle Creek and Falls, which provides
Graeagle's drinking water and feeds into the
town's Old Mill Pond. Some cabins have sleeping lofts or second bedrooms, making them
particularly attractive to families. Others permit
casting a fishing line right from their deck.

Fine dining is available to non-guests as
well in **Firewoods** *(D daily; $$$. Reservations*
required.), which serves California mountain
cuisine and housemade soups and breads.
Anglers who catch a fish can arrange for the
chef to clean and cook it.

Pullman House Inn
256 Commercial St., in Portola, (530) 832-0107;
http://users.psln.com/pullman. 6 rooms; $.
Continental breakfast. No pets.

Built in 1910 as a boarding house for rail-
road workers, this B&B sports a railroad theme.
A model train runs on tracks attached to the
perimeter of the breakfast room ceiling, and
stunning locomotive paintings done by local
artist Ken Roller hang on the walls. Pullman
memorabilia is displayed throughout. A deck
permits sitting and watching the arrivals and
departures of trains on the nearby tracks.

River Pines Resort
8296 Hwy. 89, in Blairsden, (800) 696-2551,
(530) 836-0313; www.riverpines.com. 65 units; $-$$.
Some kitchens. Continental breakfast in winter.
Heated pool (seasonal); hot tub.

This old-fashioned motel is the kind of
place where guests gather fallen pinecones and
line them up in a row beside the door of their
cabin. Guests can park right in front of their
unit, and rooms have knotty-pine paneling and
soothing views of the surrounding pines.
Housekeeping cottages require a 3-night
minimum stay in summer.

The adjacent **Coyote Bar & Grill**
((530) 836-2002. D Tu-Sun; $$; closed Jan-Feb.)
serves Southwestern-style cuisine.

Sardine Lake Resort
Off Gold Lake Rd., 15 mi. S of Graeagle; summer
(530) 862-1196; winter (530) 862-1363. 9 cabins; $.

Once upon a time, this spectacularly scenic
spot was called Emerald Lake—until a mule
named Sardine fell in and miners renamed it in
her honor. It offers a dramatic view of the crag-
gy Sierra Buttes. Though the cabins here are so
popular that it is neigh on impossible for new
guests to get a reservation—there is a story
about one couple going through a divorce who
considered who got their annual reservation
here to be more important than who got the
dog—it *is* possible to come here and fish or
have an elegant dinner in the cozy **dining room**
(D mid-May-mid-Oct. Reservations required.).

WHERE TO EAT

Grizzly Grill
250 Bonta St., in Blairsden (530) 836-1300;
www.grizzlygrill.com. D daily; closed M-Tu in winter;
$$. Reservations advised.

Contemporary American cuisine is the
specialty in this tasteful, upscale venue.
A particularly good baby greens salad with
honey-roasted walnuts and crumbled bleu
cheese is among the appetizers, and assorted
pastas, meats, and fish comprise the entrees.
An antique bar and comfortable lounge area
furnished with lodgepole pine furniture invites
lingering.

The Log Cabin
64 E. Sierra Ave., in Portola, (530) 832-5243.
D W-Sat; $$. Reservations accepted.

The knotty-pine interior here is cozy, with
china plates decorating the walls and comfort-
able wooden booths for seating. American
steaks, hamburgers, and spaghetti are stars on
the eclectic menu.

The Village Baker
340 Bonta St., in Blairsden, (530) 836-4064.
Daily 6-2.

This spacious old-time bakery is definitely
the place to go for delicious European-style
pastries and breads, not to mention espresso
drinks.

880 SOUTH

OAKLAND

A LITTLE BACKGROUND

Though this much-maligned city usually loses in the struggle with San Francisco for media attention, it does have a "there there." (Although Gertrude Stein, who lived here as a child, is often quoted as having said about this city, "There is no there there," in reality it seems that she was referring to what remained of her demolished childhood house.) Interesting facts about this surprising city: It is the West Coast headquarters for the federal government; it has the country's third-largest Chinatown (or Asia Town as it is called here); the Human Wave—the synchronized movement of sports fans in stadiums—was "invented" in Oakland during the seventh-inning stretch of the final playoff game between the Oakland Athletics and New York Yankees on October 15, 1981; it is the most ethnically diverse city in the U.S., with at least 81 different languages and dialects spoken.

VISITOR INFORMATION

Oakland Convention & Visitors Bureau
463 11th St., (510) 839-9000; www.oaklandcvb.com.

GETTING THERE

Located approximately 10 miles east of San Francisco. From San Francisco, cross the Bay Bridge, taking Highway 580 south into Oakland.

ANNUAL EVENTS

Tulip Bloom at Mountain View Cemetery
March-April. 5000 Piedmont Ave., (510) 658-2588; www.oaklandhistory.com/files/hmvc1.html.
Tour: 2nd Sat of month, 10am; free.
More than 22,000 Dutch tulips bloom each spring in the cemetery gardens here. Drive or take a stroll through this 220-acre classic cemetery designed in 1863 by Frederick Law Olmsted, designer of Golden Gate Park. In 1865, Jane Waer, in plot 1, was the first person buried here. Since then, more than 165,000 people have joined her, and there's room for more. Anybody who is anyone in the history of the Bay Area is buried here. Serpentine paved walkways thread through the picturesque tombstones, including those of architects Julia Morgan and Bernard Maybeck and artist

Thomas Hill. Don't miss either the ornately decorated main mausoleum or "Millionaires' Row," where steel magnate Henry J. Kaiser, banker Charles Crocker, and several Ghirardelli chocolatiers rest in small Victorian family mausoleums with spectacular views of San Francisco and Oakland. Two pyramids and an assortment of stone angels round out the visual delights. This is also a bird-watcher's paradise and home to plenty of feral cats.

Open Studios
June. (510) 763-4361; www.proartsgallery.org. Free.

For this combination gallery exhibit and self-guided tour of artists' workplaces throughout the East Bay, more than 500 artists open their studios, workshops, lofts, and homes to meet with the public. Many offer works for sale.

Woodminster Summer Musicals
June-September. In Joaquin Miller Park, (510) 531-9597; www.woodminster.com. $23-$38, under 16 free with adult; parking $5.

It's difficult to imagine a more pleasant way to spend a balmy summer evening than at a live performance here. Witnessing the deepening of the evening and the slow appearance of the stars adds to the overall enjoyment of the production on stage. The amphitheater seats approximately 1,500 people on individually molded seats, all with good views. Pre-theater picnic tables are set up in redwood groves outside the theater.

Black Cowboy Parade
October. On 14th St. near City Hall; www.oaklandblackcowboyassociation.org. Free.

The only such event in the U.S., this parade commemorates the contributions made by African Americans and other minorities to building the American West. A festival follows in De Fremery Park.

WHAT TO DO

Chabot Space & Science Center
10000 Skyline Blvd., in Joaquin Miller Park, (510) 336-7300; www.chabotspace.org. Full facility: W-Thur 10-5, F-Sat 10-10, Sun 12-5; in summer Tu-Thur 10-5, Fri-Sat 10-10, Sun 12-5. $13, 65+ & 4-12 $9.

Begun in 1883 as the Oakland Observatory, this facility was originally located downtown. It served as the official timekeeping station for the entire Bay Area from 1885 through 1915, measuring time with its transit telescope. Now it has the largest, most technologically advanced planetarium west of NYC. Facilities include a domed-screen MegaDome theater *($8, 65+ & 4-12 $7.)*, an assortment of hands-on exhibits, and an observatory with three telescopes that is open free on Fridays and Saturday nights from dusk to 10 p.m.

Dunsmuir Historic Estate
2960 Peralta Oaks Ct., near 106th St. exit off I-580 east, (510) 615-5555; www.dunsmuir.org. Mansion & grounds: 1st Sun 12-3. Mansion tour: W at 11 & 12; Easter-Sept only; $5, 62+ & 6-13 $4. Grounds open for strolling year-round, Tu-F 10-4; free.

Built in 1899, this renovated 37-room neoclassical Revival mansion is furnished with period antiques. It features a Tiffany-style dome and 10 fireplaces. Visitors can picnic and stroll on the 50 acres of grounds. Of special interest are a grotto, a drained but rustically beautiful swimming pool, and a peaceful duck and swan pond. The horror film *Burnt Offerings* and the James Bond thriller *A View to a Kill* were both filmed here.

Cultural entertainment is scheduled on Family Sundays. Each December the grounds are transformed into a wonderland for **Holidays at Dunsmuir**, and the house is decked out in appropriate finery. Other annual special events include a **Spring Festival**, and a **Scot's Faire** in July with Highland games and more.

Fortune Cookie Factory Tour

261 12th St./Harrison St., (510) 832-5552. M-Thur 10-3. $1.

The A&K Wong Inc. bakery still hand-folds its cookies. It also makes unusual fruit-flavored fortune cookies and permits customers to insert their own original messages. Drop-in tours last about 15 minutes and include a small bag of cookies.

Jack London Square

(866) 295-9853, (510) 645-9292; www.jacklondon square.com.

Situated on the inlet of the Oakland Estuary, this entertainment complex borders the city's huge commercial shipping area. People come here to stroll the spacious modern walkways closed to cars, to browse a variety of shops, and to dine in myriad restaurants. Also, boat-watching (on the estuary) and train-watching (slow-moving trains pass regularly on the tracks at the area's northern edge) is enjoyable, and nightlife is lively.

• Alameda/Oakland Ferry

(510) 522-3300; www.eastbayferry.com. Schedule & fares vary.

Board the ferry here for Alameda. San Francisco destinations are the Ferry Building, Pier 41, the Giants' AT&T Park, and Angel Island State Park.

• Heinold's First and Last Chance Saloon

48 Webster St., (510) 839-6761; www.heinoldsfirs tandlastchance.com. Daily noon-midnight. Must be age 21+.

Built in 1883 from the remnants of a whaling ship, this tiny, informal, funky bar with a tilted floor pays tribute to the area's waterfront past. Jack London, a longtime Oakland resident, was a regular customer during the period when he was an oyster fisherman here. Though somewhat menacing in appearance (it is impossible to see in through the thick windows), this saloon makes a good spot to wet a dry whistle and is a National Literary Landmark. While here, notice the still-functioning gas lamps and a clock that stopped at 5:18 a.m. during the 1906 earthquake.

Jack London's Cabin is across the way. Moved here in 1970, this rustic one-room hovel is the top half of the cabin believed to have housed London when he prospected in Canada's Yukon Territory during the 1897 Klondike gold rush. The bottom half is in Dawson City in Canada's Yukon Territory.)

• Port of Oakland Tours

(510) 627-1302; www.portofoakland.com. May-Oct; schedule varies; reservations required. Free.

Sponsored by the Port of Oakland, these 75-minute tours take participants alongside port operations in the Oakland Estuary and into the Outer Harbor area.

• USS *Potomac*

Berthed at N end of Jack London Square. Visitor Center at 540 Water St./Clay St., (510) 627-1215; www.usspotomac.org. Dockside tour: W & F 10:30-2:30, Sun 1-4; $7, 60+ $5, under 12 free. Narrated history cruise: 1st & 3rd Thur, 2nd & 4th Sat of month,

mid-April-mid-Nov, weather permitting; $40, 60+ $35, under 12 $20; advance purchase advised.

This 165-foot-long, all-steel vessel served as President Franklin Delano Roosevelt's "floating White House." Having undergone a 12-year, $5 million restoration, it is now a National Historic Landmark. The 2-hour ride begins ashore with a background video and the chance to study some historical photos, including one of Elvis Presley (who once owned the yacht) presenting it to his friend Danny Thomas for St. Jude's Hospital. More photos testify to the degeneration from its original purpose of chasing rumrunners into being used for drug running, and its eventual sinking near Treasure Island. Governor Ronald Reagan passed legislation to restore her and, happily, with the help of the Port of Oakland and many dedicated volunteers, she now operates as a public museum. FDR, who was confined to a wheelchair and suffered from sinusitis, preferred the *Potomac* to the White House on sultry summer days. He relaxed on this simple, but comfortable, ship as he led the country through the Great Depression and World War II. Aboard, visitors can see his surprisingly small and simply furnished cabin and his private elevator mounted within a false smokestack (it may be used by visitors in wheelchairs). The radio room, pilothouse, and various guest rooms are also open for inspection. The cruise goes out of the estuary, past the gigantic maritime crane horses that urban legend says inspired George Lucas's similar-looking snow walkers in *The Empire*

Strikes Back, on past Treasure Island, and then around Alcatraz. A favorite spot to settle in is the lower fantail deck lounge in back, with a seat so deep that the legs of loungers must be stretched out straight. A complimentary light snack is provided.

Lakeside Park/Lake Merritt

Entrance at Grand & Bellevue aves., (510) 238-7275; www.oaklandnet.com/parks. Free; parking $3 Sat-Sun.

This beautiful expanse of water is the hub of a variety of activities and is encircled in the evening by a lovely necklace of lights. Fed by both salt water from the bay and fresh water from streams in the hills, it is approximately 18 feet deep.

• Camron-Stanford House

1418 Lakeside Dr./14th St., (510) 444-1876; www.cshouse.org. 3rd W of month, 1-5. $5, seniors $4, 12-18 $3; free 1st Sun of month.

Restored and furnished in period fashion, this 1876 Italianate-style Victorian is on the western edge of Lake Merritt. Tours begin with a short film on Oakland's history.

• Children's Fairyland

699 Bellevue Ave./Grand Ave., (510) 452-2259; www.fairyland.org. Daily 10-4 in summer; W-Sun in spring & fall; F-Sun in winter; puppet show at 11, 2, 4. $6, under 1 free; magic key $2.

Designed especially for children age 8 and under, this non-profit facility was the country's first educational storybook theme park when it opened in 1950. In fact, Disneyland is patterned after it. Mother Goose rhymes and fairy tales come to life in more than 30 fantasy sets, some of which hold live animals. Among the attractions are an Alice in Wonderland card maze and a variety of slides—including one down a dragon's back. Rides on the Jolly Trolly and on a mini-carousel and -Ferris wheel are included. All ages can view an award-winning puppet show at the oldest continuously operating puppet theater in the U.S. Mature trees provide shade, and a picnic area, fast-food stand, and packaged birthday party are also available. No adult is admitted without a child, and no child is admitted without an adult.

For the annual Halloween **Jack-O-Lantern Jamboree**, families are encouraged to come in costume.

• Lake Merritt Boating Center

568 Bellevue Ave./near Grand Ave., (510) 238-2196;
www.oaklandnet.com/parks. Daily 11-3:30, Mar-Sept;
F-Sun Oct-Feb; open later in summer. Boat rentals
$8+/hr.

A variety of vessels are for rent, including rowboats, sailboats, and pedal boats.

Romantic gondolas operated by opera-singing gondoliers are for hire at about half the price they'd go for in Venice through **Gondola Servizio** *((866) 737-8494, (510) 663-6603; www.gondolacruise.com. $45+/couple. Reservations required.)*.

• Lakeside Garden Center

666 Bellevue Ave., at N end of lake, (510) 763-8409;
www.oaklandnet.com/parks. W-F 11-3, Sat 10-4,
Sun 12-4. Free.

In addition to fuchsia and bulb gardens, a Japanese garden, a citrus garden, and an herb garden for the blind and disabled are found here. A Bonsai and Suiseki Display Garden exhibits an assortment of suiseki viewing stones and 50 bonsai trees—among them a 400-year-old Japanese black pine that was brought to the U.S. for the 1915 Panama Pacific International Exposition in San Francisco, and a Dalmyo oak that is the oldest in cultivation in the U.S. A community garden is available free to anyone who wants to grow their own pesticide-free produce.

• Rotary Nature Center/ Lake Merritt Wildlife Refuge

600 Bellevue Ave./Perkins St., at N end of lake,
(510) 238-3739; www.oaklandnet.com/parks.
Center: Daily 10-5. Free.

The nature center has a nature/science library for children to use when researching school reports. The wildlife refuge dates to 1870 and is the first and oldest in the country. Among the birds seen here regularly are egrets, mallards, Canada geese, and herons. The daily feeding is at 3:30 p.m.

Morcom Amphitheater of Roses

700 Jean St./Grand Ave., (510) 238-3187;
www.oaklandnet.com/parks. Daily dawn-dusk. Free.

Not far from Lake Merritt, this peaceful garden is designed in traditional Florentine style with terraces and a classic reflecting pool. Sections are devoted to pastel roses and antique roses, and a children's garden features miniature roses. A wedding site designed with a color scheme of white, beige, and pink is reputed to bring good luck. Bloom is best June through October, and benches throughout invite picnicking.

Museum of Children's Art (MOCHA)

538 9th St./Washington St.,(510) 465-8770;
www.mocha.org. Tu-F 10-5, Sat-Sun 12-5. Free.

This gallery displays East Bay children's art as well as the occasional national and international exhibit. Drop-In Art classes are scheduled regularly for parents and kids.

Oakland Ice Center

519 18th St./San Pablo Ave., (510) 268-9000;
www.oaklandice.com. Schedule varies. $7.50, 55+ &
under 13 $6.50, skate rental $2.50.

This Olympic-size rink has a variety of programs and packages.

Oakland Museum of California

1000 Oak St./10th St., (888) OAK-MUSE,
(510) 238-2200; www.museumca.org. W-Sat 10-5,
Sun 12-5, 1st F to 9. $8, 65+ & 6-17 $5; free 2nd Sun
of month; parking $1/hr.

This beautifully designed tri-level museum is the only one in the state focusing on the art, natural sciences, and history of California. Opened in 1969, it is recognized for both its innovative shows and its architecture featuring terraced gardens and a center courtyard. The Natural Sciences Gallery walks visitors across a miniature representation of the state, complete with appropriate plant and animal life. Near the museum store, visitors can rest on a surprisingly comfortable circular sculpture fashioned from a large slice of a giant redwood burl and view colorful koi in a lily pond outside. An airy cafe features reasonably priced lunches and snacks and has huge picture windows overlooking the gardens.

Each March, the museum is benefited by a **White Elephant Sale** *((510) 839-5919. Free.)*. This truly mammoth rummage sale offers just about anything imaginable, as well as many things unimaginable. In April or May, volunteers collect fresh specimens for display at the annual **California Wildflower Show**, and in December, the annual **Fungus Fair** celebrates the beauty of fungi with a display of more than 1,000 local specimens.

Three "kids" get acquainted at the Petting Zoo

Oakland Zoo

9777 Golf Links Rd., off Hwy. 580, in Knowland Park, (510) 632-9525; www.oaklandzoo.org. Daily, 10-4, weather permitting; Skyride Sat-Sun, daily in summer; kiddie rides open at 11. $9.50, 55+ & 2-12 $6; Skyride $2; parking $6.

The Malayan sun bear exhibit here is the largest in the U.S. Naturalistic habitats mix several animals together. The Skyride chairlift offers a good view of the outstanding African Veldt enclosure, with its watering hole for giraffes and vultures, and is the only way to view the bison and tule elk. Kids love the Children's Zoo, with its grassy petting area for goats and sheep and its awesome fruit bat exhibit, and a kiddie ride area outside the zoo entrance includes a roller coaster, carousel, and train.

Paramount Theatre

2025 Broadway/21st St., (510) 893-2300; www.paramounttheatre.com. Tour: 1st & 3rd Sat at 10am; $5; must be age 10+.

Built in 1931, this magnificently restored art deco landmark is at its best during an actual performance. It boasts a magnificent old Wurlitzer organ (the second largest west of the Mississippi), which is sometimes played before performances. Live ballet, symphony, and theater performances are also scheduled.

Pardee Home Museum

672 11th St./Castro St., across from Preservation Park, (510) 444-2187; www.pardeehome.org. Tour W, F, Sat at 12, 1, 2, 3; reservations advised. $5, under 13 free.

Home to three generations of the Pardee family, this house was lived in by Enoch Pardee (mayor of Oakland in the mid-1870s) and his son, George C. Pardee (mayor of Oakland in the early 1890s and then governor of California from 1903 to 1907). More than 50,000 pieces of family memorabilia and historical artifacts are displayed just as they were left when the home was donated, and all the furniture is original to the house. A unique Carleton Watkins light fixture hangs in the downstairs hallway. The expansive grounds hold a lovely mature coastal redwood.

Parkway Speakeasy Theater

1834 Park Blvd./E. 18th St., near Lake Merritt, (510) 814-2400; www.speakeasytheaters.com. Daily; schedule varies. $5-$7; must be age 21+, except Sat-Sun matinees. No cards.

In this classic movie house, viewers sit on comfortable couches while munching on thin-crust pizza and enjoying a brew with a view of first-run, second-run, and classic flicks. Popcorn with *real* butter is also on the menu. Mondays are Baby Brigade night, when infants under

1 year are admitted free and their attendant noises are welcome.

Preservation Park
13th St./Martin Luther King Jr. Way, (510) 874-7580; www.preservationpark.com. Free.

This group of 16 exquisite Victorian houses was originally scheduled to be demolished by Highway 980, but they were saved when a public outcry caused the freeway to be moved over a block. They represent five distinct domestic architectural styles from 1870 to 1910. Those on the north side of the street are in their original positions, while the rest were moved in from other parts of the city. Houses are rented to non-profits and small businesses for office space. The 2-block area is beautifully landscaped with posh lawns, palms, and pines, plus one gorgeous 19th-century fountain. A cafe in one house serves weekday lunch.

Redwood Regional Park
7867 Redwood Rd., (510) 482-6024; www.ebparks.org/parks/redwood. Daily 5am-10pm. $5/vehicle; $2/dog.

This unassuming park is full of surprises. It holds a grove of second-growth redwood trees—a remnant of the solid redwood forest found here in Oakland long ago, which was harvested to build homes in San Francisco—and has the only fish ladder in the Bay Area where rainbow trout spawn.

Spectator sports
At McAfee Coliseum and Oracle Arena, 7000 Coliseum Way, Hegenberger Rd. exit off I-880.

• **Baseball. Oakland Athletics**
(510) 638-GOAS; www.oaklandathletics.com. Apr-Oct.

• **Basketball. Golden State Warriors**
(888) GSW-HOOP; www.warriors.com. Nov-Apr.

• **Football. Oakland Raiders**
(800) RAIDERS, (510) 569-2121; www.raiders.com. Aug-Dec.

Temescal Regional Park
6500 Broadway Terrace/Hwys. 13 & 24, (510) 652-1155; www.ebparks.org/parks/temescal. Daily 5am-10pm. $5/vehicle Sat-Sun; $2/dog. Swim area: Daily 11-6 in summer, Sat-Sun Apr-Oct; $3, 62+ & under 16 $2.

Opened as a recreation area in 1936, this scenic 48-acre park offers swimming, fishing, jogging, and hiking. Facilities include a rose garden, two children's play areas, and a 13-acre artificial lake with a roped-off swimming area and raft. A lifeguard is on duty at the swim area, and vending machines, picnic tables, and barbecue pits are available.

Yoshi's
510 Embarcadero West/Washington St., (510) 238-9200; www.yoshis.com. M-Sat at 8 & 10, Sun at 2 & 8. $10-$28; no age min.

This jazz club attracts the circuit elite, and the audience can order light snacks and sushi during the show. Alternatively, a California-Japanese restaurant, complete with a tatami room and separate sushi bar, is also available.

WHERE TO STAY

Oakland Marriott City Center
1001 Broadway, (800) 228-9290, (510) 451-4000; www.marriott.com./oakdt. 21 stories, 491 rooms; $$-$$$. Heated pool; hot tub; fitness room. Restaurant. No pets. Self-parking $22, valet $26.

Casting a dramatic profile on the downtown skyline, this centrally located, angular building is Oakland's only high-rise, full-service luxury hotel. It connects to the Oakland Convention Center and is one of the few hotels in the Bay Area with a kosher kitchen.

Washington Inn
495 10th St./Washington St., (510) 452-1776; www.thewashingtoninn.com. 4 stories; 47 rooms; $$. Full breakfast M-F, continental Sat-Sun; restaurant. No pets. No parking.

Located across the street from the Oakland Convention Center, this landmark building was Oakland's first hotel. It features turn-of-the-century decor, and photos of old Oakland hang in the welcoming, high-ceilinged lobby.

Waterfront Hotel
10 Washington St., at Jack London Square, (800) 729-3638, (510) 836-3800; www.jdvhotels.com/waterfront. 5 stories; 145 rooms; $$$-$$$+. Heated pool; fitness room. Restaurant; room service. No pets. Valet parking $20.

This contemporary hotel offers an atmosphere of casual luxury and features a glass-enclosed swimming pool deck overlooking the

Oakland City Center

estuary. More than half of the rooms have water views. The San Francisco ferry docks adjacent, and the hotel operates a free BART shuttle.

WHERE TO EAT

À Côté
5478 College Ave./Taft Ave., (510) 655-6469;
www.acoterestaurant.com. D daily; $$.
No reservations.

Who doesn't like sitting in a dimly lit room buzzing with excitement? Choose the bar, some smaller side tables, a central communal table, or an outdoor patio in this casual bistro. The ever-changing menu consists of rustic French, Spanish, and Mediterranean small plates meant to be shared. All seem to be winners, but the don't-misses include pommes frites with aioli, house-marinated olives, and any of the flatbreads. A selection of cheeses and a long list of wines and spirits add to the hum. Designated drivers aren't denied drink delights—try a tasty Gewurztraminer grape juice served up in a martini glass. Delicious desserts might include a Meyer lemon-curd tart or a plate of profiteroles stuffed with banana-nut ice cream.

Bay Wolf
3853 Piedmont Ave./40th St., (510) 655-6004;
www.baywolf.com. L M-F, D daily; $$$. Reservations advised.

One of the region's very best restaurants, this veteran bistro has been around for more than 30 years now. Serving a Mediterranean-inspired menu and famous for its duck dishes, it operates out of a simple but cozy remodeled

Victorian house sporting paintings by internationally recognized local artists. The menu changes every 3 weeks, highlighting the food of a different region and making use of the season's bounty. Starters might include a subtly spiced puréed cauliflower soup or a vibrantly colored citrus-beet salad. The sublime, silky, duck liver flan that is the kitchen's signature dish is always available. Desserts are worth saving space for, but when little room remains, try a plate of sweets that hopefully will include a chocolate-covered, liqueur-soaked cherry and a tiny gingerbread angel. Brunch is served only once each year, on Mother's Day.

Bittersweet
5427 College Ave./Taft St., (510) 654-7159;
www.bittersweetchocolatecafe.com. Tu-Thur 8-7, F 8-9,
Sat 9-9, Sun 9-6, closed M.

This friendly cafe is famous for really good hot chocolate. Choose from a blend of dark chocolates, a classic sweet milk chocolate, a spicy chili version, and a sweeter one especially for kids. And don't overlook the chocolate chai. Want something cold? Try chocolate Thai iced tea or an old-fashioned chocolate milk. Seating is limited to a few communal tables inside and benches outside, but everything is easy to carry away. Some baked goods and an array of chocolate bars from around the world are also available.

Cactus Taqueria
5642 College Ave., (510) 658-6180;
www.cactustaqueria.com. L-D daily.

For description, see page 291.

Caffé 817
817 Washington St./9th St., downtown,
(510) 271-7965; www.caffe817.com. B-L M-Sat; $.
Reservations for 6+.

For breakfast, this sleek, modern, very Italian paninoteca (sandwich bar) prepares a perfectly poached organic egg, squeezes a vibrantly colorful glass of blood orange juice, and brews superb coffees using a state-of-the-art espresso machine and Illy beans imported from Trieste. Note that "a latte" is made with filtered coffee and served French-style in a big bowl, whereas "a regular latte" is made with espresso and served in a tall glass. Lunch items include assorted housemade soups, polentas, salads, and panini. Add to these choices sun-brewed iced tea, Tuscan wines, fresh juices, and Italian Moretti beer from the Tyrolian area of Udine, and life is good. A picnic box can be prepared with a call by 2 p.m. the day before needed. All this and walls graced by the work of local artists, too!

Caffé Verbena
1111 Broadway/11th St., downtown, (510) 465-9300; www.caffeverbena.com. L-D M-F; $$. Reservations advised.

Tucked away in an office building lobby, this spot features a low-key bar and wide-open dining room with some comfy booths. The busy kitchen whips up tasty fare that includes great artichoke fritters with lemon aioli and a wild mushroom pizza. Main courses include bouilla-baisse, achiote-roasted chicken, and flat iron steak with green peppercorn sauce. To wash it down, choose from cocktails and a large selection of wines and beers.

Everett & Jones Barbeque
126 Broadway/2nd St., near Jack London Square, (510) 663-2350; www.eandjbbq.com. L-D daily; $. Reservations accepted.

This family-owned and -run, full-service restaurant is a sit-down-and-stay-a-while branch of a popular take-out storefront. Former Oakland Raiders coach John Madden says it's "the greatest"; former mayor Jerry Brown calls it "the premier restaurant in Oakland"; and Whoopi Goldberg says,"Ummm—goood!" Lunch portions of chicken, ribs, homemade beef links, and the house-specialty beef brisket come with potato salad, wheat bread, and the tasty, award-winning house sauce in a choice of mild, medium, or hot (and they *do* mean *hot*). Dinner portions are bigger and include a choice of fresh housemade greens, yams, potato salad, and baked beans, plus either corn bread or wheat bread. It all washes down nicely with a Brothers Brewing Company beer produced locally by the only African American-owned microbrewery in the country. Desserts include sweet potato, pecan, and peach pies, and lemon, chocolate (actually white cake with chocolate frosting), and "sock-it-to-me" cakes.

Fentons Creamery
4226 Piedmont Ave./Entrada Ave., (510) 658-7000; www.fentonscreamery.com. B F-Sun, L-D daily; $. No reservations.

Enormous portions of housemade 12% to 14% butterfat ice cream is the name of the game at this well-established ice cream parlor, in business here since 1922 and remodeled in 2003 after a devastating fire. Favorite flavors for Fentons freaks looking for a fix are toasted almond and Swiss milk chocolate. Many of the sundaes are big enough to share among several people. If all those people eating out of one bowl is unappealing, ask for extra bowls. Drinks include milkshakes served in old-fashioned metal canisters as well as sodas, floats, and sherbet freezes. The menu also offers soups and salads, hamburgers, and an assortment of sandwiches, including the delicious house specialty—fresh crab salad on grilled sour-dough. Seating is in a large, open room with some booths around the perimeter and an atmospheric sea of old-fashioned marble-top tables and wire-back chairs in the center.

Great Wall Chinese Vegi Restaurant
6247 College Ave./63rd St., (510) 658-8458. L-D daily; $. Reservations accepted.

The surroundings here are comfortable and fresh and the service is fast and courteous. In addition to vegan "meats" and fresh vegetables, seafood is on the menu. Favorites include hot-and-sour soup, Szechuan "chicken," eggplant or green beans with spicy garlic sauce, sweet and sour pork, and kung pao vegetables. Sauces are generally quite tasty, and chow fun dishes and brown rice are available. Both egg and garlic can be omitted upon request.

Huynh Vietnamese Cuisine
381 15th St./Franklin St., downtown, (510) 832-5238; www.huynhrestaurant.com. L M-F; $. No reservations.

The large, open, curry-yellow dining room here is furnished with jack wood tables and chairs made by the owner's family in Viet Nam (customers can place special orders). Portions are generous and service is fast. Among the outstanding Vietnamese items are deep-fried imperial rolls, lotus root salad topped with peanuts and a side of shrimp crackers, hot-and-sour soup, Vietnamese coconut milk-shrimp curry, and a vegetarian special of tofu sautéed with eggplant and onions in spicy plum sauce. Pho noodle dishes, rice plates, and exotic French iced black coffee and lotus leaf hot tea are also on the exceptional menu.

Il Pescatore

57 Jack London Square, (510) 465-2188; www.ilpescatoreristorante.com. L-D daily, Sat-SunBr; $$. Reservations advised.

This atmospheric, bustling, remotely ark-shaped restaurant serves a variety of garlic-laden Italian seafood dishes. Though waiters don spiffy white shirts with black vests and ties, customers dress casually. Garlicky baked Dungeness crab, positioned attractively on large clamshells, is a great appetizer. Entrees include a delicious, delicate fresh filet of sole covered in a light egg batter and sautéed with white wine, lemon juice, and capers. The extensive, mouth-watering menu offers more seafood choices, plus meats, pastas, and vegetarian items—all accompanied by steamed fresh chard and pasta tubes in a light tomato sauce. A slab of liquor-soaked housemade tiramisu provides a just right, not-too-sweet ending.

Italian Colors

2220 Mountain Blvd./Park Blvd., Montclair area, (510) 482-8094. L W-F, D daily; $$. Reservations advised.

This attractively decorated neighborhood restaurant features warm peach-colored walls and a large, high-ceilinged open dining room. Outdoor patio dining, with a view of the hills, is an option in warm weather. Diners young and old alike are provided crayons with which to express themselves on the butcher paper-covered tables—after all, this *is* California. This amenity is also a nod to the restaurant's name and to the fact that it is a great place for kids. Though the menu of Italian-style California cuisine changes seasonally, particularly delicious items have included a bruchetta starter topped with a variety of mushrooms, a delicate Green Scarves lasagna made with thin layers of pasta atop a cheese-cream sauce, a perfect sea bass, and a succulent herb-roasted chicken. Sicily is the focus of the menu specials on Monday nights. Pizzas and housemade desserts—order the gooey warm chocolate cake in advance as it takes 20 minutes to prepare—are also on the menu.

Kincaid's

1 Franklin St., at Jack London Square, (510) 835-8600; www.kincaids.com. L-D daily, Sat-SunBr; $-$$. Reservations accepted.

The ideal spot for a fresh fish lunch here is at a waterside table in the room fitted with a magnificent 15-foot-tall teak bar. Kayakers, canoers, and motorboaters outside provide constant entertainment. Delicious wedges of house-made sesame pan bread come with meals.

Le Cheval

1007 Clay St./10th St., downtown, (510) 763-8957; www.lecheval.com. L M-Sat, D daily; $. Reservations advised.

This cavernous dining room stretches over half a block and positively roars with animated diners. Large windows provide an even more open feeling, and namesake horses are prominent in the decor. Especially tasty selections on the classic French-Vietnamese menu include lemon grass chicken, curry-spicy Singapore-style thin noodles with veggies, soy sauce rice, and clay pot prawns with mushrooms. Bananas flambé makes a spectacular dessert. Service is super fast.

Nan Yang

6048 College Ave./Claremont Ave., (510) 655-3298. L-D Tu-Sun; $. Reservations for 4+.

The Bay Area's first Burmese restaurant, this restive spot opened in 1983 and includes the refined touch of cloth napkins. The extensive selection of vegetarian items includes a crunchy Burmese ginger salad composed of 16 ingredients—among them shredded ginger and cabbage, toasted yellow split peas, fava beans, and peanuts—all mixed together at the table by the server. Also exceptional on the enticing menu are a green papaya salad with Burmese dressing, a savory curried smoked eggplant, an appetizer of batter-fried tropical squash with a tomato-garlic sauce, and flavorful curried garlic noodles served with succulent chicken and crisp lettuce.

Oakland Grill

301 Franklin St./3rd St., near Jack London Square, (510) 835-1176. B-L daily; $. No reservations.

Situated in the produce district, this down-to-earth spot is a cheery haven for a satisfying meal and a good cup of coffee. The excellent breakfasts are served all day. Three-egg omelettes and two-egg "scramlets" are available with an extensive choice of fillings and are prepared with egg whites upon request. They come with a side of baking powder biscuits and home fries. Hot cakes, French toast, crêpes, and eggs Benedict are also options. Lunch brings on a hamburger and veggie burger, a French dip sandwich, and a variety of salads. Being selected by *Travel & Leisure* as one of the country's top 100 restaurants in 1995 obviously refers to the food, not the ambiance.

Oliveto

5655 College Ave./Shafter Ave., (510) 547-5356; www.oliveto.com. L M-F, D daily; $$$. Reservations advised.

Delicious, simple dishes made with the freshest seasonal ingredients have included a blood orange-avocado butter lettuce salad and a flavorful pan-roasted halibut entree. A seasonal soup, freshly made pastas, and an assortment of side dishes are always available at dinner. Do leave room for dessert, as they are exceptional: Meyer lemon éclairs with lemon-caramel sauce and pistachios, persimmon pudding, simple tangelo sherbet.

Should the classy upstairs restaurant be completely booked, as it often is, opt for a less expansive, and less expensive, meal in the cozy downstairs **cafe**.

Picnic Pick-Ups

• A. G. Ferrari Foods

4001 Piedmont Ave./40th St., (510) 547-7222; www.agferrari.com; M-F 9-9, Sat 9-8, Sun 10-7:30. Also at 6119 La Salle Ave., (510) 339-9716; M-Sat 9-9, Sun 10-6:30.

For description, see page 295.

• Gregoire

4001 Piedmont Ave. #B/40th St., (510) 547-3444; www.gregoirerestaurant.com. Daily 11-9; $$.

For description, see page 295.

• Ratto's International Market & Deli

821 Washington St./9th St., downtown, (510) 832-6503. M-F 9-5:30, Sat 10:30-5.

In business since 1897, this deli operates out of a lovely turn-of-the-20th-century brick building stocked with bins of beans, bulk spices, hanging sausages, garlic braids, and fresh breads. There is sauerkraut from Germany, pepper from India, and morel mushrooms from France. A deli counter provides countless sandwich possibilities, and a picnic box can be pre-packed by reservation.

• Rockridge Market Hall

5655 College Ave./Keith Ave., (510) 250-6000; www.rockridgemarkethall.com. Open daily.

Specialty stalls include **The Pasta Shop** (*(510) 547-4005. M-F 9-8, Sat 9-7, Sun 10-6.*) for deli items and a variety of fresh pastas, as well as more for produce, wine, and flowers.

Quinn's Lighthouse

1951 Embarcadero Cove (16th Ave. exit off I-880), (510) 536-2050; www.quinnslighthouse.com. L-D daily, SunBr; $$. Reservations advised.

Quinn's operates out of the remodeled Oakland Harbor Lighthouse in an industrial corner of town. Built in 1890 and replaced by an automatic beacon in 1966, it was purchased from the Coast Guard for just $1 and moved here in 1965 by the world's largest ocean-going crane. The novelty of the setting makes dining here fun. Roasted peanuts are complimentary in the casual Upper Deck Pub, and, to the delight of children, it's okay to throw the shells on the floor. Relaxing on the upstairs deck overlooking the quiet estuary with a fancy drink and some garlic bread is highly recommended. The menu in the downstairs Yacht Club Dining Room includes seafood, pastas, and a variety of burgers, as well as a delicious jambalaya.

Scott's Seafood

2 Broadway, at Jack London Square, (510) 444-3456; www.scottseastbay.com. L-D daily, SunBr; $$$. Reservations advised. Valet parking.

With window tables overlooking the estuary and live background music emanating from the bar, this upscale fish house is a great place for a celebration. In addition to fresh seafood, the extensive menu also offers some pastas and steaks. A New Orleans-style Sunday brunch features complimentary champagne and live jazz.

Soi4 Bangkok Eatery

5421 College Ave./Taft St., (510) 655-0889; www.soifour.com. L M-F, D M-Sat; $$. Reservations advised.

In this stylish spot sporting high ceilings and sleek decor, all tables have a sidewalk view through floor-to-ceiling windows. The menu offers a sophisticated take on Bangkok street food ("soi" means "street" in Thai) and is filled with hits. If sharing, start with soup of the day and a few skewers—the usual satays plus eggplant, beef balls, and portabella mushroom versions are options—followed by one shared entree per diner selected from noodles, sautés, and curries. Favorites are yellow curry with chicken and potatoes, sautéed Asian eggplant and tiger prawns, and spicy wide rice noodles with chicken and basil.

Szechwan Restaurant

366 8th St./Franklin St., in Chinatown, (510) 832-7878. L M-F, D daily; $. Reservations accepted.

All the usual suspects are found on this extensive menu: crispy fried won tons, noisy sizzling rice soup, spicy hot-and-sour soup, Chinese burrito-like mu shu dishes, and dramatic sizzling iron platters. Personal favorites include crispy dry-braised green beans in a garlicky sauce with minced pork, and the house special chow fun—a colorful, fragrant hodgepodge of meats and vegetables mixed with addictive wide, flat rice noodles. Chinese brunch items are also on the lunch menu. Different than the more common dim sum breakfast specialties, they include Chinese-style donuts, onion pancakes, and almond jelly.

XOX Truffles

6126 La Salle Ave./Moraga Ave., in Montclair, (510) 339-9XOX; www.xoxtruffles.com. M-Sat 10-7; $.

For description, see page 86.

ALAMEDA

A LITTLE BACKGROUND

Once a peninsula off Oakland, Alameda became an island in 1902 when a canal was dredged through marshland between the two cities so that shipping facilities could expand. The Naval Air Station closed in 1997. The community remains little known by tourists and is a particularly pleasant place for lunch and shopping along **Park Street** *(www.shopparkstreet.com).*

VISITOR INFORMATION

Alameda Chamber of Commerce

1416 Park Ave., (510) 522-0414; www.alameda chamber.com.

GETTING THERE

15 miles east of San Francisco. Cross the Bay Bridge and take I-880 south to the Alameda tunnel exit near Jack London Square.

Ferry service is available in San Francisco from the Ferry Building and Pier 41, and in Oakland from Jack London Square *((510) 522-3300; www.eastbayferry.com.).*

WHAT TO DO

Alameda Point Antiques & Collectibles Fair

At end of Main St., (510) 522-7500; www.antiques bythebay.net. 1st Sun of month, 9-3, $5, under 16 free; early admission 6-7:30 $15, 7:30-9 $10. Free parking & shuttle. No pets.

More than 800 booths spread out over the former Alameda Naval Air Station's main runway. In addition to antiques and old stuff galore, shoppers enjoy a sweeping view of San Francisco and the bay. Items sold here are required by management to be at least 20 years old. Food vendors offer a tantalizing selection.

Crown Memorial State Beach

www.ebparks.org/parks/crown_beach. $5/vehicle.

This beach runs for 2½ miles and has a bicycle trail bordered by dunes. Though no lifeguards are on duty, the water is warm and shallow and great for wading.

Crab Cove Visitor Center *(1252 McKay Ave./Central Ave., at, (510) 521-6887; www.ebparks.org/parks/vc/crab_cove. W-Sun 10-5. Free.)* is dedicated to helping people understand the area's rich marine environment. It has a saltwater aquarium and features exhibits about the area's past as the "Coney Island of the West." Nature classes for families and children are scheduled regularly. An adjacent marine reserve has picnic tables and large, grassy expanses that are perfect for flying kites.

Farther down the shoreline, the **Elsie Roemer Bird Sanctuary** saltwater marsh attracts shorebirds and waterfowl.

An annual **Sand Castle/Sculpture Contest** is scheduled on the first high-tide Saturday in June.

Rosenblum Cellars Winery and Tasting Room
2900 Main St., (510) 865-7007; www.rosenblum cellars.com. Tasting daily 11-6; tour by appt.

Almost as unlikely as finding a farm in Berkeley is finding a winery in Alameda—especially out by the docks of the Oakland Estuary. Located within a large warehouse in the historic circa 1910 Todd Shipyard Building, the winery's upstairs tasting room features a gorgeous view of the Bay Bridge and San Francisco. The winery is known for its rich Rhone reds and Zinfandels. Three open houses—with live music, hors d'oeuvres, and a tasting of all wines—are scheduled annually. Note that the ferry docks right next door.

St. George Spirits
2601 Monarch St., (510) 769-1601; www.stgeorgespirits.com. Tasting W-Sat 12-7, Sun 12-6; tour Sat-Sun at 1.

A variety of European-style eaux-de-vie can be tasted at this distillery, which was the first in the U.S. to make absinthe since Prohibition.

USS *Hornet* Museum
707 W. Hornet Ave., Pier 3, Alameda Point,
(510) 521-8448; www.uss-hornet.org. Daily 10-5. $14,
65+ $12, 5-17 $6.

Stretching the length of three football fields and reaching 11 stories high, this immense vessel served as an aircraft carrier from 1943 to 1970. She is now a National Historic Landmark. The oil-fired *Hornet* was known as the "Grey Ghost" during World War II and could outrun anything. She holds an unequaled combat record for destroying enemy aircraft and sinking enemy ships. She survived 59 air attacks without getting hit, and was the primary recovery vessel for the Apollo 11 and 12 moon missions in 1969. Nowadays, vets lead fascinating tours, and a dynamite view of San Francisco is enjoyed from the flight deck. Great photo ops abound.

On Living Ship Day (the third Saturday of the month) the radar tower turns, the loudspeakers spit out messages, and the extraordinarily fast airplane elevator carries fighter planes up and down from the hold to the deck. Big Band Dance programs are sometimes scheduled.

WHERE TO STAY

Marina Village Inn
1151 Pacific Marina, at end of Triumph Dr.,
(800) 345-0304, (510) 523-9450;
www.marinavillage inn.com. 51 rooms; $-$$.
Heated pool. Continental breakfast.

In this quiet waterfront hotel, all rooms have either a private deck or balcony.

Webster House Bed & Breakfast Inn
1238 Versailles Ave., (510) 523-9697, (954) 586-7718;
http://websterhouse2.home.comcast.net/˜webster-
house2. 3 rooms, 1 cottage; $$. Some gas fireplaces.
Afternoon tea; full breakfast. No pets.

This 1854 Gothic-Revival predates Victorians and is Alameda's oldest house. The house was constructed in New York, then brought around the Horn in sections via clipper ship and assembled in Alameda. It is an easy walk to the beach. Vegetarian or vegan meals and other special diets are available by request.

Afternoon tea and dinner is served daily by appointment; non-guests are welcome.

WHERE TO EAT

Boniere Bakery
1417 Park St./Central Ave., (510) 522-0110;
www.boniere.com. M-Sat 7-6; $.

This oldest continuously operating bakery in California (since 1878) whips up European-style pastries, housemade chocolates, and dough to go. Everything is made from scratch, using real eggs and fresh fruit.

Burma SuperStar
1345 Park St./Alameda Ave., (510) 522-6200;
www.burmasuperstar.com. L-D daily; $.
No reservations.

Exotic Burmese cuisine is on the menu in this contemporary dining room with high ceilings and a wall of windows. A salad platter that is mixed at the table is always a choice starter, and the crunchy tea leaf salad is superb (dried shrimp powder is served on the side, just in case). A variety of curries are available, and most dishes can be made vegetarian by request.

La Pinata #3
1440 Park St., (510) 769-9110; www.lapinata.com.
B-L-D daily, SunBr; $.

Mexican food is served in large portions in a festive atmosphere at this wildly popular spot. Portions are large and the menu includes carne asada, layered enchiladas, carnitas, fajitas, chimichangas, pollo a la diablo, tamales, and seafood. The bar has a selection of more than 300 100% Blue Agave tequilas—the largest selection in Northern California—and makes great margaritas. Mexican breakfast is served all day.

Ole's Waffle Shop
1507 Park St./Santa Clara Ave., (510) 522-8108. B-L-D daily; $. No reservations.

Always packed, this old-fashioned spot has a counter and comfy booths. Breakfast is served all day, but many folks come here for the burgers, steaks, and deep-fried broasted chicken. Biscuits and gravy are also on the menu, along with Jell-O and tapioca pudding.

Speisekammer
2424 Lincoln Ave./Park St., (510) 522-1300; www.speisekammer.com. L F-Sun, D daily; $$. Reservations for 6+.

Pronounced "shpy-say-kummer," which means "pantry" in German, this pleasant spot serves well-executed German specialties such as sausages, venison, potato pancakes with housemade applesauce, schnitzels, and spatzle. German beers are on tap (and available in everything from 3-ounce sample flights to the 2-liter "boot"), and dessert choices include apple strudel and Black Forest cake. A biergarten patio in front is available in good weather. Free live music is scheduled Thursday through Saturday evenings. The first Friday of the month is Pirate Night, featuring seafaring songs, and everyone is invited to come dressed as pirates.

Tucker's Super Creamed Ice Cream
1349 Park St., (510) 522-4960; www.tuckersicecream.com. Sun-M 12-9:30, Tu-Thur 11-9:30, F-Sat 11-11; $.

Operating in a historic building, this Park Street institution has been here since 1941. More than 33 flavors of ice cream, sorbets, and sherbets are available, and fresh fudge, waffle cones, and cakes are made fresh daily. A rear patio with a sheltering jacaranda tree and a fountain is open in good weather.

FREMONT

A LITTLE BACKGROUD

In its heyday, from 1912 to 1916, the Niles district of town was the largest film studio in Northern California. Charlie Chaplin made some of his earliest silent films here—*The Champion* and *The Tramp*. More recently, Fremont has been declared the best city in America to raise a child in.

WHAT TO DO

Ardenwood Historic Farm
34600 Ardenwood Blvd., off Hwy. 84, (510) 796-0663; www.ebparks.org. Thur, F, Sun 10-4; $5, 62+ $4, 4-17 $3.50; admission includes horse-drawn railroad & house tour. Also open Tu, W, Sat 10-4; $2, under 18 free. House tour: (510) 791-4196; Thur-Sun 11-3; get tickets at train station; additional fee on Sat; must be age 6+.

Situated in a fragrant eucalyptus grove, this 205-acre farm was named after a forested area described in Shakespeare's *As You Like It*. It is one of the few historic farm parks in the West and allows visitors to step back in time for a view of 1880s farm life. The old farm buildings, crop fields, and antique farm equipment have all been restored, and on some days the

Horse-drawn narrow-gauge railroad

admission fee includes a ride on a novel horse-drawn narrow-gauge railroad. Throughout the park, staff in period costumes demonstrate typical Victorian farm chores that vary with the season but might include grinding corn, rope making, or washing clothes. Visitors are encouraged to pitch in. A blacksmith demonstrates his craft Thursday-Sunday. Children especially enjoy rolling around on the grassy expanses. Sometimes they can see baby farm animals, and sometimes rugs are hung out on the line for them to beat clean.

Hourly tours are given of the restored **Patterson House**—a white gingerbread Victorian farmhouse furnished with period antiques that are original to the house.

Supplement a picnic with farm fare from the **Farmyard Cafe** and, in season, with organic vegetables sold at the park entrance.

Coyote Hills Regional Park

8000 Patterson Ranch Rd., (510) 795-9385; www.ebparks.org/parks/coyote_hills. Daily 8-8; Nov-Mar, 8-6. Visitor Center: Tu-Sun 9:30-5. $5/vehicle, $2/dog.

The Visitor Center features an Ohlone Indian display, and an Indian archaeological site is sometimes accessible. The park has 15 miles of trails, plus a boardwalk trail through a freshwater cattail marsh. Picnic tables are available.

Mission San Jose De Guadalupe

43300 Mission Blvd./Washington Blvd., (510) 657-1797; www.missionsanjose.org. Daily 10-5. By donation.

Marking the center of the oldest community in the East Bay, this mission was founded in 1797 and is 14th in the chain of California missions. It is also known as Old Mission San Jose and was the only mission built in the East Bay. Though little remains of the original structure, part of the original adobe monastery wing now holds exhibits. Of particular note are the peaceful graveyard and the beautiful interior of the 1809 New England Gothic-style St. Joseph's Church.

New United Motor Manufacturing

45500 Fremont Blvd., (510) 498-5765; www.nummi.com. Tu-F at 10, 1. Free. Must be age 10+. Reservations required.

This 75-minute tour begins with a video and includes a tram ride through the Toyota assembly plant. Reservations are taken up to 3 months in advance.

Niles Canyon Railway Museum

6 Kilkare Rd., in Sunol, (925) 862-9063; www.ncry.org. Every Sun Apr-Aug; 1st & 3rd Sun, Jan-Mar, Sept, & Oct; at 10:30, 12, 1:30, 3. By donation: $10, 62+ $8, 4-12 $5.

Operating on abandoned Southern Pacific Lines rail, refurbished oil-burning and steam engines and World War II-era diesel locomotives follow the original route of the 1869 transcontinental railroad. They hiss and chug through a woodsy gorge while pulling a variety of vintage cars between Sunol and Niles. Old train cars and locomotives in the process of being meticulously restored by members of the Pacific Locomotive Association are also seen from the train. The 13-plus-mile round trip takes an hour. Just a caboose or the entire train can be chartered for a special occasion. Wildflower Trains run in April and May, and decorated Santa Trains run most evenings in December.

Niles Essanay Silent Film Museum & Edison Theater

37417 Niles Blvd., (510) 494-1411; www.nilesfilm museum.org. Movies: Sat at 7:30pm; by donation, $5. Tour of theater: Sat-Sun 12-4; free.

More than 350 movies were produced in Niles, but only about 50 still exist. This museum and theater operate within the historical Essanay silent film studio that once produced movies starring Charlie Chaplin and Broncho Billy Anderson—the first cowboy movie star. A silent film with live piano accompaniment is shown every Saturday night. Tours of historic Niles are sometimes offered.

At the annual **Broncho Billy Silent Film Festival** (*June. $7-$10.*) screenings of movies filmed in the area are enhanced by film seminars and tours of Niles. The annual **Charlie Chaplin Days** (*June. Free.*) involves lookalike contests, impersonators, penny carnival games, and screenings of movies that Charlie Chaplin filmed in the area.

WHERE TO EAT

Little Sichuan Express
34420-G Fremont Blvd., (510) 608-0585. L-D daily; $.
For description, see page 171.

Salang Pass
37462 Fremont Blvd./Central St., (510) 795-9200; www.salangpass.com. L-D Tu-Sun; $$. Reservations accepted.

Fremont has the largest population of Afghanis outside of Afghanistan. Located in the Little Kabul neighborhood, this comfortable restaurant specializes in Afghan cuisine. Seating is on the floor in a tented area with floor cushions or at regular Western tables. Particularly tasty entrees include ground-meat or lamb kabobs, fish curry, mantoo (a sort of ravioli filled with ground beef), and a borta baked eggplant dish. All dinners come with a western salad and bolani (traditional unleavened Afghan flat bread served with a delicious cilantro dipping sauce). Dough (a yogurt drink flavored with cucumber and mint) makes a tart and refreshing accompaniment, and baklavah is the perfect dessert.

Tyme for Tea & Co.
37501 Niles Blvd./H St., (510) 790-0944; www.tymefortea.com. M-F 12-3, Sat-Sun 11-4; $$. Reservations advised.

Henry James once said, "There are few hours in life more agreeable than the hour dedicated to the ceremony known as afternoon tea." True. Sydney Smith said, "Thank God for tea! What would the world do without tea?—how did it exist? I am glad I was not born before tea." True again. Operating in an alcove within an antique shop and making good use of doilies, mismatched vintage silverware, and charming bone china tea cups, this tearoom offers respite from the day's tribulations. A bathtub full of borrowable hats invites diners to fancy up their outfit. The full Victoria Tea includes loose leaf tea (herbals and decafs available) or coffee (this *is* the U.S., *not* England), a scone with crème frâiche plus lemon curd and preserves, and assorted tea sandwiches and pastries. Smaller spreads are also available. Should there be a wait, browse the shop's well-priced collection. Allow time to visit the myriad antique shops that line the street for several blocks.

Udupi Palace
5988 New Park Mall Rd., in Newark, (510) 794-8400; www.udupipalaceca.com. L-D daily; $.
For description, see page 297.

Vung Tau 3
6092 Mowry Ave., in Cedar Shopping Center, in Newark, (510) 793-8299; www.vungtaurestaurant.com. L-D Tu-Sun; $. Reservations accepted.

Located in a mall filled with Asian restaurants and shops, this spot serves authentic Vietnamese cuisine in a comfortable coffee shop atmosphere. Delicious options from the extensive menu include a tasty Panang curry, a specialty red curry chicken, and a flat sheet rice noodle topped with either butterflied grilled prawns or onion-beef and served with a plate of undressed fresh herbs and salad makings. Noodle soups and rice plates are good one-plate choices. The large drink menu includes a Thai iced tea with a frozen scoop of milk and also unusual shakes—durian (a strange-tasting Asian fruit), avocado, green bean.

LIVERMORE WINE COUNTRY

A LITTLE BACKGROUND

Surprisingly, out here in Livermore just past the tract homes, more than 40 wineries are busy making darn good wines. They're less touted only because they aren't in Sonoma-Napa, and many continue to offer free tasting. It's even still possible to buy a home here with a vineyard that is maintained by a winery.

But, of course, there's no need to actually move to Livermore to enjoy the bounty. Just come for a visit. Check winery websites ahead, because some offer two-for-one tasting coupons; and consider joining a wine club, because members often get free tasting and other perks.

The challenge is to prepare an itinerary. Figure on three or four wineries a day, maximum. And vary the program. For instance, try one big winery, one midsized venue selected maybe just because the name is intriguing, and also one out-of-the-way place. Alternatively, just go where the wind blows you.

VISITOR INFORMATION

Tri-Valley Convention & Visitors Bureau
349 Main St. #203, Pleasanton, (888) 874-9253, (925) 846-8910; www.trivalleycvb.com.

This bureau covers Pleasanton, Livermore, Dublin, and San Ramon.

Livermore Valley Winegrowers Association
3585 Greenville Rd. #4, (925) 447-WINE; www.livermorewine.com.

GETTING THERE

Located 45 miles east of San Francisco, 10 miles east of Fremont. Be sure to secure a map from the visitors bureau, as the roads here can be a confusing maze.

WHAT TO DO

Del Valle Regional Park
7000 Del Valle Rd., (925) 373-0332; www.ebparks.org. Daily 6am-9pm through Labor Day. $6/vehicle, $2/dog, canoe rental $10/hr.

Pleasant Lake Del Valle is great for swimming and fishing, and horseback riders, mountain bikers, and hikers are welcome along its banks. Windsurfing and sailboat lessons are available, and boats and bikes can be rented. Lifeguards are on duty in summer at two beaches. Picnic tables and campsites are available.

Livermore Centennial Light Bulb
4550 East Ave., in Livermore Fire Station #6, (925) 454-2361; www.centennialbulb.org. By appt.

This light bulb has burned here since 1901. It is declared the oldest known working light bulb by the *Guinness Book of World Records*.

WINERIES

Bent Creek Winery
5455 Greenville Rd., (925) 989-9610; www.bentcreekwinery.com. Tasting F-Sun 12-5; no tour.

The tasting room here is set back in among vineyards, with an oak-dotted ridge as a backdrop. The winery makes reds—owner Pat Heineman describes their most popular wine, Petite Sirah, as "a monster"—and two ports. A sheltered patio provides both tables for picnicking and a great view.

Charles R Vineyards
8195 Crane Ridge Rd., (925) 454-3040; www.charlesrvineyards.com. Tasting F-Sun 12-4:30; tour by appt.

Located on an old mining trail, this winery is definitely way out there. The winery makes both reds and whites as well as a Portuguese-style dessert wine, and it provides a scenic picnic area.

Concannon Vineyard
4590 Tesla Rd., (800) 258-9866, (925) 456-2505; www.concannonvineyard.com. Tasting daily 11-4:30; tour by appt.

Established in 1883, Concannon is one of the oldest continuously operating wineries in the country, and it was among the first to make big reds. Spokesman Jim Ryan says, "We do environmentally friendly things because it makes a better wine." Most of the wines are sold only at the winery, but the Petite Syrah is available in all 50 states and 17 foreign countries. Wines are contained in heavier than usual bottles featuring a pressed image of the property's front gate. Tasting occurs in a barn-like brick-and-redwood room, and picnic tables are available under an arbor of table grapes that are at their sweetest in September.

Garré Vineyard and Winery
7986 Tesla Rd., (925) 371-8200; www.garrewinery.com. Tasting Sat-Sun 11:30-4:30; no tour. Cafe: L daily, D F-Sun; $$.

One of the larger small wineries, Garré specializes in small lots of high quality wine and uncommon Bordeaux blends. Two bocce ball courts are available, and cooking demonstrations are sometimes scheduled in the cafe.

La Rochelle

*5443 Tesla Rd., (925) 243-6442; www.lrwine.com.
Tasting daily 12-4:30; no tour.*

This winery focuses on Pinot Noir. A flight tasting paired with a food platter is offered in its relaxing tasting room; reservations are not necessary.

The Steven Kent Winery

*5443 Tesla Rd., (925) 243-6440; www.stevenkent.com.
Tasting daily 12-4:30; no tour.*

Incredibly enthusiastic owner-winemaker Steven Mirassou makes a delicious "Merrillie" Chardonnay and Vincere. Picnic tables are shaded by several olive trees.

Tamas Estates

*5489 Tesla Rd., (925) 456-2380;
www.tamasestates.com. Tasting daily 11-4:30; no tour.*

This winery produces only Italian wines, including Pinot Grigio and Barbera. The Sangiovese, an easy-to-drink red table wine, is particularly tasty. All the wines are bottled with a trendy, Very Now screw cap.

Wente Vineyards

*5050 Arroyo Rd., (925) 456-2405;
www.wentevineyards.com. Tasting daily 11-6:30;
cave tour Sat-Sun at 1 & 3, reservation required.*

The area's largest winery, Wente claims to be "California's oldest family-owned and continuously operated winery," with fourth- and fifth-generation Wentes carrying on the business. In addition to making a killer 2004 Crane Ridge Merlot—it is smooth and gives a big buzz—Wente schedules summer concerts under the stars (in the past, Ringo Starr, Huey Lewis, and Seal have played here), offers an 18-hole public golf course designed by Greg Norman, and has an excellent restaurant with tree-shaded terraces that are heavenly in good weather. And it has a *real* cork tree on the property.
The Estate Winery Tasting Room *(5565 Tesla Rd., (925) 456-2300. Tasting daily 11-4:30; tours daily at 11, 1, 2, 3.)* is nearby and is where the winery began.

WHERE TO STAY

Purple Orchid Inn Resort & Spa

*4549 Cross Rd., (800) 353-4549, (925) 606-8855;
www.purpleorchid.com. 8 rooms; $$-$$$+.
Pool; 2 hot tubs; 1 tennis court; golf driving range;
full-service spa.*

Getting here is via a soothing rural drive past wineries galore. This property abuts scenic vineyard-covered hillsides amid horse and sheep ranches. It is surrounded by 18 acres of olive trees.

WHERE TO EAT

Campo di Bocce

*175 E. Vineyard Ave., (925) 249-9800;
www.campodibocce.com. L-D Sun-Thur; $-$$.
Bocce: $10/person/1½ hr. Reservations advised.*

Delicious Italian fare mingles here with bocce ball—the game that "takes five minutes to learn, a lifetime to master." This hooting-and-hollering spot has eight inside and outside courts, as well as inside and outside dining.

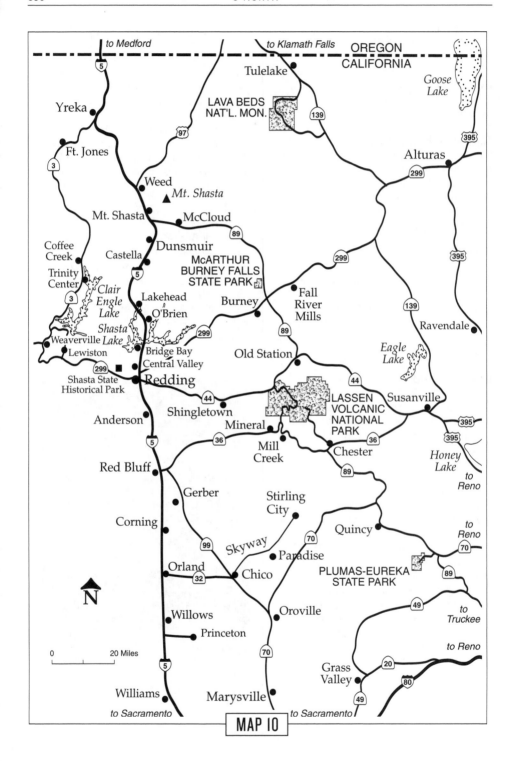

MAP 10

5 NORTH

WILLIAMS

WHERE TO STAY NEARBY

Wilbur Hot Springs
For description, see page 257.

WHERE TO EAT

Granzella's
451 Sixth St., (800) 759-6104, (530) 473-5583; www.granzellas.com. B,L,D daily; $.
Popular with travelers and locals alike, this complex burned to the ground in 2007. But it's back: an Italian restaurant; a deli (which claims to have the largest selection of imported beer in Northern California); a shop selling baked goods and bargain-priced local olives; a bar with a collection of mounted trophies, including a giant polar bear.
The **Inn** *((800) 643-8614, (530) 473-3310. 43 rooms; $-$$. Unheated pool, hot tub. Continental breakfast.)* is particularly popular with duck hunters in season.

WILLOWS

A LITTLE BACKGROUND

I-5 between Sacramento and Redding parallels one North America's great wildlife migration routes. Known as the **Pacific Flyway**, it runs the length of the Central Valley, where the birds find plenty of food and water. Once composed of oak woodlands, grasslands and marshes, this area now grows rice, nuts, fruits, and vegetables.

WHAT TO DO

Wildlife refuges
(530) 934-2801; www.fws.gov/sacramento valleyrefuges.

• Colusa National Wildlife Refuge
Hwy. 20 exit, 15 mi. S of town, just N of Williams.
This refuge is about 7 miles off the freeway. It has a 3-mile gravel loop drive, a viewing platform, and a 1-mile walking trail.

• Sacramento National Wildlife Refuge
Norman Rd./County Road 68 exit, 5 mi. S of town. Visitor Center: Daily 9-4 during Nov-Feb migration; M-F Mar-Oct. $3/vehicle.
This refuge has a 6-mile auto tour, a viewing platform, and a 2-mile walking trail.

CHICO

A LITTLE BACKGROUND

Though many residents of this charming small town prefer to play it down, Chico is most famous for its party school, Chico State—the second-oldest university in the state. Both *Playboy* and MTV have acknowledged this claim to fame. And indeed, lots of students are seen around town, which is not particularly surprising since downtown streets dead-end at the campus. Still, in spite of the fact that Chico is first and foremost Party Central, much more to see and do awaits visitors here. It is no wonder that Chico is also referred to as "the crown jewel of the north valley," and many movies were filmed here, among them *Gone with the Wind* and Clint Eastwood's *The Outlaw Josey Wales*.

VISITOR INFORMATION

Butte County Cultural Tourism
805 Whispering Winds Lane, (530) 228-2860; www.experiencebuttecounty.com.

Chico Chamber of Commerce
300 Salem St., (800) 852-8570, (530) 891-5556; www.chicochamber.com.

GETTING THERE

Located 85 miles north of Sacramento via Highway 99, and 180 miles northeast of San Francisco via I-5 to Highway 32 east, and 22 miles east of I-5.

ANNUAL EVENTS

Endangered Species Faire
May. (530) 891-6424; www.endangeredspeciesfaire.org. Free.
    Interactive educational activities, live animal presentations, and musical performances combine to make this an enjoyable event.

WHAT TO DO

Bidwell Mansion State Historic Park
525 The Esplanade, downtown, (530) 895-6144; www.parks.ca.gov. Mansion tour: Tu-F 12-4, Sat-Sun 10-4, on the hr. $4, 5-17 $2.

    An early pioneer, General John Bidwell arrived in California in 1841 and founded Chico in 1860. He built this 3-floor, 26-room Italianate Victorian mansion in 1868. Its cavernous rooms have 14-foot ceilings and provide a cooling break in summer. Interesting features include eight slate fireplaces painted to look like marble and a third-floor ballroom, which because the owners were Presbyterians was never used for that purpose. Shockingly, the house once was used as a Chico State dormitory. A gigantic Southern magnolia tree planted out front in 1863 is now taller than the house, and an adjacent carriage house displays several antique coaches and wagons.

Bidwell Park
(530) 895-4972; www.ci.chico.ca.us/parks/Bidwell_Park.asp. Daily to sunset, opening hr. varies. Free.
    The third-largest city park in the U.S. (Phoenix's South Mountain Park is the largest, Los Angeles' Griffith Park is second), this 3,670-acre park was the movie stand-in for Sherwood Forest in the original 1938 *Adventures of Robin Hood*. Among its numerous trails is the ½-mile-long World of Trees Independence Trail nature path that winds through a former U.S. Forest Service tree nursery and is accessible to both the physically and visually challenged. Most of the park is closed to cars and so is particularly enjoyable on a bicycle, which can be rented downtown. In summer, Chico Creek is dammed to form several swimming holes. Imaginative Caper Acres playground located at the south end has a nursery rhyme theme, and a stables rents horses.
    Chico Creek Nature Center *(1968 E. 8th St., (530) 891-4671; www.bidwellpark.org. Tu-Sun 11-4. By donation.)* displays living examples of area wildlife and operates a children's program.

California State University, Chico (Chico State)
2nd St./Hazel St., (800) 542-4426, (530) 898-6835; www.csuchico.edu. Guided campus tours; schedule varies; free; reservations advised.
    Founded in 1887, this beautiful campus has several art galleries, an anthropology museum, and a rose garden.

Chico Museum

141 Salem St., (530) 891-4336;
www.chicomuseum.org. W-Sun 12-4. By donation; $2,
children $1.

Housed in an architecturally interesting former Carnegie Library dating from 1904, this gem of a museum focuses on Chico's history and culture. Collection highlights include the town's original Chinese Taoist Temple and some exceptional Maidu and Yahi Indian baskets.

National Yo-Yo Museum

320 Broadway, in Bird in Hand store, (530) 893-0545;
www.nationalyoyo.org. M-Sat 10-6, Sun 12-5. Free.

More than 2,000 yo-yos are displayed here. Among them is the world's largest—a 256-pound wooden behemoth that requires an 80-foot crane to operate.

The **National Yo-Yo Championships** are hosted here annually in October.

Satava Art Glass Studio

819 Wall St., (530) 345-7985; www.satava.com.
Tu-F 9-2. Free.

Using ancient techniques to create nature-themed glass pieces, Richard Satava has been blowing vividly colored artworks at his studio here since 1977. His ethereal jellyfish pieces sell

for between $400 and $10,000. Less expensive items are also available in the gift shop inside a converted house. Watching him in action out back in his cool, open-air studio is fascinating. There, surrounded by mature black bamboo and a giant fig tree, Rick and crew perform their finely orchestrated glass-blowing dance to vintage Beatles tunes and squawking jays.

WHERE TO STAY

The Grateful Bed

1462 Arcadian Ave./W. 5th Ave., (530) 342-2464;
www.thegratefulbed.net. 4 rooms; $$. No TVs.
Full breakfast. No pets.

On a tree-lined residential street near downtown, this lovely 1905 Victorian farm-house features beautifully decorated rooms. Suite Dreams is a standout, with a king-size iron bed and oversize bath with clawfoot tub and twin pedestal sinks. The three-course candlelight breakfast sometimes includes decadent white chocolate scones.

Holiday Inn

685 Manzanita Ct., 4 mi. from downtown,
(800) 310-2491, (530) 345-2491;
www.holiday-inn.com. 5 stories; 172 rooms; $.
Evening snack M-Thur; restaurant. Unheated pool;
hot tub; fitness room.

Located on the quieter outskirts of town, this full-service hotel provides a complimentary shuttle to the airport.

Music Express Inn

1145 El Monte Ave./Hwy. 32, 2 mi. from downtown,
(530) 891-9833; www.northvalley.net/musicexpress.
9 rooms; $. Full breakfast. Unheated pool.

Out on the edge of town near where Highways 32 and 99 intersect, this simple inn offers rooms are in several converted houses and has a fence out front that is usually loaded with gorgeous roses. It combines the best of a motel and B&B: Guests can park in front of their room motel-style and also enjoy a made-to-order breakfast B&B-style. The owner conducts music lessons in the main house and operates a popular music camp here in summer, hence the name. Don't miss seeing her 1916 Steinway reproducing grand that plays 500 pieces of music just as the artist originally performed them (Martha Stewart has a 1926 model).

WHERE TO EAT

Shubert's Ice Cream & Candy

178 E. 7th St./Main St., (530) 342-7163;
www.shuberts.com. M-F 9:30-10, Sat-Sun 11-10; $.

On a hot summer day in Chico, nothing beats an ice cream cone. Family-owned since 1938 and now a town landmark, this shop dispenses to-die-for housemade ice cream and candies. There's no place to sit inside, but get a cone—consider a simple Chico mint, a Mount Shasta (chocolate ice cream with coconut and marshmallow swirls), or a fabulous Turtle (caramel ice cream with pecans and chocolate swirl)—and sit on a bench out front, just licking lazily and watching the world go by.

Sierra Nevada Taproom & Restaurant

1075 E. 20th St., just W of Hwy. 99 at 20th St. exit,
(530) 345-2739; www.sierranevada.com. L-D Tu-Sun,
SunBr; $. Tour M-F & Sun at 2:30, Sat continuously
12-3; self-guided tour daily 10-6.

This renowned brewery is the country's seventh largest. It has a stylish taproom and restaurant situated inside a large room accented with polished copper and gleaming wood. This brewpub serves up its famous Pale Ale and other housemade beers (a sampler is available) as well as a deliciously executed, modestly priced menu featuring expected items such as beer-battered fish & chips and a hamburger. More exotic fare is also available, including an Asian noodle salad and an assortment of wood-fire oven pizzas with chi-chi toppings. In nice weather, the outside patio is primo and the perfect place to try a milkshake made with the brewery's own malt. Mustards and malt vinegar made with house beers make good souvenirs.

Thursday Night Market

Broadway/3rd St., downtown, (530) 345-6500;
www.downtownchico.net. Thur 6-9pm; Apr-Sept only.

For this weekly event, the streets are lined with vendors displaying handmade goods and farm-fresh produce, and shops and restaurants stay open later than usual. Children's activities and entertainers provide diversion for everyone.

Tres Hombres Restaurant

100 Broadway/1st St., downtown, (530) 342-0425.
L-D daily; $-$$. Reservations for 8+.

Popular with students, this restaurant serves a selection of Mexican items in John Bidwell's former storehouse and office. In a large, open, brick-walled room with comfy booths and roomy tables, this happening place's menu offers the expected as well as more imaginative items such as tequila-lime paella and pasta. The excellent fajitas dish is large enough for two people with average appetites to share. A cheeseburger is an option, and margaritas come in many styles, including non-alcoholic fresh fruit versions.

PARADISE

VISITOR INFORMATION

Paradise Ridge Chamber of Commerce

5550 Skyway #1, (888) 845-2769, (530) 877-9356;
www.paradisechamber.com.

GETTING THERE

From Chico, this mountain hamlet is an easy 11-mile drive up a scenic hill via Skyway/Highway 134. On the way, watch both for fields dotted with big rocks left from when Mt. Lassen blew in prehistoric times and for historical Chinese walls fitted together without mortar. The town sign reads, "May you find Paradise to be all its name implies."

ANNUAL EVENTS

Johnny Appleseed Days

October. (530) 877-9356; www.paradisechamber.com.
Free.

Though only one orchard is left in this former apple producing area, people come from all over to celebrate everything apple. Demonstrations, crafts, a pancake breakfast, and, of course, lots of apple pie are part of the fun. This festival has been held since 1880.

WHAT TO DO

Antiquing

This town has more than 20 well-priced antiques shops, most of them on the main drag. Some are in old historical houses sporting pampered resident cats and atmospheric old-time music. One of the most extensive inventories is in the **Skyway Antique Mall** (*6118*

Skyway, (530) 877-6503; www.skywayantique
mall.com. M-Sat 10-5, Sun 12-5.), where
25 dealers display their finds.

Gold Nugget Museum

502 Pearson Rd., (530) 872-8722;
www.goldnuggetmuseum.com. W-Sun 12-4. Free.

Visitors here can walk through a replica
mine and view a reproduction of the largest
gold nugget ever discovered in North America—
a 54-pound monster found here in 1859.
A miniature covered bridge and a one-room
schoolhouse are found on the shady grounds
outside, and a blacksmith shop and gold panning sluices operate on summer weekends.

Days of Living History occurs each year in
September and includes crafts demonstrations,
hands-on activities, and food booths.

Honey Run Covered Bridge

Take downhill road directly across street from Skyway
Antique Mall at 6118 Skyway, (530) 895-0911;
www.colmanmuseum.com/coveredbridge.html.

Built across Butte Creek in 1894, this is the
only covered bridge in the U.S. with three different roof levels. Though closed to traffic, it
provides a lovely stroll. (A horse and buggy
scene was shot here for the 1955 film Friendly
Persuasion.)

An annual fund-raising **Pancake Breakfast**
(June. (530) 342-9197.) raises money for a local
school and museum and permits the opportunity to dine on the bridge. Arts and crafts
projects and live music are part of the down-
home atmosphere.

From here, it's 5 miles back to Chico on a
road that passes through 1,000-foot-deep Butte
Creek Canyon gorge—called "Little Grand
Canyon" by locals.

WHERE TO EAT

Stirling City Hotel

16975 Skyway, 17 mi. from town, up scenic Skyway, in
Stirling City, (530) 873-0858; www.stirlingcity.info/
schotel.shtml. Schedule varies; $. Reservations
required.

The picturesque mountain town of
Stirling City retains its original wooden
walkways from when it was action central for
logging. Though it has a population of
only 371, logging continues.

Afternoon tea is served in this 1903 building, as is lunch, dinner, and weekend brunch—
all by advance reservation. Diners are assured
tasty fare. Owner-chef-cookbook author
Charlotte Ann Hilgeman says she only makes
dishes she likes "because I might have to eat the
leftovers."

The **B&B** (6 rooms. $-$$. Afternoon snack;
full breakfast. No pets.) part of the hotel consists
of simple, cozy, and blessedly un-cutesy guest
rooms. They are decorated with vintage
furniture and chenille bedspreads and share
bathrooms.

Across the street, manicured **Clotilde
Merlo Park** ((530) 873-1658. Thur-Sun 10-7;
May-Oct only. Free.) has several koi-filled
ponds, nature trails, and a lovely outdoor
chapel.

CORNING

GETTING THERE

This small town is 170 somewhat flat, dreary
miles from San Francisco, punctuated only by
the occasional sighting of an unusual migrating
bird. It is the I-5 mid-point between Los
Angeles and Portland.

WHAT TO DO

Olive Pit

2156 Solano St., (800) OLIVE-PIT, (530) 824-4667;
www.olivepit.com. Daily 7am-8pm, in summer to 9.

In the town that is the center of the olive
industry in Northern California, everything
olive is found here. Taste a vast variety of
flavored olives (the best being the greens stuffed
with pimento and almond), pick up some car
snacks, or chow down on fast food.

RED BLUFF

A LITTLE BACKGROUND

After passing over a crest just before town,
a verdant valley unfolds backed by the magnificent mountain range dominated by Mount
Shasta.

VISITOR INFORMATION

Red Bluff/Tehama County Chamber of Commerce

100 Main St., (800) 655-6225, (530) 527-6220; www.redbluffchamberofcommerce.com.

ANNUAL EVENTS

South Shasta Model Railroad

Held every other year; April-May; Sun. In Gerber, 12 mi. S of town, (530) 385-1389. $5, 5-12 $3.

This miniature ¼-inch O-gauge reproduction of the 100-mile Southern Pacific Railroad line from Gerber to Dunsmuir operates in the basement of a private farmhouse. It includes 16 handmade steam locomotives, 100 cars, and more than 900 feet of track. Visitors can also ride on a 2-foot-gauge steam train and visit a museum of antique farm equipment.

Honey Bee Festival

September. In Palo Cedro, (530) 547-3676; www.palocedrohoneybeefestival.com. Free.

The town buzzes with excitement during this happy event, which includes a pancake breakfast, food booths, and bee-related stuff.

WHAT TO DO

Coleman National Fish Hatchery

24411 Coleman Fish Hatchery Rd., in Anderson, 16 mi. E of I-5, (530) 365-8622; www.fws.gov/redbluff/coleman.html. Daily 7:30am-dusk. Free.

The huge Chinook, or king salmon, flap their way out of Battle Creek and up the fish ladder here four times each year. See the fall run spawn October through mid-December; the late fall run spawn January through March; the winter run spawn May through July; and the spring run spawn August through September. Steelhead trout spawn January through March. Fingerlings can be seen in holding tanks in the hatchery building. This is the largest salmon hatchery in the U.S.

A **Salmon Festival** occurs here each October.

Kelly-Griggs House Museum

1248 Jefferson St., (530) 527-1129. Thur-Sun 1-4. By donation.

This restored 1880s Victorian is just off the freeway. While here, pick up a self-guiding map to local Victorian homes.

William B. Ide Adobe State Historic Park

21659 Adobe Rd., (530) 529-8599; www.parks.ca.gov. Daily 8-5. $4/vehicle.

Located on the outskirts of town beside the Sacramento River, this authentically furnished one-room adobe was the home of early California settler William B. Ide—the Republic of California's first and only president. Other buildings in the 3-acre park are an adobe smokehouse, a carriage shed for old buggies, and a small corral. This is a great spot for a picnic.

LASSEN VOLCANIC NATIONAL PARK AND AREA

A LITTLE BACKGROUND

Considered to be an active volcano that is now dormant, imposing 10,457-foot Lassen Peak last erupted in 1915. (It is one of only two active volcanoes on the U.S. mainland. The other is Mt. St. Helens in Washington state, which last erupted in 1980. A curious fact is that they both erupted in the month of May.) It is thought to be the largest plug dome volcano in the world.

McArthur-Burney Falls

The best time to visit is July through September, when the 30-mile road through the park is least likely to be closed by snow. Visitors can take several self-guided nature walks and attend campfire talks in summer. Children age 7 through 12 can participate in the Junior Ranger program (see page 468), and those age 4 through 6 can participate in the Chipmunk Club (contact the Loomis Museum for information). In winter, ranger-led snowshoe walks are scheduled. For skiing information, see page 456.

Boardwalks supplement the trail through popular **Bumpass Hell** (it is named after its discoverer Kendall Bumpass, who severely burned his leg when he fell into a boiling mud pot), which is the largest geothermal feature in the park and sports geological oddities such as boiling springs and mud pots, pyrite pools, and noisy fumaroles. The trail covers 3 miles and takes 2 or 3 hours round trip to walk. The park also offers more than 150 miles of backcountry trails, including a 17-mile section of the Pacific Crest Trail.

The park's **Loomis Museum** *((530) 595-4444 x5180. Daily 9-5, June-Aug only. Free.)*, which is located inside a lovely old stone building at Manzanita Lake, has an orientation video and exhibits dramatic photos of the 1915 eruption.

A free park newsletter/map orients visitors and lists daily activities. Campsites are available.

Park admission is $10 per vehicle.

VISITOR INFORMATION

Park Headquarters
38350 Hwy. 36, in Mineral, (530) 595-4444; www.nps.gov/lavo. M-F 8-4:30.

Lassen County Chamber of Commerce
601 Richmond Rd., in Susanville, (530) 257-4323; www.lassencountychamber.org.

GETTING THERE

Take Highway 36 east from Red Bluff, or Highway 44 east from Redding.

WHAT TO DO

Fort Crook Museum
43030 Fort Crook Museum Rd., on Hwy. 299, in Fall River Mills, (530) 336-5110; www.ftcrook.org. Tu-Sun 12-4; May-Oct only. Free.

Composed of a 3-story main building and eight outer buildings, this large complex displays six rooms of antique furniture, a collection of early farm implements and Native American artifacts, the old Fall River jail, a one-room schoolhouse from Pittville, a pioneer log cabin, and more.

McArthur-Burney Falls Memorial State Park
24898 Hwy. 89, in Burney, (530) 335-2777; www.parks. ca.gov. Daily 8-4; Apr-Sept to 11. $6/vehicle.

A lovely 1-mile nature trail winds past the soothing rush of the 129-foot waterfall here (Theodore Roosevelt called it the eighth wonder of the world), allowing for closer inspection of the volcanic terrain for which this area is known. Paddleboats can be rented at man-made Lake Britton, where facilities include picnic tables, a sandy beach, and a wading area for children. Swimming is allowed only in designated areas, as the lake has a steep drop-off. Campsites and camping cabins are available.

A boat is needed to reach isolated **Ahjumawi Lava Springs State Park**, which features one of the largest systems of freshwater springs in the world. Descendants of the Native American Ahjumawi tribe reside in the area. Twelve miles away, the town of Burney offers motels and supermarkets.

Spattercone Crest Trail

½ mi. W of Old Station, across from Hat Creek Campground. Free.

This 2-mile, self-interpretive trail winds past a number of volcanic spatter cones, lava tubes, domes, and blowholes. It takes about 2 hours to walk and is most comfortably hiked in early morning or late afternoon.

Subway Cave

1 mi. N of Old Station, near junction of Hwys. 44 & 89, (530) 336-5521. Free.

Lava tubes formed here about 2,000 years ago, when the surface of a lava flow cooled and hardened while the liquid lava beneath the hard crust flowed away. This cave, which is actually a lava tube, winds for about ¼ mile. Always a cool 46 degrees, it makes a good place to visit on a hot afternoon. However, it is completely unlighted inside, so visitors are advised to bring along a powerful lantern. Allow time for a picnic in the lovely surrounding woods. Just north of here, Mt. Lassen starts showing up in the rearview mirror, and Mt. Shasta looms ahead.

WHERE TO STAY

Little lodging is found here, but many forest campsites are available on a first-come, first-served basis. Bear in mind that this area is remote and does not offer many big-city facilities or supermarkets.

Drakesbad Guest Ranch

At end of Warner Valley Rd., 17 mi. from Chester, (530) 529-1512 x120; www.drakesbad.com. 19 units; $$$+; closed Oct-May. No TVs. Hot springs pool. Includes 3 meals. No pets.

Located at the end of the road—the last 3 miles of which is dirt—in a secluded, scenic mountain valley within the national park, this rustic resort was a hot springs spa in the mid-1800s. It has been a guest ranch since the turn of the 19th century and is now the only one located within a national park. Most of the rustic cabins, bungalows, and lodge rooms have no electricity, so kerosene lanterns provide light. The ranch is within easy hiking distance of some of Lassen's thermal sights: 1 mile from the steaming fumaroles at Boiling Springs Lake; 2 miles from the bubbling sulfurous mud pots at Devil's Kitchen. Guests can rent horses from the ranch stables for guided rides into these areas. All this and a good trout fishing stream, too! Day visitors should call ahead for horse or dining reservations, which include complimentary use of the 90- to 100-degree hot springs-fed pool. Overnight guests should book a year in advance.

Fall River Hotel

24860 Main St., in Fall River Mills, (530) 336-5550; www.fallriverhotel.com. 17 rooms; $. One mini-kitchen. Restaurant.

They keep things simple in these parts. This inn provides cozy comfort, with antique furniture and handmade quilts, but it's not hard to tell the building dates to 1935. And we wouldn't want it any other way. It will be clear that the world has gone to hell in a hand basket when a Ritz opens in the area.

Dinner in the **restaurant** *(B&D daily; $-$$. Reservations advised.)* includes a salad and a glass of house wine and is quite a bargain. Seating is in either a small area with booths and counter stools, or in a more formal dining room with a fireplace built from river rock boulders.

Hat Creek Resort

On Hwy. 89 just N of Hwy. 44, in Old Station, 11 mi. from N entrance to Lassen Park, (800) 568-0109, (530) 335-7121; www.hatcreekresortrv.com. 17 units; $-$$. Cabins closed in winter. Some kitchens.

These bargain motel rooms and old-time housekeeping cabins—with linoleum floors and homemade curtains—are located beside rushing Hat Creek, which is considered to be one of the finest fly-fishing streams in the western U.S. Guests can fish in the creek, roast marshmallows over an open fire, and check out the stars at night.

KOA Kampground
7749 KOA Rd., in Shingletown, 5 mi. S of Hwy. 44, 21 mi. from Lassen, (800) KOA-3403, (530) 474-3133; www.koa.com.

Facilities include a playground, pool, petting zoo, and general store. For more description, see page 467.

St. Bernard Lodge
44801 Hwy. 36, 15 mi. E of Mineral, 10 mi. E of south entrance to Lassen park, 10 mi. W of Chester, in Mill Creek, (530) 258-3382; www.stbernardlodge.com. 7 rooms; $. All shared baths. Continental breakfast; restaurant. No pets.

Old World charm dresses up the cozy knotty-pine interior of this 1920s German inn situated at just under 5,000 feet. One of the two shared bathrooms sports a large clawfoot tub (all rooms have a sink), and antiques and historic memorabilia are displayed throughout. The owners maintain a crystal-clear pond filled with their pet rainbow trout, which guests may feed in the morning. Stables and horse boarding are available, but no horse rentals. Campsites are also available.

The **dining room** *(F D, Sat B-L-D, Sun B-L; $-$$. Reservations required.)* is illuminated by oil-burning lamps, and lace tablecloths cover the tables. The BLT and burger are exceptional and are served on a housemade whole wheat bun with a side of really good big fries; iced tea is served in a gigantic 16-ounce beer stein.

Wild Horse Sanctuary
On Wilson Hill Rd., in Shingletown, 5 mi. S of Hwy. 44, 21 mi. from Lassen, (530) 335-2241; www.wildhorsesanctuary.org. 5 cabins; $435/person/ 1 nt., $535/person/2 nts.; trips Apr-Oct only; viewing year-round, W & Sat 10-3. Unsuitable for children under 14. No TVs; shared bath house. All meals included.

This protected preserve for wild mustangs and burros is the only wild horse sanctuary in the nation. Guests ride out of a base camp to observe the 200-plus population in their natural habitat. Meals are served by an open campfire, and overnight accommodations are in new, but rustic, cabins overlooking Vernal Lake. The price includes everything.

LAVA BEDS NATIONAL MONUMENT

A LITTLE BACKGROUND

This 46,000-acre national monument is located in the middle of nowhere. It has a campground, but the nearest motels and restaurants are far away in Tulelake. There is nowhere to buy food within many miles of the monument, so it is a good idea to pack-in picnic supplies. In fact, this could be where the expression "out in the tules" originated. The area also buzzes with insects, is a haven for rattlesnakes, and sometimes has plague warnings posted. Still, it is an unusual place that is well worth a visit.

The Visitors Center at the southern entrance offers a good orientation. Historically, this area was the site of the 1872 Modoc War—the only major Indian war fought in California. Geologically, the area is of interest because of its concentration of lava tube caves.

Park admission is $10 per vehicle.

VISITOR INFORMATION

Monument Headquarters
(530) 667-8100; www.nps.gov/labe.

GETTING THERE

Go north from Lassen Volcanic National Park on Highway 89 to Highway 299. Continue north on Highway 139, taking it through sparsely populated forest and farmland. The monument is approximately 115 miles northeast of Mt. Shasta City/Highway 5.

WHAT TO DO

Caves
Located a short walk from the **Visitors Center** *(Daily 8:30-5; in summer 8-6.)*, Mushpot Cave has interpretive displays and is the only

lighted cave here. A 2-mile loop road leads to 13 caves developed for easy access, including some with descriptive names such as Blue Grotto, Sunshine, and Natural Bridge. The 71-step staircase at Skull Cave descends 80 feet to an ice floor, and some of Catacombs must be crawled through. Lanterns are available to borrow.

Tule Lake Wildlife Refuge and Lower Klamath National Wildlife Refuge
4 mi. S of Oregon border; www.fws.gov/klamath basinrefuges. Visitor Center: 4009 Hill Rd., in Tulelake, (530) 667-2231; M-F 8-4:30, Sat-Sun 10-4; free.

The gravel road north out of the monument passes through the Tule Lake portion of this scenic area, which is the largest wetlands west of the Mississippi. These refuges are home to a variety of interesting birds that are easily viewed from a car. In winter, they have the densest concentration of bald eagles in the U.S. south of Alaska.

REDDING

A LITTLE BACKGROUND

Built on the Sacramento River, this down-to-earth city anchors the area's outdoor recreation venues. Its stores are convenient for stocking up before heading out on a boating, fishing, hunting, or hiking trip. Redding was once home to the country's largest covered street mall, but no more. The roof is being dismantled and the area is now a pleasant outdoor shopping streetscape. The city claims to be the second-sunniest city in the U.S. (Yuma, Arizona is first). Note that it gets hot here in summer. *Real* hot.

VISITOR INFORMATION

Redding Convention & Visitors Bureau
777 Auditorium Dr., (800) 874-7562, (530) 225-4100; www.visitredding.org.

Shasta-Cascade Wonderland Association
1699 Hwy. 273, in Anderson, 7 mi. S of town, (800) 474-2782, (530) 365-7500; www.shastacascade.org.

GETTING THERE

Located 30 miles north of Red Bluff, and 210 miles north of San Francisco.

WHAT TO DO

Shasta State Historic Park
On Hwy. 299, 10 mi. W of I-5, in Old Shasta, (530) 243-8194; www.parks.ca.gov. Free. Courthouse Museum: W-Sun 10-5; $2, under 6 $1; includes same-day admission to Weaverville Joss House S.H.P.

Prosperous and bustling during the Gold Rush, this gold-mining ghost town is now an interesting museum of restored buildings and picturesque ruins located on either side of the highway. In the 1861 **Courthouse Museum**, a lovely eclectic collection of California art spanning 1850 through 1950 is displayed Louvre-like— crowded together tightly on the walls. A collection of Modoc Indian baskets and of antique weapons is also displayed. A gallows is just outside the completely restored courtroom, and a basement jail with heavy-duty ironwork and a ghost hologram is 13 steps down. A large picnic area with tables, a barn, and grassy expanses is adjacent, and across the highway the old Blumb Bakery, though no longer operating commercially, still has its massive brick oven and sometimes serves up inexpensive baked goods and drinks. Also across the street, the delightful Litsch Store is refitted and stocked to look as it did way back when and is sometimes open for tours. More than 30% of the objects displayed are original to the store, and the rest are convincing replicas.

Turtle Bay Exploration Park
840 Sundial Bridge Dr., (800) TURTLEBAY, (530) 243-8850; www.turtlebay.org. Tu-Sun 9-5; daily in summer. $13, 65+ $9, 4-15 $6. No dogs.

Stop in at the Visitor Center for an orientation to this diverse, spread-out facility situated on the banks of the Sacramento River. It is composed of several venues—all focusing on life along the river.

The **Turtle Bay Museum**'s displays run the gamut from a bevy of Wintu Indian baskets to a collection of atmospheric aquariums filled with local river fish and turtles. Particularly popular with kids is the reproduction of an oak tree with a window in the floor through which they can peer down at its root structure. Resembling a 19th-century logging mill, Paul Bunyan's Forest Camp has exhibits about the region's logging days plus an extensive collection of live California snakes. A creative outside play area has a tree stump maze, an osprey nest climbing structure, and a giant log slide; a live butterfly and bird exhibit is open May through September.

Turtle Bay Cafe *(www.turtlebaycafe.com. L W-M to 5pm; May-Sept, L-D daily to 10pm; $.)* has outdoor seating overlooking the new all-white, harp-shaped, pedestrians-only **Sundial Bridge** *(www.visitredding.com/ sundial.cfm. Daily 6am-midnight.)* designed by avant-garde Spanish architect Santiago Calatrava—one of the world's premier bridge designers. Made from steel, glass, and granite, it is designed so that no part of it is in the water disturbing the Sacramento River's delicate salmon spawning grounds. It features a surface of opaque glass panels that permits viewing the fish below, and its pylon forms the world's largest working sundial. Access to the cafe and bridge is free.

The bridge connects the main facility to the 200-acre **McConnell Arboretum and Gardens**, which features 20 acres of display gardens that include a children's garden, a medicinal garden, and several unique water features.

WHERE TO STAY

Motel Row
Chains galore are situated along Hilltop Drive. A few standouts are:

• Best Western Hilltop Inn
2300 Hilltop Dr., (800) 336-4880, (530) 221-6100; www.thehilltopinn.com. 114 rooms; $-$$. Heated pool, children's pool; hot tub. Full breakfast; restaurant; limited room service. No pets.

This contemporary motel provides guests with passes to a nearby health club.

A step above the usual motel restaurant, **C. R. Gibbs American Grill** *((530) 221-2335; www.crgibbs.com.)* operates off the lobby. Items on the expansive menu include pizza from a wood-fired oven and rotisserie chicken, as well as a superb French-dip sandwich and delicious fish tacos. The bar is known for its selection of beers and martinis but also serves up sodas and milkshakes and features live music in the

evening April through October. The patio is primo in good weather.

• Motel 6
1640 Hilltop Dr., 3 mi. SE of town, (800) 4 MOTEL 6, (530) 221-1800; www.motel6.com. 80 rooms; $. Unheated pool (seasonal).

This chain has three branches in town.

TRINITY ALPS

A LITTLE BACKGROUND

Densely forested and home to 55 lakes and streams, the Trinity Alps Wilderness is the second-largest designated wilderness in California. It is prime camping country, and there's not much to do here except relax and perhaps fish, boat, or hike. The area is the only county in the state with no freeway and no stop lights. Promisingly, James Hilton, author of *Lost Horizon*, said in 1941 that Weaverville was as close as he had come to a real-life Shangri-La.

VISITOR INFORMATION

Trinity County Chamber of Commerce
215 S. Main St. (Hwy. 99), in Weaverville, (800) 487-4648, (530) 623-6101; www.trinitycounty.com.

WHAT TO DO

Jake Jackson Museum & History Center and Trinity County Historical Park
508 Main St., in Weaverville, (530) 623-5211; www.trinitymuseum.org. Daily 10-5, May-Oct; Tu-Sat 12-4, Nov-Apr. By donation.

Using mining equipment, old bottles, and photographs, this museum traces Trinity County's history. Exhibits include a reconstructed blacksmith shop and miner's cabin. Outside, a creek-side picnic area beckons, and a full-size steam-powered stamp mill, located on the block just below the museum, is operated on holidays.

Weaverville Joss House State Historic Park
404 Main St., in Weaverville, (530) 623-5284; www.parks.ca.gov. Tours W-Sun 10-4; on hr. $2, under 17 free. Includes same-day admission to Courthouse Museum at Shasta S.H.P.

Located in a shaded area beside a creek, this Chinese Taoist temple provides cool respite on a hot summer day. Built in 1874 on the site of a previous temple that burned to the ground, it is still used for worship and is the oldest continuously used Chinese temple in the state.

WHERE TO STAY

Coffee Creek Ranch
Off Hwy. 3, in Coffee Creek, 40 mi. N of Weaverville, (800) 624-4480, (530)266-3343; www.coffee creekranch.com. 15 cabins; $$$+; closed Dec-Mar. No TVs; wood-burning fireplaces & stoves. Heated pool (seasonal); children's wading pool; hot tub; fitness room. Includes all meals; restaurant.

Private one-and two-bedroom cabins here are surrounded by trees. Activities include horse-drawn hayrides, movies, steak frys, outdoor games, square and line dancing, archery, rifle and trap shoot using guns, panning for gold, and supervised activities for children 3 to 17. Horseback riding is included in the price.

Trinity Alps Resort
1750 Trinity Alps Rd., in Trinity Center, 12 mi. N of Weaverville, (530) 286-2205; www.trinityalps resort.com. 43 cabins; $$-$$$; closed Oct-Apr. No TVs; all kitchens. 1 tennis court. Restaurant.

Arranged especially to please families, this 90-acre resort is composed of rustic 1920s cabins with sleeping verandas—all scattered along rushing Stuart Fork River. Guests provide their own linens or pay additional to rent them. Simple pleasures include crossing the river on a suspension bridge, hanging out at the general store, and enjoying dinner on a patio overlooking the river at **Bear's Breath Bar & Grill**. Scheduled activities include square dancing, bingo, and evening movies. Hiking and fishing are popular activities, and kids can ride their bikes endlessly. Cabins have a 1-week minimum in summer and a 3-night minimum in spring and fall.

Trinity Lake Resorts & Marinas
45810 Hwy. 3, in Trinity Center, 15 mi. N of Weaverville, (530) 286-2225; www.trinitylakeresort.com. 12 cabins; $-$$; closed Nov-Feb. No TVs; all kitchens. Restaurant.

This quiet spot offers lodging in a cabin in the woods or on a houseboat on Trinity Lake. Guests provide their own bedding and linens. The marina also rents boats, houseboats, and slips, and the bar and restaurant offer a terrific view of the lake.

SHASTA LAKE AREA

A LITTLE BACKGROUND

The drive around this lake's circumference is 360 miles, and because it is a reservoir it has no beaches. The Forest Service has eliminated all private docks on the lake, and restrictions have stopped development here since the 1970s.

GETTING THERE

Located approximately 235 miles north of San Francisco.

WHAT TO DO

Lake Shasta Caverns
20359 Shasta Caverns Rd., in Lakehead, (800) 795-CAVE, (530) 238-2341; www.lakeshastacaverns.com. Tours daily; schedule varies. $20, 3-15 $12.

Discovered in 1878, these limestone and marble caverns didn't open for tours until 1964. The 2-hour tour begins with a 15-minute catamaran cruise across the McCloud arm of Lake Shasta. Then visitors board a bus for a scenic, winding ride up the steep mountainside to the caverns. In this case, getting there really is half the fun. Nature trails, picnic facilities, and a snack bar are available.

Shasta Dam

*16349 Shasta Dam Blvd., in Shasta Lake City, 5 mi.
off Hwy. 5, (530) 275-4463; www.usbr.gov/mp/ncao/
shasta/tour.html. Tours daily, in winter at 9, 11, 1, 3;
in summer at 9, 10:15, 11:30, 1, 2:15, 3:30. Free.*

Constructed from 1938 to 1945 and
measuring 602 feet high and 3,460 feet long,
this is the second-largest dam in the U.S. and
it has one of the highest center-overflow
spillways in the world (it's three times higher
than Niagara Falls!). The guided 1-hour tour
includes an elevator ride 428 feet deep into the
dam's depths and a view of the spillway and
power plant.

WHERE TO STAY

Tsasdi Resort

*19990 Lakeshore Dr., in Lakehead, 25 mi. N of
Redding on Sacramento Arm of lake, 3 mi. off I-5,
(800) 995-0291, (530) 238-2575;
www.tsasdiresort.com. 20 cabins; $$-$$$. All
kitchens. Heated pool.*

Pronounced "sauz-dee," this family-
friendly resort is tucked into a peaceful
black-oak forest with a filtered view of Shasta
Lake. Situated across the street (it is actually a
country lane with little traffic) from the lake,
updated housekeeping cabins have knotty-pine
interiors with high beamed ceilings and private
decks. Many can accommodate large families.
Facilities include volleyball and basketball
courts, a general store with a pool table and
video games, and a private boat dock that
guests can also fish from. Folks tend to come
back every year, often for the same week, so
reserve as early as possible. There is a 2-night
minimum September through May, and a
1-week minimum in summer.

Houseboats

Lake Shasta has the largest fleet of
commercial houseboats in the world. For more
information, see page 465.

Motel Row

Inexpensive motels are located at Bridge
Bay and in the Lakehead area.

WHERE TO EAT

Tail O' the Whale Restaurant

*10300 Bridge Bay Rd, at Bridge Bay Resort (for
description, see p. 465), 10 mi. N of Redding,
(530) 275-3021; www.sevencrown.com/lakes/lake_
shasta/bridge_bay/restaurants.htm. B-L daily,
D W-Sun; $$. Reservations accepted.*

Situated up on a knoll, this longtime
restaurant has a following. Hatch cover tables,
seemingly held up by thick ropes, provide a
pleasant pine-filtered lake view. The crisp tap
water comes right from the lake, so no need to
order bottled. Best menu bets are surf & turf,
fried chicken, chicken-fried steak, housemade
meatloaf, fish & chips, and a hamburger.
Heartier appetites favor steak or chicken picatta,
and Friday and Saturday nights feature a prime
rib special.

DUNSMUIR

A LITTLE BACKGROUND

Surrounded by a million acres of forest and
wilderness, this wildly scenic town is touted as
"the home of the best water on Earth." And,
indeed, pure spring water from Mt. Shasta
glaciers is delivered to the city via lava tubes
and then piped to every tap in town. One of the
hamlet's 10 always-flowing public drinking
fountains is in a sheltered spot by the side of
the two-lane road through town. It is reminis-
cent of restorative fountains seen in small spa
towns in Germany's Black Forest.

The town's history is the railroad. At the
turn of the 19th century, it was a division point
on the railroad and a popular resort area.
By the 1920s, things were really booming.
Celebrities stopped here by the trainload,
including Clark Gable and Babe Ruth, and
the town's California Theatre was a movie
palace. Then, in the 1950s steam locomotives
were phased out, drastically hurting the area's
economy. And in 1961, I-5 bypassed
Dunsmuir—a mixed blessing that allowed the
town to retain its charm.

Fishing is good year round on the area's
Upper Sacramento River.

VISITOR INFORMATION

Dunsmuir Chamber of Commerce and Visitor's Center

5915 Dunsmuir Ave., (800) DUNSMUIR, (530) 235-2177; www.dunsmuir.com.

WHAT TO DO

Brown Trout Gallery & Cafe

5841 Sacramento Ave., (800) 916-4278, (530) 235-0754; www.browntroutgallery.com. Shop: M-Sat 7-3, Sun 8-3; in summer, M-F 7-5, Sun 8-5. Cafe: B-L daily; $.

Located off the main drag, down by the town's historic rail yard, this boutique purveys interesting crafts and art. Of special note is a stream running underneath that can be seen and heard through a hole in the floor. A cafe serves up tasty meals and coffees.

Castle Crags State Park

Castle Creek Rd., in Castella, 10 mi. S of town; (530) 235-2684; www.parks.ca.gov. Daily sunrise-sunset. $6/vehicle.

Mile-high, snaggle-tooth granite peaks dominate this 6,000-acre park. Hiking trails, picnic areas, and swimming holes are available. For a smashing picnic spot with a view of the crags and Mt. Shasta, drive up the narrow one-lane road leading to Vista Point. The 1-mile Indian Creek Nature Trail loop has gentle slopes and provides an easy leg stretch. Campsites are available.

Dunsmuir Hardware

5836 Dunsmuir Ave., (530) 235-4539; www.dunsmuirhardware.com. M-Sat 8:30-5:30, Sun 10-4.

The town's oldest retail business, this historic hardware store has changed its name and location through the years but has been operating since 1894. It's been in this 1912 brick building since 1962 and is *the* place to buy everything from a fishing pole to a Merle Haggard CD (the singer lives in the area). Nails are still sold by the pound and rope by the foot. Gold panning supplies are stocked, too. The store features a high tin ceiling, natural wood floor, and ceiling fans, and a display of antique tools lines the walls.

Hedge Creek Falls

On Dunsmuir Ave., at N end of town; www.dunsmuir.com/visitor/outdoor.php. Free.

The short, easy path leading to the falls follows the Sacramento River. Once there, it is possible to walk behind the base of the falls, and picnicking is lovely. A table, gazebo, and one of the town's free-flowing water faucets are provided at the trailhead. Legend has it that the notorious Gold Rush-era bandit Black Bart once used the area as a hideout.

WHERE TO STAY

Cave Springs Resort

4727 Dunsmuir Ave., (888) 235-2721, (530) 235-2721; www.cavesprings.com. 25 units; $. Unheated pool (heated in summer); hot tub; 1 tennis court. Restaurant.

Situated on the outskirts of town, just above the river, this old-time mountain resort seems like something out of a time warp. It offers simple motel rooms, cabins, and RV accommodations, and facilities on the spacious, cedar-sheltered grounds include a playground and bocce ball court.

Railroad Park Resort

100 Railroad Park Rd., 1 mi. S of town, (800) 974-RAIL, (530) 235-4440; www.rrpark.com. 27 units; $$. Some kitchens. Unheated pool; hot tub. Restaurant (closed Nov-Mar).

Guests here can sleep in either an authentic antique caboose or a deluxe, handicapped-accessible boxcar. Each is furnished with antiques, and some have clawfoot tubs and bunk beds. Four cabins and some creek-side campsites are also available. The nearby Cascade Mountains and their granite Castle Crags Spires can be viewed while frolicking in the pool, and prime rib and seafood dinners are served inside an authentic dining car that is converted into a **restaurant** *((530) 235-4611)*.

WHERE TO EAT

Cafe Maddalena

5801 Sacramento Ave., (530) 235-2725; www.cafemaddalena.com. D Thur-Sun; $$; closed Jan-Mar. Reservations advised.

Located across the street from the old train station, this well-loved restaurant has a cozy

Railroad Park Resort

interior lined with knotty-pine walls. The talented chef-owner hails from Sardinia and takes pride in whipping up authentic, well-executed Italian dishes that would be extraordinary anywhere, but seem especially so here, so far from a major city. Menu choices might include housemade ravioli stuffed with ricotta and artichokes and topped with fresh tomato; a superb pizza topped with a mixture of spinach, oyster mushrooms, garlic, eggplant, and mozzarella (sometimes the chef even makes *fresh* mozzarella); tiramisu; and an unusual egg-less bitter lemon flan that is heaven for those watching their cholesterol.

Cornerstone Bakery and Café

5759 Dunsmuir Ave., (530) 235-4677. B-L W-M, D F-Sun; $.

Delicious housemade baked goods, soups, salads, sandwiches, and more are on the expansive menu in this cozy, coffee shop-style spot. Entertainment is added on weekends. All art hanging on the knotty-pine and butter-colored walls is for sale. Don't leave without a loaf of freshly baked bread for the road.

McCLOUD

A LITTLE BACKGROUND

Set at 3,500 feet on the west slope of Mt. Shasta, this scenic little mill town was owned by the McCloud Lumber Company from 1897 to 1965. It looks now much as it did then. The streets here are wide, and there is little traffic and plenty of trees. The area is famous for excellent fishing, and the McCloud River is the only one in California populated with the rare endangered Dolly Varden Trout (formerly known as the Bull Trout). It is also well known for square dancing and hiking.

VISITOR INFORMATION

McCloud Chamber of Commerce

205 Quincy St., (530) 964-3113; www.mccloudchamber.com.

GETTING THERE

From I-5, follow Highway 89 east for 10 miles into town.

WHAT TO DO

Shasta Sunset Dinner Train

(800) 733-2141, (530) 964-2142; www.shastasunset.com. Schedule varies. $97.50. Excursion train: Schedule varies; $12, under 12 $8.

Refurbished 1915 Illinois Central coach cars are used on the 3-hour dinner ride, which includes a four-course gourmet meal served on elegant white linen set with china and silverware. Trees, trees are everywhere, with an occasional glimpse of the mountain. On the scenic 1-hour diesel excursion to Signal Butte, passengers sit in open-air cars; one is a double-decker with antique school chairs on one level and antique benches on the other.

WHERE TO STAY

The Guest House
606 W. Colombero Dr., (866) 964-3160, (530) 964-3160; www.historicalmccloudguesthouse.com.
7 rooms; $$. Full breakfast. No pets.

Sitting above town amid 6 acres of gardens and a park-like expanse of lawn, this grand 1907 California Craftsman-style house was originally the home of the McCloud River Lumber Company's owner. It has a large veranda with a view of the mountain, where breakfast is sometimes served, and antique furnishings include an ornate pool table in the lounge. Notable past guests include President Herbert Hoover, baseball player Ty Cobb, and actress Jean Harlow, as well as several members of the Hearst family.

McCloud Hotel
408 Main St., (800) 964-2823, (530) 964-2822; www.mccloudhotel.com. 15 rooms; $$-$$$.
No TVs. Afternoon wine & appetizers; full breakfast; restaurant.

A registered national landmark, this hotel was built in 1916 on the same foundation as a prior hotel that burned down that same year. It once had 96 rooms and provided housing for mill workers and teachers, and its basement was the town library until the 1960s. Now meticulously restored, its old-fashioned lobby invites lingering over a board game or book. The individually decorated rooms are spacious and furnished with rescued and restored pieces original to the hotel and area. A canopy bed, whirlpool tub for two, and balcony are available in one suite, and breakfast can be delivered to the room. A TV lounge is set up in the gift shop.

MOUNT SHASTA CITY

A LITTLE BACKGROUND

A 14,161-foot-tall volcanic mountain that last erupted in 1786, Mount Shasta holds five glaciers and is where the Sacramento River originates. It is climbed in summer and skied in winter. Poet Joaquin Miller, who considered it the most beautiful mountain in the West, described it as "lonely as God and white as a winter moon." New Agers rank it up there with Stonehenge and the Egyptian pyramids, apparently because of its unusual energy fields, and it is considered one of the world's seven sacred mountains. Peculiar stories, involving UFOs and Bigfoot, abound in this area.

VISITOR INFORMATION

Mt. Shasta Chamber of Commerce/Visitors Bureau
300 Pine St., (800) 926-4865, (530) 926-4865; www.mtshastachamber.com.

Siskiyou County Visitors Bureau
P.O. Box 1138, Mount Shasta City 96067, (530) 926-3850; www.visitsiskiyou.org.

GETTING THERE

Located 50 miles north of Redding, and 290 miles north of San Francisco.

WHERE TO STAY

KOA Kampground
900 N. Mt. Shasta Blvd., (800) KOA-3617, (530) 926-4029; www.koa.com.

In addition to offering majestic Mt. Shasta as a backdrop, this picturesque campground has a swimming pool, volleyball courts, horseshoe pits, and a game room. For more description, see page 467.

Motel Row
Drive along Mt. Shasta Boulevard.

WHERE TO EAT

Black Bear Diner
401 W. Lake St., (530) 926-4669; www.blackbeardiner.com. B-L-D daily; $.

The first link in what has become a chain throughout the West, this diner is built on the site of former wild strawberry patches that once were frequented by both black bears and people. The menu is expansive, and the reputation is for large portions of freshly prepared diner food, served fast and at a reasonable price. Breakfast is available all day, as is black"beary" cobbler. A long counter with swivel stools is great for singles, and some booths boast a view of the mountain.

Fast-food row
Along Lake St.; take Central Mt. Shasta exit.

Even with the various logo signs fighting it out amidst the trees, the view here is weepingly beautiful. On a clear day the mysterious mountain dominates the scene, and on a cloudy day it plays peek-a-boo—tantalizing the imagination. Alas, it seems the locals take this awesome sight for granted, so in the **Burger King** they often leave empty the corner tables boasting a million-dollar view.

YREKA

VISITOR INFORMATION

Yreka Chamber of Commerce
117 W. Miner St., (530) 842-1649;
www.yrekachamber.com.

GETTING THERE

Located approximately 50 miles north of Mount Shasta, and 22 miles south of the Oregon border. This small town is positioned halfway between San Francisco and Portland, Oregon.

WHAT TO DO

Yreka Western Railroad/
Blue Goose Steam Excursion Train
300 E. Miner St., (800) YREKA-RR, (530) 842-4146;
www.yrekawesternrr.com. W-Sun at 11, June-Sept only;
special events Sept-Dec. Ticket prices vary.

A ride on this excursion train, pulled by #19, a restored 1915 Baldwin steam locomotive that had a role in the movie *Stand by Me*, treats passengers to spectacular views of Mount Shasta and the Shasta Valley. (The locomotive is nicknamed "Pancho" because it was punctured by bullets during a battle in Mexico with Pancho Villa.) After the 7-mile ride to Montague, there is an hour layover during which passengers can tour the historic town and have lunch. Seats in the steam engine cab and caboose are available at additional charge.

A 1,000-square-foot model railroad is displayed in the old depot, now operating as the **Rocky Mountain Railway & Mining Museum**.

Siskiyou County Museum
910 S. Main St., (530) 842-3836;
www.co.siskiyou.ca.us/museum. Tu-F 9-5, Sat 9-4.
By donation.

This small museum emphasizes local artifacts and history. Of special interest is the occasional exhibit featuring a local pioneer family, one of which was the Terwilligers.

A 2¼-acre **Outdoor Museum** *(9:30-4:30; May-Sept only.)* is located adjacent. Among its original and replica historic buildings are a schoolhouse, a Catholic church, a blacksmith shop, a miner's cabin, and an operating general store.

The Yreka Historic District
Along Miner St.

More than 75 19th-century homes are seen here, with most situated on the four blocks of Third Street located between Lennox and Miner. The Chamber of Commerce provides a descriptive tour brochure.

WHERE TO EAT

Grandma's House
123 E. Center St., (530) 842-5300; B-L-D daily; $.
Reservations accepted.

Cozy and welcoming, with Tiffany-style lamps and floral wallpaper, Grandma's House is just like, well, Grandma's house. It's been family-run since 1977. The breakfast menu offers goodies such as buttermilk hot cakes with housemade boysenberry syrup and is served until 1 p.m. The lunch menu, which is a large selection of sandwiches and a salad bar, is available through dinner, when housemade biscuits, fried chicken, grilled pork chops and more substantial items also become options. Do save room for a slice of housemade pie. A cookbook featuring simple recipes used in the restaurant makes a great souvenir.

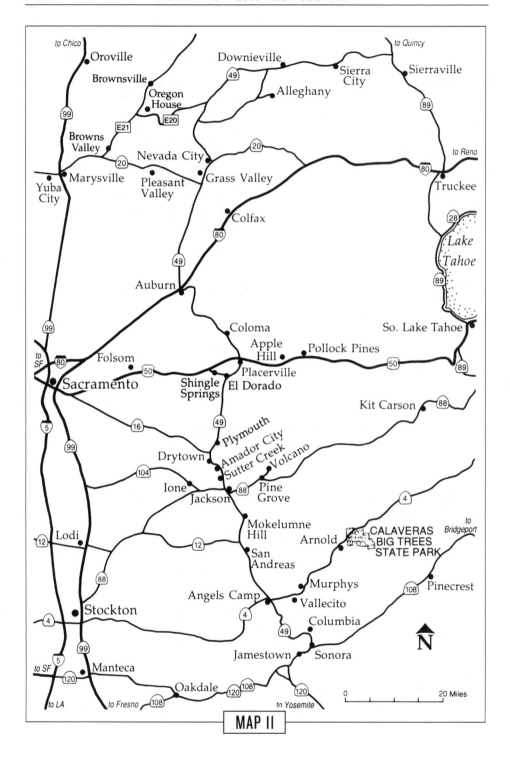

MAP II

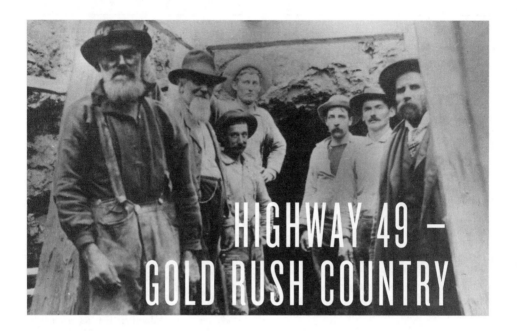

HIGHWAY 49 – GOLD RUSH COUNTRY

A LITTLE BACKGROUND

The Mother Lode, as this area is sometimes referred to (a term that is derived from a Spanish word for "riches"), stretches along the entire route of Highway 49, south from Mariposa and north through Nevada City, ending in Downieville. (On the other hand the Mother Lode *veins*, which run from Northern California to South America, surface in the area between Jamestown and Auburn and again in Nevada City.)

All the main Gold Rush towns can be visited by driving along Highway 49. But many scenic side roads lead to tiny hamlets with intriguing names such as Fiddletown and Rescue, inviting exploration.

This area provides history, adventure, and scenic beauty. Not yet heavily promoted and

packaged, it also provides many low-key and inexpensive vacation joys for the hype-weary traveler. A thorough visit could take weeks, but a satisfying one takes only a few days. For a weekend visit, don't attempt to drive the entire route. Visit one portion and then go back another time to see more.

Because the area is steeped in history, consider reading for more background information. Two classic books about the area that are also good for reading aloud are *The Celebrated Jumping Frog of Calaveras County*, by Samuel L. Clemens (Mark Twain), and *The Luck of Roaring Camp*, by Bret Harte.

Currently there is said to be another gold rush on. Many nervous people are staking claims, so caution is advised when doing any unguided panning or prospecting.

During the Gold Rush this area was filled with wineries. Its rich soil and high elevations produce excellent grapes and bold, deeply flavored wines. So be on the lookout for the nearly 100 wineries that have popped up here.

GETTING THERE

Located approximately 135 miles east of San Francisco. Take Highway 80 to Highway 580 to Highway 205 to Highway 120 to Highway 49.

JAMESTOWN

A LITTLE BACKGROUND

Filled with architecturally interesting old buildings, this historical boom town's economy is now fueled by myriad antiques shops.

WHAT TO DO

Railtown 1897 State Historic Park
Fifth St./Reservoir St., (209) 984-3953; www.csrmf.org. Daily 9:30-4:30, Apr-Oct; 10-3 Nov-Mar. Train: Sat-Sun 11-3, on the hr.; Apr-Oct only; $8, 6-12 $3. Tour: Daily 10-3, on the hr.; $2, 6-12 $1.

Be sure to arrive early enough to watch the hubbub that surrounds preparing the train for departure. The depot is full of excitement as the huge steam train rolls in and out, sounding its screaming whistle and belching a mix of fire, smoke, and steam. The Mother Lode Cannonball, a historic steam train, takes passengers on a 40-minute, 6-mile round trip to Woods Creek Siding. Several other trips are available. A tour is given of the old six-stall roundhouse turntable and machine shop, where the trains are still serviced. If it all looks familiar, that could be because many TV shows and movies have been filmed here, including *Bonanza, Little House on the Prairie, The Virginian, High Noon*, and *Pale Rider*.

WHERE TO STAY

Jamestown Hotel
18153 Main St., (800) 205-4901, (209) 984-3902; www.jamestownhotel.com. 8 rooms; $-$$. Full breakfast; restaurant.

Built in the 1850s, this hotel is furnished with Victorian antiques and has many spacious suites with sitting rooms.

A welcoming **saloon** specializes in fancy drinks, California wines, and tasty appetizers.

The National Hotel
18183 Main St., (800) 894-3446, (209) 984-3446; www.national-hotel.com. 9 rooms; $$. Unsuitable for children under 10. TVs upon request. Full breakfast; restaurant; room service.

A sense of history awaits at this really *old* hotel. Built in 1859, it has been in continuous operation ever since. In fact, it is one of the oldest continuously operating hotels in the state and is now an official historical landmark. Until 1978, rooms were rented to men only and went for $4 a night. Indoor plumbing was added in 1981. Much of the antique furniture is original to the hotel, and that which isn't is right in tune with the era. A private Soaking Room with a clawfoot tub for two—sort of an 1800s hot tub—is available to all guests. Overall, everything is far more luxurious now than anything those gold miners ever experienced.

The hotel's **restaurant** *(L-D daily, SunBr. Reservations advised.)* is an especially inviting spot for dinner after the drive in. On warm evenings, diners are seated outside on a pleasant patio. Menu strong points include fresh fish with creative sauces, a wine list with the largest selection of Gold Country wines available *anywhere*, and exceptional desserts. Just off the parlor, an old-time **saloon** features its original redwood long bar with brass rail and an 1881 cash register and makes the perfect spot for a nightcap.

WHERE TO EAT

Smoke Cafe
18191 Main St., (209) 984-3733. L-D Tu-Sun; $-$$. No reservations.

Located within a modern Santa Fe-style building with soft stucco edges and lots of tile, this popular spot specializes in Mexican cuisine. Among the many items on the menu are pollo de mole poblano, chili verde, and a hamburger.

SONORA

A LITTLE BACKGROUND

Once known as the "Queen of the Southern Mines," when it was the richest and wildest town in the southern Mother Lode, this city still bustles and is a popular stopover spot for skiers and other travelers on their way to vacation cabins and recreation. Because it is a crossroads, it has been built up more than most Gold Rush towns and is far from quiet. However, off the main thoroughfares, a taste of the old Sonora of Victorian homes and quiet streets can still be found. It is interesting to note that in Spanish "tuolumne" means "stone houses."

VISITOR INFORMATION

Tuolumne County Visitors Bureau
*542 W. Stockton Rd., (800) 446-1333,
(209) 533-4420; www.tcvb.com.*

ANNUAL EVENTS

Mother Lode Round-Up Parade
May. www.motherloderoundup.com. Free.
This is the state's second-largest parade per number of entrants (the Rose Parade in Pasadena is first). A rodeo is also part of the weekend fun.

Fall colors drive
Take Highway 108 about 30 to 35 miles east of town for a dazzling display of fall leaf colors. This entire area is populated with aspen and is usually vibrant with color after the first frost, which generally happens in early October. Beginning in late October, colorful leaves are seen right in town.

WHAT TO DO

Mark Twain's Cabin
Off Hwy. 49, midway betw. town & Angels Camp.
Built on Jackass Hill, this rickety replica of Twain's cabin is constructed around the original chimney. It can be viewed from the outside only. Twain lived here in 1864 and '65, when he wrote *The Celebrated Jumping Frog of Calaveras County* and *Roughing It.*

Tuolumne County Museum & History Center
*158 W. Bradford Ave., (209) 532-1317;
www.tchistory.org. Sun-F 10-4, Sat 10-3:30. Free.*
Located inside a jail built in 1866, this museum displays Gold Rush-era relics that include pioneer firearms and gold specimens. Picnic tables are available.

WHERE TO STAY

Gunn House Motel
*286 S. Washington St., (209) 532-3421;
www.gunnhousehotel.com. 21 rooms; $-$$. Heated pool (seasonal). Full breakfast. No pets.*
Built in 1850, this adobe house was once the residence of Dr. Lewis C. Gunn. It later

became the offices for the *Sonora Herald*—the area's first newspaper. Rooms are restored and furnished with antiques.

COLUMBIA STATE HISTORIC PARK

A LITTLE BACKGROUND

In her prime, with more than 6,000 people calling her home, Columbia was one of the largest mining towns in the southern Mother Lode. Her nickname, "Gem of the Southern Mines," was reference to the $87 million-plus in gold mined here (a figure calculated when gold was $35 an ounce).

This reconstructed Gold Rush town has been a state historic park since 1945. It is open daily from 9 to 4:30, and admission is free. Streets are blocked off to all but foot traffic and an occasional stagecoach. A museum introduces visitors to the town's history, and more exhibits are scattered among the many restored historic buildings.

In fact, the whole town is basically a living museum. Private concessionaires operate modern versions of businesses that were here in the 1800s. The town saloon pours cold mugs of beer and old-fashioned, root beer-like sarsaparilla. A blacksmith ekes out a living practicing his craft in a ramshackle shed, and a candy kitchen uses 100-year-old recipes and antique equipment to turn out such old-time favorites as horehound, rocky road, and almond bark. Customers in the photography studio don Gold Rush-era clothing for portraits, which are taken with vintage camera equipment but developed with quick modern processes. Visitors can even tour a still-operating gold mine and learn to pan for gold in a salted sluice.

If it all looks familiar, note that *High Noon* and episodes of *Little House on the Prairie* were filmed here.

VISITOR INFORMATION

Columbia State Historic Park
*22708 Broadway St., (209) 588-9128;
www.parks.ca.gov. Daily 10-5. Free.*

Columbia California Chamber of Commerce

P.O. Box 1824, Columbia 95310, (209) 536-1672; www.columbiacalifornia.com.

ANNUAL EVENTS

Victorian Promenade and Egg Hunt

March or April; on Easter Sunday. (209) 536-1672; www.columbiagazette.com/easter.html. Free.

Participants don their best 1880s attire and fanciest hat for this historical Easter parade.

Fireman's Muster

May. (209) 536-1672; www.columbiagazette.com/muster.html. Free.

Volunteer fire crews from the western U.S. test their skills in historical fire fighting. There is a parade on Saturday and a dance that night.

A Miners Christmas

December; first 2 weekends. (209) 588-9128; www.columbiagazette.com/miners.html. Free.

St. Nick arrives by stagecoach each day, and roasted chestnuts, hot camp coffee, and hot apple cider are among the culinary treats.

WHAT TO DO

Quartz Mountain Carriage Co.

(209) 588-0808; www.qmcarriage.com. Schedule varies. Stage: $5-$9, under 3 free.

Ride in an authentic stagecoach and experience travel as many gold-seekers did years ago.

WHERE TO STAY

City Hotel

22768 Main St., (800) 532-1479, (209) 532-1479; www.cityhotel.com. 10 rooms; $$; closed 1st 2 wks. in Jan. No TVs; all shared baths. Continental breakfast; restaurant; limited room service. No pets.

This 1856 hotel provides overnight lodging in keeping with the town's historic flavor. Rooms are restored and furnished with Victorian antiques from the collection of the California State Parks Department. Guests are encouraged to congregate in the parlor in the evening for sherry, conversation, and games. To make the trek down the hall to the bath more civilized, guests are loaned a wicker basket packed with shower cap, slippers, robe, soap, and shampoo.

The hotel **restaurant** *(D Tu-Sun, SunBr; $$. Reservations advised.)* serves elegant regional cuisine, and four-course seasonal dinners are an option. The cozy **What Cheer Saloon**, which retains its original cherry-wood bar that traveled around the Horn from New England, adjoins.

Columbia Gem Motel

22131 Parrotts Ferry Rd., 1 mi. from park, (866) 436-6685, (209) 532-4508; www.columbiagem.com. 11 units; $-$$.

Small log cabins are scattered here through an attractive pine tree setting. Motel rooms are also available.

Fallon Hotel

On Washington St., (800) 532-1479, (209) 532-1470; www.cityhotel.com. 14 rooms; $-$$; closed 1st 2 wks. in Jan. No TVs; many shared bathrooms. Continental breakfast; restaurant. No pets.

This historic hotel, dating from 1857, is beautifully restored to its Victorian grandeur. Many of the furnishings are original to the hotel. Several large second-floor rooms with balconies are perfect for families. The hotel is operated in similar style as the City Hotel and is under the same management.

The **Fallon Ice Cream Parlor** dishes up goodies on the main floor.

Located in the rear of the Fallon Hotel, the historic **Fallon House Theatre** *(209) 532-3120; www.sierrarep.com. W-F at 7; Sat at 8; W, Sat, Sun at 2. $20-$22. Advance purchase advised.)* has been operating since the 1880s. The second-longest continually operating playhouse in California, it stages both first-run and classic dramas and musicals and employs both professional and student talent. The semi-professional Sierra Repertory Theatre stages eight major productions each year.

ANGELS CAMP

A LITTLE BACKGROUND

Taking its name from George Angel, who founded it as a trading post in 1848, this quiet little burg is thought to be the town Bret Harte wrote of in *Luck of Roaring Camp*, and it is where Mark Twain first heard the story that he fabricated into *The Celebrated Jumping Frog of Calaveras County*. The sidewalks sport plaques celebrating high-jumping frogs from past competitions, and, of course, all kinds of souvenir frogs are available in gift shops. It is interesting to note that in Spanish "calaveras" means "skulls."

VISITOR INFORMATION

Calaveras County Chamber of Commerce
1211 S. Main St., (209) 736-2580; www.calaveras.org.

Calaveras Visitors Bureau
1192 S. Main St., (800) 225-3764, (209) 736-0049; www.gocalaveras.com.

ANNUAL EVENTS

Jumping Frog Jubilee
May; 3rd weekend. (209) 736-2561; www.frogtown.org. $5-$9.

Most contestants bring their own frog to enter in this historic contest, but rental frogs are also available on site. In 1986, Rosie the Ribiter set the current world's record by landing—after three leaps—21 feet 5¾ inches from the starting pad. She earned her jockey $1,500. The prize money is usually won by frog jockeys who are serious about the sport and bring 50 to 60 frogs. So far, a rental frog has never won.

The **Calaveras County Fair** is part of the fun and features carnival rides, livestock exhibits, a rodeo, a destruction derby, headliner entertainers, and fireworks.

Moaning Cavern
5350 Moaning Cave Rd., in Vallecito, 4 mi. W of town, (866) 762-2837, (209) 736-2708; www.moaning cavern.com. Daily 10-5; in summer 9-6. $14.25, 3-12 $7.15; gemstone mining & gold panning $5+.

Gold miners first explored this cavern in 1851, and Native Americans had revered the site for centuries before that because of the haunting, moaning sounds coming from the cave's entrance. In fact, the oldest human remains in the U.S. were found here at the bottom of the main chamber. A 45-minute tour descends a

100-foot-high spiral staircase into the deepest public cavern chamber in California. A cool 61 degrees, it is big enough to hold the Statue of Liberty from toes to torch!

A **rappel tour** *($65. Must be age 12+.)* allows a 165-foot rope descent into the cave. Twin **zip lines** provide a thrilling ¼-mile ride at speeds of more than 40 m.p.h. Nature trails, picnic tables, and campsites are also available.

WHAT TO DO

Angels Camp Museum & Carriage House
753 S. Main St., (209) 736-2963;
www.angelscamp.gov/museum.htm. Daily 10-3,
Mar-Dec; Sat-Sun only, Jan-Feb. $3, 6-12 $1.

A repository of Gold Rush memorabilia, this museum displays an extensive mineral and rock collection, a blacksmith shop, and a carriage barn filled with vintage wagons and buggies.

WHERE TO EAT

There is only one recommended restaurant for this town. Could this have something to do with Mark Twain's description of some "day-before-yesterday dishwater" coffee and "hellfire" soup suffered long ago at the Hotel Angels?

Picnic Pick-Ups

• The Pickle Barrel
1225 S. Main St., (209) 736-4704;
www.pickle-barrel.com. Tu-Sun 11-4, Thur-F to 8pm.

This friendly Italian deli packs picnic supplies to go and provides tables for those who decide to stay. Sandwiches are made with meats grilled on the back patio.

Informal picnic areas are found by the river, and scenic **Utica Park** has sheltered picnic tables and a large children's play area.

MURPHYS

A LITTLE BACKGROUND

Nicknamed "Queen of the Sierra," this town once was the source of gold strike after gold strike and made the founding Murphy brothers rich, and it is believed that Joaquin Murieta began his outlaw ways here. Nowadays it is definitely a happening place, with lots of boutiques, art galleries, restaurants, and winery tasting rooms. A map to the town's sights and buildings—many of which were constructed of lava stone and stucco after a tragic fire in 1859—is available from merchants and at the check-in desk in Murphys Hotel.

ANNUAL EVENTS

Bear Valley Music Festival
July. In Bear Valley; (800) 458-1618, (209) 753-2574;
www.bearvalleymusic.org. $25+.

Held high in the Sierra in a circus-style red-and-white-striped tent, this festival presents a musical smorgasbord.

WHAT TO DO

Calaveras Big Trees State Park
1170 E. Hwy. 4, in Arnold, 15 mi. E of town,
(209) 795-2334; www.parks.ca.gov. Daily sunrise-
sunset. Visitor Center: (209) 795-3840; daily
(schedule varies). $6/vehicle.

This ancient forest houses the mammoth, and now rare, giant sequoia variety of redwood. The Big Trees North Grove Trail is a choice trek for families with young children and provides the chance to see the Discovery Tree stump that once was used as a dance floor. Other trails are available, as are campsites and picnic tables and barbecue facilities. A cross-country ski trail is maintained in winter, and a horseback-riding concession operates in summer. Also in warm weather, the Beaver Creek Picnic Area has a good wading area for children. Picnic provisions can be picked up in Arnold, where there are delis, markets, and restaurants.

Mercer Caverns

1665 Sheep Ranch Rd., off Hwy. 4, 1.5 mi. N of town, (209) 728-2101; www.mercercaverns.com. Daily 10-4:30; in summer, Sun-Thur 9-5, F-Sat 9-6. $12, 5-12 $7. No pets.

Discovered more than 100 years ago, in 1885, this well-lighted, 55-degree limestone cavern takes about an hour to tour. It is said to be the longest continually operating commercial cavern in the state. The tour descends stairs to a depth of 161 feet and stops in 10 areas. Baby strollers are not permitted. Gemstone mining is also available.

Murphys Black Bart Theatre

580 S. Algiers, (209) 728-8842; www.murphysblackbartplayers.com. F-Sat in Apr, July-Aug, Nov; 8pm. $15, 55+ & under 13 $12. Reservations advised.

The Black Bart Players perform musicals, melodramas, mysteries, comedies, and classics here.

Old Timers Museum

470 Main St., (209) 728-1160. F-Sun 11-4; in winter Sat-Sun only. Free.

Dating from 1856, this is the oldest stone building in town, and it is interesting to note that the stones were fitted together without mortar. The museum it houses displays Gold Rush-era memorabilia.

WINERIES

Prior to Prohibition, there were more wineries in this area than anywhere else in the state.

Ironstone Vineyards

1894 Six Mile Rd., (209) 728-1251; www.ironstonevineyards.com. Tasting daily 10-6; tour daily at 11:30, 1:30, 3:30.

A replica of an 1859 gold stamp mill, this modern winery is the area's largest and is known for its Chardonnays and Merlots. Its oak-and-stone tasting room overlooks the vineyards and features an oak tasting bar built in 1907 and shipped here around the Horn. An operating sluice once used to separate gold from gravel and the world's largest gold-leaf crystalline specimen—it weighs 44 pounds—are displayed along with Gold Rush artifacts that include a mining car and gold scales. Guided half-hour tours visit the aging caverns blasted from the hard rock after which the winery is named. Also, a historic 769-pipe theater organ accompanies scheduled silent films, and in spring visitors can view a stunning display of more than 250,000 daffodils. A deli will pack up box lunches to go or to eat on site in the dramatic lakeside picnic area.

Milliaire Winery

276 Main St., (209) 728-1658; www.milliairewinery.com. Tasting daily 11-5; no tour.

Operating out of a converted 1930s gas station, this tiny winery is known for its intense, full-bodied wines and is the local Zinfandel expert (one luscious version is made from 100-year-old Ghirardelli vines). Three delicious dessert wines are also produced: late harvest Zinfandel, Zinfandel Port, and Semillon.

Stevenot Winery

2690 San Domingo Rd., 4 mi. from town, 1 mi. past Mercer Caverns, (209) 728-3436; www.stevenot winery.com. Tasting daily 11-5; tour by appt.

Located back in a canyon on the site of the first swimming pool in Calaveras County, this winery operates in a cluster of vintage buildings. The tasting room, which was once the home of founder Barden Stevenot, features a large native-limestone fireplace surrounded by windows overlooking the winery. Alaska House—a replica Gold Rush cabin with a sod roof and split-log walls—is now a private tasting room. The winery is recognized for being among the first in California to produce lesser-known Mediterranean varietals, including Tempranillo, Verdelho, and Albarino. Picnic tables are sheltered under a grape arbor and have a view of the surrounding vineyards.

In summer, **Murphys Creek Theatre** (*(209) 728-8422; www.murphyscreektheatre.org. $12-$18.*) presents live outdoor performances in an intimate grassy amphitheatre.

WHERE TO STAY

Dunbar House, 1880
271 Jones St., (800) 692-6006, (209) 728-2897; www.dunbarhouse.com. 4 rooms; $$-$$$. Unsuitable for children under 10. All gas-burning stoves. Afternoon snack; full breakfast. No pets.

Surrounded by a white-picket fence, this restored Italianate-style house was the filming location for the TV series *Seven Brides for Seven Brothers*. Rooms are decorated with antiques, lace, and down comforters. Guests are greeted each afternoon with cookies, munchies, and assorted beverages, and each room holds a complimentary bottle of wine and an evening appetizer plate. The aim here is to surprise and please guests at every turn. It is a bit like being welcomed back into the womb. Among the pleasures: towel warmers, candles, ceiling fans, a CD player, live orchids, bathrobes and slippers, and the comfiest of pillows and bedding. A large, well-tended century-old garden features native roses and is equipped with a soothing fountain, couch swing, and hammock. Robins, blue jays, hummingbirds, big black bumblebees, and even woodpeckers frequent it. Horse-drawn buggy rides through town can be arranged.

Murphys Historic Hotel
457 Main St., (800) 532-7684, (209) 728-3444; www.murphyshotel.com. 29 rooms; $. Some TVs & shared baths. Continental breakfast; restaurant.

Built in 1856 (as a stage stop for travelers on their way to see the Sequoia trees in Big Trees State Park just up the road in Arnold) and a historical landmark since 1948, this very old hotel provided lodging for such Gold Rush-era luminaries as U.S. Grant, J.P. Morgan, Mark Twain, Horatio Alger, Susan B. Anthony, and gentleman bandit Black Bart—each of whom has a room they actually stayed in named for them. Modern motel rooms, with no legends attached, are available adjacent to the hotel. Though the hotel rooms are immeasurably more interesting, they have one drawback: The noisy hotel saloon, reputed to be the best in the Mother Lode, is kept jumping until the wee hours by townspeople and travelers alike. Those who want to sleep should opt for a less interesting, but quiet, motel room. More than $5.5 million in gold was taken out of the property behind the hotel.

The hotel **restaurant** *(B-L-D daily; $-$$. Reservations advised.)* is popular with locals. Menu choices consist of hearty, made-from-scratch American country and continental fare—the specialty of the house is fried chicken and prime rib—and portions tend to be large.

WHERE TO EAT

Murphys Grille
380 Main St., (209) 728-8800. L Sat-Sun, D Thur-Tu, also closed Thur Nov-Mar; $$$. Reservations advised.

Popular with locals, this casual fine-dining venue has a particularly nice front patio. The menu emphasizes classical grilled fare and local wines.

The Peppermint Stick
454 Main St., (209) 728-3570. Sun-Thur 11-8; daily in summer; $. No reservations.

When it was built in 1893, this building served as the town icehouse. Now it is a cheerful ice cream parlor serving old-fashioned sodas and sundaes, trendy coffees, soups, and sandwiches. Everything can be packed to go.

SAN ANDREAS

A LITTLE BACKGROUND

Often mistaken as the home of the infamous San Andreas fault, this town was named after the Catholic parish of Saint Andrew. It is home to the state's largest cashmere goat ranch, which is the only custom cashmere dehairer outside of China.

WHAT TO DO

Calaveras County Museum
30 N. Main St., (209) 754-4658; www.calaverascohistorical.com. Daily 10-4. $3, 60+ $2, under 12 $1.

Items on display upstairs in this restored 1867 courthouse include Miwok Indian and Gold Rush artifacts. Among the nicely organized exhibits is a full-size display of a Gold Rush-era general store. The jail cell Black Bart once occupied is downstairs in a rustic courtyard landscaped with native California plants and trees (after he was released, he disappeared and was never heard from again).

California Cavern

9565 Cave City Rd., off Mountain Ranch Rd., in Mountain Ranch, 9 mi. E of town, (866) 762-2837, (209) 736-2708; www.californiacavern.com. Sat-Sun 10-4; daily 10-5 in summer. $14.25, 3-12 $7.15; gemstone mining $5+.

First opened to the public in 1850, this 55-degree cavern is now a state historic landmark. The nearly level Trail of Lights tour takes 60 to 80 minutes and follows the footsteps of John Muir, Mark Twain, and Bret Harte.

A more strenuous Middle Earth Expedition (*$148. Must be age 16+. Reservations required.*) through the unlighted portion of the cavern involves wading through deep mud, climbing rocks and a 60-foot ladder, squeezing through small passages, crossing 200-foot-deep lakes on rafts, and viewing breathtaking formations unequaled in any other cavern in the West.

WHERE TO STAY

Black Bart Inn & Motel

55 W. Saint Charles St., (209) 754-3808; www.blackbartinn.com. 65 rooms; $; some shared baths. Unheated pool. 2 restaurants. No pets.

This lodging facility is named after the infamous highwayman, Black Bart, whose career ended in this town. He robbed 29 stagecoaches between 1875 and 1883, always using an unloaded gun. Rooms are available in both a vintage hotel and in a more modern motel located adjacent.

MOKELUMNE HILL

WHERE TO STAY

Hotel Leger

8304 Main St., (209) 286-1401; www.hotelleger.com. 13 rooms; $-$$. Some wood-burning fireplaces & shared baths. Unheated pool (seasonal). Continental breakfast; restaurant.

Once considered among the most luxurious of Gold Rush hotels, this 1879 lodging still provides comfortable rooms with period antiques and cozy comforters. Many have a sitting area and balcony access, and all are furnished with tasteful period pieces. ("Leger" is pronounced as the original French owners pronounced it—"la-JAY.")

California Cuisine Restaurant (*L Sat-Sun, D Thur-M.*), a historic **saloon**, and a billiards parlor operate on the ground floor.

JACKSON

A LITTLE BACKGROUND

Two important gold-bearing quartz mines are located just north of this busy town. The Argonaut and Kennedy mines had some of the deepest vertical shafts in the world, extending more than 5,000 feet into the ground.

VISITOR INFORMATION

Amador County Chamber of Commerce & Visitors Bureau

571 S. Hwy. 49, (800) 649-4988, (209) 223-0350; www.amadorcountychamber.com.

It is interesting to note that in Spanish "amador" means "lover of gold."

ANNUAL EVENTS

Italian Picnic and Parade

June; 1st weekend. At Italian Picnic Grounds; (209) 223-0350; www.italiansociety.net. Free admission; parking $2. No pets.

Every year since 1882, the public has been invited to this festive event sponsored by the Italian Benevolent Society of Amador County. The fun includes kiddie rides, dancing, a parade down Highway 49 in Sutter Creek, and an all-you-can-eat barbecue.

WHAT TO DO

Amador County Museum

225 Church St., (209) 223-6386. W-Sun 10-4. By donation. Scale models operate Sat-Sun 11-3, on the hr.; $1, under 8 free.

Located within the 1859 red brick Armstead Brown House, this museum displays scale models of the Kennedy Mine tailing wheels and head frame and of the North Star Mine stamp mill. A brightly painted wooden train engine, which was once a prop on TV's *Petticoat Junction*, is parked permanently out back.

Jackson Rancheria Casino & Hotel

*12222 New York Ranch Rd., (800) 822-WINN,
(209) 223-1677; www.jacksoncasino.com. Open 24
hours. Casino visitors must be age 18+. 7 restaurants.
No pets.*

In this windowless gambling behemoth,
owned by the Jackson Rancheria Band of
Miwuk Indians, a Minor's Camp Arcade
welcomes children ages 12 through 17 (and
children 7 through 11 who are with a parent or
guardian). Note that no alcohol is served, or
allowed, on the premises.

Raging River Restaurant offers dining
beside a soothing, man-made river running
right through the casino, and the **hotel**
(4 stories; 100 rooms; $-$$$+.) offers convenient
lodging.

Kennedy Gold Mine

*Near intersection of Hwys. 49 & 88, (209) 223-9542;
www.kennedygoldmine.com. Tours Sat-Sun 10-3,
Mar-Oct only. $9, 6-12 $5.*

One of the richest gold mines in the
world, this mine produced more than
$34.2 million worth of gold from 1880 to 1942.
At 5,912 feet deep, it also was once the deepest
mine in North America. During the guided
surface tours, visitors can try panning for
gold and view several mining buildings, the
125-foot-high metal head frame, and a display
of mining equipment.

Kennedy Mine Tailing Wheels Park

*On Jackson Gate Rd., 1 mi. N of town. Daily dawn to
dusk. Free.*

Unique to the Gold Country, four huge
58-foot-diameter wheels—built in 1912 to lift
waste gravel, or "tailings," into flumes so that
they could be carried to a holding area—can be
viewed by taking a short walk on well-marked
trails on either side of the road. Two of the
wheels have already collapsed. Better hurry to
see this site before time takes its toll on the
other two. The Kennedy Mine can be seen from
here. Picnic tables are available.

Wine tasting

• **Amador Vintners' Association**
*(888) 655-8614, (209) 245-6992;
www.amadorwine.com.*

Many wineries are located in this area,
with a heavy concentration occurring around
the nearby town of Plymouth.

National Hotel

*2 Water St., (209) 223-0500. 4 stories; 25 rooms;
$-$$. Some TVs & shared baths. Restaurant.*

This hotel claims to be the oldest in continuous operation (since 1862) in California.
Some room decor is modest, as are the prices,
while others are a little more flamboyant—the
Bordello Suite, the John Wayne Suite—and a
tad more expensive. Prior guests have included
every California governor since 1862, two
Presidents (Garfield and Hoover), and John
Wayne. The ancient bar has a cheery pub
atmosphere.

Roaring Camp

*In Pine Grove, 10 mi. from town, (209) 296-4100;
www.roaringcampgold.com. 20 cabins; $600/wk./
couple; closed Oct-Apr. Shared modern bath house.
Restaurant.*

Guests leave their cars behind and make
the 1-hour trip into the remote canyon here via
truck. They stay in this former mining camp in
rustic prospector cabins without electricity and
must bring all their own gear and food (campsites are also available). Recreation consists of
swimming, fishing, and panning for gold in the
Mokelumne River, as well as hiking and perhaps
collecting rocks. Guests may keep all found
gold. A saloon, short-order restaurant, and general store are available when guests get tired of
roughing it. Weekly stays run Sunday to Sunday.
One-day tours are also available. On Saturday
evenings, a group of diners is trucked in for
a riverside steak cookout; weekly guests are
invited to join this event at no charge.

SUTTER CREEK

Seven gold mines were once located on this
quiet Main Street. Now it is lined with modern
gold mines—antiques shops.

Sutter Creek Visitor's Center

*(800) 400-0305, (209) 267-1344;
www.suttercreek.org.*

WHAT TO DO

Sutter Gold Mine

13660 Hwy. 49, N of town toward Amador City, (866) 762-2837, (209) 736-2708; www.suttergold.com. M-F 10-4, Sat-Sun 10-5; in summer 9-5. Tours: On the hr.; $17.50, 4-13 $11.50; must be age 4+. Gemstone mining & gold panning $5+.

Made up of 16 historic mines that produced more than 1.3 million ounces of gold, this is the first active gold-mining operation in the area since the Central Eureka Mine closed in the late 1940s. After donning hard hats, a "boss buggy" (a jeep-like safari-car shuttle) takes participants down Indiana Jones-style about 450 feet underground into the belly of the beast for a walking tour, and later returns everyone to the surface. Panning for gold can be done without taking the tour, and viewing a movie about gold mining is free. Picnic facilities are available.

WHERE TO STAY

The Foxes Inn of Sutter Creek

77 Main St., (800) 987-3344, (209) 267-5882; www.foxesinn.com. 7 rooms; $$-$$$+. Some gas fireplaces. Full breakfast. No pets.

Built in 1857, this New England-style farmhouse is located in the center of town. Guests are welcomed in the parlor with a refreshing glass of lemonade. Rooms are comfortable and decorated unfussily with a mixture of antiques, canopied beds, and contemporary comforts. Baths are large and tastefully tiled, and some have clawfoot tubs. As might be expected, a tasteful leitmotif of foxes occurs throughout. Breakfast is cooked-to-order and delivered to the room on an antique silver tea service.

Grey Gables Inn

161 Hanford St., (800) 473-9422, (209) 267-1039; www.greygables.com. 8 rooms; $$. Unsuitable for children under 12. All fireplaces. Afternoon tea; evening snack; full breakfast. No pets.

Bringing a touch of England to the area, this inn resembles an English country manor. Guest rooms are named for English poets such as Byron, Browning, and Shelley. Each is furnished with antiques and an armoire, and some have clawfoot tubs. In English fashion, afternoon tea is served on lovely china in the formal parlor, and breakfast can be taken either in the social atmosphere of the dining room or in the privacy of the guest room.

Sutter Creek Inn

75 Main St., (209) 267-5606; www.suttercreekinn.com. 18 rooms; $-$$. Unsuitable for children. Some TVs & wood-burning fireplaces. Afternoon snack; full breakfast. No pets.

Opened as an inn in 1966, this 1859 Greek Revival structure was one of the first B&Bs west of the Mississippi and has staked its claim as the first in California. Rooms are available in the house as well as in six vintage out buildings. As guests arrive each day, homemade lemonade and cookies are served in the garden, and a full sit-down breakfast is served family-style at long tables in the dining room and kitchen. Each room has its own charm—one has a closet filled with books, another has a clawfoot tub. For those who have been longing to spend the night swinging in a bed suspended from the ceiling by chains, this inn fulfills that and other yearnings. Some visitors have even seen a friendly ghost, although it has been more than 25 years since the last sighting. Croquet and hammocks beckon from the garden.

WHERE TO EAT

Susan's Place

15 Eureka St., (209) 267-0945; www.susansplace.com. L-D Thur-Sun.

Situated just off Main Street, this popular spot has a welcoming vine-covered courtyard that is especially inviting on a warm day. The unusual menu features build-your-own pastas, cheese-sausage boards, and Amador County wines.

Sutter Creek Ice Cream Emporium

51 Main St., (209) 267-0543;
www.suttercreekragtime.com. Sun-Thur 10-8,
F-Sat 9-10; in winter Sun-Thur 10-6, F-Sat 9-9; $.

This old-fashioned soda fountain sells ice cream specialties and more than ten kinds of housemade fudge. Sandwiches, tamales, and corn dogs are also available, plus a wall full of candy. The owner sometimes bangs out a ragtime tune or two on a 1919 Milton Piano.

The annual **Sutter Creek Ragtime Festival** occurs here on the second weekend in August.

VOLCANO

A LITTLE BACKGROUND

The scenic, rural drive here from Sutter Creek is ill marked, poorly paved, and best maneuvered during daylight. And experience indicates that directions and information obtained around these parts are often vague or misleading, leaving plenty of room for error and making a good map worth its weight in gold.

Because this tiny town is built in a depression on top of limestone caves, it is green year-round. Sleepy and quiet now, it was a boomtown during the Gold Rush and well known for its boisterous dance halls and saloons. It also opened the state's first public library.

ANNUAL EVENTS

Daffodil Hill

Mid-March until bloom is over in April. 18310 Rams Horn Grade, off Shake Ridge Rd., 3 mi. N of town, (209) 296-7048. Schedule varies. Free. No pets.

Originally planted in the 1850s by a Dutch settler, then added to and maintained by Grandma McLaughlin, this 6-acre garden boasts more than 300 varieties of bulb. There are many, many daffodils, with a few tulips and hyacinths mixed in, too. McLaughlin's grandchildren and great-grandchildren plant additional bulbs every year. Currently more than 300,000 bloom together each spring, making for a spectacular display. Peacocks, chickens, and sheep wander the grounds, and there is a picnic area with tables. It is a pleasant surprise that this seasonal extravaganza of bloom is so non-commercial.

WHAT TO DO

Black Chasm

15701 Pioneer-Volcano Rd., (866) 762-2837,
(209) 736-2708; www.blackchasmcavern.com.
M-F 10-4, Sat-Sun 10-5; in summer daily 9-5. $14.25,
3-12 $7.15; gemstone mining & gold panning $5+.

This 45-minute cave tour visits the Colossal Room, which measures 100 feet across and 150 feet deep and provides glimpses of the deep lakes far below, and the Landmark Room, which features a spectacular display of twisting, looping helictite crystals. The caves are a cool 57 degrees.

Indian Grinding Rock State Historic Park

14881 Pine Grove-Volcano Rd., in Pine Grove,
(209) 296-7488; www.parks.ca.gov. Daily dawn-dusk.
Museum: M-F 11-3, Sat-Sun 10-4. $6/vehicle.

The largest of the grinding rocks here is a huge flat bedrock limestone measuring 175 feet by 82 feet. It has more than 1,185 mortar holes and approximately 363 petroglyphs (rock carvings)—all made by Native Americans who ground their acorns and other seeds here with pestles. A reconstructed Miwok village contains a ceremonial roundhouse, a covered hand-game area, several cedar-bark houses, and an Indian game field. Additional facilities include a self-guided nature trail and the **Chaw'se Regional Indian Museum**, which orients visitors with a video show and interpretive displays. Picnic facilities and campsites—including a group site of seven authentic u'macha bark houses—are available.

A **"Big Time" Miwok Celebration** is scheduled each September.

"Old Abe" Volcano Blues Cannon

Located in the center of town in a protected shelter, this cannon helped win the Civil War without firing a single shot! Cast of bronze and brass in Boston in 1837 and weighing 737 pounds, it somehow reached San Francisco and was smuggled to Volcano in 1863. The town used it to control renegades drawn here in search of quick wealth. For the complete story, ask around town.

Soldiers' Gulch Park

Rocky terrain, a gurgling stream, and scenic stone ruins—including the façades of several ancient buildings—provide a picturesque backdrop against which to enjoy a picnic or just a few moments of quiet contemplation.

Volcano Theatre Company

(209) 296-2525; www.volcanotheatre.org. F-Sat at 8 & some Sun at 2; Apr-Nov. $9-$15. Reservations required.

The first little theater group to form in California was the Volcano Thespian Society in 1854. Performances are held in the intimate 50-seat Cobblestone Theater, except in summer, when they occur in an outdoor amphitheater. Children are welcome.

WHERE TO STAY

St. George Hotel

16104 Main St., (209) 296-4458; www.stgeorgehotel.com. 20 rooms; $-$$; closed part of Jan. No TVs; some shared baths. Continental breakfast; restaurant.

Rooms are available in either the solidly constructed main hotel, built in 1862, or in bungalows built almost a hundred years later in 1961. For safety reasons, families with children under 12 must stay in the newer rooms located around the corner, their consolation being a private bathroom. A cottage is also available.

In the hotel, a cozy memorabilia-crammed **saloon** *(Thur-Sun.)* and a parlor area with fireplace and games invite relaxing. The hotel **restaurant** *(D Thur-Sun, SunBr; $-$$. Reservations advised.)* serves creative California cuisine.

AMADOR CITY

A LITTLE BACKGROUND

With a population of 202, this is the smallest incorporated city in the state. Basically it is a crook in the road lined with a series of interesting antiques shops inside atmospheric historical buildings—some with brick walls and iron doors.

WHERE TO STAY

Imperial Hotel

14202 Old Hwy. 49, (209) 267-9172; www.imperialamador.com. 9 rooms; $$-$$$. Some gas fireplace stoves. Breakfast; restaurant. No pets.

This beautifully restored historic brick building opened as a hotel in 1879, closed in 1927, then reopened in 1988. Outside it features iron doors and shutters, and the attractively decorated, high-ceilinged interior conveys a touch of artistic flair with contemporary art, colorful fabrics, and an assortment of lovely antiques. A secluded stone patio provides a restful garden retreat. Six guest rooms are in this building, and three suites with canopy beds are in a cottage across the road.

The cozy **restaurant** *(L Sat-Sun, D W-Sun; $$-$$$. Reservations advised.)* offers a brief, eclectic menu of delicious Mediterranean-style fare and mostly local wines, and the completely restored old-time **Oasis Bar** is especially inviting for an after-dinner drink.

WHERE TO EAT

Buffalo Chips Emporium

14179 Hwy. 49, (209) 267-0570. B-L W-Sun; $. No cards.

Some folks buy just a simple cone here and then sit outside on one of the weathered benches to leisurely watch the busy world drive by. Others prefer to sit inside what was once the town's Wells Fargo Bank and indulge in a fancy fountain item. Many of the antique decorations are for sale.

DRYTOWN

A LITTLE BACKGROUND

Once home to 27 saloons, Drytown is now known for its equally abundant antiques shops—and not much else.

EL DORADO

WHERE TO EAT

Poor Red's

*6221 Main St., (530) 622-2901; www.poorreds
bbq.com. L F-Sun, D daily; $. No reservations.*

Judging just from the outside of this 1852
building, which looks to be an unsavory bar,
this former Wells Fargo stage stop might easily
be passed by. But then weary travelers would
miss the experience of dining on exquisite ham,
ribs, chicken, and steak—all cooked over an
open oak-wood pit and served in generous portions. Because this restaurant is very popular
and also very small, weekend dinner waits can
run more than an hour. Some patrons pass that
time downing Gold Cadillacs at the old-time
horseshoe bar. (It is interesting to note that
Poor Red's is the largest user of Galliano in
North America—Galliano being the main ingredient in those Gold Cadillacs invented here in
1948.) Some pass it studying the mural behind
the bar that depicts the town as it appeared in
the late 1800s. Some pass it feeding the jukebox.
And yet others beat the wait by ordering
take-out.

PLACERVILLE

A LITTLE BACKGROUND

Placerville, which in Spanish means "the golden
one," was once known as Hangtown because
hangings here were so common.

This is where the Hangtown Fry—made
with eggs, bacon, and oysters—originated. The
town's **Hangman's Tree** bar *(305 Main St.,
(530) 622-3878.)* is built on top of the legendary
hanging tree's stump and sometimes has a controversial, life-like dummy hanging from a rope
out front.

Railroad magnate Mark Hopkins, meat-
packer Philip Armour, and automobile-maker
John Studebaker all got their financial starts
here.

VISITOR INFORMATION

El Dorado County Visitors Authority

*542 Main St., (800) 457-6279, (530) 621-5885;
www.visit-eldorado.com.*

ANNUAL EVENTS

Wagon Train celebration

June. www.hwy50wagontrain.com.

Horse-drawn wagons travel to town down
Highway 50 from Carson City via Lake Tahoe.

Apple Hill®

*September-December. (530) 644-7692;
www.applehill.com. Daily 9-6.*

On a mountain ridge east of town, the
Apple Hill® tour route follows a historic path
originally blazed out in 1857 by Pony Express
riders. Each fall, 56 apple ranches along this
route sell a wide variety of tree-fresh apples at
bargain prices, and they're *crunchy* because
they're *fresh*! An impressive selection of homemade apple goodies can also be purchased:
fresh-pressed apple cider, hard cider, apple
wine, spicy apple butter, caramel apples, apple
jelly, dried apples, apple cake, apple sundaes,
apple syrup, and, of course, apple pie. Many of
the farms have picnic facilities, and some have
snack bars. A few also have hiking trails, fishing
ponds, pony rides, train rides, and live jazz. Six
wineries and a brewery are also located here.

Cherry season begins in June, and
Christmas tree farms open the day after
Thanksgiving.

WHAT TO DO

El Dorado County Historical Museum

*104 Placerville Dr., at El Dorado County
Fairgrounds, 2 mi. W of town (530) 621-5865;
www.co.el-dorado.ca.us/museum. W-Sat 10-4,
Sun 12-4. By donation.*

Historic exhibits in this "great hall" include
a Wells Fargo stagecoach and a wheelbarrow
made by John Studebaker in the days before he
manufactured cars.

Fountain-Tallman Museum

524 Main St., (530) 626-0773. W-Sun 10-4. Free.

Located in an atmospheric 1852 soda
works building, this museum documents the
town history. Downstairs are Gold Rush artifacts; upstairs is Victorian furniture.

Gold Bug Park & Mine

*Off Bedford Ave., 1 mi. N of town, (530) 642-5207;
www.goldbugpark.org. Daily 8:30-5. Mine: Daily 10-4,
Apr-Oct; Sat-Sun 12-4, Nov-Mar; $5, 10-17 $3, 3-9 $2.*

Visitors can take a self-guided tour through a cool ¼-mile-long lighted mine shaft, see a working model of a stamp mill inside an authentic stamp mill building (these were used to crush granite to extract the gold), picnic at creek-side tables, and hike in rugged 61-acre Gold Bug Park.

WINERIES

Boeger Winery
1709 Carson Rd. (Schnell School Rd. exit off Hwy. 50), (800) 655-2634, (530) 622-8094; www.boeger winery.com. Tasting daily 10-5; no tour.

A winery operated here from the 1860s through the 1920s. During Prohibition, it became a pear farm, becoming a winery again in the early 1970s. The tasting room was formerly in the farm's old stone cellar but now is in a brand new structure. The property has a redwood grove and pond, and shaded stream-side picnic tables beckon.

Sierra Vista Vineyards and Winery
4560 Cabernet Way, (800) WINE-916, (530) 622-7221; www.sierravistawinery.com. Tasting daily 10-5; tour by appt.

Enjoy a magnificent view of the entire Crystal Range of the Sierra Nevada while picnicking at this pleasant Pleasant Valley winery.

SIDE TRIPS

SHINGLE SPRINGS

A LITTLE BACKGROUND

Named for a cool spring that surfaced near a shingle mill here in 1849, this rural area is now—just as it was then—the perfect spot to set up camp.

VISITOR INFORMATION

Shingle Springs/
Cameron Park Chamber of Commerce
3300 Coach Lane #B7, in Cameron Park, (530) 677-8000; www.sscpchamber.org.

GETTING THERE

Located 9 miles west of Placerville via Highway 50.

WHERE TO STAY

KOA Kampground
4655 Rock Barn Rd., (800) KOA-4197, (530) 676-2267; www.koa-placerville.com.

Facilities include a fishing pond. For more description, see page 467.

FOLSOM

A LITTLE BACKGROUND

This small town is a quick, easy stop. Restored Gold Rush-era homes and buildings line historic Sutter Street; many are now inhabited by antique shops and unique boutiques. A new rapid transit light rail runs along the original route of the first railroad west of the Mississippi, connecting Folsom to Sacramento.

VISITOR INFORMATION

Folsom Tourism Bureau
200 Wool St., (800) 377-1414, (916) 985-2698; www.visitfolsom.com.

Pick up information about the town here. The chamber's office is located inside the town's old train depot, which was the terminus of the first passenger railroad west of the Rockies (it ran between Sacramento and Folsom).

GETTING THERE

Located off Highway 50, 20 miles west of Placerville, and 22 miles east of Sacramento.

ANNUAL EVENTS

Folsom Live!
September. (916) 985-5555; www.folsomlive.com. $30, under 2 free.

The historical area of town is closed to traffic for this fun event that is well attended by locals. Venues for the live jazz, country, and rock include bars and restaurants, plus a large outdoor stage for bigger name entertainment.

WHAT TO DO

Folsom City Zoo Sanctuary

403 Stafford St./Natoma St., in Folsom City Lions Park, (916) 351-3527; www.folsomzoo.com. Tu-Sun 10-4, in summer 9-3. $4, 55+ & 5-12 $3; train $2.

This small zoo provides refuge for injured, orphaned, and non-releasable North American animals and a few exotics. Newer enclosures hold North American black bears, mountain lions, and a wolf-hybrid.

Outside the zoo gates, in the park, the **Folsom Valley Railway**—a small, 12-inch narrow-gauge steam train that formerly ran in Berkeley's Tilden Park—now takes riders on a happy 10-minute ride.

Folsom History Museum

823 Sutter St., (916) 985-2707; www.folsomhistorymuseum.org. W-Sun 11-4; daily Aug-Sept. $3, 12-18 $2.

This museum tells the town's Gold Rush story, invites a weigh-in on an old-fashioned scale, and has gold-panning demonstrations on Sundays. Exhibits change frequently.

The historic **Railroad Turntable** *((916) 985-6031; www.fedshra.org. Sat-Sun 11-4. Free.),* which rests on its original granite pivot stone, operates nearby.

Folsom Lake State Recreation Area

7806 Folsom-Auburn Rd., (916) 988-0205; www.parks.ca.gov. Daily 6am-9pm; mid-Oct-Mar, 7-7. $3-$7/vehicle.

Among the activities to be enjoyed in this 18,000-acre park are hiking, biking, running, picnicking, horseback riding, water-skiing, boating, and fishing. Campsites are available.

Negro Bar—the historic name for the area here where African-Americans struck gold in 1849—is a super-scenic bend in the river and a prime put-in spot. Kayak rentals are available through **Adventure Sports Kayak Rentals** *((916) 971-1800; www.kayakcity.com. Sat-Sun May-mid-Oct.).* You can also swim here and picnic at tables sheltered by mature trees, and a bike trail is nearby.

Folsom Powerhouse State Historic Park

7806 Folsom-Auburn Rd., (916) 985-4843; www.parks.ca.gov. W-Sun 12-4. Free.

Built in 1895, this was the first and largest hydro-electric generating plant west of the Mississippi. It operated until 1952, when the Folsom Dam hydro-electric plant began operating. It is a great spot for kids to explore, with a "busy table" of experiments inside and a large park with sheltered picnic tables overlooking Lake Natoma outside.

Folsom Prison Museum

Prison Rd./Natoma St., in Lincoln, (916) 985-2561 x4589. Daily 10-4. $1, under 12 free.

Located just inside the prison visitor's gate, this small museum documents the history of this massive granite maximum security prison. Displays include an intriguing collection of confiscated weapons and also a copy of Johnny Cash's record album that made the prison famous with the lyrics, "I'm stuck in Folsom Prison, and time keeps draggin' on." Opened in 1880, the prison is the state's second-oldest and holds about 3,880 prisoners. Some say it just might be the prettiest little prison in the west. Inmates have been making California license plates here since 1947.

Some residents are gifted at making other things, too, and a **gift shop** stocked with inmate crafts and staffed by trustees (prisoners who are trustworthy and close to parole) operates across the street.

Nimbus Fish Hatchery

Hazel Ave./Hwy.50, (916) 358-2884; www.dfg.ca.gov/fish/Hatcheries/Nimbus/index.asp. Daily 10-3. Free.

This is a working hatchery, so something fishy is usually happening. Kazillions of fingerlings are always busy growing in the tanks. In fall, when the Chinook salmon return from the ocean, a fish ladder is opened, and steelhead trout show up in the winter. Fish food can be purchased for a nickel, and a Visitor Center features educational exhibits.

Each October, the **American River Salmon Festival** *(www.salmonfestival.net. Free; parking $8; free valet bike parking.)* features live music and barbecued salmon.

Snooks Chocolate Factory

731 Sutter St., (800) 957-6665, (916) 985-0620; www.snookscandies.com. Daily 11-8, F-Sat to 9:30.

Drop into this candy shop to view a candy-making demonstration and to do some tasting. Don't miss the candy machine that spits out hand-made chocolates like that one in the famous *I Love Lucy* episode. Though everything is yummy, the fresh peanut brittle and the old-fashioned fudge are spectacular.

WHERE TO STAY

The Bradley House
606 Figueroa St., (916) 355-1962; www.bradleyhousebandb.us. 4 rooms; $-$$. Full breakfast.

Spacious rooms and expansive porches and gardens make this Victorian farm house a comfortable place to rest.

Lake Natoma Inn
702 Gold Lake Dr., 800-808-LAKE, (916) 351-1500; www.lakenatomainn.com. 138 rooms; $-$$$+. Some fireplaces. Heated pool; hot tub; 2 saunas; fitness center. Restaurant; room service.

Located just a block from historic Sutter Street and from bike and walking trails, this comfortable lodging also has a 9-hole putting green.

WHERE TO EAT

Balcony Bistro
801½ Sutter St., (916) 353-0733; www.balcony bistro.com. L Tu-F, D Tu-Sat, Sat-SunBr; $-$$$. Reservations advised.

With a warm, open dining room featuring brick walls hung with original art, this informal spot serves up some tasty, well-priced fare fare. Fresh fish, creative pastas (anyone for a pear and walnut version?), and classics—roasted duck confit—are sometimes options on the changing menu.

Before or after dining, wander through the art gallery and studio operating off one side.

Lake Forest Cafe
13409 Folsom Blvd., (916) 985-6780; www.lakeforest cafe.com. B-L W-Sun; $. No reservations.

Among the breakfast items served in this comfy little house are 43 kinds of omelettes, a variety of Jewish specialties, and freshly baked giant cinnamon rolls. Some breakfast items are also available at lunch.

COLOMA

A LITTLE BACKGROUND

This is where James Marshall, a sawmill foreman who worked for Captain John Sutter, discovered gold in 1848. The entire town is now a National Historic Landmark.

WHAT TO DO

Marshall Gold Discovery State Historic Park
On Hwy. 49, (530) 622-3470; www.parks.ca.gov. Daily 8-sunset; museum: Daily 10-3, in summer 10-4:30. $5/vehicle.

This lovely 265-acre park encompasses 70% of the town. It contains a reconstruction of the original **Sutter's Mill** (where the Gold Rush began) as well as picnic facilities, nature trails, and Gold Rush-era buildings and artifacts. An exact replica of the piece of gold Marshall found is displayed in the museum (the original is at the Smithsonian in Washington, D.C.).

The **James W. Marshall Monument** is located on a hill overlooking the town. Marshall's grave is also there, and a statue depicts him pointing to the spot where he discovered gold.

Whitewater Connection
See page 466.

The office and base camp for this white water rafting outfit is located adjacent to the state park. Participants on American River trips can camp out at the outfitter's riverside facility. Half-day, full-day, and overnight trips are scheduled daily from mid-April through September; longer trips are also available.

AUBURN

VISITOR INFORMATION

Auburn Area Chamber of Commerce
601 Lincoln Way, (530) 885-5616;
www.auburnchamber.net.

Placer County Visitors Council
13411 Lincoln Way, (866) PLACER-1, (530) 887-2111;
www.visitplacer.com.

It is interesting to note that in Spanish "placer" means "surface mining." A **California Welcome Center** is also housed here.

ANNUAL EVENTS

Mountain Mandarin Festival
November; weekend before Thanksgiving.
At the Gold Country Fairgrounds, (916) 663-1918;
www.mandarinfestival.com. $5, under 16 free;
parking $5.

Everything Mandarin is celebrated, plus musicians and dancers entertain and more than 225 vendors offer crafts and holiday decorations. Tasty treats include pandas (Mandarin slices dipped in dark and white chocolate), Mandarin BBQ pork and Brie, pear and Mandarin salad, and Mandarin milkshakes.

WHAT TO DO

Bernhard Museum Complex
291 Auburn-Folsom Rd., (530) 889-6500. Tu-Sun 11-4. Free.

Docent-led tours are available of the Greek Revival-style Bernhard Residence, a restored Victorian farmhouse built in 1851 and furnished with Victorian antiques. A restored historic winery and reconstructed carriage barn are also on the site.

Gold Country Museum
1273 High St., at Gold Country Fairgrounds, (530) 889-6500. Tu-Sun 11-4. Free.

Located within a building constructed of logs and stones, this old-time museum emphasizes mining exhibits. Visitors can walk through a 48-foot-long mine shaft and view a working model of a stamp mill. Local Maidu Indian artifacts and an extensive doll collection are displayed.

Placer County Museum/Courthouse
101 Maple St., (530) 889-6500. Daily 10-4. Free.

Located on the echoing first floor of the landmark Placer County Courthouse (the entrance is at ground level under the formal steps that are reminiscent of an Aztec temple), this museum's exhibits include a Native American habitat, a restored circa 1915 sheriff's office, and the Pate Collection of Native American Art featuring more than 400 artifacts from throughout the U.S. The jail serves as a gallery, and a spectacular 52-piece gold collection worth more than $350,000 is displayed in a vault in the gift shop. Kids particularly enjoy a hands-on telegraph and telephone display.

WHERE TO STAY

Motel Row
Many motels are located at the top of the hill on Lincoln Way and across the freeway on Bowman Road.

WHERE TO EAT

Auburn Alehouse
289 Washington St., (530) 885-2537;
www.auburnalehouse.com. L-D daily; $-$$. No cards.

Until 2007, this building held the state's oldest family-owned bar and restaurant, which had served Cantonese fare since 1906. It was also the setting for the movie *Phenomenon.* Now, after major restoration, it holds a brewpub with an extensive menu and a nice outdoor patio. Try the Fool's Gold Ale, a Kobe Beef Burger, and the tasty bread pudding.

Awful Annie's
160 Sacramento St., (530) 888-9857;
www.awfulannies.com. B-L-D daily; $.
Reservations for 5+.

Everything about this tiny spot is appealing—the lace-covered windows, the large outdoor deck, the all-day breakfast menu. The kitchen is famous for blackberry and cream cheese-stuffed French toast and Grandma's bread pudding with brandy sauce, and the lunch menu includes scads of salads, sandwiches, and burgers. Truth be told, Annie's is awful good.

Cafe Delicias
1591 Lincoln Way, (530) 885-2050; www.cafe-delicias.com. L-D W-M; $.

Located in one of the town's oldest buildings, this casual Mexican restaurant serves especially good flautas and housemade tamales.

Ikedas
13500 Lincoln Way (¼ mi. E of Auburn Ravine-Foresthill exit off I-80), (530) 885-4243; www.ikedas.com. Daily 8-7; in summer to 9; $. No cards.

Since the 1950s, the casual Burger Bar here has been serving travel-weary diners fast-food fare: fresh-ground hamburgers, hot dogs, rice bowls, burritos, deep-fried whole mushrooms, fruit pie, fresh fruit salad, frozen yogurt, 10 flavors of hot chocolate, and thick fresh fruit milkshakes. An adjacent produce market sells terrific car snacks, among them giant cashews and pistachios, both of which are grown in the area.

GRASS VALLEY

A LITTLE BACKGROUND

It was here, in what was once the richest gold-bearing region in the state, that gold mining became a well-organized industry. Many advanced mining techniques were developed and first used here.

VISITOR INFORMATION

Grass Valley/Nevada County Chamber of Commerce
248 Mill St., (800) 655-4667, (530) 273-4667; www.grassvalleychamber.com. M-F 9-5, Sat 10-3.

Because of its location inside a replica of the home once occupied by scandalous Gold Rush personality Lola Montez, this office is worth visiting in person.

ANNUAL EVENTS

Bluegrass Festival
June. (916) 989-0993; www.fathersdayfestival.com. $30+, 13-18 $13+. No pets.

Cornish Christmas
December. (530) 272-8315; www.downtowngrassvalley.com. Free.

Experience an old-time Christmas at this event celebrating the traditions of the Cornish miners who settled this Gold Rush town. Visitors can taste traditional food and drink, hear period music, and dance in the traffic-free downtown streets.

WHAT TO DO

Empire Mine State Historic Park
10791 E. Empire St., (530) 273-8522; www.parks. ca.gov. Daily 10-5; in summer 9-6. $3, 6-16 $1. Cottage & mineyard tours each +$1.50; cottage tour, Sat-Sun 12-3:30, May-Oct; mine tour, schedule varies.

Once the largest and richest hard rock mine in the state, the Empire Mine operated for more than a century—from 1850 to 1956. Though it still holds millions of dollars worth of gold, the ore is too expensive to extract. The mine is now an 805-acre state park. Of special interest is the stone **Bourn Cottage** (also known as the Empire Cottage), which was designed and built as a summer home for William Bowers Bourn II by his hunting buddy, Willis Polk, in 1897. It is in the style of an English country manor and features hand-planed heart-redwood walls. The surrounding 13 acres of formal gardens feature an antique rose garden planted in 1905, several fountains, and a reflecting pool. The mineyard illustrates many facets of the business and allows visitors to look down a lighted mine shaft. Among the approximately 12 miles of hiking trails are self-guided backcountry paths and an easy 2-mile loop Hardrock Trail. Picnicking is not permitted.

Grass Valley Museum
410 S. Church St./Chapel St., (530) 272-4725; www.saintjosephsculturalcenter.org. Tu-F 12:30-3:30. By donation.

Built in 1863 as Mount Saint Mary's Convent and Orphanage, this was the state's first orphanage for non-Indian children. The

Workers being transported into Empire Mine

building now displays Gold Rush memorabilia and furnishings as well as a fully equipped doctor's office, classroom, parlor, and music room from that era.

Northstar Mine Powerhouse & Pelton Wheel Mining Museum

On Allison Ranch Rd./S end of Mill St., (530) 273-4255; www.nevadacountyhistory.org/ htmls/northstar.html. Daily 10-5; closed Oct-Apr. By donation.

Once the power house for the North Star Mine, this rustic stone building houses a collection of old photographs, mining dioramas and models, and a 30-foot-diameter, 10-ton Pelton water wheel dating from 1896—the largest such wheel ever constructed. It also displays the largest operational Cornish pump in the country.

A grassy picnic area is located across adjacent Wolf Creek.

Oregon House

35 mi. W of town (take Hwy. 20 W to Browns Valley, then Hwy. E21 N to Oregon House, then E20 E).

• Collins Lake Recreation Area

7530 Collins Lake Rd., (800) 286-0576, (530) 692-1600; www.collinslake.com. Daily sunrise-sunset, later on F. $6-10/vehicle.

Popular with fishermen, this 1,600-acre lake and recreation area has lakefront campsites, RV hook-ups, and cabins, and boat rentals are available.

• Renaissance Vineyard & Winery

12585 Rices Crossing Rd., (800) 655-3277, (530) 575-1254; www.renaissancewinery.com. Tasting M-Sat 11-3; tour by appt.

The scenic drive through the Sierra Nevada foothills required to reach this isolated valley would be worthwhile even if this special winery weren't waiting at the end. Operated by the Fellowship of Friends, a non-denominational religious group, the winery is atop a scenic hillside terraced with grapevines. It makes a limited production of Bordeaux and Rhone varietals. A picnic lunch and a gourmet olive oil tasting are available by reservation, as is a winery tour that includes the property's lovely rose garden.

South Yuba River State Park

17660 Pleasant Valley Rd., in Penn Valley, (530) 432-2546; www.parks.ca.gov. Sunrise-sunset. Visitor center: Thur-Sun 12-4; daily in summer. Free.

Facilities include a scenic riverbank picnic area and several hiking trails, and the wildflower display here seen from March through May can be spectacular.

Bridgeport Covered Bridge (*Take Hwy. 20 W 10 mi. to Pleasant Valley Rd., turn right (N) and follow south fork of Yuba River 9 mi. to Bridgeport.*) was built over the south fork of the Yuba River in 1862 and was in use until 1971. It is the longest (229 feet) single-span wood-covered bridge in the world and a state historical landmark. Not currently maintained and in shaky condition, it should be walked across with caution.

The 4-mile **Independence Trail** (*Off Hwy. 49, 6 mi. N of Nevada City, (530) 272-3823. Free.*) follows the Excelsior Canal and Flume, which was built in 1856 to carry water 25 miles downstream through the mountains to Smartville for hydraulic gold mining. The trail is level and easy for both wheelchairs and baby strollers to navigate. One section permits hikers to cross flumes suspended over deep crevices and a waterfall.

WHERE TO STAY

Holbrooke Hotel

212 W. Main St., (800) 933-7077, (530) 273-1353; www.holbrookehotel.com. 28 rooms; $$-$$$. Some gas fireplaces. Continental breakfast; restaurant.

Established in 1851, this meticulously restored Victorian grand hotel has hosted four presidents (Grant, Garfield, Cleveland, and Harrison), stagecoach robber Black Bart, and author Mark Twain. Current guests can step back in time in beautifully appointed rooms featuring brass beds and the original clawfoot tubs. Most rooms hold only two people, but a few larger rooms can accommodate a child on a rollaway bed. A century-old wrought-iron elevator cage lifts guests from floor to floor. This lodging complex, which consists of both the hotel and the 1874 **Purcell House** behind it, is conveniently located in the center of town.

Both the **Golden Gate Saloon**, which is the oldest continually operating saloon west of the Mississippi and features an ornate bar that was shipped around the Horn, and the elegant **212 Bistro** *(L-D daily, SunBr.)*, with full family amenities, operate on the main floor.

Sivananda Ashram Yoga Farm

14651 Ballantree Ln., (800) 469-9642, (530) 272-9322; www.yogafarm.org. 8 rooms; $. No TVs; all shared bathrooms. Meals included. No pets.

The bell rings here at 5:30 each morning to awaken guests. Attendance at scheduled meditation and yoga classes is mandatory. In between, guests dine on vegetarian meals and have plenty of free time to enjoy the natural surroundings of the 80-acre farm. Lodging is simple, almost austere, consisting of both dormitories and single and double rooms, and during the summer guests may bring their own tents. Day visits are available.

WHERE TO EAT

Marshall's Pasties

203 Mill St., (530) 272-2844. M-F 9:30-6, Sat 10-6; $.

Meat-and-potato turnovers were once popular lunch fare among the area's Cornish miners, who dubbed them "pasties" and carried them down into the mines in their pockets. At lunchtime, they reheated their pasties on a shovel held over candles secured in their hard hats. How about a hasty tasty pasty picnic? (Actually, "pasty" rhymes with "nasty.") Though town resident William Brooks invented the pasty-making machine now used throughout the world, here the pastries are made by hand.

Tofanelli's

302 W. Main St., (530) 272-1468; www.tofanellis.com. B-L-D daily; $-$$$. No reservations.

Located within an 1859 building with an attractive and restful brick-and-oak decor, this spot is particularly popular for breakfast. Salads, sandwiches, and several kinds of hamburgers—including a tofu burger and a veggie burger—are on the lunch menu, and all desserts are made in-house.

NEVADA CITY

A LITTLE BACKGROUND

Reputed to be the best privately preserved and restored small city in the state, this picturesque mining town is also said to contain residential and commercial buildings representative of all the major 19th-century architectural styles. Scenically situated on seven hills, the town boasts a particularly fine assortment of lovely gingerbread-style Victorian homes, and the entire downtown district is on the National Register of Historic Places. It is interesting to note that in Spanish "nevada" means "snow-covered."

VISITOR INFORMATION

Nevada City Chamber of Commerce

132 Main St., (800) 655-NJOY, (530) 265-2692; www.nevadacitychamber.com.

ANNUAL EVENTS

International Teddy Bear Convention

April. (530) 265-5804; www.teddybearcastle.com. $5, seniors $3, under 12 & bears free.

Bears from all over the world come out of hibernation for this warm, fuzzy event. Bearaphernalia and bear necessities—and luxuries—abound, and all kinds of bears are available for adoption.

4th of July Parade

July. (800) 655-4667, (530) 273-4667;
www.nevadacitychamber.com/events_fourth.htm.
Fairgrounds: $8, under 13 free; parking $3.

Held in Nevada City on even years and in
Grass Valley on odd, this old-fashioned celebration begins with a parade. Diversions follow—
food stalls, competitions, entertainment—at the
fairgrounds and, as might be expected, the day
culminates in a fireworks extravaganza.

Constitution Day Parade

September. (800) 655-NJOY, (530) 265-2692;
www.nevadacitychamber.com/events_constitution.htm.

The signing of the U.S. Constitution is
honored at this oldest and largest celebration in
the West. The parade includes marching bands,
drill teams, floats, fire engines, and equestrians,
and pre-parade activities include a re-enactment of the signing.

Fall colors

Mid-October to mid-November. (800) 655-NJOY,
(530) 265-2692; www.nevadacitychamber.com/
events_fallcolors.htm.

Victorian Christmas

December; on the 3 Wed eves & on one Sun aft.
before Christmas. (800) 655-NJOY, (530) 265-2692;
www.nevadacitychamber.com/events_victorian.htm.
Free.

The town's historic district is closed to
traffic and transformed into Christmas past,
and enchanting melodies and costumed charac-
ters take visitors to another time and place.
Enjoy tasting chestnuts roasted on an open fire,
hearing strolling minstrels and brass bands,
riding on a hay wagon, and more. Among the
possibilities: Victorian singers, bagpipers, a living nativity scene, a walking Christmas tree,
and, of course, Santa Claus.

WHAT TO DO

Firehouse No. 1 Museum

214 Main St., (530) 265-5468; www.nevadacounty
history.org/htmls/firehouse.html. F-Sun 1-4.
By donation.

Located inside a charming 1861 Victorian
firehouse, this museum is said to be haunted.
Among the intriguing pioneer memorabilia displayed are a Chinese altar, snowshoes made for

a horse, relics from the Donner Party, and a
noteworthy collection of Maidu Indian baskets.

Nevada Theatre

401 Broad St., (530) 265-6161;
www.nevadatheatre.com. Schedule & ticket prices
vary.

Opened in September of 1865 and lectured
in twice by Mark Twain, this is the oldest origi-
nal-use theater building in California. It is
refurbished to appear as it did when it first
opened and is used year-round for plays, concerts, films, and other performing arts events.

WINERIES

Indian Springs Vineyards Tasting Room

303 Broad St., (800) 375-9311, (530) 478-1068;
www.indianspringswines.com. Tasting Sun-Thur
11:30-5, F-Sat 11:30-6.

Taste premium wines produced from
grapes grown in Nevada County and other
parts of Northern California.

Nevada City Winery

321 Spring St., (800) 203-WINE, (530) 265-WINE;
www.ncwinery.com. Tasting M-Sat 12-6, Sun 12-5;
tour on Sat at 1:30.

Housed now in a historic foundry building, this winery is located only 2 blocks from
where it originated a century ago. It is known
for its Cabernets, Merlots, and Zinfandels.

WHAT TO DO NEARBY

Malakoff Diggins State Historic Park

23579 N. Bloomfield Rd., off Hwy. 49, 26 mi. NE of
town, (530) 265-2740; www.parks.ca.gov. Museum:
Sat-Sun 10-4; daily May-Sept. $6/vehicle.

Inhabited by more than 1,500 people in
the 1870s, when it was the largest hydraulic
gold-mining operation in the world, North
Bloomfield is now a ghost town. Several buildings are restored, but there are no commercial
shops. The park museum is in a former dance
hall and has an interpretive display on hydraulic
mining. Visitors can hike on numerous trails
and fish in a small lake, and picnic facilities are
available. Primitive cabins and both walk-in and
regular campsites are available. Note that the
drive from Nevada City takes just under an
hour, and the last mile into North Bloomfield is
dirt road.

Oregon Creek swimming hole

On Hwy. 49, 18 mi. N of town.

Located in the middle fork of the Yuba River, this popular spot has sandy beaches, both deep swimming and shallow wading spots, and picnic facilities.

WHERE TO STAY

National Hotel

211 Broad St., (530) 265-4551; www.thenational hotel.com. 42 rooms; $-$$. Some kitchens; 1 gas fireplace; some shared baths. Unheated pool. Restaurant; room service. No pets.

Located on the town's main street, this claims to be the oldest continuously operating hotel west of the Rockies—maybe even west of the Mississippi. Luminaries who have been guests here include Herbert Hoover, who stayed here when he was a mining engineer for the Empire Mine, and Mark Twain. Built in 1856, it is a state historical landmark and features high ceilings, cozy floral wallpapers, and old-time furniture. Families of four are accommodated in two separate rooms with a bath in between.

Plush, old-fashioned **Hoover's** *(B-L-D daily, SunBr; $-$$. Reservations advised.)*features a steak and lobster dinner menu.

Northern Queen Inn

400 Railroad Ave., (800) 226-3090, (530) 265-5824; www.northernqueeninn.com. 86 units; $-$$. Some kitchens & wood-burning stoves. Heated pool; hot tub. Restaurant.

Located on the outskirts of town beside Gold Run Creek, this pleasant lodging complex has modern motel rooms, cottages, and 2-story chalets. A small collection of full-size trains is displayed on the property, including a 1920s railbus, a 1910 wood-burning locomotive, and another engine that had roles in several classic western movies.

On the property, the **Nevada County Traction Company** *(402 Railroad Ave., (800) 226-3090 x.262, (530) 265-0896; www.depot people.com. Schedule varies. $10, 2-12 $7.)* operates a 1½-hour, 3-mile train ride in open-top excursion cars.

Piety Hill Cottages

523 Sacramento St., (800) 443-2245, (530) 265-2245; www.pietyhillcottages.com. 9 cottages; $-$$. All kitchenettes; 1 wood-burning stove. Hot tub (seasonal). Continental breakfast. No pets.

This 1930s auto court motel has one-and two-room cottages with antique furnishings. A breakfast basket is delivered to the room.

Red Castle Inn

109 Prospect St., (800) 761-4766, (530) 265-5135; www.redcastleinn.com. 4 stories; 7 rooms; $$. Unsuitable for children under 10. No TVs. Full breakfast. No pets.

Situated on a hilltop above town, this beautifully restored and poshly furnished Gothic Revival mansion was built in 1860. Said to be one of only two of this style left on the West Coast, it features gingerbread and icicle trim and has old-fashioned double brick walls. Rooms are decorated deliciously, and breakfast is an occasion. Some guests have reportedly seen the spirit of Laura Jean, who was once a governess here.

WHERE TO EAT

Cafe Mekka

237 Commercial St., (530) 478-1517. Sun-Thur 8am-10pm, F-Sat to midnight; $.

Mix-matched furniture here includes some stuffed couches and armchairs, making for a casual atmosphere. Art that is part of regularly changing shows hangs on the tall walls. Divine desserts and pastries made by the cafe's own baker include the White Bronco—chocolate cake with whipped cream filling topped with white chocolate swirls and raspberry sauce (guess what famous trial it is named for), and a board full of coffee selections keeps things perking right along.

Country Rose Café

300 Commercial St., (530) 265-6252. L-D Tu-Sun; $-$$. Reservations advised.

The charming dining room in this 1860s brick building features wood booths and rose-print tablecloths. In summer, diners can also sit in a bucolic outdoor area with a creek running through it. The inviting country-French menu includes delicious housemade soups and sand-wiches, French hot chocolate, and a great lemon chiffon pie. Classically prepared fresh fish is a house specialty.

Friar Tuck's

111 N. Pine St., (530) 265-9093; www.friartucks.com. D daily; $$. Reservations advised.

Operating in a building dating back to 1857, this popular restaurant burned to the ground in 2002. It reopened with a new take on its old look and features cozy booths, a huge state-of-the-art kitchen, and locally made fiber-optic lighting. The extensive menu offers a variety of casual fondue items—including a chocolate dessert version—as well as grilled fresh fish, rack of lamb, roasted duck, ribs, and steak.

Posh Nosh

318 Broad St., (530) 265-6064; www.myposhnosh.com. L-D Tu-Sun; $$. Reservations advised.

Operating within a historic stone building, this restaurant offers a cozy downstairs room for winter dining. In summer, a pleasant patio out back is choice. The eclectic menu offers something for everyone. Lunch consists of plenty of sandwiches and salads, while dinner brings on steak, ribs, and fresh fish.

DOWNIEVILLE

A LITTLE BACKGROUND

One of the Gold Country's best-preserved, least changed mining towns, this scenic mountain enclave is known as the gateway to the Lost Sierra. It is a surprise to come upon as Highway 49 winds through it, narrowing to one lane over the town's northern bridge. Situated where the North Yuba River and the Downie River merge, known as the Forks, it is where early miners found big gold nuggets by the bucketful. The rustic town retains its 19th-century charm with wood plank sidewalks, original brick buildings that include a white steeple church, and the ever-present soothing sound of the rushing Downie River. Main Street still has a mining supply shop and saloon, and the 1885 town gallows, used only once, still stands outside the County Courthouse.

The town is a popular destination with mountain bikers, who enjoy riding on the plentiful dirt roads. Enjoy a quick stop by picnicking among the Gold Rush artifacts in riverside Lions Memorial Park; sandwich and pizza shops are adjacent. And pick up a copy of *The Mountain Messenger* newspaper—the state's oldest continuously published weekly, since 1853.

GETTING THERE

Located 40 miles northeast of Nevada City.

WHERE TO STAY

Sierra Shangri-La

On Hwy. 49, (530) 289-3455; www.sierrashangrila.com. 11 units; $-$$$. No TVs; some kitchens & wood-burning fireplaces & stoves. No pets.

There is little to do here except commune with nature. Guests can relax, do some fishing and hiking, and enjoy the sight and sound of the Yuba River rushing past their cabin door. Some units are perched right over the river, allowing guests to fish from their deck. Eight housekeeping cottages and three B&B units are available.

SIERRA CITY

VISITOR INFORMATION

Sierra County Chamber of Commerce

P.O. Box 436, Sierra City 96125, (800) 200-4949, (530) 862-1275; www.sierracountychamber.net.

GETTING THERE

Located 60 miles northeast of Nevada City.

WHAT TO DO

Sierra County Historical Park

100 Kentucky Mine Rd., off Hwy. 49, (530) 862-1310; www.kentuckymine.org. W-Sun 10-5, June-Sept; Sat-Sun only in Oct; closed Nov-May. Mill tour at 11, 2. $5, under 18 $2.50. Museum only: $1; under 6 free.

The **Kentucky Mine Museum** offers a 45-minute guided tour through the reconstructed 1850s Kentucky Mine Stamp Mill. Participants view the original machinery, which is still intact and operable. The museum is inside a reconstructed wood-frame hotel dating from the mid-19th century. Picnic tables and barbecue facilities are available under a canopy of oak trees.

The eclectic **Kentucky Mine Concert Series** *($10-$25.)* is held on some summer Saturday evenings in an amphitheater within the complex.

WHERE TO STAY

Herrington's Sierra Pines Resort
On Hwy. 49, (800) 682-9848, (530) 862-1151; www.herringtonssierrapines.com. 21 units; $-$$; closed Dec-Mar. Some kitchens & wood-burning fireplaces. Restaurant.

Located on the north fork of the Yuba River, this lodging facility consists of duplex units and one cabin.

The **restaurant** *(B&D daily; $-$$; closed Oct-May.)* is known for its baked goods and rainbow trout, which are caught fresh each morning from the property's own trout pond.

Packer Lake Lodge
3901 Packer Lake Rd., 10 mi. N of town, (530) 862-1221; www.packerlakelodge.com. 14 cabins; $; closed Nov-Apr. No TVs; some kitchens & wood-burning stoves; some shared baths. Restaurant.

Located at the end of a road in a remote corner of the Sierra Nevada, this rustic resort has eight housekeeping cabins with sun decks overlooking Packer Lake. They are rented by the week and include use of a rowboat (no motorboats are permitted on the lake). Six sleeping cabins are available by the night. Summer dates are usually booked up several years in advance.

The **restaurant** is open for dinner to non-guests by reservation.

Salmon Lake Lodge
On Gold Lake Rd., 10 mi. N of town, (530) 852-0874; www.salmonlake.net. 14 cabins; $-$$; 1-wk. min. June-Oct; closed Nov-Apr. No TVs; some kitchens & wood-burning fireplaces & stoves; some shared baths.

Located in the glaciated high country of Sierra County, this remote resort has been in continuous operation for almost a century. Guests park their cars at the east end of Salmon Lake and are transported by a staff-operated barge across the lake. There they sleep in one of the cabins or tent-cabins and are provided free access to an assortment of boats. Some cabins are fully equipped, but guests in tent-cabins must provide their own bedding, kitchen utensils, and supplies. The experience is like luxurious camping. To ease cooking chores, guests are invited each week to a catered barbecue (additional fee) held on an island in the center of the lake.

SIERRAVILLE

GETTING THERE

Located 80 miles northeast of Nevada City, where Highway 49 meets Highway 89. Highway 89 continues north to Plumas County and south to Truckee and Lake Tahoe.

WHAT TO DO

Sierra Hot Springs
521 Campbell Hot Springs Rd., off Hwy. 89, (530) 994-3773; www.sierrahotsprings.org. Baths open 24-hrs. daily. Day-use: $15-$20, 5-12 half-price. $5 membership required. No pets.

Swimsuits are optional in the indoor and outdoor hot springs at this secluded spa. Open since the 1850s, its facilities include a sand-bottom hot pool inside a copper geodesic dome with stained glass and skylights; two cold plunges; a dry sauna; and an outdoor hot springs soaking pool with deck.

Lodging includes five private rooms and a dormitory in a rustic lodge by the springs, plus hotel rooms in town in its renovated 1909 **Globe Hotel** *(9 rooms; $-$$.)*—formerly a Chinese gambling parlor and once a brothel. Campsites are also available. Rates include unlimited use of the springs.

An organic vegetarian **restaurant** serves nightly buffet dinners *(In winter, F-Sun only; $.)*.

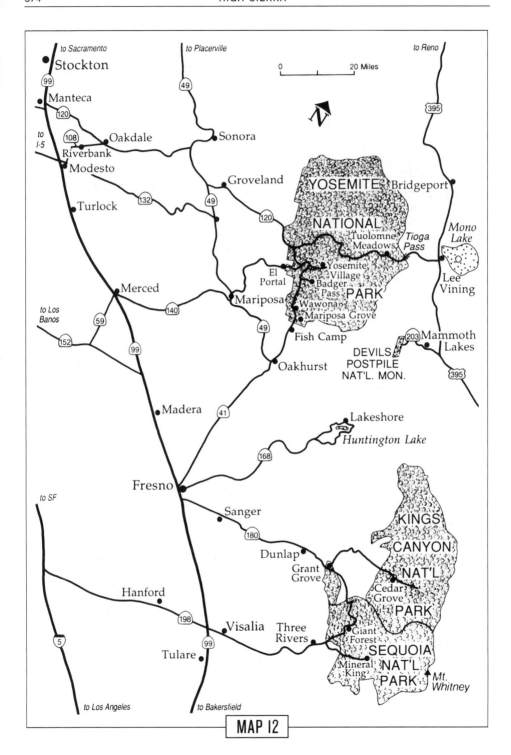

MAP 12

HIGH SIERRA

YOSEMITE NATIONAL PARK

A LITTLE BACKGROUND

Yosemite Park is a place of rest. A refuge . . . in which one gains the advantage of both solitude and society . . . none can escape its charms. Its natural beauty cleanses and warms like fire, and you will be willing to stay forever . . .

— John Muir

Yosemite is worth returning to in every season. Doing so permits enjoying the spectacular beauty of the park's dramatic seasonal changes. Most visitors see this grand national park in the summer, when it is at its busiest—with congested roads and accommodations filled to capacity. All this makes it difficult to focus on what was the original draw—the scenic, natural beauty of the High Sierra. To catch a glimpse of the Yosemite described by Muir, it is essential to visit in the off-season: in fall when the colorful foliage change is spectacular; in winter when snow blankets the valley floor; in spring when the falls are at their fullest.

Yosemite's high country was designated a national park in 1890. The valley, which was under state supervision, was added to the national park in 1906. (It is amazing to realize that the valley comprises just 1% of the park's terrain. In fact, Yosemite is as big as the state of Rhode Island.) Among the park's scenic wonders are 3,000-foot-high El Capitan—the largest piece of exposed granite in the world—and Yosemite Falls—the tallest waterfall in North America and the fifth tallest free-falling waterfall in the world.

Bear in mind that falls and rivers can be dangerous as well as beautiful. Be careful, especially when hiking with children.

A $20 per vehicle admission fee, which is good for 7 days, is collected at all park entrances. Visitors receive a copy of the *Yosemite Guide* activities newsletter and a park map. For more information, see www.YosemitePark.com.

VISITOR INFORMATION

National Park Service
Yosemite National Park 95389, (209) 372-0200; www.nps.gov/yose.

GETTING THERE

Located approximately 240 miles east of San Francisco. Take Highway 80 to Highway 580 to Highway 205 to Highway 120. To minimize the need for chains in winter, take low-elevation Highway 140 in from Merced.

STOPS ALONG THE WAY

Attractions are listed in the order encountered driving in from the San Francisco Bay Area.

Knight's Ferry Covered Bridge

18020 Sonora Rd., in Knights Ferry, 12 mi. E of Oakdale, (209) 881-3517. Visitor center M-F 8-4, Sat-Sun 10-2. Free.

Built in 1863 and measuring 330 feet long, this bridge is the longest and oldest covered bridge west of the Mississippi. It is closed to cars now, but pedestrian traffic is still permitted. A park on the highway side of the Stanislaus River provides picnicking and fishing spots. On the other side of the river is a rustic Gold Rush-era town with a general store, several restaurants, and another park.

Unguided raft and kayak rentals can be arranged through **River Journey** *((800) 292-2938, (209) 847-4671; www.riverjourney.com.).*

Groveland

This woodsy mountain town is home to the **Iron Door Saloon** *(18761 Main St. (Hwy. 120), (209) 962-8904; www.iron-door-saloon.com.),* which was built in 1853 and claims to be the oldest saloon in the state. It has a dark, cool interior with 16-foot high ceilings and a long, long bar—not to mention walls hung with stuffed buffalo and moose heads— and also serves lunch and dinner in its adjacent **Grill** and dishes up ice cream treats from its **Soda Fountain**.

In summer, the **Groveland Motel & Indian Village** *(18933 Main St., (888) 849-3529, (209) 962-7865; www.grovelandmotel.net. 27 units; $-$$$. No pets.)* gives pooped parents the option of renting a cabin for themselves and an adjacent carpeted tepee for the kids. Mobile home units are also available.

ANNUAL EVENTS

Chefs' Holidays

January & February. At The Ahwahnee.

Guest chefs give cooking presentations and prepare gala banquets.

Vintners' Holidays

November & December. At The Ahwahnee.

Two days of wine seminars hosted by esteemed wine-makers culminate in a sumptuous feast in The Ahwahnee Dining Room. Courses are especially designed to complement wines sampled in the seminars.

Bracebridge Dinner

December. At The Ahwahnee; (801) 559-4949. Usuitable for children under 8.

Since 1927, the fare at this 3-hour mock-medieval feast has been seven courses of elegant Christmas dishes. Pageantry, carols, and jesters entertain diners in between. Attending this memorable, and expensive, dinner is a pleasure not many get to enjoy.

WHAT TO DO

The Ansel Adams Gallery

In Yosemite Village, (209) 372-4413; www.anseladams.com. Daily 9-5.

Special-edition photographs by this well-known photographer are for sale here.

Bicycle rentals

Yosemite Lodge: (209) 372-1208. Curry Village: (209) 372-8319. Schedule varies. $7.50/hr., $24.50/day.

All rental bikes are old-fashioned one-speeds. A map to the 8.7-mile Yosemite Valley bike path loop is provided, and helmets are

available at no charge. Though child carriers are not available, a limited number of child trailers are.

Big Trees Tram Tour

On Hwy. 41, in Wawona, 35 mi. from valley, (209) 375-1621. Daily; schedule varies; June-Oct only. $16, 62+ $14, 5-12 $10.

Approximately 500 giant sequoias are located in the 250-acre **Mariposa Grove of Giant Sequoias**. Some measure 15 to 25 feet in diameter, and some are more than 2,000 years old. Open-air trams take visitors on a guided 75-minute tour of a 7-mile scenic loop. A 7-mile hiking trail also loops through the grove, but it is not necessary to walk the entire distance because several impressive trees are seen within the first mile. In winter, this is a choice spot for cross-country skiing.

Bus tours

(209) 372-1240. Valley floor $22, 62+ $18, 5-12 $11.50. Grand Tour: $62, 62+ $55, 5-12 $33; June-Oct only.

The Grand Tour includes Glacier Point, from which gazers enjoy a 270-degree view of the high country and a bird's-eye view of the valley 3,214 feet below.

Hiking

Participate in a ranger-guided walk or take any of the many self-guided trails. Maps can be purchased in park stores. The most popular trail is the Mist Trail to Vernal Fall, which features breathtaking vistas and a close-up view of the 317-foot-tall waterfall.

Junior Ranger Program

This program is available June through August for children ages 8 through 12. Consult the *Yosemite Guide* for details. For more description, see page 468.

Movies

Scenic movies and slide shows are scheduled some evenings. Check the *Yosemite Guide* for times and locations.

Pioneer History Center

On Hwy. 41, in Wawona, 25 mi. from valley. Daily dawn-dusk. Free.

This village of restored historic pioneer buildings dating from the late 1800s is reached by walking across an authentic covered bridge. Originally located in different areas around the park, the various structures were moved here in the 1950s and '60s. In summer, history comes to life with demonstrations of soap making, yarn spinning, rail-splitting, and other pioneer crafts, and horse-drawn carriage rides are sometimes available.

Rafting

Rentals: At Curry Village, (209) 372-8319. June-July only. $20.50, under 13 $12.50. Must weigh at least 50 lbs.

Scenic and calm is the area on the Merced River between Pines Campground and Sentinel Bridge. Raft rentals include personal flotation devices, paddles, and return shuttle.

Shuttle buses

Free.

A fleet of clean, quiet hybrid buses operate daily and make stops at convenient locations.

Winter activities

See pages 460 to 461.

Yosemite Chapel

In the Valley, (209) 372-4831.

Built in 1879, this charming structure is the oldest building in the park. Sunday services are held year-round.

Yosemite Mountaineering School

(209) 372-8344. Year-round. $117+. Must be age 10+.

Learn rock climbing at one of the finest schools in the world. Beginners learn the safety essentials for dealing with this area's granite rock and can expect to climb as high as 80 feet in the first lesson. Oddly, snow and ice climbing are offered only in summer.

Yosemite Museum

In Yosemite Village, next to Valley Visitor Center, (209) 372-0304. Daily 9-12 & 1-4. Free.

Visitors learn about the Awaneechee Indians through artifacts, cultural demonstrations, and recorded chants.

The reconstructed **Indian Village of Ahwahnee** is located behind the museum and features a self-guided trail that points out plants used by Native American residents for food, clothing, and shelter.

Yosemite Valley Stables

(209) 372-8348. Schedule varies; Apr-Oct only. Guided 2-hr. horse rides $53+. Must be age 7+ & 44" tall; max. weight 225 lbs.

Said to have the largest public riding stock in the world, this concession can arrange a custom pack or fishing trip. Mule rides are also available.

WHERE TO STAY IN THE VALLEY

(801) 559-4949; www.yosemitepark.com. Reservations essential. Some facilities open year-round. No pets.

It is especially difficult to obtain accommodations in summer and on holiday weekends. Rates for two range from $60 to $822. A bargain Midweek Ski Package is available in winter.

The Ahwahnee

123 rooms; $$$+. Some fireplaces. Heated pool; 2 tennis courts. Afternoon tea; restaurant; room service. Free valet parking.

Built in 1927 of granite blocks and concrete beams, this sedate luxury hotel is a National Historic Landmark. Its decor includes priceless Native American baskets and oriental rugs, and interesting historic photos and artwork hang on the walls. The grand Great Lounge, with a walk-in fireplace at either end, is delightful to relax in. Some cottages are available.

Campgrounds

(800) 436-7275; http://reservations.nps.gov. $. Most Apr-Oct only; several open year-round.

Curry Village

628 units; $-$$$. No TVs; some fireplaces; some shared baths. Unheated pool (seasonal). Restaurant.

Started as a summer camp, this popular option includes standard rooms, cabins, and inexpensive tent-cabins located along the Merced River that sleep up to six people (some are heated, some aren't; some provide bedding, some don't). Cabins are woodsy-rustic, and the cozy Foster Curry specialty cabin must be booked 1 year and 1 day in advance. The pool can be used by non-guests for a small fee.

Housekeeping Camp

266 units; $. No TVs; all have fire rings; all shared baths.

Cook on an outdoor pit grill and experience camping beside the Merced River without the bother of setting up a tent. Units sleep up to six people and consist of three concrete walls, a concrete floor, a canvas roof, and a canvas curtain closure. Basic furniture is provided.

Yosemite Lodge at the Falls

245 rooms; $$. Heated pool (seasonal). 3 restaurants.

These comfortable modern hotel rooms feature carpeting made of recycled soda bottles. Many have a view of the falls. The pool can be used by non-guests for a small fee.

WHERE TO STAY ELSEWHERE

High Sierra Camps

204 beds; $$; summer only. Unsuitable for children under 7. No TVs; communal bath house. B&D included; dining tent.

Five camps provide dormitory-style tent accommodations and include two meals. Guests must bring their own linens. Reservations are assigned by lottery.

Tuolumne Meadows Lodge

At park's east entrance, (209) 372-8413. 69 units; $; summer only. No TVs; all wood-burning stoves; communal bath house. Dining tent; D reservations required.

This is an all tent-cabin facility. Non-guests can eat dinner here.

Wawona Hotel

On Hwy. 41, in Wawona, 30 mi. from valley, 6 mi. inside park's south entrance, (209) 375-6556. 104 rooms; $$; open Apr-Nov & Christmas vacation; weekends only Jan-Easter. No TVs; some shared baths. Heated pool (seasonal); 1 tennis court; 9-hole golf course. Restaurant.

Built in 1879, this Victorian hotel is located near the Mariposa Grove of Giant Sequoias. A National Historic Landmark, it is said to be the oldest resort hotel in the state. Most rooms accommodate only two people; a few in the annex, added in 1918, accommodate three. Decor consists of distressed-white painted furniture, rose-print wallpaper, and old-rose fabric bedspreads, and some clawfoot tubs and connected family rooms are available. Facilities include a 1917 "swimming tank" surrounded by a white picket fence.

A **Christmas program** is scheduled annually. Details vary from year to year, but in the past it has included a stagecoach ride across the covered bridge leading to the Pioneer History Center, where all the cabins were decorated for the holidays. Santa might arrive in a horse-drawn wagon dating from the 1800s, and a

The Ahwahnee

special Christmas Eve and New Year's Eve dinner is always served.

White Wolf
On Tioga Pass, 31 mi. from the valley. 28 cabins; $; summer only. No TVs; shared bath house. Dining tent; reservations advised.

This complex consists of tent-cabins and a few cabins with private baths. Breakfast and dinner are available, and non-guests are welcome at meals.

Motel Row
Drive along Route 41 in Oakhurst.

WHERE TO EAT

All of these valley park facilities are open daily and equipped with highchairs and booster seats.

The Ahwahnee Dining Room
(209) 372-1489. B-L M-Sat, D daily, SunBr; $-$$$. Reservations essential for D.

The best time to dine in the rustic splendor of this magnificent trestle-beamed-ceiling dining room is during daylight hours, when the spectacular views of the valley afforded by the 34-foot-tall leaded-glass windows can be fully enjoyed. Dinner is expensive, and men are requested to wear a collared shirt and slacks, and women to dress accordingly. Guests of the hotel get first choice at reservations, so non-guests often must settle for either an early or late seating. Children fit in best at breakfast or lunch.

Cafeterias
Curry Pavilion, at Curry Village; Food Court, at Yosemite Lodge. B-L-D; $.

Meals here are quick and informal. Curry Village is an all-you-can-eat buffet, and Yosemite Lodge is a la carte.

Mountain Room Restaurant
At Yosemite Lodge. D; $$-$$$.

This large, open room boasts a 3-story-high ceiling and massive windows with a stunning view of Upper Yosemite Fall. The menu features fresh fish and aged beef as well as made-from-scratch soups and desserts.

Get rid of the kinks developed on the long ride in with a drink in the adjacent **Mountain**

Room Lounge. In winter, order up a s'mores kit for the kids so they can toast marshmallows in the fireplace.

Picnic Pick-Ups
Box lunches can be reserved at hotel kitchens the evening before they are needed. Supplies can also be picked up at **Degnan's Deli** and the **Village Store** in Yosemite Village.

Wawona Dining Room
30 mi. from valley, (209) 375-1425. B-L-D, SunBr; $-$$. Reservations advised for D.

The inexpensive Sunday brunch buffet is highly recommended. Served in the hotel's wonderful traditional Victorian dining room, where expansive multi-paned windows provide views of the surrounding pines, it consists of simple, satisfying fare. Breakfast or lunch during the rest of the week is also particularly pleasant.

On summer Saturdays, the chef prepares an old-fashioned, all-you-can-eat barbecue dinner out on the lawn. Steaks, hamburgers, and corn-on-the-cob are on the menu, and diners sit at tables covered with red-checkered tablecloths.

SOUTH OF THE PARK

VISITOR INFORMATION

Yosemite Sierra Visitors Bureau
41969 Hwy. 41, in Oakhurst, (559) 683-4636; www.yosemitethisyear.com.

Request a free *Visitors Guide* covering areas outside the national park.

WHAT TO DO

Yosemite Mountain Sugar Pine Railroad
56001 Hwy. 41, in Fish Camp, 4 mi. S of park's south entrance, 1-hr. drive from valley, (559) 683-7273; www.ymsprr.com. Schedule varies. Train: $17.50, 3-12 $8.75; Jenny rail cars: $13.50, 3-12 $6.75.

A reconstruction of the Madera Sugar Pine Co. Railroad that made its last run in 1931, this narrow-gauge steam train takes passengers on a 45-minute, 4-mile scenic excursion through the Sierra National Forest. Passengers get a live narration on the area's history while sitting in open-air touring cars upon logs carved out to form long benches. A stopover at the midway point to picnic or hike is an option. Moonlight rides, which include a steak barbecue and campfire program, are scheduled on Saturday evenings in summer. Smaller Jenny rail cars, powered by Model A engines, take passengers on shorter 30-minute rides along the same route when the train isn't operating. A picnic area and snack shop are available.

WHERE TO STAY & EAT

Erna's Elderberry House
48688 Victoria Ln. (Hwy. 41), in Oakhurst, 15 mi. outside park's south entrance, (559) 683-6800; www.chateausureau.com. D daily; $$$+; closed 1st 3 wks. of Jan. Reservations essential.

This stellar venue is similar to the destination restaurants found in the countryside of France. The staff prepares a different six-course, fixed-price meal every night. One meal enjoyed here in the elegantly appointed front room began with a flute of elderberry-flavored champagne. It continued with a scallop and sorrel timbale artistically positioned on a nest of pasta, and was followed by corn and cilantro soup and then fresh pears poached in Riesling. The main course was alder wood-smoked chicken sausages served with wild rice and a colorful array of vegetables. A simple, elegant salad followed. Dessert, which is served outside on a romantic candle-lit garden terrace, was a duo of Chocolate Decadence in fresh mint sauce and puff pastry filled with caramelized apples and creamed gourmand. Three wines selected to complement each dinner are offered by the glass.

Elegant lodging is available in the property's castle-like **Chateau du Sureau** *(10 rooms; $$$+, 12% gratuity added to bill. Unsuitable for children under 7. TVs by request; all wood-burning fireplaces. Unheated pool; full-service spa. Afternoon snack; full breakfast; restaurant; room service.),* which features a giant outdoor chess court and serene walking paths. Maids wearing long black dresses topped with white ruffled aprons keep things spiffy. ("Sureau" is the French word for "elderberry.")

The Redwoods In Yosemite
In Wawona, 4 mi. inside park's south entrance, (888) 225-6666; www.redwoodsinyosemite.com. 125 units; $$-$$$+. Most TVs; all kitchens; most wood-burning fireplaces or stoves.

These rustic cabins and modern homes come equipped with linens and kitchenware.

Tenaya Lodge at Yosemite
1122 Hwy. 41, in Fish Camp, 2 mi. outside park's south entrance, (888) 514-2167, (559) 683-6555; www.tenayalodge.com. 4 stories; 244 rooms; $$-$$$+. 1 indoor heated pool & hot tub, 1 outdoor heated pool & hot tub (both seasonal); 2 saunas; 2 steam rooms; fitness room. 3 restaurants; room service.

Built in 1990, this plush lodge is evocative of the park's historic Ahwahnee hotel. A majestic public lobby features a 3-story-tall open beamed ceiling and an immense stone fireplace, and all guest rooms have forest views. Guided nature walks are scheduled most mornings, weather permitting. In winter, ski and snowshoe rentals are available at the hotel, and guests can strike out on a scenic cross-country ski trail through adjacent Sierra National Forest. The resort's seasonal ice skating rink is also an option. In summer, campfire programs, wagon rides, and mountain bike rentals are added to the roster. Spa services are available year-round, and a children's program for ages 5 through 12 operates daily except Sundays in summer and on many weekends year-round *($65/day).*

EAST OF PARK

GETTING THERE

Take Highway 120 over the Tioga Pass to Highway 395.

At 9,945 feet, the scenic **Tioga Pass** *(Road conditions: (209) 372-0200. Closed in winter.)* is the highest-elevation road in California. Turn off at Crane Flat for this scenic journey. From here the legendary road climbs to 9,000 feet, where the air is clear, clean, and cool. It winds through Yosemite's high country, past magnificent mountain vistas, deep blue lakes, and soaring glacier-carved granite monoliths. Minimal food service is available along the route, but picnic spots are plentiful and spectacular; be prepared. Campsites are available.

A stop at the **Tuolumne Meadows Visitor Center** *(Daily 9-5; May-Sept only.)* to view the lovely and informative collection of wildflower identification cards is well worth the time.

Then, at the pass's crest, look for yellow Rabbit Brush, lavender Pussypaws, and scarlet Penstemons displayed stunningly against granite.

BRIDGEPORT

VISITOR INFORMATION

Bridgeport Chamber of Commerce
P.O. Box 541, Bridgeport 93417, (760) 932-7033; www.bridgeportcalifornia.com.

WHAT TO DO

Bodie State Historic Park
18 mi. N of Lee Vining, 8 mi. S of Bridgeport, (760) 647-6445; www.parks.ca.gov. Daily 8-dusk. Museum: Daily, May-Oct only. Stamp mill tour: Schedule varies, June-Oct only. $3, under 17 $1.
        Located at the end of a 13-mile side road off Highway 395, the last 3 miles of which are unpaved gravel, this 486-acre park is the largest unrestored ghost town in the West. In 1879, when 10,000 people lived here, there were 2 churches, 4 newspapers, and 65 saloons. It was reputed to be quite rowdy. A little girl who moved here in its heyday wrote in her diary, "Good, by God! We're going to Bodie." This passage has also been interpreted as "Good-bye God! We're going to Bodie." Due to fires in 1892 and 1932, only about 5% of the town structures remain. To learn more, the ranger-led walk is highly recommended. Be prepared: The town can clock in as the coldest or hottest place in the U.S. No food service or picnic facilities are available.

LEE VINING

A LITTLE BACKGROUND

This High Sierra village is at 6,500 feet.

VISITOR INFORMATION

Lee Vining Chamber of Commerce
P.O. Box 130, Lee Vining 93541, (760) 647-6629; leevining.com.

Mono County Tourism Commission
P.O. Box 603, Mammoth Lakes 93546, (800) 845-7922; www.monocounty.org.

WHAT TO DO

Mono Lake
Off Hwy. 395, (760) 647-3000; www.monolake.org.
        John Muir described this desolate area as, "A country of wonderful contrasts, hot deserts bounded by snow-laden mountains, cinder and ashes scattered on glacier-polished pavement, frost and fire working together in the making of beauty." Situated at more than 7,000 feet above sea level, Mono Lake is a high-desert sea. It is one of the largest lakes in the state and is also the second-oldest lake in North America. Mark Twain called it the "Dead Sea of the West." An ancient Ice Age lake, estimated to be at least 1 million years old, mysterious Mono Lake is twice the size of San Francisco and features an unusual terrain of pinnacles and spires formed by calcium-rich mineral deposits that spurt up from the lake bottom. It is filled with water that contains almost three times the salt found in ocean water and holds not a single fish—though tiny brine shrimp flourish. Perhaps this is what attracts the 50,000-plus vacationing seagulls that flock in during April to nest, stay into August, and then head back to the coast. The **South Tufa Area** *(On Hwy. 120, 5 mi. E of Hwy. 395. $3; under 16 free.)* is particularly nice for a walk in the late afternoon light—the best time for a comfortable temperature and to capture good photos. Fall is the ideal time for a visit. Campsites are available.

• Mono Basin Scenic Area Ranger Station & Visitor Center

Off Hwy 395, on W shore just N of Lee Vining, (760) 647-3044; www.fs.fed.us/r5/inyo. Daily 8-5 in summer; schedule varies rest of year. Free.

This center overlooks the lake and has interpretive displays that provide insight into the area. Guided nature walks are sometimes scheduled.

• Mono Lake Committee Information Center and Bookstore

On Hwy. 395/Third St., in Lee Vining, (760) 647-6595; www.monolake.org. Daily 9-5, later in summer. Free.

Get oriented here with a brief video about Mono Lake. To see the lake up close in summer, take a sunset walk *(Daily at 6 p.m. Free.)* or a naturalist-led canoe tour *(Sat-Sun at 8, 9:30, & 11am. $22. Reservations required.).*

WHERE TO STAY

Tioga Lodge Resort

54411 Hwy. 395, just N of town, (888) 647-6423, (760) 647-6423; www.tiogalodgeatmonolake.com. 14 cabins; $$; closed mid-Oct-mid-Apr. Restaurant. No pets.

Though the original lodge was destroyed by a flood in 1956, this well-maintained re-creation includes motel rooms and cabins tucked amid sheltering mature trees. The buildings holding the registration desk and the restaurant were brought down from Bodie in pieces by mules and wagons in the early 1900s and reconstructed here. A pathway and footbridge leads over a rushing stream to a section of cabins with lake-view porches; some also have clawfoot tubs.

In 1918, when the original **restaurant** *(B-L-D Tu-Sun; $.)* opened, it was an exclusive place to eat. Waiters wore tuxedos, diners dressed formally, and the tables were covered with lacey linens topped with silver candelabras. No more. The atmosphere is casual and the well-priced food is down-home delicious, especially the Mexican specialties. In nice weather, outdoor seating is an option.

Two-hour **boat tours** depart from across the street most mornings.

WHERE TO EAT

Tioga Toomey's Whoa Nelli Deli

22 Vista Point Rd., Hwy. 120/Hwy. 395, in Tioga Gas Mart, (760) 647-1088; www.thesierraweb.com/ tiogagasmart. B-L-D daily; closed Dec-Apr; $.

Fill 'er up, and yourself, too. This deli has been declared "the best restaurant in a convenience store in America." Food includes the unexpected out in these parts: world-famous fresh fish tacos, lobster taquitos, Caesar salad, six-layer carrot cake. Diners place their order then secure a spacious table out on a grassy bluff with a great view of Mono Lake.

JUNE LAKE

VISITOR INFORMATION

June Lake Loop Chamber of Commerce
P.O. Box 2, June Lake 93529, (760) 648-7584; www.junelakechamber.org.

GETTING THERE

Located 5 miles south of Lee Vining, and 18 miles north of Mammoth Lakes.

WHAT TO DO

June Lake Loop/Highway 158
    This 15-mile excursion winds past four mountain lakes set in glacial canyons. The road is lined with aspen and pines backed by high granite peaks.

WHERE TO STAY

Double Eagle Resort & Spa
5587 Boulder Dr. (Hwy. 158), (760) 648-7004; www.doubleeagleresort.com. 32 units; $$$-$$$+. All gas or wood-burning fireplaces; some kitchens. Heated indoor pool & hot tub; fitness room; full-service spa. Full breakfast (for guest rooms); restaurant.
    Located in a fragrant valley forest of aspen and pine and surrounded by granite peaks and several waterfalls, this small luxury resort is 6 hours by car to San Francisco (via Reno), to Las Vegas, and to Los Angeles. The fruit of owners Ron and Connie Black's love story, the Double Eagle was built as a retirement dream by these high school sweethearts who reconnected after divorces and made their vision of paradise come true. They are now quite busy here living happily ever after. Guest rooms are spacious and decorated in contemporary rustique, with whole-log and bent-twig furnishings. Each has a deck overlooking a tranquil catch-and-release trout pond. Two-bedroom cabins with full kitchens are also available. An indoor pool and

hot tub look out through a wall of windows at a view of jagged peaks reminiscent of Switzerland's finest. The adjacent spa's expansive menu of treatments includes a duo massage, in which two therapists choreograph a head-to-toe massage, and a forest massage, which takes place under towering pines in an enclosed gazebo open to the sounds of the forest and rushing Reverse Creek. But it's still wild enough here for one room to be named "Cinnamon Black Bear," after the bears that sometimes are seen foraging for garbage. Hiking trails, fly-fishing ponds, and horseback riding are nearby.
    The resort's dramatic **Eagle's Landing Restaurant** *((760) 648-7897. B-L-D daily; $$.)* has knotty-pine walls, a high open-beam ceiling, and mountain views from every seat. The varied dinner menu includes prime rib as well as lighter salads, pastas, and a few special heart-healthy items. Comfy oversize booths seat six, and an outdoor deck is an option in summer.

MAMMOTH LAKES

VISITOR INFORMATION

Mammoth Lakes Visitors Bureau
P.O. Box 48, Mammoth Lakes 93546, (888) GO-Mammoth; www.visitmammoth.com.

WHAT TO DO

Devil's Postpile National Monument
(760) 934-2289; www.nps.gov/depo. Daily 7am-7pm;
June-Oct only. Shuttle bus: $7, 3-15 $4.
No reservations.

This 60-foot-high formation is
constructed of polygonal basaltic columns
formed long ago by quickly cooling lava.
Visitors can take a pleasant 1-mile walk through
the monument, and a short hike leads to
101-foot-high Rainbow Falls. Campsites are
available. The road in is closed to vehicles.
Visitors are required to ride a shuttle bus from
the Mammoth Mountain Ski Area.

BISHOP

A LITTLE BACKGROUND

After this town, Hwy. 395 drops into an arid
valley with hot, dry winds. Towns are few and
small. Many artists live here because of the
light.

VISITOR INFORMATION

Bishop Area Chamber of Commerce
and Visitors Bureau
690 N. Main St., (888) 395-3952, (760) 873-8405;
www.bishopvisitor.com. M-F 10-5, Sat-Sun 10-4.

WHAT TO DO

Mountain Light Gallery
106 S. Main St., (760) 873-7700;
www.mountainlight.com. Sun-Thur 10-6, F-Sat 10-8.

Formerly owned by the late Galen Rowell,
a celebrated nature photographer, this gallery
displays and sells his photographs as well
as some by other accomplished photographers.
Related events and workshops are often
scheduled.

WHERE TO EAT

Erick Schat's Bakkery
763 N. Main St., (760) 873-7156; www.erickschats
bakery.com. Daily 6am-6pm. No reservations.

Sheepherder Bread has been baked here
continuously since 1907. Customers line up to
place orders at the sandwich bar, then select a
cool table on the front patio. Sandwiches are
big, and a cookie is included with every order.
Small children can ride one of the old-time
wooden horses.

INDEPENDENCE

WHAT TO DO

Manzanar National Historic Site
(760) 878-2194; www.nps.gov/manz. Daily 9-4:30; in
summer, 9-5:30. Free.

Following the Pearl Harbor attack in 1942,
10,000 Japanese Americans were detained in
this internment camp. The Visitor Center,
which opened in 2004, was built by internees
in 1944 as a high school auditorium. Now it is
home to state-of-the-art exhibits that are
thoughtful and enlightening as well as disturb-
ing. When the Manzanar War Relocation Center
closed after World War II in 1945, most of the
buildings were either moved elsewhere or dismantled and sold as scrap. A self-guided auto
tour weaves through the dusty remains of foun-
dations, providing plenty of food for thought.
It has become a peaceful, beautiful site, with
sagebrush and trees and the Sierra peaks in the
distance.

General Grant Tree

SEQUOIA AND KINGS CANYON NATIONAL PARKS

A LITTLE BACKGROUND

Though located just south of Yosemite National Park, about a 3-hour drive away, these two scenic national parks often are overlooked. It's a shame because they, too, offer spectacular scenery and are much less crowded.

Sequoia National Park was established in 1890. It was California's first national park and is the country's second-oldest national park (Yellowstone is the oldest). Kings Canyon National Park was established in 1940. Combined, they encompass more than 860,000 acres.

The main attraction at these parks is the enormous sequoia trees, with their vibrant cinnamon-colored bark. The trees can be viewed in both Sequoia Park's Giant Forest and Kings Canyon's Grant Grove. The largest is the **General Sherman Tree** in Sequoia National Park. It towers 275 feet high, measures 36½ feet in diameter, and is approximately 2,100 years old. This makes it higher than Niagara Falls, as

wide as a city street, and the largest living tree on the planet.

Mt. Whitney is also located in Sequoia park and, at 14,494 feet, is the highest point in the United States outside of Alaska. It can't be viewed from the park without a long hike. From the east side of the Sierra, it is a 1 to 3-day hike to its peak; from the west side it is a 7- to 9-day hike.

Admission to the parks is $20 per vehicle.

VISITOR INFORMATION

Sequoia and Kings Canyon National Parks
47050 Generals Hwy., Three Rivers 93271-9651, (559) 565-3341; www.nps.gov/seki.

GETTING THERE

Located approximately 250 miles southeast of San Francisco. Take Highway 80 to Highway 580 to Highway 99 south; then take either Highway 180 or Highway 198 east.

ANNUAL EVENTS

Trek to the Tree
December. (559) 875-4575; www.sanger.org/events.html.

The 267-foot-tall **General Grant Tree** in Kings Canyon National Park is the Nation's Christmas Tree and has been the site of an annual Christmas service since 1926. The tree was also dedicated in 1956 as a war memorial to those who have lost their lives in the armed forces, and in honor of these soldiers a wreath is placed at its base each year by members of the National Park Service. Because its first branch is 230 feet off the ground and it is situated in the middle of a forest with no electricity, the tree is not lighted. A car caravan leaves from nearby Sanger, and seats are also available by reservation on a chartered bus.

WHAT TO DO

Caves

• Boyden Cavern
74101 E. Kings Canyon Rd, in Sequoia National Forest, just outside Kings Canyon N.P., (559) 338-0959; www.boydencavern.com. Daily 10-5, June-Sept; 11-4 Apr-May & Oct-Nov. $13, 3-12 $7.

This marble cave is located in spectacular

8,000-foot-deep Kings River Canyon—the deepest canyon in the United States. The guided tour takes about 45 minutes.

• Crystal Cave
In Sequoia N.P., (559) 565-3759; www.sequoiahistory.org/cave/cave.htm. Schedule varies; May-Oct only. $11, 62+ $10, 6-12 $6.

This 48-degree marble cavern (bring a jacket) is reached via a steep ½-mile trail (allow at least 1½ hours to reach it). Note that there are no restrooms, and strollers and baby backpacks are not permitted. The guided tour takes about 50 minutes. Tickets must be purchased at a visitor center; they are not sold at the cave.

Fishing
The most popular spots are along Kings River and at the forks of the Kaweah River. A California fishing license is required. Ask about fishing regulations at park visitor centers.

Horse rentals
In Cedar Grove & Grant Grove; www.nps.gov/seki/stables.htm. Closed late fall-spring.

Junior Ranger Program
Kids can earn a badge while discovering the parks' resources and learning how to protect them. To get started, pick up a free Junior Ranger booklet in any visitor center, and follow the instructions. The program operates year-round. For more description, see page 468.

Trails
More than 800 miles of hiking trails are in these parks. The Big Trees Trail is an easy ⅔-mile loop with interpretive exhibits.

Unusual trees
Many of these trees are encountered on the drive along the 46-mile **Generals Highway** connecting the two national parks. Some require either a short walk to reach or a drive down a side road. From December through May, this highway occasionally is closed by snow.

• Senate Group and House Group of Sequoias
These are among the most symmetrically formed and nearly perfect of the sequoias. They are reached via the Congress Trail, an easy 2.1-mile walk that begins at the General Sherman Tree.

• Tunnel Log
Cars can drive through this tunnel carved in a tree that fell across the road in 1937. Note that the drive-through-tree (see photo on page 377), which was in Yosemite National Park, fell down in a 1969 snowstorm.

Visitor Centers
www.nps.gov/seki/planyourvisit/visitorcenters.htm. Lodgepole: (559) 565-4436; daily; schedule varies; closed in winter. Giant Forest Museum: (559) 565-4480; daily 8:30-4:30, in summer to 6. Kings Canyon: (559) 565-4307; in summer 8-6, in winter 9-4:30. Foothills: (559) 565-4212; daily 8-4:30, in summer to 6.

See exhibits on the area's wildlife as well as displays on Native Americans and the sequoias. Inquire here about the schedule for nature walks and evening campfire programs.

WHERE TO STAY

(559) 565-3341; www.nps.gov/seki. (866) 875-8456; www.nationalparkreservations.com.

Montecito Sequoia Lodge
This lodging is not in the parks but is on Forest Service-managed land. See page 461.

Park Lodging
Sequoia N.P.: (888) 252-5757, (559) 565-4070; www.visitsequoia.com. Kings Canyon N.P.: (866) 522-6966, (559) 335-5500; www.sequoia-kingscanyon.com. $-$$$. No TVs; some shared baths. Restaurant. Campgrounds: (877) 444-6777.

Kings Canyon has both deluxe hotel rooms and rustic cabins. The 21-room **Cedar Grove Lodge** is showing its age but has great location beside Kings River.

At Sequoia, the new 102-room **Wuksachi Lodge** offers deluxe hotel rooms in three price categories. Ranger programs are scheduled several nights each week. Arrangements can be made to backpack 11 miles into **Bearpaw High Sierra Camp**, where facilities are tent-cabins with canvas sides and wood floors. Hot showers, cots, and linens are provided, and dinner and breakfast are included. Reservations are necessary.

Campsites are available on a first-come, first-served basis. In summer, reservations are accepted for Lodgepole and Dorst campgrounds in Sequoia National Park.

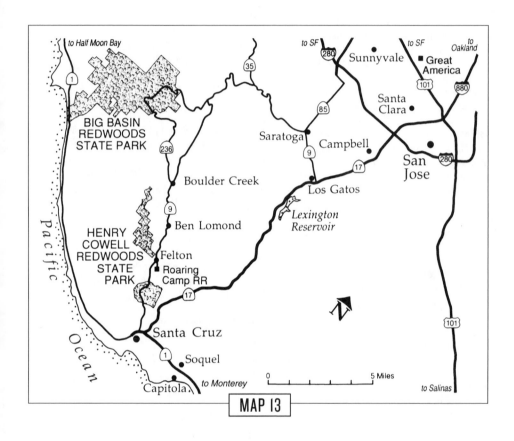

MAP 13

Roaring Camp Railroad

LOS GATOS

A LITTLE BACKGROUND

Tucked in the lush, green Santa Cruz
Mountains, this small upscale community is
known for its many boutiques and restaurants
lining Santa Cruz Avenue and Main Street. It
also claims to have 330 day of sun each year.
Originally a logging town, its name is Spanish
for "the cats," in reference to the mountain lions
that once roamed the hills in large numbers.

VISITOR INFORMATION

Los Gatos Chamber of Commerce
*349 N. Santa Cruz Ave., (408) 354-9300;
www.losgatoschamber.com.*

GETTING THERE

Located approximately 55 miles south of San
Francisco, and 10 miles south of San Jose.
Take Highway 101 to Highway 17 to the
Los Gatos exit.

WHAT TO DO

Museums of Los Gatos
*(408) 395-7375; www.museumsoflosgatos.org.
W-Sun 12-4. Free.*

• The Art Museum in the Tait Firehouse
4 Tait Ave./W. Main St., (408) 354-2646.

    Housed in a Spanish-style building dating
from 1927 that was the city's first firehouse, this
small museum displays contemporary fine arts
and hosts juried shows.

• The History Museum in the Forbes Mill Annex
75 Church St./E. Main St., (408) 395-7375.

    Located inside the town's first commercial
building–the remains of the 1854 Forbes Mill
flour mill—this tiny venue focuses on town
history.

Parks

• Oak Meadow Park
*Off Blossom Hill Rd., (408) 354-6809;
www.losgatosca.gov/index.asp?NID=910. Daily dawn-
dusk. $5/vehicle.*

    This 12-acre park has picnic facilities,
baseball diamonds, hiking trails, and a well-
equipped playground with an authentic fire
engine and airplane to climb on.

    A 1915 hand-carved English clockwise
carousel and a train pulled by a steam locomotive at the 18-inch narrow-gauge **Billy Jones
Wildcat Railroad** *((408) 395-7433;
www.bjwrr.org. Schedule varies, but always
Sat-Sun 11-3. $2/ride, under 2 free.)* are also
available.

• **Vasona Lake County Park**
333 Blossom Hill Rd., (408) 356-2729;
www.parkhere.org. Daily 8-sunset. $4/vehicle.

This 150-acre park is dominated by a huge reservoir where visitors can fish and rent row-boats or paddleboats.

At the **Youth Science Institute** *((408) 356-4945; www.youthscience.org. M-F 9-4:30. Free.),* visitors can view exhibits on water ecology and conservation, see live animals, and use barbecue facilities and a playground.

WINERIES

Byington Vineyard & Winery
2850 Bear Creek Rd., 6 mi. from Hwy. 17,
(408) 354-1111; www.byington.com. Tasting daily 11-5;
tour by appt.

Located off a winding road in the woodsy Santa Cruz Mountains, this Italianate stone winery is surrounded by manicured gardens. Sheltered, table cloth-covered picnic tables are provided that overlook vineyards, a redwood forest, and Monterey Bay. A charcoal barbecue and two grills are always available (bring your own tools), as is a bocce ball court and balls. In addition to award-winning Pinot Noirs, Chardonnays, and Cabernet Sauvignons, the winery also produces a fun little Liage and a yummy Alliage.

Testarossa Winery
300-A College Ave., 2 mi. from downtown, (408) 354-6150; www.testarossa.com. Tasting daily 11-5.

High in the hills above town, this winery is situated inside the historic 19th-century sand-stone cellars of the former Novitiate Winery. The two-foot-thick walls were hand-chiseled by the Jesuits in 1888. Now named for the current owner's nickname—testarossa means "red-head" in Italian—the winery hand-sorts its grapes and uses a gravity flow process during fermentation.

WHERE TO STAY

Hotel Los Gatos
210 E. Main St., (866) 335-1700, (408) 335-1700;
www.hotellosgatos.com. 72 rooms; $$$-$$$+. Heated
pool; hot tub; sauna; full-service spa; fitness room.
Restaurant; room service. No pets.

Located just down the street from a Ferrari/Bentley showroom, this luxurious hotel has a rustic Italian-country style. Public spaces are decorated with Mexican tiles and pottery, studded leather chairs, and ornate wood-inlayed Moroccan tables. A sort of Mediterranean hacienda, it melds the two architectural styles with a terracotta-tiled roof and spacious interior courtyards with palm trees and foun-tains. Traditional art is displayed throughout. Guest rooms are furnished luxuriously with colorful silk drapes and comforters, soft Egyptian cotton linens, and tile-and-granite bathrooms.

La Hacienda Inn
18840 Saratoga-Los Gatos Rd. (Hwy. 9),
(800) 235-4570, (408) 354-9230;
www.lahaciendainn.com. 20 rooms; $$. Some
kitchens; some wood-burning & gas fireplaces.
Heated pool (seasonal); indoor hot tub; fitness room.
Continental breakfast.

Tucked away from the main highway at the base of the Santa Cruz Mountains, the original Japanese-style inn on this site was built in 1901. This newer inn, built in 1961, has cozy rooms with 12-foot-tall redwood-beamed ceilings and pine and oak furnishings. The 4-acre site fea-tures a lushly landscaped garden with colorful flowerbeds and an expansive lawn area.

Los Gatos Garden Inn
46 E. Main St., (866) 868-8383, (408) 354-6446;
www.gardeninn.us. 28 rooms; $$. Some kitchens.
Coffee-and breakfast. No pets.

These rustic Spanish-style bungalows are in a quiet area just 2 blocks from town. Complimentary use of a nearby health club with a swimming pool is available. The claim is that Marilyn Monroe and Joe DiMaggio honeymooned here.

Should car fever strike, a souvenir can be purchased next door at **Silicon Valley Bentley/Rolls Royce.**

Los Gatos Lodge
50 Los Gatos/Saratoga Rd., (800) 231-8676,
(408) 354-3300; www.losgatoslodge.com. 128 rooms;
$$. Some kitchens & fireplaces. Heated pool
(seasonal); hot tub. Restaurant; room service.

Located on attractive, spacious grounds, this contemporary motel provides a putting green and shuffleboard area.

and good wines are poured by the glass. The creative menu changes regularly, but two particularly fabulous items include an entree of hand-rolled pasta tubes tossed with tangy fresh tomato sauce and a delicious dessert concoction called berry Masu consisting of a tower of fruit and wine-soaked cake topped with Chantilly cream. Fresh fish, grilled steak, and crispy duck might also be on the menu. A fixed-price Sunday champagne brunch features a dessert buffet and chocolate fountain.

WHERE TO EAT

Andalé Mexican Restaurant
www.andalemexican.com. 6 N. Santa Cruz Ave., (408) 395-4244; M-F 11-10, Sat 9-10, Sun 9-9. Also at 21 N. Santa Cruz Ave., (408) 395-8997; daily 11-10.

The founding location at #6 is quite small, while the #21 location is large and spacious. For more description, see page 180.

Campo di Bocce
565 University Ave., (408) 395-7650; www.campodibocce.com. L-D daily; $-$$. Bocce: $10/person/1½ hr. Reservations advised.

Located inside a converted factory, this spot features Italian dining amid indoor bocce courts paved with traditional pulverized oyster shells. To just watch, ask for a dining time when courts are reserved.

Fleur de Cocoa
39 N. Santa Cruz Ave., (408) 354-3574; www.fleurdecocoa.com. Tu-Sat 7:30-6, Sun 8-4; $.

This authentic French pâtisserie presents a case full of croissants, éclairs, and other pastries, plus housemade chocolate. A great hot chocolate is another option.

Pedro's Restaurant & Cantina
316 N. Santa Cruz Ave., (408) 354-7570; www.pedrosrestaurants.com. L-D daily; $$. Reservations advised.

This popular spot features an adobe-style interior with a bank of highly desirable enclosed booths in back. Delicious Mexican dishes are served in hefty portions. Especially tasty items include chimichangas (deep-fried flour tortillas filled with chicken and topped with guacamole and sour cream), quesadillas

Toll House
140 S. Santa Cruz Ave., 1 blk. from downtown, (800) 238-6111, (408) 395-7070; www.tollhousehotel.com. 115 rooms; $$-$$$+. Some fireplaces. Restaurant; room service. Hot tub; exercise room.

Located on the quiet end of the town's main shopping street, across the street from a grassy park square, this contemporary-style hotel was built in 1989. Its name comes from the fact that it is next door to the town's original toll house (that space is now an office building), where visitors once paid a toll to enter. Freshly baked toll-house cookies greet guests at check-in, though there is no relationship between that recipe and the hotel. Rooms feature patterned wall-to-wall carpet, wood Venetian blinds, and pleasant garden-oriented original art as well as a comfy FeatherBorne bed with leather-lined wood headboard. Most rooms have a balcony or patio, and some have a view of the area's mountains.

Situated in a spacious open room with some banquettes, sedate **Three Degrees** *(www.threedegreesrestaurant.com. B-L-D daily, SunBr; $$$.)* has a lovely outdoor dining area that is inviting in fair weather. A bar adjoins, (large folded flour tortillas filled with Jack cheese and topped with guacamole and sour cream), and chicken enchiladas topped with a fabulously tasty mole sauce made with 36 ingredients. Flautas, several tostadas, and an assortment of seafood dishes are also available, and fried ice cream is among the desserts.

SARATOGA

A LITTLE BACKGROUND

Saratoga is a smaller, quieter, and even more picturesque town than Los Gatos.

VISITOR INFORMATION

Saratoga Chamber of Commerce
14485 Big Basin Way, (408) 867-0753; www.saratogachamber.org.

ANNUAL EVENTS

Mountain Winery Groupware Technology concert series
July-October. At the Historic Mountain Winery, 14831 Pierce Rd., (408) 741-2822; www.mountainwinery.com. $25-$75; children under 5 not admitted.

The world's largest and the country's oldest winery-related music festival, this eclectic series of outdoor concerts has been held in its picturesque hilltop setting every year since 1958.

Before-show dining at the **Chateau Deck Restaurant** provides an outdoor white-tablecloth experience, while the **Vineyard Bar & Grill** provides casual outdoor elegance and beautiful views of the Silicon Valley.

WHAT TO DO

Garrod Farms Stables
22647 Garrod Rd., (408) 867-9527; www.garrodfarms.com. Daily 8:30-4:30; M-F by reservation, Sat-Sun first-come first-served. Horses $40/hr., must be age 8+; ponies $20/half-hr.

Horse trails roam over 200 acres. Shetland ponies are available for children under 8; an adult must walk them with a lead rope.

The family-owned and-operated **Cooper-Garrod Estate Vineyards** winery (22645 Garrod Rd., (408) 867-7116; www.cgv.com. Tasting M-F 12-5, Sat-Sun 11-5; tour by appt.) is also located here. It grows seven varietals on 28 acres farmed by the family for more than a century. Tasting occurs in the historic Fruit House.

Hakone Gardens
21000 Big Basin Way (Hwy. 9), (408) 741-4994; www.hakone.com. M-F 10-5, Sat-Sun 11-5. $5, 60+ & 5-17 $3.50; parking $7. Tea & cookies: Sat-Sun in summer; $5. Tea ceremony: 3rd Sun of month; $5.

Originally a private garden but now a city park, this is the oldest authentic Japanese-style residential garden in the Western Hemisphere. It is typical of a mid-17th-century residential garden and is composed of four separate areas: a Hill and Pond Garden, a Tea Garden, a Zen Garden, and a Bamboo Garden (it boasts the largest collection of Japanese bamboo in a public park in the western world). Special features include a Japanese-style house built without nails or adhesives, a pond stocked with eye-catching koi, and three authentic tea ceremony rooms. The final third of *Memoirs of a Geisha* was filmed here. A picnic area with tables is available.

Montalvo Arts Center
15400 Montalvo Rd., (408) 961-5800; www.montalvoarts.org. Schedule varies. Free.

Once the summer home of Senator James Phelan, this majestic 1912 Mediterranean-style estate is now the county center for fine arts. Performing arts events—some especially for children—are presented June through September in a natural outdoor amphitheater and year-round in an indoor Carriage House. Self-guided nature trails wind through the 175-acres of gardens.

Savannah Chanelle Vineyards
23600 Congress Springs Rd./Hwy. 9, 4 mi. from town, (408) 741-2934; www.savannahchanelle.com. Tasting daily 11-5; tour by appt.

Established in 1892, this winery has original plantings dating from 1910 and 1920. Its rustic tasting room is located at the end of a steep, woodsy back road, and it is surrounded by tall redwoods and 14 acres of vineyards that include the oldest Cabernet Franc vineyard in the state. Picnic tables are available.

WHERE TO STAY

The Inn at Saratoga

20645 Fourth St., (800) 543-5020, (408) 867-5020; www.innatsaratoga.com. 5 stories; 46 rooms; $$-$$$+. Fitness room. Afternoon snack; continental breakfast. No pets.

Set in a quiet canyon below busy Highway 9, this contemporary-style hotel's oversize guest rooms all face a forest of old eucalyptus through which winds gurgling Saratoga Creek. Afternoon wine and appetizers are served either in the cozy lobby or outdoors on a sylvan patio visited by humming birds and squirrels.

Families will appreciate that **Wildwood Park**, with its ample playground, is just across the creek.

Sanborn Park Hostel

15808 Sanborn Rd., (408) 741-0166; www.sanbornparkhostel.org. 39 beds; some private rooms.

Constructed of logs, this rustic arts and crafts-style building dates from 1908. It is located in a secluded redwood grove in the area's foothills. The naturally fragrant, quiet setting has plenty of hiking trails, plus a volleyball court and barbecue facilities.

Sanborn County Park *(www.parkhere.org. Daily 8am-sunset. $6/vehicle. No dogs.)*, within which the hostel is situated, has campsites, picnic tables, and the **Youth Science Institute** *(16055 Sanborn Rd., (408) 867-6940; www.youthscience.org. Tu-Sat 12-4:30. Free. For description, see page 390.).*

WHERE TO EAT

The Plumed Horse

14555 Big Basin Way/near Hwy. 85, (408) 867-4711; plumedhorse.com. D daily; $$$+. Reservations advised. Valet parking.

A popular venue for a long, long time, this romantic restaurant is newly redesigned. It is elegantly appointed with a Venetian plaster barrel ceiling and huge jellyfish-like light fixtures that make the sophisticated dining room glow. Drapes and carpeting subdue the sounds of the vibrant atmosphere. The contemporary California menu includes luxury items such as

Monterey abalone, pickled veal tongue, and California squab as well as some inspired vegetarian options, and a 10-course chef's tasting menu option is served at a table in a private room with a large window looking in on the kitchen action. The impressive wine collection is visible in a 3-story glass cellar that divides the bar from the dining room. But it is really all about the service—with a maitre de here, and a sommelier there, and servers surrounding a table to dramatically present everyone with their entree at the same time. Desserts are not the usual—perhaps a Baked California with huckleberry sorbet or a sweet Grand Marnier mini soufflé—and the chef sends out tiny surprises throughout.

A full **bar** with a fireplace schedules live piano music and features an enticing champagne nook with bed and a curtain for privacy.

SAN LORENZO VALLEY

A LITTLE BACKGROUND

Tucked into a dense redwood forest, this area has simple motels and cabins that are mostly relics left from a long ago heyday. Still, the abundance of tall trees, trails, and swimming holes, as well as reasonable prices, make it a choice destination for bargain-hunting vacationers.

Traveling is best done in daylight. Though the back roads are lightly traveled, they are also curvy and slow. And, of course, the forest scenery is part of the reason for coming here.

VISITOR INFORMATION

San Lorenzo Valley Chamber of Commerce

P.O. Box 661, Ben Lomond 95005, (831) 345-2084; www.slvchamber.org.

GETTING THERE

Located approximately 70 miles south of San Francisco. Take Highway 280 to Highway 85 to Highway 9. It is a beautiful drive over sun-dappled two-lane roads. On weekends, the roads are filled with bicyclists, but on weekdays, it is smooth sailing.

BOULDER CREEK

A LITTLE BACKGROUND

Back when this mountain town was home to 26 saloons, and assorted gambling houses, brothels, and hotels, residents logged "red gold"—as the centuries-old redwood trees growing here in abundance were then known.

WHAT TO DO

Big Basin Redwoods State Park
21600 Big Basin Way, 8 mi. from town, (831) 338-8860; www.parks.ca.gov. Daily sunrise-sunset. $6/vehicle.

California's first and oldest state park, Big Basin has more than 80 miles of hiking and equestrian trails in its 20,000 acres of redwood forest. The easy, canopy-shaded .6-mile Redwood Loop Trail is self-guiding and relatively flat. It leads to the park's most interesting redwoods: Mother-of-the-Forest (tallest in park at 329 feet); Father-of the-Forest (with a 66-foot circumference); and Zoo Tree (imagined animals are seen within). The trail also has a lovely stone water fountain and is dotted with log benches. Other hikes include the 10.3-mile trail leading to 65-foot-high Berry Creek Falls, and the especially popular Skyline to the Sea backpacking trail. A dramatic bloom of wild azaleas and rhododendrons is seen each spring, when globe lilies and hairy star tulips are also seen. The Nature Lodge museum features an assortment of exhibits, and a woodsy log cabin Visitor Center *(M-F 9-5.)* built in 1938 by the C.C.C. provides general information. Campfire programs are often scheduled in a huge outdoor amphitheatre with seats carved into logs. A Junior Ranger Program for children operates here (for description, see page 468). Inexpensive tent cabins can be reserved *((800) 874-TENT, (831) 338-4745; www.bigbasintentcabins.com; optional package includes food and bedding.),* and traditional campsites and hike-in campsites are also available.

San Lorenzo Valley Museum
12547 Hwy. 9, (831) 338-8382; www.slvmuseum.com. W & F-Sun 12-4. Free.

Situated within a church built completely of precious heart of redwood in 1885, this museum shows rare photographs of the area's early logging days. A recreated early-1900s kitchen and a Victorian parlor are also displayed. A self-guided walking tour brochure of historical Boulder Creek is available here.

WHERE TO STAY

Merrybrook Lodge
13420 Big Basin Way, (831) 338-6813; www.merrybrooklodge.net. 8 rooms; $-$$. Some kitchens; some wood-burning fireplaces & stoves.

Tucked among towering redwoods, some of these cottages and motel-style units overlook Boulder Creek.

WHERE TO EAT

Picnic Pick-Ups
• New Leaf Community Market
13159 Hwy. 9, (831) 338-7211; www.newleaf.com. Daily 9-9. Also at 6240 Hwy. 9, in Felton, (831) 335-7322; daily 9-9.

Everything needed for a delicious, healthy picnic—and more—is found in this popular local grocery.

Scopazzi's Restaurant
13300 Big Basin Way, (831) 338-4444; www.scopazzisrestaurant.com. L-D W-Sun; $$. Reservations advised.

This spacious, rustic mountain lodge has operated as a restaurant since 1912. Known for its Italian meals, the menu offers cannelloni, veal scaloppine, and chicken cacciatora along with fried prawns, pepper steak flambé, and quail en cocotte. Children should be pleased to see the options of a hamburger, a grilled cheese sandwich, pizza, and spaghetti.

BEN LOMOND

WHAT TO DO

Highlands Park
8500 Hwy. 9, (831) 454-7956; www.scparks.com. Daily 8-dusk. Free.

The grounds of this old estate have been transformed into a park with a playground, a skate park, two softball diamonds, three tennis courts, and picnic tables. Nature trails lead to a sandy river beach.

WHERE TO STAY

Econo Lodge
9733 Hwy. 9, (800) 676-1456, (831) 336-2292; www.stayintheredwoods.com. 21 rooms, 1 cottage; $-$$. 1 kitchen. Heated pool (seasonal). Continental breakfast.

These standard motel rooms are set back against a strand of tall redwoods. A pretty garden surrounds the large pool area, and the property is peaceful and well maintained.

Jaye's Timberlane Resort
8705 Hwy. 9, (831) 336-5479; www.jayestimberlane.com. 10 cabins; $$. All kitchens; some fireplaces. Solar-heated pool (seasonal).

These renovated cabins are scattered on spacious grounds shaded by redwoods.

WHERE TO EAT

Brookroom
11570 Hwy. 9, in Brookdale, halfway betw. Ben Lomond & Boulder Creek, (831) 338-1300; www.brookdaleinnandspa.com. D W-Sun, SunBr; $-$$$. Reservations advised.

A natural brook flows right through the center of this unique dining room that has been around almost forever. Once mentioned in "Ripley's Believe It or Not!," it must be seen to be believed. Diners sit streamside, enjoying the pleasant, continuous sound of water rushing

over stones and viewing the occasional trout. A well-priced champagne brunch buffet is available on Sundays, while dinner brings on a more expensive surf-and-turf menu. Prime Rib is a bargain on Thursdays, and live jazz begins at 5 p.m. on Sundays.

The Lodge at The Brookdale Inn & Spa
((831) 338-1300. 46 rooms; $-$$$. Indoor heated pool; full-service spa. 2 restaurants. No pets.).
Built as the headquarters for a lumber mill in 1870 and converted into a hotel in 1900, this complex features standard '50s-style motel rooms and cottages. Some family rooms and two theme suites—the Marilyn Monroe Suite and the Enchanted Forest Suite—are available. The Honeymoon Cottage is positioned over the creek, and the Mermaid Room has windows that look underwater into the pool. Pool hours vary by season and are subject to lifeguard availability.

Ciao! Bella!! Italian Restaurant
9217 Hwy. 9, (831) 336-9221; www.ciaobella benlomond.com. D daily; $$. Reservations advised.

"We are the people our parents warned us against," promises the menu. That might be referring to the slightly off-center waitstaff. They sing. They dance. They have tattoos. Funky is an understatement, but fun isn't, what with parking spaces reserved for Elvis and Fonzie and the gang. Though seating inside is cozy and atmospheric, dining outside on the deck within a natural cathedral circle of tall, tall redwood trees is not to be missed. Most importantly, the food is tasty, and each meal begins with bread and an addictive dipping sauce of fresh garlic mixed at table with olive oil and balsamic vinegar. Menu items include pasta aplenty, plus an assortment of salads and heavier meat dishes.

Tyrolean Inn
9600 Hwy. 9, (831) 336-5188; www.tyroleaninn.com. L Sun, D Tu-Sun; $$. Reservations advised.

Appearing as something right out of Germany's Black Forest, this restaurant prepares exquisite Austrian-German cuisine. Eight German beers are on tap—including a refreshing Weiss Bier cloudy with yeast. Entrees include sauerbraten and schnitzels, and among the desserts are housemade fresh apple strudel and Black Forest cake. With notice, the kitchen will prepare any venison, hare, or duck specialty dish desired. Dinner is served in a romantic, cozy dining room heated by two fireplaces. In good weather, dining is available on a patio sheltered by mature redwoods.

FELTON

WHAT TO DO

Felton Covered Bridge Park
Off Graham Hill Rd./Mt. Hermon Rd., (831) 425-1234; www.scparks.com. Daily 8am-sunset. Free.

Built over the San Lorenzo River in 1892, this redwood bridge is restored to its original condition and can be walked on. A state historical landmark, it measures 34 feet high and is the tallest covered bridge in the U.S. Facilities include a nice grassy area with picnic tables, barbecues, and a playground.

Hallcrest Vineyards
379 Felton Empire Rd., (800) OWW-WINE, (831) 335-4441; www.hallcrestvineyards.com. Tasting daily 12-5; tour by appt.

Hidden behind a ridge of mansions, this winery is noted for its Estate White Riesling. All wines in their Organic Wine Works division are made without sulfites from organically grown grapes and are vegan-friendly (some wines are processed with egg whites and gelatin). This division is one of only two federally licensed organic wine processors in the United States. Picnic tables are provided on a shady deck just outside the tasting room.

Henry Cowell Redwoods State Park
101 N. Big Tree Park Rd., off Hwy. 9, 2 mi. S of town, (831) 335-2174; www.parks.ca.gov. Daily sunrise-sunset. $6/vehicle.

A number of trails lead through this park's redwood groves, including the easy mile-long Redwood Circle Trail that visits the hollow General Fremont Tree within which the general is said to have once camped. Trail guides are available at the Nature Center. Campsites are available.

Roaring Camp & Big Trees Narrow-Gauge Railroad
On Graham Hill Rd., (831) 335-4484; www.roaringcamp.com. Schedule varies. $19.50, 3-12 $13.50; parking $7.

This 6-mile, hour-long steam train ride winds through virgin redwoods and crosses over a spectacular trestle. About the time passengers start feeling a little restless, the train makes a short stretch stop atop Bear Mountain at Cathedral Grove—an impressive circle of tall 800-year-old redwoods said to have a 3,000-year-old root system. Riders may stay for a picnic or hike and then return on a later train. Bring warm wraps. Though this area enjoys warm to hot weather in summer, it can

get chilly on the train ride. Picnic facilities are available.

Another train, the **Santa Cruz Big Trees & Pacific Railway** *($21.50, 3-12 $16.50.)*, makes two trips each day between Roaring Camp and the Santa Cruz Beach Boardwalk. The round-trip excursion takes 3 hours.

An outdoor **chuck wagon barbecue** *(Sat-Sun 12-3; May-Oct only; $-$$. Reservations advised.)* operates near the depot, and the **Red Caboose Saloon** dispenses short-order items. Be sure to save some tidbits for hungry ducks and geese in the lake.

Special events include the **Civil War Encampment and Battles** in May and a choco-late **Easter egg hunt** for kids on Easter Sunday.

WHERE TO STAY

Felton Crest Inn

780 El Solyo Heights Dr., (800) 474-4011, (831) 335-4011; www.feltoncrest.com. 4 rooms; $$$-$$$+. Unsuitable for small children. 1 wood-burning stove. Continental breakfast. No pets.

Situated up a hill, at the end of a private road in a rural residential area, this B&B is surrounded by an acre of redwoods. A contem-porary brown-shingled mountain house with mustard-yellow trim, it is reminiscent of lodgings found in Germany's Black Forest. Public spaces include a large sundeck, a shel-tered tea area with a hammock, and a cheery breakfast room. Beds are made with soft featherbeds and topped with pouffy white duvets covered with lovely cut-lace linens. It's like being on Mick's cloud. The third-floor Treetop Penthouse has a knotty-pine cathedral ceiling with exposed rafters, a stained glass window, and a private deck open to the fragrant tall trees. Deeply dark, silent nights are part of the deal.

Fern River Resort Motel

5250 Hwy. 9, (831) 335-4412; www.fernriver.com. 14 cabins; $-$$. Most kitchens; some gas fireplaces. Hot tub.

These modernized knotty-pine cabins are located on the river across from Henry Cowell Redwoods State Park. The 5-acre lot features a redwood-shaded outdoor recreation area with volleyball, tetherball, and Ping-Pong. Guests have use of a private beach on the river, and riverside picnic tables are provided.

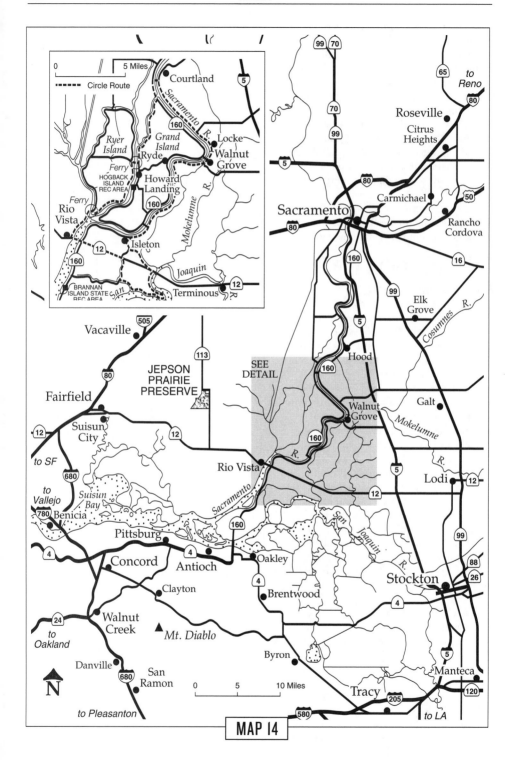

MAP 14

DELTA

A LITTLE BACKGROUND

Composed of flat land, crisscrossed by more than 700 miles of rivers and sloughs (pronounced "slews"), this agricultural area is filled with scenic roads running along raised levees. The Delta is formed by five major rivers and many more sloughs, cuts, and canals. The two largest rivers—the Sacramento and the San Joaquin—join here and flow on out to the Pacific Ocean via San Francisco Bay. Bridges abound (there are at least 70), and many can be raised to accommodate large boats. Popular for a houseboat vacation (see page 465), this area is also pleasant for just a day trip. Pack along a good detailed map, as the roads here are maze-like, and try to avoid driving at night, when the levee roads can be dangerous.

Trendy hasn't yet hit this area and might never. Food is basic, and wine is sometimes mistreated. However, locals enjoy a good time, and many eating establishments book live entertainment in the evening.

VISITOR INFORMATION

California Delta Chambers & Visitors Bureau

169 W. Brannan Island Rd., in Isleton, (916) 777-4041; www.californiadelta.org.

GETTING THERE

Located approximately 60 miles east of San Francisco. Take Highway 80 north to Highway 4 east. Continue following Highway 4 as it turns into Highway 160 (River Road) and crosses the gigantic arch that is the John A. Nejedly Bridge. Highway 160 continues north into Sacramento.

ANNUAL EVENTS

Pear Fair

July. In Courtland; (916) 775-2000; www.pearfair.com. Free; parking $10.

The Delta is the foremost pear-growing area in the country. This annual celebration of the harvest features a parade, kiddie rides, and, of course, plenty of pear foods. Contests include pear bobbing, pear pie eating, and pear peeling—in which the longest continuous peel after 10 minutes wins. A competition to find the area's largest pear is also part of the fun here in 'pear'adise.

The following towns are listed in the order in which they appear on the circle tour highlighted with broken lines on the map. Start the tour at any point. Following it takes drivers through the area's most scenic towns, across several different types of bridges, and on two car ferries.

ISLETON

A LITTLE BACKGROUND

Located at the geographic center of the Delta, this picturesque, isolated town is one of the larger in the area. Once a bustling port city with a population of more than 2,000, it is now home to only 860 people.

VISITOR INFORMATION

Isleton Chamber of Commerce
308 Second St., (916) 777-5880; www.isletoncoc.org.

ANNUAL EVENTS

Asian Celebration
March. (916) 777-5880; www.isletoncoc.org. Free.
    The town celebrates its Asian heritage with the Great March of China, lion dancers, an Asian gift bazaar, ancient cultural rites, Asian foods, and the Invitational Rickshaw Races.

Crawdad Festival
June. (916) 777-5880; www.isletoncoc.org. $5, under 13 free; parking $5.
    Benefiting the town Children's Fund, this festival features live music and entertainment, activities such as a Crawdad Race and a Crawdad Petting Zoo, and a mess of cooked crawdads for eating.

WALNUT GROVE

A LITTLE BACKGROUND

This town, which grew up on both sides of the river, is linked by the first cantilever bridge built west of the Mississippi. Most of the decaying east side of town, which holds the remnants of a Chinatown, is on the National Register of Historic Places. The west side is a well-maintained residential area.

WHERE TO EAT

Giusti's
14743 Walnut Grove-Thornton Rd., 4 mi. W of town, (916) 776-1808; www.giustis.com. L-D Tu-Sun; SunBr in summer; no D Jan-Feb; $$. No reservations. No cards.

In a rustic landmark building standing at the junction of the North Fork of the Mokelumne River and Snodgrass Slough, this restaurant has been dishing up family-style Italian dinners since 1896. For lunch, it's burgers, pastas, and steaks. The dining room overlooks the river, and the bar ceiling is covered with more than 950 baseball caps.

LOCKE

A LITTLE BACKGROUND

Said to be the only town in the country that was built entirely by and for Chinese immigrants, this tiny town dates back to 1915. Its narrow Main Street is lined with picturesque weathered wooden buildings, many of which are still inhabited. In its prime, it had more than 3,000 residents. Now the aging Chinese residents, down to only about 50, are often seen sitting on benches on the wooden walkways, just watching.

    When leaving here, continue the circle tour as indicated or backtrack to Walnut Grove, cross the river, and continue south to Ryde.

WHAT TO DO

Dai Loy Museum
On Main St., (916) 776-1661; www.locketown.com/ museum.htm. Sat-Sun 12-3. $1.25, children 75¢.
    Located within what was the town gambling hall from 1916 to 1951, this museum fills visitors in on the town's history as a Chinese outpost. The Central Gaming Hall—with its original furniture and gaming tables—and the dealers' low-ceilinged upstairs bedrooms can be

The Real McCoy

viewed, and interesting era photographs hang on the walls throughout.

WHERE TO EAT

Al's Place
13936 Main St., (916) 776-1800; www.locketown. com/als.htm. L-D daily; $-$$. No reservations.

Once a speakeasy, this restaurant's unsavory looks might cause many people to pass it by. But once through the bar, which can be rowdy even at lunchtime, diners enter a windowless back room and can seat themselves at simple Formica picnic tables with benches. In addition to a steak sandwich served with a side of tasty grilled garlic bread, which used to be the only thing on the menu, hamburgers and chicken sandwiches are now available. Jars of peanut butter and apricot jam adorn each table and are meant to be used with the steak. Parents can sometimes strike a deal with a waitress to bring extra bread so their kids can make peanut butter & jelly sandwiches. At dinner, when the place gets more crowded, the steak goes up a bit in price and is served with sides of fries, pasta, French bread, and grilled mushrooms. Chicken and pasta are also available. When leaving, stop by the bar to find out how dollar bills get stuck to the 2-story-high ceiling. The fee is $1. Stuck without a buck? An ATM is on the premises.

RYDE

WHAT TO DO

Car ferries
Free.

Catch the old-time diesel-powered, cable-guided **Howard's Landing Ferry**, also known as the *J-Mack*, off Grand Island Road. It holds about six cars, and waits are usually short. (Note that it closes down for lunch from 12 to 12:30.)

Once on Ryer Island, take Ryer Road south to the **Ryer Island Ferry**, also known as *The Real McCoy*. After crossing, follow the road into Rio Vista.

Hogback Island Recreation Area
On Grand Island Rd., www.sacparks.net. $4/vehicle.

A grassy picnic area is bounded on one side by Steamboat Slough and on the other by a boat-launching lagoon. This isn't a good swimming area, but it has access spots that are fine for getting feet wet.

WHERE TO EAT

Grand Island Mansion
13415 Grand Island Rd., in Walnut Grove, (916) 775-1705; www.grandislandmansion.com. SunBr; $$. Reservations advised.

Across the island, this spot is open only on Sunday for an opulent champagne brunch. Diners are welcome to tour the mansion and grounds.

Ryde Hotel
14340 Hwy. 160, 3 mi. S of Walnut Grove, (888) 717-RYDE, (916) 776-1318; www.rydehotel.com. SunBr; seasonal schedule; $$. Reservations advised.

Built in 1927 and once owned by actor Lon Chaney and family, this salmon-colored stucco, art deco hotel operated a basement speakeasy during Prohibition. It is claimed that Herbert Hoover, who was a Prohibitionist, announced his presidential candidacy in 1928 in this very hotel while standing, ironically, above a large stash of bootleg booze. Now beautifully restored, the hotel once again serves elegant meals in its dining room.

Guest rooms *(4 stories, 42 rooms; $-$$. Continental breakfast Sat-Sun.)* are also available.

RIO VISTA

VISITOR INFORMATION

Rio Vista Chamber of Commerce
50 N. Second St., (707) 374-2700; www.riovista.org.

WHAT TO DO

Brannan Island State Recreation Area
17645 Hwy. 160, 3 mi. S of town, (916) 777-6671; www.parks.ca.gov. Daily sunrise-sunset. Visitor Center: Sat-Sun. $5/vehicle.

Located on a knoll, this 336-acre park offers slough-side picnic and swimming areas and a short nature trail. Campsites are available.

Victorian homes
On Second St.

Second Street is also known as Millionaires' Row.

WHERE TO EAT

Foster's Bighorn
143 Main St., (707) 374-2511; www.fostersbighorn.com. L-D daily; $-$$. Reservations accepted.

Opened in 1931, this restaurant features walls lined with more than 250 mounted big game heads. The trophies include a full-grown elephant that is the largest mammal trophy in any collection in the world, the largest mounted moose head in the world, and a rare giraffe head. Gathered by the late hunter William Foster, who shot most of the wild animals himself, it is the world's largest collection of big game trophies. An attractive bar area in front leads to an open dining room with high ceilings and comfortable booths. Sandwiches and hamburgers are on the lunch menu, and steak and seafood on the dinner menu.

The Point Waterfront Restaurant

120 Marina Dr., in Delta Marina, (707) 374-5400; www.pointrestaurant.com. L-D Tu-Sun, SunBr; $$. Reservations advised on weekends.

Overlooking the Sacramento River at its widest point, this comfortable, well-maintained restaurant has many roomy booths. The lunch menu features housemade soups and sandwiches. Dinner entrees include prime rib, calamari, and chicken pasta. Photos illustrating Humphrey the Whale's well-publicized visit to the area are displayed in the entryway.

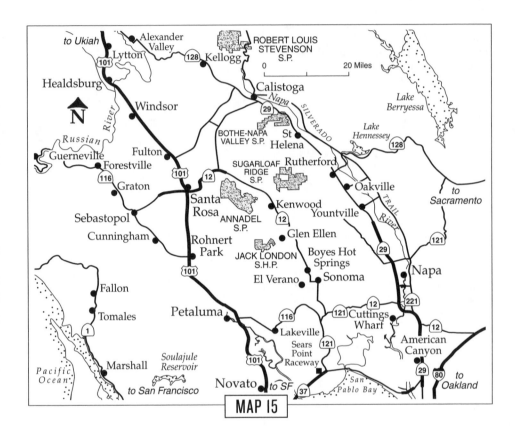

to Ukiah
Alexander Valley
Lytton
101
128 Kellogg
ROBERT LOUIS STEVENSON S.P.
0   20 Miles

Healdsburg
Calistoga
Napa
N
Russian River
Windsor
Lake Berryessa
29
BOTHE-NAPA VALLEY S.P.
St Helena
SILVERADO
Lake Hennessey
Guerneville
Fulton
Forestville
SUGARLOAF RIDGE S.P.
Rutherford
128
116 Graton
101
12
Oakville
to Sacramento
Santa Rosa
ANNADEL S.P.
Kenwood
TRAIL
12
Yountville
River
Sebastopol
Cunningham
Rohnert Park
Glen Ellen
JACK LONDON S.H.P.
Boyes Hot Springs
29
121
101
El Verano
Sonoma
Napa
Fallon
221
Petaluma
12
Tomales
116
121 Cuttings Wharf
121
1
Lakeville
Sears Point Raceway
American Canyon
Pacific Ocean
Soulajule Reservoir
Marshall
101
12
to San Francisco
Novato
to SF
37
San Pablo Bay
29 80
to Oakland

MAP 15

Wine Tasting at Bartholomew Park Winery

A LITTLE BACKGROUND

California's first wineries were appendages of the 21 Franciscan missions that were built a day's ride by horseback from each other in a chain reaching from San Diego to Sonoma. The missions produced the wine for sacramental use. Eventually the church gave up making wine, and the art passed into the realm of private enterprise.

Presently Sonoma County and Napa County are literally erupting with new small family wineries. Winemaking has become a hobby with many city folks who have bought themselves modest, and not so modest, vineyard retreats.

The most popular route for wine tasting is in the Napa Valley along Highway 29 between Oakville and Calistoga. Not far behind in popularity is scenic Highway 12 in the Sonoma Valley. When visiting these stretches of highway, which are heavily concentrated with wineries, try to remain selective. Experts suggest not planning to taste at more than four wineries in one day.

Though a visit to the Wine Country is enjoyable at any time of year, fall just might be the most beautiful season. The grapevine leaves are turning brilliant hues of gold and red, "the crush" is in full swing, and the crowds—like the hot temperatures—have subsided. Workers are seen in the fields, and gondolas laden with grapes move slowly down the highway delivering their bounty to the wineries. But because everyone is working to beat the clock, winery personnel are less available to give visitors quality time.

Young children can be difficult on a winery tour. Out of courtesy to the other tour participants—a noisy child interferes with the guide's presentation—parents might consider having a member of their party stay with the children while the others go on a tour. Most wineries don't require taking a tour before tasting. Or visit a winery with a self-guided tour. It's a nice idea to bring along some plastic wine glasses and a bottle of grape juice so children can "taste," too.

Many wineries have picnic areas. An ideal itinerary is to tour a winery, taste, and then purchase a bottle of wine to drink with a picnic lunch.

A wrinkle in the pleasure of wine tasting is that most wineries now charge for tasting. Sometimes the charge permits tasters to keep their glass as a souvenir or is applied to a wine purchase. Originally, tasting fees were imposed by smaller wineries with expensive vintages, and

their purpose seemed to be to keep the less serious tasters away, but now almost all the wineries charge. Fees change regularly, and occasionally a winery will charge one day but not the next. It's best to call ahead to determine the charge or just to expect that a fee of around $5 to $10 will be levied, more when tasting premium wines. Check websites, because some offer two-for-one tasting coupons; and consider joining a wine club, because members often get free tasting and other perks. Many wineries now also charge for tours but often include tasting in the fee.

Some tasting rooms provide vertical tastings, which portray the aging process of a varietal, and cross tastings, which show the different results that varied treatment of the same grapes can cause. Some also provide tastings paired with food. Check websites for details about these special tastings.

Carry a cooler with an ice pack to store purchases; wine is damaged by high temperatures.

ANNUAL EVENTS

Carols in the Caves
December. (707) 224-4222; www.cavemusic.com. $40; unsuitable for children under 11.

In spectacular settings, David Auerbach performs seasonal music selections using rare and unusual instruments he has collected from around the world: the panpipes of South America, the Celtic harp of Ireland, the steel drums of Trinidad. Instruments and winery sites change each year. Mr. Auerbach also performs in winery caves during the summer and fall.

WHAT TO DO

California Wine Tours
(800) 294-6386, (707) 939-7225; www.california winetours.com; 22678 Broadway, in Sonoma; also at 4075 Solano Ave., in Napa. $50+/vehicle/hr.

Customized winery tours to any region of the wine country can be arranged. Riders just sit back and relax in a stretch limo, sipping something cool from the complimentary beverage bar while leaving the driving to a classy tuxedoed professional. Printed itineraries are provided. Round-trip ferry rides from Pier 1 in San Francisco can be included for an additional fee.

SONOMA

VISITOR INFORMATION

Sonoma Valley Visitors Bureau
453 First St. East, on the plaza, (866) 996-1090, (707) 996-1090; www.sonomavalley.com.

GETTING THERE

Located approximately 45 miles north of San Francisco. Take Highway 101 to Highway 37 to Highway 121 to Highway 12.

ANNUAL EVENTS

Valley of the Moon Vintage Festival
September. (707) 996-2109; www.sonomavinfest.com. Free.

Begun in 1887 as a celebration of the harvest, this old-time event kicks off in the historic Barracks each year with an evening tasting of elite Sonoma Valley wines. Free daytime events include a Blessing of the Grapes, several parades, and a re-enactment of the Bear Flag Revolt (during the revolt American soldiers seized the town from General Vallejo, taking down the Mexican flag and raising the bear flag—which later became California's state flag). Messy grape-stomping competitions, in which one person stomps while the other holds a bottle under the spigot, are also part of the fun.

WHAT TO DO

Cornerstone Sonoma

23570 Hwy. 121, 5 mi. S of town, (707) 933-3010;
www.cornerstoneplace.com. Daily 10-5. Free. No pets.

The 22 fanciful garden spaces here are designed individually by landscape architects and artists. Modeled in part after the International Garden Festival at Chaumont-sur-Loire in France's Loire Valley and the Grand Metis in Quebec, Canada, this is the first gallery-style landscape architecture exhibit in the U.S. A children's garden and play area keeps kids busy as little bees. Shops, wine tasting rooms, and a café are located adjacent.

Depot Park Museum

270 First St. West, (707) 938-1762;
www.vom.com/depot. W-Sun 1-4:30. Free.

Operated by Sonoma Historical Society volunteers, this tiny museum is housed in a replica of the Northwestern Pacific Railroad depot and features changing historical and railroad exhibits. Adjacent Depot Park has a playground and picnic area. A bicycle path following the old railroad tracks here originates at Sebastiani Winery.

Infineon Raceway

At intersection of Hwys. 37 & 121, (800) 870-RACE,
(707) 938-8448; www.infineonraceway.com.
Schedule & ticket prices vary; closed Dec-Jan.

Facilities for car races here include a 2.52-mile course with 12 turns and a ¼-mile drag strip. Concession stands dispense fast food, and grassy hillsides provide perfect picnic perches.

Ramekins

450 W. Spain St., (707) 933-0450;
www.ramekins.com. Schedule & fees vary.

Constructed in a semi-rural setting, this unusual building of solid, 2-foot-thick rammed-earth walls holds a delightful cooking school. It features subtle, whimsical, food-related decorative touches—such as stair railings resembling asparagus stalks—and rustic light-pine furnishings. Students dice and measure and stir while learning new techniques in a well-equipped teaching kitchen. Short classes are scheduled year-round, and eating the results with fellow students is a big part of the fun.

Spacious, tastefully decorated **guest rooms** *((707) 933-0452. 6 rooms; $$-$$$. Continental breakfast.)* are available upstairs. Some have high four-poster beds. Some bathrooms are equipped with a raised stone sink placed so that its bottom is flush with the counter top, and some have open showers. Stainless steel soup ladles double as towel racks.

Sebastiani Theatre

476 First St. East, on the plaza, (707) 996-2020;
www.sebastianitheatre.com. $9, 62+ & under 13 $6;
Bargain Tuesday $6.

Built in 1933 by August Sebastiani, this restored vintage movie theater shows first-run films and also schedules live events.

Sonoma Plaza

This town square—the largest in the state and a National Historic Landmark—was designed by General Vallejo in 1834 for troop maneuvers. Basically an old-fashioned park, it is great for picnics and has a playground and tiny duck pond. City Hall, which is located here, acted as the Tuscany County Courthouse on TV's *Falcon Crest*. A Visitors Bureau is located on the east edge and is worth visiting for the discounted wine-tasting coupons alone.

Sonoma State Historic Park

On the plaza, along Spain St., (707) 938-1519;
www.parks.ca.gov. Daily 10-5. $2, under 17 free.

This extensive park preserves structures dating from the early 1800s, when General Mariano Guadalupe Vallejo, founder of Sonoma, was Mexico's administrator of Northern California.

• Barracks

(707) 939-9420.

This 2-story, whitewashed adobe building once housed Vallejo's soldiers. It now contains historical exhibits. Vallejo drilled his soldiers across the street in what is now the town square.

• Mission San Francisco Solano de Sonoma

(707) 938-9560. Tours F-Sun at 11, 12, 1, 2.

This re-created mission is next door and across the street from the Barracks. Founded in 1823 and the most northerly and last in the chain of California missions, this historic site has been through a lot. It burned to the ground twice, was the victim of a Native American uprising, and sustained serious damage in the 1906 earthquake. Then it went through a period as a saloon, a winery, and even a hennery. It now houses a museum and 1840s parish church. A collection of watercolors depicting each of California's 21 missions is on permanent display. The paintings were done in 1903 by Chris Jorgensen, who traveled from mission to mission by horse and buggy. An adobe section of the mission's original quadrangle is located near the church, which is said to host a ghost, and an impressive old prickly pear cactus forest graces the courtyard.

• Toscano Hotel and Kitchen
20 E. Spain St., (707) 938-5889. Tour: Sat-M 1-4. Free.

This beautifully restored mining-era hotel was built in 1858.

• General Vallejo's Home
At W. Third St./W. Spain St., (707) 938-9559. Self-guided tour daily; docent tour: Sat-Sun at 1, 2, 3.

Located at the end of a long, tree-shaded lane ½ mile west of the plaza, this classic 2-story Victorian Gothic has its original furnishings. Shaded picnic tables are found here along with a Victorian garden and another giant prickly pear cactus garden.

Sonoma Train Town
20264 Broadway (Hwy. 12), (707) 938-3912; www.traintown.com. F-Sun 10-5; daily in summer. Train $4.25, other rides $1.75.

A miniature steam train (a diesel engine is used on weekdays) winds through 10 acres during the 20-minute ride here. It passes through forests and tunnels and crosses both a 70-foot double-truss bridge and a 50-foot steel-girder bridge. During a 10-minute stop at a miniature 1800s mining town, where the train takes on water, riders detrain at a petting zoo inhabited by sheep, goats, ducks, and llamas. An antique merry-go-round, full-size Ferris wheel, airplane ride, snack bar, and picnic area are available at the station.

Sonoma Valley Museum of Art
551 Broadway/McDonell St., (707) 939-7862; www.svma.org. W-Sun 11-5. $5; free on Sun.

Shows change every 6 to 8 weeks at this small venue.

Vasquez House
414 First St. East, in El Paseo de Sonoma, (707) 938-0510; www.sonomaleague.org/vasquez.html. Thur-Sat 2-4:30; $. Free admission.

Built in 1856, this refurbished wood-frame house features a tearoom where visitors can relax over homemade pastries and a pot of tea.

Vintage Aircraft Company
23982 Arnold Dr., off Hwy. 121 at Sonoma Valley Airport, 2 mi. N of raceway, in Schellville, (707) 938-2444; www.vintageaircraft.com. Sat-Sun 9-5, walk in; M & W-F by appt. $175+.

A pilot here claims an aerobatic ride in an authentic 1940 Stearman biplane, once used to train World War II combat pilots, "tops any roller coaster ever built." Calmer scenic rides and glider rides are also available, and antique planes can be viewed at the airport.

WINERIES

Bartholomew Park Winery
1000 Vineyard Ln., (707) 935-9511; www.bartpark.com. Tasting daily 11-4:30; no tour.

Situated in the heart of peaceful 400-acre Bartholomew Memorial Park, this winery is a newcomer to the area. Though wine grapes were planted on the property in the early 1830s and the land once was owned by Agoston

Haraszthy, known as the father of the California wine industry (and connected with the Vallejo family), this winery has been in business just since 1994. The winery makes only 100% varietal wines and produces just 4,000 cases each year. Because production is so small, the flavorful premium wines are sold only at the winery.

Just off the tasting room, a small but interesting **museum** chronicles the property's history and current grape-growing practices. It also holds a fascinating topographical map and photographic displays of both contemporary area winemakers and of images by Victorian photographer Eadweard Muybridge dating back to the early 1870s. Visitors can picnic in a spacious area with a vineyard view, and a 3-mile hiking trail leads through a fragrant old-growth conifer forest with the promise that on a clear day you can see forever—or at least to San Francisco. Monthly jazz concerts are scheduled, and visitors are invited to help punch down the grapes during harvest.

Buena Vista Carneros Winery
18000 Old Winery Rd., (800) 926-1266, (707) 938-1266; www.buenavistawinery.com. Tasting daily 10-5; no tour.

Founded in 1857, this is California's oldest winery. Visitors park among the grapevines, and, after a short, pleasant walk in, taste wines in the welcoming old Press House (don't miss sampling the nutty cream sherry, available only at the winery). Select a favorite bottle to enjoy with a picnic outside at one of the tables shaded by stately old eucalyptus trees growing on the banks of a tiny brook. The winery shop sells a variety of picnic supplies, as well as chilled non-alcoholic Gewurztraminer grape juice. A self-guided tour is available.

Cline Cellars
24737 Arnold Dr. (Hwy. 121), 2 mi. S of plaza, (800) 546-2070, (707) 940-4030; www.clinecellars.com. Tasting daily 10-6; tour at 11, 1, 3.

Situated on the site of a former Miwok Indian village and on the original site of Mission San Francisco Solano, this winery is known for its Rhone varietals and Zinfandels. Tasting occurs in an 1850s farmhouse. Six thermal pools filled by underground mineral springs dot the property. Though once warm, they have been cool since the last big earthquake, and some now are populated with fish and turtles.

A tree-shaded picnic area amid rose bushes and ponds is located behind the farmhouse tasting room, as are cages holding a collection of birds—chickens, doves, quail, and pheasants. Also behind the tasting room is the **California Missions Museum** *((707) 939-8051; www.californiamissionsmuseum.com. Daily 11-4. Free.)*, which displays intricate handmade models of the missions made for display at the 1939 World's Fair.

Gloria Ferrer Caves & Vineyards
23555 Hwy. 121, (707) 996-7256; www.gloria ferrer.com. Tasting daily 10-4:45; tour daily at 11, 1, 3.

Located back from the highway, atop a hill in a Catalan hacienda-style building, this tasting room provides views across the vineyards. In warm weather, tasters can relax on a patio; in cooler weather, they can gaze at the view from inside, warmed by a large fireplace. The winery is part of Spain's Freixenet family, which has been making wine since the 12th century. The tour visits the man-made caves and provides insight into the making of sparkling wine.

Gundlach Bundschu Winery
2000 Denmark St. (another entrance is on Thornsberry Rd.), 3 mi. E of plaza, (707) 938-5277; www.gunbun.com. Tasting daily 11-4:30; tour F-Sun by appt.

Located off a winding, backcountry road, this pioneer winery was established in 1858. Now the great-great grandson of German founder Jacob Gundlach's partner continues the tradition. Jim Bundschu, who has been referred to as the "clown prince of wines," and his merry wine-makers produce wines they like to drink themselves—wines with intense varietal

"If you can't say 'Gundlach-Bundschu Gewurztraiminer,' you shouldn't be driving!"

character. White wines here are dry and flavorful, reds dark and complex. The Kleinberger varietal, a kind of Riesling, is produced by vines brought over in 1860. It is unique to the winery and can be purchased only here. Picnic tables perch on a small hill overlooking a pond and vineyards. When leaving, be sure to take the alternate road out. Each route provides different scenery.

Ravenswood
18701 Gehricke Rd., (888) NO-WIMPY, (707) 933-2332; www.ravenswood-wine.com. Tasting daily 10-5, later in summer; tour daily at 10:30.

A prime producer of Zinfandel, this winery's bold slogan is "no wimpy wines." A picnic area overlooks the vineyards, and a festive barbecue with live music purveys picnic lunches on summer weekends.

Sebastiani Vineyards & Winery
389 Fourth St. East, (800) 888-5532, (707) 933-3230; www.sebastiani.com. Tasting daily 10-5; tour daily at 11, 1, 3.

This winery has been owned continuously by the same family since 1904—longer than any other in the country. It is home to Northern California's first vineyard, planted in 1825 by Franciscan padres and purchased from them by Sebastiani in 1904. The winery is best known for its Symphony and Pinot Noir Blanc, which are available only here. A museum displays the world's largest collection of carved oak wine casks, and a trolley tour of town is sometimes an option. A pleasant picnic area is available.

Viansa Winery
25200 Arnold Dr. (Hwy. 121), 5 mi. S of plaza, (800) 995-4740, (707) 935-4700; www.viansa.com. Tasting daily 10-5; tour daily at 11, 2.

Built on top of a hill commanding magnificent views of the area, this winery is named for its original owners—Sam Sebastiani and his wife Vicki (the name comes from merging the first two letters of each of their first names). The beautifully crafted Tuscan-style winery building was inspired by a monastery near Farneta, Italy. Noteworthy varietals include Barbera Blanc—a light blush wine perfect for picnics—and Cabernet Sauvignon. They are sampled in the tasting room featuring a dramatic "wall of wines" behind two tasting bars. Wines are available for purchase only at the winery.

The **Italian Marketplace** food hall is designed after the mercato in Lucca, Italy, and the extraordinary food offerings *almost* overshadow the wines. Using Vicki's recipes, the kitchen staff prepares wonderful things for picnics: country pâté, torta rustica, hot-sweet mustard, focaccia bread, panini (Italian sandwiches), a triple-chocolate chunk cookie, tiramisu. More goodies include porcini mushroom tomato sauce (made with Viansa Cabernet Sauvignon) and spiced figs (made with Sonoma black mission figs and Viansa Cabernet Sauvignon using Vicki's grandmother's recipe). Some of the items are prepared with produce from the winery's own vegetable garden. On nice days, picnics can be enjoyed at a bevy of tables situated on a knoll with a panoramic view of the Sonoma and Napa valleys. On cooler days, tables are available inside.

WHERE TO STAY

El Dorado Hotel

405 First St. West, on the plaza, (800) 289-3031, (707) 996-3220; www.eldoradosonoma.com. 27 rooms; $$-$$$. Heated pool. Restaurant. No pets.

Built in 1843, this historic inn was remodeled with plenty of Mexican paver tiles and beveled glass. Each of the contemporary rooms contains a handmade four-poster bed and a goose-down comforter to chase the chill. Four separate poolside bungalows are also available.

On the first floor, the appealing **El Dorado Kitchen** *((707) 996-3030. D daily; $$$. Reservations advised.)* offers outside seating at heavy marble tables on a tiled patio dominated by a majestic old fig tree. On cooler days, the large inside dining room is equally inviting.

The Fairmont Sonoma Mission Inn & Spa

100 Boyes Blvd., in Boyes Hot Springs, 3 mi. N of plaza, (800) 441-1414, (707) 938-9000; www.fairmont.com/sonoma. 226 rooms; $$$-$$$$+. Some wood-burning fireplaces. Heated pool; sauna; full-service spa with 3 geo-thermal mineral pools & 3 mineral hot tubs; fitness room; 18-hole golf course. 2 restaurants; room service.

Built in 1927 and surrounded by 13 acres of beautifully landscaped, fragrant grounds, this sedate luxury resort's pink adobe architecture is reminiscent of the town mission. Its immense lobby is outfitted with comfortable oversize furniture and features vintage tiled floors and massive ceiling beams. Traditional rooms in the original building sport enormous closets, and the completely round turret—the most requested room—has a view of the pool and gardens. Newer contemporary-style rooms and luxury suites are also available. Though children are welcome, this is an adult-oriented resort: Children under 18 are not permitted in the spa but can use the hotel pool.

People were coming to this spot for the therapeutic 135-degree mineral waters long before the hotel was built, so it is fitting a fabulous spa should take form here. An entire day there can be used to good advantage. Start by decompressing with the Bathing Ritual: Soak first in the 92-degree Tepiderium Roman Bath; then move on to the 102-degree Caldarium hot pool; cool off under 2-foot-diameter showerheads; and finally enter the herbal steam room and then the sauna. An array of treatments is available, including the marvelous Wine Country Kur. Nicknamed "the scrub, tub, and rub," it consists of an exfoliation rub with local grape seed crush, a soak in a hot grape seed-enhanced bath, and then a massage with rich grape seed oil and lotion. Men might especially enjoy the facial designed just for them. The spa also has an outdoor pool and several private outdoor hot tubs.

Gorgeous **Santé Restaurant** *(B-D daily; $$$.)* operates just off the lobby. The seasonal menu changes regularly but might include a tasty salad with spicy pecans and blue cheese as a starter, and perhaps a horseradish-crusted grouper or a black pepper-and-coriander-crusted rack of lamb. If available, opt for the dessert of fireside s'mores, which includes housemade marshmallows, Valrhona chocolate, and a trip to the outdoor fire pit or huge lobby fireplaces.

The spacious, casual dining room of the **Big 3** *(18140 Hwy. 12, (707) 938-9000. B-L-D daily, Sat-SunBr; $-$$. Reservations advised.)* offers seating at tables and in comfy booths. The restaurant is well known for its extensive and delicious breakfast menu, which offers everything from oatmeal with raisins and brown sugar to eggs Benedict. At lunch and dinner, the menu features eclectic American foods such as sandwiches, soups and salads, a delicious hamburger, and trendy pizzas. Low-fat spa cuisine options are available in both restaurants.

Ledson Hotel

480 First St. East, on the plaza, (707) 996-9779;
www.ledsonhotel.com. 6 rooms; $$$+. Unsuitable for
children under 12. All gas fireplaces. Continental
breakfast. No pets.

This hotel dupes most people into think-
ing it is a historical building. Actually, it is a
new structure designed and built in period style
by Steve Ledson, a fifth-generation Sonoma
farmer and winemaker. A stay here makes it
clear he used only the best materials. On the
second floor, spacious guest rooms feature
plenty of architectural details—crown mold-
ings, arched doorways, Venetian plaster, elegant
black marble bathrooms—plus flip-on fireplaces
and heavy beveled-lead glass French doors
leading to a small balcony. The high beds are
made with soft, smooth, cotton Frette linens
and topped with a down comforter and piles of
pillows. After sampling a "welcome" bottle of
delicious Ledson wine, it is easy to relax away
the late afternoon.

Downstairs, the sophisticated **Harmony
Lounge** and wine bar features shiny granite
floors and coffered ceilings and is not to be
missed. Wine tasting is available all day. See also
"Ledson Winery & Vineyards," page 416.

MacArthur Place

29 E. MacArthur St., (800) 722-1866, (707) 938-2929;
www.macarthurplace.com. 64 rooms; $$-$$$+.
Heated pool; hot tub; fitness room; full-service spa.
Continental breakfast; restaurant; room service.
No pets.

Featuring a combination of restored
Victorian buildings and newly constructed
units, this historic estate has been transformed
into a luxurious country inn. Rooms are

decorated sumptuously with splendid fabrics
and furniture, and bathrooms have oversize
open showers. Guests can stroll through 6 acres
of manicured gardens and view the original
sculptures ensconced throughout, or borrow a
bike and see the sights. Upon leaving the prop-
erty, a sign indicates New York is 3,562 miles
thataway and Sonoma Plaza is 4 blocks straight
ahead. It's a no-brainer which way to go.

Saddles *((707) 933-3191. B-L-D daily; $$-*
$$$. Reservations advised.) is situated in a beau-
tifully transformed 100-year-old barn said to be
fashioned after Thomas Jefferson's at
Monticello. It has saddles for chairs in the wait-
ing area and serves good grub, including deli-
cious potato skin cups filled with salsa, exquisite
garlic bread, and really good salads. Entrees
include prime steaks, baby back ribs, roasted
chicken, a vegetarian pasta, and fresh fish. At
"The Finish Line," as the dessert menu is called,
don't miss the signature brownie mousse parfait
wrapped in a cowboy kerchief.

Sonoma Hotel

110 W. Spain St., on the plaza, (800) 468-6016,
(707) 996-2996; www.sonomahotel.com. 16 rooms;
$$-$$$. Unsuitable for children under 12. Continental
breakfast; restaurant. No pets.

Dating from the 1870s, when it was the
town social hall, this hotel's rooms feature
French Country furnishings. Some bathrooms
have clawfoot tubs. The friendly resident ghost,
a Chinese man named Fred who dresses in
coolie-style clothing, is said to roam the third
floor and has been seen late at night sweeping
the sidewalk outside.

The Girl & The Fig *((707) 938-3634;*
www.thegirlandthefig.com. L-D daily, SunBr;
$$-$$$. Reservations advised.) operates off the
lobby. A signature arugula-goat cheese-
pancetta-pecan-grilled fig salad is usually
among the menu's figgy goodies. Appetizers
might include a charcuterie platter and artisan
cheeses. A sample entree is a Liberty duck
confit with French green lentils, and desserts are
seasonal and often flavored with intriguing
herbs. The wine list favors Rhone-style varietals
from Sonoma and offers flights for comparing
and contrasting. This festive spot's back patio is
outfitted with a fountain and is primo in warm
weather.

WHERE TO EAT

Estate

400 W. Spain St., 3 blks. from plaza, (707) 933-3663; www.estate-sonoma.com. D daily; $$$. Reservations advised.

General Vallejo's third daughter, Natalia, built this Victorian in 1864 with her husband, Attilla Haraszthy, whose family grew grapes in the valley. The house is beautifully renovated and adapted, and diners have a choice of several seating spaces, plus a porch and patio area in good weather. The menu is regional Italian.

Picnic Pick-Ups

• Basque Boulangerie Cafe

460 First St. East, on the plaza, (707) 935-SOUR. B-L daily; $. No reservations.

This popular bakery makes breads galore (the rustic round loaf and wheat-walnut are both superb), as well as cookies, cakes, and pastries. Dine-in and sidewalk-side breakfast and lunch are also an option, as is a take-away picnic box tied with a ribbon (order 24 hours in advance). Everything is so delicious people are willing to wait in a usually long, long line.

• Sonoma Cheese Factory

2 W. Spain St., on the plaza, (800) 535-2855, (707) 996-1931; www.sonomacheesefactory.com. Daily 8:30-5:30.

This shop opened in 1931. It stocks hundreds of cheeses—including their famous varieties of Sonoma Jack made from old family recipes—plus cold cuts, salads, and marvelous marinated artichoke hearts. Sandwiches are made to order. A few tables are available inside, and more are outside on a shaded patio. The workings of the cheese factory can usually be observed on weekdays through large windows in the back of the shop, and cheese samples are provided for tasting.

• Sonoma Market

500 W. Napa St. #550, 4 blks. W of the plaza, (707) 996-3411; www.sonoma-glenellenmkt.com.

For description, see "Glen Ellen Village Market" on page 415.

Sunflower Café

421 First St. West, on the plaza, (707) 996-6645. B-L daily; $. No reservations.

Located within Captain Salvador Vallejo's historic 1830s adobe home, this inviting cafe offers salads, sandwiches, and coffees. Order in front, then find a chair out back in the casual patio garden planted with a large variety of native flora.

GLEN ELLEN

A LITTLE BACKGROUND

Like the curve of a scimitar blade, the Valley of the Moon stretched before them, dotted with farm houses and varied by pasture-lands, hay-fields, and vineyards. The air shimmered with heat and altogether it was a lazy, basking day. Quail whistled to their young from thicketed hillside behind the house. Once, there was a warning chorus from the foraging hens and a wild rush for cover, as a hawk, high in the blue, cast its drifting shadow along the ground.

—Jack London, *Burning Daylight*, 1910

Contrary to popular belief, Jack London, a man with an eye for landscapes, didn't coin the name "Valley of the Moon." The valley stretching north from Sonoma was referred to as "Valle de la Luna" as early as 1841. But London, who lived on a ranch here when he wasn't on the road, popularized the term—and the place—in his novels.

Now, almost a hundred years later, there are still no high-rise buildings or shopping malls here. Instead visitors are treated to unimpeded views of tree-covered hills and vineyards that appear to stretch forever. It is the perfect antidote to the congestion of civilization, and it is where food guru M.F.K. Fisher spent her last 20 years and where actress Sharon Stone is rumored to have a vacation home.

GETTING THERE

Located on Arnold Drive, 7 miles north of Sonoma via Highway 12.

WHAT TO DO

Jack London Bookstore

14300 Arnold Dr., (707) 996-2888. Thur-M 12-4:30.

To get in the mood for visiting this area, read a London classic such as *The Call of the Wild* or *Martin Eden*. Or stop in at this wee shop, which in addition to stocking rare and out-of-print books, especially those by Jack London, also has a good selection of mysteries. The proprietor can provide assistance in selecting a London title.

Jack London State Historic Park

2400 London Ranch Rd., (707) 938-5216; www.parks.ca.gov. Park: Daily 10-5, in summer to 7. Museum: Daily 10-5. $6/vehicle.

Jack London, who wrote 191 short stories and 51 books, was once one of the highest paid authors in the country. This 830-acre park contains the ruins of his 26-room Wolf House (reached via a pleasant ½-mile trail), his grave, and **The House of Happy Walls**—a museum built in his memory by his widow. Beauty Ranch includes the cottage he actually lived in as well as Pig Palace, a deluxe piggery designed by London. London's nephew donated it all to the state.

WINERIES

Benziger Family Winery

1883 London Ranch Rd., (888) 490-2739, (707) 935-3000; www.benziger.com. Tasting daily 10-5; self-guided tour daily; tram tour daily (fee), schedule varies.

Just up the hill from the little crook in the road that is Glen Ellen, this family-operated winery operates a 45-minute tram tour through their vineyards and hands-on experience with vines, grapes, and trellising techniques. The tour is followed by tasting a wide selection of wines. Additional diversions include caged peacocks and extensive picnic facilities.

B.R. Cohn Winery

15000 Sonoma Hwy. 12, (800) 330-4064, (707) 938-4064; www.brcohn.com. Tasting daily 10-5; tour avail.

Originally part of a Spanish land grant and a dairy during the '40s and '50s, this 90-acre estate is now a winery owned by Bruce R. Cohn, the manager of The Doobie Brothers band. All of the old farm buildings have been converted into winery buildings, and French Picholine olive trees planted more than 140 years ago are now farmed for premium extra-virgin olive oil. The winery's distinctive, intense Cabernets are credited to the area's unique microclimate. Several picnic areas are available, and music and theater performances are sometimes scheduled in an amphitheater.

WHERE TO STAY

Gaige House Inn

13540 Arnold Dr., (800) 935-0237, (707) 935-0237; www.thompsonhotels.com. 23 rooms; $$-$$$+. Unsuitable for children under 10. Some gas fireplaces. Heated pool (seasonal); hot tub. Afternoon & evening snack, full breakfast. No pets.

Because of this inn's 1890 Queen Anne-Italianate exterior, most guests are surprised by its fresh, understated, clean-lined, definitely un-Victorian interior. With Asian touches and gorgeous orchids throughout, the simple but elegant style is refreshing and easy to become accustomed to. Afternoon relaxation is provided by a sheltered creek-side deck and by a gorgeous pool and hot tub area with a perfectly manicured half-acre of lawn lined with flowering oleander trees. Among the most interesting rooms are the Gaige Suite, with a 12-foot ceiling, four-poster lace-canopy bed, and wraparound balcony; and the Creek Side Suite, with a Jacuzzi for two and a double-headed shower, a private porch overlooking Calabasas Creek, and a stunning tree-filled view from the bed. Also, eight newer private Japanese-style spa suites, inspired by the ancient Japanese Ryokan inns in Kyoto, each feature a 2,500-pound granite soaking tub for two overlooking Calabasas Creek; floor to ceiling sliding glass walls line each suite's private garden. A gourmet two-course breakfast is served at private tables in an airy, open room. It might include an appetizer plate of ripe fruits plus a hot plate of polenta and goat cheese topped with perfectly poached eggs and mild salsa—all served on beautifully glazed, Japanese-style rectangular plates.

WHERE TO EAT

The Fig Café & Winebar

13690 Arnold Dr./Warm Springs Rd., (707) 938-2130; www.thefigcafe.com. D daily, Sat&SunBr; $$. No reservations.

Selections from the seasonal menu include thin-crust pizza, macaroni and cheese, braised pot roast, chopped salad, duck confit, and a homey butterscotch pot de crème. Do try the Fig Royale cocktail made with champagne and Figoun liqueur, and consider bringing a favorite wine—corkage is *free!*

Glen Ellen Inn Oyster Grill & Martini Bar
13670 Arnold Dr., (707) 996-6409;
www.glenelleninn.com. L F-Tu, D daily; $$-$$$.
Reservations advised. No pets.

This modest, charming place is sort of a California-style roadhouse. Diners are seated in one of several small rooms, and in warm weather more tables are tucked into an outside sunken herb garden with a koi pond and mini-waterfall. Husband Christian Bertrand produces a non-stop parade of delicious California-fusion fare. Dinner begins with a basket of scones fresh from the oven, often delivered to the table by co-owner and wife Karen, who sometimes waits tables all by herself. Items on the dinner menu have included an exquisitely light puff pastry pocket filled with mushrooms and sausage in a brandy cream sauce, and a late harvest ravioli stuffed with the unexpected taste sensation of a mixture of pumpkin, walnuts, and sun-dried cranberries served on a bed of oven-glazed butternut squash. Save room for one of the killer desserts: perhaps a vertical chocolate mousse contained within a tall chocolate "basket," or maybe housemade vanilla ice cream topped with a marvelous caramel/toasted coconut sauce.

Newly constructed creek-side **Secret Cottages** *((707) 996-1174. 6 rooms; $$-$$$. All fireplaces.)* are painted in warm earth colors and have whirlpool tubs for two surrounded in natural stone tile.

Picnic Pick-Ups
• **Glen Ellen Village Market**
13751 Arnold Dr., (707) 996-6728;
www.sonoma-glenellenmkt.com. Daily 6am-9pm.

The perfect place to select a picnic lunch, this full-service deli prepares sandwiches to order and offers a variety of salads and desserts. Fresh local produce, cold drinks, and the usual market staples are also available.

KENWOOD

GETTING THERE

Located 3 miles north of Glen Ellen on Highway 12, which continues on into Santa Rosa.

WHAT TO DO

Morton's Warm Springs Resort
1651 Warm Springs Rd., (707) 833-5511;
www.mortonswarmsprings.com. Tu-Sun 10-5; summer only. $8, 55+ & 3-11 $7.

Long ago, these mineral springs were used by Native Americans to heal their sick. Nowadays, two large pools and one toddler wading pool are filled each day with fresh mineral water averaging 86 to 88 degrees. Lifeguards are on duty. Facilities include picnic tables and barbecue pits shaded by large oak and bay trees, a snack bar, a large grassy area for sunbathing, a softball field, horseshoe pits, a basketball court, and two volleyball courts. A teenage rec room is equipped with a jukebox, Ping-Pong tables, and pinball machines, and dressing rooms and lockers are available.

Sugarloaf Ridge State Park
2605 Adobe Canyon Rd., (707) 833-5712;
www.parks.ca.gov. Daily dawn-dusk. $6/vehicle.

Here await 25 miles of wilderness trails, a horseback-riding concession, and campsites.

The **Robert Ferguson Observatory** *((707) 833-6979; www.rfo.org. $3, under 18 free.)* schedules public programs.

WINERIES

Chateau St. Jean Vineyards and Winery
8555 Sonoma Hwy. (Hwy. 12), (800) 543-7572, (707) 833-4134; www.chateaustjean.com. Tasting daily 10-5; tour at 11, 2.

This winery specializes in white varietals. The tasting room is inside a 1920s château, and the grassy, shaded picnic area has several fountains.

Kunde Estate Winery & Vineyards
9825 Sonoma Hwy. (Hwy. 12), (707) 833-5501; www.kunde.com. Tasting daily 10:30-4:30; tour F-Sun, on the hr.

Tucked between expansive vineyards and the Sugarloaf foothills, this fourth-and fifth-generation family-owned andoperated winery produces a spicy Zinfandel from gnarled vines growing in a 28-acre vineyard planted more than 125 years ago. Tours are given of the half-mile-long aging caves, which are camouflaged by a hill planted with Syrah grapes, and a picnic area is situated by a fountain and pond under a shady grove of oak trees.

Ledson Winery & Vineyards

7335 Hwy. 12/Sonoma Hwy., 1 mi. W of town, in Santa Rosa, (707) 537-3810; www.ledson.com. Tasting daily 10-5; no tour.

Situated atop a knoll surrounded by Merlot vines, this majestic chateau-like building was originally built by Steve Ledson as his home. Steve's family has been making wine since 1862, and he continues the tradition of high quality, hands-on winemaking. The winery has three tasting bars and a well-stocked deli, and picnic tables are scattered throughout the scenic grounds. Wines are small production and mostly 100% varietals, and they are available only at the winery. Special events are held regularly. See also "Ledson Hotel," page 412.

The Wine Room

9575 Sonoma Hwy. (Hwy. 12), (707) 833-6131; www.the-wine-room.com. Tasting daily 11-5; no tour.

Tommy Smothers says, "Making wine is so close to show business. Wine, like comedy, is subjective. Either people like your wine—or your songs, or your comedy—or they don't. Each is a creative process and you're only as good as your last effort." His wines—**Smothers Winery/Remick Ridge Vineyards**—and several others are available here for tasting. Children get grape juice and pretzels while their parents taste, and a small shaded area is equipped with picnic tables.

WHERE TO STAY

Kenwood Inn & Spa

10400 Sonoma Hwy. 12, (800) 353-6966, (707) 833-1293; www.kenwoodinn.com. 30 rooms; $$$+. Unsuitable for children under 21. No TVs; all wood-burning or gas fireplaces. 2 heated pools; hot tub; full-service spa. Full breakfast.

Hugging a hillside covered with olive trees, this sensual, aesthetically pleasing Tuscan-style inn looks very much like an old Italian villa. Guests are greeted at the desk by an inviting arrangement of seasonal fruits. Painted in gray and ochre tones, the various buildings enclose a center courtyard and mix attractively with the green of the garden and the seasonal punch of color provided by orange globes hanging from persimmon trees and yellow orbs ripening on lemon bushes housed in terra-cotta pots. Fountains and archways are everywhere. Rooms are furnished with a combination of antiques and comfortable newer pieces, and the blissful beds are covered with a feather bed and topped with a lofty down comforter. Dinner is available at additional charge on weekends.

NAPA

A LITTLE BACKGROUND

Considered by most tourists to be the center of the Wine Country, this town is more accurately referred to as the "Gateway to the Wine Country." The center of its old downtown features vintage churches and buildings and is currently being renovated and developed. Its downtown area has more than 22 tasting rooms—more within walking distance of each other than anyplace else in the world—and more than 45 restaurants. A group of wineries is found south of town, but the Wine Country's heaviest concentration of wine estates is farther north. Film buffs will be interested to know that the Napa River stood in for the Mekong Delta in Francis Ford Coppola's *Apocalypse Now*.

VISITOR INFORMATION

Napa Valley Conference & Visitors Bureau
1310 Napa Town Center, (707) 226-7459; www.napavalley.com.

GETTING THERE

Located approximately 50 miles north of San Francisco. Take Highway 101 to Highway 37 to Highway 121 to Highway 12 to Highway 29.

ANNUAL EVENTS

Napa Valley Mustard Festival
February-March. (707) 944-1133; www.mustardfestival.org.

Designed to bring visitors into this area at a beautiful, unhurried time of year when the yellow mustard is blooming, this festival includes a variety of unusual events held around the Napa Valley. Events include tastings as well as art, sporting, and recipe competitions.

Auction Napa Valley
June. Events held throughout the valley; (800) 982-1371 x402, (707) 963-3388; www.napavintners.com. $250-$2,500.

Though tickets are pricey, this 3-day event usually sells out early. Its popularity is explained by the fact that many wine makers open their homes and wineries to unique events in the interest of helping to raise money for local charities. For example, one year the Rutherford Hill Winery hosted a refined candlelight dinner in their hillside caves, while Stag's Leap Wine Cellars hosted a festive Greek dinner and dancing extravaganza on their courtyard. The auction occurs during Saturday dinner at the lush Meadowood Napa Valley Resort.

WHAT TO DO

Copia
500 First St., E of Hwy.29, 3 blks. E of downtown, (888) 512-6742, (707) 259-1600; www.copia.org. W-M, 10-6. Free.

Someone made the delicious comment that without food we cannot live, without wine we cannot endure, and without art we cannot evolve. Here to cover all the bases is Copia: The American Center for Wine, Food & the Arts. Situated on 12 acres beside the Napa River, this center is named for the Roman goddess of abundance and celebrates American achievements in the culinary, winemaking, and visual arts. It was founded and mostly funded by the late Robert Mondavi and his wife, Margrit. Among interesting exterior architectural features are randompatterned fitted stone walls representing the past and a metal crescent representing the future. Though it has no permanent art collection, works on loan are displayed throughout. A long-term interactive exhibition, "Forks in the Road: Food, Wine and the American Table," offers a light-hearted yet serious look at the place of food and wine in American life today. Cooking classes, dinners, concerts, and Friday Flicks are scheduled at additional charge.

Julia's Kitchen—the late Julia Child was an honorary trustee—*((707) 265-5700. L W-M, D Thur-Sun; $$$. Reservations advised.)* is the on-site restaurant, and the **American Market Cafe** is perfect for picking up picnic supplies). Proceeds benefit this non-profit center.

di Rosa Preserve
5200 Carneros Hwy. (Hwy. 121)/near Duhig Rd., 6 mi. SW of town, (707) 226-5991; www.dirosapreserve.org. Schedule varies. Tours $10-$15; free on W. Reservations required.

The show at this expansive 217-acre museum complex begins in the parking lot, where wrought-iron sheep greet visitors. This is one of the largest regional art collections in the country, and tours last 1 to 2½ hours. So extensive is the collection of more than 2,200 pieces of local contemporary art that a tram is used to shuttle guests between the four gallery buildings: a 19th-century stone winery building that was converted into a house and now into a gallery; a tractor barn; two new architecturally striking structures. Art is also displayed outdoors among the meadows and rolling hills. The property is also a nature preserve and is a stopping point for migratory birds. It features towering oaks, a 100-year-old olive orchard, a 35-acre lake, and its own flock of peacocks.

Napa Valley Opera House

1030 Main St., downtown, (707) 22-OPERA; www.nvoh.org. Schedule & prices vary.

After being closed to public performances since 1914, this revitalized 1879 Italianate-style opera house now features informal cabaret seating in its first-floor Cafe Theatre. Upstairs, a small, contemporary-style theater boasts its original bleached redwood trim and has fixed seats that allow everyone a good view.

Napa Valley Wine Train

1275 McKinstry St., near downtown, (800) 427-4124, (707) 253-2111; www.winetrain.com. Daily; schedule varies; closed 1 wk. in Jan. $40-$140. Reservations required.

This leisurely 3-hour, 36-mile excursion takes passengers through the heart of the Wine Country. The train boasts opulently restored vintage lounge cars and a 1916 Pullman converted into a kitchen complete with a stainless-steel galley and a window-wall allowing chefs to be viewed in action. Rides include either lunch or dinner served in richly appointed dining cars outfitted with the refined pleasures of damask linen, bone china, and silver flatware. Almost everything is prepared right on the train using fresh ingredients, and the menu offers several choices in each category. One lunch enjoyed aboard included a tasty baby lettuce salad with Cambozola cheese and hazelnut-sherry vinaigrette, filet mignon with Cabernet-Roquefort sauce, and a creamy tiramisu served cutely in an oversize cappuccino cup. An inexpensive a la carte menu is available for families with young children. Some runs make a stop at a winery, and special events such as private winery tours and murder mystery dinners are often scheduled.

WINERIES

Due to a county restriction placed on most wineries that opened after 1990, many wineries in Napa County are open by appointment only. However, many tasting rooms permit visitors to sign in on the spot (call to verify). Generally, a tasting plus tour requires a reservation, but tasting alone doesn't.

Artesa Winery

1345 Henry Rd., off Hwy. 121, (707) 224-1668; www.artesawinery.com. Tasting daily 10-5; tour at 11, 2.

This spectacular Spanish-owned winery can be difficult to find but is well worth the effort. Its stunning minimalist architecture has it set right into a grassy hill that acts as a sod roof, helping insulate wines stored beneath. Visitors reach the tasting room by walking up a pyramid-like staircase on either side of a a cascading man-made water feature. Stunning panoramic views are enjoyed at the top. In the spirit of the Codorniu family's creation of the first méthode champenoise sparkling wine in Spain in 1872, the winery creates a distinctly California sparkling wine here. After sampling in the spacious tasting room or outside on the inviting deck, a mini-museum of wine-related artifacts awaits leisurely perusal.

Domaine Carneros

1240 Duhig Rd., just off Hwy. 121, 6 mi. SW of town, (800) 716-BRUT, (707) 257-0101; www.domaine carneros.com. Tasting daily 10-6; tour at 11, 1, 3.

Sitting atop a hill surrounded by vineyards, this imposing classic French château is inspired by the Château de la Marquetterie—a historic 18th-century residence in Champagne, France owned by the winery's principal founder. After climbing a *lot* of steps, visitors reach the elegant tasting salon and garden terrace. Here, information is dispensed both about the méthode champenoise procedure that produces the champagnes of French founder Taittinger and about their local sparkling wines made in the same tradition. Flavored mineral water is given to children while their parents taste.

The Hess Collection

4411 Redwood Rd., (877) 707-HESS, (707) 255-1144; www.hesscollection.com. Tasting daily 10-4; self-guided tour; gallery admission free.

Located on the slopes of Mt. Veeder, off a road that winds first through the suburbs and then through scenic woods, this remarkable winery is owned by Swiss entrepreneur Donald Hess. He grows grapes here in rocky soil on steep, terraced hillsides and turns them into premium wine. The winery is known for its Chardonnays and Cabernet Sauvignons. Built in

1903 and once the original Napa Valley home for the Christian Brothers, it has been extensively remodeled but retains the original stone walls.

The winery features an impressive 13,000-square-foot **art gallery**. Among the eclectic collection of contemporary paintings and sculptures are works by Robert Motherwell and Frank Stella and a stunning portrait by Swiss artist Franz Gertsch titled "Johanna II." The antique Underwood typewriter with a flaming carriage by Leopoldo Maier is also memorable. Later, nostalgic viewers can go to www.lynnhershman.com/doll2 to re-see a piece of art that is a blonde doll with a live cam behind her purple sunglasses. Known as CybeRoberta and created by Lynn Hershman Leeson, she observes current visitors observing her.

At various points, portholes look into rooms where steel fermentation tanks and bottling machines are located. Visitors can also view a 12-minute narrated slide presentation of the winemaking operations.

"Hommage"

Trefethen Winery
1160 Oak Knoll Ave./Hwy. 29, (800) 556-4847, (707) 255-7700; www.trefethen.com. Tasting daily 10-4:30; tour at 10:30 & 2, by appt.

Built in 1886 and now a historical landmark, the wood building here is a superb example of a gravity-flow winery. Though it can be difficult to find, it is worth the effort just to drive through the majestic gates and down an impressive private road through expansive vineyards to the tasting room.

WHERE TO STAY

Blackbird Inn
1755 First St./Jefferson St., near downtown, (888) 567-9811, (707) 226-2450; www.foursisters.com. 8 rooms; $$-$$$. Some fireplaces. Afternoon snack; full breakfast. No pets.

Situated inside a completely gutted and reworked 1920s arts and crafts-style house, this inn provides a refreshing change from froufrou. All rooms have the same subdued, masculine-style decor of dark plaid, striped, and floral fabrics. Dark mahogany wood trim is used throughout, and bathrooms are appointed with marble vanities and shiny white tiles. Iron-frame beds hold a charming row of namesake blackbirds atop the foot end.

For dinner, an easy option is just to cross the inn's back parking lot for a French meal at **La Boucane** *(1778 2nd St., (707) 253-1177.)*.

The Carneros Inn
4048 Sonoma Hwy. 12, 6 mi. SW of downtown, (888) 400-9000, (707) 299-4900; www.thecarnerosinn.com. 96 cottages; $$$+. All wood-burning fireplaces. 2 heated pools (year-round); hot tub; full-service spa; fitness room. 3 restaurants; room service. No pets.

Reached by a drive down a long, wood-fence-lined chute, this luxury resort is hidden from the highway. It appears as a sort of upscale camp for adults. Each unit here is a private cabin, and, due to an odd building code restriction and perhaps in homage to the site's former trailer park, all are built on wheels. Each has a private deck with heater, a yard, and plenty of space in between. Fixtures are top-of-the line—bathrooms feature limestone tiles, an oversize shower with three heads and a hand-held, a second outdoor shower with sunflower head, and a heated slate floor—and the decor simple—lovely cherry wood floors, puffy beds, and a flat-panel TV. Check-in, the spa, and a sleek infinity pool are all up on a hill with a sweeping vineyard view.

The Hilltop Restaurant is for guests only. It serves a daily breakfast and poolside lunch, plus a fixed-price dinner Thursday through Saturday. The more casual **Boon Fly Cafe** *((707) 299-4873. B,L,D daily; $-$$.)* is open to the public. Consisting of a large one-room, barn-like dining room with a wood floor, it serves up simple diner fare. At breakfast that includes housemade donut holes and sausage gravy over buttermilk biscuits, while lunch brings on beer-battered onion rings and thin-crusted pizza.

Embassy Suites Napa Valley

1075 California Blvd., 1½-mi. from downtown, (800) 400-0353, (800) EMBASSY, (707) 253-9540; www.napavalley.embassysuites.com. 205 suites; $$-$$$+. All mini-kitchens. Indoor heated pool & hot tub; sauna. Evening drinks; full breakfast; restaurant; room service.

This property offers suites equipped with a bedroom, a front room with sofa bed, and a galley kitchen. The full breakfast is the all-you-can-eat variety and can be enjoyed either in a pleasant indoor atrium or outside beside a pond inhabited by ducks and both black and white swans. For more description, see page 445.

Hennessey House

1727 Main St., near downtown, (707) 226-3774; www.hennesseyhouse.com. 10 rooms; $$-$$$+. Some TVs; some wood-burning & gas fireplaces. Sauna. Afternoon & evening snack; full breakfast. No pets.

Listed in the National Register of Historic Places, this 1889 Eastlake Queen Anne Victorian's exterior is painted stylishly in five different colors. Six rooms are in the main residence, four more in a carriage house. Some have oversize whirlpool tubs or clawfoot tubs; all have featherbeds. Breakfast is served under what is claimed to be Napa County's finest 19th-century, hand-painted, stamped-tin ceiling, and indeed it is magnificent.

La Residence

4066 St. Helena Hwy. N (Hwy. 29), 4 mi. N of downtown, (800) 253-9203, (707) 253-0337; www.laresidence.com. 25 rooms; $$-$$$+. Some fireplaces. Unheated pool (seasonal); hot tub. Evening snack; full breakfast.

Set back on a spacious site amid a tiny groomed vineyard, this inn's guest rooms are spread among three buildings and are decorated uniquely with designer fabrics and quality furnishings. The 1870 farmhouse Mansion features late 18th-century Revival architecture, though the guest rooms are decorated in contemporary style, while the French Barn additionally holds the reception area and breakfast room. The

newer Cellar House has large suites with fireplaces and French doors opening onto a patio. Breakfast is simply prepared and made with the best ingredients—fluffy scrambled eggs, monster buttery croissants, a perfect fresh fruit cup.

WHERE TO EAT

Alexis Baking Company and Cafe

1517 Third St., near downtown, (707) 258-1827; www.alexisbakingcompany.com. B-L daily; $. Reservations accepted for 4+.

This combination bakery/cafe is a must-stop for breads and pastries to take home, but most people wind up staying for a casual meal, too. Breakfast offerings include huevos rancheros, cornmeal pancakes, and sometimes hot cinnamon rolls. Lunch is a selection of focaccia sandwiches, housemade soups, and seasonal salads.

Cole's Chop House

1122 Main St./Pearl St., downtown, (707) 224-MEAT; www.coleschophouse.com. D daily; $$$. Reservations advised. Valet parking F-Sat.

Situated inside a vintage building made with hand-hewn native stone, this stunning space dates to 1886 and retains its original 80-foot-high open-truss ceiling and Douglas fir floors. The golden-hued plaster walls are trimmed with mahogany and brightened with antique French posters. To allow sampling more of the menu, consider sharing, especially the 16-ounce U.S.D.A. Prime corn-fed, 21-day Chicago dry-aged New York steak—it just might be the very best steak ever. Garlic mashed potatoes and a wickedly delicious pecan pie are also share-worthy, but do order separate cups of cappuccino.

Downtown Joe's

902 Main St./Second St., downtown, (707) 258-2337; www.downtownjoes.com. B-L-D daily; $. Reservations advised.

Situated within a historic building constructed in 1894, then updated in 1926 with an art deco tile façade, this centrally located brewpub serves up housemade soups, salads, pizzas, steaks, and seafood, plus a burger, ribs, and a pulled pig sandwich. Beers include Golden Thistle Bitter Ale (an English-style bitter) and a dark, full-bodied Slipknot Stout; a refreshing housemade root beer is also available. Inside seating provides a view of the Napa River; patio seating is also available. Live music is scheduled Wednesday through Saturday evenings.

Oxbow Public Market

610 First St., 3 blks. E of downtown, (707) 226-6529; www.oxbowpublicmarket.com. Daily M-Sat 9-7, Sun 10-5; sometimes later.

The marketplace features local food vendors and organic farm stands.

Among the several mini-restaurants inside is **Pica Pica Maize Kitchen** *((707) 251-3757; www.picapicakitchen.com.)* which specializes in delicious Venezuelan corn-based dishes, including a spectacularly tasty arepa flatbread sandwich stuffed with shredded skirt steak, fried plantains, and black bean paste.

Adjacent to the main market hall, **Taylor's Automatic Referesher** *(644 First St., (707) 224-6900; www.taylorsrefresher.com. Daily 10:30-9; $.)* features a shiny, contemporary diner atmosphere. The menu includes a fat hamburger on a toasted egg bun and thick milkshakes, plus local wines and an assortment of draft beers. It is a branch of the original in St. Helena (see page 428).

Around on the side, **Model Bakery** *(644 First St., (707) 259-1128; www.themodel bakery.com. M-F 6:30-6:30, Sat 7-6:30, Sun 7-6.)* dispenses freshly baked breads and pastries as well as limited picnic fare. It is another branch of an original in St. Helena (see page 428).

Tuscany

1005 First St./Main St., downtown, (707) 258-1000. L M-F, D daily; $$-$$$. Reservations advised.

This inviting restaurant operates inside a substantial, wide-open space that retains the 1855 building's original hardwood floors and brick walls. It has no trouble mixing modern and new with cozy and warm. Servers wear casual blue work shirts, and tables are covered with butcher paper. The restaurant is wildly popular with locals, and lots of families dine here. Indeed, animated diners are content to eat in the bar when the main room is full. The Mediterranean menu includes pizzas made in a wood-fired oven and both grilled and rotisserie meats.

YOUNTVILLE

VISITOR INFORMATION

Yountville Chamber of Commerce/ Visitor Center

6484 Washington St., (707) 944-0904; www.yountville.com.

WHAT TO DO

Hot air balloon rides

Tour the Napa Valley via hot air balloon. Trips average 1 hour in the air; altitude and distance depend on which way the wind blows.

• Napa Valley Aloft

6525 Washington St., in Vintage 1870, (800) 627-2759, (707) 944-4400; www.napavalleyaloft.com. $225+, 6-16 $190+. Reservations required.

This is the Wine Country's oldest balloon company, with the most experienced pilot team available. The adventure includes a post-flight sit-down breakfast enhanced with a local sparkling wine.

• Napa Valley Balloons

6975 Washington St., (800) 253-2224, (707) 944-0228; www.napavalleyballoons.com. $240, 5-9 $115 (must be at least 48"tall). Reservations required.

This business offers a similar experience.

V Marketplace

6525 Washington St., (707) 944-2451;
www.vmarketplace.com. Daily 10-5:30.

Once a winery, this lovely old brick building now houses specialty shops and restaurants.

WINERIES

Domaine Chandon

1 California Dr., (707) 944-2280; www.chandon.com.
Tasting daily 10-6; tour at 11, 1, 3, 5.

This attractive French-owned winery specializes in sparkling wines produced by the
traditional méthode champenoise. Built with
stones gathered on the site, its arched roofs
and doorways are inspired by the caves of
Champagne, France. It is reached by crossing a
bridge spanning a scenic duck pond surrounded
by beautifully landscaped grounds. The Tasting
Salon features a tasting bar overlooking the valley and provides tables and chairs both inside
and outside on a terrace. Visitors can purchase
hors d'oeuvres and taste by the glass, the flight,
or the bottle.

Though the spacious, elegant dining room
in the winery's **étoile** restaurant *((800) 736-
2892, (707) 204-7529; www.chandon.com/
restaurant. L-D Thur-M; closed Jan; $$$.
Reservations advised.)* is lovely, in good weather
the terrace is the première spot to be seated.
Menu items are designed especially to comple-
ment the winery's sparkling and varietal wines,
which are available by the glass. A signature
tasting menu pairs four courses at lunch and
seven at dinner with Chandon wines.

WHERE TO STAY

Bordeaux House

6600 Washington St., (800) 677-6370,
(707) 944-2855; www.bordeauxhouse.com. 8 rooms;
$$. Some wood-burning fireplaces. Afternoon snack;
full breakfast. No pets.

This ultra-modern building features a
curved, red brick exterior and lush French- and
English-style gardens.

Maison Fleurie

6529 Yount St., (800) 788-0369, (707) 944-2056;
www.maisonfleurienapa.com. 13 rooms; $$-$$$.
Some gas fireplaces. Heated pool (seasonal); hot tub.
Afternoon snack; full breakfast. No pets.

The rustic, vine-covered main building was
built in the center of town as a hotel in 1873. It
has 2-foot-thick brick walls, lots of terra cotta
tile, and romantic multi-paned windows.
Rooms, some of which are located in two adjacent buildings, are decorated in French country
style. Amenities include oversize pool towels,
complimentary use of mountain bikes, evening
turndown, and a morning newspaper. Cookies,
fruit, and beverages are always available, and
wine and hors d'oeuvres are served in the afternoon. Though breakfast is delightful taken in
the cozy dining room, it is delivered to the
room upon request.

Napa Valley Lodge

2230 Madison St., (888) 944-3545, (800) 368-2468,
(707) 944-2468; www.woodsidehotels.com. 55 rooms;
$$$-$$$+. Some fireplaces. Heated pool; hot tub;
sauna; fitness room. Afternoon snack; continental
breakfast. No pets.

Located on the outskirts of town, this
Spanish-style motel is across the street from a
park and playground. Each room has a private
patio or balcony, and breakfast includes
champagne.

Napa Valley Railway Inn

6523 Washington St., (800) 520-0206,
(707) 944-2000; www.napavalleyrailwayinn.com.
9 units; $$-$$$. No TVs. No pets.

Railroad enthusiasts are sure to enjoy a
night in a brass bed here. Three cabooses and
six rail cars—authentic turn-of-the-century
specimens sitting on the original town tracks—
have been whimsically converted into comfortable suites complete with private bath, sitting
area, and skylight.

Vintage Inn

6541 Washington St., (800) 351-1133, (707) 944-1112;
www.vintageinn.com. 80 rooms; $$$-$$$+. All wood-
burning fireplaces. Heated pool; hot tub; 2 tennis
courts. Afternoon tea; full breakfast.

This attractive contemporary inn is centrally located next to V Marketplace. Rooms
feature sunken spa tubs and antiques, and
bicycle rentals are available.

WHERE TO EAT

The French Laundry

6640 Washington St., (707) 944-2380; www.french laundry.com. L F-Sun, D daily; $$$; closed part of Jan. Reservations essential.

Indeed once an actual French laundry, this rustic old stone building now holds one of the Wine Country's most popular culinary gems. Owner-chef Thomas Keller offers diners both a nine-course chef's tasting menu and a nine-course vegetarian menu. The kitchen specializes in freshly prepared, innovative, labor-intensive dishes. A favorite dessert is "coffee and doughnuts"—a cappuccino semifreddo plus a cinnamon-sugar doughnut. Reservations are accepted 2 months in advance to the day. But be warned: This tiny restaurant is so popular and so difficult to get a reservation at that one busy San Francisco executive is said to have hired a temporary worker to spend the day on the phone trying to get him one!

Mustards Grill

7399 St. Helena Hwy. (Hwy. 29), (707) 944-2424; www.mustardsgrill.com. L-D daily; $$. Reservations advised.

The best place to be seated at this popular, well-established bar and grill (it's been here now for a quarter century) is on the cool, screened porch. Though tables are set with crisp white napery, the atmosphere is casual and chic and the menu imaginative. Selections include soups, salads, and sandwiches—the grilled ahi tuna with basil mayonnaise and the hamburger are particularly tasty—as well as entrees such as barbecued baby back ribs, mesquite-grilled Sonoma rabbit, and marinated skirt steak. Fresh fish specials are also available. Onion rings are thin, light, and superb, and housemade ketchup can be ordered with them. Garlic lovers can order a roasted head to spread on the complimentary baguette. Varietal wines are available by the glass, and rich desserts and specialty coffees invite lingering.

The **Cosentino Winery** (*7415 St. Helena Hwy. (Hwy. 29), (707) 944-1220; www.cosentino winery.com. Tasting daily 10-5:30; no tour.*) is located just next door. Built in 1990, this winery produced the country's first designated Meritage wine. Referred to as The Poet, it is a marvelous blend of Cabernet Sauvignon, Cabernet Franc, and Merlot.

OAKVILLE

WINERIES

Opus One

7900 St. Helena Hwy. (Hwy. 29), (800) 292-6787, (707) 944-9442; www.opusonewinery.com. Tasting daily 10-4, by appt.; tour daily at 10:30, reservations required.

The gated entrance to this exceptional winery is just north of town. A merging of American (Robert Mondavi) and French (Baron Philippe de Rothschild) winemaking skills, this exclusive label boasts a facility that is as impressive as its wine. Though from the highway it looks like a squat pyramid, up close and personal it resembles more a contemporary monastery. Constructed of Texas limestone and landscaped with a softening planting of olive trees, the winery uses gentle gravity-flow production and plants its vines in dense French Bordeaux style. This requires costly handwork and helps explain the $180 tab attached to its young bottles of Cabernet Sauvignon. A highlight of the tour is seeing the immense barrel room, which is somehow reminiscent of the pods lined up waiting to hatch in *The Body Snatchers*, only here it is great wine aging in French oak barrels that is waiting patiently to be born.

Robert Mondavi Winery

7801 St. Helena Hwy. (Hwy. 29), (888) RMONDAVI, (707) 226-1395; www.robertmondaviwinery.com. Tasting daily 10-5; tours daily, reservations advised.

In addition to simple tasting and tours, this long-lived winery offers a variety of specialty tastings and tours.

At the annual **Summer Festival at Robert Mondavi Winery** (*July & August*)**,** the entertainers (who in the past have included Ella Fitzgerald, Al Hirt, and the Preservation Hall Jazz Band—on the *same bill!*) probably enjoy the dusk concerts as much as their audience. After an intermission for wine and cheese tasting, the concerts conclude under the stars. Picnics are encouraged, and catered repasts are available by advance reservation. Ah, the pleasure of sitting on a lawn, surrounded by vineyards and rolling foothills, while listening to great jazz.

WHERE TO EAT

Picnic Pick-Ups

• Oakville Grocery Co.
7856 St. Helena Hwy. (Hwy. 29), (707) 944-8802;
www.oakvillegrocery.com. Daily 8-6.

Everything needed for a fantastic gourmet picnic is found here. Select from a vast variety of mustards, vinegars, jams, fresh fruits, beers, and natural juices, as well as cheeses, sandwiches, salads, sausages, and other deli items, plus a large assortment of enticing desserts. If the choices seem overwhelming, call 48 hours in advance to order a pre-packed picnic box, and let them select the contents.

RUTHERFORD

WINERIES

Beaulieu Vineyard

1960 St. Helena Hwy. (Hwy. 29), (800) 373-5896,
(707) 967-5230; www.bvwines.com. Tasting daily 10-5;
no tour.

Founded in 1900 by Frenchman Georges deLatour, this winery is known for its Cabernet Sauvignons and Chardonnays. It is said to be the oldest continuing winery in California.

Rubicon Estate

1991 St. Helena Hwy. (Hwy. 29), (800) RUBICON,
(707) 968-1100; www.rubiconestate.com. Tasting &
tours daily 10-5.

Founded in 1879 by a Finnish sea captain who made his fortune in the Alaskan shipping trade, this is one of the oldest wineries in the Napa Valley. It is now owned by legendary film director Francis Ford Coppola, who has owned a home on part of the property since the 1970s, and who, when the winery was up for sale, made an offer they couldn't refuse. Now, after driving down a long lane, through iron gates and past newly planted vineyards, visitors arrive at an impressive vintage estate.

In addition to a traditional tasting bar, the winery has a small **cafe** where wines can be tasted by the glass, and a terrace provides space for picnicking. Coppola's five Oscars and an authentic Tucker automobile are on view on the floor above the tasting room, and the **Centennial Museum** documents the winery's history.

A gift shop extraordinaire purveys such essentials as *The Godfather* t-shirts and enormous macaroni. This winery is known for its premium red Rubicon wine, which sells for $50 to $125 a bottle, but more affordable everyday wines are also available.

Sequoia Grove

8338 St. Helena Hwy. (Hwy. 29), (800) 851-7841,
(707) 944-2945; www.sequoiagrove.com. Tasting daily
10:30-5; tour by appt.

Family-owned and operated, this small winery gets its name from the 100-year-old cluster of tall sequoia redwoods its tasting room sits beneath. Known for its Rutherford-style Cabernet Sauvignons, it claims to be the only winery with underground production facilities. Things are *real* casual here, with several mellow dogs lounging about while tasters sample the wares.

St. Supéry Vineyards and Winery

8440 St. Helena Hwy. (Hwy. 29), (800) 942-0809,
(707) 963-4507; www.stsupery.com. Tasting daily
10-5; tour daily at 1, 3.

This French-owned winery's **Wine Discovery Center** is a super place to get an introduction to wine-making. The guided tour includes a viewing of the Queen Anne Victorian **Atkinson House**, once occupied by the winery's founder and now furnished with unusual Victorian pieces representative of the era, and an educational visit to a 1-acre demonstration vineyard where, in season, varietal grapes can be tasted. A highlight of the tour is a Smella Vision display that permits a whiff of the various scents used to describe wines (grassy, peppery, etc.). A self-guided tour is free. This winery produces award-winning Sauvignon Blancs and Cabernet Sauvignons. Children get a coloring book and crayons to occupy them while parents taste.

ST. HELENA

A LITTLE BACKGROUND

Downtown's Main Street is lined with upscale clothing and housewares boutiques, and most are inside atmospheric vintage buildings. The streetlights are antique electrolaires brought here in 1915 from San Francisco's Pan-Pacific Exposition.

VISITOR INFORMATION

St. Helena Highway, Main Street, and Highway 29 are all the same road.

St. Helena Chamber of Commerce
1010 Main St., (800) 799-6456, (707) 963-4456; www.sthelena.com.

GETTING THERE

Located approximately 15 miles north of Yountville via Highway 29.

WHAT TO DO

Bale Grist Mill State Historic Park
3369 Hwy. 29, 3 mi. N of town, (707) 963-2236; www.parks.ca.gov. Daily 10-5. $2, under 16 free.

Reached via a shaded, paved, stream-side path, this gristmill ground grain for farmers from the 1840s through the turn of the 20th century. The damp site and slow-turning millstones are reputedly responsible for the exceptional cornmeal produced here. Interpretive displays are located inside the gable-roofed granary, and the 36-foot-diameter waterwheel is restored to full operation. On weekends, a miller usually demonstrates grinding corn and wheat and it is then available for purchase. Picnic tables are provided in several shaded areas, and a 1-mile loop History Trail leads through the woods to a pioneer cemetery.

Cameo Theater
1340 Main St., (707) 963-9779; www.cameocinema.com. $8, 55+ & under 13 $6.

This tiny first-run movie theater is equipped with posh velvet seats and Dolby digital sound, making it well worth a visit. Special performances are sometimes scheduled. When offered, *Silverado Squatters*, based on the book by Robert Louis Stevenson and performed live by local resident Donald Davis, is a don't-miss.

Silverado Museum
1490 Library Ln., (707) 963-3757; www.silveradomuseum.org. Tu-Sun 12-4. Free.

Situated on the edge of a scenic vineyard, this museum contains more than 8,500 pieces of Robert Louis Stevenson memorabilia. There are paintings, sculptures, and manuscripts as well as his childhood set of lead toy soldiers. Consider a family read-in of *A Child's Garden of Verses* or *Treasure Island* before or after this visit.

WINERIES

Beringer Vineyards
2000 Main St., just N of town, (707) 967-4412; www.beringervineyards.com. Tasting daily 10-5, in summer to 6; tour daily at 10:30, 2:15, 3.

Established in 1876, this winery's Visitor Center is inside a beautiful oak-paneled, stained-glass-laden reproduction of a 19th-century German Tudor mansion known as the Rhine House. It is Napa Valley's oldest continuously operating winery, and its tour is considered one of the most historically informative. The winery is noted for its Chardonnays and Cabernet Sauvignons. Unfortunately, picnicking is not permitted on the beautifully landscaped grounds.

Charbay
4001 Spring Mountain Rd., (800) M-DISTIL, (707) 963-9327; www.charbay.com. No tasting; tour by appt.

Located off a remote scenic road, at almost 2,300 feet, this "still on the hill," as it is fondly nicknamed, is totally family-run andoperated. Co-owner Miles Karakasevic, who hails from Yugoslavia, is a 12th-generation wine maker and master distiller. Spirits are double-distilled by hand in classic Alambic pot stills. The winery is known for exceptional—and pricey—ports, brandies, and liqueurs. Among them is a grappa, a black walnut liqueur, and California's first pastis. Law prohibits tasting.

Charles Krug Winery
2800 Main St., 1.5 mi. N of town, (800) 682-KRUG, (707) 967-2200; www.charleskrug.com. Tasting daily 10:30-5; no tour.

In 1858, using a small cider press borrowed from Agoston Haraszthy at the Buena Vista Winery in Sonoma, this winery made the first commercial wines in the Napa Valley. It was also the very first to stop stomping grapes with human feet and start pressing them with machines. Now producing 16 different wines, the winery is noted most for its Cabernet Sauvignons and Chenin Blancs.

Freemark Abbey Winery

3022 St. Helena Hwy. N., 2 mi. N of town, (800) 963-9698, (707) 963-9694; www.freemarkabbey.com. Tasting daily 10-5; tour by appt.

The large, lodge-like tasting room here has oriental carpets covering its hardwood floor. Comfortable furniture arranged around a fireplace invites leisurely sampling, and a picnic area is available for purchasers of wine. The winery is noted for its Chardonnays and Cabernet Sauvignons.

Prager Winery and Port Works

1281 Lewelling Ln., 1 mi. S of town, (800) 969-PORT, (707) 963-PORT; www.pragerport.com. Tasting daily 10:30-4:30; no tour.

Located down a country lane and behind Sutter Home Winery, the valley's premier port purveyor offers a rustic, informal tasting room for sampling the wares.

B&B lodging is available.

Sutter Home Winery

277 St. Helena Hwy. S., 1 mi. S of town, (800) 967-4663, (707) 963-3104; www.sutterhome.com. Tasting daily 10-5; no tour.

Bob Trinchero—son of Mario, who bought the winery in 1947—introduced a fruity, pink-colored White Zinfandel in 1971. It took the country by storm. That inexpensive signature version is still available, but the winery now also produces some premium Chardonnays and Cabernets. The tasting room is inside a barn that housed the original winery, and the winery's showcase 1884 Victorian home is used now for private lodging. Highlights of the surrounding garden—inspired by the renowned Butchart Gardens in Victoria, B.C.—include a rose garden with more than 150 varieties and a garden of dwarf Japanese maples.

V. Sattui Winery

1111 White Ln., (800) 799-2337, (707) 963-7774; www.vsattui.com. Tasting & self-guided tour daily 9-5; in summer 9-6.

Established in San Francisco's North Beach in 1885, this winery was shut down during Prohibition then re-established in St. Helena in 1976. Family-owned for four generations, the current winemaker is the great-grandson of founder Vittorio Sattui and his goal is to take wine off the pedestal and make it user-friendly.

V. Sattui wines are sold only at the winery. Favorites include the Johannisberg Rieslings and Cabernet Sauvignons for which they are best known, as well as the nation's oldest port-style Madera and a Gamay Rouge that was once voted the best hot tub wine. All can be tasted in the stone winery building featuring 3-foot-thick walls and chiseled archways. A deli stocks housemade salads and pâtés along with what is claimed to be the largest selection of international cheeses on the West Coast, and plenty of oak-shaded tables are provided on a 2-acre picnic grounds.

WHERE TO STAY

Ambrose Bierce House

1515 Main St., downtown, (707) 963-3003; www.ambrosebiercehouse.com. 4 rooms; $$-$$$. Unsuitable for children under 12. No TVs; some fireplaces. Hot tub. Evening snack; continental breakfast. No pets.

Named for the witty author who wrote *The Devil's Dictionary* (said to be Rolling Stone Keith Richards' all-time favorite book) and who was portrayed by Gregory Peck in the movie *The Old Gringo*, this 1872 house was once Ambrose Bierce's home. One pleasantly decorated room is named after Eadweard Muybridge, who is known as the "father of the motion picture." It holds two interesting artifacts: an 1897 Eastman Kodak No. 2 Hawk-eye camera and a Smith and Wesson No. 2 that is just like the one Muybridge used in 1874 to shoot his wife's lover. Located at the north end of town, the inn is within convenient walking distance of shopping and dining.

El Bonita Motel

195 Main St., (800) 541-3284, (707) 963-3216; www.elbonita.com. 42 rooms; $$-$$$. Heated pool; hot tub; sauna.

Featuring an art deco decor, this motel has a shaded, grassy pool area and offers an alternative to classy, cutesy, and expensive Wine Country lodgings. Each room is equipped with a microwave, refrigerator, and coffee maker.

Harvest Inn

One Main St., (800) 950-8466, (707) 963-WINE; www.harvestinn.com. 74 units; $$$-$$$+. Some wood& gas-burning fireplaces. 2 heated pools; 2 hot

tubs; full-service spa. Evening wine on F & Sat; full breakfast.

If this English Tudor-style inn were a magazine, it would be a cross between *Town & Country* and *Wine Spectator*. Situated beside a working vineyard, it has 8 acres of beautifully landscaped grounds. Paths wind throughout, allowing the chance to admire the property's exceptional brickwork, and one leads to a peaceful koi pond. Tours are given on weekdays. Furnishings include antiques, and some rooms with a private terrace also have a private hot tub. Mountain bikes are available to rent.

The Ink House
1575 St. Helena Hwy./Whitehall Ln., S of town, (866) 963-3890, (707) 963-3890; www.inkhouse.com. 6 rooms; $$-$$$. Unsuitable for children under 10. Afternoon snack; full breakfast. No pets.

This 4-acre estate includes lawns, gardens, olive orchards, and a petite sirah vineyard. The top floor of the landmark 1884 Victorian is a glass-walled observatory with a spectacular 360-degree view of the surrounding vineyards; it is used as a public space for guests. The parlor has a restored 1870 pump organ that guests may use, and breakfast is served in the elegant dining room. Guest rooms are all on the second floor and are furnished with antiques. More amenities include a full size pool table and loaner 18-speed bicycles. And as if this isn't enough, *Wild in the Country* starring Elvis was filmed here in 1961. He stayed in the French Room, and a copy of the film is available for guests to view.

The Wine Country Inn
1152 Lodi Ln., (888) 465-4608, (707) 963-7077; www.winecountryinn.com. 24 rooms, 5 cottages; $$$-$$$+. Unsuitable for children under 13. No TVs; some wood-burning fireplaces. Heated pool; hot tub. Afternoon snack; full breakfast.

Built in the style of a New England inn, without a lot of fuss and frill, this attractive, quiet lodging is located back from the main highway on top of a small country hill. Rooms are decorated with floral wallpapers and tasteful antiques. Many have views of the surrounding vineyards and hills, and a few have private outdoor hot tubs. A free shuttle takes guests to local restaurants for dinner. Breakfast, which includes housemade granola and breads, is served on attractive handmade crockery.

WHERE TO EAT

The Culinary Institute of America at Greystone
2555 Main St., (707) 967-2320; www.ciachef.edu/california.

Formerly home to The Christian Brothers winery, this school is housed in a magnificent 1889 landmark building that was constructed of locally quarried volcanic tufa stone. Out front, the Cannard Herb Garden consists of seven terraces and features both an edible flower garden and an herbal tea garden. Across the street, the Organic Garden grows vegetables, fruits, and flowers—many from rare and heirloom seeds. Inside, Brother Timothy's 1,800-strong corkscrew collection is displayed, and the well-stocked **Spice Islands Marketplace** gift shop (*(707) 967-2309. Daily 10-6.*) purveys cooking accoutrements. Cooking demonstrations are scheduled. Asking questions, sampling the finished product, and taking home a recipe are all part of the package.

The atmospheric, stone-walled **Wine Spectator Greystone Restaurant** (*L-D daily; $$. Reservations advised. Free valet parking.*) affords the opportunity to see toqued student chefs scurrying about an open kitchen. Though the menu has more substantial entrees, the way to go here is to order up a selection of appetizers called Today's Temptations. Served on a tiered lazy Susan, they might include a tiny, tiny bowl of butternut squash soup or a perfect grilled shrimp with green sauce.

Gillwoods

1313 Main St., downtown, (707) 963-1788;
www.gillwoodscafe.com. B-L daily; $. No reservations.

Known for its breakfasts, this comfortable cafe has all kinds of egg dishes on the menu along with preservative-free Mother Lode bacon and toasted house-baked bread. Not to mention corned-beef hash, buttermilk pancakes, French toast, hot cereals, and granola. Salads and sandwiches are added at 11 a.m.

Martini House

1245 Spring St./Oak St., downtown, (707) 963-2233;
www.martinihouse.com. L F-Sun, D daily; $$$-$$$+.
Reservations advised.

Decorated in a sort of contemporary hunting lodge-style by co-owner Pat Kuleto—restaurateur and restaurant decorator extraordinaire and local resident—this converted 1920s bungalow is a satisfying venue. On a nice day, diners can sit at tables covered with white linens on the arbor-sheltered patio or in the front yard under mature trees. A large 75-year-old fountain populated with koi acts as a soothing kid-magnet. The wine list is excellent, and celebrity chef and co-owner Todd Humphries' daily-changing menu always is interesting. A delicious fixed-price lunch might include creamy mushroom soup, a shrimp salad, and fabulous crème fraîche ice cream with berries and wildflower-honey cake. Surprise touches include warm steamed milk in the cream pitcher and coffee served in a French presse pot. The low-ceilinged downstairs bar is worth a look-see, if only to view the acorn-mimicking light fixtures.

Picnic Pick-Ups

• Dean & Deluca

607 S. St. Helena Hwy., (707) 967-9980;
www.deandeluca.com. Daily 7:30-8.

A branch of the fabled Manhattan store in SoHo, this airy European-style market hall is impressively stocked and a gustatory delight. It is home to the Wine Country's largest cheese-aging room, and truffled butter and Devon cream are stocked along with hand-cut tortilla chips and fresh flowers. Choosing a picnic or take-home dinner from among the fresh breads, expansive array of deli items, and organic produce is a pleasure. Professional quality cookware is also for sale.

• The Model Bakery

1357 Main St., downtown, (707) 963-8192;
www.themodelbakery.com. Tu-Sat 7-6, Sun 7-4.

Among the great hand-formed breads baked in the 1920s-era brick-and-sand ovens here are pain de vin (whole-wheat sourdough made with a starter derived from Napa Valley grape yeasts), sour rye, crusty sourdough, and both sweet baguettes and rounds. Panini, mini-pizzas, and stuffed croissants make quick snacks, and old-fashioned cookies and biscotti are pleasing desserts. Coffee and espresso drinks are also available. Seating is provided for on-the-spot indulgence.

• Napa Valley Olive Oil Manufacturing Co.

835 Charter Oak Ave., (707) 963-4173. Daily 8-5; in summer to 5:30.

Everything needed for a picnic is available inside this 100-year-old barn: cheese, sausage, olives, bread sticks, focaccia, biscotti. This Old World-style Italian deli also offers a variety of pastas, sauces, and dried mushrooms, plus its own cold-pressed olive oil and homemade red wine vinegar—all placed helter-skelter in barrels and on makeshift tables. Tabs are tallied on the shopping bag, and a cigar box holds the receipts. It's really quite unusual. A shaded picnic area is provided outside.

Taylor's Automatic Refresher

933 Main St./Pope St., (707) 963-3486;
www.taylorsrefresher.com. Daily 10:30-9; $.

This 1940s drive-in diner serves juicy burgers, thick shakes made with Double Rainbow ice cream, housemade chili, hot dogs, various sandwiches and salads, and great french fries (don't miss the sweet potato fries dusted with chili spices). Seating is at umbrella-shaded outdoor picnic tables. Local wines and an assortment of draft beers are also available. A branch is in Napa (see page 421).

Terra

1345 Railroad Ave./Hunt St., downtown,
(707) 963-8931; www.terrarestaurant.com. D W-M;
$$$; closed first 2 wks. of Jan. Reservations advised.

Fronted by flower-filled planter boxes, this magical spot has a cave-like stone wall interior and offers a cool respite from the area's often warm weather. Creative dishes from owner-chef Hiro Sone combine the styles of France, northern Italy, and the Pacific Rim. They are unusual and flavorful and change periodically: radicchio salad tossed with a balsamic vinaigrette and plenty of Parmesan; broiled sake-marinated sea bass with shrimp dumplings in shiso broth; grilled salmon with red Thai curry sauce and basmati rice. Desserts can be wicked: rich, moist chocolate bread pudding with sun-dried cherries; chocolate truffle cake with espresso ice cream.

Tra Vigne
1050 Charter Oak Ave., (707) 963-4444; www.travigne restaurant.com. L-D daily; $$. Reservations advised.

Situated in a rustic stone building, this justly popular northern Italian restaurant features a stunning, wide-open, high-ceilinged room furnished with both comfortable tables and booths. Outside seating on a stone patio is inviting on warm days and evenings, when tiny lights twinkle in the mulberry trees. A round of crusty bread and olive oil for dipping are provided to enjoy while perusing the menu. Interesting housemade pastas and pizzas share the bill of fare with fresh fish, meats, and poultry, and it seems that nothing is not delicious. Antipasti items and daily specials are often intriguing, and desserts include such goodies as fresh fruit gelato and biscotti with sweet wine. Wine varietals are available by the glass and include both local and Italian selections.

Next door, **Merryvale Vineyards** *(1000 Main St., (800) 326-6069, (707) 963-7777; www.merryvale.com. Tasting daily 10-6:30; tour by appt.)* has made its home in the former Sunny St. Helena Winery—the first winery built in the Napa Valley after the repeal of Prohibition. A wine component tasting seminar is scheduled every Saturday and Sunday; reservations are necessary.

CALISTOGA

A LITTLE BACKGROUND

Calistoga sits on top of a hot underground river. Originally called "Indian Hot Springs," the town's current name is devised from a combination of California and Saratoga—a spa area in New York that was the inspiration for an early 25-cottage spa development by town founder Sam Brannan, California's first

millionaire. Two of those original town cottages remain. More of the town's history is waiting to be discovered in Robert Louis Stevenson's *The Silverado Squatters.* But when Stevenson quipped that "sightseeing is the art of disappointment," he simply couldn't have meant it to apply to this scenic area.

Calistoga is enjoying a renaissance as a popular weekend and summer retreat. Its many unpretentious spas help visitors relax, unwind, and get healthy in pools filled from hot springs. Most offer services such as mud baths, steam baths, and massages, and many make their mineral pools available for day use for a small fee.

While here, don't miss taking a mud bath, one of life's great experiences. The mud is prepared using a mixture of volcanic ash (collected from nearby Mount St. Helena), peat moss, and naturally heated mineral water. After a period of nude immersion, the bather takes a mineral bath and a steam bath, and then, swaddled in dry blankets, rests and cools. Ahhh. (A few notes: Pregnant women, people with high blood pressure or heart conditions, and children under 14 are cautioned against taking mud baths. Technicians are all licensed by the city. It's sanitary; after each use, tubs are flooded with 140-degree mineral water, the mud is turned, and new mud is added. To avoid cramping, don't eat for a while before or after.)

VISITOR INFORMATION

Calistoga Chamber of Commerce
1506 Lincoln Ave., downtown, (707) 942-6333; www.calistogafun.com.

GETTING THERE

Located approximately 10 miles north of St. Helena, and 25 miles north of Napa, via Highway 29.

WHAT TO DO

Bothe-Napa Valley State Park
3801 St. Helena Hwy. N., (707) 942-4575; www.parks.ca.gov. Daily 8-sunset. $6/vehicle. Pool: Daily 12-6, summer only; $3, 6-17 $1.

Swimming in the unheated pool is a favorite activity at this lovely park, but picnicking and hiking are also popular. Guided horseback rides and campsites are available.

Getaway Adventures/
Wine Country Bike Tours
1718 Michael Way, (800) 499-BIKE, (707) 568-3040;
www.getawayadventures.com. $149/1 day.

Guided bicycle trips visit several small
wineries and include a gourmet picnic lunch.
Overnight trips, complete with inn stays, are
also available, and airport transfer can be
arranged.

Old Faithful Geyser of California
1299 Tubbs Ln., (707) 942-6463;
www.oldfaithful geyser.com. Daily 9-5; in summer 9-6.
$8, 60+ $7, 6-12 $3.

Located in the crater of an extinct volcano,
this idyllic site is home to one of only three
geysers in the world that erupt regularly and
merit the name Old Faithful (the other two are
in Yellowstone National Park in Wyoming and
on North Island in New Zealand). The geyser
erupts approximately every 14 minutes, shooting scalding 350-degree water 60 feet into the
air. The show lasts from 3 to 4 minutes. Plenty
of picnic tables and a snack bar are available.

The Petrified Forest
4100 Petrified Forest Rd., 4 mi. W of town,
(707) 942-6667; www.petrifiedforest.org. Daily 10-5;
in summer to 7. $6, 60+ & 12-17 $5, 6-11 $3.

A self-guided ½-mile path leads through
this natural oddity, a forest that is home to the
world's largest petrified trees. An old-time
roadside attraction that has been open to the
public since 1870, it contains petrified redwood
trees that are more than 3 million years old and
as long as 126 feet. Facilities include a small
museum and picnic tables.

The Sharpsteen Museum
1311 Washington St., downtown, (707) 942-5911;
www.sharpsteen-museum.org. Daily 11-4. By donation,
$3, under 12 free.

Created by Ben Sharpsteen, a Walt Disney
Studio animator and Oscar-winning producer
(his Oscar is displayed here), this exceptionally
well-designed museum displays an elaborate
and extensive diorama of Calistoga as it
appeared in 1865 when Sam Brannan opened
the town's first spa and began its reputation as a
restorative resort area. A working model of the
Napa Valley Railroad is also displayed, and an
early kitchen, blacksmith shop, and stagecoach

round out the exhibits. The adjoining **Sam
Brannan Cottage**, one of the town's original 25,
is beautifully furnished and exemplifies the style
in which wealthy San Franciscans lived when
they vacationed here in the late 1800s.

Smith's Mount St. Helena Trout Farm
18401 Ida Clayton Rd., 14 mi. from town (call for
directions), (707) 987-3651. Sat-Sun 10-5; Mar-Sept
only. $1-$6.

All ages can enjoy fishing on this lake.
Poles and bait are free. Size determines the
charge for fish caught, and cleaning and pack-
aging are included.

WINERIES

Castello di Amorosa
4045 N. St. Helena Hwy., S of town, (707) 967-6276,
tour (707) 967-6272; www.castellodiamorosa.com.
Tasting 9:30-6, Dec-Jan 9:30-5; tour daily, must be
age 10+, reservations advised.

America's only authentically replicated
12th-century medieval Italian castle consists of
107 rooms on 7 levels, 95 of which are devoted
to wine making. Two-thirds of the castle is
underground, where wines are stored instead of
in caves. Reached by crossing an authentic
drawbridge, the castle has its own well, church,
and stables. "I just didn't know when to quit,"
says owner/winemaker Dario Sattui. "Instead
of going forward, I'm going backwards." The
walls in the great hall are covered with hand-
painted frescoes, and the castle boasts secret
passageways, a prison and dungeon torture
chamber, and, comfortingly, an escape tunnel.
Like many unusual facilities found at wineries,
it is the result of Sattui's passion for castles. And
melding it well with his other passion for wine
making, he produces here high-end wines from
primarily Italian grape varietals. A "Super
Tuscan" is among them—as is an "Il Barone"
reserve, their biggest red—and all wines are
available only on site. The tour includes a barrel
tasting and a sampling in a private tasting room.

Château Montelena Winery
1429 Tubbs Ln., (707) 942-5105; www.montelena.com.
Tasting daily 9:30-4; no tour.

Noted for its Chardonnay (which famously
won the 1976 Judgment of Paris tasting) and
Estate Cabernet Sauvignon, this castle-like

Castello di Amorosa

winery built of stone and carved into a hillside in 1882 can be difficult to find. Its Jade Lake has two islets reached via footbridge and is populated with ducks, swans, and geese. Picnicking is not permitted.

Clos Pegase

1060 Dunaweal Ln., (800) 366-8583, (707) 942-4981; www.clospegase.com. Tasting daily 10:30-5; tour at 11:30, 2.

This winery opened in 1987 amid much controversy. Even though its post-modern design by now famous Michael Graves was the winner in a contest sponsored by the San Francisco Museum of Modern Art, there were those who liked its stark stucco architecture and those who didn't. Surrounded by young vineyards, it has a surreal quality, with tall, thin cypress trees lining an outdoor walkway and modern sculpture—including pieces by Henry Moore and Richard Serra—dotting the landscape. Named after Pegasus, the winged horse of Greek mythology that gave birth to wine and art, the winery appropriately displays a collection of fine art within its caves. Among the treasure-trove dating from the 3rd century B.C. to the present are ancient vineyard tools and rare free-blown wine bottles, carafes, and glasses. An elaborate slide presentation that follows wine from the birth of the grape, through its celebration in art, and on into the present is sometimes scheduled. Picnic tables are sheltered by the shady canopy of a 300-year-old oak tree.

Frank Family Vineyards

1091 Larkmead Lane, (800) 574-9463, (707) 942-0859; www.frankfamilyvineyards.com. Tasting daily 10-5; tour Tu-Thur at 11, 1.

The massive stone edifice here was constructed in 1884 using native sandstone from the nearby hills and is on the National Register of Historic Places. Originally known as the Larkmead Winery, this winery produces small quantities and sells them only on site. Don't miss sampling the killer Zinfandel and Cabernet Sauvignons that pretty much explode on the palate, but the Chardonnay is darn good, too. The motto here is "Kiss French, Drink California," and photos of Marilyn Monroe hang in one of the tasting rooms in tribute to the fact that this was once a favorite retreat of hers. A further Hollywood connection is co-owner Rich Frank, who was once president of Disney Studios and who still is in The Business down south.

Hans Fahden Vineyards

4855 Petrified Forest Rd., (707) 942-6760; www.hansfahden.com. Tasting M-Thur 10-5, F-Sun 10-2; tour by appt.

Located on a ridge above town in the Mayacamus Mountains, this small family winery features extensive gardens, panoramic views of Mt. St. Helena, and volcanic ash wine caves—unusual in that they were dug in 1986 with a Welsh coal-mine machine and in that

Sterling Vineyards

nothing is sprayed over the interior walls. Elaborate gardens are filled with colorful blooms and feature four ponds accented with water lilies and reeds. Though there is only one picnic table (it has a spectacular view), benches abound, as do birds, bees, and bull frogs. Original owners Hans and Marie Fahden, who came here from Hamburg, Germany, purchased the property in 1912. They grew grapes until Prohibition, then prunes. Now the third generation is again growing grapes. The gold medal-winning winery produces only complex, earthy-tasting Cabernet Sauvignons and is perhaps most famous now for its weddings, which are scheduled outside of tasting times.

Schramsberg

1400 Schramsberg Rd., 4 mi. S of town, (800) 877-3623, (707) 942-4558; www.schramsberg.com. Tasting & tour by appt.

Established in 1862, this landmark winery is written about extensively by Robert Louis Stevenson in *The Silverado Squatters*. R.L.S., who called their wine "bottled poetry," was once a guest, as was Ambrose Bierce. Further recognition for its distinctive bottle-fermented sparkling wines made from hand-picked grapes came in 1972 when President Nixon and Premier Chou En-lai poured a bottle of Schramsberg Blanc de Blancs sparkling wine—the country's first commercial sparkling wine using Chardonnay—for the "Toast to Peace"

in Beijing. It is interesting to note that some of the winery buildings are constructed from redwoods grown on the property, and the Victorian house was built without nails by a shipmaker.

The informative tour goes through portions of the 2 miles of caves, taking in sections draped with ancient cobwebs and sometimes bumping into the famous "riddler," whose job it is to turn approximately 50,000 bottles each day (this is perhaps the *perfect* job for a compulsive-neurotic). After the tour, tasting occurs in a private room with participants seated at a glass table supported appropriately by an old riddling rack.

Sterling Vineyards

1111 Dunaweal Ln., (800) 726-6136, (707) 942-3345; www.sterlingvineyards.com. Tasting & self-guided tour daily 10:30-4:30.

Accessed via a 4-minute gondola ride, this winery was built to resemble a Greek monastery. It features stunning and unusual white stucco, cubist-style architecture. Spectacular views of the Napa Valley are provided throughout the self-guided tour. Tasters sit at tables either in a spacious interior room or on an outdoor terrace, and a picnic terrace with a magnificent view is also available. A package fee includes the gondola ride, the self-guided tour, and a taste of five wines (children get a juice drink).

WHERE TO STAY

Brannan Cottage Inn

109 Wapoo Ave., downtown, (707) 942-4200;
www.brannancottageinn.com. 6 rooms; $$. Unsuitable
for children under 12. Some TVs & fireplaces.
Full breakfast.

Located a pleasant 2-block walk from
town, this Greek Revival Victorian cottage built
by Sam Brannan in 1860 is listed on the
National Register of Historic Places. It is the
only original Brannan resort cottage that
remains in its original location. A large palm
tree planted by Brannan, and mentioned by
Robert Louis Stevenson in *The Silverado
Squatters*, still grows in the garden. Rooms are
named after colors and most open onto a quiet
courtyard, where breakfast is served in warm
weather. Complimentary access is provided to a
nearby mineral springs resort with hot tubs and
a swimming pool.

Calistoga Spa Hot Springs

1006 Washington St., downtown, (866) 822-5772,
(707) 942-6269; www.calistogaspa.com. 57 units; $$.
All kitchens. 4 hot spring pools; fitness room.
No pets.

This conveniently located, unpretentious,
and particularly family-friendly spa offers motel
rooms that open onto the pool area. Four
outdoor mineral water pools are available:
an 83-degree lap pool, a 90-degree children's
wading pool, a 100-degree soaking pool, and a
105-degree covered hot tub. Mud baths, mineral
baths, steam baths, and massage are available.
Non-guests can also use the facilities *(Daily
8:30am-9pm. $15-$20.).*

Chanric Inn

1805 Foothill Blvd. (Hwy. 128), (877) 281-3671,
(707) 942-4535; www.thechanric.com. 6 rooms;
$$-$$$+. Unsuitable for chidren. No TVs.
Solar-heated pool; hot tub. Full breakfast.

This 1875 Victorian is stylishly updated
with a contemporary interior of hardwood
floors, walls colored in muted shades of beige
and brown, and sleek black furniture. Large
orchids punctuate the decor. A relaxing afternoon on the expansive pool deck with a view of
the Palisades Mountains is a must. Cold beverages are always available in a large communal
area. Co-owner Ric Pielstick, who is culinary
school trained, prepares and serves a top tier
three-course brunch. Guest are seated outside
by a grapevine hedge in good weather.

Cottage Grove Inn

1711 Lincoln Ave., downtown, (800) 799-2284, (707) 942-8400; www.cottagegrove.com. 16 cabins; $$$-$$$+. Unsuitable for children under 12. All wood-burning fireplaces. Afternoon snack; continental breakfast. No pets.

Nestled in a historic elm grove, each of these individual cottages is decorated in a different theme. All are equipped with a deep whirlpool soaking tub for two and a refrigerator.

Dr. Wilkinson's Hot Springs Resort

1507 Lincoln Ave., downtown, (707) 942-4102; www.drwilkinson.com. 42 rooms; $$-$$$. Some kitchens. 1 indoor & 2 outdoor mineral pools; steam room; full-service spa.

This long-time spa features a 104-degree indoor mineral pool with a view of the nearby foothills, a cooler 92-degree outdoor mineral pool, and a refreshing 82-degree outdoor swimming pool. Though the pools are not open to non-guests, the mud baths, mineral baths, steam baths, massage, and separate facial salon are. Lodging is in fluffed-up motel units as well as in nearby cottages and a Victorian.

Indian Springs

1712 Lincoln Ave., downtown, (707) 942-4913; www.indianspringscalistoga.com. 41 units; $$-$$$+. All kitchens; some gas fireplaces. Mineral pool; full-service spa; 1 clay tennis court. No pets.

Dating back to 1910 and erected on the site of the town's first spa (built in 1860 by Sam Brannan), this resort is where Robert Louis Stevenson vacationed in 1880 and wrote part of The Silverado Squatters. It is the state's oldest continuously operating thermal pool and spa facility. Its Mission-style, Olympic-size swimming pool is filled with 90to 102-degree geyser mineral water, and this is the only spa in town offering all-ash mud baths. Lodging is in nicely refurbished 1940s housekeeping bungalows and in a lodge, and croquet and other lawn games are available on the large palm tree-studded lawn. The pool is not open to non-guests.

Mountain Home Ranch

3400 Mountain Home Ranch Rd., 6 mi. from town, (707) 942-6616; www.mountainhomeranch.com. 23 units; $-$$; closed Dec-Jan. No TVs; some kitchens & wood-burning fireplaces & stoves; some shared baths. 1 heated & 1 unheated pool; 1 tennis court. Full breakfast.

Guests at this informal rural spot can stay in modern cabins with a private deck or porch, in lodge rooms, or in rustic cabins (summer only). Summer activities include lake swimming, hiking, and fishing.

Mount View Hotel & Spa

1457 Lincoln Ave., downtown, (800) 816-6877, (707) 942-6877; www.mountviewhotel.com. 32 units; $$-$$$+. Unsuitable for children under 16. Heated pool; hot tub; full-service spa. Continental breakfast; 2 restaurants. No pets.

Built in 1918 and furnished with an eclectic mix of contemporary and antique pieces, this beautifully restored grand hotel is a National Historic Landmark. Nine theme suites are furnished with period pieces—two in art deco style—and three private cottages have their own decks and hot tubs. Breakfast is delivered to the room.

Off the lobby, JoLe ((707) 942-5938; www.jolerestaurant.com. Reservations advised.) specializes in small plates. In a cool dark room decorated with black wood and cinnamon accents, it has comfy wall banquettes as well as high seats at a prep bar by the wood-burning oven that are perfect for solo diners. Soups—roasted eggplant, cold cucumber topped with crab—and desserts—deep dish peach pie with a flaky top crust—can be spectacular. Indeed, most dishes are full flavored and well executed. The all-organic menu changes regularly.

The Pink Mansion

1415 Foothill Blvd. (Hwy. 128), (800) 238-PINK, (707) 942-0558; www.pinkmansion.com. 6 rooms; $$$-$$$+. Some fireplaces. Indoor heated pool & hot tub. Afternoon snack; full breakfast.

Nestled against a hillside on the outskirts of town, this restored 1875 Victorian mansion is painted a pleasant shade of pink. A large front porch equipped with a couch swing invites leisurely contemplation of the surroundings, and the indoor pool and hot tub provide a relaxing view of a redwood grove behind the house. Several rooms have clawfoot tubs, and a lavish breakfast is served in the elegant dining room.

WHERE TO EAT

All Seasons Cafe & Wine Shop

1400 Lincoln Ave., downtown, (707) 942-9111; www.allseasonsnapavalley.net. L F-Sun, D Tu-Sun; $$-$$$. Reservations advised.

Dress is very casual in this narrow dining room, and children are welcome and accommodated. One dinner enjoyed here began with great housemade bread and a flawless warm spinach salad prepared with pancetta, house-smoked chicken, and Feta cheese. It was followed by a perfectly roasted chicken accompanied by perfectly roasted potatoes, whole cloves of garlic, artichokes, and olives. Dessert was a memorable fresh cherry cobbler with housemade vanilla ice cream arranged artistically on a plate strewn with flower petals.

Calistoga Inn

1250 Lincoln Ave., downtown, (707) 942-4101; www.napabeer.com. L-D daily. Sat-SunBr; $-$$. Reservations advised.

Since a delightful collection of turkey platters decorates the walls here, it isn't too much of a surprise that the house specialty is big portions of old-fashioned hardwood-grilled meats

and vegetables. Fresh fish and 40-clove garlic chicken are also on the menu, and irresistible down-home desserts include both creamy peanut butter pie and housemade brownies "smushed" with vanilla ice cream and topped with hot fudge. In warm weather, diners are seated outside on a patio overlooking the Napa Valley River.

An informal **brewpub** operating in a cozy old-time bar area offers four house brews—one of them is a Pilsner-style lager (the house specialty)—and inexpensive pub food such as housemade potato chips, a variety of salads, a good hamburger, and jerk chicken.

Modest **lodging** *(18 rooms; $. All shared baths. Continental breakfast. No pets.)* is available upstairs in cozy, pleasant rooms equipped with sinks. Several sets of adjoining rooms are suitable for families.

THE SILVERADO TRAIL

A LITTLE BACKGROUND

Stretching approximately 30 miles from Napa to Calistoga, this scenic route offers a quieter, less-crowded wine tasting experience.

GETTING THERE

Located 50 miles northeast of San Francisco. Take I-880 north to Highway 29 north to Napa. Turn right on Trancas Street. After about 10 minutes, turn left at the sign onto the Silverado Trail.

WHAT TO DO

Lake Berryessa

From Napa take Hwy. 128 E, (707) 966-2111; www.usbr.gov/mp/berryessa/facts.html. Park: Daily sunrise-sunset. Visitor Center: Sat-Sun 10-4. Free.

This man-made lake is 26 miles long, 3 miles wide, and has 165 miles of shoreline. Boats and water-skis can be rented, and the swimming and fishing are excellent. Camping and lodging facilities—including houseboats—are available. A three-arch stone bridge is beneath the lake; it is the largest one west of Rockies and is all that remains of the city of Monticello that was flooded over to make the lake.

WINERIES

Jarvis Winery
2970 Monticello Rd., in Napa, 10 mi. E of town, (800) 255-5280, (707) 255-5280; www.jarviswines.com. Tasting & tour daily by appt.

Located on 1,300 acres in the scenic Mt. George area, this is the first Napa winery entirely inside a cave. The owners, who bought the property on a weekend getaway, didn't want to spoil its beauty and so cleverly hid the winery away in a 45,000-square-foot cave. Visitors park out in a meadow and walk in. Tour highlights include passing natural springs reformed into gurgling streams and cascading waterfalls; visiting the Crystal Chamber, a room with a floor of polished Brazilian granite and an impressive collection of huge purple amethysts from Brazil; and viewing the whimsical use of fiber optics throughout. Delicious wines await sampling in an elegant tasting room appointed with red velvet chairs and a red marble table; it is entered by crossing a stream on stepping stones. Good news for those who suffer from wine headaches—the winery uses minimal sulfites. And many Jarvis wines are available in half bottles.

Mumm Napa
8445 Silverado Trail, in Rutherford, (707) 967-7700; http://mummnapa.com. Tasting daily 10-5; tours 10-3, on the hr.

In good weather, tasters can sample sparkling wines while sitting under umbrellas on a patio with a magnificent view of the valley's vineyards. The winery's art galleries feature changing exhibits of fine photography as well as a permanent exhibit of Ansel Adams photographs.

Nichelini Winery
2950 Sage Canyon Rd. (Hwy. 128), 11 mi. E of Silverado Trail, in St. Helena, (800) WE-TASTE, (707) 963-0717; www.nicheliniwinery.com. Tasting Sat-Sun 10-5; self-guided tour.

Established in 1890, this historic stone winery with an outdoor tasting bar is in a gorgeous, out-of-the-way location well off the main drag and down a rural side road leading to Lake Berryessa. Pack a picnic to enjoy at tables sheltered by old, old trees, and allow some time for the seasonal bocce ball court.

Operated now by four of founder Anton Nichelini's grandchildren, it is the oldest continuously owned family winery in Napa Valley. The winery produces great Zinfandels using vines planted long, long ago by the elder Nichelini.

Pine Ridge Winery
5901 Silverado Trail, in Napa, (800) 486-0503, (707) 253-7500; www.pineridgewinery.com. Tasting daily 10:30-4:30; tour by appt.

This tasting room is a pleasant place to sample the premium Cabernets produced by this winery's Stags Leap District grapes. On tours, participants tote along tasting glasses for barrel samplings. Less time is spent among the stainless-steel tanks and barrels in the extensive caves and more time outside in the vineyard (the Demonstration Vineyard is always available for strolling).

Rutherford Hill Winery
200 Rutherford Hill Dr., in Rutherford, (800) MERLOT-1, (707) 963-1871; www.rutherfordhill.com. Tasting daily 10-5; tour at 11:30, 1:30, 3:30.

Visitors pass through massive 15-foot-tall doors as they enter the tasting room here. The tour includes viewing the most extensive wine-aging cave system in the U.S. Across the street from the tasting room, a sylvan hillside picnic area beckons with spacious tables sheltered by old oaks and a pleasant view of the valley.

WHERE TO STAY

Auberge du Soleil
180 Rutherford Hill Rd., in Rutherford, (800) 348-5406, (707) 963-1211; www.aubergedusoleil.com. 50 rooms; $$$+. All fireplaces. Heated pool (seasonal); hot tub; steam rooms; full-service spa; fitness room; 1 tennis court. Unsuitable for children under 16. Restaurant; room service. No pets.

With a name meaning literally "inn of the sun," this upscale Mediterranean-style bungalow village cascades down a peaceful wooded hillside that spreads over the 33-acre property. Each room in the four-unit cottages has a private deck (most with a panoramic view of the valley), a wood-burning fireplace, and an oversize bathtub big enough for two. Rooms are stocked with fresh fruit and snacks, and beds are made with Italian linens.

Paths crisscross the property, passing through a 5-acre **Olive Grove Sculpture Garden** featuring works by California sculptors; all pieces are for sale.

The inn's elegant French **restaurant** *(B-L-D daily; $$$-$$$+. Reservations required. Free valet parking.)* has plush indoor seating as well as more rustic, but very desirable, outside seating on a heated terrace with sweeping views of the valley. Menu items are sumptuous and full-flavored, and desserts are not boring.

Meadowood Napa Valley

900 Meadowood Ln., in St. Helena, (800) 458-8080, (707) 963-3646; www.meadowood.com. 85 units; $$$+. Some kitchens & fireplaces. 2 heated pools; 2 hot tubs; fitness room; full-service spa; 7 tennis courts (fee); 9-hole golf course. 2 restaurants; room service.

This luxury resort allows guests an escape from reality. Contemporary cottages with skylights and old-fashioned porches dot the secluded property, providing plenty of privacy, and room service will deliver a breakfast basket to the door. Facilities on the 250 acres of lush wooded grounds include a family pool, two regulation English croquet lawns, and 4½ miles of hiking trails. Bike rentals are also available.

The Restaurant at Meadowood *(D daily, SunBr; $$$. Reservations advised.)* complements its refined menu with an extensive Napa Valley wine list that is said to be the most comprehensive selection in the world. Downstairs, the slightly less formal **Grill** *(B-L-D daily; $$$.)* serves delicious California bistro fare and features a terrace overlooking the green, green golf course.

Silverado Resort

1600 Atlas Peak Rd., in Napa, 1 mi. NE of town, (800) 532-0500, (707) 257-0200; www.silveradoresort.com. 280 units; $$-$$$+. All kitchens & wood-burning fireplaces. 1 heated pool, 8 unheated pools; hot tub; sauna; fitness room; full-service spa; 17 tennis courts (fee); 2 18-hole golf courses. 2 restaurants; room service.

Once part of General Vallejo's Rancho Yajome (he gave the property to his daughter as a wedding gift), this 1,200-acre resort has the largest tennis complex in Napa Valley. Its heart is a gracious 1875 mansion, where guests are greeted and registered and within which are the resort's two restaurants. Accommodations are in individually owned condominiums, and the location, architectural style, and decor of each vary. Some units are available on the grounds adjacent to the mansion, allowing an easy walk to most of the facilities, while larger condos— some open right onto the golf course—are farther away and require a 1 or 2-mile drive. Facilities include jogging trails, bicycle rentals, and two golf courses designed by Robert Trent Jones, Jr.

The 16,000-square-foot spa is fashioned after a classic Roman bath and is the largest spa facility in the Wine Country. It has a couples massage room with skylight and fireplace and is equipped with saunas, steam baths, whirlpool tubs, a heated pool, a fitness center, and a snack bar.

The **Royal Oak** *(D W-Sun; $$$. Reservations required.)* serves mesquite-grilled steaks and seafood, while the more casual **Grill at Silverado** *(B-L-D daily; $$.)* serves casual fare and offers a soothing view of the golf course.

Silver Rose Inn & Spa

351 Rosedale Rd., in Calistoga, (800) 995-9381, (707) 942-9581; www.silverrose.com. 20 rooms; $$-$$$+. No TVs; some fireplaces. 1 hot spring pool; 1 hot tub; full-service spa; putting green. Continental breakfast. No pets.

Sitting amid acres of vineyards and mountains, this peaceful enclave provides serene views. Architecture is contemporary, with massive stone fireplaces and rustic beams in the public rooms. Many rooms feature up-close vineyard-side views and in-room whirlpool tubs for two. The property's original building, the Inn on the Knoll, has an impressive public room and is just a few steps from the spa. The large pool is shaped like a wine bottle, and the pool, hot tub, and spa tubs are all fed by underground hot springs.

Silver Rose Cellars *(Tasting Thur-M 10-5; no tour.)* is also on the property.

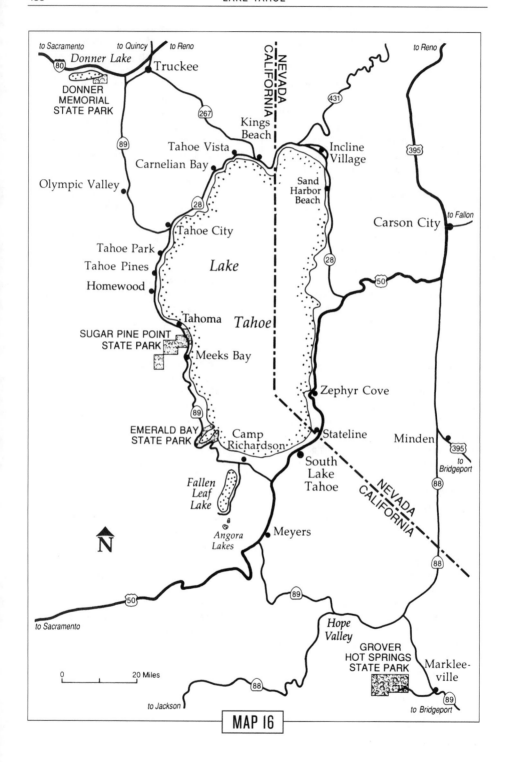

MAP 16

SOUTH LAKE TAHOE

A LITTLE BACKGROUND

*. . . At last the Lake burst upon us—a noble sheet
of blue water lifted six thousand three hundred
feet above the level of the sea, and walled in by a
rim of snowclad mountain peaks that towered
aloft full three thousand feet higher still!*

*It was a vast oval. As it lay there with the
shadows of the great mountains brilliantly
photographed upon its surface, I thought it must
surely be the fairest picture the whole earth
affords . . .*

—Mark Twain

Lake Tahoe lies two-thirds in California and
one-third in Nevada. It is the largest (192-
square-miles surface) and deepest (1,645 feet)
alpine lake in North America and the third
largest in the world. At 6,227 feet above sea
level, its crystal-clear, deep-blue summer
waters provide a striking contrast with the
extensive green forests and majestic mountains
encircling it.

Once a remote area, Tahoe is now a popular and well-equipped vacation destination
offering a wide range of recreational activities
along with its spectacular scenery. Swimming,
hiking, boating, tennis, golf, bicycling, horseback riding, river rafting, camping, fishing,
water-skiing, and backpacking are among the
summer outdoor activities to be enjoyed. In
winter, the skiing is excellent.

On the Nevada side, gambling is another
big attraction. A lodging shuttle service provides
transportation to the casinos, and some lodgings have discount casino coupons for their
guests. In addition, the casinos offer on-demand
pick-up shuttle service from most lodgings.

Children may go into a casino with adults
but are not allowed to "loiter" (not even babies
in backpacks!) or play the slot machines.
Fortunately, childcare is relatively easy to find in
this area. Many lodgings maintain a list of local
sitters, and childcare centers that take drop-ins
are listed in the Yellow Pages. Also, the Lake
Tahoe Visitors Authority provides a free list of
day care providers.

In addition to having more slot machines
than any other casino at Lake Tahoe, Harrah's
has an unsupervised **Arcade** for children
*((800) 648-3773. M-Thur 12-8, F 12-10, Sat 10-
10, Sun 10-8. Admission free.)* that is equipped
with the latest video and arcade games, as well
as some old classics, and is a safe, well-lighted,
smokeand alcohol-free environment. Sure beats
sitting on the curb reading comic books like
some people did when they were kids.

VISITOR INFORMATION

All addresses in this section are in the city of South Lake Tahoe unless otherwise noted.

Lake Tahoe Visitors Authority
169 Hwy. 50; (800) AT-TAHOE (lodging reservations referral service); (775) 588-5900; www.bluelaketahoe.com.

GETTING THERE

Located approximately 200 miles north of San Francisco. Take Highway 80 to Highway 50 to the lake.

STOPS ALONG THE WAY

I-80 North
See pages 278 through 310.

Folsom
See pages 363 through 365.

Poor Red's
See page 362.

Placerville
See pages 362 through 363.

ANNUAL EVENTS

Lights on the Lake
July 4; (530) 544-5050. Free.
This spectacular show is the largest and best synchronized fireworks display west of the Mississippi. Each shell is choreographed and computer-synchronized to a radio broadcast soundtrack. More than 100,000 people watch it each year.

Fall colors
October.
The area around Kirkwood Mountain Resort (see page 459) is home to groves of aspen. Hope Valley, north of Kirkwood on Highway 89, is particularly colorful.

WHAT TO DO

Angora Lakes Trail
On Spring Creek Rd., off Hwy. 89.

Take the road to Fallen Leaf Lake, which passes a waterfall, and then turn left at the sign to Angora Lakes. It is an easy ½-mile hike from the end of the road to the lakes, where quiet picnic and swimming spots await.

Around the lake
• By car
A leisurely drive around the 72-mile perimeter of Lake Tahoe takes about 3 hours, but allow all day. Tempting places to stop for picnicking, swimming, and exploring abound.

• On foot
(775) 298-0012; www.tahoerimtrail.org.
The well-marked 165-mile **Tahoe Rim Trail** circles the lake in the surrounding mountain tops and passes through part of Desolation Wilderness. It has nine trailheads, is designed for both day trekkers and overnight hikers, and a 1½-mile section is wheelchair accessible.

Beaches and biking
• Pope Beach and **Baldwin Beach**
On Hwy. 89, between the Y & Emerald Bay, (530) 544-5994; www.fs.fed.us/r5/ltbmu/recreation/beaches. Daily 8-sunset; closed in winter. $5/vehicle.

M.S. Dixie & Tahoe Queen

These beaches are primo. This same stretch of highway has several bike rental facilities and a nice bike trail.

Boat rentals

• Tahoe Sports
(888) 542-2111, (530) 542-2111; www.tahoesports.com.

With seven locations, this is the largest rental company in the area. Everything from powerboats and personal watercraft to skis and snowboards are available.

Boat tours

• Lake Tahoe Cruises
900 Ski Run Blvd., (800) 23-TAHOE, (530) 543-6191; www.zephyrcove.com. Basic cruise: $41+, 3-11 $20+; parking $8. Reservations advised.

• M.S. Dixie II
760 Hwy. 50, in Zephyr Cove, Nevada, 4 mi. N of Stateline. Schedule varies; May-Oct only.

A replica of a cotton barge used on the Mississippi River in the 1920s, this three-deck paddle wheel steamer cruises to Emerald Bay. She is the largest boat on the lake and boasts a glass-bottom viewing window. Dinner cruises with live music for dancing and breakfast/ brunch cruises are available at additional charge.

• Tahoe Queen
900 Ski Run Blvd. Schedule varies.

This slightly smaller paddle wheeler also cruises to Emerald Bay and also has a large window in its floor for underwater viewing.

• Woodwind II
760 Hwy. 50, in Zephyr Cove, Nevada, (888) 867-6394, (775) 588-3000; www.sailwoodwind.com. Schedule varies; Apr-Oct only. $32, 60+ $28, 3-12 $15. Reservations advised.

Only 35 passengers fit on this 55-foot catamaran with two underwater observation windows. The basic cruise sails the west shore. More expensive and extensive tours are available, including one to Thunderbird Lodge Historic Site.

Camp Richardson Corral and Pack Station
On Hwy. 89 N., (530) 541-3113. Daily; schedule varies; June-Sept only. Guided rides $35/hr. Must be age 6+. Reservations required.

Operated by the same family since 1934, this stables has breakfast rides *($50)*, dinner rides *($70)*, and wagon rides *($25, under 3 free)*. Fishing trips, overnight pack trips, and spot pack trips can be arranged, and sleigh rides are available December through March when there is enough snow.

Casino showrooms

Big name entertainment is always booked into these showrooms. Call ahead for reservations at the early or late cocktail shows. Seats are assigned. Children 6 and older are usually admitted, but it depends on the show's content.

• Harrah's South Shore Room

(800) HARRAHS, (800) 786-8208, (775) 588-6611; www.southshoreroom.com.

• Harveys Cabaret

(800) HARVEYS, (775) 588-2411; www.totalrewardstahoe.com. No smoking.

Holding just 288 seats, this is said to be the only mini-showroom in the world. There are no bad seats.

• Horizon Golden Cabaret

(800) 648-3322, (775) 588-6211; www.horizoncasino.com.

Another entertainment option here is the **Stadium Cinemas**, where eight screens show first-run movies.

• MontBleu Theatre

(888) 829-7630, (775) 588-3515; www.montbleuresort.com.

Gondola at Heavenly

Hwy. 50/Park Ave., (800) HEAVENLY, (775) 586-7000; www.skiheavenly.com. Schedule varies. $30, 13-18 & 65+ $26, 5-12 $20.

These eight-passenger gondolas take 12 minutes to climb 2.4 miles up Monument Peak to an observation deck that is 3,000 feet above lake level—and more than 9,000 feet above sea level—on the California side. Views are magnificent. The first stop features a viewing deck with telescopes and picnic tables, plus an assortment of dining venues and shops. Farther up, at the second and last stop, are hiking trails and **Adventure Peak Grill**, which serves mountain barbecue.

Grover Hot Springs State Park

3415 Hot Springs Rd., 4 mi. E of Markleeville, 35 mi. SE of town, (530) 694-2248; www.parks.ca.gov. Daily 11-8 in summer; schedule varies rest of year. $5, under 17 $2.

Beautifully situated in a valley meadow ringed by pine-covered slopes, this hot springs park features a 3-foot deep, 104-degree mineral pool filled by six nonsulfurous springs,

and a 70- to 80-degree fresh-water pool. The pools are well maintained, and lifeguards are on duty. The number of bathers permitted is limited so sometimes there is a wait, and swimsuits are always required. Short hiking trails, picnic facilities, and campsites are also available. In winter, this is a popular après-ski destination.

Lake Tahoe Historical Society Museum

3058 Lake Tahoe Blvd. (Hwy. 50), (530) 541-5458. Thur-M 10-3, summer only. $2, under 13 $1.

The history of Lake Tahoe's south shore is chronicled here.

Magic Carpet Golf

2455 Lake Tahoe Blvd. (Hwy. 50), (530) 541-3787. Daily in summer; as weather permits in winter.

This is the kind of colorful miniature course that has giant plaster dinosaurs and a new theme at each hole. Choose from either 19- or 28-hole rounds.

Tahoe Trout Farm

1023 Blue Lake Ave., off Hwy. 50, (530) 541-1491. Daily 10-5; June-Aug only. Charge determined by size of fish caught.

Though there is, of course, no challenge to catching trout here, there are some compelling reasons to give it a try: No license in required; bait and tackle are furnished free; and there is no limit. Anglers are almost guaranteed to go home with tasty dinner fare. Even young children, who frustrate easily, will probably succeed in catching a fish. (But do bear in mind that some children are appalled at just the *idea* of catching a fish—let alone actually *eating* it.)

Tallac Historic Site

Off Hwy. 89, 3 mi. W of Hwy. 50, (530) 541-5227; www.tahoeheritage.org. Daily dawn-dusk; museum: Daily 10-4, summer only. Free.

Composed of three early-20th-century summer estates, this 74-acre site is crisscrossed with fragrant, pine needle-littered paths leading to themed outbuildings—a laundry, a dairy, a boathouse—and to an arboretum. House tours are sometimes available for a fee. Picnic tables and barbecues are provided, and beautiful sandy beaches invite exploration. Cultural and historical programs, including afternoon teas

Tallac Historic Site

and special children's activities, are sometimes scheduled.

A **Great Gatsby Festival** occurs here each August. Celebrating the area's partying past, this festival brings history to life with era arts and crafts demonstrations, plus some old-fashioned fun and games.

Taylor Creek Visitor Center
Off Hwy. 89, 4 mi. W of Hwy. 50, (530) 543-2674; www.fs.fed.us/r5/ltbmu/recreation/visitor-center. Daily 8-5:30; closed Nov-May. Free.

Taylor Creek Stream Profile Chamber

Interpretive programs and guided nature walks are scheduled regularly. Self-guided trails include Smokey's Trail, which teaches kids about campfire safety, and the Lake of the Sky Trail, which leads to the lake's shore. Rainbow Trail winds through a meadow, past Taylor Creek, and on to the Stream Profile Chamber—where the life in a real mountain stream is viewed from underwater.

Visit in October to see the annual run of the Kokanee salmon and to take part in the annual **Kokanee Salmon Festival**.

Vikingsholm
On Hwy. 89, in Tahoma, (530) 525-7277; www.vikingsholm.com. Tours daily 10-4; closed Oct-May. $5, 6-17 $3.

Butterflies, waterfalls, and wildflowers are encountered on the steep 1-mile trail that descends to this magnificent 39-room, sod-roof Swedish castle home built in 1928. Constructed completely by hand using native materials, it was completed in one summer. Baby strollers are not permitted on the tour. The house is part of **Emerald Bay State Park** *((530) 541-3030; www.parks.ca.gov.).* Picnic tables are available, and swimming is permitted in an area with a sandy beach.

Vikingsholm

Winter activities
See pages 459 through 460.

WHERE TO STAY
LAKEFRONT

Best Western Timber Cove Lodge Marina Resort
3411 Lake Tahoe Blvd. (Hwy. 50), (800) 972-8558, (530) 541-6722; www.timbercovetahoe.com. 262 rooms; $-$$$. Heated pool (year-round); hot tub; fitness room. Continental breakfast; 2 restaurants; room service.

This well-situated motel has a private beach, full marina, and pier, and many of the rooms have lake views.

Historic Camp Richardson Resort
1900 Jameson Beach Rd., off Hwy. 89, 2½ mi. W of Hwy. 50, (800) 544-1801, (530) 541-1801; www.camp richardson.com. 37 rooms, 42 cabins (1-wk. min.); $$. Some TVs & kitchens. Continental breakfast; restaurant. Parking $5. No pets. Day use $7/vehicle.

Spread over 150 lake-side acres leased from the U.S. Forest Service, this complex exudes a nostalgic 1930s Old Tahoe charm. Lodging is in

a historic hotel, a beach motel, and rustic cabins spread amid tall pines. An inexpensive Kid's Kamp operates in summer for ages 5 through 15 (children must be accompanied by an adult), and woodsy campsites are also available. It is home to the longest floating pier on the lake and rents boats, kayaks, and more.

The lakeside **Beacon Bar & Grill** is famous for its Rum Runner drink, and in summer, the **Ice Cream Parlor**, which is across the highway, is *the* place to cool off.

In winter, this is the only place where people can ski along the lake's shoreline on groomed and marked cross-country ski trails. Lessons and rentals are available. A horse-drawn sleigh can be hired to deliver sledders to the resort's hill, and cross-country and snowshoe bonfire parties are held on Friday nights.

Inn By the Lake
3300 Lake Tahoe Blvd. (Hwy. 50), (800) 877-1466, (530) 542-0330; www.innbythelake.com. 100 rooms; $$-$$$+. Some kitchens; 1 wood-burning fireplace. Heated pool; hot tub, sauna. Continental breakfast.

Located in a grove of pine trees across the street from the lake, this attractive contemporary hotel offers comfortable, quiet accommodations.

Royal Valhalla on the Lake
4104 Lakeshore Blvd., (800) 999-4104, (530) 544-2233; www.tahoeroyalvalhalla.com. 80 units; $$. Some kitchens. Heated pool (seasonal); hot tub. Continental breakfast. No pets.

Pick from one-, two-, or three-bedroom units, many of which have a lake view and balcony. Guests have use of a private beach, and the lodge is within walking distance of the casinos.

Tahoe Beach & Ski Club
3601 Lake Tahoe Blvd. (Hwy.50), 1 mi. S of casinos, (530) 541-6220; www.tahoebeachandski.com. 128 rooms; $$-$$$+. All kitchens. Heated pool; 2 hot tubs; 2 saunas; fitness room; 1 tennis court. Restaurant. No pets.

This lakeside hotel has 400 feet of private beach with volleyball and horseshoe courts. It also offers an on-site activities program for the entire family and a game room with a pool table.

A **Marie Callenders** restaurant is just next door.

Tahoe Lakeshore Lodge & Spa

930 Bal Bijou, 1 mi. S of casinos, (800) 448-4577, (530) 541-2180; www.tahoelakeshorelodge.com. 45 rooms, 23 condos; $-$$$+. Some kitchens; wood-burning & gas fireplaces. Heated pool (seasonal); hot tub; sauna; spa. Continental breakfast. No pets.

This simple, comfortable motel is right on the sand, and every room has a lake view, fireplace, and chunky lodge-pine furnishings. Each room also has a private patio or balcony overlooking the property's 500-foot-long stretch of private beach. Condominiums are adjacent.

WHERE TO STAY
CASINOS

The major casinos offer large numbers of luxury hotel rooms.

• **Harrah's Lake Tahoe Casino & Hotel**
(800) 648-3773; www.harrahs.com/our_casinos/ tah. $$-$$$+.

• **Harveys Lake Tahoe Casino & Resort**
(800) HARVEYS, (775) 588-2411; www.totalrewardstahoe.com.

• **Horizon Casino Resort Lake Tahoe**
(800) 648-3322, (775) 588-6211; www.horizoncasino.com/main.php.

• **MontBleu Resort Casino & Spa**
55 Hwy. 50, (800) 648-3322, (775) 586-3515; www.montbleuresort.com.

WHERE TO STAY
CONDOS AND HOMES

Lakeland Village
Beach and Mountain Resort

3535 Lake Tahoe Blvd. (Hwy. 50), (800) 822-5969, (800) 646-2779, (530) 544-1685; www.lakeland-village.com. 207 units; $-$$$+. All kitchens & wood-burning or gas fireplaces. 2 heated pools (1 seasonal); children's wading pool (seasonal); 2 hot tubs; sauna; fitness room; 2 tennis courts (fee).

Though located beside a bustling highway, this condominium complex manages to retain a secluded, restive atmosphere. Some units are lakefront; all are within a short walk. Amenities include a private beach, a children's playground, paddleboat rentals, and a free shuttle to the casinos.

Rental agencies

These services rent privately owned condominiums, cabins, and houses. The rate is determined by the number of bedrooms and type of accommodation, plus cleaning fee and tax.

• **Accommodation Station**
(800) 344-9364, (530) 542-5850; www.tahoelodging.com. 85+ units; $$-$$$+. All kitchens & fireplaces.

• **Lake Tahoe Accommodations**
(800) 544-3234; www.tahoeaccommodations.com. 400+ units; $$-$$$+.

WHERE TO STAY
OTHER

Embassy Suites Lake Tahoe
Hotel & Ski Resort

4130 Lake Tahoe Blvd. (Hwy. 50), (877) 497-8483, (800) EMBASSY, (530) 544-5400; www.embassy tahoe.com. 9 stories; 400 rooms; $$-$$$+. Indoor heated pool; hot tub; sauna; steam room; fitness room. Evening cocktails; full breakfast; 3 restaurants; room service. No pets. Valet parking $20.

This link in the popular Embassy Suites chain features a nightclub and a 7-story-tall indoor atrium with waterfalls. Winter amenities include on-site ski rental, repair, and storage, plus next-day lift ticket sales and a complimentary shuttle to the Heavenly Mountain ski area. And, as an ad for the hotel declares, ". . . you don't have to gamble to get a free breakfast and free drinks": An all-you-can-eat breakfast and evening cocktails are complimentary to guests. But for those who *do* want to gamble, Harrah's is right next door.

Tahoe Seasons Resort

3901 Saddle Rd., (800) 540-4874, (530) 541-6700; www.tahoeseasons.com. 8 stories; 183 units; $$-$$$$+. Some gas fireplaces. Heated pool; hot tub; tennis court (seasonal). Restaurant; room service. No pets. Free valet parking.

Each unit here is a spacious suite equipped with a microwave and refrigerator as well as an oversize whirlpool bathtub big enough for two. And since it is located across the street from the Heavenly Valley ski area, skiers who stay here can just walk there in the morning. No chains. No parking hassles. But if someone in the party doesn't want to ski, it's possible to get a room with a view of the slopes so they can stay cozy in front of a fireplace and just watch. The resort also provides on-site ski rentals and both chain installation and removal services.

Motel Row

Highway 50 into town is lined with motels. However, this might be changing. South Lake Tahoe's redevelopment plan, which focuses on upgrading rather than expanding, dictates that for every new hotel room built, 1.31 old rooms must be removed.

WHERE TO STAY
FARTHER AWAY

Sorensen's Resort

See page 459.

Zephyr Cove Resort

760 Hwy. 50, in Zephyr Cove, Nevada, 4 mi. N of Stateline, (800) 23-TAHOE, (775) 589-4907, (775) 588-6644; www.zephyrcove.com. 28 cabins, 4 rooms; $$-$$$$+. Some kitchens & wood-burning fireplaces. Restaurant.

Located in a lovely forested area by the lake, these rustic cabins and lodge rooms have access to a beach, marina with boat rentals, stables, and arcade. Campsites are also available. Do reserve early; cabins usually book up a year in advance.

WHERE TO EAT

The Cantina Bar & Grill

765 Emerald Bay Rd., ¼ mi. W of Hwy. 50, (530) 544-1233; www.cantinatahoe.com. L-D daily; $-$$. No reservations.

There is usually a wait to be seated in this festive and popular spot, but that's no reason to stay away. Waiting time can be passed sitting in the bar with a pitcher of margaritas (kids can order tasty niña coladas) and some nachos. Menu standouts include carnitas (roasted pork), any of the giant burritos, and fresh fish. Southwestern dishes and wraps are also available.

Casinos

For some of the best food in this area, try the casino restaurants and buffets. Favorites include:

• Harrah's

(800) HARRAHS, (775) 588-6611; www.totalrewards.com.

• Forest Buffet

x2194. B-L M-Sat, D daily, SunBr; $-$$. No reservations.

Located on the 18th floor, this classy restaurant provides spectacular lake and mountain views, plus outstanding food at a reasonable price.

• The 19 Kitchen Bar

Hip and high—on the 19th floor, this spot serves appetizers, salads, and "Shake & Cake"—an espresso-malt shake made in a martini shaker and served with warm chocolate brownie cake.

• The Summit

x2196. D only; schedule varies; $$$. Reservations advised.

Located on the 16th and 17th floors in what was originally the Star Suite, where rich and famous headliners once were put up, this elegant spot offers heady views and a new menu of refined cuisine every day. Items are beautifully presented, and service is impeccable. One meal enjoyed here began with crispy-crusted mini baguettes and sweet butter shaped like roses. An appetizer of chilled gulf shrimp was arranged in a red seafood sauce swirled with horseradish hearts, and a salad of baby lettuces was arranged in a scooped-out tomato so that it resembled a bouquet. The entree was a perfect rack of lamb with an anise crust and a side of mashed potatoes sprinkled with truffles, followed by a dessert Frangelico soufflé with a hazelnut-praline crème frâiche.

• Harveys
(800) HARVEYS, (775) 588-2411; www.totalrewardstahoe.com.
• Cabo Wabo Cantina
x2461. L-D daily.

Menu highlights include tableside made-to-order guacamole, fish tacos, and fajitas. Specialty drinks made with Sammy Hagar's signature tequila and ongoing videos of his band keep things rocking. Beach attire is welcome.

• Hard Rock Cafe
x6597; www.hardrock.com. L-D daily.

For description, see page 72.

The Fresh Ketch
2435 Venice Dr., (530) 541-5683; www.thefreshketch.com. L-D daily; $$. Reservations advised.

Located at the Tahoe Keys Marina—the lake's only protected inland marina—this restaurant offers water views and fresh seafood. In addition to a daily special, the menu has scampi, calamari steak topped with anchovy butter, cioppino, king crab legs, and live Maine lobster. Non-fish items include steaks and hamburgers, and dessert brings on Key lime and hula pies.

Heidi's
3485 Lake Tahoe Blvd. (Hwy.50), (530) 544-8113. B-L daily; $. No reservations.

Breakfast is served all day in this cozy, casual restaurant. The menu includes pancakes, French toast, crêpes, Belgian waffles, and omelettes—as well as just about any other breakfast item imaginable—and orange juice is fresh-squeezed in the kitchen. At lunch, a variety of sandwiches, hamburgers, and salads are added to the menu.

NORTH LAKE TAHOE

VISITOR INFORMATION

North Lake Tahoe Visitors & Convention Bureau
P.O. Box 1757, Tahoe City 96145, (800) 462-5196, (530) 581-8703; www.gotahoenorth.com.

GETTING THERE

Located approximately 210 miles north of San Francisco. Take Highway 80 to Truckee, then Highway 267 south to the lake.

The Chicago-bound **Amtrak train** *((800) 872-7245; www.amtrak.com.)* leaves Emeryville daily at 8:10 a.m. and arrives in Truckee at 1:38 p.m.

ANNUAL EVENTS

Lake Tahoe Shakespeare Festival
July-August. At Sand Harbor State Park, in Nevada; (888) 32-SHOWS, (775) 832-1616; www.laketahoeshakespeare.com. $14-$72.

"Bard on the Beach," a nickname bestowed by fond locals, is the biggest event of the summer at the lake. Bring a picnic, a blanket, and some low-leg beach chairs. Food is also available for purchase.

Lake Tahoe Wooden Boat Week
August. (530) 581-4700; www.laketahoeconcours.com. $25-$30, under 12 free.

The Tahoe Yacht Club hosts this annual extravaganza celebrating Tahoe's classic wood boats. Festivities include a Concours d'Elegance. Proceeds support local charitable and cultural organizations, and most events are open to the public.

STOPS ALONG THE WAY

Along I-80 North
See pages 278 through 310.

Auburn
See pages 366 through 367.

Grass Valley
See pages 367 through 369.

Nevada City
See pages 369 through 372.

WHAT TO DO

Best beaches

• Sand Harbor State Park
In Nevada, 4 mi. S of Incline Village, (775) 831-0494; www.parks.nv.gov/lt.htm. $8/vehicle. No pets.

This is a perfect beach. The sand is clean and fine, lifeguards are usually on duty, and there are plenty of parking spaces and picnic tables.

• Tahoe City Commons Beach
In Tahoe City; stairway across from 510 North Lake Blvd.; parking lot behind Tahoe City Fire Station; (530) 583-3796; www.tahoecitypud.com/parksrec/beaches.shtml#1. Free.

This family beach boasts a large grassy area and a lakefront playground.

• William Kent Beach
2½ mi. S of Tahoe City, (530) 583-3642. Free.

Parking is difficult, but this small, rocky beach is worth the hassle. Campsites are available.

Bike trails
One begins in Tahoe City, following the shoreline and the Truckee River. Bike rentals are available in Tahoe City and at other locations along the lake.

Fishing charters
Get a fishing license and the names of captains at one of the local sporting goods shops. The captain usually supplies bait and tackle.

Gatekeeper's Museum
130 West Lake Blvd., in Tahoe City, (530) 583-1762; www.northtahoemuseums.org. Daily 11-5, June-Sept; W-Sun 11-5, May & Sept; Sat-Sun 11-3, Oct-Apr. $3, 55+ $2, 6-12 $1.

Situated lakeside, this museum is inside a replica 1910 lodge pole-pine log cabin originally inhabited by a succession of keepers whose job it was to raise and lower the gates of the dam. Displays include Native American artifacts and Lake Tahoe memorabilia.

An annex holds the **Marion Steinbach Indian Basket Museum**, which displays more than 800 Native American baskets, dolls, and other artifacts that represent the work of more than 50 tribes.

The surrounding 3½-acre **William B. Layton Park** is equipped with picnic tables and barbecue facilities.

High Camp Bath & Tennis Club
In Olympic Valley; www.squaw.com. Cable car: (530) 583-6985; daily 10-9; $22, 65+ & 13-15 $17, 4-12 $6; after 5pm, $12, 4-12 $5. Recreational facilities additional.

Located at 8,200 feet and reached via a scenic aerial cable car ride, this facility includes an Olympic-size outdoor ice-skating rink, two tennis courts, a pool and hot tub, and the **1960 Winter Olympic Museum**. Several restaurants are also here.

A lovely, though difficult, 1.3-mile hike to Shirley Lake begins at the cable car building. Hikers pass waterfalls and huge boulders while following Squaw Creek about 1.7 miles farther down to the base area.

Sugar Pine Point State Park

On west shore, in Tahoma, 9 mi. S of Tahoe City,
(530) 525-7232, in summer (530) 525-7982;
www.parks.ca.gov. Daily 8-dusk. $6/vehicle. Mansion:
Tours 11-4, on the hr.; July-Aug only; $5, 6-17 $3.

In this gorgeous, peaceful setting, the
3-story 1902 Queen Anne **Hellman-Ehrman
Mansion** has 16 rooms open for public viewing.
The General Phipps Cabin, built in 1872 of
hand-split logs, is also on the property. A magnificent beach invites swimming and sunning.
Picnic tables, hiking trails, and a 1930s tennis
court are available, and campsites are open
year-round. In winter, cross-country skiing and
ranger-led snowshoe walks join the agenda
(see page 459).

Thunderbird Lodge

5000 Hwy.28., 2 mi. S of Sand Harbor State Park,
(800) GO-TAHOE, (775) 832-8750; www.thunderbird
lodge.org. Tour schedule varies; May-Oct only;
reservations required; must be age 6+. By shuttle bus
from north shore: (800) 468-2463, (775) 832-1606;
$39, 6-11 $19. By boat from south shore:
(888) 867-6394, (775) 588-1881; www.tahoeboatcruis-
es.com; $110, 6-11 $55.

Built in 1936 by eccentric San Franciscan
George Whittell, Jr., this secluded estate sits on
140 forested lakeside acres. It is considered a
remarkable example of the Old Tahoe architectural style, and its name means "eternal happi-
ness." Native Americans were taught the various
trades and then did most of the stone masonry
and hand-wrought ironwork. Unusual features
include an Elephant House (for George's pet
Indian elephant, Mingo), a 600-foot underground tunnel carved through granite and leading to the mustard-colored boathouse, and a
man-made waterfall. Salacious stories tell of
showgirls and secret passages. The boat tour
sails round-trip from the south shore and
includes lunch.

Truckee River Bridge

At junction of Hwys. 89 & 28 (the Y), in Tahoe City.

The only outlet from the lake, the dam
below this bridge has gates that control the flow
of water into the river. Spectators gather here to
view and feed the giant rainbow trout that congregate beneath the bridge (they favor bread
and crackers). The nickname "**Fanny Bridge**"
comes from the sight that develops as people
bend over the bridge railing to view the fish.

"Fanny Bridge"

Truckin' on the Truckee/river rafting

Begins at the Y in Tahoe City. Daily 8:30-3:30;
June-Oct only. Rates vary.

What better way to spend a sunny summer
alpine day than floating down the peaceful
Truckee River a la Huckleberry Finn? All that's
needed is a swimsuit, water-friendly shoes, and
some sun lotion. Packing along a picnic and
cold drinks is also a good idea, and a daypack
keeps hands free for paddling. White-water
enthusiasts—stay away! This 4-mile, 3-hour
adventure is so tame that portable toilets are
placed strategically along the riverbank.

Tahoe City concessionaires offer a package
that includes raft, life jacket, paddles, and return
ride. It is first-come, first-served, so arrive
before 11 a.m. to avoid crowds and to get an
early-bird discount.

The trip ends at **River Ranch Lodge**
(2285 River Rd., off Hwy. 89, (866) 991-9912,
(530) 583-4264; www.riverranchlodge.com.),
where the restaurant prepares an outdoor
barbecue lunch on an expansive deck overlooking the river; lodging is also available.
A 3½-mile off-road bicycle trail runs along the
river here from River Ranch into Tahoe City.

Watson Cabin Curios

560 North Lake Blvd., in Tahoe City, (530) 583-8717;
www.northtahoemuseums.org. Sat-Sun 12-4;
W-M 12-4, July & Aug. Free.

Built in 1908 and 1909, this log cabin is
the oldest building in town still on its original
site. Furnished as it was in 1909, it illustrates
turn-of-the-19th-century life.

Winter activities

See pages 458 through 459.

WHERE TO STAY
CONDOS ON THE LAKE

Rates in condos vary tremendously depending on number of people, length of stay, and time of year, and most do not include the booking fee or cleaning fee. Most units are equipped with kitchens and TVs, and many are privately owned.

Brockway Springs

9200 Brockway Springs Dr., in Kings Beach, (530) 546-4201; www.brockwaysprings.com. 47 rental units. Most wood-burning fireplaces. Heated pool; children's wading pool; sauna; fitness room; 2 tennis courts. No pets.

Most units here have stone fireplaces and balconies overlooking the lake. The resort features ½ mile of private lakefront and a pool filled with hot thermal waters.

Chinquapin

3600 North Lake Blvd., in Tahoe City, (800) 732-6721, (530) 583-6991; www.chinquapin.com. 172 rental units. All TVs, kitchens, & fireplaces. Heated pool (seasonal); 2 saunas; 7 tennis courts.

The oneto four-bedroom units here feature vaulted, beamed ceilings, natural rock fireplaces, and lake views. Some of these units also have private saunas, and all are equipped with washers and dryers. Additional resort amenities include two private beaches, boating facilities, a fishing pier, and a 1-mile paved beachfront path.

Coeur du Lac

136 Juanita Dr., in Incline Village, Nevada, (800) 869-8308, (775) 832-4475. Heated pool (seasonal); indoor hot tub; sauna.

Located 1 block from the lake, this attractive complex also has a recreation center.

WHERE TO STAY
CONDOS FARTHER OUT

Carnelian Woods

5005 North Lake Blvd., in Carnelian Bay, ¼ mi. from lake, (877) NLT-ahoe, (530) 546-5547; www.carnelianwoods.com. 30 rental units. Recreation center with heated pool (seasonal); 2 hot tubs; 2 saunas; 3 tennis courts.

Further amenities include sports facilities and bicycle rentals. In winter, a 2-mile cross-country ski course and a snow play area are available.

Granlibakken Conference Center & Lodge

End of Granlibakken Rd., in Tahoe City, 1 mi. from lake, (800) 543-3221, (530) 583-4242; www.granlibakken.com. 190 rental units. Some kitchens & fireplaces. Heated pool, children's wading pool (seasonal); hot tub; sauna; 6 tennis courts. Full breakfast. No pets.

Situated in a 74-acre forested valley, this resort also has a jogging trail. In winter, it maintains a ski and snow play area (see also page 458).

Kingswood Village

1001 Commonwealth Ave., off Hwy. 267, in Kings Beach, ¾ mi. from lake, (800) 646-0809, (530) 546-2501; www.kingswoodcondos.com. 60 rental units. All gas or wood-burning fireplaces. Heated pool (seasonal); hot tub; sauna; 3 tennis courts.

Amenities here include access to a private lakefront beach club.

Northstar-at-Tahoe

On Northstar Dr., off Hwy. 267, in Truckee, (800) GO-NORTH, (530) 562-1010; www.northstarattahoe.com. 6 mi. from lake. 260 rental units; $-$$$+. Most kitchens & wood-burning fireplaces. 2 heated

pools (seasonal); 3 hot tubs; 2 saunas; fitness room; 10 clay tennis courts; 18-hole golf course. 5 restaurants.

In addition to condos, hotel rooms and homes are available. A complimentary shuttle bus makes it unnecessary to use a car within the complex. Facilities include Tahoe's largest mountain bike park—with 100 miles of trails— and also a pedestrian village with retail stores and restaurants and free scenic chairlift rides. See also page 458.

Squaw Valley Lodge

201 Squaw Peak Rd., in Olympic Valley, 10 mi. from lake, (800) 549-6742, (530) 583-5500; www.squawvalleylodge.com. 178 rental units; $$-$$$+. All kitchens, some gas fireplaces. Heated pool (seasonal); 3 indoor & 2 outdoor hot tubs; sauna; steam room; full-service spa; fitness room; 2 tennis courts. No pets.

Claiming to be "just 84 steps from the Squaw Valley tram," this resort is convenient for both skiers and non-skiers. Staying here avoids a congested early morning commute to Squaw's parking lot. When ready to ski, it is possible to just walk, or even ski, to the lifts. For non-skiers, a room facing the slopes allows complete warmth and comfort while watching the rest of the group whiz by. The pool here is treated with gentle-on-the-eyes bromine instead of chlorine.

WHERE TO STAY
OTHER

Cal-Neva Resort

2 Stateline Rd., in Crystal Bay, Nevada, (800) CAL-NEVA, (775) 832-4000; www.calnevaresort.com. 9 stories; 190 rooms, 10 cabins; $-$$. Heated pool; indoor hot tub; full-service spa; 2 tennis courts (free). Restaurant; room service. Free valet parking.

This resort straddles California and Nevada. In fact, a line runs right through the pool depicting where the property divides— allowing guests to swim in two states. In its 1940s heyday, it was a popular playground for mobsters and stars, who favored the property's private chalets (Marilyn Monroe stayed in #3, Frank Sinatra in #5). Today, all guests get a lake view.

When Sinatra owned 65% of "the joint" in the 1960s, he had a secret tunnel built so he could get from his cabin to the lodge without any fuss. Today, visitors can take a stroll in it as part of a tour (Fe&Sat from 6pm. $8.) that also tells of illicit affairs, money laundering, and much, much more.

A drink in the **Circle Bar**—with its lake view and German 7,000-piece stained-glass dome—and a visit to the immense knotty-pine Indian Room—which features a granite boulder fireplace and displays interesting artifacts—are de rigueur.

A small **casino** (it is the oldest legal gambling facility in the U.S.) and a large video arcade are also on the premises.

Hyatt Regency Lake Tahoe Resort, Spa and Casino

111 Country Club Dr./Lakeshore, in Incline Village, Nevada, (800) 233-1234, (775) 832-1234; www.laketahoehyatt.com. 12 stories; 424 rooms; $$-$$$+. Some fireplaces. Heated pool; 2 hot tubs; fitness room; full-service spa. 4 restaurants; room service.

Guests here have a choice between a room in a 12-story high-rise, in a 3-story annex, or in a lakeside cottage, and Lady Luck can be tested 24 hours a day in the 13,000-square-foot casino. Of special note is the resort's magnificent private beach, complete with beach boys who set up lounge chairs and umbrellas wherever desired. In summer, guests can relax with the water lapping at the shore just beneath their toes, causing one to ponder, "Can it get any better than this?" The pool is designed like a lagoon, and jet skis and paddleboats can be rented at an adjacent marina. At night, an oceanfront fire pit equipped with comfortable chairs and a hammock invites lingering under the tall pines. During ski season, free shuttle service is provided to nearby ski areas, and both ski rentals and discounted lift tickets can be purchased on the premises. The Camp Hyatt program for children ages 3 through 12 operates on weekends year-round and daily during summer and holidays (fee).

The imposing **Lone Eagle Grille** features Old Tahoe-style atmosphere, with massive wood-beamed ceilings, gigantic fireplaces made of local rock, and large windows with lake views. Lunch is soups and salads, pastas and pizzas, and plenty of tempting desserts. The dinner menu offers updated surf-and-turf and a good Caesar salad. **Cutthroat's Saloon**'s wooden floors are littered with peanut shells, and food is served on camping-style tin plates and beer comes in big Mason jars. Cocktails include a flaming Toasted Marshmallow (Stoli Vanilla, butterscotch liqueur, Frangelico, and cream), a Girl Scout Cookie (peppermint schnapps, creme de cacoa, and cream), and a Beehive (honey liqueur, brandy, and lemon juice). Bottoms up!

Mourelatos Lakeshore Resort

6834 North Lake Blvd., in Tahoe Vista, (800) TAHOE-81, (530) 546-9500; www.mlrtahoe.com. 32 units; $$-$$$+. Some kitchens & fireplaces. 2 hot tubs. No pets.

At this lakefront lodging, a small pine forest opens onto a private beach on the lake, and a children's playground is available in summer. All units have a lake views, and some open right onto the beach.

Resort at Squaw Creek

400 Squaw Creek Rd., in Olympic Valley, (800) 3CREEK3, (530) 583-6300; www.squawcreek.com. 9 stories; 403 rooms; $$$-$$$+. Some kitchens & gas fireplaces. 2 heated pools; 1 children's wading pool; 4 hot tubs; sauna;
fitness room; full-service spa; 2 tennis courts (fee); 18-hole golf course. 5 restaurants; room service.

This sleek, black-toned, high-rise hotel is almost invisible tucked up against a mountain. Two-story windows in the lobby provide a magnificent valley view. The majestic property is impressively landscaped and features a 250-foot man-made waterfall feeding a rushing stream that cascades over boulders. One of the pools has a twisting 120-foot-long waterslide, and the toddler pool includes a large sandy beach for extra diversion. The Mountain Buddies children's program operates year-round for ages 4 through 13 (fee).

Bicycles can be rented for a scenic ride beside the Truckee River, and a fly fishing center is on property. In winter, ski-in/ski-out access is available to Squaw Valley, and cross-country skiing, snowshoe tours, an ice-skating pavilion, and dog-sledding tours are available.

Motel Row

Last-minute lodging can usually be found among the numerous motels and cabins lining the lake in Kings Beach and Tahoe Vista. Chances are best, of course, on weekdays and in the off-season.

WHERE TO EAT

Lakehouse Pizza

120 Grove Ct., in Tahoe City, (530) 583-2222.
L-D daily; $. No reservations.

This casual spot offers lakefront views and
a choice of sitting either inside or outside on a
deck. Menu choices include pizza, sandwiches,
salads, hamburgers, and exceptionally good
housemade potato chips. Though the schedule
varies, an extensive breakfast menu is served in
an area known as the **Eggschange**.

Sunnyside Steakhouse & Lodge

1850 West Lake Blvd., in Tahoe City, (800) 822-2-SKI,
(530) 583-7200; www.sunnysideresort.com. D daily;
also L in summer; $$-$$$+. Reservations advised.

It's hard to beat a summer meal here,
especially when eaten outside on the huge
deck—the largest on the lake—while watching
sailboats.

Overnight **lodging** *(23 rooms; $$-$$$.*
Some fireplaces. Continental breakfast.) is also
available. All rooms have private decks and
most have lake views.

Wolfdale's Cuisine Unique

640 North Lake Blvd., Tahoe City, (530) 583-5700;
www.wolfdales.com. D W-M; daily July-Aug; $$$.
Reservations advised.

The attractive circa 1880 house this
restaurant is located within is the town's oldest.
It was floated over on a barge from the Nevada
side of the lake at the turn of the 19th century
and was converted into a restaurant in the
1960s. Colorful art decorates the walls, and a
bit of the lake and a lot of trees provide a nice
view. Talented owner-chef Douglas Dale
combines Asian and European cooking tech-
niques to produce high-flavor, low-fat fresh fish
and meat entrees—all artistically arranged and
served with yeasty house-baked herb rolls.
The appetizers and desserts are also exceptional.
Adding to the aesthetics of this dining
experience, everything is served on lovely
handmade pottery designed especially to
enhance the food.

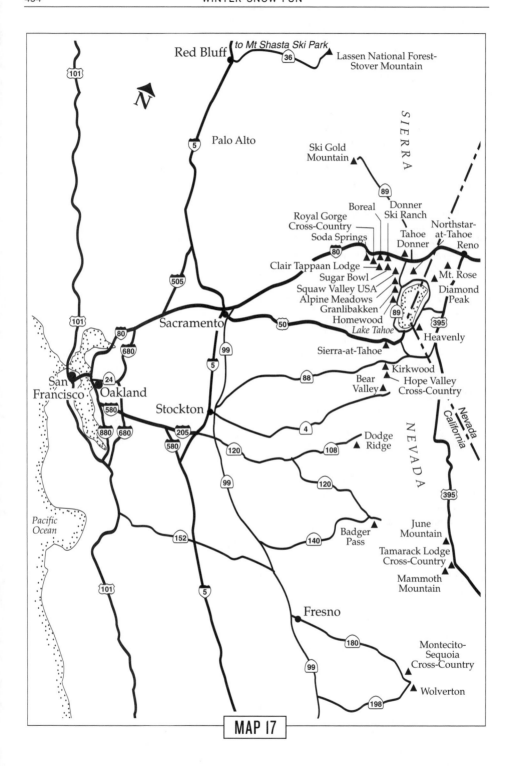

MAP 17

WINTER SNOW FUN

A LITTLE BACKGROUND

Downhill Skiing

Downhill ski areas are plentiful in Northern California. The season runs from the first snow, usually in late November, through the spring thaw in April. Several resorts are known for staying open longer.

Lifts usually operate daily from 9 a.m. to 4 p.m. To avoid parking problems and long lines for lift tickets and rentals, arrive early. On-site equipment rentals are usually available and convenient, and lift tickets are often discounted mid-week. Many resorts now post tickets prices and daily weather reports at their website.

The least crowded times at the resorts are the three weeks after Thanksgiving, the first two weeks in January, and late in the season. The two weeks around Christmas are ridiculous.

Those who know say it is worthwhile to buy ski equipment if someone skis more than 10 days per season. Otherwise, it is financially beneficial to rent. Avoid buying children plastic skis; they break easily.

Most ski areas now have at least one terrain park, where man-made snow formations—halfpipes, tabletops, etc.—allow snowboarders to practice tricky moves.

Cross-country Skiing

Cross-country skiing becomes more popular each year. This might be due to advantages it has over downhill skiing: no lift tickets to purchase; less expensive equipment; is considered safer; can be enjoyed in groups; allows escape from crowds. However, the sport also has several disadvantages: requires more stamina; is less exhilarating.

Specialized cross-country centers offer equipment rentals, maintained trails with maps, and warming huts. Some centers also offer lodging, guided tours, snowshoeing, and the option of downhill facilities.

Children age 4 and older are usually taught in classes with their parents, but some centers have special children's classes. Parents who have the strength can carry younger children in a backpack or pull them along in a "pulk."

It is a good idea for beginners to rent equipment and take a few lessons to learn safety guidelines and basic skiing techniques. Once the basics are learned, this sport can be practiced just about anywhere there is a foot of snow.

The state **SNO-PARK** program *((916) 324-1222; www.ohv.parks.ca.gov. $5/1 day, $25/season pass Nov.1-May30.)* makes it easier to park at popular trail heads and snow play areas.

Snow Play

Toboggans, saucers, inner tubes, and sleds are the equipment for snow play. For safety's sake, take note that sleds are lots of fun to use but extremely hazardous. Truck inner tubes are also dangerous because the rider is high off the ground with nothing to hold on to and no way to steer.

When people do not pay attention to safety rules, snow play can become dangerous. (I once had the wind knocked out of me by an antsy bear of a man who didn't wait for me and my young child to come to a stop before he pushed off down the same hill in his saucer. After the collision he said, "Sorry. But you shouldn't have been there." I'm sure worse stories are waiting to be told.)

Most ski resorts have an informal snow play area. Some commercial snow play areas allow people to bring their own equipment, but others require that equipment be rented on-site.

Dress for cold, wet weather. Wear wool when possible, and pack a change of clothes. Always wear gloves to protect hands from sharp, packed snow and boots to protect feet.

The high-speed fun of snowmobiling provides an exciting adventure. Many snowmobile concessions provide protective clothing and equipment. Though not inexpensive, especially for a family, it is an exhilarating, memorable experience.

In the following listings, difficulty of terrain at downhill ski resorts is specified in percentages: %B (beginner), %I (intermediate), %A (advanced). For more detailed information about

the ski resorts—including details about childcare, lodging, and lift ticket prices—go to the respective website or to www.skitown.com/resortguide.

SHASTA-CASCADE

Lassen National Forest—Stover Mountain
On Forest Service Road 316A, at Hwy. 36/Hwy. 89, 3 mi. SW of Chester, (530) 258-3987; Sat-Sun only. Downhill only. 25%B, 50%I, 25%A.

California's "undiscovered National Park" is an excellent area for families and beginners and it has one of the country's longest rope tows. The scenery includes hot steam vents and mud pots.

Mt. Shasta Board & Ski Park
104 Siskiyou Ave., in Mt. Shasta, 10 mi. E of Mt. Shasta City, (800) SKI-SHASTA, (530) 926-8610; www.skipark.com. Downhill and cross-country. 20%B, 55%I, 25%A.

Night skiing is available at this low-key, family-oriented ski area, and all trails are open to snowboarders.

DONNER SUMMIT

Boreal Mountain Resort
Castle Peak exit off Hwy. I-80, 10 mi. W of Truckee, (530) 426-3666; www.borealski.com. Downhill only. 30%B, 55%I, 15%A. Lodging on premises, (530) 426-1012.

Known for being relatively inexpensive and convenient to the Bay Area, this resort offers night skiing and is the first and only all-mountain terrain park in Northern California. Slopes are especially good for beginners and intermediates, and skiers of all ability levels can ride on the same chairs together. A Shared Pass allows two parents to buy just one ticket if they want to take turns skiing and babysitting their children.

Clair Tappaan Lodge
In Norden, 19940 Donner Pass Rd. (old Hwy. 40), 3 mi. E of Norden/Soda Springs exit off Hwy. I-80, (800) 679-6775, (530) 426-3632; www.ctl.sierra club.org. Cross-country only.

This area is said to be the snowiest in the continental U.S. Both the massive timbered lodge, which was built by volunteers in 1934, and the groomed track system are owned and operated by the Sierra Club. Lodging is dormitory-style with bunk beds, and, as at hostels, guests bring their own bedding and everyone is expected to do a chore. Programs and workshops are scheduled throughout the year.

Donner Ski Ranch

19320 Donner Pass Rd., in Norden, off Hwy. 40, 3 mi. from the Norden/Soda Springs exit off Hwy. I-80, (530) 426-3635; www.donnerskiranch.com. Downhill only. 25%B, 50%I, 25%A. Lodging on premises.

Best for beginners and intermediates, this area offers no frills.

Royal Gorge Cross Country Ski Resort

9411 Hillside Dr., in Soda Springs, 1 mi. from Soda Springs/Norden exit off Hwy. I-80, near Donner Pass, (800) 666-3871, (800) 500-3871, (530) 426-3871; www.royalgorge.com. Cross-country only. Lodging on premises.

Modeled after Scandinavian ski resorts, this was the first cross-country ski resort in California. The overnight **Wilderness Lodge** here is not accessible by road. Guests are brought in by snowcat-drawn sleigh and leave by skiing the 2 miles back out. Accommodations are rustic. In the old 1920s hunting lodge, everyone shares the same toilet areas. Sleeping facilities are tiny roomettes, each with either a double bed or a bunk bed and a curtain-covered doorway, and several three-bed rooms for families. Bathing facilities—showers, a sauna, and an outdoor hot tub—are located in an adjacent building reached by a short trek through the snow. Some private cabins are also available. The food, however, is remarkably civilized. A chef works full-time in the kitchen preparing attractive, tasty, and bountiful French repasts. Oh, yes—the skiing. Guests may ski whenever they wish, and the capable staff gives lessons each morning and guided tours each afternoon. Guided moonlight ski tours are scheduled after dinner. The nightly fee includes everything except equipment, which can be rented on site.

Royal Gorge also operates a more accessible B&B, **Rainbow Lodge** *((530) 426-3661)*, nearby.

The cross-country ski center is open to non-guests and features the largest cross-country track system in the U.S. Facilities include ten warming huts, four trail-side cafes, and four surface lifts. The Rainbow Interconnect Trail provides 8 miles of scenic downhill cross-country skiing; shuttle buses return skiers to the trailhead. A program is available for skiers with disabilities.

Soda Springs Mountain Resort

In Soda Springs, at Soda Springs exit off Hwy. I-80, 4 mi. W of Donner Summit, (530) 426-3901; www.ski sodasprings.com. Downhill only. 30%B, 50%I, 20%A.

Built on the former site of one of the first Sierra ski resorts, this ski area is among the closest to the Bay Area and is particularly well designed for beginners. A children's snow park includes bunny-slope chair lifts, inner tube merry-go-rounds, and mini snowmobiles.

Sugar Bowl Ski Resort

629 Sugar Bowl Rd., in Norden, off Hwy. 40, 2 mi. E of Soda Springs exit off Hwy. I-80, (530) 426-9000; www.sugarbowl.com. Downhill only. 17%B, 45%I, 38%A. Lodging on premises.

Exuding a 1930s Tyrolean charm, this ski resort is one of the Sierra's oldest and had the first chairlift in the state. It is known for short lift lines, good runs at all ability levels, and the deepest snow at Tahoe. Skiers park and ride a rustic gondola across the valley to the snowbound village.

Tahoe Donner

11603 Slalom Way, in Truckee, off Hwy. I-80; www.skitahoedonner.com. Downhill: (530) 587-9444. 40%B, 60%I. Cross-country: 15275 Alder Creek Rd., (530) 587-9484; www.tdxc.com.

This small resort with wide-open bowls is especially good for families. The number of lift tickets sold each day is limited, assuring that it never gets overcrowded. Snow-biking a la the Beatles in *Help!* was introduced in 1998.

The cross-country ski center offers lighted night skiing and schedules special tours: Ski With Santa, Morning Nature Tour, Sauna Tour, Donner Trail Tour.

SNOW PLAY

Western SkiSport Museum

At Castle Peak exit off Hwy. I-80, (530) 426-3313 x110; www.auburnskiclub.org. F-Sun 10-4, Dec-mid-Apr only. Free.

See just how cumbersome that charming old-time ski equipment really was. This museum chronicles the history of skis in the West from gold camp days—when long-board skis were used by pioneers to help open this mountain area—to current times. Vintage ski films are shown upon request.

NEVADA

Diamond Peak Ski Resort
1210 Ski Way, in Incline Village, off Hwy. 28, (775) 832-1177; www.diamondpeak.com. Downhill only. 18%B, 46%I, 36%A.

This well-sheltered, family-oriented resort is especially good on inclement days. It is the area's first and only ski resort to use the European-style easy-loading "Launch Pad" system—similar to a moving walkway—on its quad chairlifts.

Mt. Rose-Ski Tahoe
22222 Mt. Rose Hwy., in Reno, on Hwy. 431, 11 mi. NE of Incline Village, (800) SKI-ROSE, (775) 849-0704; www.skirose.com. Downhill only. 30%B, 30%I, 40%A.

At 8,260 feet, this is the highest base elevation at Tahoe.

NORTH LAKE TAHOE

Alpine Meadows Ski Resort
2600 Alpine Meadows Rd., in Tahoe City, off Hwy. 89, 6 mi. N of town, (800) 441-4423, (530) 583-4232; www.skialpine.com. Downhill only. 25%B, 40%I, 35%A.

Situated on U.S. Forest Service land, Alpine is acclaimed for its snow quality and is usually open well into May.

The **Tahoe Adaptive Ski School** *((530) 581-4161)* for people with disabilities operates here.

Granlibakken
725 Granlibakken Rd., in Tahoe City, 1 mi. S of town, (800) 543-3221, (530) 581-7333; www.granlibakken.com. 50%B, 50%I.

This small ski area is protected from the wind and caters to beginners and families with small children. It is the oldest ski resort at Tahoe and has the least expensive lift ticket.

Downhill, cross-country, snowboarding, and snowshoeing are all accommodated. See also page 450.

Homewood Mountain Resort
5145 West Lake Blvd., in Homewood, off Hwy. 89, 6 mi. S of Tahoe City, (530) 525-2992; www.ski homewood.com. Downhill only. 15%B, 50%I, 35%A.

The slopes here are ideal for intermediates and families and provide panoramic views of Lake Tahoe.

Northstar-at-Tahoe
Off Hwy. 267, 6 mi. S of Truckee, (800) GO-NORTH; www. northstarattahoe.com. Downhill: (530) 562-1010. 25%B, 50%I, 25%A. Cross-country: (530) 562-2475. Lodging on premises.

This attractive ski area is reputed to be the least windy at Tahoe. Catering to families, it is good for beginners and excellent for intermediates. Organized activities are scheduled throughout the week, and free 1½-hour introductory tours—in which participants are introduced to the resort and given a history of the area—are given daily at 10 a.m. A new village features shops, restaurants, and a skating rink. See also page 451.

Squaw Valley USA
1960 Squaw Valley Rd., in Olympic Valley, off Hwy. 89, 5 mi. N of Tahoe City, (888) SNOW-321, (800) 545-4350, (530) 583-6985; www.squaw.com. Downhill & cross-country. 25%B, 45%I, 30%A. Lodging on premises.

Squaw Valley made its name in 1960 when it was home to the VIII Winter Olympic Games. Today it is a top ski area known internationally for open slopes and a predictably generous snowfall, which usually permits it to stay open into May. Expert skiers consider it the best ski resort in the state because it has the steepest, most challenging slopes. Indeed, there are good slopes for every ability level. A special area for children ages 3 through 12 is equipped with two rope tows and a Magic Carpet. A snowtubing area with a dedicated lift and sled hill are available, and night skiing is available mid-December through mid-March. Ice-skating, dining, and a mountaintop swimming pool and hot tub (summer only) are available at High Camp, elevation 8,200 feet.

SNOW PLAY

Carnelian Woods condominiums
See page 450.

SnowFest!
(530) 583-7167; www.tahoesnowfestival.com.

Held for 10 days each year in March, this is the largest winter carnival in the West. One activity is a fireworks display over the slopes at Squaw Valley followed by the awe-inspiring sight of scores of torch-bearing skiers making a twisting descent down Exhibition Run. Other popular events include The Great Ski Race (a 30-kilometer Nordic ski competition) and the Polar Bear Swim (a race in chilly Lake Tahoe).

Snow hikes
Sugar Pine Point State Park, P.O. Box 266, Tahoma 96142, (530) 525-9528; www.parks.ca.gov. Dec-Mar only, depending on snow.

Request a schedule of free ranger-led snowshoe and cross-country hikes in Lake Tahoe area state parks by sending a stamped, self-addressed, legal size envelope to the above address. Winter campsites are available.

SOUTH LAKE TAHOE

Heavenly Mountain Resort
In South Lake Tahoe, (800) 2-HEAVEN, (775) 586-7000; www.skiheavenly.com. Downhill only. 20%B, 45%I, 35%A.

Situated in two states, this is the largest, and one of the most scenic, ski areas in the country. Runs on the California side offer breathtaking views of Lake Tahoe. This resort is rated as having the best intermediate skiing in California. It also has exhilarating expert slopes and has the longest descent—5½ miles—in the West. A new gondola—California's longest—travels the 2½ miles from Stateline to Heavenly in under 12 minutes.

Kirkwood Mountain Resort
1501 Kirkwood Meadows Dr., in Kirkwood, on Hwy. 88, 30 mi. S of South Lake Tahoe, (800) 967-7500, (209) 258-6000; www.kirkwood.com. Downhill, & cross-country (209) 258-7248. 15%B, 50%I, 35%A. Lodging on premises.

This very large, uncrowded family resort is reputed to have the deepest snow in North America. It is often snowing here when it is raining at other Tahoe ski areas. Ice skating, tubing, dogsledding, and snowmobiling is available, and the cross-country area offers guided snowshoe adventures and night hikes.

Sierra-at-Tahoe Snowsport Resort
1111 Sierra-at-Tahoe Rd., in Twin Bridges, on Hwy. 50, 12 mi. W of South Lake Tahoe, (530) 659-7453; www.sierraattahoe.com. Downhill only. 25%B, 50%I, 25%A.

This ski area is known for its wind-protected slopes and tree skiing and is reputed to be particularly popular with college students and families with teenagers. Free shuttles are available from South Lake Tahoe.

Sorensen's and Hope Valley Resorts
14255 Hwy. 88, in Hope Valley, 16 mi. S of Lake Tahoe, (800) 423-9949, (530) 694-2203; www.sorensensresort.com. Cross-country only. Lodging on premises.

Small and informal, this historic spot is a great place for families. The resort is open year-round, with a sauna and cafe among its facilities. In summer, it offers a family-oriented fly-fishing school and history tours of the Emigrant and Pony Express trails.

Lodging is available in 33 cabins, most of which have housekeeping kitchens and 10 of which are authentic log cabins. Some are newish log cabins equipped with kitchenettes and wood-burning fireplaces; others are older and smaller. Smoking is not permitted, and rooms have no TV.

SNOW PLAY

Borges Carriage and Sleigh Rides
On Hwy. 50 next to Caesar's Tahoe casino, in Stateline, (800) 726-RIDE, (775) 588-2953; www.sleighride.com. Daily 10-sunset, weather permitting. $20, 2-10 $10.

Take a ride around a meadow in an old-fashioned "one-horse open sleigh." Five handmade sleighs are used, ranging from a cozy two-seater to a 20-passenger super model. Sleighs are pulled by either a 2,000-pound Blonde Belgian horse or a rare American-Russian Baskhir Curly.

Hansen's Resort

1360 Ski Run Blvd./Needle Peak Rd., 3 blks. from Heavenly ski area, in South Lake Tahoe, (530) 544-3361; www.hansensresort.com. Daily 9-5; Dec-mid-March. $10, 5-9 $5.

Facilities include a saucer hill and a packed toboggan run with banked turns. All equipment is furnished. Lodging in secluded cabins is available.

Husky Express dog sled tours

In Hope Valley, 25 mi. S of South Lake Tahoe, (775) 782-3047; www.highsierra.com/sst. Adults & children over 60 lbs. $100/1 hr., children under 60 lbs. $50, under 3 free. Reservations required.

As the sled swooshes over the scenic trails and through the trees on these enjoyable excursions, the frisky, well-tempered huskies seem to be having as much fun as their passengers. As does the "musher," who never utters the word "mush" but instead hollers "Hike!" or "Let's Go!" Two sleds are available, and each can carry two adults or a combination of kids and adults that does not exceed 375 pounds.

CENTRAL SIERRA

Badger Pass

In Yosemite National Park, off Hwy. 41 on Glacier Point Rd., 23 mi. from the valley; www.badgerpass.com. Downhill: (209) 372-8432. 35%B, 50%I, 15%A. Cross-country: (209) 372-8444.

Badger Pass opened in 1935, making it California's first—and oldest—organized ski area. A prime spot for beginners and intermediates and especially popular with families, it has a natural bowl with gentle slopes that provide

shelter from wind. A free shuttle bus delivers valley guests to the slopes. A bargain Midweek Ski Package and free ranger-led snowshoe walks *($3 snowshoe maintenance fee. Must be age 10+.)* are available. A good place to snowshoe without a guide is in the Mariposa Grove of Giant Sequoias.

Cross-country skiing is arranged through **Yosemite Nordic Ski Center**—the oldest cross-country ski school on the West Coast. Survival courses, snow camping, and overnight tours that include lodging and meals are also available.

Bear Valley Mountain Resort

On Hwy. 4/Hwy. 207, 45 mi. E of Angels Camp, in Bear Valley. Downhill: (209) 753-2301; www.bearvalley.com. 30%B, 40%I, 30%A.

Intermediate or better skiers staying in this secluded resort village can ski the 3-mile Home Run trail back to the resort area at the end of the day. A bus takes skiers to and from the village lodgings and the slopes. Bear is one of the biggest ski areas in the state and generally has short lift lines. However, that Ski Bare campaign must have caught people's attention: Now there are lines where once there were none. The resort is popular with families and especially good for beginners and intermediates.

Bear Valley Adventure Company *((209) 753-2834; www.bearvalleyxc.com)* is not affiliated with the downhill resort. It offers cross-country skiing, snowshoeing, and a **sledding hill** for ages 3 through 12 *(Must rent sled, $8; child must be accompanied by adult.).* Stays at ski-in snowbound cabins can be arranged.

The old days

*Yosemite's first ski lift (skier's stood skis upright in center of "upski,"
then sat down beside them to be pulled up the hill via funicular cable)*

Dodge Ridge

*In Pinecrest, off Hwy. 108, 32 mi. E of Sonora,
(209) 965-3474; www.dodgeridge.com. Downhill only.
20%B, 40%I, 40%A.*

This low-key, family-oriented ski area is
known for short lift lines. It is also the ski resort
nearest to the Bay Area.

Montecito Sequoia Resort

*63410 Generals Hwy., in Sequoia National Forest,
betw. Kings Canyon & Sequoia National Parks,
(800) 227-9900, (650) 967-8612; www.mslodge.com.
Cross-country only. Lodging on premises. No pets.*

Skiers here enjoy breathtaking ski tours
and snowshoe walks through groves of giant
sequoias. A children's program is included, and
parents can rent a pulk sled to pull babies and
toddlers along with them. Because of its high-
altitude location at 7,500 feet, this resort usually
retains its snow and stays open for skiing
through spring. Lodge guests have plenty to do
besides skiing. In the lodge, they feast on
"California fresh" cuisine and have access to
snacks around the clock. Board games, Ping-
Pong, and a library of movies provide entertainment. Outside activities include snow sculpture, igloo building, and ski football. An ice-
skating session on the naturally frozen lake is
also a possibility, as is a soak in the outdoor hot
tub overlooking the Great Western Divide or a
romp in the snowboard area or a run down the
chute on the tow-enhanced tubing and sledding
hills. But just resting in front of the massive
stone fireplaces is also an option. See also
pages 387 and 465.

SNOW PLAY

Long Barn Lodge Ice Rink

*In Long Barn, off Hwy. 108, 23 mi. E of Sonora,
(800) 310-3533, (209) 586-3533; www.longbarn.com.
$7, skates $2.*

Located behind a bar and restaurant built
in 1925, this rink is covered but has two sides
open to the outdoors.

Yosemite Outdoor Ice Rink

*In Curry Village, (209) 372-8319;
www.yosemitepark.com. Daily; Nov-Mar. $8,
under 12 $6, skate rental $3.*

Ice skate in the shadow of Glacier Point
and enjoy a spectacular view of Half Dome at
the same time at this scenic outdoor rink. Folks
have been doing just that here since 1930.

MISCELLANEOUS ADVENTURES

FAMILY CAMPS

Most adults remember the good old days when they were kids and got to go away to summer camp, and most adults think those days are gone for good. Well, they're not. A vacation at a family camp can bring it all back.

Family camps provide a reasonably priced, organized vacation experience. They are sponsored by city recreation departments, university alumni organizations, and private enterprise. The city and private camps are open to anyone, but some university camps require a campus affiliation.

And it isn't necessary to have children to attend. One year at one camp, a couple was actually *honeymooning*!, and elderly couples whose children are grown occasionally attend, too. Family reunions sometimes are held at a camp, and clubs and groups of friends often book in at the same time.

Housing varies from primitive platform tents and cabins without electricity, plumbing, or bedding to comfortable campus dormitory apartments with daily maid service. Locations vary from the mountains to the sea. Predictably, costs also vary with the type of accommodations and facilities. Some camps allow stays of less than a week, but most require a weeklong

commitment. Children usually are charged at a lower rate according to age.

Most family camps operate during the summer months only. Fees usually include meal preparation and clean up, special programs for children, and recreation programs for everyone. Activities can include river or pool swimming, hiking, fishing, volleyball, table tennis, badminton, hayrides, tournaments, campfires, crafts programs, songfests, tennis, and horseback riding.

Each camp has its own special appeal, but all offer an informal atmosphere where guests can really unwind. Often more than half the guests return the following year. Repeat guests and their camp friends tend to choose the same week each year.

For detailed rate information, itemization of facilities, session dates, and route directions, contact the camp reservation offices directly and request a descriptive brochure. Reserve early to avoid disappointment.

CITY/GROUP CAMPS

Berkeley Tuolumne Camp
Berkeley Camps Office, Berkeley, (510) 981-5140; www.ci.berkeley.ca.us/camps. Located on the south fork of the Tuolumne River, near Yosemite National

Park. Daily rates. Platform tents without electricity; provide own bedding; community bathrooms; family-style meals. Programs for toddlers-6, 6-12, & teens. Swimming in river; evening programs; breakfast hikes.

Camp Concord

City of Concord Community & Recreation Services, Concord, (925) 671-3273; www.campconcord.org. Located near Camp Richardson at South Lake Tahoe. Daily rates. Tent camping, cabins with electricity; provide own bedding; community bathrooms; cafeteria-style meals. Horseback riding & river rafting at additional fee.

Camp Mather

San Francisco Rec. and Park Dept., San Francisco, (415) 831-2715; www.parks.sfgov.org. Located on the rim of the Tuolumne River gorge near Yosemite National Park. Daily rates. Cabins with electricity; provide own bedding; community bathrooms; cafeteria-style meals. Playground area; program for age 6+. Unheated pool; lake swimming; tennis courts; horseback riding (fee).

Camp Sacramento

Dept. of Parks and Rec., Sacramento, (916) 808-6169, Oct-May (916) 808-6098; www.cityofsacramento.org/parksandrecreation/campsac. Located in the El Dorado National Forest, 17 mi. S of Lake Tahoe. Daily & weekly rates. Cabins with electricity; provide own bedding; community bathrooms; cafeteria-style meals. Programs for all ages.

Co-op Camp Sierra

Berkeley, (888) 708-CAMP, (510) 595-0873; www.coopcamp.com. Located in a pine forest between Huntington & Shaver Lakes, 65 mi. NE of Fresno. Daily & weekly rates. Cabins with electricity, lodge rooms, or bring own tent; provide own bedding; community bathrooms; family-style meals. Special activities for teens; playground & crafts program for younger children. Discussion groups and workshops for adults.

Feather River Camp

Oakland, (510) 336-CAMP; www.featherrivercamp.com. Located in the Plumas National Forest, N of Lake Tahoe near Quincy. Daily rates. Cabins & platform tents with electricity; provide own bedding; community bathrooms; family-style meals. Play area & activities for ages 2-5; program for age 6+. Theme weeks.

San Jose Family Camp

Dept. of Parks, Rec. & Neighborhood Services, San Jose, (408) 871-3820; www.sanjoseca.gov/prns/familycamp.asp. Located in Stanislaus National Forest, 30 mi. from Yosemite National Park. Daily rates; tent cabins without electricity (electricity avail. at additional fee); provide own bedding; community bathrooms. Cafeteria-style meals. Play area; program for age 3+. Dammed-off river pool.

Silver Lake Camp

Dept. of Parks and Rec., Stockton, (209) 937-8285; www.stocktongov.com/parks/silverlake/silverlake.cfm. Located 40 mi. S of Lake Tahoe. Daily rates. Platform tents & cabins with electric lights; provide own bedding; community bathrooms; cafeteria-style meals. Program for toddlers & older children. Swimming in lake; horseback riding nearby.

PRIVATE ENTERPRISE CAMPS

Coffee Creek Ranch

See page 342.

Emandal Farm

See page 260.

Montecito Sequoia High Sierra Family Vacation Camp

(800) 227-9900, (650) 967-8612; www.mslodge.com. Located in Sequoia National Forest, betw. Kings Canyon & Sequoia national parks. Weekly rates. Lodge rooms with private bathrooms; rustic cabins with

community bathrooms; bedding provided. Buffet meals. Parent-child program for babies 6 mo.-23 mo.; programs for age 2+. Tennis courts; lake swimming; heated pool; hot tub; sailing; canoeing; boating; archery; fishing; riflery; golf cage; extra fee for mountain biking, water-skiing, & horseback riding. See also page 461.

UNIVERSITY CAMPS

Lair of the Golden Bear

Sponsored by California Alumni Assoc. at U.C. Berkeley, (888) CAL-ALUM, (510) 642-0221; www.lairofthebear.org. Located in Stanislaus National Forest, in Pinecrest. Weekly/weekend rates. Tent cabins with electricity; provide own bedding; community bathrooms; family-style meals. Organized activities for ages 2+. 3 heated pools; tennis courts; softball; hiking; art activities.

These three separate, but contiguous, camps—**Camp Blue, Camp Gold,** and **Camp Oski**—operate side by side. Each has its own staff and facilities.

HOUSEBOATS

Living in a houseboat for a few days is an unusual way to get away from it all. It is possible to dive off the boat for a refreshing swim, fish for dinner while sunbathing, and dock in a sheltered, quiet cove for the night.

Houseboats are equipped with kitchens and flush toilets. Most rental agencies require that renters bring their own bedding, linens, and groceries, but almost everything else is provided on the floating hotel, including life jackets.

Rates vary quite dramatically depending on the time of year, the size and quality of the boat, and how many people are in the party. Summer rentals are most expensive, and a group of six to ten people gets the best rates. Weekly rates begin at around $1,120 for a small boat in off season and go up. Fuel is additional. Most facilities offer midweek specials and 3-day weekends; some offer a Thanksgiving special that includes the turkey and pumpkin pie. During the off-season, rates drop by approximately one-third, and some facilities will rent their boats for just a day. Contact rental facilities directly for current stock and rates.

DELTA

Paradise Point Marina

8095 Rio Blanco Rd., in Stockton, (800) 752-9669, (209) 952-1000; www.sevencrown.com.

LAKE OROVILLE

Bidwell Canyon Marina

801 Bidwell Canyon Rd., in Oroville, (800) 637-1767, (530) 589-3165; www.gobidwell.com.

Lake Oroville Marina

In Oroville, (800) 255-5561, (530) 877-2414; www.foreverresorts.com.

Lake Oroville State Recreation Area

In Oroville, (800) 444-7275, (530) 538-2200; www.parks.ca.gov. $100/night.

Floating campsites have fully equipped kitchens, bathrooms, and sleeping space for up to 15 people.

For more information on this area contact:
Oroville Area Chamber of Commerce

1789 Montgomery St., (800) 655-GOLD, (530) 538-2542; www.oroville-city.com.

LAKE SHASTA

Bridge Bay Resort and Digger Bay Marina

(800) 752-9669; www.sevencrown.com. Bridge Bay: 10300 Bridge Bay Rd., off Hwy. 5 below Pit River Bridge, in Redding, (530) 275-3021. Digger Bay: End of Digger Bay Rd., in Central Valley, (530) 275-3072.

This resort also has motel rooms, housekeeping units, and the Tail O' the Whale restaurant (see page 343).

Holiday Harbor
20061 Shasta Caverns Rd., in O'Brien,
(800) 776-BOAT, (530) 238-2383;
www.lakeshasta.com.

Packers Bay Marina
16814 Packers Bay Rd., in Lakehead, (800) 331-3137,
(530) 275-5570; www.packersbay.com.

TRINITY LAKE

Trinity Lake Resorts & Marinas
See page 342.

RIVER TRIPS

The adventure of rafting down an unpredictable river offers a real escape for the harried, city-weary participant. But don't expect it to be relaxing. Participants help with setting up and breaking camp, and sometimes they are exposed mercilessly to the elements. While usually not dangerous when done with experienced guides, an element of risk is involved. Still, most partic-ipants walk away ecstatic and addicted to the experience.

The outfitter provides shelter, food, and equipment for the trip. Participants need only bring sleeping gear and personal items. Some day trips and overnight runs are available. Seasons and rivers vary with each company.

Most outfitters offer special trips for fami-lies with young children. The minimum age requirement for children ranges from 4 to 8. For details, contact the tour operators directly.

For information on more California river out-fitters, contact **California Outdoors** *((800) 552-3625; www.caloutdoors.org.).*

The American River Touring Association
In Groveland, (800) 323-ARTA, (209) 962-7873;
www.arta.org.

ECHO River Trips
In Hood River, Oregon, (800) 652-3246,
(541) 386-2271; www.echotrips.com.

Kern River Outfitters
In Wofford Heights (in Southern California),
(800) 323-4234, (760) 376-1455;
www.kernrafting.com.

This company caters to families with campfire games and songs and other activities.

Mariah Wilderness Expeditions
In Lotus, (800) 4-MARIAH, (530) 626-6049;
www.mariahwe.com.

This is California's only woman-owned and -operated white water raft and wilderness company. Family trips are accompanied by a professional storyteller and include both female and male guides.

O.A.R.S.
In Angels Camp, (800) 3-GO-OARS, (209) 736-4677;
www.oars.com.

Turtle River Rafting Company
In Mt. Shasta, (800) 726-3223, (530) 926-3223;
www.turtleriver.com.

Among the special trips are personal growth workshops and family river trips.

Whitewater Connection
In Coloma, (800) 336-7238, (530) 622-6446;
www.whitewaterconnection.com.

This outfitter offers rafting trips on four different rivers throughout California.

Whitewater Voyages
In El Sobrante, (800) 400-RAFT, (510) 222-5994;
www.whitewatervoyages.com.

If that guide looks familiar, she might be Kelly Wiglesworth of *Survivor* TV fame, who works as a guide for this outfitter. Several dis-counted Clean-Up Trips are scheduled each year. Participants get the same amenities as on any other trip but are expected to pick up any debris they encounter.

PACK TRIPS

Packing equipment onto horses or mules allows for a much easier and more comfortable trek into the wilderness than does backpacking.

Campers need simply choose the type of pack trip desired. On a spot pack trip, the packers will load the animals with gear, take them to a prearranged campsite, unload the gear, and return to the pack station with the pack animals. They return to repack the gear on the day campers are scheduled to leave. Campers can either hike or ride on horses to the campsite. If riding, campers usually have a choice of keeping the horses at the campsite or of having the packers take them back out. If keeping the horses, campers should be experienced with horses and need to arrange in advance for a corral and feed. Children who haven't had at least basic riding instruction should not be included on such a trip.

A more rugged trip (where the campsite is moved each day) or an easier trip (with all expenses and a guide included) can also usually be arranged with the packer.

This is not an inexpensive vacation. Prices will vary according to which options are selected. Often there are special rates for children, who must be at least 5 years old to participate. Trips are usually available only in the summer.

One of the biggest and most organized packers is **Red's Meadow Pack Station** (*Mammoth Lakes, (800) 292-7758, (760) 934-2345; www.redsmeadow.com.*). Trips include horses, saddles, and meals. Day rides can be arranged, and special family trips, horse drives, and wagon rides are scheduled.

For general information and a list of packers, contact the **Eastern High Sierra Packers Association** (*c/o Bishop Area Chamber of Commerce & Visitors Bureau, 690 N. Main St., Bishop 93514, (888) 395-3952, (760) 873-8405; www.bishopvisitor.com.*).

CAMPING

Because there are excellent resources available on campgrounds, this book mentions only briefly those that fit into the text.

Making reservations

• State Park campgrounds
(800) 444-7275; www.reserveamerica.com (campsite info: www.parks.ca.gov). Reservations advised. Fee.

Reservations can be made by phone from 2 days to 7 months in advance.

• California National Parks
(800) 365-2267; www.recreation.gov. Fee.

• KOA Kampgrounds
www.koa.com; (406) 248-7444.

In this book, these sites are listed in each section under "Where to Stay." An inexpensive Kamping Kabin is a great option for those who don't own a tent, yet long for an outdoors camping vacation. These rustic one-room cabins provide all the fun and excitement of camping out with all the security and comfort of sleeping in. Each sleeps four and is equipped with a double bed plus kid-pleasing bunk beds. A two-room cabin sleeps six. Campers need bring only sleeping bags and cooking gear. Some locations also have Kamping Kottages, complete with fully equipped kitchenette and bathroom. Tents and RVs are, of course,

welcome here. Most of the campgrounds in the KOA chain have swimming pools, and some offer additional recreational facilities. To get a free KOA Directory, stop in at any KOA Kampground, visit the website, or send $6 for shipping to: KOA Directory, P.O. Box 30558, Billings, MT 59114.

Camping references

• California-Nevada CampBook
This book and its companion maps list camping facilities and fees. They are available free to California State Automobile Association members.

• California State Parks Camping Reservation Guide
(800) 777-0369, (916) 653-6995.
This informative free brochure provides campground details on all state parks, reserves, recreation areas, and historic parks.

MISCELLANY

Cal Adventures
Dept. of Recreational Sports, University of California, Berkeley, (510) 642-4000; www.oski.org.
Adventure trips include sailing, sea kayaking, windsurfing, and more. Day classes and special programs for children in grades 3 through 12 are also available.

Coastwalk
Sebastopol, (800) 550-6854, (707) 829-6689; www.coastwalk.org. $50+/day.
Organized summer hikes in California's coastal counties range from 2 to 9 days, with camping gear shuttled by vehicle. The goals of this non-profit organization are to nurture an awareness of the coastal environment and to promote development of a continuous California Coastal Trail.

Green Tortoise
San Francisco, (800) TORTOISE, (415) 956-7500; www.greentortoise.com.
Travel on this groovy, laid-back, alternative bus line at bargain rates. The clientele on summer trips tends to be the under-30s crowd, and winter trips to Mexico attract mature travelers, but all ages are welcome on all trips. Trips are

available to almost anywhere on this continent, including cross-country trips with stops at national parks and trips to Baja. Usually the scenic route, which is not necessarily the most direct route, is followed. Overnight accommodations are sometimes on the bus, which is a sleeper coach, and sometimes at a campsite or in a hostel. The jack-of-all-trades bus drivers often organize cookouts, and they get out and fix breakdowns themselves. Back in the '70s passengers sometimes got out and pushed when necessary, but the new buses have eliminated that. All in all, a trip on this bus line is really a *trip.*

Hostelling International—USA (American Youth Hostels), Golden Gate Council
San Francisco, (415) 863-1444; www.norcalhostels.org. No pets.
The idea behind hostelling is to save money, so accommodations are simple. Traditionally women bunk in one dormitory-style room, men in another, but nowadays many hostels also have separate rooms for couples and families. Most hostels provide bedding and towels to guests at no charge or a nominal fee, and bathrooms and kitchens are shared. Fees are low, ranging from $20 to $30 per person per night, and children under 13 with a parent are half of that; fees for separate rooms are slightly more. Note that some hostels close during the day, usually from 10 to 4:30. Call for a free brochure detailing the hostels in Northern California. (In *Weekend Adventures*, hostels are included in "Where to Stay" sections.) For toll-free reservations using a credit card as a deposit, call (888) GO-HIUSA. After prompting, enter the first three letters of the hostel's city. Members get a discount at most hostels and receive a newsletter and handbook describing U.S. hostels.

Junior Ranger Program
At state parks, (916) 653-8959; www.parks.ca.gov. A similar program operates in national parks.
Designed for children ages 7 through 12, the Junior Ranger program is most active in summer. It includes nature walks and activities related to learning more about the particular park and helps kids discover the rich natural and cultural heritage of California's state and national parks. Sessions last about an hour, and

awards are presented as children progress. A child can begin the program at one park and continue at a later date in another location. To join the national parks program, kids promise, "I pledge to do what I can to protect and preserve the plants, animals, and history of our National Parks." Why, some Junior Rangers have even grown up to become *real* park rangers.

Reno Fun Train

(800) 783-0783, (925) 945-8938; www.keyholidays.com. Schedule & prices vary; Jan-Mar only. Must be age 21+.

This rolling cocktail party includes a bar car, a dance car with a live band, and a sightseeing dome car. Passengers are encouraged to bring along snacks and drinks, and one meal is provided in each direction. The package includes lodging for two nights in Reno, transfers to some hotels, and a coupon book. The train takes on passengers in Emeryville, Martinez, Suisun, and Sacramento. A Reno Snow Train operates mid-week.

"Fun Rick" welcomes guests aboard

Sierra Club Outings

San Francisco, (415) 977-5522; www.outings.sierraclub.org.

Of the more than 350 global outdoor adventures scheduled each year, close to 20% are in California. Trips last from 4 to 8 days and typically include lodging and meals. Shorter day and overnight trips are organized by local Sierra Club chapters *(www.sierraclub.org/outings/ chapter).*

INDEXES

OCTOBER

NOVEMBER

DECEMBER

ALPHABETICAL INDEX

HAVE KIDS?

MILES OF SMILES:
101 GREAT CAR GAMES & ACTIVITIES

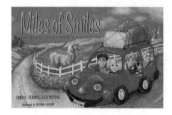

Anyone who has ever been trapped in a hot car with bored kids is well aware that the world needs a sure-fire way of easing the resulting tensions. This clever book fills that need. In fact, according to one enthusiastic user it just "may be the ultimate solution for back seat squabbling." The book is filled with games and activities that have travel-related themes. Ninety-seven require just your minds and mouths to play, and the other four need only simple props: a penny, a pencil, and some crayons. A helpful index categorizes each game and activity according to age appropriateness, and humorous illustrations that kids can color add to everyone's enjoyment. *128 pages. $8.95.*

To order direct, call Carousel Press.
(510) 527-5849

WEEKEND ADVENTURES UPDATE: THE BLOG

Updates to this 9th edition of *Weekend Adventures in San Francisco & Northern California,* as well as some completely new adventures, are periodically posted at our website. Get notified of new postings by signing up for the free *Weekend Adventures* Update blog at:

www.carousel-press.com